JOHN MARSHALL AS CHIEF JUSTICE
From the portrait by Jarvis

THE LIFE
OF
JOHN MARSHALL

BY
ALBERT J. BEVERIDGE

VOLUMES I AND II
1755–1801

BOSTON AND NEW YORK
HOUGHTON MIFFLIN COMPANY
The Riverside Press Cambridge

The Riverside Press
CAMBRIDGE · MASSACHUSETTS
PRINTED IN THE U.S.A.

THE LIFE OF JOHN MARSHALL

VOLUME I

FRONTIERSMAN, SOLDIER, LAWMAKER

1755–1788

PREFACE

The work of John Marshall has been of supreme importance in the development of the American Nation, and its influence grows as time passes. Less is known of Marshall, however, than of any of the great Americans. Indeed, so little has been written of his personal life, and such exalted, if vague, encomium has been paid him, that, even to the legal profession, he has become a kind of mythical being, endowed with virtues and wisdom not of this earth.

He appears to us as a gigantic figure looming, indistinctly, out of the mists of the past, impressive yet lacking vitality, and seemingly without any of those qualities that make historic personages intelligible to a living world of living men. Yet no man in our history was more intensely human than John Marshall and few had careers so full of movement and color. His personal life, his characteristics and the incidents that drew them out, have here been set forth so that we may behold the man as he appeared to those among whom he lived and worked.

It is, of course, Marshall's public work with which we are chiefly concerned. His services as Chief Justice have been so lauded that what he did before he ascended the Supreme Bench has been almost entirely forgotten. His greatest opinions, however, cannot be fully understood without considering his previous life and experience. An account of Marshall the frontiersman, soldier, legislator, lawyer, politician, diplomat, and statesman, and of the conditions he faced in each of these capacities, is essential to a comprehension of Marshall the constructive jurist and of the problems he solved.

In order to make clear the significance of Marshall's public activities, those episodes in American history into which his life was woven have been briefly stated. Although to the historian these are twice-told tales, many of them are not fresh in the minds of the reading public. To say that Marshall took this or that position with reference to the events and questions of his time, without some explanation of them, means little to any one except to the historical scholar.

In the development of his career there must be some clear understanding of the impression made upon him by the actions and opinions of other men, and these, accordingly, have been considered. The influence of his father and of Washington upon John Marshall was profound and determinative, while his life finally became so interlaced with that of Jefferson that a faithful account of the one requires a careful examination of the other.

Vitally important in their effect upon the conduct and attitude of Marshall and of the leading characters of his time were the state of the country, the condition of the people, and the tendency of popular thought. Some reconstruction of the period has, therefore, been attempted. Without a background, the picture and the figures in it lose much of their significance.

The present volumes narrate the life of John Marshall before his epochal labors as Chief Justice began. While this was the period during which events prepared him for his work on the bench, it was also a distinctive phase of his career and, in itself, as important as it was picturesque. It is my purpose to write the final part as soon as the nature of the task permits.

For reading one draft of the manuscript of these volumes I am indebted to Professor Edward Channing, of Harvard University; Dr. J. Franklin Jameson, of the Carnegie Foundation for Historical Research; Professor William E. Dodd, of Chicago University; Professor James A. Woodburn, of Indiana University; Professor Charles A. Beard, of Columbia University; Professor Charles H. Ambler, of Randolph-Macon College; Professor Clarence W. Alvord, of the University of Illinois; Professor D. R. Anderson, of Richmond College; Dr. H. J. Eckenrode, of Richmond College; Dr. Archibald C. Coolidge, Director of the Harvard University Library; Mr. Worthington C. Ford, of the Massachusetts Historical Society; and Mr. Lindsay Swift, Editor of the Boston Public Library. Dr. William G. Stanard, of the Virginia Historical Society, has read the chapters which touch upon the colonial period. I have availed myself of the many helpful suggestions made by these gentlemen and I gratefully acknowledge my obligations to them.

Mr. Swift and Dr. Eckenrode, in addition to reading early drafts of the manuscript, have read the last draft with particular care and I have utilized their criticisms. The proof has been read by Mr. Swift and the comment of this finished critic has been especially valuable.

I am indebted in the highest possible degree to Mr. Worthington C. Ford, of the Massachusetts Historical Society, who has generously aided me with his profound and extensive knowledge of manuscript sources and of the history of the times of which this work treats. His sympathetic interest and whole-hearted helpfulness have not only assisted me, but encouraged and sustained me in the prosecution of my labors.

In making these acknowledgments, I do not in the least shift to other shoulders the responsibility for anything in these volumes. That burden is mine alone.

I extend my thanks to Mr. A. P. C. Griffin, Assistant Librarian, and Mr. Gaillard Hunt, Chief of the Manuscripts Division, of the Library of Congress, who have been unsparing in their efforts to assist me with all the resources of that great library. The officers and their assistants of the Virginia State Library, the Boston Public Library, the Library of Harvard University, the Manuscripts Division of the New York Public Library, the Massachusetts Historical Society, the Pennsylvania Historical Society, and the Virginia Historical Society have been most gracious in affording me all the sources at their command.

I desire to express my appreciation for original material furnished me by several of the descendants and collateral relatives of John Marshall. Miss

Emily Harvie, of Richmond, Virginia, placed at my disposal many letters of Marshall to his wife. For the use of the book in which Marshall kept his accounts and wrote notes of law lectures, I am indebted to Mrs. John K. Mason, of Richmond. A large number of original and unpublished letters of Marshall were furnished me by Mr. James M. Marshall, of Front Royal, Virginia, Mr. Robert Y. Conrad, of Winchester, Virginia; Mrs. Alexander H. Sands, of Richmond, Virginia; Miss Sallie Marshall, of Leeds, Virginia; Mrs. Claudia Jones, and Mrs. Fannie G. Campbell of Washington, D.C.; Judge J. K. M. Norton, of Alexandria, Virginia; Mr. A. Moore, Jr., of Berryville, Virginia; Dr. Samuel Eliot Morison, of Boston, Massachusetts, and Professor Charles William Dabney, of Cincinnati, Ohio. Complete copies of the highly valuable correspondence of Mrs. Edward Carrington were supplied by Mr. John B. Minor, of Richmond, Virginia, and by Mr. Carter H. FitzHugh, of Lake Forest, Illinois. Without the material thus generously opened to me, this narrative of Marshall's life would have been more incomplete than it is and many statements in it would, necessarily, have been based on unsupported tradition.

Among the many who have aided me, Judge James Keith, of Richmond, Virginia, until recently President of the Court of Appeals of Virginia; Judge J. K. M. Norton and the late Miss Nannie Burwell Norton of Alexandria, Virginia; Mr. William Marshall Bullitt, of Louisville, Kentucky; Mr. Thomas Marshall Smith, of Baltimore, Maryland; Mr. and Mrs. Alexander H. Sands; Mr. W. P. Taylor and Dr. H.

Norton Mason, of Richmond, Virginia; Mr. Lucien Keith, Mr. William Horgan, and Mr. William C. Marshall, of Warrenton, Virginia; Judge Henry H Downing and Mr. Aubrey G. Weaver, of Front Royal, Virginia, have rendered notable assistance in the gathering of data.

The large number of citations has made abbreviations necessary. At the end of each volume will be found a careful explanation of references, giving the full title of the work cited, together with the name of the author or editor, and a designation of the edition used.

The index has been made by Mr. David Maydole Matteson, of Cambridge, Massachusetts, and his careful work has added to whatever of value these volumes possess.

Albert J. Beveridge

CONTENTS

LIST OF ABBREVIATED TITLES MOST FREQUENTLY CITED

All references here are to the List of Authorities at the end of this volume.

Beard: *Econ. I. C. See* Beard, Charles A. Economic Interpretation of the Constitution of the United States.

Beard: *Econ. O. J. D. See* Beard, Charles A. Economic Origins of Jeffersonian Democracy.

Bruce: *Econ. See* Bruce, Philip Alexander. Economic History of Virginia in the Seventeeth Century.

Bruce: *Inst. See* Bruce, Philip Alexander. Institutional History of Virginia in the Seventeeth Century.

Cor. Rev.: Sparks. *See* Sparks, Jared. Correspondence of the Revolution.

Eckenrode: *R. V. See* Eckenrode, H. J. The Revolution in Virginia.

Eckenrode: *S. of C. and S. See* Eckenrode, H. J. Separation of Church and State in Virginia.

Jefferson's *Writings:* Washington. *See* Jefferson, Thomas. Writings. Edited by H. A. Washington.

Monroe's *Writings:* Hamilton. *See* Monroe, James. Writings. Edited by Stanislaus Murray Hamilton.

Old Family Letters. See Adams, John. Old Family Letters. Edited by Alexander Biddle.

Wertenbaker: *P. and P. See* Wertenbaker, Thomas J. Patrician and Plebeian in Virginia; or the Origin and Development of the Social Classes of the Old Dominion.

Wertenbaker: *V. U. S. See* Wertenbaker, Thomas J. Virginia Under the Stuarts, 1607–1688.

Works: Adams. *See* Adams, John. Works. Edited by Charles Francis Adams.

Works: Ford. *See* Jefferson, Thomas. Works. Federal Edition. Edited by Paul Leicester Ford.

Works: Hamilton. *See* Hamilton, Alexander. Works. Edited by John C. Hamilton.

Works: Lodge. *See* Hamilton, Alexander. Works. Federal Edition. Edited by Henry Cabot Lodge.

Writings: Conway. *See* Paine, Thomas. Writings. Edited by Moncure Daniel Conway.

Writings: Ford. *See* Washington, George. Writings. Edited by Worthington Chauncey Ford.

Writings: Hunt. *See* Madison, James. Writings. Edited by Gaillard Hunt.

Writings: Smyth. *See* Franklin, Benjamin. Writings. Edited by Albert Henry Smyth.

Writings: Sparks. *See* Washington, George. Writings. Edited by Jared Sparks.

THE LIFE OF JOHN MARSHALL

THE LIFE OF JOHN MARSHALL

CHAPTER I

ANCESTRY AND ENVIRONMENT

Often do the spirits of great events stride on before the events and in to-day already walks to-morrow. (Schiller.)

I was born an American; I will live an American; I shall die an American. (Webster.)

"The British are beaten! The British are beaten!" From cabin to cabin, from settlement to settlement crept, through the slow distances, this report of terror. The astounding news that Braddock was defeated finally reached the big plantations on the tidewater, and then spread dismay and astonishment throughout the colonies.

The painted warriors and the uniformed soldiers of the French-Indian alliance had been growing bolder and bolder, their ravages ever more daring and bloody.[1] Already the fear of them had checked the thin wave of pioneer advance; and it seemed to the settlers that their hereditary enemies from across the water might succeed in confining British dominion in America to the narrow strip between the ocean and the mountains. For the royal colonial authorities had not been able to cope with their foes.[2]

[1] For instance, the Indians massacred nine families in Frederick County, just over the Blue Ridge from Fauquier, in June, 1755. (*Pennsylvania Journal and Weekly Advertiser*, July 24, 1755.)

[2] Marshall, i, 12–13; Campbell, 469–71. "The Colonial contingents were not nearly sufficient either in quantity or quality." (Wood, 40.)

But there was always the reserve power of Great Britain to defend her possessions. If only the home Government would send an army of British veterans, the colonists felt that, as a matter of course, the French and Indians would be routed, the immigrants made safe, and the way cleared for their ever-swelling thousands to take up and people the lands beyond the Alleghanies.

So when at last, in 1755, the redoubtable Braddock and his red-coated regiments landed in Virginia, they were hailed as deliverers. There would be an end, everybody said, to the reign of terror which the atrocities of the French and Indians had created all along the border. For were not the British grenadiers invincible? Was not Edward Braddock an experienced commander, whose bravery was the toast of his fellow officers?[1] So the colonists had been told, and so they believed.

They forgave the rudeness of their British champions; and Braddock marched away into the wilderness carrying with him the unquestioning confidence of the people.[2] It was hardly thought necessary for any Virginia fighting men to accompany him; and that haughty, passionate young Virginia soldier, George Washington (then only twenty-three years of age, but already the chief military figure of the Old Dominion), and his Virginia rangers were invited to

[1] Braddock had won promotion solely by gallantry in the famous Coldstream Guards, the model and pride of the British army, at a time when a lieutenant-colonelcy in that crack regiment sold for £5000 sterling. (Lowdermilk, 97.)

[2] "The British troops had been looked upon as invincible, and preparations had been made in Philadelphia for the celebration of Braddock's anticipated victory." (*Ib.*, 186.)

accompany Braddock more because they knew the country better than for any real aid in battle that was expected of them. "I have been importuned," testifies Washington, "to make this campaign by General Braddock, . . . conceiving . . . that the . . . knowledge I have . . . of the country, Indians, &c. . . . might be useful to him." [1]

So through the ancient and unbroken forests Braddock made his slow and painful way.[2] Weeks passed; then months.[3] But there was no impatience, because everybody knew what would happen when his scarlet columns should finally meet and throw themselves upon the enemy. Yet this meeting, when it came, proved to be one of the lesser tragedies of history, and had a deep and fateful effect upon American public opinion and upon the life and future of the American people.[4]

Time has not dulled the vivid picture of that disaster. The golden sunshine of that July day; the pleasant murmur of the waters of the Monongahela; the silent and somber forests; the steady tramp,

[1] Washington to Robinson, April 20, 1755; *Writings:* Ford, i, 147.

[2] The "wild desert country lying between fort Cumberland and fort Frederick [now the cities of Cumberland and Frederick in Maryland], the most common track of the Indians, in making their incursions into Virginia." (Address in the Maryland House of Delegates, 1757, as quoted by Lowdermilk, 229–30.) Cumberland was "about 56 miles beyond our [Maryland] settlements." (*Ib.*) Cumberland "is far remote from any of our inhabitants." (Washington to Dinwiddie, Sept. 23, 1756; *Writings:* Ford, i, 346.) "Will's Creek was on the very outskirts of civilization. The country beyond was an unbroken and almost pathless wilderness." (Lowdermilk, 50.)

[3] It took Braddock three weeks to march from Alexandria to Cumberland. He was two months and nineteen days on the way from Alexandria to the place of his defeat. (*Ib.*, 138.)

[4] "All America watched his [Braddock's] advance." (Wood, 61.)

tramp of the British to the inspiriting music of their regimental bands playing the martial airs of England; the bright uniforms of the advancing columns giving to the background of stream and forest a touch of splendor; and then the ambush and surprise; the war-whoops of savage foes that could not be seen; the hail of invisible death, no pellet of which went astray; the pathetic volleys which the doomed British troops fired at hidden antagonists; the panic; the rout; the pursuit; the slaughter; the crushing, humiliating defeat! [1]

Most of the British officers were killed or wounded as they vainly tried to halt the stampede.[2] Braddock himself received a mortal hurt.[3] Raging with battle lust, furious at what he felt was the stupidity and cowardice of the British regulars,[4] the youthful Washington rode among the fear-frenzied Englishmen, striving to save the day. Two horses were shot under him. Four bullets rent his uniform.[5] But, crazed with fright, the Royal soldiers were beyond human control.

Only the Virginia rangers kept their heads and their courage. Obeying the shouted orders of their young commander, they threw themselves between the terror-stricken British and the savage victors;

[1] For best accounts of Braddock's defeat see Bradley, 75–107; Lowdermilk, 156–63; and Marshall, i, 7–10.

[2] "Of one hundred and sixty officers, only six escaped." (Lowdermilk, footnote to 175.)

[3] Braddock had five horses killed under him. (*Ib.*, 161.)

[4] "The dastardly behavior of the Regular [British] troops," who "broke and ran as sheep before hounds." (Washington to Dinwiddie, July 18, 1755; *Writings:* Ford, i, 173–74.)

[5] Washington to John A. Washington, July 18, 1755. (*Ib.*, 176.)

and, fighting behind trees and rocks, were an ever-moving rampart of fire that saved the flying remnants of the English troops. But for Washington and his rangers, Braddock's whole force would have been annihilated.[1] Colonel Dunbar and his fifteen hundred British regulars, who had been left a short distance behind as a reserve, made off to Philadelphia as fast as their panic-winged feet could carry them.[2]

So everywhere went up the cry, "The British are beaten!" At first rumor had it that the whole force was destroyed, and that Washington had been killed in action.[3] But soon another word followed hard upon this error — the word that the boyish Virginia captain and his rangers had fought with coolness, skill, and courage; that they alone had prevented the extinction of the British regulars; that they alone had come out of the conflict with honor and glory.

Thus it was that the American colonists suddenly came to think that they themselves must be their own defenders. It was a revelation, all the more impressive because it was so abrupt, unexpected, and dramatic, that the red-coated professional soldiers were not the unconquerable warriors the colonists

[1] "The Virginia companies behaved like men and died like soldiers . . . of three companies . . . scarce thirty were left alive." (Washington to Dinwiddie, July 18, 1755; *Writings:* Ford, i, 173–74.)

[2] Lowdermilk, 182–85; and see Washington's *Writings:* Ford, i, footnote to 175. For account of battle and rout see Washington's letters to Dinwiddie, *ib.*, 173–76; to John A. Washington, July 18, 1755, *ib.*; to Robert Jackson, Aug. 2, 1755, *ib.*, 177–78; also see Campbell, 472–81. For French account see Hart, ii, 365–67; also, Sargent: *History of Braddock's Expedition.*

[3] Washington to John A. Washington, July 18, 1755; *Writings:* Ford, i, 175.

had been told that they were.[1] From colonial "mansion" to log cabin, from the provincial "capitals' to the mean and exposed frontier settlements, Braddock's defeat sowed the seed of the idea that Americans must depend upon themselves.[2]

As Bacon's Rebellion at Jamestown, exactly one hundred years before Independence was declared at Philadelphia, was the beginning of the American Revolution in its first clear expression of popular rights,[3] so Braddock's defeat was the inception of that same epoch in its lesson of American military self-dependence.[4] Down to Concord and Lexington, Great Bridge and Bunker Hill, the overthrow of the King's troops on the Monongahela in 1755 was a theme of common talk among men, a household legend on which American mothers brought up their children.[5]

Close upon the heels of this epoch-making event, John Marshall came into the world. He was born in

[1] "The Defeat of Braddock was totally unlooked for, and it excited the most painful surprise." (Lowdermilk, 186.)

[2] "After Braddock's defeat, the Colonists jumped to the conclusion that all regulars were useless." (Wood, 40.)

[3] See Stanard: *Story of Bacon's Rebellion.* Bacon's Rebellion deserves the careful study of all who would understand the beginnings of the democratic movement in America. Mrs. Stanard's study is the best brief account of this popular uprising. See also Wertenbaker: *V. U. S.*, chaps. 5 and 6.

[4] "The news [of Braddock's defeat] gave a far more terrible blow to the reputation of the regulars than to the British cause [against the French] itself." (Wood, 61.)

[5] "From that time [Braddock's defeat] forward the Colonists had a much less exalted opinion of the valor of the royal troops." (Lowdermilk, 186.) The fact that the colonists themselves had been negligent and incompetent in resisting the French or even the Indians did not weaken their newborn faith in their own prowess and their distrust of British power.

a little log cabin in the southern part of what now is Fauquier County, Virginia (then a part of Prince William), on September 24, 1755,[1] eleven weeks after Braddock's defeat. The Marshall cabin stood about a mile and a half from a cluster of a dozen similar log structures built by a handful of German families whom Governor Spotswood had brought over to work his mines. This little settlement was known as Germantown, and was practically on the frontier.[2]

Thomas Marshall, the father of John Marshall, was a close friend of Washington, whom he ardently admired. They were born in the same county, and their acquaintance had begun, apparently, in their boyhood.[3] Also, as will presently appear, Thomas Marshall had for about three years been the companion of Washington, when acting as his assistant in surveying the western part of the Fairfax estate.[4] From that time forward his attachment to Washington amounted to devotion.[5]

Also, he was, like Washington, a fighting man.[6] It seems strange, therefore, that he did not accom-

[1] *Autobiography.*

[2] Campbell, 494. "It is remarkable," says Campbell, "that as late as the year 1756, when the colony was a century and a half old, the Blue Ridge of mountains was virtually the western boundary of Virginia." And see Marshall, i, 15; also, *New York Review* (1838), iii, 330. For frontier settlements, see the admirable map prepared by Marion F. Lansing and reproduced in Channing, ii.

[3] Humphrey Marshall, i, 344–45. Also Binney, in Dillon, iii, 283.

[4] See *infra*, chap. II.

[5] Humphrey Marshall, i, 344–45.

[6] He was one of a company of militia cavalry the following year, (Journal, H.B. (1756), 378); and he was commissioned as ensign Aug. 27, 1761. (Crozier: *Virginia Colonial Militia*, 96.) And see *infra*, chaps. III and IV.

pany his hero in the Braddock expedition. There is, indeed, a legend that he did go part of the way.[1] But this, like so many stories concerning him, is untrue.[2] The careful roster, made by Washington of those under his command,[3] does not contain the name of Thomas Marshall either as officer or private. Because of their intimate association it is certain that Washington would not have overlooked him if he had been a member of that historic body of men.

So, while the father of John Marshall was not with his friend and leader at Braddock's defeat, no man watched that expedition with more care, awaited its outcome with keener anxiety, or was more affected by the news, than Thomas Marshall. Beneath no rooftree in all the colonies, except, perhaps, that of Washington's brother, could this capital event have made a deeper impression than in the tiny log house in the forests of Prince William County, where John Marshall, a few weeks afterwards, first saw the light of day.

Wars and rumors of wars, ever threatening danger, and stern, strong, quiet preparation to meet whatever befell — these made up the moral and intellectual atmosphere that surrounded the Marshall cabin before and after the coming of Thomas and Mary

[1] Paxton, 20.

[2] A copy of a letter (MS.) to Thomas Marshall from his sister Elizabeth Marshall Martin, dated June 15, 1755, referring to the Braddock expedition, shows that he was at home at this time. Furthermore, a man of the quality of Thomas Marshall would not have left his young wife alone in their backwoods cabin at a time so near the birth of their first child, when there was an overabundance of men eager to accompany Braddock.

[3] Washington MSS., Lib. Cong.

Marshall's first son. The earliest stories told this child of the frontier[1] must have been those of daring and sacrifice and the prevailing that comes of them.

Almost from the home-made cradle John Marshall was taught the idea of American solidarity. Braddock's defeat, the most dramatic military event before the Revolution,[2] was, as we have seen, the theme of fireside talk; and from this grew, in time, the conviction that Americans, if united,[3] could not only protect their homes from the savages and the French, but defeat, if need be, the British themselves.[4] So thought the Marshalls, father and mother; and so they taught their children, as subsequent events show.

It was a remarkable parentage that produced this child who in manhood was to become the master-builder of American Nationality. Curiously enough, it was exactly the same mingling of human elements that gave to the country that great apostle of the rights of man, Thomas Jefferson. Indeed, Jefferson's mother and Marshall's grandmother were first cousins. The mother of Thomas Jefferson was Jane

[1] Simon Kenton, the Indian fighter, was born in the same county in the same year as John Marshall. (M'Clung: *Sketches of Western Adventure*, 93.)

[2] Neither the siege of Louisburg nor the capture of Quebec took such hold on the public imagination as the British disaster on the Monongahela. Also, the colonists felt, though unjustly, that they were entitled to as much credit for the two former events as the British.

[3] The idea of unity had already germinated. The year before, Franklin offered his plan of concerted colonial action to the Albany conference. (*Writings:* Smyth, i, 387.)

[4] Wood, 38–42.

Randolph, daughter of Isham Randolph of Turkey Island; and the mother of John Marshall was Mary Randolph Keith, the daughter of Mary Isham Randolph, whose father was Thomas Randolph of Tuckahoe, the brother of Jefferson's maternal grandfather.

Thus, Thomas Jefferson was the great-grandson and John Marshall the great-great-grandson of William Randolph and Mary Isham. Perhaps no other couple in American history is so remarkable for the number of distinguished descendants. Not only were they the ancestors of Thomas Jefferson and John Marshall, but also of "Light Horse Harry" Lee, of Revolutionary fame, Edmund Randolph, Washington's first Attorney-General, John Randolph of Roanoke, George Randolph, Secretary of War under the Confederate Government, and General Robert E. Lee, the great Southern military leader of the Civil War.[1]

The Virginia Randolphs were one of the families of that proud colony who were of undoubted gentle descent, their line running clear and unbroken at least as far back as 1550. The Ishams were a somewhat older family, their lineage being well established to 1424. While knighthood was conferred upon one ancestor of Mary Isham, the Randolph and Isham families were of the same social stratum, both being of the English gentry.[2] The

[1] For these genealogies see Slaughter: *Bristol Parish*, 212; Lee: *Lee of Virginia*, 406 *et seq.*; Randall, i, 6–9; Tucker, i, 26. See Meade, i, footnote to 138–39, for other descendants of William Randolph and Mary Isham.

[2] *Va. Mag. Hist. and Biog.*, iii, 261; xviii, 86–87.

Virginia Randolphs were brilliant in mind, physically courageous, commanding in character, generally handsome in person, yet often as erratic as they were gifted.

When the gentle Randolph-Isham blood mingled with the sturdier currents of the common people, the result was a human product stronger, steadier, and abler than either. So, when Jane Randolph became the wife of Peter Jefferson, a man from the grass roots, the result was Thomas Jefferson. The union of a daughter of Mary Randolph with Thomas Marshall, a man of the soil and forests, produced John Marshall.[1]

Physically and mentally, Peter Jefferson and Thomas Marshall were much alike. Both were powerful men of great stature. Both were endowed with rare intellectuality.[2] Both were hard-working, provident, and fearless. Even their occupations were the same: both were land surveyors. The chief difference between them was that, whereas Peter Jefferson appears to have been a hearty and con-

[1] The curious sameness in the ancestry of Marshall and Jefferson is found also in the surroundings of their birth. Both were born in log cabins in the backwoods. Peter Jefferson, father of Thomas, "was the third or fourth white settler within the space of several miles" of his cabin home, which he built "in a small clearing in the dense and primeval forest." (Randall, i, 11.) Here Jefferson was born, April 2, 1743, a little more than twelve years before John Marshall came into the world, under like conditions and from similar parents.

Peter Jefferson was, however, remotely connected by descent, on his mother's side, with men who had been burgesses. His maternal grandfather, Peter Field, was a burgess, and his maternal great-grandfather, Henry Soane, was Speaker of the House of Burgesses. But both Peter Jefferson and Thomas Marshall were "of the people" as distinguished from the gentry.

[2] Morse, 3; and Story, in Dillon, iii, 330.

vivial person,[1] Thomas Marshall seems to have been self-contained though adventurous, and of rather austere habits. Each became the leading man of his county[2] and both were chosen members of the House of Burgesses.[3]

On the paternal side, it is impossible to trace the origin of either Peter Jefferson[4] or Thomas Marshall farther back than their respective great-grandfathers, without floundering, unavailingly, in genealogical quicksands.

Thomas Marshall was the son of a very small planter in Westmoreland County, Virginia. October 23, 1727, three years before Thomas was born, his father, John Marshall "of the forest," acquired by deed, from William Marshall of King and Queen County, two hundred acres of poor, low, marshy land located on Appomattox Creek.[5] Little as the value of land in Virginia then was, and continued to be for three quarters of a century afterwards,[6] this particu-

[1] Randall, i, 7. Peter Jefferson "purchased" four hundred acres of land from his "bosom friend," William Randolph, the consideration as set forth in the deed being, "Henry Weatherbourne's biggest bowl of arrack punch"! (*Ib.*)

[2] Peter Jefferson was County Lieutenant of Albemarle. (*Va. Mag. Hist. and Biog.*, xxiii, 173–75.) Thomas Marshall was Sheriff of Fauquier.

[3] Randall, i, 12–13; and see *infra*, chap. II.

[4] Tucker, i, 26.

[5] Records of Westmoreland County, Deeds and Wills, viii, 1, 276.

[6] *Ib.* Seventy years later La Rochefoucauld found land adjoining Norfolk heavily covered with valuable timber, close to the water and convenient for shipment, worth only from six to seven dollars an acre. (La Rochefoucauld, iii, 25.) Virginia sold excellent public land for two cents an acre three quarters of a century after this deed to John Marshall "of the forest." (Ambler, 44; and see Turner, Wis. Hist. Soc., 1908, 201.) This same land which William Marshall deeded to John Marshall nearly two hundred years ago is now valued at only from ten to twenty dollars an acre. (Letter of Albert Stuart,

lar tract seems to have been of an especially inferior quality. The deed states that it is a part of twelve hundred acres which had been granted to "Jno. Washington & Thos. Pope, gents . . . & by them lost for want of seating."

Here John Marshall "of the forest" [1] lived until his death in 1752, and here on April 2, 1730, Thomas Marshall was born. During the quarter of a century that this John Marshall remained on his little farm, he had become possessed of several slaves, mostly, perhaps, by natural increase. By his will he bequeaths to his ten children and to his wife six negro men and women, ten negro boys and girls, and two negro children. In addition to "one negro fellow named Joe and one negro woman named Cate" he gives to his wife "one Gray mair named beauty and side saddle also six hogs also I leave her the use of my land During her widowhood, and afterwards to fall to my son Thomas Marshall and his heirs forever." [2] One year later the widow, Elizabeth Marshall, deeded half of this two hundred acres to her son Thomas Marshall.[3]

Deputy Clerk of Westmoreland County, to author, Aug. 26, 1913.) In 1730 it was probably worth one dollar per acre.

[1] A term generally used by the richer people in referring to those of poorer condition who lived in the woods, especially those whose abodes were some distance from the river. (Statement of W. G. Stanard, Secretary of the Virginia Historical Society and Dr. H. J. Eckenrode of Richmond College, and formerly Archivist of the Virginia State Library.) There were, however, Virginia estates called "The Forest." For example, Jefferson's father-in-law, John Wayles, a wealthy man, lived in "The Forest."

[2] Will of John Marshall "of the forest," made April 1, 1752, probated May 26, 1752, and recorded June 22, 1752; Records of Westmoreland County, Deeds and Wills, xi, 419 *et seq*. (Appendix II.)

[3] *Ib.*, 421.

Such was the environment of Thomas Marshall's birth, such the property, family, and station in life of his father. Beyond these facts, nothing positively is known of the ancestry of John Marshall on his father's side. Marshall himself traces it no further back than his grandfather. "My Father, Thomas Marshall, was the eldest son of John Marshall, who intermarried with a Miss Markham and whose parents migrated from Wales, and settled in the county of Westmoreland, in Virginia, where my Father was born." [1]

It is probable, however, that Marshall's paternal great-grandfather was a carpenter of Westmoreland County. A Thomas Marshall, "carpenter," as he describes himself in his will, died in that county in 1704. He devised his land to his son William. A William Marshall of King and Queen County deeded to John Marshall "of the forest," for five shillings, the two hundred acres of land in Westmoreland County, as above stated.[2] The fair inference is that this William was the elder brother of John "of the forest" and that both were sons of Thomas the "carpenter."

Beyond his paternal grandfather or at furthest his great-grandfather, therefore, the ancestry of John Marshall, on his father's side, is lost in the fogs of uncertainty.[3] It is only positively known that

[1] *Autobiography*. Marshall gives the ancestry of his wife more fully and specifically. See *infra*, chap. v.

[2] Will of Thomas Marshall, "carpenter," probated May 31, 1704; Records of Westmoreland County, Deeds and Wills, iii, 232 *et seq.* (Appendix I.)

[3] Most curiously, precisely this is true of Thomas Jefferson's paternal ancestry.

his grandfather was of the common people and of moderate means.[1]

[1] There is a family tradition that the first of this particular Marshall family in America was a Royalist Irish captain who fought under Charles I and came to America when Cromwell prevailed. This may or may not be true. Certainly no proof of it has been discovered. The late Wilson Miles Cary, whose authority is unquestioned in genealogical problems upon which he passed judgment, decided that "the Marshall family begins absolutely with Thomas Marshall, 'Carpenter.'" (The Cary Papers, MSS., Va. Hist. Soc. The *Virginia Magazine of History and Biography* is soon to publish these valuable genealogical papers.)

Within comparatively recent years, this family tradition has been ambitiously elaborated. It includes among John Marshall's ancestors William le Mareschal, who came to England with the Conqueror; the celebrated Richard de Clare, known as "Strongbow"; an Irish king, Dermont; Sir William Marshall, regent of the kingdom of England and restorer of Magna Charta; a Captain John Marshall, who distinguished himself at the siege of Calais in 1558; and finally, the Irish captain who fought Cromwell and fled to Virginia as above mentioned. (Paxton, 7 *et seq.*)

Senator Humphrey Marshall rejected this story as "a myth supported by vanity." (*Ib.*) Colonel Cary declares that "there is no evidence whatever in support of it." (Cary Papers, MSS.) Other painstaking genealogists have reached the same conclusion. (See, for instance, General Thomas M. Anderson's analysis of the subject in *Va. Mag. Hist. and Biog.*, xii, 328 *et seq.*)

Marshall himself, of course, does not notice this legend in his *Autobiography*; indeed, it is almost certain that he never heard of it. In constructing this picturesque genealogical theory, the kinship of persons separated by centuries is assumed largely because of a similarity of names. This would not seem to be entirely convincing. There were many Marshalls in Virginia no more related to one another than the various unrelated families by the name of Smith. Indeed, *maréchal* is the French word for a "shoeing smith."

For example, there lived in Westmoreland County, at the same time with John Marshall "of the forest," another John Marshall, who died intestate and the inventory of whose effects was recorded March 26, 1751, a year before John Marshall "of the forest" died. These two John Marshalls do not seem to have been kinsmen.

The only prominent person in Virginia named Marshall in 1723–34 was a certain Thomas Marshall who was a member of the colony's House of Burgesses during this period; but he was from Northampton County. (Journal, H.B. (1712–23), xi; *ib.* (1727–40), viii, and 174.) He does not appear to have been related in any way to John "of the forest."

Concerning his paternal grandmother, nothing definitely is established except that she was Elizabeth Markham, daughter of Lewis Markham, once Sheriff of Westmoreland County.[1]

John Marshall's lineage on his mother's side, however, is long, high, and free from doubt, not only through the Randolphs and Ishams, as we have seen, but through the Keiths. For his maternal grand-

There were numerous Marshalls who were officers in the Revolutionary War from widely separated colonies, apparently unconnected by blood or marriage. For instance, there were Abraham, David, and Benjamin Marshall from Pennsylvania; Christopher Marshall from Massachusetts; Dixon Marshall from North Carolina; Elihu Marshall from New York, etc. (Heitman, 285.)

At the same time that John Marshall, the subject of this work, was captain in a Virginia regiment, two other John Marshalls were captains in Pennsylvania regiments. When Thomas Marshall of Virginia was an officer in Washington's army, there were four other Thomas Marshalls, two from Massachusetts, one from South Carolina, and one from Virginia, all Revolutionary officers. (*Ib.*)

When Stony Point was taken by Wayne, among the British prisoners captured was Lieutenant John Marshall of the 17th Regiment of British foot (see Dawson, 86); and Captain John Marshall of Virginia was one of the attacking force. (See *infra*, chap. IV.)

In 1792, John Marshall of King and Queen County, a boatswain, was a Virginia pensioner. (*Va. Hist. Prs.*, v, 544.) He was not related to John Marshall, who had become the leading Richmond lawyer of that time.

While Hamilton was Secretary of the Treasury he received several letters from John Marshall, an Englishman, who was in this country and who wrote Hamilton concerning the subject of establishing manufactories. (Hamilton MSS., Lib. Cong.)

Illustrations like these might be continued for many pages. They merely show the danger of inferring relationship because of the similarity of names, especially one so general as that of Marshall.

[1] The Cary Papers, *supra*. Here again the Marshall legend riots fantastically. This time it makes the pirate Blackbeard the first husband of Marshall's paternal grandmother; and with this freebooter she is said to have had thrilling and melancholy experiences. It deserves mention only as showing the absurdity of such myths. Blackbeard was one Edward Teach, whose career is well authenticated (Wise, 186.) Colonel Cary put a final quietus on this particular tale, as he did on so many other genealogical fictions.

father was an Episcopal clergyman, James Keith, of the historic Scottish family of that name, who were hereditary Earls Marischal of Scotland. The Keiths had been soldiers for generations, some of them winning great renown.[1] One of them was James Keith, the Prussian field marshal and ablest of the officers of Frederick the Great.[2] James Keith, a younger son of this distinguished family, was destined for the Church;[3] but the martial blood flowing in his veins asserted itself and, in his youth, he also became a soldier, upholding with arms the cause of the Pretender. When that rebellion was crushed, he fled to Virginia, resumed his sacred calling, returned to England for orders, came back to Virginia[4] and during his remaining years performed his priestly duties with rare zeal and devotion.[5] The motto of the Keiths of Scotland was "Veritas Vincit," and John Marshall adopted it. During most of his life he wore an amethyst with the ancient Keith motto engraved upon it.[6]

When past middle life the Scottish parson married Mary Isham Randolph,[7] granddaughter of William Randolph and Mary Isham. In 1754 their

[1] See Douglas: *Peerage of Scotland* (1764), 448. Also Burke: *Peerage* (1903), 895; and *ib.* (1876). This peerage is now extinct. See Burke: *Extinct Peerages*.

[2] For appreciation of this extraordinary man see Carlyle's *Frederick the Great*.

[3] Paxton, 30.

[4] From data furnished by Justice James Keith, President of the Court of Appeals of Virginia.

[5] Paxton, 30; and see Meade, ii, 216.

[6] Data furnished by Thomas Marshall Smith of Baltimore, Md.

[7] With this lady the tradition deals most unkindly and in highly colored pictures. An elopement, the deadly revenge of outraged brothers, a broken heart and resulting insanity overcome by gentle

daughter, Mary Randolph Keith, married Thomas Marshall and became the mother of John Marshall. "My mother was named Mary Keith, she was the daughter of a clergyman, of the name of Keith, who migrated from Scotland and intermarried with a Miss Randolph of James River" is Marshall's comment on his maternal ancestry.[1]

Not only was John Marshall's mother uncommonly well born, but she was more carefully educated than most Virginia women of that period.[2] Her father received in Aberdeen the precise and methodical training of a Scottish college;[3] and, as all parsons in the Virginia of that time were teachers, it is certain that he carefully instructed his daughter. He was a deeply religious man, especially in his latter years, — so much so, indeed, that there was in him a touch of mysticism; and the two marked qualities of his daughter, Mary, were deep piety and strong intellectuality. She had, too, all the physical hardiness of her Scottish ancestry, fortified by the active and useful labor which all Virginia women of her class at that time performed.

treatment, only to be reinduced in old age by a fraudulent Enoch Arden letter apparently written by the lost love of her youth — such are some of the incidents with which this story clothes Marshall's maternal grandmother. (Paxton, 25–26.)

[1] *Autobiography.*

[2] In general, Virginia women at this time had very little education (Burnaby, 57.) Sometimes the daughters of prominent and wealthy families could not read or write. (Bruce: *Inst.*, i, 454–55.) Even forty years after John Marshall was born, there was but one girls' school in Virginia. (La Rochefoucauld, iii, 227.) In 1789, there were very few schools of any kind in Virginia, it appears. (Journal, H.B. (Dec. 14, 1789), 130; and see *infra*, chap. VI.)

[3] Paxton, 30. Marischal College, Aberdeen, was founded by George Keith, Fifth Earl Marischal (1593).

So Thomas Marshall and Mary Keith combined unusual qualities for the founding of a family. Great strength of mind both had, and powerful wills; and through the veins of both poured the blood of daring. Both were studious-minded, too, and husband and wife alike were seized of a passion for self-improvement as well as a determination to better their circumstances. It appears that Thomas Marshall was by nature religiously inclined; [1] and this made all the greater harmony between himself and his wife. The physical basis of both husband and wife seems to have been well-nigh perfect.

Fifteen children were the result of this union, every one of whom lived to maturity and almost all of whom rounded out a ripe old age. Every one of them led an honorable and successful life. Nearly all strongly impressed themselves upon the community in which they lived.

It was a peculiar society of which this prolific and virile family formed a part, and its surroundings were as strange as the society itself. Nearly all of Virginia at that time was wilderness, [2] if we look upon it with the eyes of to-day. The cultivated parts were given over almost entirely to the raising of tobacco, which soon drew from the soil its virgin strength; and the land thus exhausted usually was abandoned to the forest, which again soon covered it. No use was made of the commonest and most

[1] See *infra*, chap. II. When Leeds Parish was organized, we find Thomas Marshall its leading vestryman. He was always a stanch churchman.

[2] Jones, 35; Burnaby, 58. But see Maxwell in *William and Mary College Quarterly*, xix, 73–103; and see Bruce: *Econ.*, i, 425, 427, 585, 587.

obvious fertilizing materials and methods; new spaces were simply cleared.[1] Thus came a happy-go-lucky improvidence of habits and character.

This shiftlessness was encouraged by the vast extent of unused and unoccupied domain. Land was so cheap that riches measured by that basis of all wealth had to be counted in terms of thousands and tens of thousands of acres.[2] Slavery was an even more powerful force making for a kind of lofty disdain of physical toil among the white

[1] "Though tobacco exhausts the land to a prodigious degree, the proprietors take no pains to restore its vigor; they take what the soil will give and abandon it when it gives no longer. They like better to clear new lands than to regenerate the old." (De Warville, 439; and see Fithian, 140.)

The land produced only "four or five bushels of wheat per acre or from eight to ten of Indian corn. These fields are never manured, hardly even are they ploughed; and it seldom happens that their owners for two successive years exact from them these scanty crops. . . . The country . . . everywhere exhibits the features of laziness, of ignorance, and consequently of poverty." (La Rochefoucauld, iii, 106–07, describing land between Richmond and Petersburg, in 1797; and see Schoepf, ii, 32, 48; and Weld, i, 138, 151.)

[2] Burnaby, 45, 59. The estate of Richard Randolph of Curels, in 1742 embraced "not less than forty thousand acres of the choicest lands." (Garland, i, 7.) The mother of George Mason bought ten thousand acres in Loudoun County for an insignificant sum. (Rowland, i, 51.) The Carter plantation in 1774 comprised sixty thousand acres and Carter owned six hundred negroes. (Fithian, 128.) Compare with the two hundred acres and few slaves of John Marshall "of the forest," *supra*.

Half a century later the very best lands in Virginia with valuable mines upon them sold for only eighteen dollars an acre. (La Rochefoucauld, iii, 124.) For careful account of the extent of great holdings in the seventeenth century see Wertenbaker: *P. and P.*, 34–35, 97–99. Jefferson in 1790 owned two hundred slaves and ten thousand acres of very rich land on the James River. (Jefferson to Van Staphorst, Feb. 28, 1790; *Works:* Ford, vi, 33.) Washington owned enormous quantities of land, and large numbers of slaves. His Virginia holdings alone amounted to thirty-five thousand acres. (Beard: *Econ. I. C.*, 144.)

people.[1] Black slaves were almost as numerous as white free men.[2] On the great plantations the negro quarters assumed the proportions of villages;[3] and the masters of these extensive holdings were by example the arbiters of habits and manners to the whole social and industrial life of the colony. While an occasional great planter was methodical and industrious,[4] careful and systematic methods were rare. Manual labor was, to most of these lords of circumstance, not only unnecessary but degrading. To do no physical work that could be avoided on the one hand, and on the other hand, to own as many slaves as possible, was, generally, the ideal of members of the first estate.[5] This spread to the classes below, until it became a common ambition of white men throughout the Old Dominion.

While contemporary travelers are unanimous upon this peculiar aspect of social and economic conditions in old Virginia, the vivid picture drawn by Thomas Jefferson is still more convincing. "The whole com-

[1] Burnaby, 54.

[2] In the older counties the slaves outnumbered the whites; for instance, in 1790 Westmoreland County had 3183 whites, 4425 blacks, and 114 designated as "all others." In 1782 in the same county 410 slave-owners possessed 4536 slaves and 1889 horses. (*Va. Mag. Hist. and Biog.*, x, 229–36.)

[3] Ambler, 11. The slaves of some planters were valued at more than thirty thousand pounds sterling. (Fithian, 286; and Schoepf, ii, 38; also, Weld, i, 148.)

[4] Robert Carter was a fine example of this rare type. (See Fithian, 279–80.)

[5] Burnaby, 53–54 and 59. "The Virginians . . . are an indolent haughty people whose thoughts and designs are directed solely towards p[l]aying the lord, owning great tracts of land and numerous troops of slaves. Any man whatever, if he can afford so much as 2–3 [two or three] negroes, becomes ashamed of work, and goes about in idleness, supported by his slaves." (Schoepf, ii, 40.)

merce between master and slave," writes Jefferson, "is a perpetual exercise of the most boisterous passions, the most unremitting despotism on the one part, and degrading submissions on the other. Our children see this and learn to imitate it. . . . Thus nursed, educated, and daily exercised in tyranny . . . the man must be a prodigy who can retain his manners and morals undepraved. . . . With the morals of the people their industry also is destroyed. For in a warm climate, no man will labour for himself who can make another labour for him. . . . Of the proprietors of slaves a very small proportion indeed are ever seen to labour." [1]

Two years after he wrote his "Notes on Virginia" Jefferson emphasized his estimate of Virginia society. "I have thought them [Virginians] as you found them," he writes Chastellux, "aristocratical, pompous, clannish, indolent, hospitable . . . careless of their interests, . . . thoughtless in their expenses and in all their transactions of business." He again ascribes many of these characteristics to "that warmth of their climate which unnerves and unmans both body and mind." [2]

From this soil sprang a growth of habits as noxious as it was luxuriant. Amusements to break the monotony of unemployed daily existence took the form of horse-racing, cock-fighting, and gambling.[3]

[1] "Notes on Virginia"; *Works:* Ford, iv, 82–83. See La Rochefoucauld, iii, p. 161, on Jefferson's slaves.

[2] Jefferson to Chastellux, Sept. 2, 1785; *Thomas Jefferson Correspondence*, Bixby Collection: Ford, 12; and see Jefferson's comparison of the sections of the country, *ib.* and *infra,* chap. VI.

[3] "Many of the wealthier class were to be seen seeking relief from the vacuity of idleness, not merely in the allowable pleasures of the

Drinking and all attendant dissipations were universal and extreme;[1] this, however, was the case in all the colonies.[2] Bishop Meade tells us that even the clergy indulged in the prevailing customs to the neglect of their sacred calling; and the church itself was all but abandoned in the disrepute which the conduct of its ministers brought upon the house of God.[3]

chase and the turf, but in the debasing ones of cock-fighting, gaming, and drinking." (Tucker, i, 18; and see La Rochefoucauld, iii, 77; Weld, i, 191; also *infra*, chap. VII, and references there given.)

[1] Jones, 48, 49, and 52; Chastellux, 222–24; also, translator's note to *ib.*, 292–93. The following order from the Records of the Court of Rappahannock County, Jan. 2, 1688 (*sic*), p. 141, is illustrative: —

"It having pleased Almighty God to bless his Royall Mahst. with the birth of a son & his subjects with a Prince of Wales, and for as much as his Excellency hath sett apart the 16th. day of this Inst. Janr'y. for solemnizing the same. To the end therefore that it may be don with all the expressions of joy this County is capable of, this Court have ordered that Capt. Geo. Taylor do provide & bring to the North Side Courthouse for this county as much Rum or other strong Liquor with sugar proportionable as shall amount to six thousand five hundred pounds of Tobb. to be distributed amongst the Troops of horse, Compa. of foot and other persons that shall be present at the Sd. Solemnitie. And that the said sum be allowed him at the next laying of the Levey. As also that Capt. Samll. Blomfield provide & bring to the South side Courthouse for this county as much Rum or other strong Liquor Wth. sugar proportionable as shall amount to three thousand five hundred pounds of Tobb. to be distributed as above att the South side Courthouse, and the Sd. sum to be allowed him at the next laying of the Levey."

And see Bruce: *Econ.*, ii, 210–31; also Wise, 320, 327–29. Although Bruce and Wise deal with a much earlier period, drinking seems to have increased in the interval. (See Fithian, 105–14, 123.)

[2] As in Massachusetts, for instance. "In most country towns . . . you will find almost every other house with a sign of entertainment before it. . . . If you sit the evening, you will find the house full of people, drinking drams, flip, toddy, carousing, swearing." (John Adams's *Diary*, describing a New England county, in 1761; *Works*: Adams, ii, 125–26. The Records of Essex County, Massachusetts, now in process of publication by the Essex Institute, contain many cases that confirm the observation of Adams.)

[3] Meade, i, 52–54; and see Schoepf, ii, 62–63.

Yet the higher classes of colonial Virginians were keen for the education of their children, or at least of their male offspring.[1] The sons of the wealthiest planters often were sent to England or Scotland to be educated, and these, not infrequently, became graduates of Oxford, Cambridge, and Edinburgh.[2] Others of this class were instructed by private tutors.[3] Also a sort of scanty and fugitive public instruction was given in rude cabins, generally located in abandoned fields. These were called the Old Field Schools.[4]

More than forty per cent of the men who made deeds or served on juries could not sign their names, although they were of the land-owning and better educated classes;[5] the literacy of the masses, especially that of the women,[6] was, of course, much lower.

An eager desire, among the "quality," for reading brought a considerable number of books to the homes of those who could afford that luxury.[7] A few

[1] Wise, 317–19; Bruce: *Inst.*, i, 308–15.

[2] Bruce: *Inst.*, i, 317–22; and see especially, *Va. Mag. Hist. and Biog.*, ii, 196 *et seq.*

[3] *Ib.*, 323–30; also Fithian, 50 *et seq.*

[4] Bruce: *Inst.*, i, 331–42. [5] *Ib.*, 452–53.

[6] *Ib.*, 456–57. Bruce shows that two thirds of the women who joined in deeds could not write. This, however, was in the richer section of the colony at a much earlier period. Just before the Revolution Virginia girls, even in wealthy families, "were simply taught to read and write at 25/ [shillings] and a load of wood per year — A boarding school was no where in Virginia to be found." (Mrs. Carrington to her sister Nancy; MS.) Part of this letter appears in the *Atlantic Monthly* series cited hereafter (see chap. v); but the teacher's pay is incorrectly printed as "pounds" instead of "shillings." (*Atlantic Monthly*, lxxxiv, 544–45.)

[7] Bruce: *Inst.*, i, 402–42; and see Wise, 313–15. Professor Tucker says that "literature was neglected, or cultivated, by the small number who had been educated in England, rather as an accomplishment and a mark of distinction than for the substantial benefits it confers." (Tucker, i, 18.)

libraries were of respectable size and two or three were very large. Robert Carter had over fifteen hundred volumes,[1] many of which were in Latin and Greek, and some in French.[2] William Byrd collected at Westover more than four thousand books in half a dozen languages.[3] But the Carter and Byrd libraries were, of course, exceptions. Byrd's library was the greatest, not only in Virginia, but in all the colonies, except that of John Adams, which was equally extensive and varied.[4]

Doubtless the leisure and wealth of the gentry, created by the peculiar economic conditions of the Old Dominion, sharpened this appetite for literature and afforded to the wealthy time and material for the gratification of it. The passion for reading and discussion persisted, and became as notable a characteristic of Virginians as was their dislike for physical labor, their excessive drinking, and their love of strenuous sport and rough diversion.

There were three social orders or strata, all contemporary observers agree, into which Virginians were divided; but they merged into one another so that the exact dividing line was not clear.[5] First, of course, came the aristocracy of the immense plantations. While the social and political dominance of this class was based on wealth, yet some of its members were derived from the English gentry, with, perhaps, an occasional one from a noble family in the

[1] Fithian, 177. [2] See catalogue in *W. and M. C. Q.*, x and xi.

[3] See catalogue in Appendix A to Byrd's *Writings:* Bassett.

[4] See catalogue of John Adams's Library, in the Boston Public Library.

[5] Ambler, 9; and see Wise, 68–70.

mother country.[1] Many, however, were English merchants or their sons.[2] It appears, also, that the boldest and thriftiest of the early Virginia settlers, whom the British Government exiled for political offenses, acquired extensive possessions, became large slave-owners, and men of importance and position. So did some who were indentured servants;[3] and, indeed, an occasional transported convict rose to prominence.[4]

But the genuine though small aristocratic element gave tone and color to colonial Virginia society. All, except the "poor whites," looked to this supreme group for ideals and for standards of manners and conduct. "People of fortune . . . are the pattern of all behaviour here," testifies Fithian of New Jersey, tutor in the Carter household.[5] Also, it was, of course, the natural ambition of wealthy planters and those who expected to become such to imitate the life of the English higher classes. This was much truer in Virginia than in any other colony; for she had been more faithful to the Crown and to the

[1] Trustworthy data on this subject is given in the volumes of the *Va. Mag. Hist. and Biog.*; see also *W. and M. C. Q.*

[2] Wertenbaker: *P. and P.*, 14–20. But see William G. Stanard's exhaustive review of Mr. Wertenbaker's book in *Va. Mag. Hist. and Biog.*, xviii, 339–48.

[3] "One hundred young maids for wives, as the former ninety sent. One hundred boys more for apprentices likewise to the public tenants. One hundred servants to be disposed among the old planters which they exclusively desire and will pay the company their charges" (*Virginia Company Records*, i, 66; and see Fithian, 111.)

[4] For the understanding in England at that period of the origin of this class of Virginia colonists see Defoe: *Moll Flanders*, 65 *et seq.* On transported convicts see *Amer. Hist. Rev.*, ii. 12 *et seq.* For summary of the matter see Channing, i, 210–14, 226–27.

[5] Fithian to Greene, Dec. 1, 1773; Fithian, 280.

royal ideal than had her sisters. Thus it was that the Old Dominion developed a distinctively aristocratic and chivalrous social atmosphere peculiar to herself,[1] as Jefferson testifies.

Next to the dominant class came the lesser planters. These corresponded to the yeomanry of the mother country; and most of them were from the English trading classes.[2] They owned little holdings of land from a few hundred to a thousand and even two thousand acres; and each of these inconsiderable landlords acquired a few slaves in proportion to his limited estate. It is possible that a scanty number of this middle class were as well born as the best born of the little nucleus of the genuine aristocracy; these were the younger sons of great English houses to whom the law of primogeniture denied equal opportunity in life with the elder brother. So it came to pass that the upper reaches of the second estate in the social and industrial Virginia of that time merged into the highest class.

At the bottom of the scale, of course, came the poverty-stricken whites. In eastern Virginia this was the class known as the "poor whites"; and it was more distinct than either of the two classes above it. These "poor whites" lived in squalor, and without the aspirations or virtues of the superior orders. They carried to the extreme the examples of

[1] Fithian to Peck, Aug. 12, 1774; Fithian, 286–88; and see Professor Tucker's searching analysis in Tucker, i, 17–22; also see Lee, in Ford: *P. on C.*, 296–97. As to a genuinely aristocratic *group*, the New York patroons were, perhaps, the most distinct in the country.

[2] Wertenbaker: *P. and P.*, 14–20; also *Va. Mag. Hist. and Biog.*, xviii, 339–48.

idleness given them by those in higher station, and coarsened their vices to the point of brutality.[1] Near this social stratum, though not a part of it, were classed the upland settlers, who were poor people, but highly self-respecting and of sturdy stock.

Into this structure of Virginia society Fate began to weave a new and alien thread about the time that Thomas Marshall took his young bride to the log cabin in the woods of Prince William County where their first child was born. In the back country bordering the mountains appeared the scattered huts of the pioneers. The strong character of this element of Virginia's population is well known, and its coming profoundly influenced for generations the political, social, industrial, and military history of that section. They were jealous of their "rights," impatient of restraint, wherever they felt it, and this was seldom. Indeed, the solitariness of their lives, and the utter self-dependence which this forced upon them, made them none too tolerant of law in any form.

These outpost settlers furnished most of that class so well known to our history by the term "backwoodsmen," and yet so little understood. For the heroism, the sacrifice, and the suffering of this "advance guard of civilization" have been pictured

[1] For accounts of brutal physical combats, see Anburey, ii, 310 *et seq.* And for dueling, though at an earlier period, see Wise, 329–31. The practice of dueling rapidly declined; but fighting of a violent and often repulsive character persisted, as we shall see, far into the nineteenth century. Also, see La Rochefoucauld, Chastellux, and other travelers, *infra*, chap. VII.

by laudatory writers to the exclusion of its other and less admirable qualities. Yet it was these latter characteristics that played so important a part in that critical period of our history between the surrender of the British at Yorktown and the adoption of the Constitution, and in that still more fateful time when the success of the great experiment of making out of an inchoate democracy a strong, orderly, independent, and self-respecting nation was in the balance.

These American backwoodsmen, as described by contemporary writers who studied them personally, pushed beyond the inhabited districts to get land and make homes more easily. This was their underlying purpose; but a fierce individualism, impatient even of those light and vague social restraints which the existence of near-by neighbors creates, was a sharper spur.[1] Through both of these motives, too, ran the spirit of mingled lawlessness and adventure. The physical surroundings of the backwoodsman nourished the non-social elements of his character. The log cabin built, the surrounding patch of clearing made, the seed planted for a crop of cereals only large enough to supply the household needs — these almost ended the backwoodsman's agricultural activities and the habits of regular industry which farming requires.

While his meager crops were coming on, the backwoodsman must supply his family with food from the stream and forest. The Indians had not yet retreated so far, nor were their atrocities so remote,

[1] Schoepf, i, 261; and see references, *infra*, chap. VII.

that fear of them had ceased;[1] and the eye of the backwoodsman was ever keen for a savage human foe as well as for wild animals. Thus he became a man of the rifle,[2] a creature of the forests, a dweller amid great silences, self-reliant, suspicious, non-social, and almost as savage as his surroundings.[3]

But among them sometimes appeared families which sternly held to high purposes, orderly habits, and methodical industry;[4] and which clung to moral and religious ideals and practices with greater tenacity than ever, because of the very difficulties of their situation. These chosen families naturally became the backbone of the frontier; and from them came the strong men of the advanced settlements.

[1] After Braddock's defeat the Indians "extended their raids . . . pillaging and murdering in the most ruthless manner . . . The whole country from New York to the heart of Virginia became the theatre of inhuman barbarities and heartless destruction." (Lowdermilk, 186.)

[2] Although the rifle did not come into general use until the Revolution, the firearms of this period have been so universally referred to as "rifles" that I have, for convenience, adopted this inaccurate term in the first two chapters.

[3] "Their actions are regulated by the wildness of the neighbourhood. The deer often come to eat their grain, the wolves to destroy their sheep, the bears to kill their hogs, the foxes to catch their poultry. This surrounding hostility immediately puts the gun into their hands, . . . and thus by defending their property, they soon become professed hunters; . . . once hunters, farewell to the plough. The chase renders them ferocious, gloomy, and unsociable; a hunter wants no neighbour, he rather hates them. . . . The manners of the Indian natives are respectable, compared with this European medley. Their wives and children live in sloth and inactivity . . . You cannot imagine what an effect on manners the great distance they live from each other has. . . . Eating of wild meat . . . tends to alter their temper. . . . I have seen it." (Crèvecœur, 66–68.) Crèvecœur was himself a frontier farmer. (*Writings:* Sparks, ix, footnote to 259.)

[4] "Many families carry with them all their decency of conduct, purity of morals, and respect of religion; but these are scarce." (Crèvecœur, 70.) Crèvecœur says his family was one of these.

Such a figure among the backwoodsmen was Thomas Marshall. Himself a product of the settlements on the tidewater, he yet was the personification of that spirit of American advance and enterprise which led this son of the Potomac lowlands ever and ever westward until he ended his days in the heart of Kentucky hundreds of miles through the savage wilderness from the spot where, as a young man, he built his first cabin home.

This, then, was the strange mingling of human elements that made up Virginia society during the middle decades of the eighteenth century — a society peculiar to the Old Dominion and unlike that of any other place or time. For the most part, it was idle and dissipated, yet also hospitable and spirited, and, among the upper classes, keenly intelligent and generously educated. When we read of the heavy drinking of whiskey, brandy, rum, and heady wine; of the general indolence, broken chiefly by fox-hunting and horse-racing, among the quality; of the coarser sport of cock-fighting shared in common by landed gentry and those of baser condition, and of the eagerness for physical encounter which seems to have pervaded the whole white population,[1] we wonder at the greatness of mind and soul which grew from such a social soil.

Yet out of it sprang a group of men who for ability, character, spirit, and purpose, are not outshone and have no precise counterpart in any other company of illustrious characters appearing in like space of time

[1] This bellicose trait persisted for many years and is noted by all contemporary observers.

and similar extent of territory. At almost the same point of time, historically speaking, — within thirty years, to be exact, — and on the same spot, geographically speaking, — within a radius of a hundred miles, — George Mason, James Madison, Patrick Henry, Thomas Jefferson, John Marshall, and George Washington were born. The life stories of these men largely make up the history of their country while they lived; and it was chiefly their words and works, their thought and purposes, that gave form and direction, on American soil, to those political and social forces which are still working out the destiny of the American people.

CHAPTER II

A FRONTIER EDUCATION

"Come to me," quoth the pine tree,
"I am the giver of honor." (Emerson.)

I do not think the greatest things have been done for the world by its bookmen. Education is not the chips of arithmetic and grammar. (Wendell Phillips.)

JOHN MARSHALL was never out of the simple, crude environment of the near frontier for longer than one brief space of a few months until his twentieth year, when, as lieutenant of the famous Culpeper Minute Men, he marched away to battle. The life he had led during this period strengthened that powerful physical equipment which no strain of his later years seemed to impair; and helped to establish that extraordinary nervous equilibrium which no excitement or contest ever was able to unbalance.[1] This foundation part of his life was even more influential on the forming mind and spiritual outlook of the growing youth.

Thomas Marshall left the little farm of poor land in Westmoreland County not long after the death of his father, John Marshall "of the forest." This ancestral "estate" had no attractions for the enterprising young man. Indeed, there is reason for thinking that he abandoned it.[2] He lifted his first

[1] Story, in Dillon, iii, 334.

[2] The records of Westmoreland County do not show what disposition Thomas Marshall made of the one hundred acres given him by his mother. (Letter of Albert Stuart, Deputy Clerk of Westmoreland County, Virginia, to the author, Aug. 26, 1913.) He probably abandoned it just as John Washington and Thomas Pope abandoned one thousand acres of the same land. (*Supra.*)

rooftree in what then were still the wilds of Prince William County.[1] There we find him with his young wife, and there in the red year of British disaster his eldest son was born. The cabin has long since disappeared, and only a rude monument of native stone, erected by college students in recent years, now marks the supposed site of this historic birthplace.

The spot is a placid, slumberous countryside. A small stream runs hard by. In the near distance still stands one of the original cabins of Spotswood's Germans.[2] But the soil is not generous. When Thomas Marshall settled there the little watercourse at the foot of the gentle slope on which his cabin stood doubtless ran bank-full; for in 1754 the forests remained thick and unviolated about his cabin,[3] and fed the waters from the heavy rains in restrained and steady flow to creek and river channels. Amidst these surroundings four children of Thomas Marshall and Mary Keith were born.[4]

The sturdy young pioneer was not content to remain permanently at Germantown. A few years later found him building another home about thirty

[1] Westmoreland County is on the Potomac River near its entrance into Chesapeake Bay. Prince William is about thirty miles farther up the river. Marshall was born about one hundred miles by wagon road from Appomattox Creek, northwest toward the Blue Ridge and in the wilderness.

[2] Campbell, 404–05.

[3] More than forty years later the country around the Blue Ridge was still a dense forest. (La Rochefoucauld, iii, 173.) And the road even from Richmond to Petersburg, an hundred miles east and south of the Marshall cabin, as late as 1797 ran through "an almost uninterrupted succession of woods." (*Ib.*, 106; and see *infra*, chap. VII.)

[4] John, 1755; Elizabeth, 1756; Mary, 1757; Thomas, 1761.

miles farther westward, in a valley in the Blue Ridge Mountains.[1] Here the elder son spent the critical space of life from childhood to his eighteenth year. This little building still stands, occupied by negroes employed on the estate of which it forms a part. The view from it even now is attractive; and in the days of John Marshall's youth must have been very beautiful.

The house is placed on a slight rise of ground on the eastern edge of the valley. Near by, to the south and closer still to the west, two rapid mountain streams sing their quieting, restful song. On all sides the Blue Ridge lifts the modest heights of its purple hills. This valley at that time was called "The Hollow," and justly so; for it is but a cup in the lazy and unambitious mountains. When the eldest son first saw this frontier home, great trees thickly covered mountain, hill, and glade, and surrounded the meadow, which the Marshall dwelling overlooked, with a wall of inviting green.[2]

Two days by the very lowest reckoning it must have taken Thomas Marshall to remove his family to this new abode. It is more likely that three or four days were consumed in the toilsome task. The very careful maps of the British survey at that time show only three roads in all immense Prince William County.[3] On one of these the Marshalls might have made their way northward, and on another, which it probably joined, they could have traveled west-

[1] Binney, in Dillon, iii, 284.

[2] The ancient trunks of one or two of these trees still stand close to the house.

[3] British map of 1755; Virginia State Library.

ward. But these trails were primitive and extremely difficult for any kind of vehicle.[1]

Some time before 1765, then, rational imagination can picture a strong, rude wagon drawn by two horses crawling along the stumpy, rock-roughened, and mud-mired road through the dense woods that led in the direction of "The Hollow." In the wagon sat a young woman.[2] By her side a sturdy, red-cheeked boy looked out with alert but quiet interest showing from his brilliant black eyes; and three other children cried their delight or vexation as the hours wore on. In this wagon, too, were piled the little family's household goods; nor did this make a heavy load, for all the Lares and Penates of a frontier settler's family in 1760 would not fill a single room of a moderately furnished household in the present day.

By the side of the wagon strode a young man dressed in the costume of the frontier. Tall, broad-shouldered, lithe-hipped, erect, he was a very oak of a man. His splendid head was carried with a peculiar dignity; and the grave but kindly command that shone from his face, together with the brooding thoughtfulness and fearless light of his striking eyes,

[1] See La Rochefoucauld, iii, 707. These "roads" were scarcely more than mere tracks through the forests. See chap. VII, *infra*, for description of roads at the period between the close of the Revolution and the beginning of our National Government under the Constitution. Even in the oldest and best settled colonies the roads were very bad. Chalkley's *Augusta County* (*Va.*) *Records* show many orders regarding roads; but, considering the general state of highways, (see *infra*, chap. VII) these probably concerned very primitive efforts. When Thomas Marshall removed his family to the Blue Ridge, the journey must have been strenuous even for that hardship-seasoned man.

[2] She was born in 1737. (Paxton, 19.)

would have singled him out in any assemblage as a man to be respected and trusted. A negro drove the team, and a negro girl walked behind.[1]

So went the Marshalls to their Blue Ridge home. It was a commodious one for those days. Two rooms downstairs, one fifteen feet by sixteen, the other twelve by fourteen, and above two half-story lofts of the same dimensions, constituted this domestic castle. At one end of the larger downstairs room is a broad and deep stone fireplace, and from this rises a big chimney of the same material, supporting the house on the outside.[2]

Thomas and Mary Marshall's pride and aspiration, as well as their social importance among the settlers, are strongly shown by this frontier dwelling. Unlike those of most of the other backwoodsmen, it was not a log cabin, but a frame house built of whip-sawed uprights and boards.[3] It was perhaps easier to construct a one and a half story house with such materials; for to lift heavy timbers to such a height required great effort.[4] But Thomas Marshall's social, religious, and political status [5] in the newly organized County of Fauquier were the leading influences that

[1] At this time, Thomas Marshall had at least two slaves, inherited from his father. (Will of John Marshall "of the forest," Appendix I.) As late as 1797 (nearly forty years after Thomas Marshall went to "The Hollow"), La Rochefoucauld found that even on the "poorer" plantations about the Blue Ridge the "planters, however wretched their condition, have all of them one or two negroes." (La Rochefoucauld, iii, 135.)

[2] Personal inspection.

[3] Mill-sawed weather-boarding, held by cut nails, now covers the sides of the house, the original broad whip-sawed boards, fastened by wrought nails, having long since decayed.

[4] Practically all log cabins, at that time, had only one story.

[5] See *infra*.

induced him to build a house which, for the time and place, was so pretentious. A small stone "meat house," a one-room log cabin for his two negroes, and a log stable, completed the establishment.

In such an abode, and amidst such surroundings, the fast-growing family[1] of Thomas Marshall lived for more than twelve years. At first neighbors were few and distant. The nearest settlements were at Warrenton, some twenty-three miles to the eastward, and Winchester, a little farther over the mountains to the west.[2] But, with the horror of Braddock's defeat subdued by the widespread and decisive counter victories, settlers began to come into the country on both sides of the Blue Ridge. These were comparatively small farmers, who, later on, became raisers of wheat, corn, and other cereals, rather than tobacco.

Not until John Marshall had passed his early boyhood, however, did these settlers become sufficiently numerous to form even a scattered community, and his early years were enlivened with no child companionship except that of his younger brothers and sisters. For the most part his days were spent, rifle in hand, in the surrounding mountains, and by the pleasant waters that flowed through the valley of his forest home. He helped his mother, of course, with her many labors, did the innumerable chores which the day's work required, and looked after the

[1] Six more children were born while the Marshalls remained in "The Hollow": James M., 1764; Judith, 1766; William and Charles, 1767; Lucy, 1768; and Alexander, 1770.

[2] Nearly twenty years later, "Winchester was rude, wild, as nature had made it," but "it was less so than its inhabitants." (Mrs. Carrington to her sister Nancy, describing Winchester in 1777, from personal observation; MS.)

younger children, as the eldest child always must do. To his brothers and sisters as well as to his parents, he was devoted with a tenderness peculiar to his uncommonly affectionate nature and they, in turn, "fairly idolized" him.[1]

There were few of those minor conveniences which we to-day consider the most indispensable of the simplest necessities. John Marshall's mother, like most other women of that region and period, seldom had such things as pins; in place of them use was made of thorns plucked from the bushes in the woods.[2] The fare, naturally, was simple and primitive. Game from the forest and fish from the stream were the principal articles of diet. Bear meat was plentiful.[3] Even at that early period, salt pork and

[1] See Mrs. Carrington to her sister Nancy, *infra*, chap. v.

[2] John Marshall, when at the height of his career, liked to talk of these times. "He ever recurred with fondness to that primitive mode of life, when he partook with a keen relish of balm tea and mush; and when the females used thorns for pins." (Howe, 263, and see *Hist. Mag.*, iii, 166.)

Most of the settlers on the frontier and near frontier did not use forks or tablecloths. Washington found this condition in the house of a Justice of the Peace. "When we came to supper there was neither a Cloth upon ye Table nor a knife to eat with; but as good luck would have it, we had knives of our [own]." (*Writings:* Ford, i, 4.)

Chastellux testifies that, thirty years later, the frontier settlers were forced to make almost everything they used. Thus, as population increased, necessity developed men of many trades and the little communities became self-supporting. (Chastellux, 226–27.)

[3] More than a generation after Thomas Marshall moved to "The Hollow" in the Blue Ridge large quantities of bear and beaver skins were brought from the Valley into Staunton, not many miles away, just over the Ridge. (La Rochefoucauld, iii, 179–80.) The product of the Blue Ridge itself was sent to Fredericksburg and Alexandria. (See Crèvecœur, 63–65.) Thirty years earlier (1733) Colonel Byrd records that "Bears, Wolves, and Panthers" roamed about the site of Richmond; that deer were plentiful and rattlesnakes considered a delicacy. (Byrd's *Writings:* Bassett, 293, 318–19.)

salt fish probably formed a part of the family's food, though not to the extent to which such cured provisions were used by those of the back country in later years, when these articles became the staple of the border.[1]

Corn meal was the basis of the family's bread supply. Even this was not always at hand, and corn meal mush was welcomed with a shout by the clamorous brood with which the little cabin soon fairly swarmed. It could not have been possible for the Marshall family in their house on Goose Creek to have the luxury of bread made from wheat flour. The clothing of the family was mostly homespun. "Store goods," whether food, fabric, or utensil, could be got to Thomas Marshall's backwoods dwelling only with great difficulty and at prohibitive expense.[2]

But young John Marshall did not know that he was missing anything. On the contrary, he was conscious of a certain wealth not found in cities or among the currents of motion. For ever his eye looked out upon noble yet quieting, poetic yet placid, surroundings. Always he could have the in-

[1] See *infra*, chap. VII.

[2] Even forty years later, all "store" merchandise could be had in this region only by hauling it from Richmond, Fredericksburg, or Alexandria. Transportation from the latter place to Winchester cost two dollars and a half per hundredweight. In 1797, "store" goods of all kinds cost, in the Blue Ridge, thirty per cent more than in Philadelphia. (La Rochefoucauld, iii, 203.) From Philadelphia the cost was four to five dollars per hundredweight. While there appear to have been country stores at Staunton and Winchester, over the mountains (Chalkley's *Augusta County* (*Va.*) *Records*), the cost of freight to those places was prohibitive of anything but the most absolute necessities even ten years after the Constitution was adopted.

spiring views from the neighboring heights, the majestic stillness of the woods, the soothing music of meadow and stream. So uplifted was the boy by the glory of the mountains at daybreak that he always rose while the eastern sky was yet gray.[1] He was thrilled by the splendor of sunset and never tired of watching it until night fell upon the vast and somber forests. For the boy was charged with poetic enthusiasm, it appears, and the reading of poetry became his chief delight in youth and continued to be his solace and comfort throughout his long life;[2] indeed, Marshall liked to make verses himself, and never outgrew the habit.

There was in him a rich vein of romance; and, later on, this manifested itself by his passion for the great creations of fiction. Throughout his days he would turn to the works of favorite novelists for relaxation and renewal.[3]

The mental and spiritual effects of his surroundings on the forming mind and unfolding soul of this young American must have been as lasting and profound as were the physical effects on his body.[4] His environment and his normal, wholesome daily activities could not have failed to do its work in building the character of the growing boy. These and his sound, steady, and uncommonly strong parentage must, perforce, have helped to give him that courage for action, that balanced vision for judgment, and that serene outlook on life and its

[1] *Hist. Mag.*, iii, 166; Howe, 263; also, Story, in Dillon, iii, 334.
[2] Story, in Dillon, iii, 331–32. [3] *Ib.*
[4] See Binney, in Dillon, iii, 285.

problems, which were so notable and distinguished in his mature and rugged manhood.

Lucky for John Marshall and this country that he was not city born and bred; lucky that not even the small social activities of a country town drained away a single ohm of his nervous energy or obscured with lesser pictures the large panorama which accustomed his developing intelligence to look upon big and simple things in a big and simple way.

There were then no public schools in that frontier [1] region, and young Marshall went untaught save for the instruction his parents gave him. For this task his father was unusually well equipped, though not by any formal schooling. All accounts agree that Thomas Marshall, while not a man of any learning, had contrived to acquire a useful though limited education, which went much further with a man of his well-ordered mind and determined will than a university training could go with a man of looser fiber and cast in smaller mould. The father was careful, painstaking, and persistent in imparting to his children and particularly to John all the education he himself could acquire.

Between Thomas Marshall and his eldest son a mutual sympathy, respect, and admiration existed, as uncommon as it was wholesome and beneficial. "My father," often said John Marshall, "was a far

[1] "Fauquier was then a frontier county . . . far in advance of the ordinary reach of compact population." (Story, in Dillon, iii, 331; also see *New York Review* (1838), iii, 333.) Even a generation later (1797), La Rochefoucauld, writing from personal investigation, says (iii, 227–28): "There is no state so entirely destitute of all means of public education as Virginia."

abler man than any of his sons." [1] In "his private and familiar conversations with me," says Justice Story, "when there was no other listener . . . he never named his father . . . without dwelling on his character with a fond and winning enthusiasm . . . he broke out with a spontaneous eloquence . . . upon his virtues and talents." [2] Justice Story wrote a sketch of Marshall for the "National Portrait Gallery," in which Thomas Marshall is highly praised. In acknowledging the receipt of the magazine, Marshall wrote: "I am particularly gratified by the terms in which you speak of my father. If any contemporary, who knew him in the prime of manhood, survived, he would confirm all you say." [3]

So whether at home with his mother or on surveying trips with his father, the boy continually was under the influence and direction of hardy, clear-minded, unusual parents. Their lofty and simple ideals, their rational thinking, their unbending uprightness, their religious convictions — these were the intellectual companions of John Marshall's childhood and youth. While too much credit has not been given Thomas Marshall for the training of the eldest son, far too little has been bestowed on Mary Randolph Keith, who was, in all things, the equal of her husband.

Although, as we have seen, many books were brought into eastern Virginia by the rich planters, it was difficult for the dwellers on the frontier to secure any reading material. Most books had to be im-

[1] See Binney, in Dillon, iii, 285. [2] Story, in Dillon, iii, 330.
[3] Marshall to Story, July 31, 1833; Story, ii, 150.

ported, were very expensive, and, in the back country, there were no local sources of supply where they could be purchased. Also, the frontier settlers had neither the leisure nor, it appears, the desire for reading [1] that distinguished the wealthy landlords of the older parts of the colony.[2] Thomas Marshall, however, was an exception to his class in his eagerness for the knowledge to be gathered from books and in his determination that his children should have those advantages which reading gives.

So, while his small house in "The Hollow" of the Blue Ridge probably contained not many more books than children, yet such volumes as were on that frontier bookshelf were absorbed and made the intellectual possession of the reader. The Bible was there, of course; and probably Shakespeare also.[3] The only book which positively is known to have been a literary companion of John Marshall was a volume of Pope's poems. He told Justice Story that, by the time he was twelve years old (1767), he had copied every word of the "Essay on Man" and other of Pope's moral essays, and had committed to memory "many of the most interesting passages." [4] This

[1] See *infra*, chaps. VII and VIII.

[2] "A taste for reading is more prevalent [in Virginia] among the gentlemen of the first class than in any other part of America; but the common people are, perhaps, more ignorant than elsewhere." (La Rochefoucauld, iii, 232.) Other earlier and later travelers confirm this statement of this careful French observer.

[3] Story thinks that Thomas Marshall, at this time, owned Milton, Shakespeare, and Dryden. (Dillon, iii, 331.) This is possible. Twenty years later, Chastellux found Milton, Addison, and Richardson in the parlor of a New Jersey inn; but this was in the comparatively thickly settled country adjacent to Philadelphia. (Chastellux, 159.)

[4] Story, in Dillon, iii, 331, and Binney, in *ib.*, 283; *Hist. Mag.*, iii, 166.

would seem to prove that not many other attractive books were at the boyhood hands of so eager a reader of poetry and fiction as Marshall always was. It was quite natural that this volume should be in that primitive household; for, at that time, Pope was more widely read, admired, and quoted than any other writer either of poetry or prose.[1]

For those who believe that early impressions are important, and who wish to trace John Marshall's mental development back to its sources, it is well to spend a moment on that curious work which Pope named his "Essay on Man." The natural bent of the youth's mind was distinctively logical and orderly, and Pope's metred syllogisms could not but have appealed to it powerfully. The soul of Pope's "Essay" is the wisdom of and necessity for order; and it is plain that the boy absorbed this vital message and made it his own. Certain it is that even as a beardless young soldier, offering his life for his country's independence, he already had grasped the master truth that order is a necessary condition of liberty and justice.

It seems probable, however, that other books were brought to this mountain fireside. There was a limited store within his reach from which Thomas Marshall could draw. With his employer and friend, George Washington,[2] he was often a visitor at the

[1] Lang: *History of English Literature,* 384; and see Gosse: *History of Eighteenth Century Literature,* 131; also, Traill: *Social England,* v, 72; Stephen: *Alexander Pope,* 62; and see Cabot to Hamilton, Nov. 29, 1800; *Cabot:* Lodge, 299.

[2] Binney, in Dillon, iii, 283–84; Washington's ***Diary;*** MS., Lib. Cong.

wilderness home of Lord Fairfax just over the Blue Ridge. Washington availed himself of the Fairfax Library,[1] and it seems reasonable that Thomas Marshall did the same. It is likely that he carried to his Blue Ridge dwelling an occasional Fairfax volume carefully selected for its usefulness in developing his own as well as his children's minds.

This contact with the self-expatriated nobleman had more important results, however, than access to his books. Thomas Marshall's life was profoundly influenced by his early and intimate companionship with the well-mannered though impetuous and headstrong young Washington, who engaged him as assistant surveyor of the Fairfax estate.[2] From youth to manhood, both had close association with Lord Fairfax, who gave Washington his first employment and secured for him the appointment by the colonial authorities as public surveyor.[3] Washington was related by marriage to the proprietor of the Northern Neck, his brother Lawrence having married the daughter of William Fairfax. When their father died, Lawrence Washington took the place of parent to his younger brother;[4] and in his house the great landowner met George Washington, of whom he became very fond. For more than three years the youthful surveyor passed most of his time in the Blue Ridge part of the British nobleman's vast

[1] Irving, i, 45; and Lodge: *Washington*, i, 59. Many years later when he became rich, Washington acquired a good library, part of which is now in the Boston Athenæum. But as a young and moneyless surveyor he had no books of his own and his "book" education was limited and shallow.

[2] Binney, in Dillion, iii, 281–84.

[3] Irving, i, 37, 45; and Sparks, 10.

[4] Irving, i, 27.

holdings,[1] and in frequent and intimate contact with his employer. Thus Thomas Marshall, as Washington's associate and helper, came under the guidance and example of Lord Fairfax.

The romantic story of this strange man deserves to be told at length, but only a résumé is possible here. This summary, however, must be given for its bearing on the characters of George Washington and Thomas Marshall, and, through them, its formative influence on John Marshall.[2]

Lord Fairfax inherited his enormous Virginia estate from his mother, the daughter of Lord Culpeper, the final grantee of that kingly domain. This profligate grant of a careless and dissolute monarch embraced some five million acres between the Potomac and Rappahannock Rivers back to a straight line connecting the sources of these streams. While the young heir of the ancient Fairfax title was in Oxford, his father having died, his mother and grandmother, the dowager Ladies Fairfax and Culpeper, forced him to cut off the entail of the extensive Fairfax estates in England in order to save the heavily mortgaged Culpeper estates in the same country; and as compensation for this sacrifice, the noble Oxford student was promised the inheritance of this wild Virginia forest principality.

Nor did the youthful baron's misfortunes end there. The lady of his heart had promised to become his bride, the wedding day was set, the prepara-

[1] Irving, i, 46.

[2] As will appear, the Fairfax estate is closely interwoven into John Marshall's career. (See vol. II of this work.)

tions made. But before that hour of joy arrived, this fickle daughter of ambition received an offer to become a duchess instead of a mere baroness, and, throwing over young Fairfax without delay, she embraced the more exalted station offered her.

These repeated blows of adversity embittered the youthful head of the illustrious house of Fairfax against mother and grandmother, and, for the time being, all but against England itself. So, after some years of management of his Virginia estate by his cousin, William, who was in Government employ in America, Lord Fairfax himself left England forever, came to Virginia, took personal charge of his inherited holdings, and finally established himself at its very outskirts on the savage frontier. In the Shenandoah Valley, near Winchester, he built a small house of native stone and called it Greenway Court,[1] after the English fashion; but it never was anything more than a hunting lodge.[2]

From this establishment he personally managed his vast estates, parting with his lands to settlers on easy terms. His tenants generally were treated with liberality and consideration. If any land that was leased or sold did not turn out as was expected by the purchaser or lessee, another and better tract would be given in its place. If money was needed for improvements, Lord Fairfax advanced it. His excess revenues were given to the poor. So that the Northern Neck under Lord Fairfax's administration

[1] For description of Greenway Court see Pecquet du Bellet, ii, 175.
[2] Washington's *Writings:* Ford, i, footnote to 329.

became the best settled, best cultivated, and best governed of all the upper regions of the colony.[1]

Through this exile of circumstance, Fate wove another curious thread in the destiny of John Marshall. Lord Fairfax was the head of that ancient house whose devotion to liberty had been proved on many a battlefield. The second Lord Fairfax commanded the Parliamentary forces at Marston Moor. The third Lord Fairfax was the general of Cromwell's army and the hero of Naseby. So the proprietor of the Northern Neck, who was the sixth Lord Fairfax, came of blood that had been poured out for human rights. He had, as an inheritance of his house, that love of liberty for which his ancestors had fought.[2]

But much as he hated oppression, Lord Fairfax was equally hostile to disorder and upheaval; and his forbears had opposed these even to the point of helping restore Charles II to the throne. Thus the Virginia baron's talk and teaching were of liberty with order, independence with respect for law.[3]

[1] For a clear but laudatory account of Lord Fairfax see Appendix No. 4 to Burnaby, 197–213. But Fairfax could be hard enough on those who opposed him, as witness his treatment of Joist Hite. (See *infra*, chap. v.)

[2] When the Revolution came, however, Fairfax was heartily British. The objection which the colony made to the title to his estate doubtless influenced him.

[3] Fairfax was a fair example of the moderate, as distinguished from the radical or the reactionary. He was against both irresponsible autocracy and unrestrained democracy. In short, he was what would now be termed a liberal conservative (although, of course, such a phrase, descriptive of that demarcation, did not then exist). Much attention should be given to this unique man in tracing to their ultimate sources the origins of John Marshall's economic, political, and social convictions.

He loved literature and was himself no mean writer, his contributions while he was in the University having been accepted by the "Spectator."[1] His example instructed his companions in manners, too, and schooled them in the speech and deportment of gentlemen. All who met George Washington in his mature years were impressed by his correct if restricted language, his courtly conduct, and his dignified if rigid bearing. Much of this was due to his noble patron.[2]

Thomas Marshall was affected in the same way and by the same cause. Pioneer and backwoodsman though he was, and, as we shall see, true to his class and section, he yet acquired more balanced ideas of liberty, better manners, and finer if not higher views of life than the crude, rough individualists who inhabited the back country. As was the case with Washington, this intellectual and moral tendency in Thomas Marshall's development was due, in large measure, to the influence of Lord Fairfax. While it cannot be said that George Washington imitated the wilderness nobleman, yet Fairfax undoubtedly afforded his protégé a certain standard of living, thinking, and acting; and Thomas Marshall followed the example set by his fellow surveyor.[3] Thus came into the Marshall household a different atmosphere from that which pervaded the cabins of the Blue Ridge.

[1] Sparks, 11; and Irving, i, 33.

[2] For Fairfax's influence on Washington see Irving, i, 45; and in general, for fair secondary accounts of Fairfax, see *ib.*, 31–46; and Sparks, 10–11.

[3] Senator Humphrey Marshall says that Thomas Marshall "emulated" Washington. (Humphrey Marshall, i, 345.)

All this, however, did not make for his unpopularity among Thomas Marshall's distant, scattered, and humbly placed neighbors. On the contrary, it seems to have increased the consideration and respect which his native qualities had won for him from the pioneers. Certainly Thomas Marshall was the foremost man in Fauquier County when it was established in 1759. He was almost immediately elected to represent the county in the Virginia House of Burgesses;[1] and, six years later, he was appointed Sheriff by Governor Fauquier, for whom the county was named.[2] The shrievalty was, at that time, the most powerful local office in Virginia; and the fees and perquisites of the place made it the most lucrative.[3]

By 1765 Thomas Marshall felt himself sufficiently established to acquire the land where he had lived since his removal from Germantown. In the autumn of that year he leased from Thomas Ludwell Lee and Colonel Richard Henry Lee the three hundred and thirty acres on Goose Creek "whereon the said Thomas Marshall now lives." The lease was "for and during the natural lives of . . . Thomas Marshall, Mary Marshall his wife, and John Marshall his son and . . . the longest liver of them." The consideration was "five shillings current money in

[1] See *infra*.

[2] Bond of Thomas Marshall as Sheriff, Oct. 26, 1767; Records of Fauquier County (Va.), Deed Book, iii, 70. Approval of bond by County Court; Minute Book (from 1764 to 1768), 322. Marshall's bond was "to his Majesty, George III," to secure payment to the British revenue officers of all money collected by Marshall for the Crown. (Records of Fauquier County (Va.), Deed Book, iii, 71.)

[3] Bruce: *Inst.*, i, 597, 600; also, ii, 408, 570–74.

hand paid" and a "yearly rent of five pounds current money, and the quit rents and Land Tax." [1]

In 1769 Leeds Parish, embracing Fauquier County, was established.[2] Of this parish Thomas Marshall became the principal vestryman.[3] This office supplemented, in dignity and consequence, that of sheriff; the one was religious and denoted high social status, the other was civil and evidenced political importance.[4] The occupancy of both marked Thomas Marshall as the chief figure in the local government and in the social and political life of Fauquier County, although the holding of the superior office of burgess left no doubt as to his leadership. The vestries had immense influence in the civil affairs of the parish and the absolute management of the practical business of the established (Episcopal) church.[5] Among the duties and privileges of the vestry was that of selecting and employing the clergyman.[6]

The vestry of Leeds Parish, with Thomas Mar-

[1] Records of Fauquier County (Va.), Deed Book, ii, 42. There is a curious record of a lease from Lord Fairfax in 1768 to John Marshall for his life and "the natural lives of Mary his wife and Thomas Marshall his son and every of them longest living." (Records of Fauquier County (Va.), Deed Book, iii, 230.) John Marshall was then only thirteen years old. The lease probably was to Thomas Marshall, the clerk of Lord Fairfax having confused the names of father and son.

[2] Meade, ii, 218.

[3] In 1773 three deeds for an aggregate of two hundred and twenty acres "for a glebe" were recorded in Fauquier County to "Thos. Marshall & Others, Gentlemen, & Vestrymen of Leeds Parish." (Records of Fauquier County (Va.), Deed Book, v, 401, 403, 422.)

[4] The vestrymen were "the foremost men . . . in the parish . . . whether from the point of view of intelligence, wealth or social position." (Bruce: *Inst.*, i, 62; and see Meade, i, 191.)

[5] Bruce: *Inst.*, i, 62–93; and see Eckenrode: *S. C. & S.*, 13.

[6] Bruce: *Inst.*, i, 131 *et seq.*

shall at its head, chose for its minister a young Scotchman, James Thompson, who had arrived in Virginia a year or two earlier. He lived at first with the Marshall family.[1] Thus it came about that John Marshall received the first of his three short periods of formal schooling; for during his trial year the young[2] Scotch deacon returned Thomas Marshall's hospitality by giving the elder children such instruction as occasion offered,[3] as was the custom of parsons, who always were teachers as well as preachers. We can imagine the embryo clergyman instructing the eldest son under the shade of the friendly trees in pleasant weather or before the blazing logs in the great fireplace when winter came. While living with the Marshall family, he doubtless slept with the children in the half-loft[4] of that frontier dwelling.

There was nothing unusual about this; indeed, circumstances made it the common and unavoidable custom. Washington tells us that in his surveying trips, he frequently slept on the floor in the room of a settler's cabin where the fireplace was and where husband, wife, children, and visitors stretched themselves for nightly rest; and he remarks that the person was lucky who got the spot nearest the fireplace.[5]

[1] Meade, ii, 219. Bishop Meade here makes a slight error. He says that Mr. Thompson "lived at first in the family of Colonel Thomas Marshall, of Oak Hill." Thomas Marshall did not become a colonel until ten years afterward. (Heitman, 285.) And he did not move to Oak Hill until 1773, six years later. (Paxton, 20.)

[2] James Thompson was born in 1739. (Meade, ii, 219.) [3] *Ib.*

[4] Forty years later La Rochefoucauld found that the whole family and all visitors slept in the same room of the cabins of the back country. (La Rochefoucauld, iv, 595–96.)

[5] "I have not sleep'd above three nights or four in a bed, but, after walking . . . all the day, I lay down before the fire upon a little hay,

At the end of a year the embryo Scottish clergyman's character, ability, and services having met the approval of Thomas Marshall and his fellow vestrymen, Thompson returned to England for orders.[1] So ended John Marshall's first instruction from a trained teacher. His pious tutor returned the next year, at once married a young woman of the Virginia frontier, and settled on the glebe near Salem, where he varied his ministerial duties by teaching such children of his parishioners as could get to him. It may be that John Marshall was among them.[2]

In the light they throw upon the Marshall family, the political opinions of Mr. Thompson are as important as was his teaching. True to the impulses of youth, he was a man of the people, ardently championed their cause, and was fervently against British misrule, as was his principal vestryman. Five years later we find him preaching a sermon

straw, fodder or bearskin . . . with man, wife, and children, like a parcel of dogs and cats; and happy is he, who gets the berth nearest the fire." (Washington to a friend, in 1748; *Writings:* Ford, i, 7.)

Here is another of Washington's descriptions of frontier comforts: "I not being so good a woodsman as ye rest of my company, striped myself very orderly and went into ye Bed, as they calld it, when to my surprize, I found it to be nothing but a little straw matted together without sheets or any thing else, but only one thread bear [*sic*] blanket with double its weight of vermin such as Lice, Fleas, &c." (Washington's *Diary*, March 15, 1747; *ib.*, 2.) And see La Rochefoucauld, iii, 175, for description of homes of farmers in the Valley forty years later — miserable log huts "which swarmed with children." Thomas Marshall's little house was much better than, and the manners of the family were far superior to, those described by Washington and La Rochefoucauld.

[1] Meade, ii, 219.

[2] *Ib.* Bishop Meade says that Thomas Marshall's sons were sent to Mr. Thompson again; but Marshall himself told Justice Story that the Scotch parson taught him when the clergyman lived at his father's house.

on the subject so strong that a part of it has been preserved.[1]

Thus the years of John Marshall's life sped on until his eighteenth birthday. By this time Thomas Marshall's rapidly growing prosperity enabled him to buy a larger farm in a more favorable locality. In January, 1773, he purchased from Thomas Turner seventeen hundred acres adjacent to North Cobler Mountain, a short distance to the east of his first location in "The Hollow."[2] For this plantation he paid "nine hundred and twelve pounds ten shillings current money of Virginia." Here he established himself for the third time and remained for ten years.

On an elevation overlooking valley, stream, and grove, with the Blue Ridge as a near background, he built a frame house thirty-three by thirty feet, the attic or loft under the roof serving as a second story.[3] The house had seven rooms, four below and three above. One of the upper rooms is, comparatively, very large, being twenty-one by fifteen feet; and, according to tradition, this was used as a schoolroom for the Marshall children. Indeed, the structure was, for that section and period, a pretentious

[1] Meade, ii, 219. This extract of Mr. Thompson's sermon was treasonable from the Tory point of view. See *infra*, chap. III.

[2] Records of Fauquier County (Va.), Deed Book, v, 282. This purchase made Thomas Marshall the owner of about two thousand acres of the best land in Fauquier County. He had sold his Goose Creek holding in "The Hollow."

[3] The local legend, current to the present day, is that this house had the first glass windows in that region, and that the bricks in the chimney were imported from England. The importation of brick, however, is doubtful. Very little brick was brought to Virginia from England.

dwelling. This is the famous Oak Hill.[1] The house still stands as a modest wing to the large and attractive building erected by John Marshall's eldest son, Thomas, many years later.

A book was placed in the hands of John Marshall, at this time, that influenced his mind even more than his reading of Pope's poetry when a small boy. Blackstone's "Commentaries" was published in America in 1772 and one of the original subscribers was "Captain Thomas Marshall, Clerk of Dunmore County, Virginia."[2] The youthful backwoodsman read Blackstone with delight; for this legal classic is the poetry of law, just as Pope is logic in poetry. Also, Thomas Marshall saw to it that his son read Blackstone as carefully as circumstances permitted. He had bought the book for John's use as much as or more than for his own information. Marshall's parents, with a sharp eye on the calling that then brought greatest honor and profit, had determined that their eldest son should be a lawyer. "From my infancy," says Marshall, "I was destined for the bar."[3] He did not, we believe, give his attention exclusively to Blackstone. Indeed, it appears certain that his legal reading at this period was fragmentary and interrupted, for his time was taken up and his mind largely absorbed by military exercises

[1] Five more children of Thomas and Mary Marshall were born in this house: Louis, 1773; Susan, 1775; Charlotte, 1777; Jane, 1779; and Nancy, 1781. (Paxton.)

[2] This volume is now in the possession of Judge J. K. M. Norton, of Alexandria, Va. On several leaves are printed the names of the subscribers. Among them are Pelatiah Webster, James Wilson, Nathanael Greene, John Adams, and others.

[3] *Autobiography.*

and study. He was intent on mastering the art of war against the day when the call of patriotism should come to him to be a soldier.[1] So the law book was pushed aside by the manual of arms.

About this time John Marshall was given his second fragment of formal teaching. He was sent to the school of the Reverend Archibald Campbell in Westmoreland County.[2] This embryo "academy" was a primitive affair, but its solitary instructor was a sound classical scholar equipped with all the learning which the Scottish universities could give. He was a man of unusual ability, which, it appears, was the common possession of his family. He was the uncle of the British poet Campbell.[3]

The sons of this colonial parson school-teacher from Scotland became men of note and influence, one of them among the most distinguished lawyers of Virginia.[4] Indeed, it was chiefly in order to teach his two boys that Mr. Campbell opened his little school in Westmoreland.[5] So, while John Marshall attended the "academy" for only a few months, that brief period under such a teacher was worth much in methods of thought and study.

The third scanty fragment of John Marshall's education by professional instructors comes seven years later, at a time and under circumstances which make it necessary to defer a description of it.

[1] Binney, in Dillon, iii, 286.

[2] Story and Binney say that Marshall's first schooling was at Campbell's "academy" and his second and private instruction under Mr. Thompson. The reverse seems to have been the case.

[3] Meade, ii, 159, and footnote to 160.

[4] *Ib.*, 161. [5] *Ib.*

During all these years, however, young Marshall was getting another kind of education more real and more influential on his later life than any regular schooling could have given him. Thomas Marshall served in the House of Burgesses at Williamsburg[1] from 1761 until October, 1767, when he became Sheriff of Fauquier County.[2] In 1769 he was again chosen Burgess,[3] and reëlected until 1773, when he was appointed Clerk of Dunmore County.[4] In 1775 he once more appears as Burgess for Fauquier County.[5] Throughout this period, George Washington also served as Burgess from Westmoreland County. Thomas Marshall was a member of the standing committees on Trade, Religion, Propositions and Grievances, and on several special committees and commissions.[6]

[1] Journal, H.B. (1761–65), 3. Thomas Marshall was seldom out of office. Burgess, Sheriff, Vestryman, Clerk, were the promising beginnings of his crowded office-holding career. He became Surveyor of Fayette County, Kentucky, upon his removal to that district, and afterwards Collector of Revenue for the District of Ohio. (Humphrey Marshall, i, 120; and see ii, chap. v, of this work. Thomas Marshall to Adams, April 28, 1797; MS.) In holding offices, John Marshall followed in his father's footsteps.

[2] Journal, H.B. (1766–69), 147 and 257.

[3] His election was contested in the House, but decided in Marshall's favor. (*Ib.* (1761–69), 272, 290, 291.)

[4] *Ib.*, (1773–76), 9. County Clerks were then appointed by the Secretary of State. In some respects the Clerk of the County Court had greater advantages than the Sheriff. (See Bruce: *Inst.*, i, 588 *et seq.*) Dunmore County is now Shenandoah County. The Revolution changed the name. When Thomas Marshall was appointed Clerk, the House of Burgesses asked the Governor to issue a writ for a new election in Fauquier County to fill Marshall's place as Burgess. (*Ib.* (1773–76), 9.)

[5] *Ib.* (1766–69), 163.

[6] *Ib.*, 16, 71, 257; (1770–72), 17, 62, 123, 147, 204, 234, 251, 257, 274, 292; (1773–76), 217, 240.

The situations, needs, and interests of the upland counties above the line of the falls of the rivers, so different from those on the tidewater, had made the political oligarchy of the lower counties more distinct and conspicuous than ever. This dominant political force was aristocratic and selfish. It was generally hostile to the opinions of the smaller pioneer landowners of the back country and it did not provide adequately for their necessities. Their petitions for roads, bridges, and other indispensable requisites of social and industrial life usually were denied; and their rapidly growing democratic spirit was scorned with haughty disfavor and contempt.[1]

In the House of Burgesses, one could tell by his apparel and deportment, no less than by his sentiments, a member from the mountains, and indeed from anywhere above the fall line of the rivers; and, by the same tokens, one from the great plantations below. The latter came fashionably attired, according to the latest English mode, with the silk knee breeches and stockings, colored coat, ornamented waistcoat, linen and lace, buckled shoes, garters, and all details of polite adornment that the London fashion of the time dictated. The upland men were plainly clad; and those from the border appeared in their native homespun, with buckskin shirts, coonskin caps, and the queue of their unpowdered hair tied in a bag or sack of some thin material. To this upland class of Burgesses, Thomas Marshall belonged.

He had been a member of the House for four years

[1] Ambler, Introduction.

when the difference between the two Virginia sections and classes suddenly crystallized. The upper counties found a leader and fought and overcame the hitherto invincible power of the tidewater aristocracy, which, until then, had held the Government of Virginia in its lordly hand.

This explosion came in 1765, when John Marshall was ten years old. For nearly a quarter of a century the combination of the great planter interests of eastern Virginia had kept John Robinson Speaker of the House and Treasurer of the Colony.[1] He was an ideal representative of his class — rich, generous, kindly, and ever ready to oblige his fellow members of the ruling faction.[2] To these he had lent large sums of money from the public treasury and, at last, finding himself lost unless he could find a way out of the financial quagmire in which he was sinking, Robinson, with his fellow aristocrats, devised a scheme for establishing a loan office, equipping it with a million and a quarter of dollars borrowed on the faith of the colony, to be lent to individuals on personal security.[3] A bill to this effect was presented and the tidewater machine was oiled and set in motion to put it through.

As yet, Robinson's predicament was known only to himself and those upon whom he had bestowed the proceeds of the people's taxes; and no opposition was expected to the proposed resolution which would extricate the embarrassed Treasurer. But Patrick Henry, a young member from Hanover County, who had just been elected to the House of

[1] Ambler, 17–18. [2] Henry, i, 71. [3] *Ib.*, 76–77.

Burgesses and who had displayed in the famous Parsons case a courage and eloquence which had given him a reputation throughout the colony,[1] opposed, on principle, the proposed loan-office law. In a speech of startling power he attacked the bill and carried with him every member from the up counties. The bill was lost.[2] It was the first defeat ever experienced by the combination that had governed Virginia so long that they felt that it was their inalienable right to do so. One of the votes that struck this blow was cast by Thomas Marshall.[3] Robinson died the next year; his defalcation was discovered and the real purpose of the bill was thus revealed.[4]

Quick on the heels of this victory for popular rights and honest government trod another event of vital influence on American history. The British Parliament, the year before, had passed resolutions declaring the right of Parliament to tax the colonies without representation, and, indeed, to enact any law it pleased for the government and administration of British dominions wherever situated.[5] The

[1] Henry, i, 39–48.

[2] Wirt, 71 *et seq.* It passed the House (Journal, H.B. (1761–65), 350); but was disapproved by the Council. (*Ib.*, 356; and see Henry, i, 78.)

[3] The "ayes" and "noes" were not recorded in the Journals of the House; but Jefferson says, in his description of the event, which he personally witnessed, that Henry "carried with him all the members of the upper counties and left a minority composed merely of the aristocracy." (Wirt, 71.) "The members, who, like himself [Henry], represented the yeomanry of the colony, were filled with admiration and delight." (Henry, i, 78.)

[4] Wirt, 71. The incident, it appears, was considered closed with the defeat of the loan-office bill. Robinson having died, nothing further was done in the matter. For excellent condensed account see Eckenrode: *R. V.*, 16–17.

[5] Declaratory Resolutions.

colonies protested, Virginia among them; but when finally Parliament enacted the Stamp Act, although the colonies were in sullen anger, they yet prepared to submit.[1] The more eminent men among the Virginia Burgesses were willing to remonstrate once more, but had not the heart to go further.[2] It was no part of the plan or feeling of the aristocracy to affront the Royal Government openly. At this moment, Patrick Henry suddenly offered his historic resolutions, the last one a bold denial of Parliament's right to pass the Stamp Act, and a savage defiance of the British Government.[3]

Cautious members of the tidewater organization were aghast. They did not like the Stamp Act themselves, but they thought that this was going too far. The logical end of it would be armed conflict, they said; or at the very least, a temporary suspension of profitable commerce with England. Their material interests were involved; and while they hazarded these and life itself most nobly when the test of war finally came, ten years later, they were not minded to risk either business or comfort until forced to do so.[4]

But a far stronger influence with them was their hatred of Henry and their fear of the growing power of the up country. They were smarting from the defeat[5] of the loan-office bill. They did not relish the idea of following the audacious Henry and his

[1] For the incredible submission and indifference of the colonies before Patrick Henry's speech, see Henry, i, 63–67. The authorities given in those pages are conclusive.

[2] *Ib.*, 67. [3] *Ib.*, 80–81. [4] *Ib.*, 82–86.

[5] Wirt, 74–76.

democratic supporters from the hills. They resented the leadership which the "new men" were assuming. To the aristocratic machine it was offensive to have any movement originate outside itself.[1]

The up-country members to a man rallied about Patrick Henry and fought beneath the standard of principle which he had raised. The line that marked the division between these contending forces in the Virginia House of Burgesses was practically identical with that which separated them in the loan-office struggle which had just taken place. The same men who had supported Robinson were now against any measure which might too radically assert the rights of the colonies and offend both the throne and Westminster Hall. And as in the Robinson case so in the fight over Henry's Stamp Act Resolutions, the Burgesses who represented the frontier settlers and small landowners and who stood for their democratic views, formed a compact and militant force to strike for popular government as they already had struck, and successfully, for honest administration.[2]

Henry's fifth resolution was the first written American assertion of independence, the virile seed out of which the declaration at Philadelphia ten years later directly grew. It was over this resolution that Thomas Jefferson said, "the debate was most bloody";[3] and it was in this particular part of the debate that Patrick Henry made his immortal

[1] Eckenrode: *R. V.*, 5–6.

[2] "The members from the upper counties invariably supported Mr. Henry in his revolutionary measures." (Jefferson's statement to Daniel Webster, quoted in Henry, i, 87.)

[3] Henry, i, 86.

speech, ending with the famous words, "Tarquin and Cæsar had each his Brutus, Charles the First his Cromwell, and George the Third —" And as the cries of "Treason! Treason! Treason!" rang from every part of the hall, Henry, stretching himself to the utmost of his stature, thundered, "*— may profit by their example.* If *this* be treason, make the most of it." [1]

Henry and the stout-hearted men of the hills won the day, but only by a single vote. Peyton Randolph, the foremost member of the tidewater aristocracy and Royal Attorney-General, exclaimed, "By God, I would have given one [2] hundred guineas for a single vote!" [3] Thomas Marshall again fought by Henry's side and voted for his patriotic defiance of British injustice.[4]

This victory of the poorer section of the Old Dominion was, in Virginia, the real beginning of the active period of the Revolution. It was more — it

[1] Henry, i, 86, and authorities there cited in the footnote.

[2] Misquoted in Wirt (79) as "500 guineas."

[3] Jefferson to Wirt, Aug. 14, 1814; *Works:* Ford, xi, 404.

[4] It is most unfortunate that the "ayes" and "noes" were not kept in the House of Burgesses. In the absence of such a record, Jefferson's repeated testimony that the up-country members voted and worked with Henry must be taken as conclusive of Thomas Marshall's vote. For not only was Marshall Burgess from a frontier county, but Jefferson, at the time he wrote to Wirt in 1814 (and gave the same account to others later), had become very bitter against the Marshalls and constantly attacked John Marshall whom he hated virulently. If Thomas Marshall had voted out of his class and against Henry, so remarkable a circumstance would surely have been mentioned by Jefferson, who never overlooked any circumstance unfavorable to an enemy. Far more positive evidence, however, is the fact that Washington, who was a Burgess, voted with Henry, as his letter to Francis Dandridge, Sept. 20, 1765, shows. (*Writings:* Ford, ii, 209.) And Thomas Marshall always acted with Washington.

was the ending of the hitherto unquestioned supremacy of the tidewater aristocracy.[1] It marked the effective entrance of the common man into Virginia's politics and government.

When Thomas Marshall returned to his Blue Ridge home, he described, of course, the scenes he had witnessed and taken part in. The heart of his son thrilled, we may be sure, as he listened to his father reciting Patrick Henry's words of fire and portraying the manner, appearance, and conduct of that master orator of liberty. So it was that John Marshall, even when a boy, came into direct and living touch with the outside world and learned at first hand of the dramatic movement and the mighty forces that were about to quarry the materials for a nation.

Finally the epic year of 1775 arrived, — the year of the Boston riots, Paul Revere's ride, Lexington and Concord, — above all, the year of the Virginia Resolutions for Arming and Defense. Here we find Thomas Marshall a member of the Virginia Convention,[2] when once more the radicals of the up country met and defeated the aristocratic conservatives of the older counties. The latter counseled prudence. They argued weightily that the colony was not prepared for war with the Royal Power across the sea. They urged patience and the working-out of the problem by processes of conciliation and moderate devices, as those made timid by their

[1] "By these resolutions, Mr. Henry took the lead out of the hands of those who had heretofore guided the proceedings of the House." (Jefferson to Wirt, Aug. 14, 1814; *Works:* Ford, xi, 406.)

[2] *Proceedings*, Va. Conv., 1775, March 20, 3; July 17, 3, 5, 7.

own interests always do.[1] Selfish love of ease made them forget, for the moment, the lesson of Braddock's defeat. They held up the overwhelming might of Great Britain and the impotence of the King's subjects in his western dominions; and they were about to prevail.

But again Patrick Henry became the voice of America. He offered the Resolutions for Arming and Defense and carried them with that amazing speech ending with, "Give me liberty or give me death,"[2] which always will remain the classic of American liberty. Thomas Marshall, who sat beneath its spell, declared that it was "one of the most bold, animated, and vehement pieces of eloquence that had ever been delivered."[3] Once more he promptly took his stand under Henry's banner and supported the heroic resolutions with his vote and influence.[4] So did George Washington, as both had done ten years before in the battle over Henry's Stamp Act Resolutions in the House of Burgesses in 1765.[5]

Not from newspapers, then, nor from second-hand rumor did John Marshall, now nineteen years old, learn of the epochal acts of that convention. He

[1] Henry, i, 255–61; Wirt, 117–19. Except Henry's speech itself, Wirt's summary of the arguments of the conservatives is much the best account of the opposition to Henry's fateful resolutions.

[2] Wirt, 142; Henry, i, 261–66. [3] *Ib.*, 271; and Wirt, 143.

[4] In the absence of the positive proof afforded by a record of the "ayes" and "noes," Jefferson's testimony, Washington's vote, Thomas Marshall's tribute to Henry, and above all, the sentiment of the frontier county he represented, are conclusive testimony as to Thomas Marshall's stand in this all-important legislative battle which was the precursor of the iron conflict soon to come in which he bore so heroic a part. (See Humphrey Marshall, i, 344.)

[5] Washington was appointed a member of the committee provided for in Henry's second resolution. (Henry, i, 271.)

heard of them from his father's lips. Henry's inspired speech, which still burns across a century with undiminished power, came to John Marshall from one who had listened to it, as the family clustered around the fireside of their Oak Hill home. The effect on John Marshall's mind and spirit was heroic and profound, as his immediate action and his conduct for several years demonstrate.

We may be sure that the father was not deceived as to the meaning of it all; nor did he permit his family to be carried off the solid ground of reality by any emotional excitement. Thomas Marshall was no fanatic, no fancy-swayed enthusiast resolving highly in wrought-up moments and retracting humbly in more sober hours. He was a man who looked before he leaped; he counted the costs; he made up his mind with knowledge of the facts. When Thomas Marshall decided to act, no unforeseen circumstance could make him hesitate, no unexpected obstacle could swerve him from his course; for he had considered carefully and well; and his son was of like mettle.

So when Thomas Marshall came back to his Fauquier County home from the fateful convention of 1775 at Richmond, he knew just what the whole thing meant; and, so knowing, he gravely welcomed the outcome. He knew that it meant war; and he knew also what war meant. Already he had been a Virginia ranger and officer, had seen fighting, had witnessed wounds and death.[1] The same decision

[1] Thomas Marshall had been ensign, lieutenant, and captain in the militia, had taken part in the Indian wars, and was a trained soldier. (Crozier: *Virginia Colonial Militia*, 96.)

that made him cast his vote for Henry's resolutions also caused Thomas Marshall to draw his sword from its scabbard. It inspired him to do more; for the father took down the rifle from its deerhorn bracket and the hunting-knife from its hook, and placed them in the hands of his first-born. And so we find father and son ready for the field and prepared to make the ultimate argument of willingness to lay down their lives for the cause they believed in.

CHAPTER III

A SOLDIER OF THE REVOLUTION

Our liberties are at stake. It is time to brighten our fire-arms and learn to use them in the field. (Marshall to Culpeper Minute Men, 1775.)

Our sick naked, and well naked, our unfortunate men in captivity naked. (Washington, 1777.)

I have seen a regiment consisting of *thirty men* and a company of *one corporal.* (Von Steuben, 1778.)

THE fighting men of the up counties lost not a minute's time. Blood had been shed in New England; blood, they knew, must soon flow in Virginia. At once Culpeper, Orange, and Fauquier Counties arranged to raise a regiment of minute men with Lawrence Taliaferro of Orange as colonel, Edward Stevens of Culpeper as lieutenant, Thomas Marshall of Fauquier as major.[1] Out over the countryside went the word; and from mountain cabins and huts in forest clearings, from log abodes in secluded valleys and on primitive farms, the fighting yeomanry of northern Virginia came forth in answer.

In the years between Patrick Henry's two epochal appeals in 1765 and 1775, all Virginia, but particularly the back country, had been getting ready to make answer in terms of rifle and lead. "No man should scruple, or hesitate a moment, to use arms," wrote Washington in 1769.[2] Thomas Marshall's

[1] Slaughter, 107–08. This was "the first minute battalion raised within this Commonwealth." (Memorial of Thomas Marshall to the Virginia Legislature for military "emoluments"; MS. Archives, Va. St. Lib.) Appendix IV.

[2] Washington to Mason, April 5, 1769; *Writings:* Ford, ii, 263.

minister, Mr. Thompson, preached militant preparation; Parliament had deprived the colonists of "their just and legal rights" by acts which were "destructive of their liberties," thundered the parson; it had "overawed the inhabitants by British troops," loaded "great hardships" upon the people, and "reduced the poor to great want." The preacher exhorted his flock "as men and Christians" to help "supply the country with arms and ammunition," and referred his hearers, for specific information, to "the committee of this county,"[1] whose head undoubtedly was their Burgess and leading vestryman of the parish, Thomas Marshall.

When news of Concord and Lexington finally trickled through to upper Virginia, it found the men of her hills and mountains in grim readiness; and when, soon after, Henry's flaming words came to them, they were ready and eager to make those words good with their lives. John Marshall, of course, was one of the band of youths who had agreed to make up a company if trouble came. In May, 1775, these young frontiersmen were called together. Their captain did not come, and Marshall was appointed lieutenant, "instead of a better," as he modestly told his comrades. But, for his years, "a better" could not have been found; since 1773 John Marshall had received careful military instruction from his father.[2] Indeed, during the two years before his company took the field in actual warfare, the youth had devoted most of his time to preparing himself, by study and practice, for military service.[3] So these

[1] Meade, ii, 219. [2] Binney, in Dillon, iii, 286. [3] *Ib.*

embryo warriors gathered about their leader to be told what to do.[1]

Here we get the first glimpse of John Marshall's power over men. "He had come," the young officer informed his comrades of the backwoods, "to meet them as fellow soldiers, who were likely to be called on to defend their country." Their own "rights and liberties" were at stake. Their brothers in New England had fought and beaten the British; now "it is time to brighten our fire-arms and learn to use them in the field." He would show them how to do this. So the boys fell into line, and John Marshall, bringing his own gun to his shoulder, instructed them in the manual of arms. He first gave the words of command slowly and distinctly and then illustrated the movements with his own rifle so that every man of the company might clearly understand what each order meant and how to execute it. He then put the company through the drill.[2]

On this muster field we learn how John Marshall looked in his nineteenth year. He was very tall, six feet at least, slender and erect. His complexion was dark, with a faint tinge of red. His face was round — "nearly a circle." His forehead was straight and low, and thick, strong, "raven black" hair covered his head. Intense eyes "dark to blackness,"[3] of compelling power, pierced the beholder while they reassured him by the good nature which shone from

[1] Statement of eye-witness. (Binney, in Dillon, iii, 287.)

[2] *Ib.*, 288.

[3] In all descriptions of Marshall, it is stated that his eyes were black and brilliant. His portraits, however, show them as dark brown, but keen and piercing.

them. "He wore a purple or pale blue hunting-shirt, and trousers of the same material fringed with white." [1]

At this point, too, we first learn of his bent for oratory. What his father told him about the debates in the House of Burgesses, the speeches of Wythe and Lee and Randolph, and above all, Patrick Henry; what he had dreamed and perhaps practiced in the silent forests and vacant fields, here now bore public fruit. When he thought that he had drilled his company enough for the time being, Marshall told them to fall out, and, if they wished to hear more about the war, to gather around him and he would make them a speech.[2] And make them a speech he did. Before his men the youthful lieutenant stood, in his hand his "round black hat mounted with a buck's tail for a cockade," and spoke to that company of country boys of the justice of their cause and of those larger things in life for which all true men are glad to die.

"For something like an hour" he spoke, his round face glowing, the dormant lightning of his eye for the time unloosed. Lively words they were, we may be sure; for John Marshall was as ardent a patriot as the colonies could produce. He had learned the elementary truths of liberty in the school of the frontier; his soul was on fire with the burning words of Henry; and he poured forth his immature eloquence not to a company of peaceful theorists, but to a group of youths ready for the field. Its premises were freedom and independence; its conclusion was

[1] Binney, in Dillon, iii, 287–88.

[2] *Ib.*

action. It was a battle speech.[1] This fact is very important to an understanding of John Marshall's character, and indeed of the blood that flowed in his veins. For, as we shall find, he was always on the firing line; the Marshall blood was fighting blood.[2]

But it was not all labor of drill and toil of discipline, heroics of patriotic speech, or solemn preachments about duty, for the youths of John Marshall's company. If he was the most earnest, he was also, it seems, the jolliest person in the whole band; and this deserves especial note, for his humor was a quality which served not only the young soldier himself, but the cause for which he fought almost as well as his valor itself, in the martial years into which he was entering. Indeed this capacity for leavening the dough of serious purpose with the yeast of humor and diversion made John Marshall's entire personal life wholesome and nutritious. Jokes and fun were a part of him, as we shall see, whether in the army, at the bar, or on the bench.

So when, the business of the day disposed of, Lieutenant Marshall challenged his sure-eyed, strong-limbed, swift-footed companions to a game of quoits, or to run a race, or to jump a pole, we find him practicing that sport and comradeship which, luckily for himself and his country, he never outgrew. Pitch quoits, then, these would-be soldiers did, and coursed their races, and vaulted high in

[1] Binney, in Dillon, iii, 288.

[2] Not only do we find Marshalls, father and sons, taking gallant part in the Revolutionary War, but, thereafter, advocates of war with any country when the honor or interest of America was at stake.

their running jumps.[1] Faster than any of them could their commander run, with his long legs out-going and his powerful lungs out-winding the best of them. He could jump higher, too, than anybody else; and from this accomplishment he got his soldier nickname "Silver Heels" in Washington's army a year later.[2]

The final muster of the Culpeper Minute Men was in "Major Clayton's old field" hard by the county seat [3] on September 1, 1775.[4] They were clad in the uniform of the frontier, which indeed was little different from their daily apparel. Fringed trousers often of deerskins, "strong brown linen hunting-shirts dyed with leaves, . . . buck-tails in each hat, and a leather belt about the shoulders, with tomahawk and scalping-knife" made up their warlike costume.[5] By some preconcert, — an order perhaps from one of the three superior officers who had poetic as well as fighting blood in him, — the mothers and wives of this wilderness soldiery had worked on the breast of each hunting-shirt in large white letters the words "Liberty or Death," [6] with which Patrick Henry had trumpeted the purpose of hitherto inarticulate America.

Early in the autumn of 1775 came the expected call. Not long had the "shirt men,"[7] as they were styled, been drilling near the court-house of Cul-

[1] Binney, in Dillon, iii, 288. [2] *Infra*, chap. IV.

[3] Slaughter, 107–08. But Binney's informant says that it was twenty miles from the court-house. (Binney, in Dillon, iii, 286.)

[4] Slaughter, 107–08; and certificate of J. Marshall in pension claim of William Payne; MSS. Rev. War, S. F. no. 8938½, Pension Bureau.

[5] Slaughter, 107–08. [6] *Ib.* [7] Campbell, 607–14.

peper County when an "express" came from Patrick Henry.[1] This was a rider from Williamsburg, mounting swift relays as he went, sometimes over the rough, miry, and hazardous roads, but mostly by the bridle paths which then were Virginia's principal highways of land travel. The "express" told of the threatening preparations of Lord Dunmore, then Royal Governor of Virginia, and bore Patrick Henry's command to march at once for the scene of action a hundred miles to the south.

Instantly the Culpeper Minute Men were on the move. "We marched immediately," wrote one of them, "and in a few days were in Williamsburg." News of their coming went before them; and when the better-settled districts were reached, the inhabitants were in terror of them, for the Culpeper Minute Men were considered as "savage backwoodsmen" by the people of these older communities.[2] And indeed they must have looked the part, striding along armed to the teeth with the alarming weapons of the frontier,[3] clad in the rough but picturesque war costume of the backwoods, their long hair falling behind, untied and unqueued.

[1] Slaughter, 107–08; certificate of J. Marshall in pension claim of David Jameson; MSS. Rev. War, S. F. no. 5607, Pension Bureau.

[2] Only the Tories and the disaffected were frightened by these back-countrymen. Apparently Slaughter took this for granted and failed to make the distinction.

[3] "The people hearing that we came from the backwoods, and seeing our savage-looking equipments, seemed as much afraid of us as if we had been Indians," writes the chronicler of that march. But the people, it appears, soon got over their fright; for this frontier soldiery, as one of them relates, "took pride in demeaning ourselves as patriots and gentlemen, and the people soon treated us with respect and great kindness." (Slaughter, 107–08.)

When they reached Williamsburg half of the minute men were discharged, because they were not needed;[1] but the other half, marching under Colonel Woodford, met and beat the enemy at Great Bridge, in the first fight of the Revolution in Virginia, the first armed conflict with British soldiers in the colonies since Bunker Hill. In this small but bloody battle, Thomas Marshall and his son took part.[2]

The country around Norfolk swarmed with Tories. Governor Dunmore had established martial law, proclaimed freedom of slaves, and summoned to the Royal standard everybody capable of bearing arms. He was busy fortifying Norfolk and mounting cannon upon the entrenchments. Hundreds of the newly emancipated negroes were laboring upon these fortifications. To keep back the patriots until this military work should be finished, the Governor, with a force of British regulars and all the fighting men whom he could gather, took up an almost impregnable position near Great Bridge, about twenty miles from Norfolk, "in a small fort on an oasis surrounded by a morass, not far from the Dismal Swamp, accessible on either side by a long causeway." Here Dunmore and the Loyalists awaited the Americans.[3]

When the latter came up they made their camp "within gunshot of this post, in mud and mire, in a village at the southern end of the causeway." Across this the patriot volunteers threw a breastwork. But, having no cannon, they did not attack the British position. If only Dunmore would take the offen-

[1] Slaughter, 107–08. [2] *Ib.*

[3] Campbell, 633–34; Eckenrode: *R. V.*, 81, 82.

sive, the Americans felt that they would win. Legend has it that through a stratagem of Thomas Marshall, the British assault was brought on. He instructed his servant to pretend to desert and mislead the Governor as to the numbers opposing him. Accordingly, Marshall's decoy sought the enemy's lines and told Dunmore that the insurgents numbered not more than three hundred. The Governor then ordered the British to charge and take the Virginians, "or die in the attempt."[1]

"Between daybreak and sunrise," Captain Fordyce, leading his grenadiers six abreast, swept across the causeway upon the American breastworks. Marshall himself tells us of the fight. The shots of the sentinels roused the little camp and "the bravest . . . rushed to the works," firing at will, to meet the British onset. The gallant Fordyce "fell dead within a few steps of the breastwork. . . . Every grenadier . . . was killed or wounded; while the Americans did not lose a single man." Full one hundred of the British force laid down their lives that bloody December morning, among them four of the King's officers. Small as was this affair, — which was called "The Little Bunker Hill," — it was more terrible than most military conflicts in loss of life in proportion to the numbers engaged.[2]

This was John Marshall's first lesson[3] in warfare upon the field of battle. Also, the incidents of

[1] Burk, iv, 85; and Lossing, ii, 535–36.

[2] Marshall, i, 69; and Campbell, 635.

[3] Marshall to Samuel Templeman, Richmond, Sept. 26, 1832, supporting latter's claim for pension; MSS. Rev. War, S. F. no. 6204, Pension Bureau.

Great Bridge, and what went before and came immediately after, gave the fledgling soldier his earliest knowledge of that bickering and conflict of authority that for the next four years he was to witness and experience in far more shocking and dangerous guise.[1]

Within a few months from the time he was haranguing his youthful companions in "Major Clayton's old field" in Culpeper County, John Marshall learned, in terms of blood and death and in the still more forbidding aspects of jealousy and dissension among the patriots themselves, that freedom and independence were not to be wooed and won merely by high-pitched enthusiasm or fervid speech. The young soldier in this brief time saw a flash of the great truth that liberty can be made a reality and then possessed only by men who are strong, courageous, unselfish, and wise enough to act unitedly as well as to fight bravely. He began to discern, though vaguely as yet, the supreme need of the organization of democracy.

After the victory at Great Bridge, Marshall, with the Culpeper Minute Men, marched to Norfolk, where he witnessed the "American soldiers frequently amuse themselves by firing" into Dunmore's vessels in the harbor; saw the exasperated Governor imprudently retaliate by setting the town on fire; and beheld for "several weeks" the burning of Virginia's metropolis.[2] Marshall's battalion then

[1] For the conduct of the men then in supreme authority in Virginia see Wirt, 166–81; and Henry, i, 333–36; also, Campbell, 636 *et seq.*; and see Eckenrode: *R. V.*, 75.

[2] Marshall, i, 69; and see Eckenrode: *R. V.*, chap. iii, for the best account that has been given of this important episode. Dr. Ecken-

marched to Suffolk, and was discharged in March, 1776.[1]

With this experience of what war meant, John Marshall could have returned to the safety of Oak Hill and have spent, at that pleasant fireside, the red years that were to follow, as indeed so many in the colonies who then and after merely prated of liberty, actually did. But it was not in the Marshall nature to support a cause with lip service only. Father and son chose the sterner part; and John Marshall was now about to be schooled for four years by grim instructors in the knowledge that strong and orderly government is necessary to effective liberty. He was to learn, in a hard and bitter school, the danger of provincialism and the value of Nationality.

Not for long did he tarry at the Fauquier County home; and not an instant did the father linger there. Thomas Marshall, while still serving with his command at Great Bridge, was appointed by the Legislature major of the Third Virginia Regiment; and at once entered the Continental service;[2] on July 30, 1776, four months after the Culpeper Minute Men, their work finished, had been disbanded by the new State, his son was commissioned lieutenant in the same regiment. The fringed hunting-shirt and leggings, the buck-tail headgear, scalping-knife, and

rode's narrative is a complete statement, from original sources, of every phase of this initial armed conflict between the patriots and Royalists in Virginia. Also see affidavit of Marshall in pension claim of William Payne, April 26, 1832; MSS. Rev. War, S. F. no. 8938½, Pension Bureau.

[1] Affidavit of Marshall in pension claim of William Payne, April 26, 1832; MSS. Rev. War, S. F. no. 8938½, Pension Bureau.

[2] Memorial of Thomas Marshall. (*Supra*, and Appendix IV.)

tomahawk of the backwoods warrior now gave place to the buff and blue uniform, the three-cornered hat,[1] the sword, and the pistol of the Continental officer; and Major Thomas Marshall and his son, Lieutenant John Marshall, marched away to the north to join Washington, and under him to fight and suffer through four black and heart-breaking years of the Revolution.

It is needful, here, to get clearly in our minds the state of the American army at this time. What particular year of the Revolution was darkest up almost to the victorious end, it is hard to say. Studying each year separately one historian will conclude that 1776 sounded the depths of gloom; another plumbs still greater despair at Valley Forge; still another will prove that the bottom was not reached until '79 or '80. And all of them appear to be right.[2]

Even as early as January, 1776, when the war was new, and enthusiasm still warm, Washington wrote to the President of Congress, certain States having paid no attention to his application for arms: "I have, as the last expedient, sent one or two officers from each regiment into the country, with money to try if they can buy."[3] A little later he writes: "My situation has been such, that I have been obliged to use art to conceal it from my own officers."[4]

[1] This uniform was rare; it is probable, however, that Thomas Marshall procured it for himself and son. He could afford it at that time, and he was a very proud man.

[2] Chastellux found the army nearly disbanded from necessity in 1782. (Chastellux, translator's note to 60.)

[3] Washington to President of Congress, Jan. 24, 1776; *Writings*: Ford, iii, 372–73.

[4] Washington to Reed, Feb. 10, 1776; *ib.*, 413.

Congress even placed some of Washington's little army under the direction of the Committee of Safety of New York; and Washington thus wrote to that committee: "I should be glad to know how far it is conceived that my powers over them [the soldiers] extend, or whether I have any at all. Sure I am that they cannot be subjected to the direction of both"[1] (the committee and himself).

In September the Commander-in-Chief wrote to the President of Congress that the terms of enlistment of a large portion of the army were about to expire, and that it was direful work "to be forming armies constantly, and to be left by troops just when they begin to deserve the name, or perhaps at a moment when an important blow is expected."[2]

Four days later Washington again told Congress, "beyond the possibility of doubt, . . . unless some speedy and effectual measures are adopted by Congress, our cause will be lost."[3] On December 1, 1776, the army was "greatly reduced by the departure of the Maryland *Flying Camp* men, and by sundry other causes."[4] A little afterwards General Greene wrote to Governor Cooke [of Rhode Island] that "two brigades left us at Brunswick, notwithstanding the enemy were within two hours' march and coming on."[5]

Thirteen days before the Christmas night that

[1] Washington to Committee of Safety of New York, April 27, 1776; *Writings:* Ford, iv, 51–52.

[2] Washington to President of Congress, Sept. 20, 1776; *ib.*, 422.

[3] Washington to President of Congress, Sept. 24, 1776; *ib.*, 439.

[4] Washington to Major-General Lee, Dec. 1, 1776; *ib.*, v, 62.

[5] General Greene to Governor Cooke, Dec. 4, 1776; *ib.*, footnote to 62.

Washington crossed the Delaware and struck the British at Trenton, the distressed American commander found that "our little handful is daily decreasing by sickness and other causes."[1] And the very day before that brilliant exploit, Washington was compelled to report that "but very few of the men have [re]enlisted" because of "their wishes to return home, the nonappointment of officers in some instances, the turning out of good and appointing of bad in others, and the incomplete or rather no arrangement of them, a work unhappily committed to the management of their States; nor have I the most distant prospect of retaining them . . . notwithstanding the most pressing solicitations and the obvious necessity for it." Washington informed Reed that he was left with only "fourteen to fifteen hundred effective men. This handful and such militia as may choose to join me will then compose our army."[2] Such was American patriotic efficiency, as exhibited by "State Sovereignty," the day before the dramatic crossing of the Delaware.

A month earlier the general of this assemblage of shreds and patches had been forced to beg the various States for militia in order to get in "a number of men, if possible, to keep up the appearance of our army."[3] And he writes to his brother Augustine of his grief and surprise to find "the different States

[1] Washington to President of Congress, Dec. 12, 1776; *Writings:* Ford, v, 84.

[2] Washington to President of Congress, Dec. 24, 1776; *ib.*, 129–30. While Washington was desperately badly off, he exaggerates somewhat in this despondent report, as Mr. Ford's footnote (*ib.*, 130) shows.

[3] Washington to President of Congress, Nov. 11, 1776; *ib.*, 19.

so slow and inattentive. . . . In ten days from this date there will not be above two thousand men, if that number, of the fixed established regiments, . . . to oppose Howe's whole army." [1]

Throughout the war, the neglect and ineffectiveness of the States, even more than the humiliating powerlessness of Congress, time and again all but lost the American cause. The State militia came and went almost at will. "The impulse for going home was so irresistible, that it answered no purpose to oppose it. Though I would not discharge them," testifies Washington, "I have been obliged to acquiesce, and it affords one more melancholy proof, how delusive such dependencies [State controlled troops] are." [2]

"The Dependence, which the Congress have placed upon the militia," the distracted general complains to his brother, "has already greatly injured, and I fear will totally ruin our cause. Being subject to no controul themselves, they introduce disorder among the troops, whom you have attempted to discipline, while the change in their living brings on sickness; this makes them Impatient to get home, which spreads universally, and introduces abominable desertions. In short, it is not in the power of words to describe the task I have to act." [3]

[1] Washington to John Augustine Washington, Nov. 19, 1776; *Writings*: Ford, v, 38–39.

[2] Washington to President of Congress, Sept. 8, 1776; *ib.*, iv, 397.

[3] Washington to John Augustine Washington, Sept. 22, 1776; *ib.*, 429.

Nor was this the worst. Washington thus pours out his soul to his nephew: "Great bodies of militia in pay that never were in camp; . . . immense quantities of provisions drawn by men that never rendered . . . one hour's service . . . every kind of military [discipline] destroyed by them. . . . They [the militia] come without any conveniences and soon return. I discharged a regiment the other day that had in it fourteen rank and file fit for duty only. . . . The subject . . . is not a fit one to be publicly known or discussed. . . . I am wearied to death all day . . . at the conduct of the militia, whose behavior and want of discipline has done great injury to the other troops, who never had officers, except in a few instances, worth the bread they eat." [1]

Conditions did not improve in the following year, for we find Washington again writing to his brother of "militia, who are here today and gone tomorrow — whose way, like the ways of [Pr]ovidence, are almost inscrutable." [2] Baron von Steuben testifies thus: "The eternal ebb and flow of men . . . who went and came every day, rendered it impossible to have either a regiment or company complete. . . . I have seen a regiment consisting of *thirty men* and a company of *one corporal*." [3] Even Thomas Paine, the arch-enemy of anything resembling a regular or "standing" army, finally declared that militia "will not do for a long campaign." [4] Marshall thus de-

[1] Washington to Lund Washington, Sept. 30, 1776; *Writings:* Ford, iv, 457–59.

[2] Washington to John Augustine Washington, Feb. 24, 1777; *ib.*, v, 252. The militia officers were elected "without respect either to service or experience." (Chastellux, 235.)

[3] Kapp, 115. [4] *The Crisis:* Paine; *Writings:* Conway, i, 175.

scribes the predicament in which Washington was placed by the inconstancy of this will-o'-the-wisp soldiery: "He was often abandoned by bodies of militia, before their places were filled by others. . . . The soldiers carried off arms and blankets."[1]

Bad as the militia were,[2] the States did not keep up even this happy-go-lucky branch of the army. "It is a matter of astonishment," savagely wrote Washington to the President of Pennsylvania, two months before Valley Forge, "to every part of the continent, to hear that Pennsylvania, the most opulent and populous of all the States, has but twelve hundred militia in the field, at a time when the enemy are endeavoring to make themselves completely masters of, and to fix their winter quarters in, her capital."[3] Even in the Continental line, it appears, Pennsylvania's quota had "never been above one third full; and now many of them are far below even that."[4]

Washington's wrath at Pennsylvania fairly blazed at this time, and the next day he wrote to Augustine Washington that "this State acts most infamously, the People of it, I mean, as we derive little or no assistance from them. . . . They are in a manner, totally disaffected or in a kind of Lethargy."[5]

The head of the American forces was not the only patriot officer to complain. "The Pennsylvania Asso-

[1] Marshall (1st ed.), iii, 66.

[2] The militia were worse than wasteful and unmanageable; they deserted by companies. (Hatch, 72–73.)

[3] Washington to Wharton, Oct. 17, 1777; *Writings:* Ford, vi, 118–19.

[4] *Ib.*

[5] Washington to John Augustine Washington, Oct. 18, 1777; *ib.*, 126–29.

ciators [militia] . . . are deserting . . . notwithstanding the most spirited exertions of their officers," reported General Livingston in the midsummer of 1776.[1] General Lincoln and the Massachusetts Committee tried hard to keep the militia of the Bay State from going home; but, moaned Lee, "whether they will succeed, Heaven only knows."[2]

General Sullivan determined to quit the service because of abuse and ill-treatment.[3] For the same reason Schuyler proposed to resign.[4] These were not examples of pique; they denoted a general sentiment among officers who, in addition to their sufferings, beheld their future through none too darkened glasses. They "not only have the Mortification to See every thing live except themselves," wrote one minor officer in 1778, "but they see their private fortune wasting away to make fat those very Miscreants [speculators] . . . they See their Country . . . refuse to make any future provision for them, or even to give them the Necessary Supplies."[5]

Thousands of the Continentals were often practically naked; Chastellux found several hundred in an invalid camp, not because they were ill, but because "they were not covered even with rags."[6] "Our sick naked, and well naked, our unfortunate men in captivity naked"! wailed Washington in

[1] Livingston to Washington, Aug. 12, 1776; *Cor. Rev.*: Sparks, i, 275.

[2] Lee to Washington, Nov. 12, 1776; *ib.*, 305.

[3] Sullivan to Washington, March 7, 1777; *ib.*, 353–54.

[4] Schuyler to Washington, Sept. 9, 1776; *ib.*, 287.

[5] Smith to McHenry, Dec. 10, 1778; Steiner, 21.

[6] Chastellux, 44; and see Moore's *Diary*, i, 399–400; and *infra*, chap. IV.

1777.[1] Two days before Christmas of that year he informed Congress that, of the force then under his immediate command, nearly three thousand were "barefoot and otherwise naked."[2] Sickness was general and appalling. Smallpox raged throughout the army even from the first.[3] "The Regimental Surgeons are immediately to make returns . . . of all the men in their Regiments, who have not had the small Pox,"[4] read the orders of the day just after New Year's Day, in 1778.

Six years after Concord and Lexington, three hundred American soldiers, in a body, wished to join the British.[5] Stern measures were taken to prevent desertion and dishonesty and even to enforce the most ordinary duties of soldiers. "In the afternoon three of our regt were flogged; — 2 of them received one hundred lashes apiece for attempting to desert; the other received 80 for enlisting twice and taking two bounties,"[6] Wild coolly enters in his diary. And again: "This afternoon one of our men was hanged on the grand parade for attempting to desert to the enemy";[7] and "at 6 ock P.M. a soldier of Col. Gimatts Battalion was hanged."

Sleeping on duty meant "Twenty Lashes on . . .

[1] Washington to Livingston, Dec. 31, 1777; *Writings:* Ford, vi, 272.

[2] Washington to President of Congress, Dec. 23, 1777; *ib.*, 260; and see *ib.*, 267.

[3] *Pa. Mag. Hist. and Biog.*, 1890–91 (2d Series), vi, 79. Most faces among the patriot troops were pitted with this plague. Washington was deeply pockmarked. He had the smallpox in the Barbadoes when he was nineteen years old. (Sparks, 15.)

[4] Weedon, Jan. 6, 1778, 183. [5] Hatch, 135; and Kapp, 109.

[6] *Proc.*, Mass. Hist. Soc. (2d Series), vi, 93.

[7] *Ib.* Entries of desertions and savage punishment are frequent in Wild's *Diary;* see p. 135 as an example. Also see Moore's *Diary*, i, 405.

[the] bare back" of the careless sentry.[1] A soldier convicted of "getting drunk & losing his Arms" was "Sentenc'd to receive 100 Lashes on his bare back, & pay for his Arms lost." [2] A man who, in action, "turns his back on the Enemy" was ordered to be "instantly put . . . to Death" by the officers.[3] At Yorktown in May, 1781, Wayne ordered a platoon to fire on twelve soldiers who were persuading their comrades not to march; six were killed and one wounded, who was, by Wayne's command, enforced by a cocked pistol, then finished with the bayonet thrust into the prostrate soldier by a comrade.[4]

Such was the rough handling practiced in the scanty and ill-treated army of individualists which Washington made shift to rally to the patriot colors.[5] It was not an encouraging omen. But blacker still was the disorganizing effect of local control of the various "State Lines" which the pompous authority of the newborn "sovereign and independent" Commonwealths asserted.[6]

[1] Weedon, 14. [2] *Ib.*, Sept. 3, 1777, 30.

[3] *Ib.*, Sept. 15, 1777, 52. And see Sept. 6, p. 36, where officers as well as privates are ordered "instantly Shot" if they are "so far lost to all Shame as basely to quit their posts without orders, or shall skulk from Danger or offer to retreat before orders."

[4] Livingston to Webb, May 28, 1781; *Writings:* Ford, ix, footnote to 267.

[5] One reason for the chaotic state of the army was the lack of trained officers and the ignorance of the majority of common soldiers in regard to the simplest elements of drill or discipline. Many of the bearers of commissions knew little more than the men; and of such untrained officers there was an overabundance. (Hatch, 13–15.) To Baron von Steuben's training of privates as well as officers is due the chief credit for remedying this all but fatal defect. (Kapp, 126–35; also *infra*, chap. IV.)

[6] For statement of conditions in the American army throughout the war see Hatch; also, Bolton.

Into this desperate confusion came the young Virginia lieutenant. Was this the manner of liberty? Was this the way a people fighting for their freedom confronted their enemy? The dreams he had dreamed, the visions he had seen back in his Virginia mountains were clad in glories as enchanting as the splendors of their tree-clad summits at break of day — dreams and visions for which strong men should be glad of the privilege of dying if thereby they might be won as realities for all the people. And indeed at this time, and in the even deadlier days that followed, young John Marshall found strong men by his side willing to die and to go through worse than death to make their great dream come true.

But why thus decrepit, the organization called the American army? Why this want of food even for such of the soldiers as were willing and eager to fight for their country? Why this scanty supply of arms? Why this avoidable sickness, this needless suffering, this frightful waste? What was the matter? Something surely was at fault. It must be in the power that assumed to direct the patriot army. But whence came that power? From Congress? No. Congress had no power; after a while, it did not even have influence. From the States? Yes; that was its source — there was plenty of power in the States.

But what kind of power, and how displayed? One State did one thing; another State did another thing.[1] One State clothed its troops well; another

[1] The States were childishly jealous of one another. Their different laws on the subject of rank alone caused unbelievable confusion. (Hatch, 13–16. And see Watson, 64, for local feeling, and inefficiency caused by the organization of the army into State lines.)

sent no supplies at all.[1] One regiment of Maryland militia had no shirts and the men wrapped blankets about their bare bodies.[2] One day State troops would come into camp, and the next day leave. How could war be conducted, how could battles be fought and won, through such freakish, uncertain power as that?

But how could this vaunted liberty, which orators had proclaimed and which Lieutenant Marshall himself had lauded to his frontier companions in arms, be achieved except by a well-organized army, equipped, supplied, and directed by a competent central Government? This was the talk common among the soldiers of the Continental establishment in which John Marshall was a lieutenant. In less than two years after he entered the regular service, even officers, driven to madness and despair by the pusillanimous weakness of Congress, openly denounced that body; and the soldiers themselves, who saw their wounds and sufferings coming to naught, cursed that sham and mockery which the jealousy and shallowness of State provincialism had set up in place of a National Government.[3]

All through the latter half of 1776, Lieutenant

[1] Hatch says that Connecticut provided most bountifully for her men. (Hatch, 87.) But Chastellux found the Pennsylvania line the best equipped; each Pennsylvania regiment had even a band of music. (Chastellux, 65.)

[2] "The only garment they possess is a blanket elegantly twined about them. You may judge, sir, how much this apparel graces their appearance in parade." (Inspector Fleury to Von Steuben, May 13, 1778; as quoted in Hatch, 87.)

[3] Diary of Joseph Clark; *Proceedings*, N.J. Hist. Soc. (1st Series), vii, 104. The States would give no revenue to the general Government and the officers thought the country would go to pieces. (Hatch, 154.)

Marshall of the Third Virginia Regiment marched, suffered, retreated and advanced, and performed his duties without complaint. He did more. At this time, when, to keep up the sinking spirits of the men was almost as important as was ammunition, young Marshall was the soul of good humor and of cheer; and we shall find him in a few months heartening his starving and freezing comrades at Valley Forge with quip and jest, a center from which radiated good temper and a hopeful and happy warmth. When in camp Marshall was always for some game or sport, which he played with infinite zest. He was the best quoit-thrower in the regiment. His long legs left the others behind in foot-races or jumping contests.

So well did he perform his work, so highly did he impress his superior officers, that, early in December, 1776, he was promoted to be captain-lieutenant, to rank from July 31, and transferred to the Fifteenth Virginia Line.[1] Thus he missed the glory of being one of that immortal company which on Christmas night, 1776, crossed the Delaware with Washington and fell upon the British at Trenton. His father, Major Thomas Marshall, shared in that renown;[2] but the days ahead held for John Marshall his share of fighting in actual battle.

Sick, ill-fed, dirty, and ragged, but with a steady nucleus of regular troops as devoted to their great commander as they were disgusted with the hybrid arrangement between the States and Congress, Washington's army worried along. Two months before the battle of the Brandywine, the American

[1] Heitman, 285.

[2] Binney, in Dillon, iii, 284.

General informed the Committee of Congress that "no army was ever worse supplied than ours . . . our Soldiers, the greatest part of last Campaign, and the whole of this, have scarcely tasted any kind of Vegetables; had but little salt and Vinegar." He told of the "many putrid diseases incident to the Army, and the lamentable mortality," which this neglect of soldiers in the field had caused. "Soap," says he, "is another article in great demand," but not to be had. He adds, sarcastically: "A soldier's pay will not enable him to purchase [soap] by which his . . . consequent dirtiness adds not a little to the disease of the Army." [1]

Such was the army of which John Marshall was a part when it prepared to meet the well-fed, properly clad, adequately equipped British veterans under Howe who had invaded Pennsylvania. Even with such a force Washington felt it necessary to make an impression on disaffected [2] Philadelphia, and, for that purpose, marched through the city on his way to confront the enemy. For it was generally believed that the American army was as small in numbers [3] as it was wretched in equipment. A parade of eleven thousand men [4] through the Tory-infested metropolis would, Washington hoped, hearten patriot sympathizers and encourage Congress. He took pains that his troops should make the best appearance possible. Arms were scoured and the men wore

[1] Washington to Committee of Congress, July 19, 1777; *Writings:* Ford, v, 495.

[2] Washington to President of Congress, Aug. 23, 1777; *Writings:* Ford, vi, 50; also see Marshall (1st ed.), iii, 126.

[3] Marshall (1st ed.), iii, 126. [4] *Ib.*, 127.

sprigs of green in their headgear. Among the orders for the march through the seat of government it was directed: "If any Soldr. shall dare to quit his ranks He shall receive 39 Lashes at the first halting place afterwards. . . . Not a Woman[1] belonging to the Army is to be seen with the troops on their March through the City."[2]

The Americans soon came in contact with the enemy and harassed him as much as possible. Many of Washington's men had no guns. Although fewer militia came to his aid than Congress had called for, testifies Marshall, yet "more appeared than could be armed. Those nearest danger were, as usual, most slow in assembling."[3]

Upon Wayne's suggestion, Washington formed "a corps of light infantry consisting of nine officers, eight sergeants, and a hundred rank and file, from each brigade" and placed them under the command of General Maxwell who had acquired a reputation as a hard fighter.[4] Among these picked officers was Captain-Lieutenant John Marshall. Maxwell's command was thrown forward to Iron Hill. "A choice body of men" was detailed from this select light infantry and, during the night, was posted on the road along which it was believed one column of the British army would advance. The small body of Americans had no artillery and its only purpose was to annoy the enemy and retard his progress. The British under Cornwallis attacked as soon as they discovered

[1] On this subject see Waldo's poem, *Hist. Mag.*, vii, 274; and Clark's Diary, *Proc.*, N.J. Hist. Soc., vii, 102.

[2] Weedon, Aug. 23, 1777, 19.

[3] Marshall (1st ed.), iii, 127.

[4] *Ib.*, 128; and see Trevelyan, iv, 226.

Maxwell's troops. The Americans quickly were forced to retreat, having lost forty killed and wounded. Only three of the British were killed and but nineteen were wounded.[1]

This action was the first engagement in which Marshall took part after the battle of Great Bridge. It is important only as fixing the command to which he was assigned. Marshall told Justice Story that he was in the Iron Hill fight; [2] and it is certain, therefore, that he was in Maxwell's light infantry and one of the little band picked from that body of choice troops, for the perilous and discouraging task of checking the oncoming British thousands.

The American army retreated to the Brandywine, where on the 9th of September Washington stationed all his forces except the light infantry on the left of the river. The position was skillfully chosen, but vague and conflicting reports [3] of the movement of the British finally resulted in American disaster.

The light infantry was posted among the hills on the right of the stream along the road leading to Chadd's Ford, in order to skirmish with the British when they approached, and, if possible, prevent them from crossing the river. But the enemy, without much effort, drove the Americans across the Brandywine, neither side suffering much loss.[4]

[1] Marshall (1st ed.), iii, 127–29; *ib.* (2d ed.), i, 154–56; Washington to President of Congress, Sept. 3, 1777; *Writings:* Ford, vi, 64–65.

[2] Story, in Dillon, iii, 335.

[3] Washington to President of Congress, Sept. 11, 1777; *Writings:* Ford, vi, 69.

[4] Marshall (1st ed.), iii, 131; *ib.* (2d ed.), i, 156. Colonel Harrison, Washington's Secretary, reported immediately to the President of Congress that Maxwell's men believed that they killed or wounded

Washington now made his final dispositions for battle. The command to which Marshall belonged, together with other detachments under the general direction of Anthony Wayne, were placed opposite the British at Chadd's Ford. Small parties of selected men crossed over and attacked the British on the other side of the stream. In one of these skirmishes the Americans "killed a British captain with ten or fifteen privates, drove them out of the wood and were on the point of taking a field piece." But large numbers of the enemy hurried forward and again the Americans were thrown across the river. Marshall was in this party.[1]

Thomas Marshall, now colonel,[2] held the advanced position under Sullivan at the right; and his regiment did the hardest fighting and suffered the heaviest losses on that unhappy day. When Cornwallis, in greatly superior numbers, suddenly poured down upon Sullivan's division, he all but surprised the Continentals and drove most of them flying before him; [3] but Colonel Marshall and his Virginians refused to be stampeded. That regiment "main-

"at least three hundred" of the British. (Harrison to President of Congress, Sept. 11, 1777; *Writings:* Ford, vi, footnote to 68.)

[1] Marshall, i, 156. The fact that Marshall places himself in this detachment, which was a part of Maxwell's light infantry, together with his presence at Iron Hill, fixes his position in the battle of the Brandywine and in the movements that immediately followed. It is reasonably certain that he was under Maxwell until just before the battle of Germantown. Of this skirmish Washington's optimistic and excited Secretary wrote on the spot, that Maxwell's men killed thirty men and one captain "left dead on the spot." (Harrison to the President of Congress, Sept. 11, 1777; *Writings:* Ford, vi, footnote to 68.)

[2] Thomas Marshall was promoted to be lieutenant-colonel Aug. 13, 1776; and colonel Feb. 21, 1777. (Heitman, 285.)

[3] Trevelyan, iv, 230.

tained its position without losing an inch of ground until both its flanks were turned, its ammunition nearly expended, and more than half the officers and one third of the soldiers were killed and wounded." [1] Colonel Marshall had two horses shot under him. But, cut to pieces as they were, no panic appeared in this superb Virginia command and they "retired in good order." [2]

While Thomas Marshall and his Third Virginia Line were thus checking Cornwallis's assault on the right, the British charged, in dense masses, across the Brandywine, at Chadd's Ford, upon Wayne's division, to which Captain-Lieutenant John Marshall had been assigned. The Americans made a show of resistance, but, learning of the rout of their right wing, quickly gave way.[3]

"Nearly six hundred British . . . were killed or wounded; and the Americans lost eleven pieces of artillery and above a thousand men, of whom the third part were prisoners," according to the British

[1] Marshall, i, footnote to 158.

[2] *Ib.* Colonel Thomas Marshall's cool-headed and heroic conduct at this battle, which brought out in high lights his fine record as an officer, caused the Virginia House of Delegates to elect him colonel of the State Regiment of Artillery raised by that Commonwealth three months later. The vote is significant; for, although there were three candidates, each a man of merit, and although Thomas Marshall himself was not an aspirant for the place, and, indeed, was at Valley Forge when the election occurred, twice as many votes were cast for him as for all the other candidates put together. Four men were balloted for, Thomas Marshall receiving seventy-five votes and the other three candidates all together but thirty-six votes. (Journal, H.B. (Nov. 5, 1777), 27.)

[3] Marshall, i, 156; and Trevelyan, iv, 230–31. Washington reported that Wayne and Maxwell's men retreated only "after a severe conflict." (Washington to President of Congress, Sept. 11, 1777; *Writings:* Ford, vi, 69.)

statement.[1] And by their own account the Americans lost three hundred killed, six hundred wounded, and between three and four hundred prisoners.[2]

Both British and American narratives agree that the conduct of the Continental troops at Brandywine was most unequal in stanchness, discipline, and courage. John Marshall himself wrote: "As must ever be the case in new-raised armies, unused to danger and from which undeserving officers have not been expelled, their conduct was not uniform. Some regiments, especially those which had served the preceding campaign, maintained their ground with the firmness and intrepidity of veterans, while others gave way as soon as they were pressed."[3]

But the inefficiency of the American equipment gave some excuse for the fright that seized upon so many of them. For, testifies Marshall, "many of their muskets were scarcely fit for service; and being of unequal caliber, their cartridges could not be so well fitted, and consequently, their fire could not do as much execution as that of the enemy. This radical defect was felt in all the operations of the army."[4]

So ended the battle of the Brandywine, the third formal armed conflict in which John Marshall took part. He had been in skirmish after skirmish, and in all of them had shown the characteristic Marshall coolness and courage, which both father and son exhibited in such striking fashion on this September day on the field where Lafayette fell

[1] Trevelyan, iv, 232.
[2] Marshall, i, 157–58.
[3] *Ib.*; and see Irving, iii, 200–09.
[4] Marshall, i, 158–59.

wounded, and where the patriot forces reeled back under the all but fatal blows of the well-directed British regiments.[1]

It is small wonder that the Americans were beaten in the battle of the Brandywine; indeed, the wonder is that the British did not follow up their victory and entirely wipe out the opposing patriots. But it is astonishing that the American army kept up heart. They were even "in good spirits" as Washington got them in hand and directed their retreat.[2]

They were pretty well scattered, however, and many small parties and numerous stragglers were left behind. Maxwell's men, among whom was John Marshall, were stationed at Chester as "a rallying point" for the fragments which otherwise would disperse or be captured. Much maneuvering followed by both British and Americans. At sight of a detachment of the enemy approaching Wilmington, the Delaware militia "dispersed themselves," says Marshall.[3] Soon the two armies again faced one another. Marshall thus describes the situation: "The advanced parties had met, and were beginning to skirmish, when they were separated by a heavy rain, which, becoming more and more violent, rendered the retreat of the Americans a measure of absolute necessity." [4]

Through a cold and blinding downpour, over

[1] Four years afterward Chastellux found that "most of the trees bear the mark of bullets or cannon shot." (Chastellux, 118.)

[2] Washington to President of Congress, Sept. 11, 1777; *Writings:* Ford, vi, 70.

[3] Marshall (1st ed.), iii, 141, and see Washington to President of Congress, Sept. 23, 1777; *Writings:* Ford, vi, 81.

[4] Marshall, i, 160.

roads deep with mud, Captain-Lieutenant Marshall marched with his retreating comrades. All day they struggled forward, and nearly all night. They had no time to eat and little or no food, even if they had had the time. Before the break of a gray, cold, rainy September dawn, a halt was called, and an examination made of arms and ammunition. "Scarcely a musket in a regiment could be discharged," Marshall records, "and scarcely one cartridge in a box was fit for use," although "forty rounds per man had just been drawn" — this because the cartridge boxes had been ill-made and of improper material.

Gun locks were loose, declares Marshall, because flimsily put on; the muskets were scarcely better than clubs. Hardly any of the soldiers had bayonets.[1] "Never" had the patriot army been "in such imminent peril," he asserts — and all because of the inefficiency or worse of the method of supplies. Well might Washington's dilapidated troops thank Providence for the bitter weather that drenched through and through both officers and men and soaked their ammunition, for "the extreme severity of the weather had entirely stopped the British army."[2]

Yet Washington was determined to block the British march on Philadelphia. He made shift to secure some fresh ammunition[3] and twice moved his army to get in front of the enemy or, failing in that,

[1] Marshall, i, 160. When their enlistments expired, the soldiers took the Government's muskets and bayonets home with them. Thus thousands of muskets and bayonets continually disappeared. (See Kapp, 117.)

[2] Marshall, i, 160–61.

[3] *Ib.*

"to keep pace with them." [1] To check their too rapid advance Washington detached the troops under Wayne, among whom was John Marshall.[2] They found the "country was so extensively disaffected that Sir William Howe received accurate accounts of his [Wayne's] position and of his force. Major-General Grey was detached to surprise him [Wayne] and effectually accomplished his purpose." At eleven o'clock at night Grey drove in Wayne's pickets with charged bayonets, and in a desperate midnight encounter killed and wounded one hundred and fifty of his men.[3] General Smallwood, who was to have supported Wayne, was less than a mile away, but his militia, who, writes Marshall, "thought only of their own safety, having fallen in with a party returning from the pursuit of Wayne, fled in confusion with the loss of only one man." [4]

Another example, this, before John Marshall's eyes, of the unreliability of State-controlled troops;[5] one more paragraph in the chapter of fatal inefficiency of the so-called Government of the so-called United States. Day by day, week by week, month by month, year by year, these object lessons were witnessed by the young Virginia officer. They made

[1] Washington to President of Congress, Sept. 23, 1777; *Writings*: Ford, vi, 81–82.

[2] This is an inference, but a fair one. Maxwell was under Wayne; and Marshall was one of Maxwell's light infantry of picked men. (*Supra.*)

[3] Marshall, i, 161. "The British accounts represent the American loss to have been much larger. It probably amounted to at least three hundred men." (*Ib.*, footnote.)

[4] *Ib.*, and see *Pa. Mag. Hist. and Biog.*, i, 305.

[5] Marshall repeatedly expresses this thought in his entire account of the war.

a lifelong impression upon him and had an immediate effect. More and more he came to depend on Washington, as indeed the whole army did also, for all things which should have come from the Government itself.

Once again the American commander sought to intercept the British, but they escaped "by a variety of perplexing maneuvers," writes Washington, "thro' a Country from which I could not derive the least intelligence (being to a man disaffected)" and "marched immediately toward Philadelphia."[1] For the moment Washington could not follow, although, declares Marshall, "public opinion" was demanding and Congress insisting that one more blow be struck to save Philadelphia.[2] His forces were not yet united; his troops utterly exhausted.

Marching through heavy mud, wading streams, drenched by torrential rains, sleeping on the sodden ground "without tents . . . without shoes or . . . clothes . . . without fire . . . without food,"[3] to use Marshall's striking language, the Americans were in no condition to fight the superior forces of the well-found British. "At least one thousand men are bare-footed and have performed the marches in that condition," Washington informed the impatient Congress.[4] He did his utmost; that brilliant officer, Alexander Hamilton, was never so efficient; but nearly all that could be accomplished was to

[1] Washington to President of Congress, Sept. 23, 1777; *Writings:* Ford, vi, 80.

[2] Marshall, i, 162. [3] *Ib.*

[4] Washington to President of Congress, Sept. 23, 1777; *Writings:* Ford, vi, 82.

remove the military stores at Philadelphia up the Delaware farther from the approaching British, but also farther from the American army. Philadelphia itself "seemed asleep, or dead, and the whole State scarce alive. Maryland and Delaware the same," wrote John Adams in his diary.[1]

So the British occupied the Capital, placing most of their forces about Germantown. Congress, frightened and complaining, fled to York. The members of that august body, even before the British drove them from their cozy quarters, felt that "the prospect is chilling on every side; gloomy, dark, melancholy and dispiriting."[2] Would Washington never strike? Their impatience was to be relieved. The American commander had, by some miracle, procured munitions and put the muskets of his troops in a sort of serviceable order; and he felt that a surprise upon Germantown might succeed. He planned his attack admirably, as the British afterwards conceded.[3] In the twilight of a chilling October day, Washington gave orders to begin the advance.

Throughout the night the army marched, and in the early morning[4] the three divisions into which the American force was divided threw themselves upon the British within brief intervals of time. All went well at first. Within about half an hour after Sullivan and Wayne had engaged the British left wing, the American left wing, to which John Mar-

[1] *Works:* Adams, ii, 437. [2] *Ib.*
[3] *Pa. Mag. Hist. and Biog.*, xvi, 197 *et seq.*
[4] American officer's description of the battle. (*Ib.*, xi, 330.)

shall was now attached,[1] attacked the front of the British right wing, driving that part of the enemy from the ground. With battle shouts Marshall and his comrades under General Woodford charged the retreating British. Then it was that a small force of the enemy took possession of the Chew House and poured a murderous hail of lead into the huzzaing American ranks. This saved the day for the Royal force and turned an American victory into defeat.[2]

It was a dramatic struggle in which John Marshall that day took part. Fighting desperately beside them, he saw his comrades fall in heaps around him as they strove to take the fiercely defended stone house of the Tory Judge. A fog came up so thick that the various divisions could see but a little way before them. The dun smoke from burning hay and fields of stubble, to which the British had set fire, made thicker the murk until the Americans fighting from three different points could not tell friend from foe.[3] For a while their fire was directed only by the flash from what they thought must be the guns of the enemy.[4]

The rattle of musketry and roar of cannon was like "the crackling of thorns under a pot, and incessant peals of thunder," wrote an American officer in an attempt to describe the battle in a letter to his relatives at home.[5] Through it all, the Americans kept up their cheering until, as they fought, the

[1] Marshall, i, 168. [2] *Ib.*, 168–69.

[3] From an American officer's description, in *Pa. Mag. Hist. and Biog.*, xi, 330.

[4] *Ib.*, 331–32. [5] *Ib.*

defeat was plain to the most audacious of them; and retreat, with which they had grown so familiar, once more began. For nine miles the British pursued them, the road stained with blood from the beaten patriots.[1] Nearly a thousand of Washington's soldiers were killed or wounded, and over four hundred were made prisoners on that ill-fated day, while the British loss was less than half these numbers.[2]

Two months of service followed, as hard as the many gone before with which Fate had blackened the calendar of the patriot cause. Washington was frantically urged to "storm" Philadelphia: Congress wished it; a "torrent of public opinion" demanded it; even some of Washington's officers were carried off their feet and advised "the mad enterprise," to use Marshall's warm description of the pressure upon his commander.[3] The depreciation of the Continental paper money, the increasing disaffection of the people, the desperate plight of American fortunes, were advanced as reasons for a "grand effort" to remedy the ruinous situation. Washington was immovable, and his best officers sustained him. Risking his army's destruction was not the way to stop depreciation of the currency, said Washington; its value had fallen for want of taxes to sustain it and could be raised only by their levy.[4] And "the corruption and defection of the people, and their unwillingness to serve in the army of the United States,

[1] "The rebels carried off a large number of their wounded as we could see by the blood on the roads, on which we followed them so far [nine miles]." (British officer's account of battle; *Pa. Mag. Hist. and Biog.*, xvi, 197 *et seq.*)

[2] Marshall, i, 170–71. [3] *Ib.*, 181. [4] *Ib.*, 181–82.

were evils which would be very greatly increased by an unsuccessful attempt on Philadelphia." [1]

So black grew American prospects that secret sympathizers with the British became open in their advocacy of the abandonment of the Revolution. A Philadelphia Episcopal rector, who had been chaplain of Congress, wrote Washington that the patriot cause was lost and besought him to give up the struggle. "The most respectable characters" had abandoned the cause of independence, said Duché. Look at Congress. Its members were "obscure" and "distinguished for the weakness of their understandings and the violence of their tempers . . . chosen by a little, low, faction. . . . Tis you . . . only that support them." And the army! "The whole world knows that its only existence depends on you." Consider the situation: "Your harbors are blocked up, your cities fall one after the other; fortress after fortress, battle after battle is lost. . . . How fruitless the expense of blood!" Washington alone can end it. Humanity calls upon him to do so; and if he heeds that call his character "will appear with lustre in the annals of history." [2] Deeply offended, Washington sent the letter to Congress, which, however, continued to find fault with him and to urge an attack upon the British in the Capital.

Although Washington refused to throw his worn and hungry troops upon the perfectly prepared and victorious enemy entrenched in Philadelphia, he was

[1] Marshall (1st ed.), iii, 287. Marshall omits this sentence in his second edition. But his revised account is severe enough.

[2] The Reverend Jacob Duché, to Washington, Oct. 8, 1777; *Cor. Rev.*: Sparks, i, 448–58.

eager to meet the British in the open field. But he must choose the place. So when, early in December, Howe's army marched out of Philadelphia the Americans were ready. Washington had taken a strong position on some hills toward the Schuylkill not far from White Marsh. After much maneuvering by the British and effective skirmishing by detachments of the patriots,[1] the two armies came into close contact. Not more than a mile away shone the scarlet uniforms of the Royal troops. Washington refused to be lured from his advantageous ground.[2] Apparently the British were about to attack and a decisive battle to be fought. After Brandywine and Germantown, another defeat would have been ruinous.

Washington personally animated his men. Marshall, who witnessed it, thus describes the scene: "The American chief rode through every brigade of his army, delivering, in person, his orders respecting the manner of receiving the enemy, exhorting his troops to rely principally on the bayonet, and encouraging them by the steady firmness of his countenance, as well as by his words, to a vigorous performance of their duty." [3]

These words make one see, as one reads, the great Virginian in his noblest aspect — calm in the face of possible disaster, his spirit burning brightest on the

[1] Washington to President of Congress, Dec. 10, 1777; *Writings*: Ford, vi, 238–39.

[2] Clark's Diary, *Proc.*, N.J. Hist. Soc. (1st Series), vii, 102–03. "It seems that the enemy had waited all this time before our lines to decoy us from the heights we possessed." (*Ib.*)

[3] Marshall, i, 184.

very fuel of danger itself, his clear mind unclouded by what was likely to befall.

Each division, each regiment, each company, was given plain and practical orders for the expected conflict. And we may be sure that each man, private as well as officer, took heart as he looked upon the giant figure and listened to the steady directions and undismayed encouragement of his chief. Certain it is that John Marshall so felt and thought. A rare picture, this, full of life and color, that permits us to behold the growth in the young soldier's soul of that faith in and devotion to George Washington, seeds of which had been planted in his childhood days in the Blue Ridge home.

Finally the British, seeing the resolute front of the Americans and already bleeding from the fierce thrusts of Morgan's Virginia riflemen, suddenly withdrew to Philadelphia,[1] and Washington's army went into winter quarters on the hills of Valley Forge.

[1] Marshall, i, 184.

CHAPTER IV

VALLEY FORGE AND AFTER

Unless some great and capital change suddenly takes place . . . this army must inevitably starve, dissolve, or disperse. (Washington, Dec. 23, 1777.)

John Marshall was the best tempered man I ever knew. Nothing discouraged, nothing disturbed him. (Lieutenant Slaughter, of Marshall at Valley Forge.)

GAUNT and bitter swept down the winter of 1777. But the season brought no lean months to the soldiers of King George, no aloes to the Royal officers in fat and snug Philadelphia.[1] It was a period of rest and safety for the red-coated privates in the city, where, during the preceding year, Liberty Bell had sounded its clamorous defiance; a time of revelry and merry-making for the officers of the Crown. Gay days chased nights still gayer, and weeks of social frolic made the winter pass like the scenes of a warm and glowing play.

For those who bore the King's commission there were balls at the City Tavern, plays at the South-Street Theater; and many a charming flirtation made lively the passing months for the ladies of

[1] It appears that, throughout the Revolution, Pennsylvania's metropolis was noted for its luxury. An American soldier wrote in 1779: "Philada. may answer very well for a man with his pockets well lined, whose pursuit is idleness and dissipation. But to us who are not in the first predicament, and who are not upon the latter errand, it is intolerable. . . . A morning visit, a dinner at 5 o'clock — Tea at 8 or 9 — supper and up all night is the round *die in diem*. . . . We have advanced as far in luxury in the third year of our Indepeny. as the old musty Republics of Greece and Rome did in twice as many hundreds." (Tilghman to McHenry, Jan. 25, 1799; Steiner, 25.)

the Capital, as well as for lieutenant and captain, major and colonel, of the invaders' army. And after the social festivities, there were, for the officers, carousals at the "Bunch of Grapes" and all night dinners at the "Indian Queen." [1]

"You can have no idea," wrote beautiful Rebecca Franks, — herself a keen Tory, — to the wife of a patriot, "you can have no idea of the life of continued amusement I live in. I can scarce have a moment to myself. I spent Tuesday evening at Sir William Howe's, where we had a concert and dance. . . . Oh, how I wished Mr. Paca would let you come in for a week or two! . . . You'd have an opportunity of raking as much as you choose at Plays, Balls, Concerts, and Assemblies. I have been but three evenings alone since we moved to town." [2]

"My wife writes me," records a Tory who was without and whose wife was within the Quaker City's gates of felicity, "that everything is gay and happy [in Philadelphia] and it is like to prove a frolicking winter." [3] Loyal to the colors of pleasure, society waged a triumphant campaign of brilliant amusement. The materials were there of wit and loveliness, of charm and manners. Such women there were as Peggy Chew and Rebecca Franks, Williamina Bond and Margaret Shippen — afterwards the wife of Benedict Arnold and the probable cause of his fall; [4] such men as Banastre Tarleton of the Dragoons, twenty-three years old, handsome and accomplished;

[1] Trevelyan, iv, 279. [2] *Ib.*, 280. [3] *Ib.*

[4] The influence of Margaret Shippen in causing Arnold's treason is now questioned by some. (See Avery, vi, 243–49.)

brilliant Richard Fitzpatrick of the Guards; Captain John André, whose graces charmed all hearts.[1] So lightly went the days and merrily the nights under the British flag in Philadelphia during the winter of 1777–78.

For the common soldiers there were the race-course and the cock-pit, warm quarters for their abodes, and the fatness of the land for their eating. Beef in abundance, more cheese than could be used, wine enough and to spare, provisions of every kind, filled pantry and cellar. For miles around the farmers brought in supplies. The women came by night across fields and through woods with eggs, butter, vegetables, turkeys, chickens, and fresh meat.[2] For most of the farmers of English descent in that section hated the war and were actively, though in furtive manner, Tory. They not only supplied the British larder, but gave news of the condition and movements of the Americans.[3]

Not twenty miles away from these scenes of British plenty and content, of cheer and jollity, of wassail and song, rose the bleak hills and black ravines of Valley Forge, where Washington's army had crawled some weeks after Germantown. On the Schuylkill heights and valleys, the desperate Americans made an encampment which, says Trevelyan, "bids fair to be the most celebrated in the

[1] Trevelyan, iv, 281–82. [2] *Ib.*, 278–80.

[3] *Ib.*, 268–69; also Marshall, i, 215. The German countrymen, however, were loyal to the patriot cause. The Moravians at Bethlehem, though their religion forbade them from bearing arms, in another way served as effectually as Washington's soldiers. (See Trevelyan iv, 298–99.)

world's history." [1] The hills were wooded and the freezing soldiers were told off in parties of twelve to build huts in which to winter. It was more than a month before all these rude habitations were erected.[2] While the huts were being built the naked or scarcely clad [3] soldiers had to find what shelter they could. Some slept in tents, but most of them lay down beneath the trees.[4] For want of blankets, hundreds, had "to sit up all night by fires."[5] After Germantown Washington's men had little to eat at any time. On December 2, "the last ration had been delivered and consumed."[6] Through treachery, cattle meant for the famishing patriots were driven into the already over-supplied Philadelphia.[7]

The commissariat failed miserably, perhaps dishonestly, to relieve the desperate want. Two days before Christmas there was "not a single hoof of any kind to slaughter, and not more than twenty-five barrels of flour!" [8] Men died by the score from starvation.[9] Most of the time "fire cake" made of dirty, soggy dough, warmed over smoky fires, and

[1] Trevelyan, iv, 290.

[2] The huts were fourteen by sixteen feet, and twelve soldiers occupied each hut. (Sparks, 245.)

[3] "The men were literally naked [Feb. 1] some of them in the fullest extent of the word." (Von Steuben, as quoted in Kapp, 118.)

[4] *Hist. Mag.*, v, 170.

[5] Washington to President of Congress, Dec. 23, 1777; *Writings*: Ford, vi, 260.

[6] Marshall, i, 213.

[7] *Ib.*, 215.

[8] Washington to President of Congress, Dec. 23, 1777; *Writings*: Ford, vi, 258.

[9] "The poor soldiers were half naked, and had been half starved, having been compelled, for weeks, to subsist on simple flour alone and this too in a land almost literally flowing with milk and honey." (Watson's description after visiting the camp, Watson, 63.)

washed down with polluted water was the only sustenance. Sometimes, testifies Marshall himself, soldiers and officers "were absolutely without food." [1] On the way to Valley Forge, Surgeon Waldo writes: "I'm Sick — eat nothing — No Whiskey — No Baggage — Lord, — Lord, — Lord." [2] Of the camp itself and of the condition of the men, he chronicles: "Poor food — hard lodging — Cold Weather — fatigue — Nasty Cloaths — nasty Cookery — Vomit half my time — Smoak'd out of my senses — the Devil 's in it — I can't Endure it — Why are we sent here to starve and freeze — What sweet Felicities have I left at home; — A charming Wife — pretty Children — Good Beds — good food — good Cookery — all agreeable — all harmonious. Here, all Confusion — Smoke — Cold, — hunger & filthyness — A pox on my bad luck. Here comes a bowl of beef soup, — full of burnt leaves and dirt, sickish enough to make a hector spue — away with it, Boys — I'll live like the Chameleon upon Air." [3]

While in overfed and well-heated Philadelphia officers and privates took the morning air to clear the brain from the night's pleasures, John Marshall and his comrades at Valley Forge thus greeted one another: "Good morning Brother Soldier (says one to another) how are you? — All wet, I thank'e, hope you are so — (says the other)." [4] Still, these empty, shrunken men managed to squeeze some fun out of it. When reveille sounded, the hoot of an owl would come from a hut door, to be answered by like hoots

[1] Marshall (1st ed.), iii, 341.
[2] *Hist. Mag.*, v, 131.
[3] *Ib.*
[4] *Ib.*, 132.

and the cawing of crows; but made articulate enough to carry in this guise the cry of "'No meat! — No meat!' The distant vales Echo'd back the melancholy sound — 'No Meat! — No Meat!' . . . What have you for our Dinners, Boys? [one man would cry to another] 'Nothing but Fire Cake and Water, Sir.' At night — 'Gentlemen, the Supper is ready.' What is your Supper, Lads? 'Fire Cake & Water, Sir.'"

Just before Christmas Surgeon Waldo writes: "Lay excessive Cold & uncomfortable last Night — my eyes are started out from their Orbits like a Rabbit's eyes, occasion'd by a great Cold — and Smoke. What have you got for Breakfast, Lads? 'Fire Cake and Water, Sir.' The Lord send that our Commissary of Purchases may live on Fire Cake & Water till their glutted Gutts are turned to Pasteboard."

He admonishes: "Ye who Eat Pumpkin Pie and Roast Turkies — and yet Curse fortune for using you ill — Curse her no more — least she reduce you . . . to a bit of Fire Cake & a Draught of Cold Water, & in Cold Weather." [1]

Heart-breaking and pitiful was the aspect of these soldiers of liberty. "There comes a Soldier — His bare feet are seen thro' his worn out Shoes — his legs nearly naked from the tatter'd remains of an only pair of stockings — his Breeches not sufficient to cover his Nakedness — his Shirt hanging in Strings — his hair dishevell'd — his face meagre — his whole appearance pictures a person foresaken &

[1] *Hist. Mag.*, v, 132–33.

discouraged. He comes, and crys with an air of wretchedness & despair — I am Sick — my feet lame — my legs are sore — my body cover'd with this tormenting Itch — my Cloaths are worn out — my Constitution is broken — my former Activity is exhausted by fatigue — hunger & Cold! — I fail fast I shall soon be no more! And all the reward I shall get will be — 'Poor Will is dead.'" [1]

On the day after Christmas the soldiers waded through snow halfway to their knees. Soon it was red from their bleeding feet.[2] The cold stung like a whip. The huts were like "dungeons and . . . full as noisome." [3] Tar, pitch, and powder had to be burned in them to drive away the awful stench.[4] The horses "died by hundreds every week"; the soldiers, staggering with weakness as they were, hitched themselves to the wagons and did the necessary hauling.[5] If a portion of earth was warmed by the fires or by their trampling feet, it froze again into ridges which cut like knives. Often some of the few blankets in the army were torn into strips and wrapped around the naked feet of the soldiers only to be rent into shreds by the sharp ice under foot.[6] Sick men lay in filthy hovels covered only by their rags, dying and dead comrades crowded by their sides.[7]

As Christmas approached, even Washington became so disheartened that he feared that "this army

[1] *Hist. Mag.*, v, 131–32.

[2] Trevelyan, iv, 297.

[3] *Ib.* For putrid condition of the camp in March and April, 1778, see Weedon, 254–55 and 288–89.

[4] Trevelyan, iv, 298.

[5] *Ib.*

[6] Personal narrative; Shreve, *Mag. Amer. Hist.*, Sept., 1897, 568.

[7] Trevelyan, iv, 298.

must dissolve;"[1] and the next day he again warned Congress that, unless the Commissary were quickly improved, "this army must inevitably . . . starve, dissolve, or disperse."[2]

Early in 1778 General Varnum wrote General Greene that "The situation of the Camp is such that in all human probability the Army must soon dissolve. Our desertions are astonishingly great."[3] "The army must dissolve!" "The army must dissolve!" — the repeated cry comes to us like the chant of a saga of doom.

Had the British attacked resolutely, the Americans would have been shattered beyond hope of recovery.[4] On February 1, 1778, only five thousand and twelve men out of a total of more than seventeen thousand were capable of any kind of service: four thousand were unfit for duty because of nakedness.[5] The patriot prisoners within the British lines were in even worse case, if we credit but half the accounts then current. "Our brethren," records Surgeon Waldo in his diary, "who are unfortunately Prisoners in Philadelphia, meet with the most savage & inhumane treatments — that Barbarians are Capable of inflicting. . . . One of these poor unhappy men — drove to the last extreem by the rage of hunger —

[1] Washington to President of Congress, Dec. 22, 1777; *Writings*: Ford, vi, 253.

[2] Washington to President of Congress, Dec. 23, 1777; *ib.*, 257.

[3] General Varnum to General Greene, Feb. 12, 1778, Washington MSS., Lib. Cong., no. 21. No wonder the desertions were so great. It was not only starvation and death but the hunger-crazed soldiers "had daily temptations thrown out to them of the most alluring nature," by the British and Loyalists. (Chastellux, translator's note to 51.)

[4] Marshall, i, 227.

[5] *Ib.*

eat his own fingers up to the first joint from the hand, before he died. Others eat the Clay — the Lime — the Stones — of the Prison Walls. Several who died in the Yard had pieces of Bark, Wood, — Clay & Stones in their mouths — which the ravings of hunger had caused them to take in the last Agonies of Life."[1]

The Moravians in Bethlehem, some miles away from Valley Forge, were the only refuge of the stricken patriots. From the first these Christian socialists were the Good Samaritans of that ghastly winter. This little colony of Germans had been overrun with sick and wounded American soldiers. Valley Forge poured upon it a Niagara of starvation, disease, and death. One building, scarcely large enough for two hundred and fifty beds, was packed with nearly a thousand sick and dying men. Dysentery reduced burly strength to trembling weakness. A peculiar disease rotted blood and bones. Many died on the same foul pallet

[1] *Hist. Mag.*, v, 132. This is, probably, an exaggeration. The British were extremely harsh, however, as is proved by the undenied testimony of eye-witnesses and admittedly authentic documentary evidence. For their treatment of American prisoners see Dandridge: *American Prisoners of the Revolution*, a trustworthy compilation of sources. For other outrages see Clark's Diary, *Proc.*, N.J. Hist. Soc., vii, 96; Moore's *Diary*, ii, 183. For the Griswold affair see Niles: *Principles and Acts of the Revolution*, 143–44. For transportation of captured Americans to Africa and Asia see Franklin's letter to Lord Stormont, April 2, 1777; Franklin's *Writings*: Smyth, vii, 36–38; also Moore's *Diary*, i, 476. For the murder of Jenny M'Crea see Marshall, i, 200, note 9, Appendix, 25; and Moore's *Diary*, i, 476; see also Miner: *History of Wyoming*, 222–36; and British officer's letter to Countess of Ossory, Sept. 1, 1777; *Pa. Mag. Hist. and Biog.*, i, footnote to 289; and Jefferson to Governor of Detroit, July 22, 1779; *Cal. Va. St. Prs.*, i, 321. For general statement see Marshall (1st ed.), iii, 59. These are but a few of the many similar sources that might be cited.

before it could be changed. The beds were "heaps of polluted litter." Of forty of John Marshall's comrades from a Virginia regiment, which was the "pride of the Old Dominion," only three came out alive.[1] "A violent putrid fever," testifies Marshall, "swept off much greater numbers than all the diseases of the camp."[2]

Need, was there not, at Valley Forge for men of resolve so firm and disposition so sunny that they would not yield to the gloom of these indescribable months? Need, was there not, among these men, for spirits so bright and high that they could penetrate even the death-stricken depression of this fetid camp with the glow of optimism and of hope?

Such characters were there, we find, and of these the most shining of all was John Marshall of the Virginia line.[3] He was a very torch of warmth and encouragement, it appears; for in the journals and diaries left by those who lived through Valley Forge, the name of John Marshall is singled out as conspicuous for these comforting qualities.

"Although," writes Lieutenant Philip Slaughter, who, with the "two Porterfields and Johnson," was

[1] Trevelyan, iv, 299. [2] Marshall, i, 227.

[3] John Marshall's father was also at Valley Forge during the first weeks of the encampment and was often Field Officer of the Day. (Weedon.) About the middle of January he left for Virginia to take command of the newly raised State Artillery Regiment. (Memorial of Thomas Marshall; *supra.*) John Marshall's oldest brother, Thomas Marshall, Jr., seventeen years of age, was commissioned captain in a Virginia State Regiment at this time. (Heitman, 285.) Thus all the male members of the Marshall family, old enough to bear arms, were officers in the War of the Revolution. This important fact demonstrates the careful military training given his sons by Thomas Marshall before 1775 — a period when comparatively few believed that war was probable.

the messmate of John Marshall, "they were reduced sometimes to a single shirt, having to wrap themselves in a blanket when that was washed"[1] and "the snow was knee-deep all the winter and stained with blood from the naked feet of the soldiers,"[2] yet "nothing discouraged, nothing disturbed" John Marshall. "If he had only bread to eat," records his fellow officer, "it was just as well; if only meat it made no difference. If any of the officers murmured at their deprivations, he would shame them by good-natured raillery, or encourage them by his own exuberance of spirits.

"He was an excellent companion, and idolized by the soldiers and his brother officers, whose gloomy hours were enlivened by his inexhaustible fund of anecdote. . . . John Marshall was the best tempered man I ever knew,"[3] testifies his comrade and messmate.

So, starving, freezing, half blind with smoke, thinly clad and almost shoeless, John Marshall went through the century-long weeks of Valley Forge, poking fun wherever he found despondency, his drollery bringing laughter to cold-purpled lips, and, his light-hearted heroism shaming into erectness the bent backs of those from whom hope had fled. At one time it would be this prank; another time it would be a different expedient for diversion. By some miracle he got hold of a pair of silk stockings and at mid-

[1] This was the common lot; Washington told Congress that, of the thousands of his men at Valley Forge, "few men have more than one shirt, many only the moiety of one and some none at all." (Washington to President of Congress, Dec. 23, 1777; *Writings:* Ford, vi, 260.)

[2] Slaughter, 107–08.

[3] Howe, 266.

night made a great commotion because the leaves he had gathered to sleep on had caught fire and burned a hole in his grotesque finery.[1]

High spirits undismayed, intelligence shining like a lamp, common sense true as the surveyor's level — these were the qualities which at the famine camp at Valley Forge singled the boyish Virginia officer out of all that company of gloom. Just before the army went into winter quarters Captain-Lieutenant Marshall was appointed "Deputy Judge Advocate in the Army of the United States," [2] and at the same time, by the same order, James Monroe was appointed aide-de-camp to Lord Stirling, one of Washington's generals.[3]

Such was the confidence of his fellow officers and of the soldiers themselves in Marshall's judgment and fairness that they would come to him with their disputes and abide by his decision; and these tasks, it seems, the young Solomon took quite seriously. He heard both sides with utmost patience, and, having taken plenty of time to think it over, rendered his decision, giving the reasons therefor in writing.[4] So just after he had turned his twenty-second year, we find John Marshall already showing those qualities which so distinguished him in after life. Valley Forge was a better training for Marshall's peculiar abilities than Oxford or Cambridge could have been.

His superiority was apparent, even to casual ob-

[1] Slaughter, 108.

[2] Weedon, 134; also, Heitman, 285. [3] *Ib.*

[4] Description of Marshall at Valley Forge by eye-witness, in *North American Review* (1828), xxvi, 8.

servers, notwithstanding his merriment and waggishness. One of a party visiting Valley Forge said of the stripling Virginia officer: "By his appearance then we supposed him about twenty-two or twenty-three years of age. Even so early in life . . . he appeared to us *primus inter pares*, for amidst the many commissioned officers he was discriminated for superior intelligence. Our informant, Colonel Ball, of another regiment in the same line,[1] represented him as a young man, not only brave, but signally intelligent." [2]

Marshall's good humor withstood not only the horrors of that terrible winter, but also Washington's iron military rule. The Virginia lieutenant saw men beaten with a hundred stripes for attempting to desert. Once a woman was given a hundred lashes and drummed out of the army. A lieutenant was dismissed from the service in disgrace for sleeping and eating with privates, and for buying a pair of shoes from a soldier.[3] Bitter penalties were inflicted on large numbers of civilians for trying to take flour, cattle, and other provisions to the British in Philadelphia; [4] a commissary was "mounted on a horse, back foremost, without a Saddle, his Coat turn'd wrong side out his hands tied behind him & drummed out of the Army (Never more to return) by all the Drums in the Division." [5]

What held the patriot forces together at this time?

[1] Ninth Virginia. (Heitman, 72.)

[2] *North American Review* (1828), xxvi, 8.

[3] Weedon, Feb. 8, 1778, 226–27. Washington took the severest measures to keep officers from associating with private soldiers.

[4] *Ib.*, 227–28.

[5] *Ib.*, Jan. 5, 1778; 180.

George Washington, and he alone.[1] Had he died, or had he been seriously disabled, the Revolution would have ended. Had typhoid fever seized Washington for a month, had any of those diseases, with which the army was plagued, confined him, the patriot standard would have fallen forever. Washington was the soul of the American cause. Washington was the Government. Washington was the Revolution. The wise and learned of every land agree on this. Professor Channing sums it all up when he declares: "Of all men in history, not one so answers our expectations as Washington. Into whatever part of his life the historian puts his probe, the result is always satisfactory." [2]

Yet intrigue and calumny sought his ruin. From Burgoyne's surrender on through the darkest days of Valley Forge, the Conway cabal shot its filaments through Congress, society, and even fastened upon the army itself. Gates was its figurehead, Conway its brain, Wilkinson its tool, Rush its amanuensis, and certain members of Congress its accessories before the fact. The good sense and devotion of Patrick Henry, who promptly sent Washington the anonymous letter which Rush wrote to the Virginia Governor,[3] prevented that shameful plot from driving Washington out of the service of his country.

Washington had led his army to defeat after de-

[1] See Washington's affecting appeal to the soldiers at Valley Forge to keep up their spirits and courage. (Weedon, March 1, 1778, 245–46.)

[2] Channing, ii, 559.

[3] See Rush's anonymous letter to Henry and the correspondence between Henry and Washington concerning the cabal. (Henry, i, 544–51.)

feat while Gates had gained a glorious victory; Gates was the man for the hour — down, then, with the incompetent Virginian, said the conspirators. The Pennsylvania Legislature, wroth that Howe's army had not been beaten, but allowed to occupy the comfortable Capital of the State, remonstrated to Congress. That body, itself, was full of dissatisfaction with the Commander-in-Chief. Why would he not oust the British from Philadelphia? Why had he allowed Howe to escape when that general marched out to meet him? As the first step toward Washington's downfall, Congress created a new Board of War, with Gates as President; Conway was made Inspector-General.[1]

The conspirators and those whom their gossip could dupe lied about Washington's motives. His abilities, it was said, were less than ordinary; and his private conduct, went the stealthy whisper, was so bad as to prove the hypocrisy of his deportment.[2] Nor were Washington's generals spared. Greene was a sycophant, said these assassins of character; Sullivan a braggart; Stirling "a lazy, ignorant drunkard." These poisoners of reputation declared that General Knox and Alexander Hamilton were "paltry satellites" of Washington and flatterers of his vanity.[3] So cunning, subtle, and persistent were these sappers and miners of reputation that even the timely action of Patrick Henry in sending Washington Rush's unsigned attack might not have prevented the great American's overthrow; for envy of Washington's strength, suspicion of his motives, distrust of

[1] Marshall, i, 217. [2] Trevelyan, iv, 301. [3] *Ib.*, 303–04.

his abilities, had made some impression even on men like John Adams.[1]

The great American bore himself with dignity, going hardly further than to let his enemies know that he was aware of their machinations.[2] At last, however, he lashed out at Congress. Let that body look to the provisioning of the army if it expected the soldiers to fight. The troops had no food, no clothing. The Quartermaster-General had not been heard from for five months. Did his critics think "the soldiers were made of stocks and stones?" Did they think an active winter campaign over three States with starving naked troops "so easy and practicable a business? I can assure those gentlemen," writes Washington, "that it is a much easier and less distressing thing to draw remonstrances in a comfortable room by a good fireside, than to occupy a cold, bleak hill, and sleep under frost and snow, without clothes or blankets. . . . I have exposed myself to detraction and calumny" because "I am obliged to conceal the true state of the army from public view. . . . No day nor scarce an hour passes without" an officer tendering his resignation.[3]

Washington was saved finally by the instinctive faith which that part of the common people who

[1] "The idea that any one Man Alone can save us is too silly for any Body but such weak Men as Duché to harbor for a Moment." (Adams to Rush, Feb. 8, 1778; *Old Family Letters*, 11; and see Lodge: *Washington*, i, 208; also Wallace, chap. ix.)

[2] Sparks, 252; and Marshall, i, 218.

[3] Washington to President of Congress, Dec. 23, 1777; *Writings*: Ford, vi, 257–65. And see Washington's comprehensive plans for the reorganization of the entire military service. (Washington to Committee of Congress, Jan. 28, 1778; *ib.*, 300–51.)

still supported the Revolution had in their great leader, and by his soldiers' stanch devotion, which defeat after defeat, retreat hard upon the heels of preceding retreat, hunger and nakedness, wounds and sickness could not shake.

"See the poor Soldier," wrote Surgeon Waldo at Valley Forge. "He labours thro' the Mud & Cold with a Song in his mouth, extolling War & Washington." [1]

Congress soon became insignificant in numbers, only ten or twelve members attending, and these doing business or idling as suited their whim.[2] About the only thing they did was to demand that Washington strike Philadelphia and restore the members of this mimetic government to their soft, warm nests. Higher and yet more lofty in the esteem of his officers and men rose their general. Especially was this true of John Marshall for reasons already given, which ran back into his childhood.

In vain Washington implored the various States to strengthen Congress by sending their best men to this central body. Such able men as had not taken up arms for their country refused to serve in Congress. Nearly every such man "was absorbed in provincial politics, to the exclusion of any keen and intelligent interest in the central Government of his nation." [3]

Amidst the falling snow at Valley Forge, Washing-

[1] *Hist. Mag.*, v, 131.

[2] On April 10, 1778, Ædanus Burke of South Carolina broke a quorum and defied Congress. (Secret Journals of Congress, April 10, 11, 24, 25, 1778, i, 62; and see Hatch, 21.)

[3] Trevelyan, iv, 291–92.

ton thus appealed to Colonel Harrison in Virginia: "America never stood in more eminent need of the wise, patriotic, and spirited exertions of her Sons than at this period. . . . The States, separately, are too much engaged in their local concerns. . . . The States . . . have very inadequate ideas of the present danger."[1] The letter could not be sent from that encampment of ice and death for nearly two weeks; and the harassed commander added a postscript of passionate appeal declaring that "our affairs are in a more distressed, ruinous, and deplorable condition than they have been in since the commencement of the War."[2]

"You are beseeched most earnestly, my dear Col^o^ Harrison," pleaded Washington, "to exert yourself in endeavoring to rescue your Country by . . . sending your best and ablest Men to Congress — these characters must not slumber nor sleep at home in such times of pressing danger — they must not content themselves in the enjoyment of places of honor or profit in their Country [Virginia][3] while the common interests of America are mouldering and sinking into irretrievable . . . ruin, in which theirs also must ultimately be involved."[4]

With such men, Washington asserted, "party disputes and personal quarrels are the great business of the day, whilst the momentous concerns of an

[1] Washington to Harrison, Dec. 18, 1778; *Writings:* Ford, vii, 297–98.

[2] *Ib.*

[3] At this period and long after a State was referred to as "the country."

[4] Washington to Harrison, Dec. 18, 1778; *Writings:* Ford, vii, 297–98.

empire [America][1] . . . are but secondary considerations." Therefore, writes Washington, in angry exasperation, "in the present situation of things, I cannot help asking — Where is Mason — Wythe — Jefferson?"[2]

"Where is Jefferson?" wrote Washington in America's darkest hour, when the army was hardly more than an array of ragged and shoeless skeletons, and when Congress was so weak in numbers and ability that it had become a thing of contempt. Is it not probable that the same question was asked by the shivering soldiers and officers of the Continental army, as they sat about the smoking fires of their noisome huts sinking their chattering teeth into their "Fire Cake" and swallowing their brackish water? If Washington would so write, is it not likely that the men would so talk? For was not Jefferson the penman who had inscribed the Declaration of Independence, for which they were fighting, suffering, dying?

Among the Virginians especially there must have been grave questionings. Just as to John Marshall's army experience the roots of the greatest of his constitutional opinions may clearly be traced, so the beginnings of his personal estimate of Thomas Jefferson may be as plainly found in their relative situations and conduct during the same period.

John Marshall was only a few days beyond his twentieth year when, with his Culpeper Minute Men,

[1] Until after Jefferson's Presidency, our statesmen often spoke of our "empire." Jefferson used the term frequently.

[2] Washington to Harrison, Dec. 18, 1778; *Writings:* Ford, vii, 301–02.

he fought the British at Great Bridge. Thomas Jefferson at that time was thirty-two years old; but the prospect of battle on Virginia's soil did not attract him. At Valley Forge, John Marshall had just entered on his twenty-third year, and Thomas Jefferson, thirty-five years old, was neither in the army nor in Congress. Marshall had no fortune; Jefferson was rich.[1]

So, therefore, when as reserved a man as Washington had finally and with great effort trained himself to be, asked in writing, "Where is Jefferson?" is it not a reasonable inference that the Virginia officers in the familiar talk of comrades, spoke of Jefferson in terms less mild?

And, indeed, where was Thomas Jefferson? After serving in Congress, he refused point-blank to serve there again and resigned the seat to which he had been reëlected. "The situation of my domestic affairs renders it indispensably necessary that I should solicit the substitution of some other person," was the only excuse Jefferson then gave.[2] He wanted to go to the State Legislature instead, and to the State Legislature he went. His "domestic affairs" did not prevent that. In his Autobiography, written forty-four years afterward (1821), Jefferson declares that he resigned from Congress and went to the

[1] "My estate is a large one . . . to wit upwards of ten thousand acres of valuable land on the navigable parts of the James river and two hundred negroes and not a shilling out of it is or ever was under any incumbrance for debt." (Jefferson to Van Staphorst and Hubbard, Feb. 28, 1790; *Works:* Ford, vi, 33.) At the time of Valley Forge Jefferson's estate was much greater, for he had sold a great deal of land since 1776. (See Jefferson to Lewis, July 29, 1787; *ib.*, v, 311.)

[2] Jefferson to Pendleton, July, 1776; *ib.*, ii, 219–20.

State Legislature because "our [State] legislation under the regal government had many very vicious points which urgently required reformation and I thought I could be of more use in forwarding that work."[1]

So while the British revels were going on in Philadelphia and the horrors of Valley Forge appeared to be bringing an everlasting night upon American liberty, and when the desperation of the patriot cause wrung from the exasperated Washington his appeal that Virginia's ablest men should strengthen the feeble and tottering Congress, Jefferson was in the State Legislature. But he was not there merely enjoying office and exclusively engaged in party politics as Washington more than intimates. He was starting such vital reforms as the abolition of entails, the revision of the criminal code, the establishment of a free school system, the laying of the legal foundations of religious freedom.[2]

In short, Jefferson was sowing the seeds of liberalism in Virginia. But it is only human nature that breasts bearing the storm of war should not have thrilled in admiration of this civil husbandry. It was but natural that the benumbed men at Valley Forge should think the season early for the planting of State reforms, however needful, when the very ground of American independence was cold and still freezing with patriot misfortune and British success.

[1] Jefferson's *Autobiography; Works:* Ford, i, 57.

[2] Tucker, i, 92 *et seq.*; Randall, i, 199 *et seq.*; *Works:* Ford, ii, 310, 323, 324.

Virginia's Legislature might pass all the so-called laws it liked; the triumph of the British arms would wipe every one of them from the statute books. How futile, until America was free, must all this bill-drafting and reforming have appeared to the hard-driven men on the Schuylkill's Arctic hills! "Here are we," we can hear them say, "in worse case than most armies have been in the whole history of the world; here are we at Valley Forge offering our lives, wrecking our health, losing the little store we have saved up, and doing it gladly for the common American cause; and there, in safe and comfortable Williamsburg or at sumptuous Monticello, is the man who wrote our Declaration of Independence, never venturing within the sound of cannon or smell of powder and even refusing to go to Congress."

The world knows now that Jefferson was not to be blamed. He was not a man of arms, dreaded the duties of a soldier, had no stomach for physical combat.[1] He was a philosopher, not a warrior. He loved to write theories into laws that correct civil abuses by wholesale, and to promote the common good by sweeping statutes. Also, he was a born politician, skillful and adroit in party management above any man in our history.[2]

But as a man of action in rough weather, as an executive in stern times, he himself admitted his deficiency.[3] So we know to-day and better understand this great reformer, whose devotion to human

[1] Bloodshed, however, Jefferson thought necessary. See *infra*, vol. II, chap. I.

[2] See vol. II of this work.

[3] Jefferson's *Autobiography; Works:* Ford, i, 79.

rights has made men tolerant of his grave personal shortcomings. Nothing of this, however, could have occurred to the starving, shivering patriot soldiers in their awful plight at Valley Forge. Winning the war was their only thought, as always is the soldier's way.

Early in April, 1778, when, but for the victory at Saratoga, the Revolution seemed well-nigh hopeless to all but the stoutest hearts, an old and valued English friend begged Washington to give up the apparently doomed American cause. The Reverend Andrew Burnaby appealed to him for American and British reunion. "Must the parent and the child be forever at variance? And can either of them be happy, independent of the other?" The interests of the two countries are the same; "united they will constitute the fairest and happiest state in the world; divided they will be quite the reverse. It is not even possible that America should be happy, unconnected with Great Britain." In case America should win, the States will fall asunder from civil discord. The French, "that false and treacherous people," will desert the Americans. Great Britain and America have "the same interest, the same lineage, the same language, the same liberty, the same religion, connecting them." Everybody in England wants reunion; even the Government is anxious to "rectify . . . errors and misunderstandings." It is time to "heal the wounds on both sides." Washington can achieve this "divine purpose" and "thereby acquire more glory and confer more real and lasting service, both to your own country and to mankind in general than . . . ever yet happened to the lot of any one man."[1]

This subtle plea, designed to prepare the way for the British "Commission of Conciliation," neither flattered nor tempted Washington. It insulted him. He acted more vigorously than ever; and, soon afterward, his answer was delivered with cannon and bayonet on the field of Monmouth.[2]

When the winter had passed, Washington once more appealed to Congress to cease its bickering and indecision. That body was jealous of the army, he declared, whereas, said he, "We should all be considered, Congress and Army, as one people, embarked in one cause, in one interest; acting on the same principle, and to the same end" — a philosophy which a young Virginia officer was then absorbing and continued to absorb, until it became the ruling force in his life.

"No history extant," continues Washington, "can furnish an instance of an army's suffering such uncommon hardships . . . and bearing them with the same patience and fortitude. To see men without clothes to cover their nakedness, without blankets to lie on, without shoes, by which their marches might be traced by the blood from their feet, and almost as often without provisions as with them, marching through the frost and snow, and at Christmas taking up their winter quarters within a day's march of the enemy, without a house or hut to cover them, 'till they could be built, and submitting to it without a

[1] Burnaby to Washington, April 9, 1788; *Cor. Rev.*: Sparks, ii, 100–02. Washington sent no written answer to Burnaby.

[2] See *infra*.

murmur, is proof of patience and obedience which, in my opinion can scarce be paralleled."[1]

Further shaming Congress into action, Washington says that "with us . . . the officer . . . must break in upon his private fortune for present support, without a prospect of future relief"; while, with the British, company commands "are esteemed so honorable and so valuable that they have sold of late from fifteen to twenty-two hundred pounds sterling and . . . four thousand guineas have been given for a troop of dragoons."[2]

Finally came the spring of 1778. The spirits of the men rose with the budding of the trees. Games and sport alternated with drill and policing of the camp. The officers made matches for quoits, running, and jumping. Captain-Lieutenant Marshall was the best athlete in his regiment. He could vault over a pole "laid on the heads of two men as high as himself." A supply from home had reached him at last, it appears, and in it were socks. So sometimes Marshall ran races in his stocking feet. In knitting this foot apparel, his mother had made the heels of white yarn, which showed as he ran. Thus came his soldier nickname of "Silver Heels."[3]

As spring advanced, the troops recovered their

[1] Washington to Banister, April 21, 1778; *Writings:* Ford, vi, 477–87. In thus trying to arouse Congress to a sense of duty, Washington exaggerates the patience of his troops. They complained bitterly; many officers resigned and privates deserted in large numbers. (See *supra.*)

[2] *Ib.*

[3] Thayer, 12. For camp sports, see Waldo's poem, *Hist. Mag.*, vii, 272–74.

strength and, finally, were ready and eager again to meet the enemy. Washington had persuaded General Greene to accept the vital office of Quartermaster-General; and food, clothing, and munitions had somewhat relieved the situation.[1] Baron von Steuben had wrought wonders in the drill and discipline of the men and in the officers' knowledge of their technical duties.[2] "I should do injustice if I were to be longer silent with regard to the merits of the Baron de [von] Steuben" Washington told Congress, in hearty appreciation of the Prussian general's services.[3]

Another event of immense importance cheered the patriot forces and raised patriot hopes throughout America. The surrender of Burgoyne had encouraged the French statesmen to attempt the injury of England by helping the revolting colonies. On May 6, 1778, the treaty of alliance with Louis XVI was laid before Congress.[4] The miseries of the past winter were forgotten by the army at Valley Forge in the joy over the French Monarch's open championship of the American cause and his attack upon the British.[5] For it meant trained troops, ships of war, munitions, and money. It meant more — it signified, in the end, war by France upon England.

[1] Lossing, ii, 595, *et seq.*

[2] Marshall, i, 230. And see Hatch's clear account of the training given by this officer (63). To the work of Von Steuben was due the excellent discipline under fire at Monmouth. And see Kapp, already cited; and Bolton, 132. Even Belcher says that our debt to Von Steuben is as great as that to Lafayette. (Belcher, ii, 14.)

[3] Washington to President of Congress, April 30, 1778; *Writings:* Ford, vi, 507, and footnote to 505–06. And see Channing, iii, 292.

[4] See Channing, iii, 286, 288; and Marshall, i, 235, 236.

[5] Marshall, i. 237.

The hills of Valley Forge were vocal with huzzas and the roar of cannon. Songs filled the air. The army paraded. Sermons were preached. The rebound went to heights of enthusiasm equaling the former depths of despair.[1] Marshall, we may be sure, joined with his characteristic zest in the patriots' revel of happiness. Washington alone had misgivings. He feared that, because of the French alliance, Congress and the States would conclude that "we have nothing more to do" and so "relapse into a state of supineness and perfect security."[2] Precisely this occurred.

Soon, however, other inspiriting tidings came — the British, it was said, were about to quit Philadelphia. The gayety in that city had continued throughout the winter, and just before the evacuation, reached its climax in a festival of almost unbelievable opulence and splendor. Processions of flower-decked boats, choruses, spectacles, and parades crowded the day; dancing and music came with sunset, and at midnight, lighted by hundreds of wax candles, twelve hundred people sat down to a dinner of Oriental luxury served by negroes clad in the rich costumes of the East "with silver collars and bracelets."[3]

When, on June 18, the Royal forces abandoned the city, the Americans were quick in pursuit.

[1] Sparks, 267; and Moore's *Diary*, i, 48–50.

[2] Washington to McDougall, May 5, 1778; *Writings:* Ford, vii, 6. Washington was advised of the treaty with the French King before it was formally presented to Congress.

[3] Description by Major André, who took part in this amazing performance, reprinted in *American Historical and Literary Curiosities*, following plate 26. And see Moore's *Diary*, ii, 52–56.

On June 28, a day of blistering heat, the battle of Monmouth was fought. That scorching Sunday "was long remembered all over the United States as the most sultry day which had ever been endured since mankind learned to read the thermometer." [1]

It must have been very hot indeed, for Marshall himself speaks of "the intense heat"; [2] and he disliked extreme terms. Marshall was one of the advance guard [3] under Wayne, with Lee in command of the division. In a previous council of war most of the higher officers were decidedly against risking the action; but Washington overruled them and ordered Lee to attack the British force "the moment it should move from its ground." [4]

The Commander-in-Chief, with the main body of American troops, was to come to Lee's support. It is unnecessary to go over the details of Lee's unhappy blunder, his retreat, Washington's Berserker rage and stinging rebuke on the battlefield in sight and hearing of officer and private, the turning of the rout into attack, and attack into victory by the sheer masterfulness of the mighty Virginian. From ten o'clock until nightfall the conflict raged, the Americans generally successful.

The overpowering sun made the action all but insufferable. Many died from the effects of the furnace-like heat. The fighting was heavy and often

[1] Trevelyan, iv, 376.
[2] Marshall, i, 252.

[3] Marshall speaks of "one thousand select men" under Wayne; Maxwell's division was with Wayne under Lee; Marshall was in the battle, and it seems certain that he was among Wayne's "select men" as on former and later occasions.

[4] Marshall, i, 252.

hand to hand. Throughout the day Washington was the very soul of battle. His wrath at Lee's retreat unleashed the lion in him. He rode among the troops inspiring, calming, strengthening, steadying. Perhaps at no time in his life, except at Braddock's defeat, was his peculiar combination of cool-headed generalship and hot-blooded love of combat so manifest in a personal way as on this blazing June day at Monmouth.

"Never," testifies Lafayette, who commanded part of the advance and fought through the whole battle, "was General Washington greater in war than in this action. His presence stopped the retreat. His dispositions fixed the victory. His fine appearance on horseback, his calm courage, roused by the animation produced by the vexation of the morning, gave him the air best calculated to excite enthusiasm."[1]

When Washington was preparing the final stroke, darkness fell. The exhausted Americans, their clothing drenched with sweat, slept on their arms upon the field of battle, their General-in-Chief himself lying on the ground among the living, the wounded, and the dead. Somewhere on that hard-fought ground, Captain-Lieutenant John Marshall stretched himself by his comrades. Washington was determined to press the attack at break of day. But at midnight the British stole away so silently that the Americans did not hear a sound from their retreat.[2] The Americans lost eight officers and sixty-one privates killed,

[1] Lafayette to Marshall; Marshall, i, footnote to 255.

[2] Marshall, i, 254–59.

one hundred and sixty wounded, and one hundred and thirty missing. The British left more than two hundred and fifty dead upon the field.[1]

Upon Charles Lee most accounts of the battle of Monmouth have placed the brand of infamy. But John Marshall did not condemn Lee utterly. There were, it appears, two sides of the business — the difficulty of the ground, the mistake made by Scott, a reinforcement of the British rear, and other incidents.[2] These appealed even to Washington when the calm of judgment returned to him after the battle was fought and his blazing wrath had cooled; and had Lee not sent insulting letters to the Commander-in-Chief, it is probable that no further action would have been taken.[3]

Marshall had been in the fight from first to last; he had retreated unwillingly with the other five thousand men whom Lee commanded; he was a fighting man, always eager for the shock of arms; he cherished a devotion to Washington which was the ruling attachment of his life — nevertheless, Marshall felt that more was made of Lee's misconduct than the original offense deserved. Writing as the chosen biographer of Washington, Marshall gives both sides of this controversy.[4]

This incident throws light upon Marshall's temperament. Other historians in their eulogy of Wash-

[1] For descriptions of the battle of Monmouth see Washington to President of Congress, July 1, 1778; *Writings:* Ford, vii, 76–86; and to John Augustine Washington, July 4, 1778; *ib.*, 89–92. Also Marshall, i, 251–56; Trevelyan, iv, 376–80; Irving, iii, 423–34; Sparks, 272–78; Lossing, ii, 354–65.

[2] Marshall, i. 251–56. [3] *Ib.*, 257. [4] *Ib.*, 257–58.

ington, have lashed the memory of Lee naked through the streets of public scorn. Marshall refuses to join the chorus of denunciation. Instead, he states the whole case with fairness.[1]

Three days after Monmouth, he was promoted to a full captaincy;[2] and, as we have seen, he had been made Deputy Judge Advocate at Valley Forge. Holding these two offices, Marshall continued his military service.

The alliance with the French King, followed by the American success at Monmouth, lulled the patriots into an unwarranted feeling of security. Everybody seemed to think the war was over. Congress became more lethargic than ever, the States more torpid and indifferent. The British had seized the two points commanding King's Ferry on the North River, thus cutting the communication between the small American forces on opposite sides of the Hudson.[3] To restore this severed connection was important; and it was essential to arouse once more the declining interest of the people. Washington resolved to take Stony Point, the then well nigh impregnable position dominating King's Ferry from the New Jersey side.

A body of light infantry was carefully selected from all ranks. It was the flower of Washington's troops in health, stability, courage, and discipline.

[1] Girardin follows Marshall in his fair treatment of Lee. (Burk, iv, 290.)

[2] He was promoted July 1, 1778. (Heitman, 285.)

[3] The whole patriot army everywhere, except in the extreme south and west, now numbered only sixteen thousand men. (Marshall, i, 306–07.)

Upon this "*élite* of the army," says Dawson, "the safety of the Highlands and, indirectly, that of the cause of America, were dependent." [1] This corps of picked soldiers was intended for quick and desperate enterprises of extra hazard. John Marshall was one of those selected.[2] Their first notable task was to take Stony Point by assault. Anthony Wayne was placed in command. "I have much at heart," Washington told Wayne, in the capture of this position, "the importance of which . . . is too obvious to need explanation." [3]

Yet even to these men on missions of such moment, supplies came tardily and in scant quantities. Wayne's "men were almost naked." [4]

[1] The fullest and most accurate account of the capture of Stony Point, and conditions immediately preceding, is given by Dawson in his *Assault on Stony Point.*

[2] Binney, in Dillon, iii, 315–16. The care in the selection of the various commands of "light infantry," so often used by Washington after the first year of the war, is well illustrated by his orders in this case. "The officers commanding regiments," runs Washington's orders, "will be particularly careful in the choice of the men. . . . The Adjutant General is desired to pass the men . . . under critical inspection, and return all who on any account shall appear unfit for this kind of service to their regiments, to be replaced by others whom he shall approve." (Washington's Order Book, iii, 110–11; MS., Lib. Cong.)

[3] Washington to Wayne (Private and Confidential), July 1, 1779; Dawson, 18–19.

[4] Dawson, 20. Wayne's demand for sustenance and clothing, however, is amusing. "The Light Corps under my Command," writes Wayne, ". . . have had but two days fresh Provision . . . nor more than three days allowance of Rum *in twelve days,* which article I borrowed from Gen[l] McDougall with a Promise to Replace it. I owe him Seventy five Gallons — must therefore desire you to forward three Hod[ds] [hogsheads] of Rum to this place with all possible Dispatch together with a few fat sheep & ten Head of good Cattle." (Wayne to Issuing Commissary, July 9, 1779; *ib.*, 20–21.)

Wayne wrote to Washington concerning clothing: "I have an

Finally, on June 15, 1779, the time came for the storming of the fort. It was washed on three sides by the waters of the Hudson and a marsh separated it from the solid land on the west. Heavy guns were on the great hill of rock; lighter batteries were placed on its slope; two rows of abatis were farther down; and the British ships in the river commanded almost every point of attack.[1]

A party of Wayne's men was detailed to remove obstructions, capture the sentries, and, in general, prepare the way for the assault by the first detachment of the Light Infantry, which was to advance with unloaded muskets, depending exclusively on the bayonet.[2] The fort was taken by those assigned to make the initial attempt, Colonel Fleury being the first to enter the stronghold. Below at the edge of the marsh waited the major part of Wayne's little force, among whom was the future Chief Justice of the United States.

[word illegible] Prejudice in favor of an Elegant Uniform & Soldierly Appearance — . . . I would much rathar risque my life and Reputation at the Head of the same men in an Attack Clothed & Appointed as I could wish — with a Single Charge of Ammunition — than to take them as they appear in Common with Sixty Rounds of Cartridges." (Dawson, 20–21.)

Washington wrote in reply: "I agree perfectly with you." (*Ib.*, 21.)

[1] Marshall, i, 310.

[2] Wayne's order of battle was as picturesque as it was specific. Officer and private were directed "to fix a Piece of White paper in the most Conspicuous part of his Hat or Cap . . . their Arms unloaded placing their whole Dependence on the Bay[t] . . . If any Soldier presumes to take his Musket from his Shoulder or Attempt to fire or begin the battle until Ordered by his proper Officer he shall be Instantly put to death by the Officer next him. . . . Should any Soldier . . . attempt to Retreat one Single foot or Sculk in the face of danger, the Officer next to him is Immediately to put him to death." (*Ib.*, 35–38.)

If the state of Wayne's nerves is an indication, we know how the young Virginia captain felt, there in the midnight, holding himself in readiness for the order to advance. For early in the evening Wayne thus wrote to his brother-in-law: "This will not reach your eye until the Writer is no more — the Enclosed papers . . . [will] enable [you] to defend the Character and Support the Honor of the man who . . . fell in defense of his Country. . . . Attend to the Education of my Little *Son & Daughter* — I fear that their tender Mother will not Survive this Stroke."[1] But the British were overcome more easily than anybody had thought possible,[2] and, though wounded, Wayne survived to give more displays of his genuine heroism, while Providence spared John Marshall for a no less gallant and immeasurably greater part in the making of the American Nation.[3]

But the brilliant exploit went for nothing. The Americans failed to take Verplanck's Point on the eastern bank of the river and the patriot forces were still separated. Unable to spare enough men to garrison Stony Point permanently and since the Ferry remained under the British guns, Washington moved his army to the Highlands. The British at

[1] Wayne to Delaney, July 15, 1779; Dawson, 46–47.

[2] The generous and even kindly treatment which the Americans accorded the vanquished British is in striking contrast with the latter's treatment of Americans under similar circumstances. When the fort was taken, the British cried, "*Mercy, mercy, dear, dear Americans,*" and not a man was injured by the victors after he ceased to resist. (Dawson, 53; and Marshall, i, 311.)

[3] The fort was captured so quickly that the detachment to which Marshall was assigned had no opportunity to advance.

once reoccupied the abandoned fort which Wayne's men had just captured.

A detail from the Light Infantry was placed under Major Henry Lee of Virginia, who was instructed to watch the main forces of the enemy. Among Lee's flying detachment was Captain John Marshall. For three weeks this scouting expedition kept moving among the ravines, hills, and marshes, always in close touch with the British. "At Powles Hook, a point of land on the west side of the Hudson, immediately opposite the town of New York, penetrating deep into the river," [1] the enemy had erected works and garrisoned them with several hundred men. The British had made the Hook an island by digging a deep ditch through which the waters of the river flowed; and otherwise had rendered their position secure.

The daring Lee resolved to surprise and capture the defending force, and Washington, making sure of lines of retreat, approved the adventure. All night of August 18, 1779, Lee's men marched stealthily among the steep hills, passed the main body of the British army who were sleeping soundly; and at three o'clock in the morning crossed the ditch, entered the works, and carried away one hundred and fifty-nine prisoners, losing in the swift, silent effort only two killed and three wounded.[2] This audacious feat fired the spirits of the patriot forces and covered the British with humiliation and chagrin.

Here, except for a small incident in Arnold's invasion of Virginia, John Marshall's active participa-

[1] Marshall, i, 314. [2] *Ib.*, 314–16.

tion in actual warfare ended. He was sent home[1] because of the expiration of the term of enlistments of the regiments in which he had commanded and the excess of officers which this created.[2] The Revolution dragged along; misfortune and discouragement continued to beat upon the granite Washington. The support of Louis XVI was a staff upon which, substantial as it was, the people of the States leaned too heavily. Their exertions relaxed, as we have seen; Jefferson, patriot and reformer, but not efficient as an executive, was Governor of Virginia; and John Marshall waited in vain for the new command which never appeared.

On December 30, 1780, Jefferson received positive news of Arnold's invasion.[3] He had been warned by Washington that just this event was likely to occur;[4] but he had not summoned to the colors a single man of the militia, probably fifty thousand of whom were available,[5] nor taken any measures to prepare for it. Not until the hostile vessels entered Virginia waters to disembark the invading force was General Nelson sent to watch the enemy and call out the local militia of the adjacent vicinity; and not until news came that the British were on their way up the James River did the Governor summon the militia of the neighboring counties. The Royal soldiers reached

[1] The rolls show Marshall in active service as captain until December 9, 1779. (Records, War Dept.) He retired from the service February 12, 1781. (Heitman, 285.)

[2] Binney, in Dillon, iii, 290. There often were more officers of a State line than there were men to be officered; this was caused by expiring enlistments of regiments.

[3] Tucker, i, 136.

[4] Marshall, i, 418.

[5] *Ib.*, 139.

Richmond on January 4, 1781, without opposition; there Arnold burned some military factories and munitions, and returned down the river. John Marshall hastened to the point of danger, and was one of the small American force that ambushed the British some distance below Westover, but that scattered in panic at the first fire of the invaders.[1]

Jefferson's conduct at this time and especially during the subsequent invasion of the State has given an unhappy and undeserved coloring to his personal character.[2] It all but led to his impeachment by the Virginia Legislature;[3] and to this day his biographers are needlessly explanatory and apol-

[1] Marshall, i, 419; Binney, in Dillon, iii, 290.

[2] Even the frightened Virginia women were ashamed. "Such terror and confusion you have no idea of. Governor, Council, everybody scampering. . . . How dreadful the idea of an enemy passing through such a country as ours committing enormities that fill the mind with horror and returning exultantly without meeting one impediment to discourage them." (Eliza Ambler to Mildred Smith, 1781 MS. Also *Atlantic Monthly*, lxxxiv, 538–39.) Miss Ambler was amused, too, it seems. She humorously describes a boastful man's precipitate flight and adds: "But this is not more laughable than the accounts we have of our illustrious G–[overno]–r [Jefferson] who, they say, took neither rest nor food for man or horse till he reached C–[arte]–r's mountain." (*Ib.*) This letter, as it appears in the *Atlantic Monthly*, differs slightly from the manuscript, which has been followed in this note.

These letters were written while the laughing young Tarleton was riding after the flying Virginia Government, of which Eliza Ambler's father was a part. They throw peculiar light on the opinions of Marshall, who at that time was in love with this lady's sister, whom he married two years later. (See *infra*, chap. v.)

[3] An inquiry into Jefferson's conduct was formally moved in the Virginia Legislature. But the matter was not pressed and the next year the Legislature passed a resolution of thanks for Jefferson's "impartial, upright, and attentive Administration." (See Eckenrode's thorough treatment of the subject in his *Revolution in Virginia*, chap. vii. And see Tucker, i, 149–56, for able defense of Jefferson; and Dodd, 63–64; also Ambler, 37.)

ogetic in regard to this phase of his career. These incidents confirmed the unfortunate impressions of Jefferson which Marshall and nearly all the Virginia officers and soldiers had formed at Valley Forge. Very few of them afterward changed their unfavorable opinion.[1]

It was his experience, then, on the march, in camp, and on the battlefield, that taught John Marshall the primary lesson of the necessity of efficient government. Also his military life developed his real temperament, which was essentially conservative. He had gone into the army, as he himself declared, with "wild and enthusiastic notions,"[2] unlike those of the true Marshall. It did not occur to this fighting Virginia youth when, responding to Patrick Henry's call, he marched southward under the coiled-rattlesnake flag inscribed "Don't tread on me," that anything was needed except to drive the oppressor into the sea. A glorious, vague "liberty" would do the rest, thought the stripling backwoods "shirtman," as indeed almost all of those who favored the patriot cause seemed to think.[3]

[1] Monroe, Bland, and Grayson are the only conspicuous exceptions.

[2] Story, in Dillon, iii, 338.

[3] This prevalent idea is well stated in one of Mrs. Carrington's unpublished letters. "What sacrifice would not an American, or Virginian (even) at the earliest age have made for so desireable an end — young as I was [twelve years old when the war began] the Word Liberty so *continually* sounding in my ears seemed to convey an idea of everything that was desirable on earth — true that in attaining it, I was to see every present comfort abandoned; a charming home where peace and prosperous fortune afforded all the elegancies of life, where nature and art united to render our residence delightful, where my ancestors had acquired wealth, and where my parents looked forward to days of ease and comfort, all this was to be given up; but in infancy the love of change is so predominant that we lose sight of con-

And when in blue and buff, as an officer of the Continental army, he joined Washington, the boyish Virginia lieutenant was still a frontier individualist, though of the moderate type. But four years of fighting and suffering showed him that, without a strong and practical government, democracy cannot solve its giant problems and orderly liberty cannot live. The ramshackle Revolutionary establishment was, he found, no government at all. Hundreds of instances of its incredible dissensions and criminal inefficiency faced him throughout these four terrible years; and Marshall has recorded many of them.

Not only did each State do as it pleased, as we have seen, but these pompous sovereignties actually interfered in direct and fatal fashion with the Continental army itself. For example, when the soldiers of the line from one State happened to be in another State, the civil power of the latter often "attempted to interfere and to discharge them, notwithstanding the fact that they were not even citizens of that State."[1] The mutiny of underfed, poorly clothed, unpaid troops, even in the State lines; the yielding of Congress to their demands, which, though just in themselves, it was perilous to grant on compulsion;[2] the discontent of the people caused by the forcible State seizure of supplies, — a seizure which a strong National Government could not have surpassed in harshness,[3] — were still other

sequences and are willing to relinquish present good for the sake of novelty, this was particularly the case with me." (Mrs. Carrington to her sister Nancy, March, 1809; MS.; and see *infra*, chap. VIII.)

[1] Marshall, i, 355–65. [2] *Ib.*, 422–24. [3] *Ib.*, 425.

illustrations of the absolute need of an efficient central power. A few "judicious patriots" did urge the strengthening of National authority, but, writes Marshall, they were helpless to "correct that fatal disposition of power [by States and Congress] which had been made by enthusiasm uninstructed by experience." [1] Time and again Marshall describes the utter absence of civil and military correlations and the fearful results he had felt and witnessed while a Revolutionary officer.

Thus it is that, in his service as a soldier in the War for our Independence, we find the fountain-head of John Marshall's National thinking. And every succeeding circumstance of his swift-moving and dramatic life made plainer and clearer the lesson taught him on red battlefield and in fetid camp. No one can really understand Marshall's part in the building of the American Nation without going back to these sources. For, like all living things, Marshall's constructive opinions were not made; they grew. They were not the exclusive result of reasoning; they were the fruit of an intense and vivid human experience working upon a mind and character naturally cautious, constructive, and inclined to order and authority.

[1] Marshall, i, 425.

CHAPTER V

MARRIAGE AND LAW BEGINNINGS

He was always and under all circumstances an enthusiast in love. (Mrs. Carrington, of Marshall's devotion to his wife.)

It was upon a night of gentle gayety in the late winter or early spring of 1779–80 that Captain John Marshall first met Mary Ambler. When he went back to Virginia to take charge of troops yet to be raised, he visited his father, then commanding at the village of Yorktown.[1] More than a year had gone by since Colonel Marshall had left his son at Valley Forge. On this visit befell the most important circumstance of John Marshall's private life. While he was waiting for his new command, an event came to pass which relieved his impatience to prolong still further his four years of active warfare and inspired him to improve this period of enforced absence from

[1] Mrs. Carrington to her sister Nancy, 1810; *Atlantic Monthly*, lxxxiv, 546; and same to same, March, 1809; MS. Thomas Marshall was now Colonel of the Virginia State Regiment of Artillery and continued as such until February 26, 1781, when his men were discharged and he became "a reduced officer." (Memorial of Thomas Marshall, *supra*. See Appendix IV.) This valuable historical document is the only accurate account of Thomas Marshall's military services. It disproves the statement frequently made that he was captured when under Lincoln at Charleston, South Carolina, May 12, 1780. Not only was he commanding the State Artillery in Virginia at that time, but on March 28 he executed a deed in Fauquier County, Virginia, and in June he was assisting the Ambler family in removing to Richmond. (See *infra*.) If a Thomas Marshall was captured at Charleston, it must have been one of the many others of that name. There was a South Carolina officer named Thomas Marshall and it is probably he to whom Heitman refers. Heitman (ed. 1914), 381. For account of the surrender of Charleston, see McCrady, iii, 507–09.

the front, by preparing himself for his chosen profession.

Jacquelin Ambler had been one of Yorktown's wealthiest men, and his house was called a "mansion." But the war had ruined him financially;[1] and the year 1780 found the Ambler family dwelling in humble quarters. "The small retired tenement" to which reduced circumstances forced him to take his invalid wife and young children stood next door to the headquarters of Colonel Thomas Marshall. The Ambler family was under Colonel Marshall's protection, for the father's duties as State Councillor kept him at Williamsburg.[2] But the reverse of Jacquelin Ambler's fortunes did not make this little house less attractive than his "mansion" had been.

The unusual charm of his daughters rendered that modest abode very popular. Indeed, this quality of pleasing seems to have been a common possession of the Ambler family, and has become historic. It was this very Jacquelin Ambler for whom Rebecca Burwell threw over Thomas Jefferson. This Virginia belle was the love of Jefferson's youth. She was the "Campana in die,"[3] "Belinda," "Adnileb," and "R. B." of Jefferson's letters.[4] But Rebecca Bur-

[1] "Certain it is that another Revolutionary War can never happen to affect and ruin a family so completely as ours has been!" It "involved our immediate family in poverty and perplexity of every kind." (Mrs. Carrington to her sister Nancy; *Atlantic Monthly*, lxxxiv, 545–47.)

[2] *Ib.*

[3] Dog Latin and crude pun for "bell in day."

[4] Jefferson to Page and to Fleming, from Dec. 25, 1762, to March 20, 1764; *Works:* Ford, i, 434–52. In these delightful letters Jefferson tells of his infatuation, sometimes writing "Adnileb" in Greek.

"He is a boy and is indisputably in love in this good year 1763, and

well preferred Jacquelin Ambler and became his wife.[1] The Ambler daughters inherited from both mother and father that beauty, grace, and goodness which gave them their extraordinary personal appeal.

During John Marshall's visit to his father the young ladies of Yorktown saw to it that a "ball" was given. All the officers had been invited, of course; but none of them aroused such interest as did Captain John Marshall of the Eleventh Virginia Regiment of the line.

The fame of this young soldier, fresh from the war, was very bright in Virginia. His name was on the lips of all the fair attendants of the dance. They were in a quiver of expectancy at the prospect of meeting the gallant captain who had fought under the great Washington and who had proved himself a hero at Brandywine and Germantown, at Valley Forge and Monmouth.

Years afterwards, Eliza, the eldest of the Ambler daughters, described the event in a letter full of color written to her sister. "We had been accustomed to hear him [Marshall] spoken of by all as a very *paragon*," writes Mrs. Carrington, "we had often seen

he courts and sighs and tries to capture his pretty little sweetheart, but like his friend George Washington, fails. The young lady will not be captured!" (Susan Randolph's account of Jefferson's wooing Rebecca Burwell; *Green Bag*, viii, 481.)

[1] Tradition says that George Washington met a like fate at the hands of Edward Ambler, Jacquelin's brother, who won Mary Cary from the young Virginia soldier. While this legend has been exploded, it serves to bring to light the personal attractiveness of the Amblers; for Miss Cary was very beautiful, heiress of a moderate fortune, and much sought after. It was Mary Cary's sister by whom Washington was captivated. (Colonel Wilson Miles Cary, in Pecquet du Bellet, i, 24–25.)

letters from him fraught with filial and paternal affection. The eldest of fifteen children, devoted from his earliest years to his younger brothers and sisters, he was almost idolized by them, and every line received from him was read with rapture." [1]

"Our expectations were raised to the highest pitch," writes the elder sister, "and the little circle of York was on tiptoe on his arrival. Our girls particularly were emulous who should be first introduced"; but Mary Ambler, then only fourteen years old, and very diffident and retiring, astonished her sister and friends by telling them that "we were giving ourselves useless trouble; for that she, for the first time, had made up her mind to go to the ball, though she had not even been at dancing school, and was resolved to set her cap at him and eclipse us all." [2]

Great was their disappointment when finally Captain Marshall arrived. His ungainly dress, slouch hat, and rustic bearing instantly quenched their enthusiasm.[3] They had looked forward to seeing a handsome, romantic figure, brilliantly appareled, and a master of all the pleasing graces; instead they beheld a tall, loose-jointed young man, thin to gauntness, whose clothes were hanging about him as if upon a rack, and whose manners were awkward and timid to the point of embarrassment. No game was he for Cupid's bow, thought these belles of old Yorktown.

[1] Mrs. Carrington to her sister Nancy; *Atlantic Monthly*, lxxxiv, 547. Of the letters which John Marshall wrote home while in the army, not one has been preserved.

[2] *Ib.* [3] *Ib.*

"I, expecting an Adonis, lost all desire of becoming agreeable in his eyes when I beheld his awkward figure, unpolished manners, and total negligence of person"; [1] thus writes Eliza Ambler of the impression made upon her by the young soldier's disheveled aspect and unimpressive deportment. But Mary Ambler stuck to her purpose, and when John Marshall was presented to her, both fell in love at first sight. Thus began a lifelong romance which, in tenderness, exaltation, and constancy is unsurpassed in the chronicle of historic affections.

It was no longer alone the veneration for a father that kept the son in Yorktown. Day followed day, and still the gallant captain tarried. The unfavorable first judgment gave way to appreciation. He soon became a favorite at every house in the village.[2] His gift of popularity was as great, it seems, among women as among men; and at the domestic fireside as well as in the armed camp. Everybody liked John Marshall. There was a quality in him that inspired confidence. Those who at first had been so disappointed in his dress and manners soon forgot both in his wholesome charm. They found him delightfully companionable.[3] Here was preëminently a social being, they discovered. He liked people, and wanted people to like him. He was full of fun and hearty laughter; and his rare good sense and sheer manliness furnished solid foundation to his lighter qualities.

[1] Mrs. Carrington to her sister Nancy; *Atlantic Monthly*, lxxxiv, 547.

[2] *Hist. Mag.*, iii, 165. While this article is erroneous as to dates, it is otherwise accurate.

[3] *Ib.*, 167.

So every door in Yorktown was thrown open to Captain John Marshall. But in Jacquelin Ambler's house was the lodestone which drew him. April had come and the time of blossoming. On mellow afternoons, or by candlelight when the sun had set, the young lover spent as much time as the proprieties would permit with Mary Ambler, telling her of the war, no doubt; and, as her sister informs us, reading poetry by the hour.[1] Through it all he made love as hard as he could. He wooed as ardently and steadily as he had fought.[2]

The young lover fascinated the entire Ambler family. "Under the slouched hat," testifies Mary Ambler's sister, "there beamed an eye that penetrated at one glance the inmost recesses of the human character; and beneath the slovenly garb there dwelt a heart complete with every virtue. From the moment he loved my sister he became truly a brother to me. . . . Our whole family became attached to him, and though there was then no certainty of his becoming allied to us, we felt a love for him that can never cease. . . . There was no circumstance, however trivial, in which we were concerned, that was not his care."

He would "read to us from the best authors, particularly the Poets, with so much taste and feeling, and pathos too, as to give me an idea of their sublimity, which I should never have had an idea of. Thus did he lose no opportunity of blending improvement with our amusements, and thereby gave

[1] Mrs. Carrington to her sister Nancy; *Atlantic Monthly*, lxxxiv, 547.
[2] *Hist. Mag.*, iii, 167.

us a taste for books which probably we might never otherwise have had." [1]

The time had come when John Marshall must acquire a definite station in civil life. This was especially necessary if he was to take a wife; and married he would be, he had decided, whenever Mary Ambler should be old enough and would consent. He followed his parents' wishes [2] and began his preparation for the bar. He told his sweetheart of his purpose, of course, and her family "learned [of it] with pleasure." [3] William and Mary College, "the only public seminary of learning in the State," [4] was only twelve miles from Yorktown; and there the young officer attended the law lectures of George Wythe for perhaps six weeks [5] — a time so short that, in the opinion of the students, "those who finish this Study [law] in a few months, either have strong natural parts or else they know little about it." [6] Recalling a criticism of one of Marshall's "envious contemporaries" some years later, Mrs. Carrington says: "Allusion was made to his short stay at William and Mary, and that he could have gained little there." [7]

[1] Mrs. Carrington to her sister Nancy; *Atlantic Monthly*, lxxxiv, 547.

[2] *Supra*, chap. II.

[3] Mrs. Carrington to her sister Nancy; *Atlantic Monthly*, lxxxiv, 547.

[4] "Notes on Virginia": Jefferson; *Works:* Ford, iv, 65.

[5] Mrs. Carrington to her sister Nancy; *supra.* William and Mary was the first American institution of learning to adopt the modern lecture system. (Tyler: *Williamsburg*, 153.) The lecture method was inaugurated Dec. 29, 1779 (*ib.*, 174–75), only four months before Marshall entered.

[6] John Brown to Wm. Preston, Feb. 15, 1780; *W. and M. C. Q.*, ix, 76.

[7] Mrs. Carrington to her sister Nancy; MS.

It is said also that Marshall took a course in philosophy under President Madison, then the head of the little college and afterwards Bishop of Virginia; but this is unlikely, for while the soldier-student took careful notes of Wythe's lectures, there is not a word in his notebook [1] concerning any other college activity. The faculty consisted of five professors.[2] The college was all but deserted at that time and closed entirely the year after John Marshall's flying attendance.[3]

Although before the Revolution "the Necessary Expence of each Scholar *yearly* . . . [was] only 15 £ Currency," [4] one of Marshall's fellow students testifies that: "The amazing depreciation of our Currency has raised the price of Every Article so enormously that I despair'd of my Father's ability to support me here another year. . . . Board & entring under two Professors amounts to 4000^{wt} of Tobacco." [5]

[1] See *infra.*

[2] The Reverend James Madison, Professor of Natural Philosophy and Mathematics; James McClung, Professor of Anatomy and Medicine; Charles Bellini, Professor of Modern Languages; George Wythe, Professor of Law; and Robert Andrews, Professor of Moral and Intellectual Philosophy. (*History of William and Mary College,* Baltimore, 1870, 70–71.) There was also a fencing school. (John Brown to Wm. Preston, Feb. 15, 1780; *W. and M. C. Q.,* ix, 76.)

[3] *History of William and Mary College,* Baltimore, 1870, 45. "Thirty Students and three professors joined the army at the beginning of the Revolutionary War." (*Ib.,* 41.) Cornwallis occupied Williamsburg, June, 1781, and made the president's house his headquarters. (Tyler: *Williamsburg,* 168.)

[4] Fithian, 107.

[5] John Brown to Wm. Preston, Jan. 26, 1780; *W. and M. C. Q.,* ix, 75. Seventeen years later the total cost to a student for a year at the college was one hundred and fifty to one hundred and seventy dollars. (La Rochefoucauld, iii, 49–56.) The annual salary of the

The intercourse of students and faculty was extremely democratic. There was a "college table" at which the students took their meals. According to the college laws of that time, beer, toddy, and spirits and water might be served, if desired.[1] The students were not required to wear either coats or shoes if the weather was warm.[2]

At a later period the students boarded at private houses in the town.[3] Jefferson, who, several years

professors was four hundred dollars and that of the president was six hundred dollars.

[1] In Marshall's time the college laws provided that "No liquors shall be furnished or used at [the college students'] table except beer, cider, toddy or spirits and water." (*History of William and Mary College* (Baltimore, 1870), 44; and see Fithian, Feb. 12, 1774, 106–07.)

Twelve years after Marshall took his hasty law course at William and Mary College, a college law was published prohibiting "the drinking of spirituous liquors (except in that moderation which becomes the prudent and industrious student)." (*History of William and Mary College*, 44.)

In 1769 the Board of Visitors formally resolved that for professors to marry was "contrary to the principles on which the College was founded, and their duty as Professors"; and that if any professor took a wife "his Professorship be immediately vacated." (Resolution of Visitors, Sept. 1, 1769; *ib.*, 45.) This law was disregarded; for, at the time when Marshall attended William and Mary, four out of the five professors were married men.

The college laws on drinking were merely a reflection of the customs of that period. (See chaps. VII and VIII.) This historic institution of learning turned out some of the ablest and best-educated men of the whole country. Wythe, Bland, Peyton and Edmund Randolph, Taylor of Caroline, Nicholas, Pendleton, Madison, and Jefferson are a few of the William and Mary's remarkable products. Every one of the most distinguished families of Virginia is found among her alumni. (See Catalogue of Alumni, *History of William and Mary College*, 73–147. An error in this list puts John Marshall in the class of 1775 instead of that of 1780; also, he did not graduate.)

[2] *Infra*, chap. VII.

[3] La Rochefoucauld, iii, 49; and see Schoepf, ii, 79–80.

William Wirt, writing twenty-three years after Marshall's short attendance, thus describes the college: "They [Virginians] have only one publick seminary of learning. . . . This college . . . in the nig-

before Marshall's short attendance, was a student at William and Mary, describes the college and another public building as "rude, mis-shapen piles, which, but that they have roofs, would be taken for brick-kilns." [1] Chastellux, however, declares that "the beauty of the edifice is surpassed [only] by the richness of its library and that still farther, by the distinguished merit of several of the professors," and he describes the college as "a noble establishment . . . which does honour to Virginia." [2]

The youths attending William and Mary during Marshall's brief sojourn were disgusted by the indifference of the people of the vicinity toward the patriot cause. "The want of Men, Money, Provisions, & still more of Public Virtue & Patriotism is universal — a melancholy Lethargick disposition pervades all Ranks in this part of the Country, they appear as if determined to struggle no more, but to 'stand still & see what the Lord will do for them,'" wrote John Brown in July, 1780.[3]

Mr. Wythe, the professor of law, was the life of

gardly spirit of parsimony which they dignify with the name of economy, these democrats have endowed with a few despicable fragments of surveyors' fees &c. thus converting their national academy into a mere *lazaretto* and feeding its . . . highly respectable professors, like a band of beggars, on the scraps and crumbs that fall from the financial table. And, then, instead of aiding and energizing the police of the college, by a few civil regulations, they permit their youth to run riot in all the wildness of dissipation." (Wirt: *The British Spy*, 131, 132.)

[1] "Notes on Virginia": Jefferson; *Works:* Ford, iv, 69.

[2] Chastellux, 299. It is difficult to reconcile Jefferson's description of the college building with that of the French traveler. Possibly the latter was influenced by the French professor, Bellini.

[3] John Brown to Col. Wm. Preston, July 6, 1780; *W. and M. C. Q.*, ix, 80.

the little institution in this ebbing period of war-time. He established "a Moot Court, held monthly or oftener . . . Mr. Wythe & the other professors sit as Judges. Our Audience consists of the most respectable of the Citizens, before whom we plead our Causes, given out by Mr. Wythe Lawyer like I assure you." The law professor also "form'd us into a Legislative Body, Consisting of about 40 members." Wythe constituted himself Speaker of these seedling lawmakers and took "all possible pains to instruct us in the Rules of Parliament." These nascent Solons of old William and Mary drew original bills, revised existing laws, debated, amended, and went through all the performances of a legislative body.[1]

The parent chapter of the Phi Beta Kappa Society had been instituted at the college; and to this Marshall was immediately elected. "At a meeting of the Society the 18 of May, 1780, Capt. John Marshall being recommended as a gentleman who would make a worthy member of this Society was balloted for & received." [2] This is an important date; for it fixes with reasonable certainty the time of Marshall's entrance at William and Mary. He was probably the oldest of all the students; his army service made him, by far, the most interesting and notable; his extraordinary social qualities never failed to render him popular. It is, therefore, certain that he was made a member of Phi Beta Kappa

[1] John Brown to Col. Wm. Preston, July 6, 1780; *W. and M. C. Q.*, ix, 80.

[2] Records, Phi Beta Kappa Society of William and Mary College, printed in *W. and M. C. Q.*, iv, 236.

without much delay. He probably entered college about May 1.[1]

At once we find the new member appointed on the society's debating team. Two students were selected to "declaim" the question and two to "argue" it.

"Mr. Cabell & Mr. Peyton Short appointed to declaim the Question whether any form of government is more favorable to our new virtue than the Commonwealth.

"Mr. Joseph Cabell and Mr. Marshall to argue the same. An adjournment. William Short President.

"At a meeting in course Saturday June ye 3rd, 1780, Mr. President leaving ye chair with Mr. Fitzhugh to ye same. Mr. Wm Cabell according to order delivered his declamation on ye question given out. Mr. Peyton Short, being unprepared, was silent on ye occasion. Mr. Marshall, a gentleman not immediately interested, argued ye Question." [2]

But it was not debating on which John Marshall was intent, nor any other college duties. He had hard work, it appears, to keep his mind on the learned words that fell from the lips of Mr. Wythe; for on the inside cover and opposite page of the book in which he made notes of Wythe's law lectures,[3] we find in John Marshall's handwriting the words, "Miss Maria Ambler"; and again "Miss M. Ambler"; and still again, this time upside down,

[1] Dr. Lyon G. Tyler, now President of William and Mary College, thinks that this date is approximately correct.

[2] Records, Phi Beta Kappa Society of William and Mary College; printed in *W. and M. C. Q.*, iv, 236.

[3] See *infra.*

"Miss M. Ambler — J. Marshall"; and "John Marshall, Miss Polly Am."; and "John, Maria"; and "John Marshall, Miss Maria"; and "Molly Ambler"; and below this once more, "Miss M. Ambler"; on the corner of the page where the notes of the first lecture are recorded is again inscribed in large, bold letters the magic word, "Ambler." [1]

Jacquelin Ambler had been made Treasurer of State, and, early in June, 1780, the family removed from Yorktown to Richmond, stopping for a day or two in Williamsburg. While there "a ball was . . . given . . . by certain gentlemen in compliment . . . 'to the Misses Amblers.'" Eliza Ambler describes the incidents of this social event. The affair was "simple and frugal as to its viands," she writes, "but of the brilliancy of the company too much cannot be said; it consisted of more Beauty and Elegance than I had ever witnessed before. . . . I was transported with delight." Yet she could not "treat . . . the prime mover in this civility with common good manners. . . . His more successful friend Marshall, was devoted to my sister." [2]

This "ball" ended John Marshall's college studies; the lure of Mary Ambler was greater than that of learning to the none too studious captain. The abrupt ending [3] of the notes he was making of Mr. Wythe's lectures, in the midst of the course, otherwise so inexplicable, was caused by her two days' sojourn in the college town. Forthwith he followed to Rich-

[1] Marshall's Notebook; MS. See *infra*.

[2] Betsy Ambler to Mildred Smith, 1780; *Atlantic Monthly*, lxxxiv, 536.

[3] See *infra*.

mond, where, for two weeks he gayly played the part of the head of the family (acted "Pa," as Marshall quaintly expresses it), apparently in Jacquelin Ambler's absence.[1]

Although he had scarcely begun his studies at William and Mary; although his previous instruction by professional teachers was meager and fragmentary; and although his father could well afford the small expense of maintaining him at Williamsburg long enough for him to secure at least a moderate education, John Marshall never returned to college.[2] No more lectures of Professor Wythe for the young lover. He would begin his professional career at once and make ready for the supreme event that filled all his thoughts. So while in Richmond he secured a license to practice law. Jefferson was then Governor, and it was he who signed the license to the youth who was to become his greatest antagonist. Marshall then went to Fauquier County, and there, on August 28, 1780, was admitted to the bar. "John Marshall, Gent., produced a license from his Excellency the Governor to practice law and took the oaths prescribed by act of Assembly," runs the entry in the record.[3]

He waited for the recruiting of the new troops he was to command, and held himself in readiness to

[1] Marshall to his wife, *infra*.

[2] Marshall could have had at least one year at William and Mary, for the college did not close until June, 1781. Also he could have continued to attend for several weeks after he left in June, 1780; for student John Brown's letters show that the college was still open on July 20 of that year.

[3] County Court Minutes of Fauquier County, Virginia, 1773–80, 473.

take the field, as indeed he rushed to do without orders when Arnold's invasion came. But the new troops never were raised and Marshall finally left the service. "I continued in the army until the year 1781," he tells us, "when, being without a command, I resigned my commission in the interval between the invasion of Virginia by Arnold and Phillips."[1]

During this season of inaction he resolved to be inoculated against the smallpox. This was another effect which falling in love had on the young soldier; for he could, had he wished, have had this done more than once while with Washington's army.[2] He would now risk his health no longer. But the laws of Virginia made the new method of treating smallpox almost impossible.[3] So away on foot [4] went John Marshall to Philadelphia to be made proof against this disfiguring malady.

According to Marshall's own account, he covered the ground at an amazing pace, averaging thirty-five miles a day; but when he arrived, so disreputable did he appear that the tavern refused to take

[1] *Autobiography.*

[2] Marshall, with other officers, did go to Philadelphia in January or February of 1777 to be inoculated for smallpox (Marshall to Colonel Stark, June 12, 1832, supporting latter's pension claim; MSS. Rev. War, S. F. no. 7592, Pension Bureau); but evidently he was not treated or the treatment was not effective.

[3] First, the written permission to be inoculated had to be secured from all the justices of the county; next, all the neighbors for two miles around must consent — if only one of them refused, the treatment could not be given. Any physician was fined ten thousand dollars, if he inoculated without these restrictions. (Hening, ix, 371.) If any one was stricken with smallpox, he was carried to a remote cabin in the woods where a doctor occasionally called upon him. (La Rochefoucauld, iii, 79–80; also De Warville, 433.)

[4] Horses were very scarce in Virginia at this time. It was almost impossible to get them even for military service.

him in.[1] Long-bearded and slovenly clothed, with battered hat and uncouth manners, he gave the unfavorable first impression which the same causes so often produced throughout his life. This is not to be wondered at, for, writing twenty years afterward, when Marshall as Chief Justice was at the height of his career, his sister-in-law testifies that his "total negligence of person . . . often produced a blush on her [Marshall's wife's] cheek." [2] But he finally secured lodgings, was inoculated, and, made secure from the attacks of the dreaded scourge, back he fared to Virginia and Mary Ambler.

And Marshall made love as he made war, with all his might. A very hurricane of a lover he must have been; for many years afterward he declared to his wife's sister that "he looked with astonishment at the present race of lovers, so totally unlike what he had been himself." [3] In a touching letter to his wife, written almost half a century later, Marshall thus recalls the incidents of his courtship: —

"I begin with the ball at York, and with the dinner on the fish at your house the next day: I then retrace my visit to York, our splendid assembly at the Palace [4] in Williamsburg, my visit to Richmond

[1] *Southern Literary Messenger* (quoting from a statement by Marshall), ii, 183.

[2] Mrs. Carrington to her sister Nancy; *Atlantic Monthly*, lxxxiv, 547.

[3] *Ib.*, 548. A story handed down through generations of lawyers confirms Mrs. Carrington. "I would have had my wife if I had had to climb Alleghanys of skulls and swim Atlantics of blood" the legend makes Marshall say in one of his convivial outbursts. (The late Senator Joseph E. McDonald to the author.)

[4] "The Palace" was a public building "not handsome without but

where I acted Pa for a fortnight, my return the ensuing fall and the very welcome reception you gave me on your arrival from Dover, our little tiffs & makings up, my feelings while Major Dick [1] was courting you, my trip to the cottage,[2] the lock of hair, my visit again to Richmond the ensuing fall, and all the thousand indescribable but deeply affecting instances of your affection or coldness which constituted for a time the happiness or misery of my life and will always be recollected with a degree of interest which can never be lost while recollection remains." [3]

When he left the army in 1781, Marshall, although a member of the bar, found no legal business to do.[4] He probably alternated between the Oak Hill plantation in Fauquier County, where his help was sadly needed, and Richmond, where the supreme attraction drew him. Thus another year wore on. In this interval John Marshall engaged in politics, as was the custom of young gentlemen of standing and ambition; and in the fall of 1782 was elected to the House of Delegates from Fauquier County.[5] This

. . . spacious and commodious within and prettily situated." ("Notes on Virginia": Jefferson; *Works:* Ford, iv, 69.)

[1] Richard Anderson, the father of the defender of Fort Sumter. (Terhune: *Colonial Homesteads*, 97.)

[2] A country place of Edward Ambler's family in Hanover County. (See Pecquet du Bellet, i, 35.) Edward Ambler was now dead. His wife lived at "The Cottage" from the outbreak of the war until her death in 1781. (*Ib.*, 26; and Mrs. Carrington to Mrs. Dudley, Oct. 10, 1796; MS.)

[3] Marshall to his wife, Feb. 23, 1826; MS.

[4] Most of the courts were closed because of the British invasion. (Flanders, ii, 301.)

[5] *Infra*, chap. VI.

honor was a material help, not only in his career, but in his suit for the hand of Mary Ambler.

Also, membership in the Legislature required him to be, where his heart was, in Richmond, and not two months had John Marshall been in the Capital as a member of Virginia's Legislature when he was married. "In January [3d] 1783," writes Marshall, "I intermarried with Mary Willis Ambler, the second daughter of Mr. Jacquelin Ambler, then Treasurer of Virginia, who was the third son of Mr. Richard Ambler, a gentleman who had migrated from England, and settled at York Town, in Virginia." [1]

The Ambler abode in Richmond was not a romantic place for the wedding. The primitive town was so small that when the Ambler family reached it Eliza exclaimed, "*where* we are to lay our weary heads Heaven knows!" And she describes the house her father rented as "a little dwelling" so small that "our whole family can scarcely stand up altogether in it"; but Jacquelin Ambler took it because, poor as it was, it was "the only decent tenement on the hill." [2]

The elder Ambler sister thus pictures the Richmond of 1780: "This little town is made up of Scotch factors who inhabit small tenements scattered here and there from the river to the hill. Some of them look, as Colonel [Thomas] Marshall has observed, as if the poor Caledonians had brought them over on their backs, the weakest of whom being glad enough to stop at the bottom of the hill, others

[1] *Autobiography.*

[2] Betsy Ambler to Mildred Smith, 1780; *Atlantic Monthly*, lxxxiv, 537.

a little stronger proceeding higher, whilst a few of the stoutest and the boldest reached the summit."[1] Eight years after the Amblers moved to Richmond, Jefferson wrote: "The town below Shockoe creek is so deserted you cannot get a person to live in a house there rent free."[2]

But Mary's cousin, John Ambler, who, at twenty-one years of age, found himself "one of the richest men in the State of Virginia,"[3] solved the difficulty by offering his country seat for the wedding.[4] Mary Ambler was only seventeen when she became the young lawyer's bride,[5] and John Marshall was a little more than ten years older. After the bridegroom had paid the minister his fee, "he had but one solitary guinea left."[6]

This does not mean that John Marshall was without resources, but it indicates the scarcity of ready money in Virginia at the close of the war. Indeed, Marshall's father, while not yet the wealthy man he afterwards became,[7] had, as we have seen, already

[1] Betsy Ambler to Mildred Smith, 1780; *Atlantic Monthly*, lxxxiv, 537.

[2] Jefferson to Short, Dec. 14, 1788; *Works:* Ford, vi, 24. Twelve years after Marshall's marriage, there were but seven hundred houses in Richmond. (Weld, i, 188.)

[3] Pecquet du Bellet, i, 35–37. He was very rich. (See inventory of John Ambler's holdings, *ib.*) This opulent John Ambler married John Marshall's sister Lucy in 1792 (*ib.*, 40–41); a circumstance of some interest when we come to trace Marshall's views as influenced by his connections and sympathies.

[4] Mrs. Carrington to her sister Nancy; *Atlantic Monthly*, lxxxiv, 548.

[5] She was born March 18, 1766, and married January 3, 1783. (Paxton, 37.) Marshall's mother was married at the same age.

[6] Mrs. Carrington to her sister Nancy; *Atlantic Monthly*, lxxxiv, 548.

[7] Thomas Marshall's will shows that he owned, when he died, several years later, an immense quantity of land.

acquired very considerable property. He owned at this time at least two thousand acres in Fauquier County;[1] and twenty-two negroes, nine of them tithable (sixteen years old), twelve horses, and twenty-two head of cattle.[2]

When John Marshall married Miss Ambler, his father gave him one negro and three horses.[3] The following year (1784) the Tithable Book shows but five tithable negroes, eight young negroes, eight horses, and eighteen head of cattle in Thomas Marshall's name. He evidently sold his other slaves and personal property or took them with him to Kentucky. So it is likely that the slaves, horses, and cattle left behind were given to his son, together with a part of Thomas Marshall's Fauquier County farm.[4]

During the Revolution Thomas Marshall was, like most other Continental officers, in sore need of money. He tried to sell his land to Washington for cash. Washington was anxious to buy "Lands in my own Neck at (almost) any price . . . in ye way of Barter . . . for Negroes . . . or . . . for any thing else (except Breeding Mares and Stock)." But he could not pay money. He estimated, by memory, Thomas Marshall's land at £3000, at a time when, because of depreciated money and inflated prices, "a Barrl. of Corn which used to sell for 10/ will now fetch 40 — when a Barl. of Porke that formerly could be had for £3 sells for £15." So

[1] *Supra*, chap. II.
[2] Fauquier County Tithable Book, 1783–84; MS., Va. St. Lib.
[3] *Ib.* [4] See *infra*.

Washington in 1778 thought that "Marshall is not a necessitous man." When it came to trading, the father of his country was keen and suspicious, and he feared, it would seem, that his boyhood friend and comrade in arms would "practice every deception in his power in order to work me . . . up to his price." [1]

Soon after John Marshall met Mary Ambler at the "ball" at Yorktown, and just before he went to William and Mary College, his father sold this very land that Washington had refused to purchase. On March 28, 1780, Thomas Marshall conveyed to Major Thomas Massey [Massie] one thousand acres in Fauquier County for "thirty thousand pounds Currency." [2] This was a part of the seventeen hundred acres for which the elder Marshall had paid "nine hundred and twelve pounds ten shillings" seven years before.[3] The change shows the startling depreciation of Virginia currency as well as Continental paper, both of which in 1780 had reached a very low point and were rapidly going down.[4]

It reveals, too, the Marshall family's extreme need of cash, a want sorely felt by nearly everybody at this period; and the familiar fact that ownership of land did not mean the ready command of money. The year after John Marshall's marriage he wrote to James Monroe: "I do not know what to say to your scheme of selling out. If you can execute it you will have made a very capital sum, if you can

[1] Washington to Lund Washington, Aug. 15, 1778; *Writings:* Ford, vii, 151–52.

[2] Records of Fauquier County (Va.), Deed Book, vii, 533.

[3] *Supra,* chap. II.

[4] See *infra,* chap. VIII.

retain your lands you will be poor during life unless you remove to the western country, but you have secured for posterity an immense fortune"; and Marshall tells Monroe that the latter can avail himself of the knowledge of Kentucky lands possessed by the members of the Marshall family who were on the ground.[1]

Writing twenty years later of economic conditions during the period now under review, Marshall says: "Real property was scarcely vendible; and sales of any article for ready money could be made only at a ruinous loss. . . . In every quarter were found those who asserted it to be impossible for the people to pay their public or private debts." [2]

So, although his father was a very well-to-do man when John Marshall began married life, he had little or no ready money, and the son could not expect much immediate paternal assistance. Thomas Marshall had to look out for the bringing-up of a large number of other children and to consider their future; and it is this fact which probably induced him to seek fortune anew in the Kentucky wilderness after he was fifty years of age. Legend has it that Thomas Marshall made his venture on Washington's advice. At any rate, he settled, permanently, in Kentucky in the fall of 1783.[3]

[1] Marshall to Monroe, Dec. 28, 1784; Monroe MSS., vii, 832; Lib. Cong.

[2] Marshall, ii. 104.

[3] Marshall to Monroe, Dec. 12, 1783; Draper Collection, Wis. Hist. Soc. Thomas Marshall first went to Kentucky in 1780 by special permission of the Governor of Virginia and while he was still Colonel of the State Artillery Regiment. (Humphrey Marshall, i, 104, 120.) During his absence his regiment apparently became somewhat de-

The fledgling lawyer evidently expected to start upon a legal career in the county of his birth; but immediately after marrying Miss Ambler, he established himself at Richmond, where her family lived, and there began the practice of the law. While his marriage into the Ambler family was inspired exclusively by an all-absorbing love, the alliance was a fortunate one for John Marshall from the practical point of view. It gave him the support of a powerful State official and one of the best-liked men in all Virginia. A favor asked by Jacquelin Ambler was always granted if possible; and his recommendation of any one was final. The Ambler household soon became the most attractive in Richmond, as it had been in Yorktown; and Marshall's marriage to Mary Ambler gave him a social standing which, in the Virginia of that day, was a very great asset in business and politics.

The house to which he took his bride was a tiny

moralized. (Thomas Marshall to Colonel George Muter, Feb. 1781; MS. Archives, Va. St. Lib. and partly printed in *Cal. Va. St. Prs.*, i, 549.) Upon his return to Virginia, he was appointed Surveyor of a part of Kentucky, November 1, 1780. (Collins: *History of Kentucky*, i, 20.) The following year he was appointed on the commission "to examine and settle the Public Accts in the Western Country" and expected to go to Kentucky before the close of the year, but did not, because his military certificates were not given him in time. (Thomas Marshall to Governor Harrison, March 17, 1781; *Cal. Va. St. Prs.*, i, 578; and to Lieutenant-Governor Jameson, Oct. 14, 1781; *ib.*, 549.) He opened his surveyor's office in Kentucky in November, 1782. (Butler: *History of Kentucky*, 138.) In 1783 he returned to Virginia to take his family to their new home, where he remained until his death in 1802. (Paxton, 19.) Thomas Marshall was immediately recognized as one of the leading men in this western Virginia district, and was elected to the Legislature and became "Surveyor [Collector] of Revenue for the District of Ohio." (See *infra*, chaps. III and V.)

one-story affair of wood, with only two rooms; the best house the Amblers themselves could secure, as we have seen, was so small that the "whole family" could scarcely crowd into it. Three years before John Marshall and his young wife set up housekeeping, Richmond could "scarce afford one comfort in life."[1] According to Mrs. Carrington the dwelling-houses had no curtains for the windows.[2] The streets were open spaces of earth, unpaved and without sidewalks. Many years after Marshall established himself at the new and raw Virginia Capital, Main Street was still unpaved, deep with dust when dry and so muddy during a rainy season that wagons sank up to the axles. Footways had been laid only at intervals along the town's chief thoroughfare; and piles of ashes and cinders were made to serve as street-crossings, from which, if one misstepped on a dark and rainy night, he found himself deep in the mire. A small stream flowed diagonally across Main Street, flooding the surface; and the street itself ended in gullies and swamps.[3] In 1783 the little town was, of course, still more primitive.

There were no brick or stone buildings in Richmond when Marshall was married. The Capitol, itself, was an ugly structure — "a mere wooden barn" — on an unlovely site at the foot of a hill.[4] The private dwellings, scattered about, were the poor, mean, little wooden houses already described by Eliza Ambler.

[1] Betsy Ambler to Mildred Smith; *Atlantic Monthly*, lxxxiv, 537.
[2] Mrs. Carrington to Mildred Smith, Jan. 10, 1786; MS.
[3] Mordecai, 45–47.
[4] *Ib.*, 40.

Trade was in the hands of British merchants who managed to retain their commercial hold in spite of the Revolution.[1] Rough, heavy wagons drawn by four or six horses brought in the produce of the country, which included "deer and bear skins, furs, ginseng, snake-root," and even "dried rattlesnakes . . . used to make a viper broth for consumptive patients."[2] These clumsy vehicles were sometimes a month in covering less than two hundred miles.[3] Specie was the money chiefly used in the back country and the frontier tradesmen made remittances to Richmond by placing a "bag of gold or silver in the centre of a cask of melted wax or tallow . . . or [in a] bale of hemp."[4]

There was but one church building and attendance was scanty and infrequent.[5] The principal amusement was card-playing, in which everybody indulged,[6] and drinking was the common practice.[7] The town sustained but one tavern which was kept by a Neapolitan named Farmicola. This hostelry had two large rooms downstairs and two above. The beds were under the roof, packed closely together and unseparated by partitions. When the Legislature met, the inn was crowded; and "Generals, Colonels, Captains, Senators, Assembly-men, Judges, Doctors, Clerks, and crowds of Gentlemen of every weight and calibre and every hue of dress, sat alto-

[1] Mordecai, chap. ii.

[2] *Ib.*, 51–52. This was more than twenty years after Marshall and his young wife started housekeeping in Richmond.

[3] *Ib.*, 53.

[4] *Ib.*

[5] Meade, i, 140; Schoepf, ii, 62.

[6] Mordecai, chap. xxi; Schoepf, ii, 63 *et seq.*

[7] See *supra*, chaps. I and VII.

gether about the fire, drinking, smoking, singing, and talking ribaldry." [1]

Such were conditions in the town of Richmond when John Marshall hazarded his adventure into the legal profession there in 1783. But it was the seat of the State Government, and the place where the General Court of Appeals and the High Court of Chancery were located. Yet small, poor, and mean as was the Virginia Capital of that day, not even Philadelphia, New York, or Boston could boast of a more brilliant bar.

Randolph and Wickham, Innes and Ronald, Campbell and Call, and others whose distinction has made the bar of the Old Dominion historic, practiced at Richmond. And the court around which this extraordinary constellation gathered was equally eminent. Pendleton, whose intellect and industry more than supplied early defects in education, was president of the Court of Appeals; Wythe was one of the judges of the High Court of Chancery, of which he afterwards became sole chancellor; Paul Carrington and others of almost equal stature sat with Pendleton on the Supreme Bench. Later on appeared the erudite, able, and commanding Roane, who, long afterwards, when Marshall came into his own, was to be his most formidable antagonist in the clash of courts.

Among such lawyers and before a court of this high quality the young attorney from the backwoods of Fauquier County began his struggle for a share

[1] Schoepf, ii, 64. Marshall frequented this place and belonged to a club which met there. (See entries from Marshall's Account Book, *infra*.)

of legal business. He had practically no equipment except his intellect, his integrity, and his gift for inspiring confidence and friendship. Of learning in the law, he had almost none at all. He had read Blackstone, although not thoroughly;[1] but the only legal training that Marshall had received was acquired during his few weeks at William and Mary College. And in this romantic interval, as we have seen, he was thinking a good deal more about Mary Ambler than about preparing himself for his career.

We know exactly to which of Wythe's lectures Marshall had listened; for he took notes of them. He procured a thick, blank book strongly bound in calf. In this he wrote in a large, firm hand, at the top of the page, the topics of lectures which Wythe had announced he would give, leaving after each headline several pages for notes.[2] Since these notes are a full record of Marshall's only formal instruction in the law, a complete list of the subjects, together with the space allotted to each, is as important as it is interesting.

On the subject of Abatement he wrote three pages; on Accounts, two pages; on Accord and Satisfaction, one page; Actions in General, one and a half pages; Actions Local and Transitory, one fourth page; Actions Qui Tam, one and one fourth pages; Actions on the Case, three and one half pages; Agree-

[1] *Supra*, chap. II.

[2] This invaluable Marshall source is not a law student's commonplace book alphabetically arranged, but merely a large volume of blank leaves. It is six inches wide by eight in length and more than one in thickness. The book also contains Marshall's accounts for twelve years after his marriage. All reference hereafter to his receipts and expenses are from this source.

ments, three pages; Annuity and Rent Charge, two pages; Arbitrament and Award, one and one half pages; Assault and Battery, two thirds of a page; Assignment, one half page; Assumpsit, one and a half pages; Attachment, one half page; Audita Querela, one fourth page; Authority, one fourth page; Bail in Civil Causes, one half page; Bail in Criminal Causes, one and two thirds pages; Bailment, two pages; Bargain and Sale, one half page; Baron and Feme, four pages; Bastardy, three quarters page; Bills of Sale, one half page; Bills of Exceptions, one half page; Burglary, one page; Carriers, one page; Certiorari, one half page; Commitments, one half page; Condition, five and one half pages; Coparceners, one and one half pages; Costs, one and one fourth pages; Covenant, three pages; Curtesy of England, one half page; Damages, one and one half pages; Debt, one and one half pages; Descent, one and one half pages; Detinue, one half page; Devises, six and one half pages; Disseisin, two lines; Distress, one and two thirds pages; Dower, two pages; Duress, one third page; Ejectment, two and two thirds pages; Election, two thirds page; Error, two and one third pages; Escape in Civil Cases, one and one fifth pages; Estates in Fee Simple, three fourths page; Estate for Life and Occupancy, one and four fifths pages; Evidence, four pages, two lines; Execution, one and five sixths pages; Executors and Administrators, eleven pages; Extinguishment, two thirds page; Extortion, one half page; Felony, three and one sixth pages; Forcible Entry and Detainer, three fourths page; Forgery, three pages; Forfeiture, two and four fifths pages; Fraud, three pages, one line; Grants, three and three fourths pages; Guardian, two and five sixths pages; Heir and Ancestor, five pages, two lines; Idiots and Lunatics, three pages; Indictments, four pages, three lines; Infancy and Age, nine and one half pages; Information, one and one fifth pages; Injunction, one and two thirds pages; Inns and Innkeepers, two and two thirds pages; Joint Tenants and Tenants in Common, nine and one sixth pages; Jointure, three pages.

We find six pages he had reserved for notes on the subject of Juries left blank, and two blank pages follow the caption, "Justice of the Peace." But he made seventeen and two thirds pages of notes on the subjects of Leases and Terms for Years, and twelve and one half pages on the subject of Legacies. This ended his formal legal studies; for he made no notes under the remaining lecture subjects.[1]

Not an ideal preparation to attract clients, we must admit, nor to serve them well when he got them. But slender and elementary as was his store of learning, his apparel, manners, and habits were even less likely to bring business to this meagerly equipped young advocate.

Marshall made practically no money as a lawyer during his first year in Richmond. Most of his slender income seems to have been from his salary as a member of the Legislature.[2] He enters in his Account Book in 1783 (where it begins) several

[1] The notes are not only of lectures actually delivered by Wythe, but of Marshall's reading on topics assigned for study. It is probable that many of these notes were made after Marshall left college.

[2] See *infra*, chap. VI.

receipts "by my civil list warrants," and several others, "Rec[d] from Treasury." Only four fees are entered for the whole year — one for three pounds, another for two pounds, eleven shillings, one for two pounds, ten shillings, and a fourth for two pounds, eight shillings.

On the contrary, he paid one pound, two shillings, sixpence for "advice fee given the attorney for opinion on surveyors fees." He bought "one pair Spectacles" for three shillings and ninepence. His sociable nature is revealed at the beginning of his career by entries, "won at Whist 24–1–4" and "won at Whist 22/"; and again "At Backgammon 30/–1–10." Also the reverse entry, "Lost at Whist £3 14/."[1]

The cost of living in Richmond at the close of the Revolution is shown by numerous entries. Thirty-six bushels of oats cost Marshall three pounds, ten shillings, sixpence. He paid one pound for "one pair stockings"; and one pound, eighteen shillings, sixpence for a hat. In 1783 a tailor charged him one pound, eight shillings, sixpence for "making a Coat." He enters "stockings for P.[olly][2] 6 dollars." A stove "Dutch Oven" cost fourteen shillings and eightpence; and "150 bushels coal for self 7–10" (seven pounds, ten shillings).

[1] Such entries as these denote only Marshall's social and friendly spirit. At that period and for many years afterward card-playing for money was universal in Virginia (La Rochefoucauld, iii, 77; and Mordecai, ed. 1856, chap. xxi), particularly at Richmond, where the women enjoyed this pastime quite as much as the men. (*Ib.*) This, indeed, was the case everywhere among women of the best society who habitually played cards for money. (Also see Chastellux, 333–34.)

[2] Marshall's wife.

In October of the year of his marriage he paid six shillings for wine and "For rum £9–15." His entries for household expenditures for these months give an idea of the housekeeping: "Given Polly 6 dollars £4–10–6; . . . a coffe pot 4/; 1 yd. Gauze 3/6; 2 Sugar boxes £1–7–6; Candlestick &c. 3/6 1 yd. Linnen for P. 2/6; 2 pieces of bobbin 1/6; Tea pot 3/; Edging 3/6; Sugar pot 1/6; Milk 1/; Thimble 4/2; Irons 9/, . . . Tea 20/." [1]

The entries in Marshall's Account Book for the first year and a half of his married life are indiscriminately and poorly made, without dates of receipts and expenditures. Then follows a period up to June, 1785, where the days of the month are stated. Then come entries without dates; and later, the dates sometimes are given and sometimes not. Marshall was as negligent in his bookkeeping as he was in his dress. Entries in the notebook show on their face his distaste for such details. The Account Book covers a period of twelve years, from 1783 to 1795.

He was exceedingly miscellaneous in his expenses. On January 14, 1784, he enters as items of outlay: "Whist 30/" and "Whist 12/," "cow £3–12–8"

[1] The references are to pounds, shillings, and pence. Thus "3 14/" means three pounds and fourteen shillings. "30–5–10" means thirty pounds, five shillings, and tenpence; or "3/6" means three shillings, sixpence. Where the Account Book indicates the amount without the signs of denomination, I have stated the amount indicated by the relative positions of the figures in the Account Book. Computation should be by Virginia currency (which was then about three and one half dollars to the Virginia pound) and not by the English pound sterling. This is not very helpful, however, because there is no standard of comparison between the Virginia dollar of that period and the United States dollar of to-day. It is certain only that the latter has greater purchasing power than the former. All paper money had greatly depreciated at the time, however.

and "poker 6/," "To Parson 30/." This date is jammed in, plainly an afterthought, and no more dates are specified until June 7. Other characteristic entries at this time are, on one day, "Turkeys 12/ Wood 24/ Whist £18"; and on another day, "Beef 26/8 — Backgammon £6." An important entry, undated, is, "Paid the University in the hands of Mr. Tazewell for Col° Marshall as Surveyor of Fayette County 100" (pounds).[1]

On July 5, 1784, he enters among receipts "to my service in the Assembly 34–4" (pounds and shillings); and among his expenses for June 22 of that year, he enters "lost at Whist £19" and on the 26th, "Col° [James] Monroe & self at the Play 1–10"[2] (one pound, ten shillings). A week later the theater again cost him twelve shillings; and on the third he enters an outlay "to one Quarter cask wine 14" (pounds, or about fifty dollars Virginia currency). On the same day appears a curious entry of "to the play 13/" and "Pd for Col° Monroe £16–16." He was lucky at whist this month, for there are two entries during July, "won at whist £10"; and again, "won at whist 4–6" (four pounds, six shillings). He contributes to St. John's Church one pound, eight shillings. During this month their first child was born to the young couple;[3] and there are various

[1] The "University" was William and Mary College, then partly supported by a portion of the fees of official surveyors. Thomas Marshall was now Surveyor of Fayette County, Kentucky. (See *supra.*) This entry occurs several times.

[2] Such entries are frequent throughout his Account Book. During his entire life, Marshall was very fond of the theater. (See *infra*, II, chap. V; also vol. III of this work.)

[3] Thomas Marshall, born July 21, 1784. (Paxton, 90.)

entries for the immediate expenses of the event amounting to thirteen pounds, four shillings, and threepence. The child was christened August 31 and Marshall enters, "To house for christening 12/ do. 2/6."

The Account Book discloses his diversified generosity. Preacher, horse-race, church, festival, card-game, or "ball" found John Marshall equally sympathetic in his contributions. He was looking for business from all classes in exactly the same way that young lawyers of our own day pursue that object. Also, he was, by nature, extremely sociable and generous. In Marshall's time the preachers bet on horses and were pleasant persons at balls. So it was entirely appropriate that the young Richmond attorney should enter, almost at the same time, "to Mr. Buchanan 5" (pounds)[1] and "to my subscription for race £4–4";[2] "Saint Taminy 11 Dollars — 3–6"[3] (three pounds, six shillings); and still again, "paid my subscription to the ball 20/–1"; and later, "expenses at St. John's [church] 2–3" (pounds and shillings).

Marshall bought several slaves. On July 1, 1784, he enters, "Paid for Ben 90–4"[4] (ninety pounds, four shillings). And in August of that year, "paid for two Negroes £30" and "In part for two servants

[1] Buchanan was the Episcopal clergyman in Richmond at the time. (Meade, i, 29, 140.)

[2] The races at Richmond, held bi-annually, were the great social events of Virginia. (Mordecai, 178 *et seq.*)

[3] This fixes the equivalent in State dollars for Virginia pounds and shillings.

[4] He already owned one tithable negro in Fauquier County in 1783. (Fauquier County Tithable Book, 1783–84; MS., Va. St. Lib. See *supra.*)

£20." And in September, "Paid for servants £25," and on November 23, "Kate & Evan £63." His next purchase of a slave was three years later, when he enters, May 18, 1787, "Paid for a woman bought in Gloster £55."

Shoeing two horses in 1784 cost Marshall eight shillings; and a hat for his wife cost three pounds. For a bed-tick he paid two pounds, nine shillings. We can get some idea of the price of labor by the following entry: "Pd. Mr. Anderson for plaistering the house £10–2." Since he was still living in his little rented cottage, this entry would signify that it cost him a little more than thirty-five dollars, Virginia currency, to plaster two rooms in Richmond, in 1784. Possibly this might equal from seven to ten dollars in present-day money. He bought his first furniture on credit, it appears, for in the second year of his married life he enters, December "31st P^{d} Mr Mason in part for furniture 10" (pounds).

At the end of the year, "Pd balance of my rent 43–13" (pounds and shillings). During 1784, his third year as a lawyer, his fees steadily increased, most of them being about two pounds, though he received an occasional fee of from five to nine pounds. His largest single fee during this year was "From Mr. Stead 1 fee 24" (pounds).

He mixed fun with his business and politics. On February 24, 1784, he writes to James Monroe that public money due the latter could not be secured. "The exertions of the Treasurer & of your other friends have been ineffectual. There is not one shilling in the Treasury & the keeper of it could not borrow one on the faith of the government." Marshall confides to Monroe that he himself is "pressed for money," and adds that Monroe's "old Land Lady Mrs. Shera begins now to be a little clamorous. . . . I shall be obliged I apprehend to negotiate your warrants at last at a discount. I have kept them up this long in hopes of drawing Money for them from the Treasury."

But despite financial embarrassment and the dull season, Marshall was full of the gossip of a convivial young man.

"The excessive cold weather," writes Marshall, "has operated like magic on our youth. They feel the necessity of artificial heat & quite wearied with lying alone, are all treading the broad road to Matrimony. Little Steward (could you believe it?) will be married on Thursday to Kitty Haie & Mr. Dunn will bear off your old acquaintance Miss Shera.

"Tabby Eppes has grown quite fat and buxom, her charms are renovated & to see her & to love her are now synonimous terms. She has within these six weeks seen in her train at least a score of Military & Civil characters. Carrington, Young, Selden, Wright (a merchant), & Foster Webb have alternately bow'd before her & been discarded.

"Carrington 'tis said has drawn off his forces in order to refresh them & has march'd up to Cumberland where he will in all human probability be reinforced with the dignified character of Legislator. Webb has returned to the charge & the many think from their similitude of manners & appetites that they were certainly designed for each other.

"The other Tabby is in high spirits over the success of her antique sister & firmly thinks her time will come next, she looks quite spruce & speaks of Matrimony as of a good which she yet means to experience. Lomax is in his county. Smith is said to be electioneering. Nelson has not yet come to the board. Randolph is here and well. . . . Farewell, I am your J. Marshall."[1]

Small as were the comforts of the Richmond of that time, the charm, gayety, and hospitality of its inhabitants made life delightful. A young foreigner from Switzerland found it so. Albert Gallatin, who one day was to be so large a factor in American public life, came to Richmond in 1784, when he was twenty-two years old. He found the hospitality of the town with "no parallel anywhere within the circle of my travels. . . . Every one with whom I became acquainted," says Gallatin, "appeared to take an interest in the young stranger. I was only the interpreter of a gentleman, the agent of a foreign house that had a large claim for advances to the State. . . . Every one encouraged me and was disposed to promote my success in life. . . . John Marshall, who, though but a young lawyer in 1783, was almost at the head of the bar in 1786, offered to take

[1] Marshall to Monroe, Feb. 24, 1784; MS., N.Y. Pub. Lib. Compare with Jefferson's sentimental letters at the same age. Very few of Marshall's letters during this period are extant. This one to Monroe is conspicuously noticeable for unrestraint and joyousness. As unreserved as he always was in verbal conversation, Marshall's correspondence soon began to show great caution, unlike that of Jefferson, which increased, with time, in spontaneity. Thus Marshall's letters became more guarded and less engaging; while Jefferson's pen used ever more highly colored ink and progressively wrote more entertaining if less trustworthy matter.

me in his office without a fee, and assured me that I would become a distinguished lawyer." [1]

During his second year in Richmond, Marshall's practice showed a reasonable increase. He did not confine his legal activities to the Capital, for in February we find thirteen fees aggregating thirty-three pounds, twelve shillings, "Recd in Fauquier" County. The accounts during this year were fairly well kept, considering that happy-go-lucky John Marshall was the bookkeeper. Even the days of the month for receipts and expenditures are often given. He starts out with active social and public contributions. On January 18, 1785, he enters, "my subscription to Assemblies [balls] 4–4" (pounds and shillings), and "Jan. 29 Annual subscription for Library 1–8" (pound, shillings).

On January 25, 1785, he enters, "laid out in purchasing Certificates 35–4–10." And again, July 4, "Military Certificates pd for self £13–10–2 at 4 for one £3–7–7. Interest for 3 years £2–8 9." A similar entry is made of purchases made for his father; on the margin is written, "pd commissioners."

He made his first purchase of books in January, 1785, to the amount of "£4–12/." He was seized with an uncommon impulse for books this year, it appears. On February 10 he enters, "laid out in books £9–10–6." He bought eight shillings' worth of pamphlets in April. On May 5, Marshall paid "For Mason's Poems" nine shillings. On May 14, "books 17/–8" and May 19, "book 5/6"

[1] Gallatin to Maxwell, Feb. 15, 1848; Gallatin's *Writings:* Adams, ii, 659. Also see Mordecai, 94–95.

and "Blackstones Commentaries [1] 36/," and May 20, "Books 6/." On May 25, there is a curious entry for "Bringing books in stage 25/." On June 24, he purchased "Blair's Lectures" for one pound, ten shillings; and on the 2d of August, a "Book case" cost him six pounds, twelve shillings. Again, on September 8, Marshall's entries show, "books £1–6," and on October 8, "Kaim's Principles of Equity 1–4" (one pound, four shillings). Again in the same month he enters, "books £6–12," and "Spirit of Law" (undoubtedly Montesquieu's essay), twelve shillings.

But, in general, his book-buying was moderate during these formative years as a lawyer. While it is difficult to learn exactly what literature Marshall indulged in, besides novels and poetry, we know that he had "Dionysius Longinus on the Sublime"; the "Works of Nicholas Machiavel," in four volumes; "The History and Proceedings of the House of Lords from the Restoration," in six volumes; the "Life of the Earl of Clarendon, Lord High Chancellor of England"; the "Works of C. Churchill — Poems and Sermons on Lord's Prayer"; and the "Letters of Lord Chesterfield to his son." A curious and entertaining book was a condensed cyclopædia of law and business entitled "Lex Mercatoria Rediviva or The Merchant's Directory," on the title-page of which is written in his early handwriting, "John Marshall Richmond." [2] Marshall also

[1] His father must have kept, for the time being, the Blackstone purchased in 1772, although the volume later turned up in Marshall's possession.

[2] This book, with the others named, bears the signature of Mar-

had an English translation of "The Orations of Æschines and Demosthenes on the Crown." [1]

Marshall's wine bills were very moderate for those days, although as heavy as a young lawyer's resources could bear. On January 31, 1785, he bought fourteen shillings' worth of wine; and two and a half months later he paid twenty-six pounds and ten shillings "For Wine"; and the same day, "beer 4d," and the next day, "Gin 30/." On June 14 of the same year he enters, "punch 2/6," the next day, "punch 3/," and on the next day, "punch 6/." [2]

Early in this year Marshall's father, now in Kentucky and with opulent prospects before him, gave his favorite son eight hundred and twenty-four acres

shall at this period of his life. They are the only books in existence which certainly were bought by Marshall at that time, all other volumes he is positively known to have had in his library being published at a later date. All except one of those named, with others hereafter mentioned, are in the possession of Judge J. K. M. Norton, Alexandria, Virginia. The *Lex Mercatoria* is, of course, in English. It is a large book containing seven hundred seventy-five pages, seven by eight inches, firmly bound in calf. It is "compiled from many standard authorities." While it is an encyclopædia of law and business containing items such as a comparison of the values of money of all lands, it is very readable and entertaining. It is just the kind of book from which Marshall could have derived information without being wearied by research. John Adams also had a copy of Malynes's *Lex Mercatoria*, which seems to have been a common possession of commercial lawyers throughout the country.

[1] This book is now in the possession of Hon. William Marshall Bullitt, of Louisville, Kentucky.

[2] The numerous entries of this kind occurring throughout Marshall's Account Book must not be misunderstood. At that time and for many decades afterward, the habitual use of whiskey, wine, rum, brandy, etc., was the universal custom. They were bought in quantities and consumed much as ordinary table waters now are. The common people, especially those in the South, distilled their own stimulants. The people of New England relied on the great distilleries of Boston and vicinity for rum, of which they consumed enormous quantities. (See *infra*, chap. VII; also chap. II, vol. II, of this work.)

of the best land in Fauquier County.[1] So the rising Richmond attorney was in comfortable circumstances. He was becoming a man of substance and property; and this condition was reflected in his contributions to various Richmond social and religious enterprises.

He again contributed two pounds to "St Taminy's" on May 9, 1785, and the same day paid six pounds, six shillings to "My club at Farmicolas."[2] On May 16 he paid thirty shillings for a "Ball" and nine shillings for "music"; and May 25 he enters, "Jockie Club 4–4" (pounds and shillings). On July 5 he spent six shillings more at the "Club"; and the next month he again enters a contribution to "St Johns [Episcopal Church] £1–16." He was an enthusiastic Mason, as we shall see; and on September 13, 1785, he enters, "pd Mason's Ball subscription for 10" (pounds). October 15 he gives eight pounds and four shillings for an "Episcopal Meeting"; and the next month (November 2, 1785) subscribes eighteen shillings "to a ball." And at the end of the year (December 23, 1785) he enters his "Subscription to Richmond Assem. 3" (pounds).

Marshall's practice during his third year at the Richmond bar grew normally. The largest single fee received during this year (1785) was thirty-five pounds, while another fee of twenty pounds, and still another of fourteen pounds, mark the nearest approaches to this high-water mark. He had by now

[1] Records of Fauquier County (Va.), Deed Book, viii, 241, March 16, 1785.

[2] The tavern kept by Farmicola, where Marshall's club met. (See *supra*.)

in Richmond two negroes (tithable), two horses, and twelve head of cattle.[1]

He was elected City Recorder during this year; and it was to the efforts of Marshall, in promoting a lottery for the purpose, that the Masonic Hall was built in the ambitious town.[2]

The young lawyer had deepened the affection of his wife's family which he had won in Yorktown. Two years after his marriage the first husband of his wife's sister, Eliza, died; and, records the sorrowing young widow, "my Father . . . dispatched . . . my darling Brother Marshall to bring me." Again the bereaved Eliza tells of how she was "conducted by my good brother Marshall who lost no time" about this errand of comfort and sympathy.[3]

February 15, 1786, he enters an expense of twelve pounds "for moving my office" which he had painted in April at a cost of two pounds and seventeen shillings. This year he contributed to festivities and social events as usual. In addition to his subscriptions to balls, assemblies, and clubs, we find that on May 22, 1786, he paid nine shillings for a "Barbecue," and during the next month, "barbecue 7/" and still again, "barbecue 6/." On June 15, he "paid for Wine 7–7–6," and on the 26th, "corporation dinner 2–2–6." In September, 1786, his doctor's bills were very high. On the 22d of that month he

[1] Henrico County Tithable Book; Va. St. Lib. He had, of course, other slaves, horses, and cattle on his Fauquier County plantation.

[2] Christian, 28.

[3] Eliza Ambler to Mildred Smith, July 10, 1785; MS.; also printed in *Atlantic Monthly*, lxxxiv, 540–41.

paid nearly forty-five pounds for the services of three physicians.[1]

Among the books purchased was "Blair's sermons" which cost him one pound and four shillings.[2] In July he again "Pd. for St. Taminy's feast 2" (pounds). The expense of traveling is shown by several entries, such as, "Expenses up & down to & from Fauquier 4–12" (four pounds, twelve shillings); and "Expenses going to Gloster &c 5" (pounds); "expenses going to Wms.burg 7" (pounds); and again, "expenses going to and returning from Winchester 15" (pounds); and still again, "expenses going to Wms.burg 7" (pounds). On November 19, Marshall enters, "For quarter cask of wine 12–10" (twelve pounds and ten shillings). On this date we find, "To Barber 18" (shillings) — an entry which is as rare as the expenses to the theater are frequent.

He appears to have bought a house during this year (1786) and enters on October 7, 1786, "Pd Mr. B. Lewis in part for his house £70 cash & 5£ in an order in favor of James Taylor ——75"; and November 19, 1786, "Paid Mr. B. Lewis in part for house 50" (pounds); and in December he again "Pd Mr. Lewis in part for house 27–4" (twenty-seven pounds, four shillings); and (November 19) "Pd. Mr. Lewis 16" (pounds); and on the 28th, "Paid Mr. Lewis in full 26–17–1 1/4."

In 1786, the Legislature elected Edmund Ran-

[1] Drs. McClurg, Foushee, and Mackie.

[2] This book was purchased for his wife, who was extremely religious. The volume is in the possession of Judge J. K. M. Norton, Alexandria, Virginia. On the fly-leaf appears, "Mrs. Mary W. Marshall," in Marshall's handwriting. The book was also useful to Marshall for his own study of rhetoric, since Blair's sermons stood very high, at this time, as examples of style.

dolph Governor; and, on November 10, 1786, Randolph advertised that "The General Assembly having appointed me to an office incompatible with the further pursuit of my profession, I beg leave to inform my clients that John Marshall Esq. will succeed to my business in General &c."[1]

At the end of this year, for the first time, Marshall adds up his receipts and expenditures, as follows: "Received in the Year 1786 according to the foregoing accounts 508–4–10." And on the opposite page he enters [2] —

To my expenses	432		
	1	. . . .	8
	433	—	8

In 1787 Marshall kept his accounts in better fashion. He employed a housekeeper in April, Mrs. Marshall being unable to attend to domestic duties; and from February, 1787, until May of the following year he enters during each month, "Betsy Mumkins 16/." The usual expenditures were made during this year, and while Marshall neglects to summarize his income and outlay, his practice was still growing, although slowly. On December 3, 1787, his second child was born.[3]

In January of 1787 occurred the devastating Richmond fire which destroyed much of the little city; [4] and on February 7, Marshall enters among his expenses, "To my subscription to the sufferers by fire 21" (pounds).

[1] Christian, 29, 30.

[2] This unbusinesslike balancing is characteristic of Marshall.

[3] Jacquelin Ambler Marshall, Dec. 3, 1787. (Paxton, 99.) [4] *Ib.*

Marshall's name first appears in the reports of the cases decided by the Virginia Court of Appeals in 1786. In May of that year the court handed down its opinion in Hite *et al. vs.* Fairfax *et al.*[1] It involved not only the lands directly in controversy, but also the validity of the entire Fairfax title and indirectly that of a great deal of other land in Virginia. Baker, who appears to have been the principal attorney for the Fairfax claimants, declared that one of the contentions of the appellants "would destroy every title in the Commonwealth." The case was argued for the State by Edmund Randolph, Attorney-General, and by John Taylor (probably of Caroline). Marshall, supporting Baker, acted as attorney for "such of the tenants as were citizens of Virginia." The argument consumed three days, May 3 to 5 inclusive.[2]

Marshall made an elaborate argument, and since it is the first of his recorded utterances, it is important as showing his quality of mind and legal methods at that early period of his career. Marshall was a little more than thirty years old and had been practicing law in Richmond for about three years.

The most striking features of his argument are his vision and foresight. It is plain that he was acutely conscious, too, that it was more important to the settlers who derived their holdings from Lord Fairfax to have the long-disputed title settled than it was to win as to the particular lands directly in controversy. Indeed, upon a close study of the complicated records in the case, it would

[1] Call, i, 42. [2] Records of the Court of Appeals.

seem that Joist Hite's claim could not, by any possibility, have been defeated. For, although the lands claimed by him, and others after him, clearly were within the proprietary of Lord Fairfax, yet they had been granted to Hite by the King in Council, and confirmed by the Crown; Lord Fairfax had agreed with the Crown to confirm them on his part; he or his agents had promised Hite that, if the latter would remain on the land with his settlers, Fairfax would execute the proper conveyances to him, and Fairfax also made other guarantees to Hite.

But it was just as clear that, outside of the lands immediately in controversy, Lord Fairfax's title, from a strictly legal point of view, was beyond dispute except as to the effect of the sequestration laws.[1] It was assailed, however, through suggestion at least, both by Attorney-General Randolph and by Mr. Taylor. There was, at this time, a strong popular movement on foot in Virginia to devise some means for destroying the whole Fairfax title to the Northern Neck. Indeed, the reckless royal bounty from which this enormous estate sprang had been resented bitterly by the Virginia settlers from the very beginning;[2] the people never admitted the justice and morality of the Fairfax grant. Also, at this particular period, there was an epidemic of debt repudiation, evasion of contracts and other obligations, and assailing of titles.[3]

[1] The estate had been sequestered during the Revolution.

[2] Wertenbaker: *V. U. S.*, 123–26. For history of these grants, see chap. IV, vol. II, of this work.

[3] See *infra*, chap. VI.

So, while Baker, the senior Fairfax lawyer, referred but briefly to the validity of the Fairfax title and devoted practically the whole of his argument to the lands involved in the case then before the court, Marshall, on the other hand, made the central question of the validity of the whole Fairfax title the dominant note of his argument. Thus he showed, in his first reported legal address, his most striking characteristic of going directly to the heart of any subject.

Briefly reported as is his argument in Hite *vs.* Fairfax, the qualities of far-sightedness and simple reasoning, are almost as plain as in the work of his riper years: —

"From a bare perusal of the papers in the cause," said Marshall, "I should never have apprehended that it would be necessary to defend the title of Lord *Fairfax* to the Northern Neck. The long and quiet possession of himself and his predecessors; the acquiescence of the country; the several grants of the crown, together with the various acts of assembly recognizing, and in the most explicit terms admitting his right, seemed to have fixed it on a foundation, not only not to be shaken, but even not to be attempted to be shaken.

"I had conceived that it was not more certain, that there was such a tract of country as the Northern Neck, than that Lord *Fairfax* was the proprietor of it. And if his title be really unimpeachable, to what purpose are his predecessors criminated, and the patents they obtained attacked? What object is to be effected by it? Not, surely, the destruction of the grant; for gentlemen cannot suppose, that a grant made by the crown to the ancestor for services rendered, or even for affection, can be invalidated in the hands of the heir because those services and affection are forgotten; or because the thing granted has, from causes which must have been foreseen, become more valuable than when it was given. And if it could not be invalidated in the hands of the heir, much less can it be in the hands of a purchaser.

"Lord *Fairfax* either was, or was not, entitled to the territory; if he was, then it matters not whether the gentlemen themselves, or any others, would or would not have made the grant, or may now think proper to denounce it as a wise, or impolitic, measure; for still the title must prevail; if he was not entitled, then why was the present bill filed; or what can the court decree upon it? For if he had no title, he could convey none, and the court would never have directed him to make the attempt.

"In short, if the title was not in him, it must have been in the crown; and, from that quarter, relief must have been sought. The very filing of the bill, therefore, was an admission of the title, and the appellants, by prosecuting it, still continue to admit it. . . .

"It [the boundary] is, however, no longer a question; for it has been decided, and decided by that tribunal which has the power of determining it. That decision did not create or extend Lord *Fairfax's* right, but determined what the right originally was. The bounds of many patents are doubtful; the extent of many titles uncertain; but when a decision is once made on them, it removes the doubt, and ascertains what the original boundaries were. If this be a principle universally acknowledged, what can destroy its application to the case before the court?"

The remainder of Marshall's argument concerns the particular dispute between the parties. This, of course, is technical; but two paragraphs may be quoted illustrating what, even in the day of Henry and Campbell, Wickham and Randolph, men called "Marshall's eloquence."

"They dilate," exclaimed Marshall, "upon their hardships as first settlers; their merit in promoting the population of the country; and their claims as purchasers without notice. Let each of these be examined.

"Those who explore and settle new countries are generally bold, hardy, and adventurous men, whose minds, as well as bodies, are fitted to encounter danger and fatigue; their object is the acquisition of property, and they generally succeed.

"None will say that the complainants have failed; and, if their hardships and danger have any weight in the cause, the defendants shared in them, and have equal claim to countenance; for they, too, with humbler views and less extensive prospects, 'have explored, bled for and settled a, 'till then, uncultivated desert.'"[1]

Hite won in this particular case; but, thanks to Marshall's argument, the court's decision did not attack the general Fairfax title. So it was that Marshall's earliest effort at the bar, in a case of any

[1] Call, iv, 69–72.

magnitude, was in defense of the title to that estate of which, a few years later, he was to become a principal owner.[1] Indeed, both he and his father were interested even then; for their lands in Fauquier County were derived from or through Fairfax.

Of Marshall's other arguments at this period, no record exists. We know, however, from his Account Book, that his business increased steadily; and, from tradition, that he was coming to be considered the ablest of the younger members of the distinguished Richmond bar. For his services in this, his first notable case, Marshall received one hundred and nine pounds, four shillings, paid by fifty-seven clients. Among those employing the young attorney was George Washington. In the account of fees paid him in Hite *vs.* Fairfax, he enters: "Gen$^{l.}$ G. Washington 1–4" (pounds and shillings) and "A. Washington 1–4." Marshall's record of this transaction is headed: "List of fees rec'd from Ten$^{ts.}$ Fairfax Ad^{s} Hite," referring to the title of the case in the lower court.

An evidence of his growing prosperity is the purchase from Aquella and Lucy Dayson of two hundred and sixty acres of land in Fauquier County, for "one hundred and sixty pounds current money of Virginia."[2] This purchase, added to the land already given him by his father,[3] made John Marshall, at thirty-one years of age, the owner of nearly one thousand acres of land in Fauquier.

Marshall's Account Book shows his generosity

[1] *Infra*, vol. II, chap. IV.

[2] Records Fauquier County (Va.), Deed Book, X, 29.

[3] See *supra*.

toward his brothers and sisters, who remained in Virginia when Thomas Marshall went to Kentucky to establish himself. There are frequent entries of money advanced to his brothers, particularly James M., as, "Given my brother James £3–9"; or, "To my brother James £36–18," etc. Marshall's sister Lucy lived in his house until her marriage to the wealthy John Ambler.[1] The young lawyer was particularly attentive to the wants of his sister Lucy and saw to it that she had all the advantages of the Virginia Capital. In his Account Book we find many entries of expenses in her behalf; as, for example, "for Lucy £5–8–3"; and again, a few days later, "given Eliza [2] for Lucy" four pounds, sixteen shillings; and still later, "for Lucy 10–6" (ten pounds, six shillings); and, "Pd for Lucy entering into dancing school 2–2" (two pounds, two shillings).

Throughout Marshall's Account Book the entries that most frequently occur are for some expense for his wife. There is hardly a page without the entry, "given Polly" so much, or "for Polly" so much, and the entries are for liberal amounts. For instance, on January 15, 1785, he enters, "Sundries for Polly £8–6–8 1/2"; on the 18th, "Given Polly 6/"; on the 25th, "for Polly 11/ 7 1/2"; and on the 29th, "Given Polly for a hat 36/." And later, "Given Polly 56/" and "Given Polly 2–16" (pounds and shillings); and "for Polly £3." "For Polly 5–7–5"; "Sundries for Polly, 12–6" and "Left with Polly 10–4" (pounds and shillings). "Given Polly

[1] See *supra*, 166, footnote 3.
[2] Mrs. Carrington.

£1–8"; "Gloves for Polly 7/6." Such entries are very numerous.

The young wife, who had become an invalid soon after her marriage, received from her husband a devotion and care which realized poetic idealism. "His exemplary tenderness to our unfortunate sister is without parallel," testifies Mrs. Carrington. "With a delicacy of frame and feeling that baffles all description, she became, early after her marriage, a prey to an extreme nervous affliction which more or less has embittered her comfort thro' life; but this only served to increase his care and tenderness. . . . He is always and under every circumstance an enthusiast in love." [1]

Marshall's affection for his wife grew with the years and was nourished by her increasing infirmities. It is the most marked characteristic of his entire private life and is the one thing which differentiates him sharply from most of the eminent men of that heroic but, socially, free-and-easy period. Indeed, it is in John Marshall's worship of his delicate and nerve-racked wife that we find the beginnings of that exaltation of womankind, which his life, as it unrolls, will disclose.

John Marshall's respect, admiration, reverence, for woman became so notable that it was remarked by all who knew him, and remains to this day a living tradition in Richmond. It resembled the sentiment of the age of chivalry. While the touching incidents, glowing testimonials, and most of the letters that

[1] Mrs. Carrington to her sister Nancy; MS. The mother and sister of Mrs. Marshall were similarly afflicted. Mrs. Carrington frequently mentions this fact in her correspondence.

reveal this feature of Marshall's character occur more vividly after he ascended the bench,[1] the heart of the man cannot be understood as we go along without noting the circumstance in his earlier married life.

[1] See vol. III of this work.

CHAPTER VI

IN THE LEGISLATURE AND COUNCIL OF STATE

The proceedings of the Assembly are, as usual, rapidly degenerating with the progress of the session. (Madison.)

Our Assembly has been employed chiefly in rectifying the mistakes of the last and committing new ones for emendation at the next. (Washington.)

It is surprising that gentlemen cannot dismiss their private animosities but will bring them in the Assembly. (Marshall.)

In 1783, a small wooden building stood among the two or three hundred little frame houses [1] which, scattered irregularly from the river to the top of the hill, made up the town of Richmond at the close of the Revolution. It was used for "balls," public banquets, and other functions which the merriment or inclination of the miniature Capital required. But its chief use was to house the legislative majesty of Virginia. In this building the General Assembly of the State held its bi-yearly sessions. Here met the representatives of the people after their slow and toilsome journey on horseback through the dense forests and all but impassable roads from every county of the Commonwealth.[2]

The twenty years that had passed since Marshall's father entered the House of Burgesses had brought changes in the appearance and deportment of Virginia's legislative body corresponding to those in the government of the newly established State. But few elegancies of velvet coat, fine lace, silk stock-

[1] Richmond grew rapidly thereafter. The number of houses was trebled within a decade.

[2] Schoepf, ii, 55-56.

ing, and silver buckle were to be seen in the Virginia Legislature of 1783. Later these were to reappear to some extent; but at the close of the Revolution democracy was rampant, and manifested itself in clothing and manners as well as in curious legislation and strange civil convulsions.

The visitor at a session of the Old Dominion's lawmakers beheld a variegated array — one member in homespun trousers thrust into high boots; still another with the fringed Indian leggings and hunting-shirt of the frontier. Some wore great-coats, some jackets, and, in general, an ostentatious disregard of fashionable apparel prevailed, which occasional silk knee-breeches and stockings emphasized.

The looker-on would have thought this gathering of Virginia lawmakers to be anything but a deliberative body enacting statutes for the welfare of over four hundred thousand people. An eye-witness records that movement, talk, laughter went on continuously; these Solons were not quiet five minutes at a time.[1] All debating was done by a very few men.[2] The others "for most part . . . without clear . . . ideas, with little education or knowledge . . . merely . . . give their votes." [3]

Adjoining the big room where this august assembly sat, was an anteroom; and at the entrance between these two rooms stood a burly doorkeeper, who added to the quiet and gravity of the proceedings by frequently calling out in a loud voice the names of members whom constituents or visitors

[1] Schoepf, ii, 55–56. [2] *Ib.*; and see Journals. [3] *Ib.*, ii, 57.

wanted to see; and there was a constant running back and forth. The anteroom itself was a scene of conversational tumult. Horse-racing, runaway slaves, politics, and other picturesque matters were the subjects discussed.[1] Outsiders stood in no awe of these lawgivers of the people and voiced their contempt, ridicule, or dislike quite as freely as their approval or admiration.[2]

Into this assembly came John Marshall in the fall of 1782. Undoubtedly his father had much to do with his son's election as one of Fauquier County's representatives. His predominant influence, which had made Thomas Marshall Burgess, Sheriff, and Vestryman before the Revolution, had been increased by his admirable war record; his mere suggestion that his son should be sent to the House of Delegates would have been weighty. And the embryo attorney wanted to go, not so much as a step in his career, but because the Legislature met in the town where Mary Ambler lived. In addition to his father's powerful support, his late comrades, their terms of enlistment having expired, had returned to their homes and were hotly enthusiastic for their captain.[3] He was elected almost as a matter of course.

No one in that motley gathering called the House of Delegates was dressed more negligently than this young soldier-lawyer and politician from the backwoods of Fauquier County. He probably wore the short "round about" jacket, which was his favorite

[1] Schoepf, 55–56. [2] *Ib.*, 58.

[3] Story, in Dillon, iii, 337. Marshall was a prime favorite of his old comrades all his life. (*Ib.*)

costume. And among all that free-and-easy crowd no one was less constrained, less formal or more sociable and "hail-fellow, well-met" than this black-eyed, laughter-loving representative from the up country.

But no one had a sounder judgment, a more engaging personality, or a broader view of the drift of things than John Marshall. And notable men were there for him to observe; vast forces moving for him to study. Thomas Jefferson had again become a member of the House after his vindication from threatened impeachment. Patrick Henry was a member, too, and William Cabell, Richard Henry Lee, Benjamin Harrison, and other men whose names have become historic. During Marshall's later years in the Legislature, James Madison, George Mason, William Grayson, Edmund Randolph, George Nicholas, and others of like stature became Marshall's colleagues.

It took eighteen days to organize the House at the first session John Marshall attended.[1] The distance that members had to come was so great, traveling so hard and slow, that not until November 9 had enough members arrived to make a quorum.[2] Thomas Jefferson and Patrick Henry were two of the absent and several times were ordered to be taken into the custody of the sergeant-at-arms.[3] The Journal for Friday, November 8, gravely announces that "it was ordered that Mr. Thomas

[1] Journal, H.D. (Oct. Sess., 1782), 3–10.

[2] The roads were so bad and few that traveling even on horseback was not only toilsome but dangerous. (See *infra*, chap. VII.)

[3] Journal, H.D. (Oct. Sess., 1782), 4–8.

Jefferson, one of the members for Albemarle county who was taken into the custody of a special messenger by Mr. Speaker's warrant, agreeable to an order of the 28th ult., be discharged out of custody; it appearing to the House that he has good cause for his present non-attendance." [1]

Marshall must have favorably impressed the Speaker; for he was immediately appointed a member of the important Committee for Courts of Justice; [2] and two days later a member of a special committee "To form a plan of national defense against invasions"; to examine into the state of public arms, accouterments, and ammunition, and to consult with the Executive "on what assistance they may want from the Legislature for carrying the plan into execution." [3] Two days afterwards Marshall was appointed on a special committee to frame a bill to amend the ordinance of Convention.[4]

His first vote was for a bill to permit John M'Lean, who, because of illness, went to England before the outbreak of the war, and who had returned, to remain in Virginia and live with his family.[5] Marshall's next two votes before taking his place as a member of the Council of State are of no moment except as indicating the bent of his mind for honest business legislation and for a strong and effi-

[1] Journal, H.D. (Oct. Sess., 1782.), 9–10. [2] *Ib.*, 10.

[3] *Ib.*, 13–15. [4] *Ib.*, 15.

[5] *Ib.*, 22; Hening, xi, 111. The "ayes" and "noes" were taken on this bill and Marshall's vote is, of course, without any importance except that it was his first and that it was a little straw showing his kindly and tolerant disposition. Also the fact that the "ayes" and "noes" were called for — something that was very rarely done — shows the popular feeling against Englishmen.

cient militia.[1] During November, Marshall was appointed on several other committees.[2] Of these, the most important was the select committee to bring in a bill for the reorganization of the militia,[3] which reported a comprehensive and well-drawn measure that became a law.[4] He was also on the Standing Committee of Privileges and Elections.[5]

The Virginia Legislature, during these years, was not a body to inspire respect.[6] Madison had a great contempt for it and spoke with disgust of the "temper of the Legislature & the wayward course of its proceedings."[7] Indeed, the entire government of the State was an absurd medley of changing purposes and inefficiency. "Nothing," wrote Madison to Jefferson, "can exceed the confusion which reigns throughout our Revenue department. . . . This confusion indeed runs through all of our public affairs, and must continue as long as the present mode of legislating continues"; the method of drawing bills "must soon bring our laws and our Legislature into contempt among all orders of Citizens."[8]

[1] Journal, H.D. (Oct. Sess., 1782), 27–28. Marshall voted in favor of bringing in a bill for strengthening the credit account; and against postponing the consideration of the militia bill. (*Ib.*, 45.)

[2] *Ib.*, 23, 25, 27, 36, 42, 45.

[3] *Ib.*, 23.

[4] Hening, xi, 173–75.

[5] Journal, H.D., 36.

[6] "It greatly behoves the Assembly to revise several of our laws, and to abolish all such as are contrary to the fundamental principles of justice; and by a strict adherence to the distinctions between Right and Wrong for the future, to restore that confidence and reverence . . . which has been so greatly impaired by a contrary conduct; and without which our laws can never be much more than a dead letter." (Mason to Henry, May 6, 1783, as quoted in Henry, ii, 185.)

[7] *Writings:* Hunt, ii, 397. This notable fact is worthy of repetition if we are to get an accurate view of the Virginia Legislature of that day. Yet that body contained many men of great ability.

[8] Madison to Jefferson, July 3, 1784; *Writings:* Hunt, ii, 62.

Nor did Virginia's lawmakers improve for several years. Madison in 1787 advised Washington that "The proceedings of the Assembly are, as usual, rapidly degenerating with the progress of the session."[1] And the irritated soldier at Mount Vernon responded with characteristic heat that "Our Assembly has been . . . employed . . . chiefly in rectifying some of the mistakes of the last, and committing new ones for emendations at the next."[2] Washington, writing to Lafayette of American affairs in 1788, said, with disgust, that "Virginia in the very last session . . . was about to pass some of the most extravagant and preposterous edicts . . . that ever stained the leaves of a legislative code."[3]

Popular as he was with the members of the Legislature, Marshall shared Madison's opinion of their temper and conduct. Of the fall session of the Assembly of 1783, he writes to Colonel Levin Powell: "This long session has not produced a single bill of Public importance except that for the readmission of Commutables.[4] . . . It ought to be perfect as it has

[1] Madison to Washington, Dec. 14, 1787; *ib.*, v, 69–70.

[2] Washington to Madison, Jan. 10, 1788; *Writings:* Ford, xi, 208.

[3] Washington to Lafayette, April 28, 1788; *ib.*, 254. Washington wrote bitterly of State antagonism. "One State passes a prohibitory law respecting some article, another State opens wide the avenue for its admission. One Assembly makes a system, another Assembly unmakes it." (*Ib.*)

[4] Hening, xi, 299–306. This statement of Marshall's was grossly incorrect. This session of the Legislature passed several laws of the very greatest public consequence, such as the act to authorize Congress to pass retaliatory trade laws against Great Britain (*ib.*, 313); an immigration and citizenship act (*ib.*, 322–24); an act prohibiting British refugees from coming to Virginia; and a quarantine act (*ib.*, 29–31). It was this session that passed the famous act to authorize

twice passed the House. It fell the first time (after an immensity of labor and debate) a sacrifice to the difference of opinion subsisting in the House of Delegates and the Senate with respect to a money bill. A bill for the regulation of elections and inforcing the attendance of members is now on the Carpet and will probably pass.[1] . . . It is surprising that Gentlemen of character cannot dismiss their private animosities, but will bring them in the Assembly."[2]

Early in the session Marshall in a letter to Monroe describes the leading members and the work of the House.

"The Commutable bill,"[3] writes he, "has at

Virginia's delegates in Congress to convey to the United States the Northwest Territory (*ib.*, 326–28).

This remarkable oversight of Marshall is hard to account for. An explanation is that this was the year of his marriage; and the year also in which he became a resident of Richmond, started in the practice of the law there, and set up his own home. In addition to these absorbing things, his duty as a member of the Council of State took his attention. Also, of course, it was the year when peace with Great Britain was declared. Still, these things do not excuse Marshall's strange misstatement. Perhaps he underestimated the importance of the work done at this particular session.

[1] Hening, xi, 387–88. This bill became a law at the spring session of the following year. The impracticable part enforcing attendance of members was dropped. The bill as passed imposes a penalty of fifty pounds on any sheriff or other officer for failure to return certificates of elections; a forfeit of two hundred pounds upon any sheriff interfering in any election or showing any partiality toward candidates.

[2] Marshall to Powell, Dec. 9, 1783; *Branch Historical Papers*, i, 130–31.

[3] An act allowing one half of the taxes to be paid in tobacco, hemp, flour, or deerskins, and suspending distress for taxes until January, 1784. (Hening, xi, 289.) The scarcity of specie was so great and the people so poor that the collection of taxes was extremely difficult. In 1782 the partial payment of taxes in commutables — tobacco, hemp, flour, or deerskins — was introduced. This occasioned such loss to the

length pass'd and with it a suspension of the collections of taxes till the first of January next. . . . Colo. Harry Lee of the Legionary corps" is to take the place of "Col^o R. H. Lee" whose "services are lost to the Assembly forever"; and Marshall does not know "whether the public will be injur'd by the change." Since the passage of the "Commutable bill . . . the attention of the house has been so fix'd on the Citizen bill that they have scarcely thought on any other subject. . . . Col. [George] Nicholas (politician not fam'd for hitting a medium) introduced one admitting into this country every species of Men except Natives who had borne arms against the state. . . . Mr. Jones introduc'd by way of amendment, one totally new and totally opposite to that which was the subject of deliberation. He spoke with his usual sound sense and solid reason. Mr. Henry opposed him.

"The Speaker replied with some degree of acrimony and Henry retorted with a good deal of tartness but with much temper; 'tis his peculiar excellence when he altercates to appear to be drawn unwillingly into the contest and to throw in the eyes of others the whole blame on his adversary. His influence is immense." [1]

Marshall's strange power of personality which,

treasury that in May, 1783, the Commutable Acts were repealed; but within five months the Legislature reversed itself again and passed the Commutable Bill which so disgusted Marshall.

[1] Marshall to Monroe, Dec. 12, 1783; MS., Draper Collection, Wisconsin Historical Society; also printed in *Amer. Hist. Rev.*, iii, 673. This letter is not addressed, but it has been assumed that it was written to Thomas Jefferson. This is incorrect; it was written to James Monroe.

in after years, was so determining an influence on the destiny of the country, together with the combined influence of his father and of the State Treasurer, Jacquelin Ambler, Marshall's father-in-law, now secured for the youthful legislator an unusual honor. Eleven days after the House of Delegates had organized, Marshall was elected by joint ballot of the Senate and the House a member of the Council of State,[1] commonly called the Executive Council. The Journal of the Council for November 20, 1782, records: "John Marshall esquire having been elected a Member of the Privy Council or Council of State in the room of John Bannister esquire who hath resigned and producing a Certificate from under the hand of Jaq. Ambler esq[r] of his having qualified according to law; he took his seat at the board." [2]

Marshall had just turned his twenty-seventh year, and the Council of State was supposed to be made up of men of riper years and experience. Older men, and especially the judges of the courts, resented the bestowal of this distinction upon so youthful a member serving his first term. Edmund Pendleton, Judge of the High Court of Chancery and President of the Court of Appeals, wrote to Madison that: "Young Mr. Marshall is elected a Councillor. . . .

[1] Journal, H.D. (Oct. Sess., 1782), 27. It is almost certain that his father and Jacquelin Ambler were pushing him. The Speaker and other prominent members of the House had been colleagues of Thomas Marshall in the House of Burgesses and Ambler was popular with everybody. Still, Marshall's personality must have had much to do with this notable advancement. His membership in the Council cannot be overestimated in considering his great conflict with the Virginia political "machine" after he became Chief Justice. See volume III of this work.

[2] Journal of the Council of State, Nov. 20, 1782; MS., Va. St. Lib.

He is clever, but I think too young for that department, which he should rather have earned as a retirement and reward, by ten or twelve years hard service in the Assembly." [1]

The Council consisted of eight members elected by the Legislature either from the delegates or from the people at large. It was the Governor's official cabinet and a constitutional part of the executive power. The Governor consulted the Council on all important matters coming before him; and he appointed various important officers only upon its advice.[2]

The Constitution of Virginia of 1776 was the basis upon which was built one of the most perfect political machines ever constructed; and this machine in later years came to be Marshall's great antagonist. As a member of the Council of State, Marshall learned by actual experience the possible workings of this mechanism, first run by Patrick Henry, perfected by Thomas Jefferson, and finally developed to its ultimate efficiency by Spencer Roane and Thomas Ritchie.[3] Thus Marshall took part in the appointment of surveyors, justices of the peace, tobacco inspectors, and other officers; [4] and passed on requisitions from other States for the delivery of fugitive criminals.[5]

Marshall's signature to the minutes of the Coun-

[1] Pendleton to Madison, Nov. 25, 1782; quoted in Rives, i, 182.

[2] Constitution of Virginia, 1776.

[3] Dodd, in *Amer. Hist. Rev.*, xii, 776.

[4] Marshall participated in the appointment of General George Rogers Clark to the office of Surveyor of Officers' and Soldiers' lands (Journal, Ex. Council, 1784, 57; MS., Va. St. Lib.) [5] *Ib.*

cil is totally unlike that of his more mature years, as, indeed, is the chirography of his letters of that period. He signed the Council records in large and dashing hand with flourishes — it is the handwriting of a confident, care-free, rollicking young man with a tinge of the dare-devil in him. These signatures are so strangely dissimilar to his later ones that they deserve particular attention. They denote Marshall's sense of his own importance and his certainty of his present position and future prospects.

The criticisms from the judges — first expressed by Pendleton, before whom Marshall was trying to practice law — of his membership of the Executive Council continued. Because of these objections, Marshall finally resigned and at once sought another election from his native county to the House of Delegates. The accepted version of this incident is that Marshall resigned from the Executive Council because the duties of that position took too much time from his profession; and that, without his request or desire, his old neighbors in Fauquier, from "their natural pride in connecting his rising name with their county, spontaneously elected him to the Legislature." [1]

Thus does greatness, once achieved, throw upon a past career a glory that dazzles the historian's eye; and the early steps of advancement are seen and described as unasked and unwished honors paid by a discerning public to modest and retiring merit. Thus, too, research and fact are ever in collision

[1] Binney, in Dillon, iii, 291–92. This story is repeated in almost all of the sketches of Marshall's life.

with fancy and legend. The cherished story about Marshall's resignation from the Council and "spontaneous" election to the Legislature from his home county is a myth. The discontent of the judges practically forced him out of the Council and he personally sought another election from Fauquier County to the House of Delegates. Marshall himself gives the true account of these important incidents.

"I am no longer a member of the Executive [Council]," Marshall informs his friend James Monroe, "the opinion of the Judges with regard to a Councillor's standing at the bar determined me to retire from the Council board. Every person is now busied about the ensuing election." Certainly Marshall was thus occupied; for he writes Monroe that "I had made a small excursion into Fauquier to enquire into the probability of my being chosen by the people, should I offer as a candidate at the next election." Marshall tells the political news, in which he shows minute information, and finally advises Monroe that "I have been maneuvering amazingly to turn your warrants into cash if I succeed I shall think myself a first rate speculator." [1]

Marshall's personal attention [2] to his candidacy bore fruit; and for the second time he was chosen as Delegate from Fauquier, although he now lived in Henrico County.[3]

When the Legislature convened, nine days again

[1] Marshall to Monroe, April 17, 1784; MS., N.Y. Pub. Lib.

[2] His father, now in Kentucky, could no longer personally aid his son in his old home. Thus Marshall himself had to attend to his own political affairs.

[3] Marshall did not try for the Legislature again until 1787 when he sought and secured election from Henrico. (See *infra*.)

passed before enough members were in Richmond to make up a House.[1] Marshall was among the tardy. On May 13, the sergeant-at-arms was ordered to take him and other members into custody; and later in the day he and four others were brought in by that officer and "admitted to their seats on paying fees." [2]

He was at once appointed to his old place on the Committee for Courts of Justice and upon the immensely important Standing Committee on Propositions and Grievances, to which was referred the flood of petitions of soldiers and officers, the shower of applications of counties and towns for various laws and other matters of pressing local and personal concern in every part of Virginia.[3] To the cases of his old comrades in arms who applied to the Legislature for relief, Marshall was particularly attentive.[4] He became the champion of the Revolutionary veterans, most of whom were very poor men.[5]

Upon Washington's suggestion a bill was brought in for the relief of Thomas Paine by vesting in him a moderate tract of public lands. Upon the third reading it was "committed to a committee of the whole house" and there debated. Marshall, who apparently led the fight for Paine, "read in his place" several amendments. But notwithstanding Washington's plea, the immense services of Paine

[1] Journal, H.D. (Spring Sess., 1784), 5. A Robert Marshall was also a member of the House during 1784 as one of the representatives for Isle of Wight County. He was not related in any way to John Marshall.

[2] *Ib.* [3] *Ib.* [4] Story, in Dillon, iii, 335–36.

[5] As an example of the number and nature of these soldier petitions see Journal, H.D. (Spring Sess., 1784), 7, 9, 11, 16, 18, 44.

to the American cause during the Revolution, and the amendments which, obviously, met all objections, the bill was defeated.[1]

Numerous things of human interest happened during this session which show the character of the Legislature and the state of the people. An Englishman named Williamson[2] had gone to Essex County a year before by permission of the Governor, but in violation of the law against British refugees. When he refused to leave, the people tarred and feathered him and drove him out of the country in this condition.[3] The Attorney-General began prosecutions against the leaders of the mob; and the offending ones petitioned the Legislature to interfere. The petition was referred to the Committee on Propositions and Grievances[4] of which Marshall was a member. This committee reported that the petition ought to be granted "and that all irregularities committed by any citizen of this state on the person or properties of refugees previous to the ratification of the definitive treaty of peace . . . should be indemnified by law and buried in utter obliv-

[1] See chap. VIII and footnote to p. 288.

[2] Williamson was a Tory of the offensive type. He had committed hostile acts which embittered the people against him. (See *Cal. Va. St. Prs.*, ii. And see Eckenrode: *R. V.*, chap. xi, for full account of this and similar cases.)

[3] The gentle pastime of tarring and feathering unpopular persons and riding them on sharp rails appears to have been quite common in all parts of the country, for a long time before the Revolution. Men even burned their political opponents at the stake. (See instances in Belcher, i, 40–45.) Savage, however, as were the atrocities committed upon the Loyalists by the patriots, even more brutal treatment was dealt out to the latter by British officers and soldiers during the Revolution. (See *supra*, chap. IV, footnote to p. 116.)

[4] Journal, H.D. (Spring Sess., 1784), 19.

ion."[1] But when the bill came to a vote, it was defeated.[2]

It was reported to the House that a certain John Warden had insulted its dignity by saying publicly that if the House had voted against paying the British debts, some of its members had voted against paying for the coats on their backs — a charge which was offensively true. The Committee on Privileges and Elections was instructed to take this serious matter up and order the offender before it. He admitted the indiscretion and apologized for it. The committee read Warden's written acknowledgment and apology before the House and thus he was purged of the contempt of that sensitive body.[3]

A William Finnie, who had been deputy quartermaster in the military service, had purchased, at the request of the Board of War, a large quantity of boots for a corps of cavalry in active service and then on the march. Although the seller of the boots knew that they were bought for the public service, he sued Finnie and secured judgment against him, which was on the point of being executed. Finnie petitioned the Legislature that the debt be paid by the State. The Committee on Propositions and Grievances took charge of this petition, reported the facts to be as Finnie had stated them, and recommended that the debt "ought to be paid him by the public and charged to the United States."[4] But the House rejected the resolution. Incidents

[1] Journal, H.D. (Spring Sess., 1784), 23, 27.

[2] *Ib.*, 45. For thorough examination of this incident see Eckenrode: *R. V.*, chap. xi.

[3] Journal, H.D. (Spring Sess., 1784), 57.

[4] *Ib.*, 14.

like these, as well as the action of the Legislature and the conduct of the people themselves, had their influence on the radical change which occurred in Marshall's opinions and point of view during the decade after the war.

Marshall was appointed on many special committees to prepare sundry bills during this session. Among these was a committee to frame a bill to compel payment by those counties that had failed to furnish their part of the money for recruiting Virginia's quota of troops to serve in the Continental army. This bill was passed.[1]

A vote which gives us the first sight of Marshall's idea about changing a constitution was taken during this session. Augusta County had petitioned the Legislature to alter Virginia's fundamental law. The committee reported a resolution against it, "such a measure not being within the province of the House of Delegates to assume; but on the contrary, it is the express duty of the representatives of the people at all times, and on all occasions, to preserve the same [the Constitution] inviolable, until a majority of all the people shall direct a reform thereof." [2]

Marshall voted to amend this resolution by striking out the words quoted. Thus, as far as this vote indicates, we see him standing for the proposition that a form of government could be changed by convention, which was the easiest, and, indeed, at that time the only practicable, method of altering the constitution of the State. Madison also favored

[1] Hening, xi, 390. [2] Journal, H.D., 70–71.

this plan, but did nothing because of Patrick Henry's violent opposition. The subject was debated for two days and the project of a convention with full powers to make a new Constitution was overwhelmingly defeated, although nearly all of the "young men of education & talents" were for it.[1]

A few of the bills that Marshall voted for or reported from committee are worthy of note, in addition to those which had to do with those serious questions of general and permanent historic consequence to the country presently to be considered. They are important in studying the development of Marshall's economic and governmental views.

In 1784, Washington brought vividly before the Virginia Legislature the necessity of improving the means of transportation.[2] At the same time this subject was also taken up by the Legislature of Maryland. A law was passed by the Virginia Legislature for "opening and extending the navigation of the Potowmack river from tidewater to the highest place practicable on the north branch"; and Maryland took similar action. These identical laws authorized the forming of a corporation called the "Potowmack

[1] Madison to Jefferson, July 3, 1794; *Writings:* Hunt, ii, 56–57. The Constitution of 1776 never was satisfactory to the western part of Virginia, which was under-represented. Representation was by counties and not population. Also suffrage was limited to white freeholders; and this restriction was made more onerous by the fact that county representation was based on slave as well as free population. Also, the Constitution made possible the perpetuation of the Virginia political machine, previously mentioned, which afterward played a part of such vast importance in National affairs. Yet extreme liberals like the accomplished and patriotic Mason were against the Legislature turning itself into a convention to make a new one. (Mason to Henry, May 6, 1783; Henry, ii, 185.)

[2] Madison to Jefferson, Jan. 9, 1785; *Writings:* Hunt, ii, 104.

Company" with a quarter of a million dollars capital. It was given the power of eminent domain; was authorized to charge tolls "at all times forever hereafter"; and the property and profits were vested in the shareholders, "their heirs and assigns forever."[1]

John Marshall voted for this bill, which passed without opposition.[2] He became a stockholder in the corporation and paid several assessments on his stock.[3] Thus early did Marshall's ideas on the nature of a legislative franchise to a corporation acquire the vitality of property interest and personal experience.

Marshall was on the Committee for Courts of Justice during every session when he was a member of the House and worked upon several bills concerning the courts. On November 2, 1787, he was appointed upon a special committee to bring in a bill "to amend the act establishing the High Court of Chancery."[4] Three weeks later he reported this

[1] Hening, xi, 510–18. This law shows the chief articles of commerce at that time and the kind of money which might be received as tolls. The scale of equivalents in pounds sterling vividly displays the confused currency situation of the period. The table names Spanish milled pieces of eight, English milled crowns, French silver crowns, johannes, half johannes, moidores, English guineas, French guineas, doubloons, Spanish pistoles, French milled pistoles, Arabian sequins; the weight of each kind of money except Spanish pieces of eight and English and French milled crowns being carefully set out; and "other gold coin (German excepted) by the pennyweight." If any of this money should be reduced in value by lessening its weight or increasing its alloy it should be received at "its reduced value only." (*Ib.*)

[2] Madison to Jefferson, Jan. 9, 1785; *Writings:* Hunt, ii, 102. Madison gives a very full history and description of this legislation.

[3] Marshall's Account Book contains entries of many of these payments.

[4] Journal, H.D. (Nov. 1787), 27–127.

bill to the House;[1] and when the bill passed that body it was "ordered that Mr. Marshall do carry the bill to the Senate and desire their concurrence." The committee which drew this bill was made up from among the ablest men in the House: Henry, Mason, Nicholas, Matthews, Stuart, and Monroe being the other members,[2] with Marshall who was chairman.

The act simplified and expedited proceedings in equity.[3] The High Court of Chancery had been established by an act of the Virginia Legislature of 1777.[4] This law was the work of Thomas Jefferson. It contained one of the reforms so dear to his heart during that period — the right of trial by jury to ascertain the facts in equity causes. But six years' experience proved that the reform was not practical. In 1783 the jury trial in equity was abolished, and the old method that prevailed in the courts of chancery before the Revolution was reinstated.[5] With this exception the original act stood in Virginia as a model of Jeffersonian reforms in legal procedure; but under its provisions, insufferable delays had grown up which defeated the ends of justice.[6] It was to remedy this practical defect of Jefferson's

[1] Journal, H.D. (Nov. 1787), 70. [2] *Ib.*, 27.

[3] Hening, xii, 464–67. The preamble of the act recites that it is passed because under the existing law "justice is greatly delayed by the tedious forms of proceedings, suitors are therefore obliged to waste much time and expense to the impoverishment of themselves and the state, and decrees when obtained are with difficulty carried into execution." (*Ib.*)

[4] *Ib.*, ix, 389–99. [5] *Ib.*, xi, 342–44.

[6] See Jefferson's letter to Mazzei, explaining the difference between law and equity and the necessity for courts of chancery as well as courts of law. This is one of the best examples of Jefferson's calm, clear, simple style when writing on non-political subjects. (Jefferson to Mazzei, Nov., 1785; *Works:* Ford, iv, 473–80.)

monumental law that Marshall brought in the bill of 1787.

But the great matters which came before the Legislature during this period, between the ending of the war and the adoption of the Constitution, were: The vexed question of the debts owed by Virginia planters to British subjects; the utter impotence of the so-called Federal Government and the difficulty of getting the States to give it any means or authority to discharge the National debts and uphold the National honor; and the religious controversy involving, at bottom, the question of equal rights for all sects.[1]

The religious warfare [2] did not greatly appeal to Marshall, it would seem, although it was of the gravest importance. Bad as the state of religion was at the beginning of the Revolution, it was worse after that struggle had ended. "We are now to rank among the nations of the world," wrote Mason to Henry in 1783; "but whether our independence shall prove a blessing or a curse must depend upon our wisdom or folly, virtue or wickedness. . . . The prospect is not promising. . . . A depravity of manners and morals prevails among us, to the destruction of all confidence between man and man." [3] The want of public worship "increases daily; nor have

[1] For the best contemporaneous description of Virginia legislation during this period see Madison's letters to Jefferson when the latter was in Paris. (*Writings:* Hunt, i and ii.)

[2] For a thorough account of the religious struggle in Virginia from the beginning see Eckenrode: *S. of C. and S.* On the particular phase of this subject dealt with while Marshall was a member of the Virginia Legislature see *ib.*, chap. v.

[3] Mason to Henry, May 6, 1783, as quoted in Rowland, ii, 44.

we left in our extensive State three churches that are decently supported," wrote Mrs. Carrington, the sister of John Marshall's wife, a few years later.[1]

Travelers through Virginia during this period note that church buildings of all denominations were poor and mean and that most of these were falling into ruins; while ministers barely managed to keep body and soul together by such scanty mites as the few pious happened to give them or by the miserable wages they earned from physical labor.[2] These scattered and decaying little church houses, the preachers toiling with axe or hoe, formed, it appears, an accurate index of the religious indifference of the people.[3]

There were gross inequalities of religious privileges. Episcopal clergymen could perform marriage ceremonies anywhere, but ministers of the other denominations could do so only in the county where they lived. The property of the Episcopal Church came from the pockets of all the people; and the vestries could tax members of other churches as well as their own for the relief of the poor.[3] It was a curious swirl of conflicting currents. Out of it came

[1] Meade, i, footnote to 142. And see *Atlantic Monthly, supra.*

[2] Eckenrode: *S. of C. and S.*, 75. On this general subject see Meade, i, chaps. i and ii. "Infidelity became rife, in Virginia, perhaps, beyond any other portion of land. The Clergy, for the most part, were a laughing stock or objects of disgust." (*Ib.*, 52.) Even several years later Bishop Meade says that "I was then taking part in the labours of the field, which in Virginia was emphatically *servile labour.*" (*Ib.*, 27.)

"One sees not only a smaller number of houses of worship [in Virginia] than in other provinces, but what there are in a ruinous or ruined condition, and the clergy for the most part dead or driven away and their places unfilled." (Schoepf, ii, 62–63.)

[3] Henry, ii, 199–206. [4] Eckenrode: *S. of C. and S.*, 77.

the proposition to levy an assessment on everybody for the support of religion; a bill to incorporate the Episcopal Church which took away its general powers of vestry taxation, but confirmed the title to the property already held; and the marriage law which gave ministers of all denominations equal authority.[1]

Although these propositions were debated at great length and with much spirit and many votes were taken at various stages of the contest, Marshall recorded his vote but twice. He did not vote on the resolution to incorporate the Episcopal Church;[2] or to sell the glebe lands;[3] nor did he vote on the marriage bill.[4] He voted against Madison's motion to postpone consideration of the bill for a general assessment to support religion, which carried,[5] thus killing the bill. When the bill to incorporate the Episcopal Church came to a final vote, Marshall voted "aye," as, indeed, did Madison.[6]

But if Marshall took only a languid interest in the religious struggle, he was keen-eyed and active on the other two vital matters — the payment of debts, both public and private, and the arming of the Fed-

[1] Journal, H.D. (2d Sess., 1784), 19. [2] *Ib.*, 27.
[3] *Ib.*, 82. [4] *Ib.* [5] *Ib.*

[6] *Ib.*, 97. For the incorporation law see Hening, xi, 532–37; for marriage law see *ib.*, 532–35. Madison describes this law to Jefferson and excuses his vote for it by saying that "the necessity of some sort of incorporation for the purpose of holding & managing the property of the Church could not well be denied, nor a more harmless modification of it now be obtained. A negative of the bill, too, would have doubled the eagerness and the pretexts for a much greater evil, a general Assessment, which, there is good ground to believe, was parried by this partial gratification of its warmest votaries." (Madison to Jefferson, Jan. 9, 1785; *Writings:* Hunt, ii. 113.)

eral Government with powers necessary to its existence. Throughout this whole period we see the rapid and solid growth of the idea of Nationality, the seeds of which had been planted in John Marshall's soul by the fingers of military necessity and danger. Here, too, may be found the beginning of those ideas of contract which developed throughout his life and hardened as they developed until finally they became as flint. And here also one detects the first signs of the change in what Marshall himself called "the wild and enthusiastic notions" [1] with which, only a few years earlier, he had marched forth from the backwoods, to fight for independence and popular government.

Virginia planters owed an immense amount of money to British merchants. It had been the free-and-easy habit of Virginians to order whatever they wanted from England and pay for it in the produce of their fields, chiefly tobacco. The English merchants gave long credit and were always willing to extend it when the debt fell due. The Virginians, on their part, found the giving of new notes a convenient way of canceling old obligations and thus piled up mountains of debt which they found hard to remove. After the war was over, they had little means with which to discharge their long overdue accounts.[2]

[1] Story, in Dillon, iii, 338.

[2] "Virginia certainly owed two millions sterling [$10,000,000] to Great Britain at the conclusion of the war. Some have conjectured the debt as high as three millions [$15,000,000]. . . . These debts had become hereditary from father to son for many generations, so that the planters were a species of property annexed to certain mercantile houses in London. . . . I think that state owed near as much as all the rest put together." Jefferson's explanation of these obligations is ex-

During the Revolution stringent and radical laws were passed, preventing the recovery of these debts in the courts, sequestering the property and even forfeiting the estates owned by British subjects in Virginia; and a maze of acts, repealing and then reviving the statutes that prevented payment, were passed after the war had ended.[1] The Treaty between the United States and Great Britain provided as one of the conditions of peace that all these legal impediments to the recovery of British debts should be removed.[2] Failure to repeal the anti-debt legislation passed during the war was, of course, a plain infraction of this contract between the two countries; while the enactment of similar laws after the Treaty had become binding, openly and aggressively violated it.

Within two weeks after Marshall took his seat in the House in 1784, this sorely vexed question came up. A resolution was brought in "that so much of all and every act or acts of the Assembly, now in force in this commonwealth as prevents a due compliance with the stipulation contained in the definitive Treaty of Peace entered into between Great

tremely partial to the debtors, of whom he was one. (Jefferson to Meusnier, Jan. 24, 1786; *Works:* Ford, v, 28.)

Most of Jefferson's earlier debts were contracted in the purchase of slaves. "I cannot decide to sell my lands. . . . nor would I willingly sell the slaves as long as there remains any prospect of paying my debts with their labor." This will "enable me to put them ultimately on an easier footing, which I will do the moment they have paid the my] debts, . . . two thirds of which have been contracted by purchasing them." (Jefferson to Lewis, July 29, 1787; *ib.*, 311.)

[1] For Virginia legislation on this subject see Hening, ix, x, and xi, under index caption "British Debts."

[2] Definitive Treaty of Peace, 1783, art. 4.

Britain and America ought to be repealed"; but a motion to put the question to agree with this resolution was defeated by a majority of twenty. John Marshall voted to put the question.[1]

Those resisting the effort to carry out the Treaty of Peace declared that Great Britain itself had not complied with it, because the British had not surrendered the American posts retained by them at the close of the war and had not returned or paid for the slaves carried away by the British forces.[2] A fortnight after the first defeat of the movement against the anti-debt law, a resolution was laid before the House instructing Virginia's Representatives in Congress to request that body to protest to the British Government against this infraction of the Treaty and to secure reparation therefor, and stating that the Virginia Legislature would not coöperate "in the complete fulfillment of said treaty" until this was done. The intent of the resolution was that no British debts should be paid for a long time to come.

But the resolution did provide that, when this reparation was made, or when "Congress shall adjudge it indispensably necessary," the anti-debt laws "ought to be repealed and payment made to all [creditors] in such time and manner as shall consist with the exhausted situation of this Commonwealth"; and that "the further operation of all and every act or acts of the Assembly concerning escheats and forfeitures from British subjects ought to be

[1] Journal, H.D. (1st Sess.), 1784, 41.
[2] *Ib.*, 54; 72–73. The Treaty required both.

prevented."[1] An amendment was offered containing the idea that the debtors might deduct their losses from their debts, thus taking a little step toward payment. Another amendment to strengthen this was also proposed.

Had these amendments carried, the policy of an early payment of the British debts would have prevailed. Marshall voted for both as did Madison. The amendments, however, were overwhelmingly defeated.[2] The situation and point of view of the British merchants to whom these debts were due and who, depending upon the faithful performance of the Treaty, had come to Virginia to collect the money owing them, is illustrated by a petition which George F. Norton presented to the House. He was a member of the mercantile firm of Norton and Sons, of London, from whom Virginians had made purchases on credit for a generation before the war. He declared that his firm had "been compelled to pay many debts due from the said company, but he has been unable to collect any due to them, in consequence of the laws prohibiting recovery of British debts, by which he has been reduced to the greatest extremes."[3]

After the summer adjournment the irrepressible conflict between keeping or breaking the National faith once more arose. Henry, who was the champion of the debtors, had been elected Governor and

[1] Journal, H.D. (1st Sess., 1784), 74.

[2] *Ib.*, 74–75. Henry led the fight against repealing the anti-debt laws or, as he contended, against Great Britain's infraction of the Treaty.

[3] Journal, H.D. (1st Sess., 1784), 25.

was "*out of the way.*" [1] Several British merchants had proposed to accept payments of their debts in installments. Ratifications of the Treaty had been exchanged. The friends of National honor and private good faith had gathered headway. Finally a bill passed the House repealing the anti-debt laws. The Senate and the House came to an agreement.

Here arose a situation which pictures the danger and difficulty of travel in that day. Before the bill had been sent back to the House, enrolled, examined, and signed by both presiding officers, several members went across the river to spend the night at the neighboring hamlet of Manchester. It was the day before adjournment and they expected to return the next morning. But that night the river froze [2] and they could not get back. So this important measure fell through for the session.[3]

No "ayes" and "noes" were called for during this final battle, but Marshall probably took part in the debate and it is certain that he used the influence which his popularity among members gave him for the passage of this law.

"I wish with you," wrote Marshall to Monroe, in early December, "that our Assembly had never passed those resolutions respecting the British Debts which have been so much the subject of reprehension throughout the States. I wish it because it affords a pretext to the British to retain possession of the posts on the lakes but much more because I ever considered

[1] Madison to Jefferson, Jan. 9, 1785; *Writings:* Hunt, ii, 114.

[2] See Madison's vivid description of this incident; *ib.*, 116; also Henry, ii, 233.

[3] *Ib.*

it as a measure tending to weaken the federal bands which in my conception are too weak already. We are about, tho reluctantly, to correct the error."

Marshall despondently summed up the work of the session: "We have as yet done nothing finally. Not a bill of public importance, in which an individual was not particularly interested, has passed." [1]

Marshall was not a candidate for the Legislature in 1785–86, but sought and secured election in 1787, when he was sent from Henrico County, where Richmond was situated. During this hiatus in Marshall's public life another effort was made to repeal the anti-debt laws, but so bitter was the resistance that nothing was accomplished. Madison was distressed.[2] When Marshall again became a member of the General Assembly the question of the British debts was brought forward once more. This time the long-delayed bill was passed, though not until its foes had made their point about the runaway slaves and the unevacuated posts.[3]

[1] Marshall to Monroe, Dec. 2, 1784; MS., Monroe Papers, Lib. Cong.

[2] Madison to Monroe, Dec. 24, 1785; *Writings:* Hunt, ii, 205.

"Being convinced myself that nothing can be now done that will not extremely dishonor us, and embarass Cong.s my wish is that the report may not be called for at all. In the course of the debates no pains were spared to disparage the Treaty by insinuations agst Congs., the Eastern States, and the negociators of the Treaty, particularly J. Adams. These insinuations & artifices explain perhaps one of the motives from which the augmention of the foederal powers & respectability has been opposed." (Madison to Monroe, Dec. 30, 1785; *ib.*, 211.)

[3] Curiously enough, it fell to Jefferson as Secretary of State to report upon, explain, and defend the measures of Virginia and other States which violated the Treaty of Peace. (See Jefferson to the British Minister, May 29, 1792; *Works:* Ford, vii, 3–99.) This masterful statement is one of the finest argumentative products of Jefferson's brilliant mind.

A resolution was brought in that the anti-debt laws "ought to be repealed," but that any act for this purpose should be suspended until the other States had passed similar laws. An amendment was defeated for making the suspension until Great Britain complied with the Treaty. John Marshall voted against it, as did his father Thomas Marshall, who was now a member of the Virginia Legislature from the District of Kentucky.[1] Another amendment to pay the British debts "in such time and manner as shall consist with the exhausted situation of this Commonwealth" met a similar fate, both Marshalls, father and son, voting against it.[2] The resolution was then passed, the two Marshalls voting for it.[3]

Marshall was then appointed a member of the special committee to prepare and bring in a bill to carry out the resolution.[4] In a few days this bill was laid before the House. Except the extension clause, this bill was probably drawn by Marshall. It was short and to the point. It repealed everything on the statute books repugnant to the Treaty of Peace. It specifically "directed and required" the courts to decide all cases "arising from or touching said treaty" "according to the tenor, true intent, and

[1] Journal, H.D. (1787), 51. [2] *Ib.*, 52.

[3] *Ib.* James Monroe was a member of the House at this session and voted against the first amendment and for the second. On the contrary, Patrick Henry voted for the first and against the second amendment. George Mason voted against both amendments. So did Daniel Boone, who was, with Thomas Marshall, then a member of the Virginia Legislature from the District of Kentucky. On the passage of the resolution, James Monroe and Patrick Henry again swerved around, the former voting for and the latter against it.

[4] Journal, H.D. (1787), 52.

meaning of same" regardless of the repealed laws. But the operation of the law was suspended until Congress informed the Governor "that the other states in the Union have passed laws enabling British creditors to recover their debts agreeably to the terms of the treaty." [1] The bill was emphasized by a brief preamble which stated that "it is agreed by the fourth article of the treaty of peace with Great Britain that creditors on either side shall meet with no lawful impediment to the recovery of the full value in sterling money, of all bona fide debts heretofore contracted."

The opponents of the bill tried to emasculate it by an amendment that the law should not go into effect until the Governor of Virginia made public proclamation "that Great Britain hath delivered up to the United States the posts therein now occupied by British troops" and was taking measures to return the runaway slaves or to pay for them. They succeeded. Whether from agitation outside the legislative hall [2] or from the oratory of Patrick Henry, or from a greater power of the leaders in lobbying among their fellow members, a quick and radical transformation of sentiment took place. Probably all these causes joined to produce it. By a crushing

[1] Journal, H.D. (1787), 79.

[2] "If we are now to pay the debts due to the British merchants, what have we been fighting for all this while?" was the question the people "sometimes" asked, testifies George Mason. (Henry, ii, 187.) But the fact is that this question generally was asked by the people. Nothing explains the struggle over this subject except that the people found it a bitter hardship to pay the debts, as, indeed, was the case; and the idea of not paying them at all grew into a hope and then a policy.

majority of forty-nine the amendment was adopted and the bill denatured. Both John Marshall and his father voted against the amendment, as did George Mason, Benjamin Harrison, and James Monroe.[1]

Thus, in two weeks, a majority of thirty-three against this very scheme for breaking the force of the bill was changed to a majority of forty-nine in favor of it. The bill as amended passed the next day.[2] Such were the instability of the Virginia Legislature at this period and the people's bitter opposition to the payment of the debts owed to British subjects.

The effect on Marshall's mind was very great. The popular readiness to escape, if not to repudiate, contracted obligations, together with the whimsical capriciousness of the General Assembly, created grave misgivings in his mind. His youthful sympathy with the people was beginning to disappear. Just as the roots of his Nationalist views run back to Valley Forge, so do the roots of his economic-political opinions penetrate to the room in the small frame building where sat the Legislature of Virginia in the first years that followed the close of the war.

But the mockery of government exhibited by the Federal establishment at this period of chaos impressed Marshall even more than the spirit of repudiation of debts and breaking of contracts which was back of the anti-debt legislation.[3] The want of

[1] Journal, H.D. (1787), 80.

[2] Hening, xii, 528. Richard Henry Lee thought that both countries were to blame. (Lee to Henry, Feb. 14, 1785; quoted in Henry, iii, 279.)

[3] For an excellent statement regarding payment of British debts, see letter of George Mason to Patrick Henry, May 6, 1783, as quoted

the National power during the Revolution, which Marshall had seen from the "lights . . . which glanced from the point of his sword,"[1] he now saw through the tobacco smoke which filled the grimy room where the Legislature of Virginia passed laws and repealed them almost at the same time.[2] The so-called Federal Government was worse than no government at all; it was a form and a name without life or power. It could not provide a shilling for the payment of the National debt nor even for its own support. It must humbly ask the States for every dollar needed to uphold the National honor, every penny necessary for the very existence of the masquerade "Government" itself. This money the States were slow and loath to give and doled it out in miserable pittances.

Even worse, there was as yet little conception of Nationality among the people — the spirit of unity was far weaker than when resistance to Great Britain compelled some kind of solidarity; the idea of coöperation was even less robust than it was when fear of French and Indian depredations forced the colonists to a sort of common action. Also, as we shall see, a general dislike if not hostility toward all government whether State or National was prevalent.[3]

As to the National Government, it would appear that, even before the war was over, the first impulse

in Henry, ii, 186–87. But Mason came to put it on the ground that Great Britain would renew the war if these debts were not paid.

[1] Story, in Dillon, iii, 338.

[2] Hening, x, chaps. ii and ix, 409–51.

[3] For a general review of the state of the country see *infra*, chaps. VII and VIII.

of the people was to stop entirely the feeble heart that, once in a while, trembled within its frail bosom: in 1782, for instance, Virginia's Legislature repealed the law passed in May of the preceding year authorizing Congress to levy a duty on imports to carry on the war, because "the permitting any power other than the general assembly of this commonwealth, to levy duties or taxes upon the citizens of this state within the same, is injurious to its sovereignty" and "may prove destructive of the rights and liberty of the people." [1]

A year later the Legislature was persuaded again to authorize Congress to levy this duty; [2] but once more suspended the act until the other States had passed "laws" of the same kind and with a proviso which would practically have nullified the working of the statute, even if the latter ever did go into effect.[3] At the time this misshapen dwarf of a Nationalist law was begotten by the Virginia Legislature, Marshall was a member of the Council of State; but the violent struggle required to get the Assembly to pass even so puny an act as this went on under his personal observation.

When Marshall entered the Legislature for the second time, the general subject of the debts of the Confederation arose. Congress thought that the money to pay the loans from foreign Governments by which the war had been carried on, might be secured more easily by a new mode of apportioning their quotas among the thirteen States. The Articles of

[1] Hening, xi, chap. xlii, 171. [2] *Ib.*, chap. xxxi, 350.
[3] Journal, H.D., 52.

Confederation provided that the States should pay on the basis of the value of lands. This worked badly, and Congress asked the States to alter the eighth Article of Confederation so as to make the States contribute to the general treasury on a basis of population. For fear that the States would not make this change, Congress also humbly petitioned the thirteen "sovereignties" to ascertain the quantity and value of land as well as the number of people in each State.

On May 19, 1784,[1] after the usual debating, a strong set of Nationalist resolutions was laid before the Virginia House of Delegates. They agreed to the request of Congress to change the basis of apportioning the debt among the States; favored providing for the payment of a part of what each State owed Congress on the requisition of three years before; and even went so far as to admit that if the States did not act, Congress itself might be justified in proceeding. The last resolution proposed to give Congress the power to pass retaliatory trade laws.[2] These resolutions were adopted with the exception of one providing for the two years' overdue payment of the Virginia share of the requisition of Congress made in 1781.

Marshall was appointed a member of a special committee to "prepare and bring in bills" to carry out the two resolutions for changing the basis of apportionment from land to population, and for

[1] In order to group subjects such as British debts, extradition, and so forth, it is, unfortunately, essential to bring widely separated dates under one head.

[2] Journal, H.D. (1st Sess., 1784), 11–12.

authorizing Congress to pass retaliatory trade laws. George Mason and Patrick Henry also were members of this committee on which the enemies of the National idea had a good representation. Two weeks later the bills were reported.[1] Three weeks afterwards the retaliatory trade bill was passed.[2] But all the skill and ability of Madison, all the influence of Marshall with his fellow members, could not overcome the sentiment against paying the debts; and, as usual, the law was neutralized by a provision that it should be suspended until all the other States had enacted the same kind of legislation.

The second contest waged by the friends of the Nationalist idea in which Marshall took part was over the extradition bill which the Legislature enacted in the winter of 1784. The circumstances making such a law so necessary that the Virginia Legislature actually passed it, draw back for a moment the curtain and give us a view of the character of our frontiersmen. Daring, fearless, strong, and resourceful, they struck without the sanction of the law. The object immediately before their eyes, the purpose of the present, the impulse or passion of the moment — these made up the practical code which governed their actions.

Treaties of the American "Government" with the Governments of other countries were, to these wilderness subduers, vague and far-away engagements which surely never were meant to affect those on the outskirts of civilization; and most certainly could

[1] Journal, H.D. (1st Sess., 1784), 37.
[2] *Ib.*, 81; also, Hening, xi, 388.

not reach the scattered dwellers in the depths of the distant forests, even if such international compacts were intended to include them. As for the Government's treaties or agreements of any kind with the Indian tribes, they, of course, amounted to nothing in the opinion of the frontiersmen. Who were the Indians, anyway, except a kind of wild animal very much in the frontiersman's way and to be exterminated like other savage beasts? Were not the Indians the natural foes of these white Lords of the earth?[1]

Indeed, it is more than likely that most of this advance guard of the westward-marching American people never had heard of such treaties until the Government's puny attempt to enforce them. At any rate, the settlers fell afoul of all who stood in their way; and, in the falling, spared not their hand. Madison declared that there was "danger of our being speedily embroiled with the nations contiguous to the U. States, particularly the Spaniards, by the licentious & predatory spirit of some of our Western people. In several instances, gross outrages are said to have been already practiced."[2] Jay, then Secretary of State, mournfully wrote to Jefferson in Paris, that "Indians have been murdered by our

[1] "The white people who inhabited the frontier, from the constant state of warfare in which they lived with the Indians, had imbibed much of their character; and learned to delight so highly in scenes of crafty, bloody, and desperate conflict, that they as often gave as they received the provocation to hostilities. Hunting, which was their occupation, became dull and tiresome, unless diversified occasionally by the more animated and piquant amusement of an Indian skirmish." (Wirt, 257.)

[2] Madison to Jefferson, Jan. 9, 1785; *Writings:* Hunt, ii, 110–11.

people in cold blood, and no satisfaction given; nor are they pleased with the avidity with which we seek to acquire their lands."

Expressing the common opinion of the wisest and best men of the country, who, with Madison, were horrified by the ruthless and unprovoked violence of the frontiersmen, Jay feared that "to pitch our tents through the wilderness in a great variety of places, far distant from each other," might "fill the wilderness with white savages . . . more formidable to us than the tawny ones which now inhabit it." No wonder those who were striving to found a civilized nation had "reason . . . to apprehend an Indian war." [1]

To correct this state of things and to bring home to these sons of individualism the law of nations and our treaties with other countries, Madison, in the autumn of 1784, brought in a bill which provided that Virginia should deliver up to foreign Governments such offenders as had come within the borders of the Commonwealth. The bill also provided for the trial and punishment by Virginia courts of any Virginia citizen who should commit certain crimes in "the territory of any Christian nation or Indian tribe in amity with the United States." The law is of general historic importance because it was among the first, if not indeed the very first, ever passed by any legislative body against filibustering.[2]

The feebleness of the National idea at this time; the grotesque notions of individual "rights"; the weak-

[1] Jay to Jefferson, Dec. 14, 1786; *Jay:* Johnston, iii, 224.
[2] Hening, xi, 471; and Henry, ii, 217.

ness or absence of the sense of civic duty; the general feeling that everybody should do as he pleased; the scorn for the principle that other nations and especially Indian tribes had any rights which the rough-and-ready settlers were bound to respect, are shown in the hot fight made against Madison's wise and moderate bill. Viewed as a matter of the welfare and safety of the frontiersmen themselves, Madison's measure was prudent and desirable; for, if either the Indians or the Spaniards had been goaded into striking back by formal war, the blows would have fallen first and heaviest on these very settlers.

Yet the bill was stoutly resisted. It was said that the measure, instead of carrying out international law, violated it because "such surrenders were unknown to the law of nations."[1] And what became of Virginia's sacred Bill of Rights, if such a law as Madison proposed should be placed on the statute books, exclaimed the friends of the predatory backwoodsmen? Did not the Bill of Rights guarantee to every person "speedy trial by an impartial jury of twelve men of his vicinage," where he must "be confronted with the accusers and witnesses," said they?

But what did this Nationalist extradition bill do? It actually provided that men on Virginia soil should be delivered up for punishment to a foreign nation which knew not the divine right of trial by jury. As for trying men in Virginia courts and before Virginia juries for something they had done in the fastnesses of the far-away forests of the West and

[1] Madison to Jefferson, Jan. 9, 1785; *Writings:* Hunt, ii, 111.

South, as Madison's bill required, how could the accused "call for evidence in his favor"? And was not this "sacred right" one of the foundation stones, quarried from Magna Charta, on which Virginia's "liberties" had been built? [1] To be sure it was! Yet here was James Madison trying to blast it to fragments with his Nationalism!

So ran the arguments of those early American advocates of *laissez-faire*. Madison answered, as to the law of nations, by quoting Vattel, Grotius, and Puffendorf. As to the Bill of Rights, he pointed out that the individualist idealism by which the champions of the settlers interpreted this instrument "would amount to a license for every aggression, and would sacrifice the peace of the whole community to the impunity of the worst members of it." [2] Such were the conservative opinions of James Madison three years before he helped to frame the National Constitution.

Madison saw, too, — shocking treason to "liberty," — "the necessity of a qualified interpretation of the bill of rights," [3] if we were to maintain the slightest pretense of a National Government of any kind. The debate lasted several days.[4] With all the weight of argument, justice, and even common prudence on the side of the measure, it certainly would have failed had not Patrick Henry come to the rescue of it with all the strength of his influence and oratory.[5]

[1] Article VIII, Constitution of Virginia, 1776.

[2] Madison to Jefferson, Jan. 9, 1785; *Writings:* Hunt, ii, 111.

[3] *Ib.*

[4] Journal, H.D. (2d Sess., 1784), 34–41.

[5] "The measure was warmly patronized by Mr. Henry." (Madison

The bill was so mangled in committee that it was made useless and it was restored only by amendment. Yet such was the opposition to it that even with Henry's powerful aid this was done only by the dangerous margin of four votes out of a total of seventy-eight.[1] The enemies of the bill mustered their strength overnight and, when the final vote came upon its passage the next morning, came so near defeating it that it passed by a majority of only one vote out of a total of eighty-seven.[2]

John Marshall, of course, voted for it. While there is no record that he took part in the debate, yet it is plain that the contest strengthened his fast-growing Nationalist views. The extravagance of those who saw in the Bill of Rights only a hazy "liberty"

to Jefferson, Jan. 9, 1785; *Writings:* Hunt, ii, 111.) The reason of Henry's support of this extradition bill was not its Nationalist spirit, but his friendship for the Indians and his pet plan to insure peace between the white man and the red and to produce a better race of human beings; all of which Henry thought could be done by intermarriages between the whites and the Indians. He presented this scheme to the House at this same session and actually carried it by the "irresistible earnestness and eloquence" with which he supported it. (Wirt, 258.)

The bill provided that every white man who married an Indian woman should be paid ten pounds and five pounds more for each child born of such marriage; and that if any white woman marry an Indian they should be entitled to ten pounds with which the County Court should buy live stock for them; that once each year the Indian husband to this white woman should be entitled to three pounds with which the County Court should buy clothes for him; that every child born of this Indian man and white woman should be educated by the State between the age of ten and twenty-one years, etc., etc. (*Ib.*)

This amazing bill actually passed the House on its first and second reading and there seems to be no doubt that it would have become a law had not Henry at that time been elected Governor, which took him "*out of the way,*" to use Madison's curt phrase. John Marshall favored this bill.

[1] Journal, H.D. (2d Sess., 1784), 41. [2] *Ib.*

which hid evil-doers from the law, and which caused even the cautious Madison to favor a "qualified interpretation" of that instrument, made a lasting impression on Marshall's mind.

But Marshall's support was not wholly influenced by the prudence and Nationalism of the measure. He wished to protect the Indians from the frontiersmen. He believed, with Henry, in encouraging friendly relations with them, even by white and red amalgamation. He earnestly supported Henry's bill for subsidizing marriages of natives and whites [1] and was disappointed by its defeat.

"We have rejected some bills," writes Marshall, "which in my conception would have been advantageous to the country. Among these, I rank the bill for encouraging intermarriages with the Indians. Our prejudices however, oppose themselves to our interests, and operate too powerfully for them." [2]

During the period between 1784 and 1787 when Marshall was out of the Legislature, the absolute need of a central Government that would enable the American people to act as a Nation became ever more urgent; but the dislike for such a Government also crystallized. The framing of the Constitution by the Federal Convention at Philadelphia in 1787 never could have been brought about by any abstract notions of National honor and National power, nor by any of those high and rational ideas of government which it has become traditional to

[1] See note 5, p. 239, *ante*.

[2] Marshall to Monroe, Dec., 1784; MS. Monroe Papers, Lib. Cong.; also partly quoted in Henry, ii, 219.

ascribe as the only source and cause of our fundamental law.

The people at large were in no frame of mind for any kind of government that meant power, taxes, and the restrictions which accompany orderly society. The determination of commercial and financial interests to get some plan adopted under which business could be transacted, was the most effective force that brought about the historic Convention at Philadelphia in 1787. Indeed, when that body met it was authorized only to amend the Articles of Confederation and chiefly as concerned the National regulation of commerce.[1]

Virginia delayed acting upon the Constitution until most of the other States had ratified it. The Old Dominion, which had led in the Revolution, was one of the last Commonwealths to call her Convention to consider the "new plan" of a National Government. The opposition to the proposed fundamental law was, as we shall see, general and determined; and the foes of the Constitution, fiercely resisting its ratification, were striving to call a second general Convention to frame another scheme of government or merely to amend the Articles of Confederation.

To help to put Virginia in line for the Constitution, John Marshall, for the third time, sought election to the Legislature. His views about government had now developed maturely into a broad, well-defined Nationalism; and he did not need the spur of the wrathful words which Washington had been

[1] See *infra*, chap. IX.

flinging as far as he could against the existing chaos and against everybody who opposed a strong National Government.

If Marshall had required such counsel and action from his old commander, both were at hand; for in all his volcanic life that Vesuvius of a man never poured forth such lava of appeal and denunciation as during the period of his retirement at Mount Vernon after the war was over and before the Constitution was adopted.[1]

But Marshall was as hot a Nationalist as Washington himself. He was calmer in temperament, more moderate in language and method, than his great leader; but he was just as determined, steady, and fearless. And so, when he was elected to the Legislature in the early fall of 1787, he had at heart and in mind but one great purpose. Army life, legislative experience, and general observation had modified his youthful democratic ideals, while strengthening and confirming that Nationalism taught him from childhood. Marshall himself afterwards described his state of mind at this period and the causes that produced it.

"When I recollect," said he, "the wild and enthusiastic notions with which my political opinions of that day were tinctured, I am disposed to ascribe my devotion to the Union and to a government competent to its preservation, at least as much to casual

[1] One of the curious popular errors concerning our public men is that which pictures Washington as a calm person. On the contrary, he was hot-tempered and, at times, violent in speech and action. It was with the greatest difficulty that he trained himself to an appearance of calmness and reserve.

circumstances as to judgment. I had grown up at a time when the love of the Union, and the resistance to the claims of Great Britain were the inseparable inmates of the same bosom; when patriotism and a strong fellow-feeling with our suffering fellow-citizens of Boston were identical; when the maxim, 'United we stand, divided we fall,' was the maxim of every orthodox American.

"And I had imbibed these sentiments so thoroughly that they constituted a part of my being. I carried them with me into the army, where I found myself associated with brave men from different States, who were risking life and everything valuable in a common cause, believed by all to be most precious; and where I was confirmed in the habit of considering America as my country, and Congress as my government. . . . My immediate entrance into the State Legislature opened to my view the causes which had been chiefly instrumental in augmenting those sufferings [of the army]; and the general tendency of State politics convinced me that no safe and permanent remedy could be found but in a more efficient and better organized General Government."[1]

On the third day of the fall session of the Virginia Legislature of 1787, the debate began on the question of calling a State Convention to ratify the proposed National Constitution.[2] On October 25 the debate came to a head and a resolution for calling a State Convention passed the House.[3] The debate

[1] Story, in Dillon, iii, 338, 343.
[2] Journal, H.D. (Oct. Sess., 1787), 7. [3] *Ib.*, 11, 15.

was over the question as to whether the proposed Convention should have authority either to ratify or reject the proposed scheme of government entirely; or to accept it upon the condition that it be altered and amended.

Francis Corbin, a youthful member from Middlesex, proposed a flat-footed resolution that the State Convention be called either to accept or reject the "new plan." He then opened the debate with a forthright speech for a Convention to ratify the new Constitution as it stood. Patrick Henry instantly was on his feet. He was for the Convention, he said: "No man was more truly federal than himself." But, under Corbin's resolution, the Convention could not propose amendments to the Constitution. There were "errors and defects" in that paper, said Henry. He proposed that Corbin's resolution should be changed so that the State Convention might propose amendments [1] as a condition of ratification.

The debate waxed hot. George Nicholas, one of the ablest men in the country, warmly attacked Henry's idea. It would, declared Nicholas, "give the impression" that Virginia was not for the Constitution, whereas "there was, he believed, a decided majority in its favor." Henry's plan, said Nicholas, would throw cold water on the movement to ratify the Constitution in States that had not yet acted.

George Mason made a fervid and effective speech for Henry's resolution. This eminent, wealthy, and cultivated man had been a member of the Philadel-

[1] *Pennsylvania Packet*, Nov. 10, 1787; Pa. Hist. Soc.

phia Convention that had framed the Constitution; but he had refused to sign it. He was against it for the reasons which he afterwards gave at great length in the Virginia Convention of 1788.[1] He had "deeply and maturely weighed every article of the new Constitution," avowed Mason, and if he had signed it, he "might have been justly regarded as a traitor to my country. I would have lost this hand before it should have marked my name to the new government." [2]

At this juncture, Marshall intervened with a compromise. The Constitutionalists were uncertain whether they could carry through Corbin's resolution. They feared that Henry's plan of proposing amendments to the Constitution might pass the House. The effect of such an Anti-Constitutional victory in Virginia, which was the largest and most populous State in the Union, would be a blow to the cause of the Constitution from which it surely could not recover. For the movement was making headway in various States for a second Federal Convention that should devise another sytsem of government to take the place of the one which the first Federal Convention, after much quarreling and dissension, finally patched up in Philadelphia.[3]

So Marshall was against both Corbin's resolution and Henry's amendment to it; and also he was for the ideas of each of these gentlemen. It was plain, said Marshall, that Mr. Corbin's resolution was open to the criticism made by Mr. Henry. To be sure, the

[1] *Infra*, chaps. XI and XII.

[2] *Pennsylvania Packet*, Nov. 10, 1787; also see in Rowland, ii, 176.

[3] *Infra*, chaps. IX, XII; and also Washington to Lafayette, Feb. 7, 1788; *Writings:* Ford, xi, 220.

Virginia Convention should not be confined to a straight-out acceptance or rejection of the new Constitution; but, on the other hand, it would never do for the word to go out to the other States that Virginia in no event would accept the Constitution unless she could propose amendments to it. He agreed with Nicholas entirely on that point.

Marshall also pointed out that the people of Virginia ought not to be given to understand that their own Legislature was against the proposed Constitution before the people themselves had even elected a Convention to pass upon that instrument. The whole question ought to go to the people without prejudice; and so Marshall proposed a resolution of his own "that a Convention should be called and that the new Constitution should be laid before them for their free and ample discussion." [1]

Marshall's idea captured the House. It placated Henry, it pleased Mason; and, of course, it was more than acceptable to Corbin and Nicholas, with whom Marshall was working hand in glove, as, indeed, was the case with all the Constitutionalists. In fact, Marshall's tactics appeared to let every man have his own way and succeeded in getting the Convention definitely called. And it did let the contending factions have their own way for the time being; for, at that juncture, the friends of the new National Constitution had no doubt that they would be able to carry it through the State Convention unmarred by amendments, and its enemies were equally certain that they would be able to defeat or alter it.

[1] *Pennsylvania Packet*, Nov. 10, 1787; Pa. Hist. Soc.

Marshall's resolution, therefore, passed the House "unanimously."[1] Other resolutions to carry Marshall's resolution into effect also passed without opposition, and it was "ordered that two hundred copies of these resolutions be printed and dispersed by members of the general assembly among their constituents; and that the Executive should send a copy of them to Congress and to the Legislature and Executive of the respective states."[2] But the third month of the session was half spent before the Senate passed the bill.[3] Not until January 8 of the following year did it become a law.[4]

In addition, however, to defining the privileges of the members and providing money for its expenses, the bill also authorized the Convention to send representatives "to any of the sister states or the conventions thereof which may be then met," in order to gather the views of the country "concerning the great and important change of government which hath been proposed by the federal convention."[5] Thus the advocates of a second general Convention to amend the Articles of Confederation or frame another Constitution scored their point.

So ended the first skirmish of the historic battle soon to be fought out in Virginia, which would determine whether the American people should begin their career as a Nation. Just as John Marshall was among the first in the field with rifle,

[1] Journal, H.D. (Oct. Sess., 1787), 15. [2] *Ib.*
[3] *Ib.*, 95. [4] *Ib.* (Dec., 1787), 143, 177.
[5] Hening, xii, 462–63.

tomahawk, and scalping-knife, to fight for Independence, so, now, he was among those first in the field with arguments, influence, and political activities, fighting for Nationalism.

CHAPTER VII

LIFE OF THE PEOPLE: COMMUNITY ISOLATION

An infant people, spreading themselves through a wilderness occupied only by savages and wild beasts. (Marshall.)

Of the affairs of Georgia, I know as little as of those of Kamskatska. (James Madison, 1786.)

"LEAN to the right," shouted the driver of a lumbering coach to his passengers; and all the jostled and bethumped travelers crowded to that side of the clumsy vehicle. "Left," roared the coachman a little later, and his fares threw themselves to the opposite side. The ruts and gullies, now on one side and now on the other, of the highway were so deep that only by acting as a shifting ballast could the voyagers maintain the stage's center of gravity and keep it from an upset.[1]

This passageway through the forest, called a "road," was the thoroughfare between Philadelphia and Baltimore and a part of the trunk line of communication which connected the little cities of that period. If the "road" became so bad that the coach could not be pulled through the sloughs of mud, a new way was opened in the forest; so that, in some places, there were a dozen of such cuttings all leading to the same spot and all full of stumps, rocks, and trees.[2]

The passengers often had to abandon this four-wheeled contraption altogether and walk in the mud;

[1] Weld, i, 37–38; also, Morris, ii, 393–94. [2] Weld, i, 38.

and were now and again called upon to put their shoulders to the wheels of the stage when the horses, unaided, were unable to rescue it.[1] Sometimes the combined efforts of horses and men could not bring the conveyance out of the mire and it would have to be left all night in the bog until more help could be secured.[2] Such was a main traveled road at the close of the Revolutionary War and for a long time after the Constitution was adopted.

The difficulty and danger of communication thus illustrated had a direct and vital bearing upon the politics and statesmanship of the times. The conditions of travel were an index to the state of the country which we are now to examine. Without such a survey we shall find ourselves floating aimlessly among the clouds of fancy instead of treading, with sure foothold, the solid ground of fact. At this point, more perhaps than at any other of our history, a definite, accurate, and comprehensive inventory of conditions is essential. For not only is this phase of American development more obscure than any other, but the want of light upon it has led to vague consideration and sometimes to erroneous conclusions.

We are about to witness the fierce and dramatic struggle from which emerged the feeble beginnings of a Nation that, even to-day, is still in the making; to behold the welter of plan and counterplot, of scheming and violence, of deal and trade, which finally resulted in the formal acceptance of the Constitution with a certainty that it would be modified, and, to some extent, mutilated, by later

[1] Baily's *Journal* (1796–97), 108. [2] *Ib.*, 109–10.

amendments. We are to listen to those "debates" which, alone, are supposed to have secured ratification, but which had no more, and indeed perhaps less effect than the familiar devices of "practical politics" in bringing about the adoption of our fundamental law.

Since the victory at Yorktown a serious alteration had taken place in the views of many who had fought hardest for Independence and popular government. These men were as strong as ever for the building of a separate and distinct National entity; but they no longer believed in the wisdom or virtue of democracy without extensive restrictions. They had come to think that, at the very best, the crude ore of popular judgment could be made to enrich sound counsels only when passed through many screens that would rid it of the crudities of passion, whimsicality, interest, ignorance, and dishonesty which, they believed, inhered in it. Such men esteemed less and less a people's government and valued more and more a good government And the idea grew that this meant a government the principal purpose of which was to enforce order, facilitate business, and safeguard property.

During his early years in the Legislature, as has appeared, Marshall's opinions were changing. Washington, as we shall see, soon after peace was declared, lost much of his faith in the people; Madison arrived at the opinion that the majority were unequal to the weightier tasks of popular rule; and Marshall also finally came to entertain the melancholy fear that the people were not capable of self-government. Indeed, almost all of the foremost men of the period now under review were brought to doubt the good sense or sound heart of the multitude. The fires of Jefferson's faith still burned, and, indeed, burned more brightly; for that great reformer was in France and neither experienced nor witnessed any of those popular phenomena which fell like a drenching rain upon the enthusiasm of American statesmen at home for democratic government.

This revolution in the views of men like Washington, Madison, and Marshall was caused largely by the conduct of the masses, which, to such men, seemed to be selfish, violent, capricious, vindictive, and dangerous. The state of the country explains much of this popular attitude and disposition. The development of Marshall's public ideas cannot be entirely understood by considering merely his altered circumstances and business and social connections. More important is a review of the people, their environment and condition.

The extreme isolation of communities caused by want of roads and the difficulties and dangers of communication; the general ignorance of the masses; their childish credulity, and yet their quick and acute suspicion springing, largely, from isolation and lack of knowledge; their savage and narrow individualism, which resisted the establishment of a central authority and was antagonistic to any but the loosest local control; their envy and distrust of the prosperous and successful which their own economic condition strengthened, if, indeed, this circumstance did not create that sullen and dangerous state of mind — an understanding of all these elements of American life at that time is vital if we are to trace the development of Marshall's thinking and explore the origins of the questions that confronted our early statesmen.

The majority of the people everywhere were poor; most of them owed debts; and they were readily influenced against any man who favored payment, and against any plan of government that might compel it. Also, the redemption of State and Continental debts, which was a hard and ever-present problem, was abhorrent to them. Much of the scrip had passed into the hands of wealthy purchasers. Why, exclaimed the popular voice, should this expedient of war be recognized? Discharge of such public obligations meant very definite individual taxes. It was as easy to inflame a people so situated and inclined as it was hard to get accurate information to them or to induce them to accept any reasoning that made for personal inconvenience or for public burdens.

Marshall could not foresee the age of railway and telegraph and universal education. He had no vision of a period when speedy and accurate information would reach the great body of our population and the common hearthstone thus become the place of purest and soundest judgment. So it is impossible to comprehend or even apprehend his intellectual metamorphosis during this period unless we survey the physical, mental, and spiritual state of the country. How the people lived, their habits, the extent of their education, their tendency of thought, and, underlying all and vitally affecting all, the means or rather want of means of communication — a knowledge of these things is essential to an understanding of the times.[1] The absence of roads and the condition of the few that did exist were thoroughly characteristic of the general situation and, indeed, important causes of it. It becomes indispensable, then, to visualize the highways of the period and to picture the elements that produced the thinking and acting of the larger part of the people. Many examples are necessary to bring all this, adequately and in just proportion, before the eye of the present.

When Washington, as President, was on his way to meet Congress, his carriage stuck in the mud, and only after it had been pried up with poles and pulled out by ropes could the Father of his Country proceed on his journey;[2] and this, too, over the principal highway of Maryland. "My nerves have not yet quite recovered the shock of the *wagon*," wrote Samuel Johnston of a stage trip from Baltimore to New York two years after our present Government

[1] Professor Beard, in his exposition of the economic origins of the Constitution, shows that nearly all of the men who framed it were wealthy or allied with property interests and that many of them turned up as holders of Government securities. (Beard: *Econ. I. C.*, chap. v.) As a matter of fact, none but such men could have gone to the Federal Convention at Philadelphia, so great were the difficulties and so heavy the expenses of travel, even if the people had been minded to choose poorer and humbler persons to represent them: at any rate, they did not elect representatives of their own class until the Constitution was to be ratified and then, of course, only to State Conventions which were accessible.

[2] Weld, i, 47–48.

was established.[1] Richard Henry Lee objected to the Constitution, because, among other things, "many citizens will be more than three hundred miles from the seat of this [National] government";[2] and "as many assessors and collectors of federal taxes will be above three hundred miles from the seat of the federal government as will be less."[3]

The best road throughout its course, in the entire country, was the one between Boston and New York; yet the public conveyance which made regular trips with relays of horses in the most favorable season of the year usually took an entire week for the journey.[4] The stage was "shackling"; the horses' harness "made of ropes"; one team hauled the stage only eighteen miles; the stop for the night was made at ten o'clock, the start next morning at half-past two; the passengers often had to "help the coachman lift the coach out of the quagmire."[5]

Over parts even of this, the finest long highway in the United States, the stage had to struggle against rocks and to escape precipices. "I knew not which to admire the most in the driver, his intrepidity or dexterity. I cannot conceive how he avoided twenty times dashing the carriage to pieces,"[6] testifies a traveler. In central Massachusetts, the roads "were intolerable" even to a New Englander; and "the

[1] Johnston to Iredell, Jan. 30, 1790; McRee, ii, 279.

[2] "Letters of a Federal Farmer," no. 2; Ford: *P. on C.*, 292.

[3] *Ib.*, no. 3, 302.

[4] De Warville made a record trip from Boston to New York in less than five days. (De Warville, 122.) But such speed was infrequent.

[5] Josiah Quincy's description of his journey from Boston to New York in 1794. (Quincy: *Figures of the Past*, 47–48.)

[6] De Warville, 138–39.

country was sparsely inhabited by a rude population."[1] In Rhode Island not far from Providence the traveler was forced to keep mounting and dismounting from his horse in order to get along at all.[2] Dr. Taylor, in the Massachusetts Convention of 1788, arguing for frequent elections, said that it would take less than three weeks for Massachusetts members of Congress to go from Boston to Philadelphia.[3]

Farmers only a short distance from New York could not bring their produce to the city in the winter because the roads were impassable.[4] Up State, in Cooper's Otsego settlement, "not one in twenty of the settlers had a horse and the way lay through rapid streams, across swamps or over bogs. . . . If the father of a family went abroad to labour for bread, it cost him three times its value before he could bring it home."[5] As late as 1790, after forty thousand acres in this region had been taken up "by the poorest order of men . . . there were neither roads nor bridges"; and about Otsego itself there was not even "any trace of a road."[6] Where Utica now stands, the opening through the wilderness, which went by the name of a road, was so nearly impassable that a horseback traveler could make no

[1] Watson, 266.

[2] "The road is execrable; one is perpetually mounting and descending and always on the most rugged roads." (Chastellux, 20.)

[3] Elliott, ii, 21–22.

[4] "In December last, the roads were so intollerably bad that the country people could not bring their forage to market, though *actually offered the cash on delivery*." (Pickering to Hodgdon; *Pickering:* Pickering, i, 392.)

[5] Cooper, 1875–86, as quoted in Hart, iii, 98.

[6] *Ib.*

more than two miles an hour over it. Rocks, stumps, and muddy holes in which the horse sank, made progress not only slow and toilsome, but dangerous.[1]

Twenty days was not an unusual time for ordinary wagons, carrying adventurous settlers to the wilderness west of the Alleghanies, to cross Pennsylvania from Philadelphia to Pittsburg;[2] and it cost a hundred and twenty dollars a ton to haul freight between these points.[3] Three years after our present Government was established, twenty out of twenty-six lawsuits pending in Philadelphia were settled out of court "rather than go ninety miles from Phil$^{\underline{a}}$ for trial."[4]

Talleyrand, journeying inland from the Quaker City about 1795, was "struck with astonishment" at what he beheld: "At less than a hundred and fifty miles distance from the Capital," he writes, "all trace of men's presence disappeared; nature in all her primeval vigor confronted us. Forests old as the world itself; decayed plants and trees covering the very ground where they once grew in luxuriance." And Talleyrand testifies that the fields, only a few miles' walk out of the "cities," had been "mere wildernesses of forest" at the time the Constitution was adopted.[5]

[1] Watson, 270. Along one of the principal roads of New York, as late as 1804, President Dwight discovered only "a few lonely plantations" and he "occasionally found a cottage and heard a distant sound of an axe and of a human voice. All else was grandeur, gloom, and solitude." (Halsey: *Old New York Frontier*, 384.)

[2] Hart, iii, 116.

[3] *Mag. Western Hist.*, i, 530.

[4] Justice Cushing to Chief Justice Jay, Oct. 23, 1792; *Jay:* Johnston, iii, 450.

[5] *Memoirs of Talleyrand:* Broglie's ed., i, 176–77.

"The length and badness of the roads from hence [Mount Vernon] to Philadelphia" made Washington grumble with vexation and disgust;[1] and Jefferson wrote of the President's Southern tour in 1791: "I shall be happy to hear that no accident has happened to you in the bad roads . . . that you are better prepared for those to come by lowering the hang [body] of your carriage and exchanging the coachman for two postilions . . . which [are] . . . essential to your safety." [2]

No more comfortable or expeditious, if less dangerous, was travel by boat on the rivers. "Having lain all night in my Great Coat and Boots in a berth not long enough for me," chronicles Washington of this same Presidential journey, "we found ourselves in the morning still fast aground." [3]

So difficult were the New Jersey roads that the stout and well-kept harness with which Washington always equipped his horses was badly broken going through New Jersey in 1789.[4] "The roads [from Richmond to New York] thro' the whole were so bad that we could never go more than three miles an hour, some times not more than two, and in the night, but one," wrote Jefferson [5] in March, 1790.

A traveler starting from Alexandria, Virginia, to visit Mount Vernon, nine miles distant, was all day on the road, having become lost, in the "very thick

[1] Washington to Jay, Nov. 19, 1790; *Jay:* Johnston, iii, 409.

[2] Jefferson to Washington, March 27, 1791; *Cor. Rev.*: Sparks, iv, 366.

[3] Washington's *Diary:* Lossing, Feb. 25, 1791.

[4] Washington to Jay, Dec. 13, 1789; *Jay:* Johnston, iii, 381.

[5] Jefferson to T. M. Randolph, March 28, 1790; *Works:* Ford, vi, 36.

woods." So confusing was the way through this forest that part of this time he was within three miles of his destination.[1] Twelve years after our present Government was established James A. Bayard records of his journey to the Capital: "Tho' traveling in the mail stage . . . we were unable to move at more than the rate of two or three miles an hour."[2]

Throughout Virginia the roads were execrable and scarcely deserved the name. The few bridges usually were broken.[3] The best road in the State was from Williamsburg, the old Capital, to Richmond, the new, a distance of only sixty-three miles; yet, going at highest speed, it required two days to make the trip.[4] Traveling in Virginia was almost exclusively by horseback; only negroes walked.[5] According to Grigsby, the familiar vision in our minds of the picturesque coach comfortably rolling over attractive highways, with postilions and outriders, which we now picture when we think of traveling in old Virginia, is mostly an historical mirage; for, says Grigsby, "coaches were rarely seen. There were thousands of respectable men in the Commonwealth who had never seen any other four-wheeled vehicle than a wagon and there were thousands who had never seen a wagon" at the time when the Constitution was ratified.[6]

If horseback journeys were sore trials to the rider, they were desperately hard and sometimes fatal to

[1] Weld, i, 91.
[2] Bayard to Rodney, Jan. 5, 1801; *Bayard Papers:* Donnan, ii, 118.
[3] Schoepf, ii, 46. [4] *Ib.*, 78. [5] *Ib.*, 45. [6] Grigsby, i, 26.

the poor brute that carried him. In crossing unfordable rivers on the rude ferryboats, the horses' legs frequently were broken or the animals themselves often killed or drowned.[1] From Fredericksburg to Alexandria the roads were "frightfully bad."[2] As late as 1801 the wilderness was so dense just above where the City of Washington now stands that Davis called it "the wilds of the Potomac." In most parts of Virginia a person unacquainted with the locality often became lost in the forests.[3] South of Jamestown the crude and hazardous highways led through "eternal woods."[4]

A short time before the Revolution, General Wilkinson's father bought five hundred acres on the present site of the National Capital, including the spot where the White House now stands; but his wife refused to go there from a little hamlet near Baltimore where her family then lived, because it was so far away from the settlements in the backwoods of Maryland.[5] A valuable horse was stolen from a Virginia planter who lived one hundred and forty miles from Richmond; but, although the thief was known, the expense of going to the Capital with witnesses was double the value of the horse, and so the planter pocketed his loss.[6] It cost more to transport tobacco from Augusta County, Virginia, to market than the tobacco was worth, so difficult and expensive was the carriage.[7]

A sergeant in a Virginia regiment during the Rev-

[1] Weld, i, 170. [2] Watson, 60. [3] Davis, 372. [4] Schoepf, ii, 95.

[5] Wilkinson: *Memoirs*, i, 9–10. The distance which General Wilkinson's mother thought "so far away" was only forty miles.

[6] Schoepf, ii, 53. [7] Zachariah Johnson, in Elliott, iii, 647.

olutionary War, living in a part of the State which at present is not two hours' ride from the Capital, petitioned the House of Delegates in 1790 for payment of his arrears because he lived so far away from Richmond that he had found it impossible to apply within the time allowed for the settlement of his accounts in the regular way.[1] In 1785 the price of tobacco on the James River or the Rappahannock, and in Philadelphia varied from twenty to ninety-five per cent, although each of these places was "the same distance from its ultimate market," [2] so seriously did want of transportation affect commerce. "The trade of this Country is in a deplorable Condition . . . the loss direct on our produce & indirect on our imports is not less than 50 per ct.," testifies Madison.[3]

Only in the immediate neighborhood of Philadelphia, Boston,[4] or New York, neither of which "cities" was as large as a moderate-sized inland town of to-day, were highways good, even from the point of view of the eighteenth century. In all other parts of America the roads in the present-day sense did not exist at all. Very often such trails as had been made were hard to find and harder to keep after they had been found. Near the close of the Revolution, Chastellux became tangled up in the woods on his way to visit Jefferson at Monticello "and travelled a long time without seeing any habitation." [5]

[1] Journal, H.D. (1790), 13.

[2] Madison to Lee, July 7, 1785; *Writings:* Hunt, ii, 149–51.

[3] *Ib.*

[4] Boston was not a "city" in the legal interpretation until 1822.

[5] Chastellux, 225. "The difficulty of finding the road in many parts of America is not to be conceived except by those strangers who

Whoever dared to take in North Carolina what, at present, would be a brief and pleasant jaunt, then had to go through scores of miles of "dreary pines" in which the traveler often lost his way and became bewildered in the maze of the forest.[1] Again, the wanderer would find himself in a desolation of swamp and wood without the hint of a highway to follow out of it; and sleeping on the ground beneath the trees of this wilderness, with only wild animals about him, was, for the ordinary traveler, not an uncommon experience.[2]

Even when the road could be traced, bears would follow it, so much was it still a part of their savage domain.[3] The little traveling possible when the weather was good was sometimes entirely suspended for days after a rain or snowfall, even out of a "city" like Baltimore.[4] Six years after the Constitution

have travelled in that country. The roads, which are through the woods, not being kept in repair, as soon as one is in bad order, another is made in the same manner, that is, merely by felling trees, and the whole interior parts are so covered that without a compass it is impossible to have the least idea of the course you are steering. The distances, too, are so uncertain as in every county where they are not measured, that no two accounts resemble each other. In the back parts of Pennsylvania, Maryland, and Virginia, I have frequently travelled thirty miles for ten, though frequently set right by passengers and negroes." (*Ib.* Translator's note.)

[1] Smyth, *Tour of the United States*, i, 102–103.

[2] Watson, 40. "Towards the close of the day I found myself entangled among swamps amid an utter wilderness, and my horse almost exhausted in my efforts to overtake Harwood. As night closed upon me I was totally bewildered and without a vestige of a road to guide me. Knowing the impossibility of retracing my steps in the dark, through the mazes I had traversed, I felt the necessity of passing the night in this solitary desert . . . in no trifling apprehension of falling a prey to wild beasts before morning." (*Ib.*)

[3] *Ib.*

[4] "I waited at Baltimore near a week before I could proceed on my

was adopted, Talleyrand found the buildings of that ambitious town "disput[ing] the ground with trees whose stumps have not yet been removed." [1]

Such were the means of communication of a people scattered over a territory of almost half a million square miles. The total population of the United States was about three and a quarter millions; the same part of the country to-day has a population of not far from fifty-five millions. Including cities, and adding to these the more thickly settled portions adjoining them, there were not in the original States seven men, women, and children, all told, to the square mile. If we add Kentucky, Tennessee, Ohio, Illinois, and Indiana, into which the restless settlers already were moving, the people then living in the United States were fewer than five persons to the square mile.

The various little clusters of this scanty and widely separated population were almost entirely out of touch one with another. Inhabitants were scattered through those far-flung stretches called the United States, but they were not a people. Scarcely any communication existed between them; while such a thing as mail service was unknown to all but a comparatively few thousands. It required six days and sometimes nine to carry mail between Boston and New York. As late as 1794 a letter of Jefferson, then in Charlottesville, Virginia, to Madison at Philadelphia, reached the latter nine days after it

journey the roads being rendered impassable." (Baily's *Journal* (1796–97), 107.)

[1] *Memoirs of Talleyrand:* Broglie's ed., i, 177.

was sent; and another letter between the same correspondents was eight days on the journey.[1]

Yet this was unusually expeditious. One month later, on January 26, 1795, Madison wrote Jefferson that "I have received your favor of Dec[r] 28, but [not] till three weeks after the date of it."[2] Summer, when the post-riders made better time, seemed not greatly to increase the dispatch of mail; for it took more than a month for a letter posted in New York in that season of the year to reach an accessible Virginia county seat.[3] Letters from Richmond, Virginia, to New York often did not arrive until two months after they were sent.[4] But better time was frequently made and a letter between these points was, commonly, hurried through in a month.[5]

Many weeks would go by before one could send a letter from an interior town in Pennsylvania. "This Uniontown is the most obscure spot on the face of the globe. . . . I have been here seven or eight weeks without one opportunity of writing to the land of the living," complains a disgusted visitor.[6] A letter posted by Rufus King in Boston, February 6, 1788, to Madison in New York was received February 15;[7] and although anxiously awaiting news, Madison

[1] Madison to Jefferson, Dec. 21, 1794; *Writings:* Hunt, vi, 227.

[2] Madison to Jefferson, Jan. 26, 1795; *ib.*, 230.

[3] "Your favor of July 6 having been address[d] to Williamsburg, instead of *Orange C. Ho[u]se,* did not come to hand till two days ago." (Madison to Livingston, Aug. 10, 1795; *ib.*, vi, 234.)

[4] Lee to Henry, May 28, 1789; Henry, iii, 387.

[5] Lee to Henry, Sept. 27, 1789; Henry, iii, 402.

[6] Ephraim Douglass to Gen. James Irvine, 1784; *Pa. Mag. Hist. and Biog.*, i, 50.

[7] Madison to Washington, Feb. 15, 1788; and King to Madison, Feb. 6, 1788; *Writings:* Hunt, v, footnote to p. 100.

had not, on February 11, heard that Massachusetts had ratified the Constitution, although that momentous event had occurred five days before.[1] New York first learned of that historic action eight days after it was taken.[2] But for the snail-like slowness of the post, the Constitution would certainly have been defeated in the Virginia Convention of 1788.[3]

Transatlantic mail service was far more expeditious considering the distance; a letter from Jay in London reached Wolcott at Philadelphia in less than eight weeks.[4] But it sometimes required five months to carry mail across the ocean;[5] even this was very much faster than one could travel by land in America. Four weeks from Cowes, England, to Lynnhaven Bay, Virginia, was a record-breaking voyage.[6]

Such letters as went through the post-offices were opened by the postmasters as a matter of course, if these officials imagined that the missives contained information, or especially if they revealed the secret or familiar correspondence of well-known public men.[7] "By passing through the post-office they [letters] should become known to all" men, Wash-

[1] Madison to Washington, Feb. 11, 1788; *Writings:* Hunt, v, 99.

[2] Madison to Washington, Feb. 15, 1788; *ib.*, 100.

[3] The Randolph-Clinton Correspondence; see *infra*, chap. x.

[4] Jay to Wolcott, mailed June 23, and received by Wolcott Aug. 16, 1794; Gibbs, i, 157.

[5] *Ib.*, 160.

[6] Jefferson to Short, Nov. 21, 1789; *Works:* Ford, vi, 20.

[7] So notorious was this practice that important parts of the correspondence of the more prominent politicians and statesmen of the day always were written in cipher. Jefferson, Madison, and Monroe appear to have been especially careful to take this precaution. (See Washington's complaint of this tampering with the mails in a letter

ington cautioned Lafayette in 1788.[1] In 1791, the first year of the Post-Office under our present Government, there were only eighty-nine post-offices in the entire country.[2] "As late as 1791 there were only six post-offices in New Jersey and none south of Trenton." [3]

Yet letters were the principal means by which accounts of what was happening in one part of the country were made known to the people who lived in other sections; and this personal correspondence was by far the most trustworthy source of information, although tinctured as it naturally was by the prejudice of the writer and often nothing but report of mere rumor.

Newspapers were few in number and scanty in news. When the Constitution was adopted, not many regularly issued newspapers were printed in the whole country. Most of these were published in Philadelphia, Boston, New York, and in two or three of the other larger towns. Only ten papers were printed in Connecticut, one of the best informed and best served of all the States, and of these several soon expired;[4] in Ridgefield, with twelve hundred inhabitants, there were but four newspaper subscribers.[5] In 1784, Virginia had only one newspaper, published at Richmond twice a week.[6]

to Fairfax, June 25, 1786; *Writings:* Sparks, ix, 175.) Habitual violation of the mails by postmasters continued into the first decades of the nineteenth century.

[1] Washington to Lafayette, Feb. 7, 1788; *Writings:* Ford, xi, 218.

[2] Kettell, in *Eighty Years' Progress*, ii, 174.

[3] *Pa. Mag. Hist. and Biog.*, ix, 444.

[4] *Am. Ant. Soc. Pubs.*, xxiii, Part ii, 254–330.

[5] Goodrich, i, 61.

[6] Schoepf, ii, 61; see note, *ib.* Even this journal died for want of subscribers.

These papers carried scarcely any news and the little they published was often weeks and sometimes months old, and as uncertain as it was stale. "It is but seldom that I have an opportunity of peeping into a newspaper," wrote "Agricola" to the Salem (Massachusetts) "Gazette," September 13, 1791, "and when it happens it is commonly a stale one of 2 or 3 weeks back; but I lately met with your fresh Gazette of August 30th — may be I shan't see another for months to come."[1] "Newspaper paragraphs, unsupported by other testimony, are often contradictory and bewildering," wrote Washington of so big, important, and exciting news as the progress of Shays's Rebellion.[2] On the same day Washington complained to General Knox that he was "bewildered with those vague and contradictory reports which are presented in the newspapers."[3]

But what this pygmy press lacked in information it made up in personal abuse. Denunciation of public men was the rule, scandal the fashion. Even the mild and patient Franklin was driven to bitter though witty protest. He called the press "THE SUPREMEST COURT OF JUDICATURE," which "may judge, sentence, and condemn to infamy, not only private individuals, but public bodies, &c. with or without inquiry or hearing, *at the court's discretion*." This "Spanish Court of Inquisition," asserts Frank-

[1] Salem *Gazette*, Sept. 13, 1791; Hist. Col., Topsfield (Mass.) Hist. Soc., iii, 10.

[2] Washington to Humphreys, Dec. 26, 1786; *Writings:* Ford, xi, 98–103.

[3] Washington to General Knox, Dec. 26, 1786; *ib.*, 103–05.

lin, works "in the dark" and so rapidly that "an honest, good Citizen may find himself suddenly and unexpectedly accus'd, and in the same Morning judg'd and condemn'd, and sentence pronounced against him, that he is a *Rogue* and a *Villian*."

"The liberty of the press," writes Franklin, operates on citizens "somewhat like the *Liberty of the Press* that Felons have, by the Common Law of England, before Conviction, that is, to be *press'd* to death or hanged." "Any Man," says he, "who can procure Pen, Ink, and Paper, with a Press, and a huge pair of BLACKING BALLS, may commissionate himself" as a court over everybody else, and nobody has any redress. "For, if you make the least complaint of the *judge's* [editor's] conduct, he daubs his blacking balls in your face wherever he meets you, and, besides tearing your private character to flitters marks you out for the odium of the public, as an *enemy to the liberty of the press*." Franklin declared that the press of that day was supported by human depravity.

Searching for a remedy which would destroy the abuse but preserve the true liberty of the press, Franklin finally concludes that he has found it in what he calls "the *liberty of the cudgel*." The great philosopher advised the insulted citizen to give the editor "a good drubbing"; but if the public should feel itself outraged, it should restrain itself and, says Franklin, "in moderation content ourselves with tarring and feathering, and tossing them [editors] in a blanket." [1]

[1] *Writings:* Smyth, x, 36 *et seq.* This arraignment of the press by

Even Jefferson was sometimes disgusted with the press. "What do the foolish printers of America mean by retailing all this stuff in our papers? — As if it were not enough to be slandered by one's enemies without circulating the slanders among his friends also."[1] An examination of the newspapers of that period shows that most of the "news" published were accounts of foreign events; and these, of course, had happened weeks and even months before.

Poor, small, and bad as the newspapers of the time were, however, they had no general circulation many miles from the place where they were published. Yet, tiny driblets trickled through by the belated posts to the larger towns and were hastily read at villages where the post-riders stopped along the way. By 1790 an occasional country newspaper appeared, whose only source of news from the outside world was a fugitive copy of some journal published in the city and such tales as the country editor could get travelers to tell him: whether these were true or false made not the slightest difference — everything was fish that came to his net.[2]

America's first journalist was written when Franklin was eighty-three years old and when he was the most honored and beloved man in America, Washington only excepted. It serves not only to illuminate the period of the beginning of our Government, but to measure the vast progress during the century and a quarter since that time.

[1] Jefferson to Mrs. Adams, Paris, Sept. 25, 1785; *Works:* Ford, iv, 465.

[2] "Country Printer," in Freneau, iii, 60. Freneau thus describes the country editor of that day: —

> "Three times a week, by nimble geldings drawn,
> A stage arrives; but scarcely deigns to stop,
> Unless the driver, far in liquor gone,
> Has made some business for the black-smith-shop;

Common schools in the present-day understanding of the term did not exist. "There was not a grammar, a geography, or a history of any kind in the school," testifies Samuel G. Goodrich[1] (Peter Parley) of Ridgefield, Connecticut; and this at a time when the Constitution had been adopted and our present Government was in operation. "Slates & pencils were unknown, paper was imported, scarce and costly"; most pupils in New England "cyphered

Then comes this printer's harvest-time of news,
Welcome alike from Christians, Turks, or Jews.

"Each passenger he eyes with curious glance,
And, if his phiz be mark'd of courteous kind,
To conversation, straight, he makes advance,
Hoping, from thence, some paragraph to find,
Some odd adventure, something new and rare,
To set the town a-gape, and make it stare.

"All is not Truth ('tis said) that travellers tell —
So much the better for this man of news;
For hence the country round, that know him well,
Will, if he prints some lies, his lies excuse.
Earthquakes, and battles, shipwrecks, myriads slain —
If false or true — alike to him are gain.

. . . .

"Ask you what matter fills his various page?
A mere farrago 'tis, of mingled things;
Whate'er is done on Madam Terra's stage
He to the knowledge of his townsmen brings:
One while, he tells of monarchs run away;
And now, of witches drown'd in Buzzard's bay.

"Some miracles he makes, and some he steals;
Half Nature's works are giants in his eyes;
Much, very much, in wonderment he deals, —
New-Hampshire apples grown to pumpkin size,
Pumpkins almost as large as country inns,
And ladies bearing, each, — three lovely twins."

Freneau was himself a country printer in New Jersey, after editing the *National Gazette* in Philadelphia. Thus the above description was from his personal experience and in a town in a thickly settled part, on the main road between New York and Philadelphia.

[1] Goodrich, i, 38.

on birch bark"; and a teacher who could compute interest was considered "great in figures." [1] "The teacher was not infrequently a person with barely education enough to satisfy the critical requirements of some illiterate committeemen. . . . The pay was only from three to five dollars a month, and two months during the winter season was the usual term." [2] The half-dozen small but excellent colleges and the few embryonic academies surrounded by forests, where educated and devout men strove to plant the seeds of institutions of learning, could not, altogether, reach more than a few hundred pupils.

"*Anthony McDonald* teaches boys and girls their grammar tongue; also Geography terrestrial and celestial — Old hats made as good as new." So read the sign above the door of McDonald's "school" in Virginia, a dozen years after Washington was elected President.[3] For the most part children went untaught, except in "the three R's," which, in some mysterious manner, had been handed down from father to son. Yet in the back settlements it was common to find men of considerable property who could not read or write; and some of those who could make out to read did not know whether the earth was round or flat.[4] There were but thirty students at Virginia's historic college in 1795. Weld dined

[1] A letter from Salem Town about 1786–87; in *American Journal of Education*, xiii, 738.

[2] Van Santvoord: *Memoirs of Eliphalet Nott*, 19. [3] Davis, 333.

[4] "Many cannot read or write, and many that can, know nothing of geography and other branches. The country is too thinly settled to carry out a system of common schools." (Howe, 153, speaking of western Virginia about 1830.)

with President Madison, of William and Mary's, and several of the students were at the table. Some of these young seekers after culture were without shoes, some without coats; and each of them rose and helped himself to the food whenever he liked.[1]

Parts of the country, like the Mohawk Valley in New York, were fairly settled and well cultivated.[2] In the more thickly inhabited parts of New England there were order, thrift, and industry.[3] The houses of the most prosperous farmers in Massachusetts, though "frequently but one story and a garret," had "their walls papered"; tea and coffee were on their tables when guests appeared; the women were clad in calicoes and the men were both farmers and artisans.[4] Yet on the road from Boston to Providence houses were seen already falling into decay; "women and children covered with rags." [5] In Newport, Rhode Island, idle men loafed on the street corners, houses were tumbling down from negligence, grass grew in the public square, and rags were stuffed into the windows.[6]

In Connecticut the people were unusually prosperous; and one enthusiastic Frenchman, judging that State from the appearance of the country around Hartford, exclaimed: "It is really the Paradise of

[1] Weld, i, 168. But President Tyler says that the boys Weld saw were grammar-school pupils.

[2] Watson, 269.

[3] Chastellux, 319–20.

[4] De Warville, 126–27.

[5] *Ib.*, 145 and 450.

[6] *Ib.*, 145. All travelers agree as to the wretched condition of Rhode Island; and that State appears to have acted as badly as it looked. "The . . . infamous [scenes] in Rhode Island have done inexpressable injury to the Republican character," etc. (Madison to Pendleton, Feb. 24, 1787; *Writings:* Hunt, ii, 319.)

the United States."[1] Weld found that, while the "southeast part of . . . Pennsylvania is better cultivated than any other part of America, yet the style of farming is . . . very slovenly. . . . The farmer . . . in England . . . who rents fifty acres . . . lives far more comfortably in every respect than the farmer in Pennsylvania, or any other of the middle states, who owns two hundred acres."[2]

In the homes of Quaker farmers near Philadelphia, however, the furniture was of black walnut, the beds and linen white and clean, the food varied and excellent.[3] Yet a settler's house in the interior of Pennsylvania was precisely the reverse, as the settler himself was the opposite of the industrious and methodical Quaker husbandman. A log cabin lighted only by the open door, and with the bare earth for a floor, housed this pioneer and his numerous family. Often he was a man who had lost both fortune and credit and therefore sought regions where neither was necessary. When neighbors began to come in such numbers that society (which to him meant government, order, and taxes) was formed, he moved on to a newer, more desolate, and more congenial spot. Mostly hunter and very little of a farmer, he with his nomad brood lived "in the filth of his little cabin," the rifle or rod, and corn from the meager clearing, supplying all his wants except that of whiskey, which he always made shift to get.

One idea and one alone possessed this type — the idea of independence, freedom from restraint. He

[1] De Warville, 132.
[2] Weld, i, 113.
[3] De Warville, 186–87.

was the high priest of the religion of do-as-you-like. He was the supreme individualist, the ultimate democrat whose non-social doctrine has so cursed modern America. "He will not consent to sacrifice a single natural right for all the benefits of government,"[1] chronicles a sympathetic observer of these men.

Freneau, a fervent admirer of this shiftless and dissolute type, thus describes him and his home: —

> "Far in the west, a paltry spot of land,
> That no man envied, and that no man owned,
> A woody hill, beside a dismal bog —
> This was your choice; nor were you much to blame;
> And here, responsive to the croaking frog,
> You grubbed, and stubbed,
> And feared no landlord's claim."[2]

Nor was hostility to orderly society confined to this class. Knox wrote Washington that, in Massachusetts, those who opposed the Constitution acted "from deadly principle levelled at the existence of all government whatever."[3]

The better class of settlers who took up the "farms" abandoned by the first shunners of civilization, while a decided improvement, were, nevertheless, also improvident and dissipated. In a poor and

[1] De Warville, 186 and 332. See La Rochefoucauld's description of this same type of settler as it was several years after De Warville wrote. "The Dwellings of the new settlers . . . consist of huts, with roofs and walls which are made of bark and in which the husband, wife and children pass the winter wrapped up in blankets. . . . Salt pork and beef are the usual food of the new settlers: their drink is water and whiskey." (La Rochefoucauld, i, 293–96.)

[2] Freneau, iii, 74.

[3] Knox to Washington, Feb. 10, 1788; *Writings:* Ford, xi, footnote to 229. And see *infra*, chap. VIII.

slip-shod fashion, they ploughed the clearings which had now grown to fields, never fertilizing them and gathering but beggarly crops. Of these a part was always rye or corn, from which whiskey was made. The favorite occupation of this type was drinking to excess, arguing politics, denouncing government, and contracting debts.[1] Not until debts and taxes had forced onward this second line of pioneer advance did the third appear with better notions of industry and order and less hatred of government and its obligations.[2]

In New England the out-push of the needy to make homes in the forests differed from the class just described only in that the settler remained on his clearing until it grew to a farm. After a few years his ground would be entirely cleared and by the aid of distant neighbors, cheered to their work by plenty of rum, he would build a larger house.[3] But meanwhile there was little time for reading, small opportunity for information, scanty means of getting it;

[1] De Warville, 187. In 1797, La Rochefoucauld speaks of "the credulity and ignorance of the half-savage sort of people who inhabit the back settlements." (La Rochefoucauld, i, 293.)

[2] "A relaxation is observable among all orders of society. Drunkenness is the prevailing vice, and with few exceptions, the source of all other evils. A spirit, or rather a habit, of equality is diffused among this people as far as it possibly can go. . . . The inhabitants exhibit to strangers striking instances both of the utmost cleanliness and excessive nastiness." (La Rochefoucauld, i, 125.)

During Washington's second term as President, La Rochefoucauld thus describes manners in western Pennsylvania: "They are much surprised at a refusal to sleep with one, two, or more men, in the same bed, or between dirty sheets, or to drink after ten other persons out of the same dirty glass. . . . Whiskey mixed with water is the common drink in the country." (*Ib.*)

[3] *Ib.*, i, 293–96. See *infra*, note 4, pp. 281–82.

and mouth-to-mouth rumor was the settler's chief informant of what was happening in the outside world. In the part of Massachusetts west of the Connecticut Valley, at the time the Constitution was adopted, a rough and primitive people were scattered in lonesome families along the thick woods.[1]

In Virginia the contrast between the well-to-do and the masses of the people was still greater.[2] The social and economic distinctions of colonial Virginia persisted in spite of the vociferousness of democracy which the Revolution had released. The small group of Virginia gentry were, as has been said, well educated, some of them highly so, instructed in the ways of the world, and distinguished in manners.[3] Their houses were large; their table service was of plate; they kept their studs of racing and carriage horses.[4] Sometimes, however, they displayed a grotesque luxury. The windows of the mansions, when broken, were occasionally replaced with rags; servants sometimes appeared in livery with silk stockings thrust into boots;[5] and again dinner would be served by naked negroes.[6]

[1] Watson, 266.

[2] "You see [in Maryland and Virginia] real misery and apparent luxury insulting each other." (De Warville, 159.)

[3] Chastellux, 279, and translator's note.

[4] Anburey, ii, 331–32. [5] De Warville, 242.

[6] "Soon after entering Virginia, and at a highly respectable house, I was shocked . . . at seeing for the first time, young negroes of both sexes, from twelve even to fifteen years old, not only running about the house but absolutely tending table, as naked as they came into the world. . . . Several young women were at the table, who appeared totally unmoved." (Watson, 33.) Watson's statement may perhaps be questionable; a livelier description, however, was given with embellishments, some years later. (See translator's note to Chastellux, 245; and see Schoepf, ii, 47.)

The second class of Virginia people were not so well educated, and the observer found them "rude, ferocious, and haughty; much attached to gaming and dissipation, particularly horse-racing and cock-fighting"; and yet, "hospitable, generous, and friendly." These people, although by nature of excellent minds, mingled in their characters some of the finest qualities of the first estate, and some of the worst habits of the lower social stratum. They "possessed elegant accomplishments and savage brutality." [1] The third class of Virginia people were lazy, hard-drinking, and savage; yet kind and generous.[2] "Whenever these people come to blows," Weld testifies, "they fight just like wild beasts, biting, kicking, and endeavoring to tear each other's eyes out with their nails"; and he says that men with eyes thus gouged out were a common sight.[3]

The generation between the birth of Marshall and the adoption of the Constitution had not modified the several strata of Virginia society except as to apparel and manners, both of which had become worse than in colonial times.

Schoepf found shiftlessness [4] a common characteristic; and described the gentry as displaying the baronial qualities of haughtiness, vanity, and idleness.[5] Jefferson divides the people into two sections as regards characteristics, which were not entirely creditable to either. But in his comparative estimate Jefferson is far harsher to the Southern population

[1] Anburey, ii, 331–32. [2] *Ib.*, 332–33.

[3] Weld, i, 192. See Weld's description of "gouging." And see Fithian's interesting account; Fithian, 242–43.

[4] Schoepf, ii, 89. [5] *Ib.*, 91–95.

of that time than he is to the inhabitants of other States; and he emphasizes his discrimination by putting his summary in parallel columns.

"While I am on this subject," writes Jefferson to Chastellux, "I will give you my idea of the characters of the several States.

In the North they are	In the South they are
cool	fiery
sober	voluptuary
laborious	indolent
persevering	unsteady
independent	independent
jealous of their own liberties, and just to those of others	zealous for their own liberties, but trampling on those of others
interested	generous
chicaning	candid
superstitious and hypocritical in their religion	without attachment or pretensions to any religion but that of the heart.

"These characteristics," continues Jefferson, "grow weaker and weaker by graduation from North to South and South to North, insomuch that an observing traveller, without the aid of the quadrant may always know his latitude by the character of the people among whom he finds himself."

"It is in Pennsylvania," Jefferson proceeds in his careful analysis, "that the two characters seem to meet and blend, and form a people free from the extremes both of vice and virtue. Peculiar circumstances have given to New York the character which climate would have given had she been placed on the South instead of the north side of Pennsylvania. Perhaps too other circumstances may have occasioned in Virginia a transplantation of a particular vice foreign to its climate." Jefferson finally concludes: "I think it for their good that the vices of their character should be pointed out to them that they may amend them; for a malady of either body or mind once known is half cured."[1]

A plantation house northwest of Richmond grumblingly admitted a lost traveler, who found his sleeping-room with "filthy beds, swarming with bugs" and cracks in the walls through which the sun shone.[2] The most bizarre contrasts startled the observer — mean cabins, broken windows, no bread, and yet women clad in silk with plumes in their hair.[3] Eight years after our present National Government was established, the food of the people living in the Shenandoah Valley was salt fish, pork, and greens; and the wayfarer could not get fresh meat except at Staunton or Lynchburg,[4] notwithstanding the surrounding forests filled with game or the domestic animals which fed on the fields where the forests had been cleared away.

Most of the houses in which the majority of Virginians then lived were wretched;[5] Jefferson tells us,

[1] Jefferson to Chastellux, Sept. 2, 1785; *Thomas Jefferson Correspondence*, Bixby Collection: Ford, 12; and see Jefferson to Donald, July 28, 1787; Jefferson's *Writings:* Washington, ii, 193, where Jefferson says that the qualities of Virginians are "indolence, extravagance, and infidelity to their engagements."

[2] Weld, i, 199.

[3] Schoepf, ii, 34. This strange phenomenon was witnessed everywhere, even in a place then so far remote as Maine. "Elegant women come out of log or deal huts [in Maine] all wearing fashionable hats and head dresses with feathers, handsome cloaks and the rest of their dress suitable to this." (La Rochefoucauld, ii, 314.)

[4] *Ib.*, 89; and Weld, i, 199, 236. The reports of all travelers as to the want of fresh meat in the Valley are most curious. That region was noted, even in those early days, for its abundance of cattle.

[5] *Ib.*, 144.

speaking of the better class of dwellings, that "it is impossible to devise things more ugly, uncomfortable, and happily more perishable." "The poorest people," continues Jefferson, "build huts of logs, laid horizontally in pens, stopping the interstices with mud. . . . The wealthy are attentive to the raising of vegetables, but very little so to fruits. . . . The poorer people attend to neither, living principally on . . . animal diet." [1]

In general the population subsisted on worse fare than that of the inhabitants of the Valley.[2] Even in that favored region, where religion and morals were more vital than elsewhere in the Commonwealth, each house had a peach brandy still of its own; and it was a man of notable abstemiousness who did not consume daily a large quantity of this spirit. "It is scarcely possible," writes Weld, "to meet with a man who does not begin the day with taking one, two, or more drams as soon as he rises." [3]

Indeed, at this period, heavy drinking appears to have been universal and continuous among all classes throughout the whole country [4] quite as much

[1] "Notes on Virginia": Jefferson; *Works:* Ford, iv, 69; and see Weld, i, 114, for similar diet in Pennsylvania. [2] *Ib.*, 183–84.

[3] Weld, i, 206. "Sigars and whiskey satisfy these good people who thus spend in a quarter of an hour in the evening, the earnings of a whole day. The landlord of the Inn has also a distillery of whiskey," writes La Rochefoucauld, in 1797, of the mountain people of Virginia. He thus describes the houses and people living in the valley towards Staunton: "The habitations are in this district more numerous than on the other side of the Blue Mountains, but the houses are miserable; mean, small log houses, inhabited by families which swarm with children. There exists here the same appearance of misery as in the back parts of Pennsylvania." (La Rochefoucauld, iii, 173–76.)

[4] "It took a good deal of New England rum to launch a 75 ton

as in Virginia. It was a habit that had come down from their forefathers and was so conspicuous, ever-present and peculiar, that every traveler through America, whether native or foreign, mentions it time and again. "The most common vice of the inferior class of the American people is drunkenness," writes La Rochefoucauld in 1797.[1] And Washington eight years earlier denounced "drink which is the source of all evil — and the ruin of half the workmen in this country."[2] Talleyrand, at a farmer's house in the heart of Connecticut, found the daily food to consist of "smoked fish, ham, potatoes, strong beer and brandy."[3]

Court-houses built in the center of a county and often standing entirely alone, without other buildings near them, nevertheless always had attached to them a shanty where liquor was sold.[4] At country taverns which, with a few exceptions, were poor

schooner . . . to raise a barn . . . or to ordain a regular minister. . . . Workingmen in the fields, in the woods, in the mills and handling logs and lumber on the river were supplied with regular rations of spirits." (Maine Hist. Soc. Col. (2d Series), vi, 367–68.)

The rich people of Boston loved picnic parties in the near-by country, at which was served "Punch, warm and cold, before dinner; excellent beef, Spanish and Bordeaux wines, cover their tables . . . Spruce beer, excellent cyder, and Philadelphia porter precede the wines." (De Warville, 58.) This inquiring Frenchman called on Hancock, but found that he had a "marvelous gout which dispenses him from all attentions and forbids the access to his house." (*Ib.*, 66.) As to New England country stores, "you find in the same shop, hats, nails, liquors." (*Ib.*, 127.)

[1] La Rochefoucauld, iv, 577.

[2] Washington to Green (an employee) March 31, 1789; *Writings:* Ford, xi, 377.

[3] *Memoirs of Talleyrand:* Broglie's ed., i, footnote to 181; and see Talleyrand's description of a brandy-drinking bout at this house in which he participated.

[4] Schoepf, ii, 47.

and sometimes vile,[1] whiskey mixed with water was the common drink.[2] About Germantown, Pennsylvania, workingmen received from employers a pint of rum each day as a part of their fare;[3] and in good society men drank an astonishing number of "full bumpers" after dinner, where, already, they had imbibed generously.[4] The incredible quantity of liquor, wine, and beer consumed everywhere and by all classes is the most striking and conspicuous feature of early American life. In addition to the very heavy domestic productions of spirits,[5] there were imported in 1787, according to De Warville, four million gallons of rum, brandy, and other spirits; one million gallons of wine; three million gallons of molasses (principally for the manufacture of rum); as against only one hundred and twenty-five thousand pounds of tea.[6]

Everybody, it appears, was more interested in sport and spending than in work and saving. As in colonial days, the popular amusements continued to be horse-racing and cock-fighting; the first the peculiar diversion of the quality; the second that of the baser sort, although men of all conditions of society attended and delighted in both.[7] But the horse-

[1] Watson, 252.
[2] Chastellux, 224; see also 243.
[3] La Rochefoucauld, iv, 119.
[4] *Ib.*, 590.
[5] See *infra*, II, chap. II.
[6] De Warville, 262.
[7] Watson, 261–62. "The indolence and dissipation of the middling and lower classes of white inhabitants in Virginia are such as to give pain. . . . Horse-racing, cock-fighting, and boxing-matches are standing amusements, for which they neglect all business." (*Ib.*; and see Chastellux, 292, translator's note. Also see Chastellux's comments on the economic conditions of the Virginians, 291–93.) For habits of Virginians nearly twenty years after Watson wrote, see La Rochefoucauld, iii, 75–79.

racing and the cock-fighting served the good purpose of bringing the people together; for these and the court days were the only occasions on which they met and exchanged views. The holding of court was an event never neglected by the people; but they assembled then to learn what gossip said and to drink together rather than separately, far more than they came to listen to the oracles from the bench or even the oratory at the bar; and seldom did the care-free company break up without fights, sometimes with the most serious results.[1]

Thus, scattered from Maine to Florida and from the Atlantic to the Alleghanies, with a skirmish line thrown forward almost to the Mississippi, these three and a quarter millions of men, women, and children, did not, for the most part, take kindly to government of any kind. Indeed, only a fraction of them had anything to do with government, for there were no more than seven hundred thousand adult males among them,[2] and of these, in most States, only property-holders had the ballot. The great majority of the people seldom saw a letter or even a newspaper; and the best informed did not know what was going on in a neighboring State, although anxious for the information.

"Of the affairs of Georgia, I know as little as of

[1] "The session assembles here, besides the neighboring judges, lawyers, and parties whose causes are to be tried, numbers of idle people who come less from desire to learn what is going forward than to drink together," says La Rochefoucauld; and see his picturesque description of his arrival at the close of court day at Goochland Court-House. (La Rochefoucauld, iii, 126–29.)

[2] One man to every five men, women, and children, which is a high estimate.

those of Kamskatska," wrote Madison to Jefferson in 1786.[1] But everybody did know that government meant law and regulation, order and mutual obligation, the fulfillment of contracts and the payment of debts. Above all, everybody knew that government meant taxes. And none of these things aroused what one would call frantic enthusiasm when brought home to the individual. Bloated and monstrous individualism grew out of the dank soil of these conditions. The social ideal had hardly begun to sprout; and nourishment for its feeble and languishing seed was sucked by its overgrown rival.

Community consciousness showed itself only in the more thickly peopled districts, and even there it was feeble. Generally speaking and aside from statesmen, merchants, and the veterans of the Revolution, the idea of a National Government had not penetrated the minds of the people. They managed to tolerate State Governments, because they always had lived under some such thing; but a National Government was too far away and fearsome, too alien and forbidding for them to view it with friendliness or understanding. The common man saw little difference between such an enthroned central power and the Royal British Government which had been driven from American shores.

To be sure, not a large part of the half-million men able for the field[2] had taken much of any militant part in expelling British tyranny; but these

[1] Madison to Jefferson, Aug. 12, 1786; *Writings:* Hunt, ii, 261.

[2] Randolph in the Virginia Constitutional Convention estimated that the colonies could have put four hundred thousand soldiers in the field. (Elliott, iii, 76–77.)

"chimney-corner patriots," as Washington stingingly described them, were the hottest foes of British despotism — after it had been overthrown. And they were the most savage opponents to setting up any strong government, even though it should be exclusively American.

Such were the economic, social, and educational conditions of the masses and such were their physical surroundings, conveniences, and opportunities between the close of the War for Independence and the setting-up of the present Government. All these facts profoundly affected the thought, conduct, and character of the people; and what the people thought, said, and did, decisively influenced John Marshall's opinion of them and of the government and laws which were best for the country.

During these critical years, Jefferson was in France witnessing government by a decaying, inefficient, and corrupt monarchy and nobility, and considering the state of a people who were without that political liberty enjoyed in America.[1] But the vagaries, the changeableness, the turbulence, the envy toward those who had property, the tendency to repudiate debts, the readiness to credit the grossest slander or to respond to the most fantastic promises, which the newly liberated people in America were then displaying, did not come within Jefferson's vision or experience.

[1] It is a curious fact, however, that in his journey through France Jefferson observed no bad conditions, but, on the whole, his careful diary states that he found the people "well clothed and well fed," as Professor Hazen expresses it. For impartial treatment of this subject see Hazen, 1–21.

Thus, Marshall and Jefferson, at a time destined to be so important in determining the settled opinions of both, were looking upon opposite sides of the shield. It was a curious and fateful circumstance and it was repeated later under reversed conditions.

CHAPTER VIII

POPULAR ANTAGONISM TO GOVERNMENT

Mankind, when left to themselves, are unfit for their own government (George Washington, 1786.)

There are subjects to which the capacities of the bulk of mankind are unequal and on which they must and will be governed by those with whom they happen to have acquaintance and confidence. (James Madison, 1788.)

I fear, and there is no opinion more degrading to the dignity of man, that these have truth on their side who say that man is incapable of governing himself. (John Marshall, 1787.)

"GOVERNMENT, even in its best state," said Mr. Thomas Paine during the Revolution, "is but a necessary evil." [1] Little as the people in general had read books of any kind, there was one work which most had absorbed either by perusal or by listening to the reading of it; and those who had not, nevertheless, had learned of its contents with applause.

Thomas Paine's "Common Sense," which Washington and Franklin truly said did so much for the patriot cause,[2] had sown dragon's teeth which the

[1] *Writings:* Conway, i, 69 *et seq.*

[2] "*Common Sense* had a prodigious effect." (Franklin to Le Veillard, April 15, 1787; *Writings:* Smyth, ix, 558.) "Its popularity was unexampled. . . . The author was hailed as our angel sent from Heaven to save all from the horrors of Slavery. . . . His pen was an appendage [to the army] almost as necessary and formidable as its cannon." (Cheetenham, 46–47, 55.) In America alone 125,000 copies of *Common Sense* were sold within three months after the pamphlet appeared. (Belcher, i, 235.)

"Can nothing be done in our Assembly for poor Paine? Must the merits of *Common Sense* continue to glide down the stream of time unrewarded by this country? His writings certainly have had a powerful effect upon the public mind. Ought they not, then, to meet an adequate return?" (Washington to Madison, June 12, 1784; *Writings:* Ford, x, 393; and see Tyler, i, 458–62.) In the Virginia Legislature Marshall introduced a bill for Paine's relief. (*Supra*, chap. VI.)

author possibly did not intend to conceal in his brilliant lines. Scores of thousands interpreted the meaning and philosophy of this immortal paper by the light of a few flashing sentences with which it began. Long after the British flag disappeared from American soil, this expatriated Englishman continued to be the voice of the people;[1] and it is far within the truth to affirm that Thomas Paine prepared the ground and sowed the seed for the harvest which Thomas Jefferson gathered.

"Government, like dress, is the badge of lost innocence; the palaces of kings are built on the ruins of the bowers of paradise." And again, "Society is produced by our wants, and government by our wickedness."[2] So ran the flaming maxims of the great iconoclast; and these found combustible material.

Indeed, there was, even while the patriots were fighting for our independence, a considerable part of the people who considered "all government as dissolved, and themselves in a state of absolute liberty, where they wish always to remain"; and they were strong enough in many places "to prevent any courts being opened, and to render every attempt to administer justice abortive."[3] Zealous bearers, these, of the torches of anarchy which Paine's burn-

[1] Graydon, 358.

[2] *Common Sense:* Paine; *Writings:* Conway, i, 61. Paine's genius for phrase is illustrated in the *Crisis,* which next appeared. "These are the times that try men's souls"; "Tyranny like hell, is not easily conquered"; "The summer soldier and the sunshine patriot," are examples of Paine's brilliant gift.

[3] Moore's *Diary,* ii, 143–44. Although this was a British opinion, yet it was entirely accurate.

ing words had lighted. Was it not the favored of the earth that government protected? What did the poor and needy get from government except oppression and the privilege of dying for the boon? Was not government a fortress built around property? What need, therefore, had the lowly for its embattled walls?

Here was excellent ammunition for the demagogue. A person of little ability and less character always could inflame a portion of the people when they could be assembled. It was not necessary for him to have property; indeed, that was a distinct disadvantage to the Jack Cades of the period.[1] A lie traveled like a snake under the leaves and could not be overtaken;[2] bad roads, scattered communities, long distances, and resultant isolation leadened and

[1] "They will *rise* and for lack of argument, say, Mr Speaker, this measure will never do, the *People* Sir, will never bear it. . . . These small Politicians, returned home, . . . tell their Constituents such & such measures are taking place altho' I did my utmost to prevent it — The People must take care of themselves or they are undone. Stir up a County Convention and by Trumpeting lies from Town to Town get one [a convention] collected and Consisting of Persons of small Abilities — of little or no property — embarrass'd in their Circumstances — and of no great Integrity — and these Geniouses vainly conceiving they are competent to regulate the affairs of State — make some hasty incoherant Resolves, and these end in Sedition, Riot, & Rebellion." (Sewell to Thatcher, Dec., 1787; *Hist. Mag.* (2d Series), vi, 257.)

[2] More than a decade after the slander was set afoot against Colonel Levin Powell of Loudoun County, Virginia, one of the patriot soldiers of the Revolution and an officer of Washington, that he favored establishing a monarchy, one of his constituents wrote that "detraction & defamation are generally resorted to promote views injurious to you. . . . Can you believe it, but it is really true that the old & often refuted story of your predilection for Monarchy is again revived." (Thomas Sims to Colonel Levin Powell, Leesburg, Virginia, Feb. 5 and 20, 1801; *Branch Historical Papers*, i, 58, 61.)

delayed the feet of truth. Nothing was too ridiculous for belief; nothing too absurd to be credited.

A Baptist preacher in North Carolina was a candidate for the State Convention to pass upon the new National Constitution, which he bitterly opposed. At a meeting of backwoodsmen in a log house used for a church, he told them in a lurid speech that the proposed "Federal City" (now the District of Columbia) would be the armed and fortified fortress of despotism. "'This, my friends,' said the preacher, 'will be walled in or fortified. Here an army of 50,000, or, perhaps 100,000 men, will be finally embodied and will sally forth, and enslave the people who will be gradually disarmed.'" A spectator, who attempted to dispute this statement, narrowly escaped being mobbed by the crowd. Everything possible was done to defeat this ecclesiastical politician; but the people believed what he said and he was elected.[1]

So bizarre an invention as the following was widely circulated and generally believed as late as 1800: John Adams, it was said, had arranged, by intermarriage, to unite his family with the Royal House of Great Britain, the bridegroom to be King of America. Washington, attired in white clothing as a sign of conciliation, called on Adams and objected; Adams rebuffed him. Washington returned, this time dressed in black, to indicate the solemnity of

[1] Watson, 262–64. This comic prophecy that the National Capital was to be the fortified home of a standing army was seriously believed by the people. Patrick Henry urged the same objection with all his dramatic power in the Virginia Convention of 1788. So did the scholarly Mason. (See *infra*, chaps. XI and XII.)

his protest. Adams was obdurate. Again the Father of his Country visited the stubborn seeker after monarchical relationship, this time arrayed in full regimentals to show his earnestness; Adams was deaf to his pleas. Thereupon the aged warrior drew his sword, avowing that he would never sheathe it until Adams gave up his treasonable purpose; Adams remained adamant and the two parted determined enemies.[1]

Such are examples of the strange tales fed to the voracious credulity of the multitude. The attacks on personal character, made by setting loose against public men slanders which flew and took root like thistle seed, were often too base and vile for repetition at the present day, even as a matter of history; and so monstrous and palpably untruthful that it is difficult to believe they ever could have been circulated much less credited by the most gossip-loving.

Things, praiseworthy in themselves, were magnified into stupendous and impending menaces. Revolutionary officers formed "The Society of the Cincinnati" in order to keep in touch with one another, preserve the memories of their battles and their campfires, and to support the principles for which they had fought.[2] Yet this patriotic and fraternal order was, shouted the patriots of peace, a plain attempt to establish an hereditary nobility on which a new tyranny was to be builded. Jefferson, in Paris, declared that "the day . . . will certainly come, when a single fibre of this institution will produce an

[1] Graydon, 392–93.
[2] *Memorials of the Society of the Cincinnati*, 1790, 3–24.

hereditary aristocracy which will change the form of our governments [Articles of Confederation] from the best to the worst in the world." [1]

Ædanus Burke,[2] one of the Justices of the Supreme Court of South Carolina, wrote that the Society of the Cincinnati was "deeply planned"; it was "an hereditary peerage"; it was "planted in a fiery hot ambition, and thirst for power"; "its branches will end in Tyranny . . . the country will be composed only of two ranks of men, the patricians, or nobles, and the rabble." [3] In France, Mirabeau was so aroused by Burke's pamphlet that the French orator wrote one of his own. Mirabeau called the Cincinnati "that nobility of barbarians, the price of blood, the off-spring of the sword, the fruit of conquest." "The distinction of Celts and Ostrogoths," exclaimed the extravagant Frenchman, "are what they claim for their inheritance." [4]

The "Independent Chronicle" of Boston was so excited that it called on "legislators, Governors, and magistrates *and their* ELECTORS" to suppress the Cincinnati because it "is concerted to establish a

[1] Jefferson to Washington, Nov. 14, 1786; *Works:* Ford, v, 222–23; and see Jefferson's denunciation of the Cincinnati in Jefferson to Madison, Dec. 28, 1794; *ib.*, viii, 156–57. But see Jefferson's fair and moderate account of the Cincinnati before he had learned of its unpopularity in America. (Jefferson to Meusnier, June 22, 1786; *ib.*, v, 50–56.)

[2] The same who broke the quorum in the Continental Congress. (*Supra*, chap. IV.)

[3] Burke: *Considerations on the Society of the Order of Cincinnati;* 1784.

[4] Mirabeau: *Considerations on the Order of Cincinnati;* 1786. Mirabeau here refers to the rule of the Cincinnati that the officer's eldest son might become a member of the order, as in the Military Order of the Loyal Legion of the present time.

complete and perpetual *personal* discrimination between" its members "and the whole remaining body of the people who will be styled Plebeians."[1]

John Marshall was a member of this absurdly traduced patriotic fraternity. So were his father and fellow officers of our War for Independence. Washington was its commander. Were the grotesque charges against these men the laurels with which democracy crowned those who had drawn the sword for freedom? Was this the justice of liberty? Was this the intelligence of the masses? Such must have been the queries that sprang up in the minds of men like Marshall. And, indeed, there was sound reason for doubt and misgiving. For the nightmares of men like Burke and Mirabeau were pleasant dreams compared with the horrid visions that the people conjured.

Nor did this popular tendency to credit the most extraordinary tale, believe the most impossible and outrageous scandal, or accept the most impracticable and misshapen theory, end only in wholesome hatred of rank and distinction. Among large numbers there was the feeling that equality should be made real by a general division of property. Three years after peace had been established, Madison said he "strongly suspected" that many of the people contemplated "an abolition of debts public & private, and a new division of property."[2] And Jay thought that "a reluctance to taxes, an

[1] As quoted in Hudson: *Journalism in the United States*, 158.

[2] Madison to James Madison, Nov. 1, 1786; *Writings:* Hunt, ii, 278.

impatience of government, a rage for property, and little regard to the means of acquiring it, together with a desire for equality in all things, seem to actuate the mass of those who are uneasy in their circumstances."[1] The greed and covetousness of the people is also noted by all travelers.[2]

Very considerable were the obligations "public and private" which Madison wrote his father that he "strongly suspected" a part of the country intended to repudiate. The public debt, foreign and domestic, of the Confederation and the States, at the close of the Revolutionary War, appeared to the people to be a staggering sum.[3] The private debt aggregated a large amount.[4] The financial situation was chaos. Paper money had played such havoc with specie that, in Virginia in 1786, as we have seen, there was not enough gold and silver to pay current taxes.[5] The country had had bitter experience with a fictitious medium of exchange. In Virginia by 1781 the notes issued by Congress "fell to 1000 for 1," records Jefferson, "and then expired, as it had done in other States, without a single groan."[6]

Later on, foreigners bought five thousand dollars

[1] Jay to Jefferson, Oct. 27, 1786; *Jay:* Johnston, iii, 212.

[2] See Weld, i, 114–15, as a fair example of foreign estimate of this American characteristic at that period.

[3] See chap. II, vol. II, of this work.

[4] Private debts which Virginia planters alone owed British merchants were "20 or 30 times the amount of all money in circulation in that state." (Jefferson to Meusnier, Jan. 24, 1786; *Works:* Ford, v, 17–18; and see Jefferson to McCaul, April 19, 1786; *ib.*, 88.)

[5] "It cannot perhaps be affirmed that there is gold & silver en[o] in the Country to pay the next tax." (Madison to Monroe, June 4, 1786; *Writings:* Hunt, ii, 245.)

[6] Jefferson to Meusnier, Jan. 24, 1786; *Works:* Ford, v, 27.

of this Continental scrip for a single dollar of gold or silver.[1] In Philadelphia, toward the end of the Revolution, the people paraded the streets wearing this make-believe currency in their hats, with a dog tarred and covered with paper dollars instead of feathers.[2] For land sold by Jefferson before paper currency was issued he "did not receive the money till it was not worth Oak leaves."[3]

Most of the States had uttered this fiat medium, which not only depreciated and fluctuated within the State issuing it, but made trade between citizens of neighboring States almost impossible. Livingston found it a "loss to shop it in New York with [New] Jersey Money at the unconscionable discount which your [New York] brokers and merchants exact; and it is as damnifying to deal with our merchants here [New Jersey] in that currency, since they proportionably advance the price of their commodities."[4] Fithian in Virginia records that: "In the evening I borrowed of *Ben Carter* 15/ — I have plenty of money with me but it is in Bills of Philadelphia Currency and will not pass at all here."[5]

Virginia had gone through her trial of financial fiction-for-fact, ending in a law fixing the scale of depreciation at forty to one, and in other unique

[1] Jefferson to Meusnier, Jan. 24, 1786: *Works:* Ford, v, 27.

[2] Moore's *Diary*, ii, 425–26. The merchants of Philadelphia shut their shops; and it was agreed that if Congress did not substitute "solid money" for paper, "all further resistance to" Great Britain "must be given up." (*Ib.*)

[3] Jefferson to McCaul, April 19, 1786; *Works:* Ford, v, 90; also to Wm. Jones, Jan. 5, 1787; *ib.*, 247. — "Paiment was made me in this money when it was but a shadow."

[4] Livingston to Jay, July 30, 1789; *Jay:* Johnston, iii. 373–74.

[5] Fithian, 91.

and bizarre devices;[1] and finally took a determined stand against paper currency.[2] Although Virginia had burned her fingers, so great was the scarcity of money that there was a formidable agitation to try inflation again.[3] Throughout the country there once more was a "general rage for paper money."[4] Bad as this currency was, it was counterfeited freely.[5] Such coin as existed was cut and clipped until Washington feared that "a man must travel with a pair of money scales in his pocket, or run the risk of receiving gold of one fourth less by weight than it counts."[6]

If there was not money enough, let the Government make more — what was a government for if not for that? And if government could not make good money, what was the good of government? Courts were fine examples of what government meant — they were always against the common people. Away with them! So ran the arguments and appeals of the demagogues and they found an answer in the breasts of the thoughtless, the ignorant, and the uneasy. This answer was broader than the

[1] Virginia's paper money experiment was the source of many lawsuits in which Marshall was counsel. See, for example, Pickett *vs.* Claiborne (Call, iv, 99–106); Taliaferro *vs.* Minor (Call, i, 456–62).

[2] The House of Delegates toward the end of 1786 voted 84 to 17 against the paper money resolution. (Madison to James Madison, Nov. 1, 1786; *Writings:* Hunt, ii, 277.)

[3] "The advocates for paper money are making the most of this handle. I begin to fear exceedingly that no efforts will be sufficient to parry this evil." (Madison to Monroe, June 4, 1786; *ib.*, 245.)

[4] Madison to Jefferson, Aug. 12, 1786; *ib.*, 259.

[5] "Enclosed are one hundred Dollars of new Emmission Money which Col. Steward desires me to have exchanged for Specie. Pray, inform him they are all counterfeit." (Gerry to King, April 7, 1785; King, i, 87.)

[6] Washington to Grayson, Aug. 22. 1785; *Writings:* Ford, x, 493–94.

demand for paper money, wider than the protest against particular laws and specific acts of administration. This answer also was, declared General Knox, "that the property of the United States . . . ought to be the common property of all. And he that attempts opposition to this creed is an enemy to equity and justice, and ought to be swept from off the face of the earth." Knox was convinced that the discontented were "determined to annihilate all debts, public and private." [1]

Ideas and purposes such as these swayed the sixteen thousand men who, in 1787, followed Daniel Shays in the popular uprising in Massachusetts against taxes, courts, and government itself.[2] "The restlessness produced by the uneasy situation of individuals, connected with lax notions concerning public and private faith, and erroneous[3] opinions which confound liberty with an exemption from legal control, produced . . . unlicensed conventions, which, after voting on their own constitutionality, and assuming the name of the people, arrayed themselves against the legislature," was John Marshall's summary of the forces that brought about the New England rebellion.

The "army" of lawlessness, led by Shays, took the field, says Marshall, "against taxes, and against the administration of justice; and the circulation of

[1] Knox to Washington, Oct. 28, 1786; *Writings:* Hunt, ii, footnote to p. 407–08.

[2] Minot: *History of the Insurrections in Massachusetts in 1786* (2d ed.), 1810.

[3] Printed in the first edition (1807) "enormous" — a good example of the haste of the first printing of Marshall's *Life of Washington*. (See vol. III of this work.)

a depreciated currency was required, as a relief from the pressure of public and private burdens, which had become, it was alleged, too heavy to be borne. Against lawyers and courts the strongest resentments were manifested; and to such a dangerous extent were these dispositions indulged, that, in many instances, tumultuous assemblages of people arrested the course of law, and restrained the judges from proceeding in the execution of their duty."

"The ordinary recourse to the power of the country was found insufficient protection," records Marshall, "and the appeals made to reason were attended with no beneficial effect. The forbearance of the government was attributed to timidity rather than moderation, and the spirit of insurrection appeared to be organized into a regular system for the suppression of courts."[1] Such was Marshall's analysis of the Northern convulsion; and thus was strengthened in him that tendency of thought started at Valley Forge, and quickened in the Virginia House of Delegates.

"It rather appears to me," wrote David Humphries to Washington, in an attempt to explain the root of the trouble, "that there is a licentious spirit prevailing among many of the people; a levelling principle; and a desire of change; with a wish to annihilate all debts, public and private."[2] Unjust taxes were given as the cause of the general dislike of government, yet those who composed the mobs erupting from this crater of anarchy, now located in New England, paid few or no taxes.

[1] Marshall, ii, 117. [2] *Ib.*, 118.

"High taxes are the ostensible cause of the commotions, but that they are the real cause is as far remote from truth as light from darkness," asserts Knox. "The people who are the insurgents have never paid any, or but very little taxes," testifies this stanch Revolutionary officer. "But," continues Knox, "they see the weakness of the government. They feel at once their own poverty, compared with the opulent, and their own force, and they are determined to make use of the latter, in order to remedy the former." [1]

This condition brought to a head a distrust of the good sense, justice, and moderation of the people, which had been forming in the minds of many of the best and ablest men of the time.[2] "The knaves and fools of this world are forever in alliance," was the conclusion reached in 1786 [3] by Jay, who thought that the people considered "liberty and licentiousness" as the same thing.[4] The patient but bilious Secretary of State felt that "the wise and the good never form the majority of any large society, and it seldom happens that their measures are uniformly adopted, or that they can always prevent being overborne themselves by the strong and almost never-ceasing union of the wicked and the weak." [5] The cautious Madison was equally doubtful of the peo-

[1] Knox to Washington, Oct. 28, 1786; *Writings:* Hunt, ii, footnote to 408.

[2] Shays's Rebellion was only a local outburst of a general feeling throughout the United States. Marshall says, "those causes of discontent . . . existed in every part of the union." (Marshall, ii, 117.)

[3] Jay to Jefferson, Oct. 27, 1786; *Jay:* Johnston, iii, 213.

[4] Jay to Reed, Dec. 12, 1786; *ib.*, 222.

[5] Jay to Price, Sept. 27, 1786; *ib.*, 168.

ple: "There are subjects to which the capacities of the bulk of mankind are unequal and on which they must and will be governed by those with whom they happen to have acquaintance and confidence" was Madison's judgment.[1]

Washington, black with depression, decided and bluntly said "that mankind, when left to themselves, are unfit for their own government." Lee had suggested that Washington use his "influence" to quiet the disorders in New England; but, flung back Washington, "*Influence* is no *government*. Let us have one by which our lives, liberties, and properties will be secured, or let us know the worst at once. . . . To be more exposed in the eyes of the world, and more contemptible than we already are, is hardly possible."[2]

"No morn ever dawned more favorably than ours did; and no day was ever more clouded than the present. . . . We are fast verging to anarchy,"[3] cried the great captain of our war for liberty. The wings of Washington's wrath carried him far. "Good God!" cried he, "Who, besides a Tory, could have foreseen, or a Briton predicted" the things that were going on! "The disorders which have arisen in these States, the present prospect of our affairs . . . seems to me to be like the vision of a dream. My mind can scarcely realize it as a thing in actual existence. . . . There are combustibles in every State, which a spark might set fire to."[4]

[1] Madison to Randolph, Jan. 10, 1788; *Writings:* Hunt, v, 81.
[2] Washington to Lee, Oct. 31, 1786; *Writings:* Ford, xi, 76–77.
[3] Washington to Madison, Nov. 5, 1786; *ib.*, 81.
[4] Washington to Knox, Dec. 26, 1786; *ib.*, 103–04. And Washing-

choed his old commander's views. The s youth were fading, his confidence in leclining. He records for us his altered "These violent, I fear bloody, dissensions Massachusetts] I had thought inferior in d virtue to no one in the union, added to the ong tendency which the politics of many eminent characters among ourselves have to promote private and public dishonesty, cast a deep shade over the bright prospect which the revolution in America and the establishment of our free governments had opened to the votaries of liberty throughout the globe. I fear, and there is no opinion more degrading to the dignity of man, that these have truth on their side who say that man is incapable of governing himself."[1] Thus wrote Marshall in 1787, when he was not yet thirty-two years old.

But Jefferson in Paris was beholding a different picture that strengthened the views which he and Marshall held in common when America, in arms, challenged Great Britain. "The Spirit of resistance to government is so valuable on certain occasions that I wish it to be always kept alive. It will often be exercised when wrong, but better so than not to be exercised at all. I like a little rebellion now & then. It is like a storm in the atmosphere." So wrote Jefferson after the Massachusetts insurrection had been quelled.[2]

ton wrote to Lafayette that "There are seeds of discontent in every part of the Union." (*Writings:* Sparks, ix, 263.)

[1] Marshall to James Wilkinson, Jan. 5, 1787; *Amer. Hist. Rev.*, xii, 347–48.

[2] Jefferson to Mrs. Adams, Feb. 22, 1787; *Works:* Ford, v, 263.

The author of our Declaration of Independence was tasting the delights of the charming French Capital at this time, but he also was witnessing the shallowness and stupidity of the peculiarly weak royalty and nobility; and although it was this same Royal Government that had aided us with men and money in our struggle to throw off the yoke of England, Jefferson's heart grew wrathful against it and hot for popular rule in France. Yet in the same apostrophe to rebellion, Jefferson declares that the French people were too shallow for self-rule. "This [French] nation," writes Jefferson, "is incapable of any serious effort but under the word of command." [1]

After having had months to think about it, this enraptured enthusiast of popular upheaval spread his wings and was carried far into crimson skies. "Can history produce an instance of rebellion so honourably conducted?" exclaimed Jefferson, of the Massachusetts anarchical outburst, nearly a year after it had ended; and continued thus: —

"God forbid! we should ever be 20 years without such a rebellion. . . . What country can preserve its liberties if their rulers are not warned from time to time that their people preserve the spirit of resistance? Let them take arms! . . . What signify a few lives lost in a century or two? The tree of liberty must be refreshed from time to time with the blood of patriots & tyrants. It is its natural manure." [2]

Thus did his contact with a decadent monarchy on the one hand and an enchanting philosophy on

[1] Jefferson to Mrs. Adams, Feb. 22, 1787; *Works:* Ford, v, 263.
[2] Jefferson to Smith, Nov. 13, 1787; *ib.*, 362.

the other hand, help to fit him for the leadership of American radicalism. No better training for that mission could have been afforded. French thought was already challenging all forms of existing public control; it was a spirit Gamaliel which found in Jefferson an eager Saul at its feet; and American opinion was prepared for its doctrines. In the United States general dislike and denunciation of the established governments had uncovered the feeling against government itself which lay at the root of opposition to any stronger one.

The existing American system was a very masterpiece of weakness. The so-called Federal Government was like a horse with thirteen bridle reins, each held in the hands of separate drivers who usually pulled the confused and powerless beast in different directions. Congress could make treaties with foreign nations; but each of the States could and often did violate them at will. It could borrow money, but could not levy taxes or impose duties to pay the debt. Congress could get money only by making humble requests, called "requisitions," on the "sovereign" Commonwealths. It had to depend upon the whims of the various States for funds to discharge principal and interest of public obligations; and these springs of revenue, when not entirely dry, yielded so little that the Federal establishment was like to die of financial thirst.[1]

[1] "The payments from the States under the calls of Congress have in no year borne any proportion to the public wants. During the last year . . . the aggregate payments . . . fell short of 400,000 doll[rs], a sum neither equal to the interest due on the foreign debts, nor even to the current expenses of the federal Government. The greatest part of

The requisitions of Congress upon the various States for money to pay the National obligations to foreign creditors were usually treated with neglect and often with contempt by those jealous and pompous "Sovereignties." "Requisitions are a perfect nullity where thirteen sovereign, independent, disunited States are in the habit of discussing and refusing compliance with them at their option. Requisitions are actually little better than a jest and a by-word throughout the land. If you tell the legislatures they have violated the treaty of peace, and invaded the prerogatives of the confederacy, they will laugh in your face." [1] Thus raged Washington. "Congress cannot command money" even to redeem Americans held in slavery in Algiers,[2] testified the powerless and despondent Secretary of State. Indeed, Congress amounted to so little that the delegates from many States often refused to attend.[3]

Though debts were great and financial confusion

this sum too went from Virg[a], which will not supply a single shilling the present year." (Madison to Jefferson, March 18, 1786; *Writings:* Hunt, ii, 228.)

[1] Washington to Jay, Aug. 1, 1786; *Writings:* Ford, xi, 54–55.

[2] Jay (Secretary of State under the Confederation) to Jefferson, Dec. 14, 1786; *Jay:* Johnston, iii, 223.

[3] "We are wasting our time & labour in vain efforts to do business" (because of State delegates not attending), wrote Jefferson in 1784. (Jefferson to Washington, March 15, 1784; *Works:* Ford, iv, 266.) And at the very climax of our difficulties "a sufficient number of States to do business have not been represented in Congress." (Jay to Wm. Carmichael, Jan. 4, 1786; *Jay:* Johnston, iii, 225.) During half of September and all of October, November, December, January, and February, nine States "have not been represented in congress"; and this even after the Constitution had been adopted. (Jay to Jefferson, March 9, 1789; *Jay:* Johnston, iii, 365.)

maddening, they furnished no solid excuse for the failure of the States to enable Congress to preserve American honor by the payment of our admitted National debt. Jay reviewed the situation and showed that "the resources of the country . . . notwithstanding all appearances to the contrary, are abundant. . . . Our country is fertile, abounding in useful productions, and those productions in demand and bearing a good price." [1] The general opinion appears to have been that the people did not want to support the Government.

"The treasury is empty, though the country abounds in resources, and our people are far more unwilling than unable to pay taxes," wrote Jay, early in 1787.[2] Madison excused his support of the bill authorizing tobacco to be taken for specie in payment of taxes, upon the ground that it "could not be rejected without . . . exciting some worse project of

[1] Jay to Jefferson, Dec. 14, 1786; *Jay:* Johnston, iii, 223–24. And Melancton Smith declared that "the farmer cultivates his land and reaps the fruit. . . . The merchant drives his commerce and none can deprive him of the gain he honestly acquires. . . . The mechanic is exercised in his art, and receives the reward of his labour." (1797–98; Ford: *P. on C.*, 94.) Of the prosperity of Virginia, Grigsby says, "our agriculture was most prosperous, and our harbors and rivers were filled with ships. The shipping interest . . . was really advancing most rapidly to a degree of success never known in the colony." (Grigsby, i, footnote to p. 82; and see his brilliant account of Virginia's prosperity at this time; *ib.*, 9–19.) "The spirit of industry throughout the country was never greater. The productions of the earth abound," wrote Jay to B. Vaughan, Sept. 2, 1784. (*Jay:* Johnston, iii, 132.)

[2] Jay to John Adams, Feb. 21, 1787; *Jay:* Johnston, iii, 235. Jay thought that the bottom of the trouble was that "relaxation in government and extravagance in individuals create much public and private distress, and much public and private want of good faith." (*Ib.*, 224.)

a popular cast";[1] and "by a fear that some greater evil under the name of relief to the people would be substituted."[2] Debt "made it extremely inconvenient to most people to submit to a regular government," was the conclusion Rutledge finally reached.[3]

But, whatever the cause, the States did not act. Washington thought it a combination of the scheming of demagogues and the ignorance and dishonesty of the people. "I think there is more wickedness than ignorance mixed in our councils. . . . Ignorance and design are difficult to combat. . . . To be so fallen! so lost! . . . Virtue, I fear has in a great degree taken its departure from our land and the want of a disposition to do justice is the source of the national embarrassments; for, whatever guise or colorings are given to them, this I apprehend is the origin of the evils we now feel."[4] Such was Washington's cry of despair four years after he had wrested American liberty from Great Britain.

Look where one will among the class of men of whom Washington was the highest representative, one finds that they believed the fountain head of the country's desperate conditions to be in the people

[1] Madison to Jefferson, Dec. 4, 1786; *Writings:* Hunt, ii, 293. "This indulgence to the people as it is called & considered was so warmly wished for out of doors, and so strenuously pressed within that it could not be rejected without danger of exciting some worse project of a popular cast." (*Ib.*)

[2] Madison to Washington, Dec. 24, 1786; *ib.*, 301. "My acquiescence in the measure was against every general principle which I have embraced, and was extorted by a fear that some greater evil under the name of relief to the people would be substituted." (*Ib.*)

[3] Rutledge to Jay, May 2, 1789; *Jay:* Johnston, iii, 368.

[4] Washington to Jay, May 18, 1786; *Writings:* Ford, xi, 31–32.

themselves. Jay put this opinion in a nutshell when he said, "The mass of men are neither wise nor good."[1] Not that these leaders despaired that an American People would finally be evolved who should realize the exalted expectations of the patriot leaders of the Revolution; not that out of the flux of popular heedlessness and dishonor, indifference and disorder, idleness and avarice, the nobler qualities of human nature would not, in the end, bring forth a nation and rule it for the happiness and well-being of its people. But they thought that only a strong government could fashion the clay and breathe into its nostrils the breath of life. "Virtue, like the other resources of a country, can only be drawn to a point and exerted by strong circumstances ably managed, or a strong government ably administered," said Jay.[2]

The shield of all this turmoil and baseness was the State Governments. "Their unreasonable jealousy of that body [Congress] and of one another . . . will, if there is not a change in the system, be our downfall as a nation," exclaimed Washington only a few months after peace had been established.[3] It was the States, he declared, which made the Federal establishment "a half-starved, limping government, that appears to be always moving upon crutches and tottering at every step."[4]

It was the States which always were thwarting every plan for the general welfare; the States which

[1] Jay to Washington, June 27, 1786; *Jay:* Johnston, iii, 204.
[2] *Ib.*, 205.
[3] Washington to Harrison, Jan. 18, 1784; *Writings:* Ford, x, 345.
[4] *Ib.*

were forever impairing the National obligations; the States which bound hand and foot the straw man of the central power, clothed it in rags and made it a mere scarecrow of government. And it was State pride, prejudice, and ignorance which gave provincial demagogues their advantage and opportunity. The State Governments were the "people's" Governments; to yield State "sovereignty" was to yield the "people's" power over their own affairs, shouted the man who wished to win local prominence, power, and office.

Those who did not want to pay taxes and who disliked much government of any kind felt that they could make shift with mere State establishments.[1] "A thirst for power, and the bantling, I had liked to have said monster for sovereignty, which have taken such fast hold of the States individually, will, when joined by the many whose personal consequence in the control of State politics will in a manner be annihilated, form a strong phalanx against"[2] the National Constitution, prophesied the leader of the Revolution.

But it was not alone the powerlessness of the Federal Government to keep the National faith, plighted by solemn treaties with foreign Governments; or to uphold the National honor by paying debts made to win American independence, that wrought that bloodless revolution[3] which produced the Constitution. Nor was it the proud and far-

[1] See Madison's masterful summary of the wickedness, weakness, and folly of the State Governments in *Writings:* Hunt, ii, 361–69.

[2] Washington to Jay, March 10, 1787; *Writings:* Ford, xi, 125.

[3] See *supra*, chap. VI.

seeing plans of a few great minds whose heart's desire was to make the American People a Nation.

Finance, commerce, and business assembled the historic Philadelphia Convention; although it must be said that statesmanship guided its turbulent councils. The senseless and selfish nagging at trade in which the States indulged, after peace was declared, produced a brood of civil abuses as noisome as the military dangers which State control of troops had brought forth during the Revolution. Madison truly said that "most of our political evils may be traced up to our commercial ones." [1] The States passed tariff laws against one another as well as against foreign nations; and, indeed, as far as commerce was concerned, each State treated the others as foreign nations.[2] There were retaliations, dis-

[1] Madison to Jefferson, March 18, 1786; *Writings:* Hunt, ii, 228. "Another unhappy effect of a continuance of the present anarchy of our commerces will be a continuance of the unfavorable balance on it, which by draining us of our metals, furnishes pretexts for the pernicious substitution of paper money, for indulgencies to debtors, for postponements of taxes." (*Ib.*)

[2] Virginia carefully defined her revenue boundaries as against Pennsylvania and Maryland; and provided that any vessel failing to enter and pay duties as provided by the Virginia tariff laws might be seized by any person and prosecuted "one half to the use of the informer, and the other half to the use of the commonwealth." (Va. Statutes at Large (1785), chap. 14, 46.)

Virginia strengthened her tariff laws against importations by land. "If any such importer or owner shall unload any such wagon or other carriage containing any of the above goods, wares, or merchandise brought into this state by land without first having entered the same as directed above, every such wagon or other carriage, together with the horses thereto belonging and all such goods wares and merchandise as shall be brought therein, shall be forfeited and recovered by information in the court of the county; two-thirds to the informer and one-third toward lessening the levy of the county where such conviction shall be made." (*Ib.*)

Even Pennsylvania, already the principal workshop of the country,

criminations, and every manner of trade restrictions and impediments which local ingenuity and selfishness could devise.

The idea of each State was to keep money from going outside its borders into other States and to build up its own business and prosperity at the expense of its neighbors.[1] States having no seaports were in a particularly hard case. Madison picturesquely describes their unhappy plight: "New Jersey placed between Phil^a^ & N. York, was likened to a cask tapped at both ends; And N. Carolina, between Virg^a^ & S. Carolina to a patient bleeding at both Arms."[2] Merchants and commercial bodies were at their wits' end to carry on business and petitioned for a general power over commerce.[3]

The commercial view, as stated by Madison, was

while enacting an avowedly protective tariff on "Manufactures of Europe and Other foreign parts," included "cider, malted barley or grain, fish, salted or dried, cheese, butter, beef, pork, barley, peas, mustard, manufactured tobacco" which came, mostly, from sister States. The preamble declares that the duties are imposed to protect "the artisans and mechanics of this state" without whose products "the war could not have been carried on."

In addition to agricultural articles named above, the law includes "playing cards, hair powder, wrought gold or silver utensils, polished or cut stones, musical instruments, walking canes, testaments, psalters, spelling books or primers, romances, novels and plays, and horn or tortoise shell combs," none of which could be called absolutely indispensable to the conduct of the war. The preamble gives the usual arguments for protective tariffs. It is the first protective tariff law, in the present-day sense, ever passed. (Pa. Statutes at Large (1785), 99.)

[1] Even at the present time the various States have not recovered from this anti-National and uneconomic practice, as witness the tax laws and other statutes in almost every State designed to prevent investments by the citizens of that State in industries located in other States. Worse, still, are the multitude of State laws providing variable control over railways that are essentially National.

[2] *Writings:* Hunt, ii, 395.

[3] Marshall (1st ed.), v, 76–79.

that "the National Government should be armed with positive and compleat authority in all cases which require uniformity; such as the regulation of trade, including the right of taxing both exports & imports, the fixing the terms and forms of naturalization, &c., &c."

Madison then lays down this extreme Nationalist principle as the central article of his political faith: "Over and above this positive power, a negative *in all cases whatsoever* on the legislative acts of the States, as heretofore exercised by the Kingly prerogative, appears to me to be absolutely necessary, and to be the least possible encroachment on the State jurisdictions. Without this defensive power, every positive power that can be given on paper will be evaded & defeated. The States will continue to invade the National jurisdiction, to violate treaties and the law of nations & to harass each other with rival and spiteful measures dictated by mistaken views of interest."[1]

Too much emphasis cannot be put upon the fact that the mercantile and financial interests were the weightiest of all the influences for the Constitution; the debtors and agricultural interests the strongest groups against it. It deserves repetition, for a proper understanding of the craft and force practiced by both sides in the battle over ratification, that those who owed debts were generally against the Constitution and practically all to whom debts were due

[1] Madison to Washington, April 16, 1787; *Writings:* Hunt, ii, 345–46. This ultra-Nationalist opinion is an interesting contrast to Madison's States' Rights views a few years later. (See *infra*, vol. II, chaps. II, III, and IV.)

were for the new Government. "I have little prospect of bringing Banks [a debtor] to terms as the Law of this State now stands," wrote a Virginia agent of a creditor, "but I hope when the New Federal constitution is adopted that the Laws will be put upon a better footing. . . . Three fourths of the people that oppose it [the Constitution] are those that are deeply in debt & do not wish to pay." [1]

London merchants were very anxious for a new order of things. "I hope ere long your Federal Government will be established, and that honest Men will again have the Assendency in your Country, for without such a change it must ever remain a poor place to live in," was the opinion of a business man living in the British Capital.[2]

A few weeks after Virginia ratified the Constitution, Minton Collins reported to his principal about a person named Banks, who, says Collins, "begins to be a little alarmed from the adoption of the Federal Constitution. I hope it will alarm every such R[asca]l. He had run his rig long enough for he boasts of being worth from 150,000£ to 200,000 pounds; this is not bad for a man that six years ago could scarcely raise a suit of clothes to his back." [3]

Marshall was becoming a prosperous lawyer and his best clients were from the mercantile interests. His family relationships were coming to be more and more with the property classes. He had no ambition

[1] Minton Collins at Richmond to Stephen Collins at Philadelphia, May 8, 1788; MS., Lib. Cong.

[2] Sam Smith in London to Stephen Collins in Philadelphia, July 21, 1788; *ib.*

[3] Minton Collins to Stephen Collins, Aug. 9, 1788; *ib.*

for a political career, which might have given to his thinking and conclusions a "more popular cast," to use Madison's contemptuous phrase. Thus Marshall's economic and political convictions resulting from experience and reasoning were in harmony with his business connections and social environment.

Undoubtedly he would have taken the same stand had none of these circumstances developed; his constructive mind, his conservative temperament, his stern sense of honor, his abhorrence of disorder and loose government, his army experience, his legislative schooling, his fidelity to and indeed adoration of Washington, would have surely placed him on the side of the Constitution. Still, the professional and social side of his life should not be ignored, if we are to consider fully all the forces which then surrounded him, and which, with ever-growing strength, worked out the ultimate Marshall.

Jefferson, in France, experienced only the foreign results of the sharp and painful predicament which John Marshall was sadly witnessing in America. While not busy with the scholars and society of the French Capital, Jefferson had been engaged in the unhappy official task of staving off our French creditors and quieting, as well as he could, complaints of our trade regulations and other practices which made it hard and hazardous for the French to do business with us.[1] He found that "the nonpaiment of our

[1] "Vergennes complained, and with a good deal of stress, that they did not find a sufficient dependence on arrangements taken with us. This was the third time, too, he had done it. . . . He observed too, that the administration of justice with us was tardy, insomuch that their merchants, when they had money due to them within our States,

debts and the want of energy in our government . . . discourage a connection with us"; [1] and "want of punctuality & a habitual protection of the debtor" prevented him from getting a loan in France to aid the opening of the Potomac.[2] All this caused even Jefferson to respond to the demand for unifying the American Government as to foreign nations; but he would not go further. "Make the States one as to every thing connected with foreign nations, & several as to everything purely domestic," counseled Jefferson while the Constitutional Convention was quarreling at Philadelphia.[3]

But he did not think badly of the weakness of the Articles of Confederation which so aroused the disgust, anger, and despair of Washington, Madison, Jay, and other men of their way of thinking, who were on the ground. "With all the imperfections of our present government [Articles of Confederation]," wrote Jefferson in Paris, in 1787, "it is without comparison the best existing or that ever did exist"; [4] and he declared to one of his French friends that "the confederation is a wonderfully perfect instrument." [5] Jefferson found but three serious defects in the Articles of Confederation: no general rule for admitting States; the apportionment of the State's

considered it as desperate; and that our commercial regulations, in general, were disgusting to them." (Jefferson's Report; *Works:* Ford, iv, 487.)

[1] Jefferson to Stuart, Jan. 25, 1786; *ib.*, v, 74.

[2] Jefferson to Madison, Dec. 16, 1786; *ib.*, v, 230.

[3] Jefferson to Carrington, Paris, Aug. 4, 1787; *ib.*, 318; also 332; and Jefferson to Wythe, Sept. 16, 1787; *ib.*, 340.

[4] Jefferson to Carrington, Paris, Aug. 4, 1787; *ib.*, 318.

[5] Jefferson to Meusnier, Jan. 24, 1786; *ib.*, 8.

quota of money upon a land instead of a population basis; and the imperfect power over treaties, import duties, and commerce.[1]

He frankly said: "I am not a friend to a very energetic government"; and he thought that "our governments will remain virtuous for many centuries" — but added with seer-like vision: "as long as . . . there shall be vacant lands in America."[2] Jefferson wished the United States "to practice neither commerce nor navigation, but to stand with respect to Europe precisely on the footing of China."[3] Far from thinking that the low state of our credit was a bad thing for us, he believed that its destruction would work an actual benefit to America. "Good will arise from the destruction of our credit," he asserted in a letter to Stuart written from Paris in 1786. "I see nothing else which can restrain our disposition to luxury, and the loss of those manners which alone can preserve republican government."[4]

We have now seen the state of the country and the condition of the people, their situation and habits, their manner of life and trend of feeling. We have witnessed the change thus wrought in the leading men during this period, so destructive of confidence in the wisdom or virtue of majorities, at least on first impulse and without abundant time for reflection and second thought. Thus we have measured,

[1] Jefferson to Meusnier, Jan. 24, 1786; *Works:* Ford, v, 8.

[2] Jefferson to Madison, Dec. 20, 1787; *ib.*, 373–74. Jefferson concluded, prophetically, that when the people "get piled upon one another, in large cities, as in Europe, they will become as corrupt as Europe." (*Ib.*)

[3] Jefferson to Hogendorp, Oct. 13, 1785; *ib.*, iv, 469.

[4] Jefferson to Stuart, Jan. 25, 1786; *ib.*, v, 74.

with some degree of accuracy, the broad and well-marked space that separated the hostile forces which were to meet in what was for the moment a decisive conflict when Virginia's Constitutional Convention should assemble at Richmond.

In one camp the uninformed and credulous, those who owed debts and abhorred government, with a sprinkling among them of eminent, educated, and well-meaning men who were philosophic apostles of theoretical liberty; and in the other camp men of property and lovers of order, the trading and moneyed interests whose first thought was business; the veterans of the Revolution who had learned on the battlefield the need of a strong central Government; and, here and there, a prophetic and constructive mind who sought to build a Nation. John Marshall was one of the latter; and so he promptly took his place by the side of his old general and leader in the camp of the builders.

At last the supreme hour is striking. The Virginians, about to assemble in State Convention, will determine the fate of that unauthorized and revolutionary plan for a National Government,[1] the National Constitution. The movement for a second general Convention to have another try at framing a Constitution has made distinct progress by the time the Virginia representatives gather at the State Capital.[2] There is widespread, positive, and growing resentment at the proposed new form of government;

[1] See *infra*, chap. IX.

[2] For a careful study of this important but neglected subject see Professor Edward Payson Smith's paper in Jameson, 46–115.

and if Virginia, the largest and most populous of the States, rejects it, the flames of opposition are certain to break out in every part of the country. As Washington asserts, there is, indeed, "combustible material" everywhere.

Thus it is that the room where Virginia's Convention is about to meet in June, 1788, will become the "bloody angle" in the first great battle for Nationalism. And Marshall will be there, a combatant as he had been at Great Bridge and Brandywine. Not for John Marshall the pallid rôle of the trimmer, but the red-blooded part of the man of conviction.

CHAPTER IX

THE STRUGGLE FOR RATIFICATION

The plot thickens fast. A few short weeks will determine the political fate of America. (Washington.)

On Sunday, June 1, 1788, the dust lay deep in the streets of the little town of Richmond. Multitudes of horses were tethered here and there or stabled as best the Virginia Capital's meager accommodations permitted. Cavalcades of mounted men could be seen from Shockoe Hill, wending their way over the imperfect earthen roads from every direction to the center of interest.[1] Some of these had come hundreds of miles and arrived in the garb of the frontier, pistol and hanger at belt.[2] Patrick Henry, prematurely old at fifty-two, came in a one-horse, uncovered gig; Pendleton, aged, infirm, and a cripple, arrived in a phaeton.[3]

As we have seen, it was very hard for members of Virginia's Legislature to get to the seat of the State Government even from counties not far distant; and a rainy season, or even one week's downpour during the latter part of May, would have kept large numbers of the members of the Virginia Convention from reaching their destination in time and perhaps have decided the impending struggle[4] before it

[1] Grigsby, i, 25.

[2] Travelers from the District of Kentucky or from the back settlements of Virginia always journeyed fully armed, in readiness to defend themselves from attack by Indians or others in their journey through the wilderness.

[3] Grigsby, i, 27–28.

[4] *Ib.*, 25.

began. The year's great social and sporting event added to the throng and colored the dark background of political anxiety and apprehension with a faint tinge of gayety.[1]

Although seven months had elapsed since the Federal Convention had finished its work, there was, nevertheless, practically no accurate knowledge among the people of the various parts of the "New Plan" of government. Even some members of the Virginia State Convention had never seen a copy of the Constitution until they arrived in Richmond to deliberate upon it and decide its fate.[2] Some of the most inquiring men of this historic body had not read a serious or convincing argument for it or against it.[3] "The greater part of the members of the [Virginia] convention will go to the meeting without information on the subject," wrote Nicholas to Madison immediately after the election of delegates.[4]

One general idea, however, had percolated through the distances and difficulties of communication to the uninformed minds of the people — the idea that the new Constitution would form a strong, consolidated National Government, superior to and dominant over the State Governments; a National Sovereignty overawing State Sovereignties, dangerous to

[1] The Jockey Club was holding its annual races at Richmond when the Constitutional Convention of 1788 convened. (Christian, 31.)

[2] Grigsby, i, 31.

[3] Humphrey Marshall, from the District of Kentucky, saw for the first time one number of the *Federalist*, only after he had reached the more thickly peopled districts of Virginia while on his way to the Convention. (*Ib.*, footnote to 31.)

[4] George Nicholas to Madison, April 5, 1788; *Writings:* Hunt, v, footnote to p. 115.

if not entirely destructive of the latter; a general and powerful authority beyond the people's reach, which would enforce contracts, collect debts, impose taxes; above all, a bayonet-enforced rule from a distant point, that would imperil and perhaps abolish "liberty." [1]

So a decided majority of the people of Virginia were against the proposed fundamental law; [2] for, as in other parts of the country, few of Virginia's masses wanted anything stronger than the weak and ineffective Government of the State and as little even of that as possible. Some were "opposed to any system, was it even sent from heaven, which tends to confirm the union of the States." [3] Madison's father reported the Baptists to be "generally opposed to it"; and the planters who went to Richmond to sell their tobacco had returned foes of the "new plan" and had spread the uprising against it among others "who are no better acquainted with the necessity of adopting it than they themselves." [4] At first the friends of the Constitution deceived themselves into thinking that the work of the Philadelphia Convention met with approval in Virginia; but they soon found that "the tide next took a sudden and strong turn in the opposite direction." [5] Henry wrote to

[1] "The most common and ostensible objection was that it [the Constitution] would endanger state rights and personal liberty — that it was too strong." (Humphrey Marshall, i, 285.)

[2] Tyler, i, 142. Grigsby estimates that three fourths of the people of Virginia were opposed to the Constitution. (Grigsby, i, footnote to 160.)

[3] Lee to Madison, Dec. 1787; *Writings:* Hunt, v, footnote to p. 88,

[4] Madison's father to Madison, Jan. 30, 1788; *Writings:* Hunt, v, footnote to p. 105.

[5] Madison to Jefferson, Feb. 19, 1788; *ib.*, 103.

Lamb that "Four-fifths of our inhabitants are opposed to the new scheme of government"; and he added that south of the James River "I am confident nine-tenths are opposed to it." [1]

That keen and ever-watchful merchant, Minton Collins, thus reported to the head of his commercial house in Philadelphia: "The New Federal Constitution will meet with much opposition in this State [Virginia] for many pretended patriots has taken a great deal of pains to poison the minds of the people against it. . . . There are two Classes here who oppose it, the one is those who have power & are unwilling to part with an atom of it, & the others are the people who owe a great deal of money, and are very unwilling to pay, as they are afraid this Constitution will make them *Honest Men* in spite of their teeth." [2]

And now the hostile forces are to meet in final and decisive conflict. Now, at last, the new Constitution is to be really *debated;* and debated openly before the people and the world. For the first time, too, it is to be opposed in argument by men of the highest order in ability, character, and standing — men who cannot be hurried, or bullied, or shaken, or bought. The debates in the Virginia Convention of 1788 are the only masterful discussions on *both* sides of the controversy that ever took place.

While the defense of the Constitution had been very able in Pennsylvania and Massachusetts (and

[1] Henry to Lamb, June 9, 1788; Henry, ii, 342.

[2] Minton Collins to Stephen Collins, March 16, 1788; Collins MSS., Lib. Cong.

later in New York was to be most brilliant), the attack upon it in the Virginia Convention was nowhere equaled or approached in power, learning, and dignity. Extravagant as the assertion appears, it nevertheless is true that the Virginia contest was the only real *debate* over the whole Constitution. It far surpassed, especially in presenting the reasons against the Constitution, the discussion in the Federal Convention itself, in weight of argument and attractiveness of presentation, as well as in the ability and distinction of the debaters.

The general Federal Convention that framed the Constitution at Philadelphia was a secret body; and the greatest pains were taken that no part of its proceedings should get to the public until the Constitution itself was reported to Congress. The Journals were confided to the care of Washington and were not made public until many years after our present Government was established. The framers of the Constitution ignored the purposes for which they were delegated; they acted without any authority whatever; and the document, which the warring factions finally evolved from their quarrels and dissensions, was revolutionary.[1] This capital fact

[1] Even Hamilton admitted this. "The framers of it [the Constitution] will have to encounter the disrepute of having brought about a revolution in government, without substituting anything that was worthy of the effort; they pulled down one Utopia, it will be said, to build up another." (Hamilton to Washington, Sept., 1788; Hamilton's *Works:* Lodge, ix, 444; and also in Jefferson, *Writings:* Ford, xi, footnote to 330.) Martin Van Buren describes the action of the Federal Convention that framed the Constitution, in "having . . . set aside the instructions of Congress by making a new Constitution . . . an heroic but lawless act." (Van Buren, 49–50.)

Professor Burgess does not overstate the case when he declares :

requires iteration, for it is essential to an understanding of the desperate struggle to secure the ratification of that then unpopular instrument.

"Not one legislature in the United States had the most distant idea when they first appointed members for a [Federal] convention, entirely commercial . . . that they would without any warrant from their constituents, presume on so bold and daring a stride," truthfully writes the excitable Gerry of Massachusetts in his bombastic denunciation of "the fraudulent usurpation at Philadelphia."[1] The more reliable Melancton Smith of New York testifies that "previous to the meeting of the Convention the subject of a new form of government had been little thought of and scarcely written upon at all. . . . The idea of a government similar to" the Constitution "never entered the minds of the legislatures who appointed the Convention and of but very few of the members who composed it, until they had assembled and heard it proposed in that body."[2]

"Had the idea of a total change [from the Confederation] been started," asserts the trustworthy Richard Henry Lee of Virginia, "probably no state would have appointed members to the Convention. . . . Probably not one man in ten thousand in the United States . . . had an idea that the old ship [Confederation] was to be destroyed. Pennsylvania

"Had Julius or Napoleon committed these acts [of the Federal Convention in framing and submitting the Constitution], they would have been pronounced *coups d'état*." (Burgess, i, 105.)

Also see Beard: *Econ. I. C.*, 217–18.

[1] Ford: *P. on C.*, 14. [2] *Ib.*, 100–01.

appointed principally those men who are esteemed aristocratical. . . . Other States . . . chose men principally connected with commerce and the judicial department." Even so, says Lee, "the non-attendance of eight or nine men" made the Constitution possible. "We must recollect, how disproportionately the democratic and aristocratic parts of the community were represented" in this body.[1]

This "child of fortune,"[2] as Washington called the Constitution, had been ratified with haste and little or no discussion by Delaware, New Jersey, Connecticut, and Georgia. The principal men in the first three Commonwealths felt that the Constitution gave those States large commercial advantages and even greater political consequence;[3] and Georgia, with so small a population as to be almost negligible, felt the need of some strong Government to defend her settlers against the Indians. It is doubtful whether many of the people of these four States had read the Constitution or had heard much about it, except that, in a general way, they were to be better off under the new than under the old arrangement.

[1] Ford: *P. on C.*, 284-85. And see Jameson, 40-49.

[2] Washington to Lafayette, Sept. 18, 1788; *Writings:* Sparks, ix, 265.

[3] Connecticut, New Jersey, and Delaware had practically no ports and, under the Confederation, were at the mercy of Massachusetts, New York, and Pennsylvania in all matters of trade. The Constitution, of course, remedied this serious defect. Also, these smaller States had forced the compromise by which they, with their comparatively small populations, were to have an equal voice in the Senate with New York, Pennsylvania, and Virginia, with their comparatively great populations. And therefore they would have practically equal weight in the law- and treaty-making power of the Government. This was the most formidable of the many rocks on which the Federal Convention all but broke up.

Their ratification carried no weight other than to make up four of the nine States necessary to set the new system in motion.

In other States its friends had whipped up all possible speed. Not a week had passed after the Federal Convention had laid the proposed Constitution before Congress when a resolution was introduced in the Legislature of Pennsylvania for the election, within five weeks,[1] of delegates to a State Convention to ratify the "New Plan." When its opponents, failing in every other device to delay or defeat it, refused to attend the sessions, thus breaking a quorum, a band of Constitutionalists "broke into their lodgings, seized them, dragged them though the streets to the State House and thrust them into the Assembly room with clothes torn and faces white with rage." And there the objecting members were forcibly kept until the vote was taken. Thus was the quorum made and the majority of the Legislature enabled to "pass" the ordinance for calling the Pennsylvania State Convention to ratify the National Constitution.[2] And this action was taken before the Legislature had even received from Congress a copy of that document.

[1] One proposition was to call the State Convention "within *ten* days." (See "Address of the Minority of the Pennsylvania Convention," in McMaster and Stone, 458.)

[2] *Ib.*, 3–4; and see *ib.*, 75. An excuse for these mob methods was that the Legislature previously had resolved to adjourn *sine die* on that very day. This would put off action until the next session. The Anti-Constitutionalists urged — with entire truthfulness — that even this delay would give the people too little time to inform themselves upon the "New Plan" of government, as it was called, which the Convention was to pass upon in the people's name. "Not one in twenty know anything about it." (Mr. Whitehall in debate in the Legislature; *ib.*, 32.)

The enemies in Pennsylvania of the proposed National Government were very bitter. They said that the Legislature had been under the yoke of Philadelphia — a charge which, indeed, appears to be true. Loud were the protests of the minority against the feverish haste. When the members of the Pennsylvania Convention, thus called, had been chosen and had finished their work, the Anti-Constitutionalists asserted that no fair election had really taken place because it "was held at so early a period and want of information was so great" that the people did not know that such an election was to be held; and they proved this to their own satisfaction by showing that, although seventy thousand Pennsylvanians were entitled to vote, only thirteen thousand of them really had voted and that the forty-six members of the Pennsylvania Convention who ratified the Constitution had been chosen by only sixty-eight hundred voters. Thus, they pointed out, when the State Convention was over, that the Federal Constitution had been ratified in Pennsylvania by men who represented less than one tenth of the voting population of the State.[1]

[1] McMaster and Stone, 459–60. This charge was wholly accurate. Both sides exerted themselves to carry the "election." The Anti-Constitutionalists declared that they stood for "the principles of the Revolution"; yet, asserts Graydon, who was at Reading at the time, they sought the support of the Tories; the country lawyers were opposed to the "New Plan" and agreed not "to practice or accept any office under the Constitution"; but the Constitutionalists promised "prothonotaryships, attorney generalships, chief justiceships, and what not," and the hostile attorneys "were tempted and did eat." Describing the spirit of the times, Graydon testifies that "pelf was a better goal than liberty and at no period in my recollection was the worship of Mammon more widely spread, more sordid and disgusting."

Everybody who wanted it had a military title, that of major being

Indeed, a supporter of the Constitution admitted that only a small fraction of the people did vote for members of the Pennsylvania State Convention; but he excused this on the ground that Pennsylvanians seldom voted in great numbers except in contested elections; and he pointed out that in the election of the Convention which framed the State's Constitution itself, only about six thousand had exercised their right of suffrage and that only a little more than fifteen hundred votes had been cast in the whole Commonwealth to elect Pennsylvania's first Legislature.[1]

The enemies of the proposed plan for a National Government took the ground that it was being rushed through by the "aristocrats"; and the "Independent Gazetteer" published "The humble address of the *low born* of the United States of America, to their fellow slaves scattered throughout the world," which sarcastically pledged that "we, the *low born*, that is,

"the very lowest that a dasher of any figure would accept." To "clap on a uniform and a pair of epaulettes, and scamper about with some militia general for a day or two" was enough to acquire the coveted rank. Thus, those who had never been in the army, but "had played a safe and calculating game" at home and "attended to their interests," were not only "the men of mark and consideration," but majors, colonels, and generals as well. (Graydon, 331–33.)

Noting, at a later time, this passion for military titles Weld says: "In every part of America a European is surprised at finding so many men with military titles . . . but no where . . . is there such a superfluity of these military personages as in the little town of Staunton; there is hardly a decent person in it . . . but what is a colonel, a major, or a captain." (Weld, i, 236–37.)

Such were the conditions in the larger towns when the members of the Pennsylvania Convention were chosen. The small vote cast seems to justify the charge that the country districts and inaccessible parts of the State did not even know of the election.

[1] McMaster and Stone, 503–04.

all the people of the United States, except 600 or thereabouts, *well born,*" would "allow and admit the said 600 *well born* immediately to establish and confirm this most noble, most excellent, and truly divine constitution." [1]

James Wilson, they said, had been all but mobbed by the patriots during the Revolution; he never had been for the people, but always "strongly tainted with the spirit of *high aristocracy.*" [2] Yet such a man, they declared, was the ablest and best person the Constitutionalists could secure to defend "that political monster, the proposed Constitution"; "a monster" which had emerged from "the thick veil of secrecy." [3]

When the Pennsylvania State Convention had assembled, the opponents of the Constitution at once charged that the whole business was being speeded by a "system of precipitancy." [4] They rang the changes on the secret gestation and birth of the Nation's proposed fundamental law, which, said Mr. Whitehill, "originates in mystery and must terminate in despotism," and, in the end, surely would annihilate the States.[5] Hardly a day passed that the minority did not protest against the forcing tactics of the majority.[6] While much ability was displayed on both sides, yet the debate lacked dignity, courtesy, judgment, and even information. So scholarly a man as Wilson said that "Virginia has

[1] McMaster and Stone, 173–74.

[2] *Independent Gazetteer; ib.*, 183–84.

[3] *Ib.*, 184–85.

[4] Pennsylvania Debates, in McMaster and Stone, 231. Elliott prints only a small part of these debates.

[5] *Ib.*, 283–85.

[6] *Ib.*, 219.

no bill of rights"; [1] and Chief Justice McKean, supported by Wilson, actually declared that none but English-speaking peoples ever had known trial by jury.[2]

"Lack of veracity," "indecent," "trifling," "contempt for arguments and person," were a few of the more moderate, polite, and soothing epithets that filled Pennsylvania's Convention hall throughout this so-called debate. More than once the members almost came to blows.[3] The galleries, filled with city people, were hot for the Constitution and heartened its defenders with cheers. "This is not the voice of the people of Pennsylvania," shouted Smilie, denouncing the partisan spectators. The enemies of the Constitution would not be "intimidated," he dramatically exclaimed, "were the galleries filled with bayonets." [4] The sarcastic McKean observed in reply that Smilie seemed "mighty angry, merely because somebody was pleased." [5]

Persons not members of the Convention managed to get on the floor and laughed at the arguments of those who were against the Constitution. Findley was outraged at this "want of sense of decency and order." [6] Justice McKean treated the minority with contempt and their arguments with derision. "*If the sky falls, we shall catch larks; if the rivers run dry, we shall catch eels*," was all, said this conciliatory

[1] McMaster and Stone, 253.

[2] Findley covered them with confusion in this statement by citing authority. Wilson irritably quoted in retort the words of Maynard to a student: "Young Man! I have forgotten more law than ever you learned." (*Ib.*, 352–64.)

[3] *Ib.*, 361–63.

[4] *Ib.*, 365.

[5] *Ib.*

[6] *Ib.*, 419.

advocate of the Constitution, that its enemies' arguments amounted to; they made nothing more than a sound "like *the working of small beer.*"[1]

The language, manners, and methods of the supporters of the Constitution in the Pennsylvania Convention were resented outside the hall. "If anything could induce me to oppose the New Constitution," wrote a citizen signing himself "Federalist," "it would be the indecent, supercilious carriage of its advocates towards its opponents."[2]

While the Pennsylvania State Convention was sitting, the Philadelphia papers were full of attacks and counter-attacks by the partisans of either side, some of them moderate and reasonable, but most of

[1] McMaster and Stone, 365.

[2] *Ib.*, 453. The conduct of the Pennsylvania supporters of the Constitution aroused indignation in other States, and caused some who had favored the new plan of government to change their views. "On reception of the Report of the [Federal] Convention, I perused, and admir'd it; — Or rather, like many who still *think* they admire it, I loved Geo. Washington — I venerated Benj. Franklin — and therefore concluded that I must love and venerate all the works of their hands; — . . . . The honest and uninformed *freemen* of America entertain the same opinion of those two gentlemen as do European *slaves* of their Princes, — '*that they can do no wrong.*'"

But, continues Wait, "on the unprecedented Conduct of the Pennsylvania Legislature [and Convention] I found myself Disposed to lend an ear to the arguments of the opposition — not with an expectation of being convinced that the new Constitution was defective; but because I thought the minority had been ill used; and I felt a little curious to hear the particulars," with the result that "I am dissatisfied with the proposed Constitution." (Wait to Thatcher, Jan. 8, 1788; *Hist. Mag.* (2d Series), vi, 262; and see *infra.*)

Others did not, even then, entertain Mr. Wait's reverence for Washington, when it came to accepting the Constitution because of his support. When Hamilton asked General Lamb how he could oppose the Constitution when it was certain that his "good friend Genl. Washington would . . . be the first President under it," Lamb "reply'd that . . . after him Genl. Slushington might be the next or second president." (Ledlie to Lamb; MS., N.Y. Hist. Soc.)

them irritating, inflammatory, and absurd. A well-written petition of citizens was sent to the Convention begging it to adjourn until April or May, so that the people might have time to inform themselves on the subject: "The people of Pennsylvania have not yet had sufficient time and opportunity afforded them for this purpose. The great bulk of the people, from the want of leisure from other avocations; their remoteness from information, their scattered situation, and the consequent difficulty of conferring with each other" did not understand the Constitution, declared this memorial.

"The unaccountable zeal and precipitation used to hurry the people into premature decision" had excited and alarmed the masses, "and the election of delegates was rushed into before the greater part of the people . . . knew what part to take in it." So ran the cleverly drawn indictment of the methods of those who were striving for ratification in Pennsylvania.[1] In the State Convention, the foes of the Constitution scathingly denounced to the very last the jamming-through conduct of its friends; and just before the final vote, Smilie dared them to adjourn that the sense of the people might be taken.[2]

Even such of the people as could be reached by the newspapers were not permitted to be enlightened by the Convention "debates"; for reports of them were suppressed.[3] Only the speeches of James Wilson and Chief Justice McKean, both ardent advocates of the Constitution, were allowed to be published.[4]

[1] McMaster and Stone, 432–35.
[2] *Ib.*, 424. [3] *Ib.*, 14–15. [4] *Ib.*

But although outnumbered two to one, cuffed and buffeted without mercy in debate, scoffed at and jeered at by the people of the Quaker City, the minority was stiff-necked and defiant. Their heads were "bloody but unbowed." Three days after the vote for ratification, forty-six "ayes" to twenty-three "nays," had been taken, the minority issued an address to their constituents.[1] It relates the causes which led to the Federal Convention, describes its members, sets forth its usurpation of power, details the efforts to get popular support for the Constitution even "whilst the gilded chains were forging in the secret conclave."

The address recounts the violence by which the State Convention was called, "not many hours" after the "New Plan" had "issued forth from the womb of suspicious secrecy"; and reaffirms the people's ignorance of the Constitution, the trifling vote, the indecorous, hasty, "insulting" debate. It gives the amendments asked for by the minority, and finally presents most if not all the arguments which before had been or since have been advanced against the Constitution, and especially the National principle which pervades it.

The powers given Congress would produce "one consolidated government, which, from the nature of things, will be an *iron handed despotism*"; the State Governments would be annihilated; the general welfare clause would justify anything which "*the will and pleasure* of congress" dictated; that National body, "with complete and unlimited power over

[1] "Address of the Minority"; McMaster and Stone, 454–83.

the *purse* and the *sword*," could [1] by taxation "command the whole or any part of the property of the people" — imposts, land taxes, poll taxes, excises, duties — every kind of tax on every possible species of property and written instrument could be laid by the "monster" of National power. By the Judiciary provided in the Constitution "the rich and wealthy suitors would eagerly lay hold of the infinite mazes, perplexities and delays . . . and the poor man being plunged in the bottomless pit of legal discussion" could not get justice.[2]

Two coördinate "sovereignties," State and National, "would be contrary to the nature of things"; the Constitution without a bill of rights "would of itself necessarily produce a despotism"; a standing army might be used to collect the most burdensome taxes and with it "an ambitious man . . . may step up into the throne and seize upon absolute power" [3] — such are the broad outlines of the document with which the undismayed enemies of the Constitution began their campaign against it among the people of Pennsylvania after the Convention had ratified it.

The wrath of the Pennsylvania foes of the Constitution fed and grew upon its own extravagance. The friends of the "New Plan" tried to hold a meeting in Carlisle to rejoice over its ratification; but the crowd broke up their meeting, wrecked their cannon, and burned the Constitution in the very bonfire which the Constitutionalists had prepared to celebrate its victory. Blows were struck and violence

[1] "Address of the Minority"; McMaster and Stone, 466.
[2] *Ib.*, 469–70.
[3] *Ib.*, 480.

done.[1] For almost a year, an Anti-Constitutionalist paper in Philadelphia kept up the bombardment of the Constitution and its advocates, its gunner being a writer signing himself "Centinel." [2] His ammunition was a mixture of argument, statement, charge, and abuse, wrapped up in cartridge paper of blistering rhetoric. The Constitution was, wrote "Centinel," a "spurious brat"; "the evil genius of darkness presided at its birth" and "it came forth under the veil of mystery." [3]

Should the small fraction of the people who had voted for the members of the Pennsylvania State Convention bind the overwhelming majority who had not voted, asked "Centinel." No, indeed! The people, wrote he with pen of gall, had nothing but contempt for the "solemn mummery" that had been acted in their name.[4] As to the citizens of Philadelphia, everybody understood, asserted "Centinel," that the "spirit of independency" was dead within *their* breasts; Philadelphia merchants, as was well known, were mere vassals to a commercial "colossus" (Robert Morris) who held the city in "thraldom." [5]

"Mankind in the darkest ages, have never been so insulted," cried "Centinel," as the men of Pennsylvania had been by this "flagrant . . . audacious . . .

[1] See various contemporary accounts of this riot reprinted in McMaster and Stone, 486–94.

[2] The authorship of the "Letters of Centinel" remains unsettled. It seems probable that they were the work of Eleazer Oswald, printer of the *Independent Gazetteer*, and one George Bryan, both of Philadelphia. (See *ib.*, 6–7, and footnote.)

[3] "Letters of Centinel," no. 4, *ib.*, 606.

[4] *Ib.*, 620.

[5] *Ib.*, 625.

conspiracy [the Constitution] against the liberties of a free people." [1] The whole thing, he declared, was a dastardly plot. The conspirators had disarmed the militia, kept out of the mails such newspapers as had dared to voice the "people's rights"; [2] and "all intercourse between the patriots of America is as far as possible cut off; whilst on the other hand the conspirators have the most exact information, a common concert is everywhere evident; they move in unison." [3]

The Constitutionalists were not content with their vile work in thrusting upon Pennsylvania "the empire of delusion," charged "Centinel," [4] but their agents were off for Virginia to do the like there.[5] The whole world knew, said he, that the Constitutionalists had rushed the Constitution through in Pennsylvania; [6] and that the "immaculate convention [that framed the Constitution] . . . contained a number of the principal public defaulters," [7] chief of whom was Robert Morris, who, though a bankrupt in the beginning of the Revolution, had, by "peculation and embezzlement of the public property," accumulated "the immense wealth he has dazzled the world with since." [8]

If only the address of Pennsylvania's heroic minority, "Centinel" lamented, had reached Boston in time, it would "have enabled patriotism to triumph" there; but, of course, the "*high born*" Constitutionalist managers of post-offices kept it back.[9] Was not

[1] McMaster and Stone, 624.
[2] *Ib.*, 630, 637, 639, 642, 653, 655.
[3] *Ib.*, 629. [4] *Ib.*, 641. [5] *Ib.*, 631; and see *infra*, chap. XI.
[6] *Ib.*, 639. [7] *Ib.*, 658 [8] *Ib.*, 661. [9] *Ib.*, 667.

the scandal so foul, asked "Centinel," that, on the petition of Philadelphia printers, Pennsylvania's Legislature appealed to Congress against the suppression of the mails?[1] Of course Philadelphia was for "this system of tyranny"; but three fourths of the people in the eastern counties and nineteen twentieths of those in the middle, northern, and western counties were against it.[2]

The grape and canister which its enemies poured upon the Constitution and its friends in Pennsylvania brought an answering fire. The attacks, said the Constitutionalists, had been written by "hireling writers" and "sowers of sedition"; their slanders showed "what falsehoods disappointed ambition is capable of using to impose upon the public." According to the Constitutionalists, their opponents were "incendiaries" with "infamous designs."[3] "If every lie was to be punished by clipping, as in the case of other forgeries, not an ear would be left amongst the whole party," wrote a Constitutionalist of the conduct of the opposition.[4]

But the Constitutionalists were no match for their enemies in the language of abuse, recklessness in making charges, or plausibility in presenting their case. Mostly they vented their wrath in private correspondence, which availed nothing. Yet the letters of business men were effective in consolidating the commercial interests. Also they illuminate the situation.

[1] McMaster and Stone, 667. [2] *Ib.*, 668.

[3] "A Real Patriot," in *Independent Gazetteer*, reprinted in McMaster and Stone, 524.

[4] "Gomes," in *ib.*, 527.

"That restless firebrand, the Printer of your city [Oswald, editor of the "Independent Gazetteer"], is running about as if driven by the Devil," wrote a New York merchant to a Philadelphia business correspondent, "seemingly determined to do all the mischief he can; indeed, in my opinion he is an actual incendiary & ought to be the object of legal restraint. He is in his own person a strong argument of the necessity of speedily adopting the new System & putting it into immediate motion." [1]

And "firebrands," indeed, the Anti-Constitutionalists prove themselves in every possible way.

Madison was alarmed. He writes to Jefferson that the "minority . . . of Pennsylvania has been extremely intemperate and continues to use very bold and menacing language." [2] Little did Madison then foresee that the very men and forces he now was fighting were laying the foundation for a political party which was to make him President. Far from his thought, at this time, was the possibility of that antipodal change which public sentiment and Jefferson's influence wrought in him two years later. When the fight over the Constitution was being waged, there was no more extreme Nationalist in the whole country than James Madison.

So boiled the stormy Pennsylvania waters through which the Constitution was hastened to port and such was the tempest that strained its moorings after it was anchored in the harbor of ratification.

In Massachusetts, "all the men of abilities, of

[1] H. Chapman to Stephen Collins, June 20, 1788; MS., Lib. Cong. Oswald, like Thomas Paine, was an Englishman.

[2] Madison to Jefferson, Feb. 19, 1788; *Writings:* Hunt, v, 102.

property and of influence,"[1] were quite as strong for the Constitution as the same class in Pennsylvania; but, impressed by the revolt against the tactics of hurry and force which the latter had employed, the Constitutionalists of the Bay State took an opposite course. Craft, not arrogance, was their policy. They were "wise as serpents," but appeared to be "as harmless as doves." Unlike the methods of the Pennsylvania Constitutionalists, they were moderate, patient, conciliatory, and skillful. They put up Hancock for President of the Convention, in order, as they said, "that we might have advantage of [his] . . . name — whether capable of attending or not."[2]

The Massachusetts adversaries of the Constitution were without a leader. Among them "there was not a single character capable of uniting their wills or directing their measures."[3] Their inferiority greatly impressed Madison, who wrote to Pendleton that "there was scarce a man of respectability" among them.[4] They were not able even to state their own case.

[1] Madison to Jefferson, Feb. 19, 1788; *Writings:* Hunt, v, 101.

[2] Gore to Thatcher, June 9, 1788; *Hist. Mag.* (2d Series), vi, 263. This was a very shrewd move; for Hancock had not yet been won over to the Constitution; he was popular with the protesting delegates, and perhaps could not have been defeated had they made him their candidate for presiding officer; the preferment flattered Hancock's abnormal vanity and insured the Constitutionalists against his active opposition; and, most of all, this mark of their favor prepared the way for the decisive use the Constitutionalist leaders finally were able to make of him. Madison describes Hancock as being "weak, ambitious, a courtier of popularity, given to low intrigue." (Madison to Jefferson, Oct. 17, 1788; *Writings:* Hunt, v, 270.)

[3] Madison to Jefferson, Feb. 19, 1788; *Writings:* Hunt, v, 101.

[4] Madison to Pendleton, Feb. 21, 1788; *ib.*, 108.

"The friends of the Constitution, who in addition to their own weight . . . represent a very large proportion of the good sense and property of this State, have the task not only of answering, but also of stating and bringing forward the objections of their opponents," wrote King to Madison.[1] The opponents admitted this themselves. Of course, said they, lawyers, judges, clergymen, merchants, and educated men, all of whom were in favor of the Constitution, could make black look white; but "if we had men of this description on our side" we could run these foxes to earth.[2] Mr. Randall hoped "that these great men of eloquence and learning will not try to *make* arguments to make this Constitution go down, right or wrong. . . . It takes the best men in this state to gloss this Constitution. . . . Suppose . . . these great men would speak half as much against it, we might complete our business and go home in forty-eight hours." [3]

The election of members to the Massachusetts Convention had shown widespread opposition to the proposed establishment of a National Government. Although the Constitutionalists planned well and worked hard, some towns did not want to send delegates at all; forty-six towns finally refused to do so and were unrepresented in the Convention.[4] "Bidde-

[1] King to Madison, Jan. 27, 1788; King, i, 316.

[2] *Ib.*, 317.

[3] Elliott, ii, 40.

[4] Harding, 48. These towns were bitterly opposed to the Constitution. Had they sent delegates, Massachusetts surely would have rejected the Constitution; for even by the aid of the deal hereafter described, there was a very small majority for the Constitution. And if Massachusetts had refused to ratify it, Virginia would, beyond the possibility of a doubt, have rejected it also. (See *infra*, chaps. x,

ford has backsliden & fallen from a state of Grace to a state of nature, met yesterday & a dumb Devil seized a Majority & they voted not to send, & when called on for a Reason they were dumb, *mirabile dictu!*" [1] King Lovejoy was chosen for Vassalborough; but when the people learned that he would support the Constitution they "called another Meeting, turned him out, & chose another in his room who was desidedly against it." [2]

The division among the people in one county was: "The most reputable characters . . . on . . . *the right* side [for the Constitution] . . . but the middling & common sort . . . on the opposite"; [3] and in another county "the Majority of the Common people" were opposed,[4] which seems to have been generally true throughout the State. Of the sentiment in Worcester, a certain E. Bangs wrote: "I could give you but a very disagreeable account: The most of them entertain such a dread of arbitrary power, that they are afraid even of limited authority. . . . Of upwards of 50 members from this county not more than 7 or 8 delegates are" for the Constitution, "& yet some of them are good men — Not all [Shays's] insurgents I assure you." [5]

Judge Sewall reported from York that the dele-

xi, and xii.) And such action by Massachusetts and Virginia would, with absolute certainty, have doomed the fundamental law by which the Nation to-day exists. Thus it is that the refusal of forty-six Massachusetts towns to send representatives to the State Convention changed the destiny of the Republic.

[1] Hill to Thatcher, Dec. 12, 1787; *Hist. Mag.* (2d Series), vi, 259.

[2] Lee to Thatcher, Jan. 23, 1788; *ib.*, 266–67.

[3] *Ib.*, 267.

[4] *Ib.*

[5] Bangs to Thatcher, Jan. 1, 1788; *Hist. Mag.* (2d Series), vi, 260.

gates there had been chosen "to Oppose the Business. . . . Sanford had one meeting and Voted not to Send any — But Mr. S. come down full charged with Gass and Stirred up a 2nd Meeting and procured himself Elected, and I presume will go up charged like a Baloon." [1] Nathaniel Barrell of York, a successful candidate for the Massachusetts Convention, "behaved so indecently before the Choice, as extorted a severe Reprimand from Judge Sewall, and when chosen modestly told his Constituents, he would sooner loose his Arm than put his Assent to the new proposed Constitution, it is to be feared many of his Brethern are of his mind." [2]

Barrell explained to Thatcher: "I see it [the Constitution] pregnant with the fate of our libertys . . . I see it entails wretchedness on my posterity — Slavery on my children; . . . twill not be so much for our advantage to have our taxes imposed & levied at the pleasure of Congress as [by] the method now pursued. . . . a Continental Collector at the head of a standing army will not be so likely to do us justice in collecting the taxes . . . I think such a Government impracticable among men with such high notions of liberty as we americans." [3]

The "Address of the Minority" of Pennsylvania's Convention had reached a few men in Massachusetts, notwithstanding the alleged refusal of the post-office to transmit it; and it did some execution. To Thomas B. Wait it "was like the Thunder of Sinai —

[1] Sewall to Thatcher, Jan. 5, 1788; *Hist. Mag.* (2d Series), vi, 260–61.
[2] Savage to Thatcher, Jan. 11, 1788; *ib.*, 264.
[3] Barrell to Thatcher, Jan. 15, 1788; *ib.*, 265.

its lightenings were irresistible" to him. He deplored the "darkness, duplicity and studied ambiguity . . . running thro' the whole Constitution," which, to his mind, made it certain that "as it now stands but very few individuals do or ever will understand it. . . . The vast Continent of America cannot long be subjected to a Democracy if consolidated into one Government — you might as well attempt to rule Hell by Prayer."[1]

Christopher Gore condensed into one sentence the motives of those who favored the Constitution as the desire for "an honorable & efficient Govt. equal to the support of our national dignity — & capable of protecting the property of our citizens."[2]

The spirit of Shays's Rebellion inspired the opponents of the Constitution in Massachusetts. "Many of the [Shays's] insurgents are in the Convention," Lincoln informed Washington; "even some of Shays's officers. A great proportion of these men are high in the opposition. We could hardly expect any thing else; nor could we . . . justly suppose that those men, who were so lately intoxicated with large draughts of liberty, and who were thirsting for more would . . . submit to a Constitution which would further take up the reins of Government, which, in their opinion, were too straight before."[3]

Out of three hundred and fifty-five members of

[1] Wait to Thatcher, Jan. 8, 1788; *Hist. Mag.* (2d Series), vi, 261. Wait was an unusually intelligent and forceful editor of a New England newspaper, the *Cumberland Gazette*. (*Ib.*, 258.)

[2] Gore to Thatcher, Dec. 30, 1787; *ib.*, 260.

[3] Lincoln to Washington, Feb. 3, 1788; *Cor. Rev.*: Sparks, iv, 206.

the Massachusetts Convention, one hundred and sixty-eight held out against the Constitution to the very last, uninfluenced by the careful, able, and convincing arguments of its friends, unmoved by their persuasion, unbought by their promises and deals.[1] They believed "that some injury is plotted against them — that the system is the production of the rich and ambitious," and that the Constitution would result in "the establishment of two orders in Society, one comprehending the opulent and great, the other the poor and illiterate." [2] At no time until they won over Hancock, who presided over the Massachusetts Convention, were the Constitutionalists sure that a majority was not against the new plan.

The struggle of these rude and unlearned Massachusetts men against the cultured, disciplined, powerful, and ably led friends of the Constitution in that State was pathetic. "Who, sir, is to pay the debts of the yeomanry and others?" exclaimed William Widgery. "Sir, when oil will quench fire, I will believe all this [the high-colored prophesies of the Constitutionalists] and not till then . . . I cannot see why we need, for the sake of a little meat, swallow a great bone, which, if it should happen to stick in our throats, can never be got out." [3]

Amos Singletary "wished they [the Constitutionalists] would not play round the subject with their fine stories like a fox round a trap, but come to it." [4] "These lawyers," said he, "and men of learning and moneyed men, that talk so finely, and gloss over

[1] See *infra*. [2] King to Madison, Jan. 27, 1788; King, i, 317.
[3] Elliott, ii, 105–06. [4] *Ib.*, 101.

matters so smoothly, to make us poor illiterate people swallow down the pill, expect to get into Congress themselves; they expect to be the managers of this Constitution, and get all the power and all the money, into their own hands, and then they will swallow up all us little folks like the great *Leviathan;* . . . yes, just as the whale swallowed up *Jonah.*" [1] Replying to the Constitutionalist argument that the people's representatives in Congress would be true to their constituents, Abraham White said that he "would not trust a 'flock of Moseses.'" [2]

The opposition complained that the people knew little or nothing about the Constitution — and this, indeed, was quite true. "It is strange," said General Thompson, "that a system which its planners say is so plain, *that he that runs may read it*, should want so much explanation." [3] "Necessity compelled them to hurry," [4] declared Widgery of the friends of the Constitution. "Don't let us go too fast. . . . Why all this racket?" asked the redoubtable Thompson.[5] Dr. John Taylor was sure that Senators "once chosen . . . are chosen forever."[6]

Time and again the idea cropped out of a National Government as a kind of foreign rule. "I beg the indulgence of this honorable body," implored Samuel Nason, "to permit me to make a short apostrophe to Liberty. O Liberty! thou greatest good! thou fairest property! with thee I wish to live — with thee I wish to die! Pardon me if I drop a tear on the peril to which she is exposed: I cannot, sir, see this

[1] Elliott, ii, 102.
[2] *Ib.*, 28.
[3] *Ib.*, 96.
[4] *Ib.*, 94.
[5] *Ib.*, 80.
[6] *Ib.*, 48.

brightest of jewels tarnished — a jewel worth ten thousand worlds; and shall we part with it so soon? O no."[1] And Mr. Nason was sure that the people would part with this brightest of jewels if the Constitution was adopted. As to a standing army, let the Constitutionalists recall Boston on March 5, 1770. "Had I a voice like Jove," cried Nason, "I would proclaim it throughout the world; and had I an arm like Jove, I would hurl from the globe those villains that would dare attempt to establish in our country a standing army."[2]

These "poor, ignorant men," as they avowed themselves to be, were rich in apostrophes. The reporter thus records one of General Thompson's efforts: "Here the general broke out in the following pathetic apostrophe: 'O my country, never give up your annual elections! Young men, never give up your jewel.'"[3] John Holmes showed that the Constitution gave Congress power to "institute judicatories" like "that diabolical institution, the *Inquisition*." "*Racks*," cried he, "and *gibbets*, may be amongst the most mild instruments of their [Congress's] discipline."[4] Because there was no religious test, Major Thomas Lusk "shuddered at the idea that Roman Catholics, Papists, and Pagans might be introduced into office, and that Popery and the Inquisition may be established in America":[5] and Singletary pointed out that under the Constitution a "Papist, or an Infidel, was as eligible as . . . a Christian."[6]

[1] Elliot, ii, 133.
[2] *Ib.*, 136–37.
[3] *Ib.*, 16.
[4] *Ib.*, 111.
[5] *Ib.*, 148.
[6] *Ib.*, 44.

Thus the proceedings dragged along. The overwhelming arguments of the advocates of the Constitution were unanswered and, apparently, not even understood by its stubborn foes. One Constitutionalist, indeed, did speak their language, a farmer named Jonathan Smith, whom the Constitutionalist managers put forward for that purpose. "I am a plain man," said Mr. Smith, "and get my living by the plough. I am not used to speak in public, but I beg leave to say a few words to my brother ploughjoggers in this house"; and Mr. Smith proceeded to make one of the most effective speeches of the Convention.[1] But all to no purpose. Indeed, the pleadings and arguments for the Constitution seemed only to harden the feeling of those opposed to it. They were obsessed by an immovable belief that a National Government would destroy their liberties; "and," testifies King, "a distrust of men of property or education has a more powerful effect upon the minds of our opponents than any specific objections against the Constitution."[2]

Finally, in their desperation, the Constitutionalist managers won Hancock,[3] whose courting of the insurgents in Shays's Rebellion had elected him Gov-

[1] Elliott, ii, 102–04. Mr. Thatcher made the best summary of the unhappy state of the country under the Confederation. (*Ib.*, 141–48.)

[2] King to Madison, Jan. 20, 1788; King, i, 314.

[3] Rives, ii, 524–25. "To manage the cause against them (the jealous opponents of the Constitution) are the present and late governor, three judges of the supreme court, fifteen members of the Senate, twenty-four among the most respectable of the clergy, ten or twelve of the first characters at the bar, judges of probate, high sheriffs of counties, and many other respectable people, merchants, &c., Generals Heath, Lincoln, Brooks, and others of the late army." (Nathaniel Gorham to Madison, quoted in *ib.*)

ernor. He had more influence with the opposition than any other man in New England. For the same reason, Governor Bowdoin's friends, who included most of the men of weight and substance, had been against Hancock. By promising the latter their support and by telling him that he would be made President if Washington was not,[1] the Constitutionalist leaders induced Hancock to offer certain amendments which the Massachusetts Convention should recommend to Congress along with its ratification of the Constitution. Hancock offered these proposals as his own, although they were drawn by the learned and scholarly Parsons.[2] Samuel Adams, hitherto silent, joined in this plan.

Thus the trick was turned and the Massachusetts Convention ratified the Constitution a few days later by a slender majority of nineteen out of a vote of three hundred and fifty-five.[3] But not without bitter protest. General Thompson remarked that "he could not say amen to them [the amendments], but they might be voted for by some men — he did not say Judases."[4] The deal by which the Constitutionalists won Hancock was suspected, it appears, for Dr. Charles Jarvis denied that "these amendments have been artfully introduced to lead to a decision

[1] "Hancock has committed himself in our favor. . . . You will be astonished, when you see the list of names that such an union of men has taken place on this question. Hancock will, hereafter, receive the universal support of Bowdoin's friends; *and we told him, that, if Virginia does not unite, which is problematical, he is considered as the only fair candidate for President*." (King to Knox, Feb. 1, 1788; King, i, 319. The italics are those of King.)

[2] *Ib.*, ii, 525.

[3] Elliott, ii, 178–81.

[4] *Ib.*, 140.

which would not otherwise be had." [1] Madison in New York, watching the struggle with nervous solicitude, thought that the amendments influenced very few members of the Massachusetts opposition because of "their objections being levelled against the very essence of the proposed Government." [2] Certainly, those who changed their votes for ratification had hard work to explain their conversion.

Nathaniel Barrell, who had pledged his constituents that he would part with his arm rather than vote for the "Slavery of my children," had abandoned his vow of amputation and decided to risk the future bondage of his offspring by voting for the Constitution. In trying to justify his softened heroism, he said that he was "awed in the presence of this august assembly"; he knew "how little he must appear in the eyes of those giants of rhetoric, who have exhibited such a pompous display of declamation"; but although he did not have the "eloquence of Cicero, or the blaze of Demosthenian oratory," yet he would try to explain. He summarized his objections, ending with his wish that "this Constitution had not been, in some parts of the continent, hurried on, like the driving of Jehu, very furiously." So he hoped the Convention would adjourn, but if it would not — well, in that case, Mr. Barrell would brave the wrath of his constituents and vote for ratification with amendments offered by Hancock.[3]

[1] Elliott, ii, 153.
[2] Madison to Randolph, April 10, 1788; *Writings:* Hunt, v, 117.
[3] Elliott, ii, 159–61.

Just as the bargain with Hancock secured the necessary votes for the Constitution in the Massachusetts Convention, so did the personal behavior of the Constitutionalists forestall any outbreak of protest after ratification. "I am at Last overcome," wrote Widgery, "by a majority of 19, including the president [Hancock] whose very Name is an Honour to the State, for by his coming in and offering Som Amendments which furnished many with Excuses to their Constituants, it was adopted to the great Joy of all Boston." [1] The triumphant Constitutionalists kept up their mellowing tactics of conciliation after their victory and with good results, as appears by Mr. Widgery's account.

The "great bone" which had been thrust into his throat had not stuck there as he had feared it would. The Constitutionalists furnished materials to wash it down. "After Taking a parting Glass at the Expense of the Trades men in Boston we Disolved"; [2] but not before the mollified Widgery announced that the Constitution "had been carried by a majority of wise and understanding men. . . . After expressing his thanks for the civility which the inhabitants of this town [Boston] have shown to the Convention, . . . he concluded by saying that he should support the . . . Constitution" with all his might.[3]

"One thing I mus menchen," relates Widgery, "the Gallerys was very much Crowded, yet on the Desition of so emportant a Question as the present you might have heard a Copper fall on the Gallery

[1] Widgery to Thatcher, Feb. 8, 1788; *Hist. Mag.* (2d Series), vi, 270.
[2] *Ib.*
[3] Elliott, ii, 218.

floor, their was Sush a profound Silance; on thirs Day we got throw all our Business and on Fry Day, there was a federal Ship Riged and fix^{d} on a Slead, hald by 13 Horses, and all Orders of Men Turn^{d} out and formed a procession in the following ordor Viz first the Farmers with the plow and Harrow Sowing grain, and Harrowing it in as they went Som in a Cart Brakeing and Swingeing Flax . . . Tradesmen of all sorts, . . . the Bakers [with] their Bread peal . . . the Federal Ship ful Riged . . . the Merchants . . . a nother Slead, Halled by 13 Horses on which was a Ship yard, and a Number of smaul Ships &c. on that. in this order thay march^{d} to the House of Each of their Delegates in the Town of Boston, and returned to Fanuels Aall where the Merchants gave them 3 or 4 Hogsheads of Punch and as much wine cake & cheese as they could make way with . . . one thing more Notwithstanding my opposition to the Constitution, and the anxiety of Boston for its adoption I most Tel you I was never Treated with So much politeness in my Life as I was afterwards by the Treadesmen of Boston Merchants & every other Gentleman." [1]

Thus did the Massachusetts Constitutionalists take very human and effective measures to prevent such revolt against the Constitution, after its ratification, as the haughty and harsh conduct of their Pennsylvania brothers had stirred up in the City and State of Brotherly Love. "The minority are in good temper," King advises Madison; "they have the

[1] Widgery to Thatcher, Feb. 8, 1788; *Hist. Mag.* (2d Series), vi, 270–71.

magnanimity to declare that they will devote their lives and property to support the Government." [1] While there was a little Anti-Constitutionalist activity among the people after the Convention adjourned, it was not virulent. Gerry, indeed, gave one despairing shriek over departing "liberty" which he was sure the Constitution would drive from our shores; but that lament was intended for the ears of New York. It is, however, notable as showing the state of mind of such Anti-Constitutionalists as the Constitution's managers had not taken pains to mollify.

Gerry feared the "Gulph of despotism. . . . On these shores freedom has planted her standard, diped in the purple tide that flowed from the veins of her martyred heroes" which was now in danger from "the deep-laid plots, the secret intrigues, . . . the bold effrontery" of those ambitious to be aristocrats, some of whom were "speculating for fortune, by sporting with public money." Only "a few, a very few [Constitutionalists] . . . were . . . defending their country" during the Revolution, said Gerry. "Genius, Virtue, and Patriotism seems to nod over the vices of the times . . . while a supple multitude are paying a blind and idolatrous homage to . . . those . . . who are endeavouring . . . to betray the people . . . into an acceptance of a most complicated system of government; marked on the one side with the *dark*, *secret* and *profound intrigues* of the statesman, long practised in the purlieus of despotism; and on the other, with the ideal projects

[1] King to Madison, Feb. 6, 1788; King, i, 320.

of *young ambition*, with its wings just expanded to soar to a summit, which imagination has painted in such gawdy colours as to intoxicate the *inexperienced votary* and send *him* rambling from State to State, to collect materials to construct the ladder of preferment." [1]

Thus protested Gerry; but if the people, in spite of his warnings, *would* "give their voices for a voluntary dereliction of their privileges" — then, concluded Gerry, "while the statesman is plodding for power, and the courtier practicing the arts of dissimulation without check — while the rapacious are growing rich by oppression, and fortune throwing her gifts into the lap of fools, let the sublimer characters, the philosophic lovers of freedom who have wept over her exit, retire to the calm shades of contemplation, there they may look down with pity on the inconsistency of human nature, the revolutions of states, the rise of kingdoms, and the fall of empires." [2]

Such was the resistance offered to the Constitution in Massachusetts, such the debate against it, the management that finally secured its approval with recommendations by that Commonwealth,[3] and the after effects of the Constitutionalists' tactics.

[1] Gerry, in Ford: *P. on C.*, 1–23.

[2] *Ib.*, 23. When a bundle of copies of Gerry's pamphlet was received by the New York Anti-Constitutionalists in Albany County, they decided that it was "in a style too sublime and florid for the common people in this part of the country." (*Ib.*, 1.)

[3] During the debates the *Boston Gazette* published the following charge that bribery was being employed to get votes for the Constitution: —

BRIBERY AND CORRUPTION ! ! !

"The most diabolical plan is on foot to corrupt the members of the Convention, who oppose the adoption of the new Constitution. Large

In New Hampshire a majority of the Convention was against the Constitution. "Almost every man of property and abilities . . . [was] for it," wrote Langdon to Washington; but "a report was circulated . . . that the liberties of the people were in danger, and the great men . . . were forming a plan for themselves; together with a thousand other absurdities, which frightened the people almost out of what little senses they had." [1]

Very few of the citizens of New Hampshire knew anything about the Constitution. "I was surprised to find . . . that so little information respecting the Constitution had been diffused among the people," wrote Tobias Lear. "The valuable numbers of *Pub-*

sums of money have been brought from a neighboring state for that purpose, contributed by the wealthy. If so, is it not probable there may be collections for the same accursed purpose nearer home? CENTINEL." (Elliott, ii, 51.)

The Convention appointed a committee to investigate (*ib.*); it found that the charge was based on extremely vague rumor. (Harding, 103.) There the matter appears to have been dropped.

More than eighty years afterward, Henry B. Dawson, the editor of the *Historical Magazine*, a scholar of standing, asserted, personally, in his publication: "It is very well known — indeed, the son and biographer of one of the great leaders of the Constitutionalists in New York has frankly admitted to us — that *enough members of the Massachusetts Convention were bought with money* from New York *to secure the ratification of the new system by Massachusetts.*" (*Hist. Mag.* (2d Series), vi, 268, footnote, referring to Savage's letter to Thatcher telling of the charge in the *Boston Gazette.*)

Professor Harding discredits the whole story. (Harding, 101–05.) It is referred to only as showing the excited and suspicious temper of the times.

[1] Langdon to Washington, Feb. 28, 1788; *Cor. Rev.*: Sparks, iv, 212. "At least three fourths of the property, and a large proportion of the abilities in the State are friendly to the proposed system. The opposition here, as has generally been the case, was composed of men who were involved in debt." (Lear to Washington, June 22, 1788; *ib.*, 224–25.)

lius are not known. . . . The debates of the Pennsylvania and Massachusetts Conventions have been read by but few persons; and many other pieces, which contain useful information have never been heard of."[1]

When the New Hampshire Convention assembled, "a great part of whom had positive instructions to vote against it," the Constitutionalists, after much argument and persuasion, secured an adjournment on February 22 until June.[2] Learning this in New York, nine days later, Madison wrote Pendleton that the adjournment had been "found necessary to prevent a rejection."[3] But, "notwithstanding our late Disappointments and Mortification," the New Hampshire Constitutionalists felt that they would win in the end and "make the people happy in spight of their teeth."[4]

When, therefore, Virginia's great Convention met on June 2, 1788, the Nation's proposed fundamental law had not received deliberate consideration in any quarter; nor had it encountered weighty debate from those opposed to it. New York's Convention was not to assemble until two weeks later and that State was known to be hostile. The well-arranged plan was working to combine the strength of the leading enemies of the Constitution in the various States so that a new Federal Convention should be called.[5]

[1] Lear to Washington, June 2, 1788; *Cor. Rev.*: Sparks, iv, 220.

[2] Langdon to King, Feb. 23, 1788; King, i, 321–22.

[3] Madison to Pendleton, March 3, 1788 (*Writings:* Hunt, v, 110), and to Washington, March 3, 1788 (*ib.*, 111); and to Randolph; March 3, 1788 (*ib.*, 113).

[4] Langdon to King, May 6, 1788; King, i, 328.

[5] Washington to Lafayette, Feb. 7, 1788; *Writings:* Ford, xi, 220.

"Had the influence of character been removed, the intrinsic merits of the instrument [Constitution] would not have secured its adoption. Indeed, it is scarcely to be doubted, that in some of the adopting States, a majority of the people were in the opposition," writes Marshall many years afterwards in a careful review of the thorny path the Constitution had had to travel.[1] Its foes, says Marshall, were "firmly persuaded that the cradle of the constitution would be the grave of republican liberty." [2]

In Virginia's Convention, the array of ability, distinction, and character on both sides was notable, brilliant, and impressive. The strongest debaters in the land were there, the most powerful orators, and some of the most scholarly statesmen. Seldom, in any land or age, has so gifted and accomplished a group of men contended in argument and discussion at one time and place. And yet reasoning and eloquence were not the only or even the principal weapons used by these giant adversaries. Skill in political management, craft in parliamentary tactics, intimate talks with the members, the downright "playing of politics," were employed by both sides. "Of all arguments that may be used at the convention," wrote Washington to Madison, more than four months before the Convention, "the most prevailing one . . . will be that nine states *at least* will have acceded to it." [3]

[1] Marshall, ii, 127. [2] *Ib.*
[3] Washington to Madison, Jan. 10, 1788; *Writings:* Ford, xi, 208

CHAPTER X

IN THE GREAT CONVENTION

There is no alternative between the adoption of it [the Constitution] and anarchy. (Washington.)

I look on that paper as the most fatal plan that could possibly be conceived to enslave a free people. (Henry.)

More, much more, went forward in the Virginia struggle than appeared upon the surface. Noble as was the epochal debate in Virginia's Constitutional Convention, it was not so influential on votes of the members as were other methods[1] employed by both sides. Very practical politicians, indeed, were these contending moulders of destiny.

Having in mind the Pennsylvania storm; with the picture before them of the delicate and skillful piloting by which alone the Constitution had escaped the rocks in the tempestuous Massachusetts seas; with the hurricane gathering in New York and its low thunders heard even from States that had ratified — the Virginia Constitutionalists took no chances, neglected no precaution. Throughout the country the Constitutionalists were now acting with disciplined dispatch.

Intelligence of the New Hampshire Convention, of their success in which the Constitutionalists finally had made sure, was arranged to be carried by swift riders and relays of horses across country to Hamilton in New York; and "any expense which you may incur will be cheerfully repaid," King

[1] Though "practical," these methods were honorable, as far as the improper use of money was concerned.

assured Langdon.[1] As to Virginia, Hamilton wrote Madison to send news of "*any decisive* question . . . if favorable . . . by an express . . . with pointed orders to make all possible diligence, by changing horses etc."; assuring Madison, as King did Langdon, that "all expense shall be thankfully and liberally paid." [2]

The Constitutionalists, great and small, in other States were watching Virginia's Convention through the glasses of an infinite apprehension. "I fear that overwhelming torrent, Patrick Henry," General Knox confided to King.[3] Even before Massachusetts had ratified, one Jeremiah Hill thought that "the fate of this Constitution and the political Salvation of the united States depend cheifly on the part that Virginia and this State [Massachusetts] take in the Matter." [4] Hamilton's lieutenant, King, while in Boston helping the Constitutionalists there, wrote to Madison: "You can with difficulty conceive the real anxiety experienced in Massachusetts concerning your decision." [5] "Our chance of success depends on you," was Hamilton's own despairing appeal to the then leader of the Southern Constitutionalists. "If you do well there is a gleam of hope; but certainly I think not otherwise." [6] The

[1] King to Langdon, June 10, 1788; King, i, 331.

[2] Hamilton to Madison, May 19, 1788; *Works:* Lodge, ix, 430. See also *ib.*, 432.

[3] Knox to King, June 19, 1788; King, i, 335.

[4] Hill to Thatcher, Jan. 1, 1788; *Hist. Mag.* (2d Series), vi, 261.

[5] King to Madison, May 25, 1788; King, i, 329.

[6] Hamilton to Madison, June 27, 1788; *Works:* Lodge, ix, 436. Virginia had ratified the Constitution two days before Hamilton wrote this letter, but the news did not reach New York until long afterward.

worried New York Constitutionalist commander was sure that Virginia would settle the fate of the proposed National Government. "God grant that Virginia may accede. The example will have a vast influence."[1]

Virginia's importance justified the anxiety concerning her action. Not only was the Old Dominion preëminent in the part she had taken in the Revolution, and in the distinction of her sons like Henry, Jefferson, and Washington, whose names were better known in other States than those of many of their own most prominent men; but she also was the most important State in the Confederation in population and, at that time, in resources. "Her population," says Grigsby, "was over three fourths of all that of New England; . . . not far from double that of Pennsylvania; . . . or from three times that of New York . . . over three fourths of all the population of the Southern States; . . . and more than a fifth of the population of the whole Union." [2]

The Virginia Constitutionalists had chosen their candidates for the State Convention with painstaking care. Personal popularity, family influence, public reputation, business and financial power, and everything which might contribute to their strength with the people, had been delicately weighed. The people simply would not vote against such men as Pendleton, Wythe, and Carrington; [3] and these and

[1] Hamilton to Madison, June 8, 1788; *Works:* Lodge, ix, 432–34.

[2] Grigsby, i, 8. About three eighths of Virginia's population were slaves valued at many millions of dollars.

[3] Grigsby, i, footnote to 50; also 32; and see examples given by Judge Scott, in Scott, 235–38.

others like them accordingly were selected by the Constitutionalists as candidates in places where the people, otherwise, would have chosen antagonists to the Constitution.

More than one fourth of the Virginia Convention of one hundred and seventy members had been soldiers in the Revolutionary War; and nearly all of them followed Washington in his desire for a strong National Government. Practically all of Virginia's officers were members of the Cincinnati; and these were a compact band of stern supporters of the "New Plan."[1] Some of the members had been Tories, and these were stingingly lashed in debate by Mason; but they were strong in social position, wealth, and family connections, and all of them were for the Constitution.[2]

No practical detail of election day had been overlooked by the Constitutionalists. Colonel William Moore wrote to Madison, before the election came off: "You know the disadvantage of being absent at elections. . . . I must therefore entreat and conjure you — nay, command you, if it were in my power — to be here."[3] The Constitutionalists slipped in members wherever possible and by any device.

Particularly in Henrico County, where Richmond was situated, had conditions been sadly confused. Edmund Randolph, then Governor of the State, who next to Washington was Virginia's most conspicuous delegate to the Federal Convention, had refused to sign the Constitution and was, therefore, popularly

[1] Grigsby, i, footnote to 36; and see 29, 62, 339.

[2] Henry, ii, 339; and Rowland, ii, 223 *et seq.*

[3] Rives, ii, 549.

supposed to be against it. October 17, 1787, he wrote a letter to the Speaker of the House of Delegates explaining his reasons for dissent. He approved the main features of the proposed plan for a National Government but declared that it had fatal defects, should be amended before ratification, a new Federal Convention called to pass upon the amendments of the various States, and, thereafter, the Constitution as amended again submitted for ratification to State Conventions.[1] Randolph, however, did not send this communication to the Speaker "lest in the diversity of opinion I should excite a contest unfavorable to that harmony with which I trust that great subject will be discussed." [2] But it was privately printed in Richmond and Randolph sent a copy to Washington. On January 3, 1788, the letter was published in the *Virginia Gazette* together with other correspondence. In an additional paragraph, which does not appear in Randolph's letter as reproduced in Elliott, he said that he would "regulate himself by the spirit of America" and that he would do his best to amend the Constitution prior to ratification, but if he could not succeed he would accept the "New Plan" as it stood.[3] But he had declared to Richard Henry Lee that "either a monarchy or aristocracy will be generated" by it.[4]

[1] Randolph to the Speaker of the House of Delegates, Oct. 10, 1787; Elliott, i, 482–91; also Ford: *P. on C.*, 261–76.

[2] Randolph to Page and others, Dec. 2, 1787; *American Museum*, iii, 61 *et seq.*

[3] *Ib.*

[4] Lee to Randolph, Oct. 16, 1787; Elliott, i, 503. Upon the publication of this correspondence a young Richmond attorney, Spencer Roane, the son-in-law of Patrick Henry, in an article signed "Plain

Thus Randolph to all appearances occupied middle ground. But, publicly, he was in favor of making strenuous efforts to amend the Constitution as a condition of ratification, and of calling a second Federal Convention; and these were the means by which the Anti-Constitutionalists designed to accomplish the defeat of the "New Plan." The opponents of the proposed National Government worked hard with Randolph to strengthen his resolution and he gave them little cause to doubt their success.[1]

But the Constitutionalists were also busy with the Governor and with greater effect. Washington wrote an adroit and persuasive letter designed to win him entirely over to a whole-hearted and unqualified advocacy of the Constitution. The question was, said Washington, the acceptance of the Constitution or "a dissolution of the Union." [2] Madison,

Dealer," published in the *Virginia Gazette*, attacked Randolph for inconsistency. "Good God! How can the first magistrate and father of a pure republican government . . . before his proposed plan of amendment has been determined upon, declare that he will accept a Constitution which is to beget a monarchy or an aristocracy? . . . Can he foretell future events? How else can he at this time discover what the 'spirit of America' is? . . . How far will this principle carry him? Why, . . . if the dominion of Shays, instead of that of the new Constitution, should be generally accepted, and become 'the spirit of America,' his Excellency would turn Shayite." (Plain Dealer to Randolph, Feb. 13, 1788; Ford: *Essays on the Constitution*, 385; also *Branch Hist. Papers*, 47.) Roane's letter is important as the first expression of his hostility to the Constitution. He was to become the determined enemy of Marshall; and, as the ablest judge of the Virginia Court of Appeals, the chief judicial foe of Marshall's Nationalism. (See vol. III of this work.)

[1] "The importunities of some to me in public and private are designed to throw me unequivocally and without condition, into the opposition." (Randolph to Madison, Feb. 29, 1788; Conway, 101.)

[2] Washington to Randolph, Jan. 8, 1788; *Writings:* Ford, XI, 204–06.

in a subtle mingling of flattery, argument, and insinuation, skillfully besought his "dear friend" Randolph to come out for the Constitution fully and without reserve. If only Randolph had stood for the Constitution, wrote Madison, "it would have given it a decided and unalterable preponderancy," and Henry would have been "baffled."

The New England opposition, Madison assured Randolph, was from "that part of the people who have a repugnance in general to good government . . . a part of whom are known to aim at confusion and are suspected of wishing a reversal of the Revolution. . . . Nothing can be further from your [Randolph's] views than the principles of the different sets of men who have carried on their opposition under the respectability of your name." [1]

Randolph finally abandoned all opposition and resolved to support the Constitution even to the point of resisting the very plan he had himself proposed and insisted upon; but nobody, with the possible exception of Washington, was informed of this Constitutionalist master-stroke until the Convention met; [2] and, if Washington knew, he kept the secret. Thus, although the Constitutionalists were not yet sure of Randolph, they put up no candidate against him in Henrico County, where the people were very much opposed to the Constitution. To

[1] Madison to Randolph, Jan. 10, 1788; *Writings:* Hunt, v, 79–84; and see same to same, Jan. 20, 1788 (*ib.*, 86–88); and March 3, 1788 (*ib.*, 113–14).

[2] "If he [Randolph] approves it at all, he will do it feebly." (Washington to Lafayette, April 28, 1788; *Writings:* Ford, xi, 255; and see Madison to Jefferson, April 22, 1788; *Writings:* Hunt, v, 121.)

have done so would have been useless in any event; for Randolph could have been elected almost unanimously if his hostility to the proposed Government had been more vigorous, so decided were the people's dislike and distrust of it, and so great, as yet, the Governor's popularity. He wrote Madison a day or two before the election that nothing but his personal popularity "could send me; my politicks not being sufficiently strenuous against the Constitution." [1] The people chose their beloved young Governor, never imagining that he would appear as the leading champion of the Constitution on the Convention floor and actually oppose amending it before ratification.[2]

But the people were not in the dark when they voted for the only candidate the Constitutionalists openly brought out in Henrico County. John Marshall was for the proposed National Government, outright and aboveboard. He was vastly concerned. We find him figuring out the result of the election in northern Virginia and concluding "that the question will be very nice." [3] Marshall had been made the Constitutionalist candidate solely because of his personal popularity. As it was, even the people's confidence in him barely had saved Marshall.

"Marshall is in danger," wrote Randolph; "but F. [Dr. Foushee, the Anti-Constitutionalist candidate] is not popular enough on other scores to be

[1] Randolph to Madison, Feb. 29, 1788; quoted in Conway, 101.

[2] "Randolph was still looked upon as an Anti-Federalist by the uninitiated." But his "position . . . was evidently no secret to Washington." (Rowland, ii, 210. See also *ib.*, 225, 227, 231.)

[3] *Ib.*

elected, altho' he is perfectly a Henryite."[1] Marshall admitted that the people who elected Randolph and himself were against the Constitution; and declared that he owed his own election to his individual strength with the people.[2] Thus two strong champions of the Constitution had been secured from an Anti-Constitutionalist constituency; and these were only examples of other cases.

The Anti-Constitutionalists, too, straining every nerve to elect their men, resorted to all possible devices to arouse the suspicions, distrust, and fears of the people. "The opposition to it [the Constitution] . . . is addressed more to the passions than to the reason," declared Washington.[3]

Henry was feverishly active. He wrote flaming letters to Kentucky that the Mississippi would be lost if the new plan of government were adopted.[4] He told the people that a religious establishment would be set up.[5] The Reverend John Blair Smith, President of Hampden Sidney College, declared that Henry "has descended to lower artifices and management . . . than I thought him capable of."[6] Writing to Hamilton of the activities of the opposition, Washington asserted that "their assiduity stands unrivalled";[7] and he informed Trumbull

[1] Randolph to Madison, Feb. 29, 1788; Conway, 101. [2] Scott, 160.

[3] Washington to Carter, Dec. 14, 1787; *Writings:* Ford, xi, footnote to 210.

[4] Smith to Madison, June 12, 1788; Rives, ii, footnote to p. 544.

[5] *Ib.* "The Baptist interest . . . are highly incensed by Henry's opinions and public speeches." (Randolph to Madison, Feb. 29, 1788; Conway, 101.)

[6] Smith to Madison, June 12, 1788; Rives, ii, 544.

[7] Washington to Hamilton, Nov. 10, 1787; *Writings:* Ford, xi, footnote to p. 181.

that "the opponents of the Constitution are indefatigable."[1]

"Every art that could inflame the passions or touch the interests of men have been essayed; — the ignorant have been told that should the proposed government obtain, their lands would be taken from them and their property disposed of; — and all ranks are informed that the prohibition of the Navigation of the Mississippi (their favorite object) will be a certain consequence of the adoption of the Constitution."[2]

Plausible and restrained Richard Henry Lee warned the people that "by means of taxes, the government may command the whole or any part of the subjects' property";[3] and that the Constitution "promised a large field of employment to military gentlemen, and gentlemen of the law; and in case the government shall be executed without convulsions, it will afford security to creditors, to the clergy, salary-men and others depending on money payments."[4]

Nor did the efforts of the Virginia opponents of a National establishment stop there. They spread

[1] Washington to Trumbull, Feb. 5, 1788; *Writings:* Ford, 212. From the first Washington attributed much of the opposition throughout the country to the fact that popular leaders believed that the new National Government would lessen their importance in their respective States. "The governors elect or to be elected, the legislators, with a long tribe of others whose political importance will be lessened if not annihilated" were, said Washington, against a strong central Government. (Washington to Knox, Feb. 3, 1787; Sparks, ix, 230; and see Graydon, 340.)

[2] Washington to Lincoln, April 2, 1788; *ib.*, xi, footnote to 239–40.

[3] "Letters of a Federal Farmer," no. 3; Ford: *P. on C.*, 301.

[4] *Ib.*, no. 5, 319.

the poison of personal slander also. "They have attempted to vilify & debase the characters who formed" the Constitution, complained Washington.[1] These cunning expedients on one side and desperate artifices on the other were continued during the sitting of the Virginia Convention by all the craft and guile of practical politics.

After the election, Madison reported to Jefferson in Paris that the Northern Neck and the Valley had elected members friendly to the Constitution, the counties south of the James unfriendly members, the "intermediate district" a mixed membership, with Kentucky divided. In this report, Madison counts Marshall fifth in importance of all Constitutionalists elected, and puts only Pendleton, Wythe, Blair, and Innes ahead of him.[2]

When the Convention was called to order, it made up a striking and remarkable body. Judges and soldiers, lawyers and doctors, preachers, planters, merchants, and Indian fighters, were there. Scarcely a field fought over during the long, red years of the Revolution but had its representative on that historic floor. Statesmen and jurists of three generations were members.[3]

From the first the Constitutionalists displayed better tactics and discipline than their opponents, just as they had shown greater skill and astuteness in selecting candidates for election. They arranged everything beforehand and carried their plans out

[1] Washington to Armstrong, April 25, 1788; *Writings:* Ford, xi, 252; and to Petit, Aug. 16, 1788; *ib.*, 300.

[2] Madison to Jefferson, April 22, 1788; *Writings:* Hunt, v, 120–22.

[3] Grigsby, i, 34–35; and footnote to 49.

with precision. For the important position of President of the Convention, they agreed on the venerable Chancellor, Edmund Pendleton, who was able, judicial, and universally respected. He was nominated by his associate, Judge Paul Carrington, and unanimously elected.[1]

In the same way, Wythe, who was learned, trusted, and beloved, and who had been the teacher of many members of the Convention, was made Chairman of the Committee of the Whole. The Anti-Constitutionalists did not dare to oppose either Pendleton or Wythe for these strategic places. They had made the mistake of not agreeing among themselves on strong and influential candidates for these offices and of nominating them before the Constitutionalists acted. For the first time in Virginia's history, a shorthand reporter, David Robertson, appeared to take down a stenographic report of the debates; and this innovation was bitterly resented and resisted by the opposition[2] as a Constitutionalist maneuver.[3] Marshall was appointed a member of the committee[4] which examined the returns of the elections of members and also heard several contested election cases.[5]

At the beginning the Anti-Constitutionalists did not decide upon a plan of action — did not carefully weigh their course of procedure. No sooner had rules been adopted, and the Constitution and official

[1] Grigsby, i, 64–66; and Elliott, iii, 1.

[2] Rowland, ii, 222.

[3] Henry, ii, 345. So angered were the Anti-Constitutionalists that they would not correct or revise Robertson's reports of their speeches. (*Ib.*)

[4] Elliott, iii, 1. [5] *Ib.*, 5–6; also, Journal of the Convention, 7–11.

documents relating to it laid before the Convention, than their second tactical mistake was made; and made by one of their very ablest and most accomplished leaders. When George Mason arose, everybody knew that the foes of the Constitution were about to develop the first move in their order of battle. Spectators and members were breathless with suspense. Mason was the author of Virginia's Constitution and Bill of Rights and one of the most honorable, able, and esteemed members of the Legislature.

He had been a delegate to the Federal Convention and, with Randolph, had refused to sign the Constitution. Sixty-two years old, his snow-white hair contrasting with his blazing dark eyes, his commanding stature clad in black silk, his full, clear voice deliberate and controlled, George Mason was an impressive figure as he stood forth to strike the first blow at the new ordinance of Nationality.[1] On so important a subject, he did not think any rules should prevent "the fullest and clearest investigation." God's curse would be small compared with "what will justly fall upon us, if from any sinister views we obstruct the fullest inquiry." The Constitution, declared Mason, should be debated, "clause by clause," before any question was put.[2]

[1] Grigsby, i, 69–70. In the descriptions of the dress, manners, and appearance of those who took part in the debate, Grigsby's account has been followed. Grigsby took infinite pains and gave many years to the gathering and verifying of data on these picturesque subjects; he was personally intimate with a large number of the immediate descendants of the members of the Convention and with a few who were eye-witnesses; and his reconstruction of the scenes in the Convention is believed to be entirely accurate.

[2] Elliott, iii, 3.

The Constitutionalists, keen-eyed for any strategic blunder of their adversaries, took instant advantage of Mason's bad generalship. Madison suavely agreed with Mason,[1] and it was unanimously resolved that the Constitution should be "discussed clause by clause through all its parts,"[2] before any question should be put as to the instrument itself or any part of it. Thus the opposition presented to the Constitutionalists the very method the latter wished for, and had themselves planned to secure, on their own initiative.[3] The strength of the foes of the proposed National Government was in attacking it as a whole; their weakness, in discussing its specific provisions. The danger of the Constitutionalists lay in a general debate on the large theory and results of the Constitution; their safety, in presenting in detail the merits of its separate parts.

While the fight over the Constitution was partly an economic class struggle, it was in another and a larger phase a battle between those who thought nationally and those who thought provincially. In hostile array were two central ideas: one, of a strong National Government acting directly on men; the other, of a weak confederated league merely suggesting action to States. It was not only an economic

[1] Mason's clause-to-clause resolve was, "contrary to his expectations, concurred in by the other side." (Madison to Washington, June 4, 1788; *Writings:* Hunt, v, footnote to 124.) And see Washington's gleeful report to the New York Constitutionalists of Mason's error: "This [Mason's resolve] was as unexpected as acceptable to the federalists, and their ready acquiescence seems to have somewhat startled the opposite side for fear they had committed themselves." (Washington to Jay, June 8, 1788; *Writings:* Ford, xi, 271.)

[2] Elliott, iii, 4.

[3] Grigsby, i, 77.

contest, but also, and even more, a conflict by those to whom "liberty" meant unrestrained freedom of action and speech, against those to whom such "liberty" meant tumult and social chaos.

The mouths of the former were filled with those dread and sounding words "despotism" and "arbitrary power"; the latter loudly denounced "enemies of order" and "foes of government." The one wanted no bits in the mouth of democracy, or, at most, soft ones with loose reins and lax hand; the other wished a stout curb, stiff rein, and strong arm. The whole controversy, on its popular side, resounded with misty yet stirring language about "liberty," "aristocracy," "tyranny," "anarchy," "licentiousness"; and yet "debtor," "creditor," "property and taxes," "payment and repudiation," were heard among the more picturesque and thrilling terms. In this fundamental struggle of antagonistic theories, the practical advantage for the hour was overwhelmingly with those who resisted the Constitution.

They had on their side the fears of the people, who, as has appeared, looked on all government with suspicion, on any vital government with hostility, and on a great central Government as some distant and monstrous thing, too far away to be within their reach, too powerful to be resisted, too high and exalted for the good of the common man, too dangerous to be tried. It was, to the masses, something new, vague, and awful; something to oppress the poor, the weak, the debtor, the settler; something to strengthen and enrich the already strong and opulent, the merchant, the creditor, the financial interests.

True, the people had suffered by the loose arrangement under which they now lived; but, after all, had not they and their "liberties" survived? And surely they would suffer even more, they felt, under this stronger power; but would they and their "liberties" survive its "oppression"? They thought not. And did not many of the ablest, purest, and most trusted public characters in the Old Dominion think the same? Here was ammunition and to spare for Patrick Henry and George Mason, Tyler and Grayson, Bland and Harrison — ammunition and to spare, with their guns planted on the heights, if they could center their fire on the Constitution as a single proposition.

But they had been sleeping and now awoke to find their position surrendered, and themselves compelled, if Mason's resolutions were strictly followed, to make the assault in piecemeal on detached parts of the "New Plan," many of which, taken by themselves, could not be successfully combated. Although they tried to recover their lost ground and did regain much of it, yet the Anti-Constitutionalists were hampered throughout the debate by this initial error in parliamentary strategy.[1]

And now the Constitutionalists were eager to push the fighting. The soldierly Lee was all for haste. The Anti-Constitutionalists held back. Mason protested "against hurrying them precipitately." Harrison said "that many of the members had not yet arrived."[2] On the third day, the Convention went

[1] For a discussion of this tactical blunder of the opponents of the Constitution, see Grigsby, i, 72.

[2] Elliott, iii, 4.

into committee of the whole, with the astute and venerable Wythe in the chair. Hardly had this brisk, erect little figure — clad in single-breasted coat and vest, standing collar and white cravat, bald, except on the back of the head, from which unqueued and unribboned gray hair fell and curled up from the neck[1] — taken the gavel before Patrick Henry was on his feet.

Henry moved for the reading of the acts by authority of which the Federal Convention at Philadelphia had met,[2] for they would show the work of that Convention to be illegal and the Constitution the revolutionary creature of usurped power. If Henry could fix on the advocates of stronger law and sterner order the brand of lawlessness and disorder in framing the very plan they now were championing, much of the mistake of yesterday might be retrieved.

But it was too late. Helped from his seat and leaning on his crutches, Pendleton was recognized by Wythe before Henry could get the eye of the chair to speak upon his motion; and the veteran jurist crushed Henry's purpose before the great orator could make it plain. "We are not to consider," said Pendleton, "whether the Federal Convention exceeded their powers." That question "ought not to influence our deliberations." Even if the framers of the Constitution had acted without authority, Virginia's Legislature afterwards had referred it to the people who had elected the present Convention to pass upon it.[3] Pendleton's brief

[1] Grigsby, i, 75. [2] Elliott, iii, 6. [3] *Ib.*

speech was decisive; [1] Henry withdrew his motion; the preamble and the first two sections of the first article of the Constitution were laid before the committee and the destiny-determining debate began.

The Constitutionalists, who throughout the contest never made a mistake in the men they selected to debate or the time when they should speak, had chosen skillfully the parliamentary artillerist to fire their opening gun. They did not wait for the enemy's attack, but discharged the first shot themselves. Quickly there arose a broad, squat, ungainly man, "deformed with fat," shaggy of brow, bald of head, gray-eyed, with a nose like the beak of an eagle, and a voice clear and emotionless.[2] George Nicholas had been a brave, brilliant soldier and was one of the ablest and best-equipped lawyers in the State. He was utterly fearless, whether in battle on the field or in debate on the floor. His family and connections were powerful. In argument and reasoning he was the equal if not the superior of Madison himself; and his grim personality made the meek one of Madison seem tender in comparison. Nothing could disconcert him, nothing daunt his cold courage. He probably was the only man in the Convention whom Henry feared.[3]

Nicholas was glad, he said, that the Convention was to act with the "fullest deliberation." First he thrust at the method of the opposition to influence members by efforts outside the Convention itself; and went on with a clear, logical, and informed exposition of the sections then under consideration.

[1] Grigsby, i, 77. [2] *Ib.*, 79. [3] *Ib.*, 78, 79, 140, 141, 246, 247.

He ended by saying "that he was willing to trust his own happiness, and that of his posterity, to the operation of that system." [1]

The Constitution's enemies, thus far out-pointed by its perfectly trained and harmonious supporters, could delay no longer. Up rose the idol and champion of the people. Although only fifty-two years old, he had changed greatly in appearance since the days of his earlier triumphs. The erect form was now stooped; spectacles now covered the flashing eyes and the reddish-brown hair was replaced by a wig, which, in the excitement of speech, he frequently pushed this way and that. But the wizard brain still held its cunning, the magic tongue which, twenty-three years ago had trumpeted Independence, still wrought its spell.[2] Patrick Henry began his last great fight.

What, asked Henry, were the reasons for this change of government? A year ago the public mind was "at perfect repose"; now it was "uneasy and disquieted." "A wrong step now . . . and our republic may be lost." It was a great consolidated Government that the Constitutionalists proposed, solemnly asserted Henry. What right, he asked, had the framers of the Constitution to say, "*We, the people*, instead of *We, the states*"? He demanded the cause of that fundamental change. "Even from that illustrious man [Washington] who saved us by his valor, I would have a reason for his conduct." The Constitution-makers had no authority except to amend the old system under which the people were

[1] Elliott, iii, 7–21. [2] Grigsby. i. 76.

getting along very well. Why had they done what they had no power to do? [1]

Thus Henry put the Constitutionalists on the defensive. But they were ready. Instantly, Randolph was on his feet. He was thirty-seven years of age, fashioned on noble physical lines, with handsome face and flowing hair. His was one of Virginia's most distinguished families, his connections were influential, and he himself was the petted darling of the people. His luxuriant mind had been highly trained, his rich and sonorous voice gave an added charm to his words.[2] He was the ostensible author[3] of the plan on the broad lines of which the Constitution finally had been built. His refusal to sign it because of changes which he thought necessary, and his conversion to the extreme Constitutionalist position, which he now, for the first time, was fully to disclose, made him the strongest single asset the Constitutionalists had acquired. Randolph's open, bold, and, to the public, sudden championship of the Constitution was the explosion in the opposition's camp of a bomb which they had hoped and believed their own ammunition.

Never before, said Randolph, had such a vast event come to a head without war or force. It might well be feared that the best wisdom would be unequal to the emergency and that passion might prevail over reason. He warned the opposition that the chair "well knows what is order, how to command obedience, and that political opinions may be as

[1] Elliott, iii, 21–23. [2] Grigsby, i, 83–84.

[3] Madison was the real designer of the Virginia plan. (Rives, ii, chap. xxvii.)

honest on one side as on the other." Randolph then tried to explain his change. "I had not even the glimpse of the genius of America," said he of his refusal to sign the report of the Federal Convention. But it was now so late that to insist on amendments before ratification would mean "inevitable ruin to the Union";[1] and he would strike off his arm rather than permit that.

Randolph then reviewed the state of the country under the Confederation: Congress powerless, public credit ruined, treaties violated, prices falling, trade paralyzed, "and justice trampled under foot." The world looks upon Americans "as little wanton bees, who had played for liberty, but had no sufficient solidity or wisdom" to keep it. True, the Federal Convention had exceeded its authority, but there was nothing else to be done. And why not use the expression "We, the people"? Was the new Government not for them? The Union is now at stake, and, exclaimed he, "I am a friend to the Union."[2]

The secret was out, at last; the Constitutionalists' *coup* was revealed. His speech placed Randolph openly and unreservedly on their side. "The Governor has . . . thrown himself fully into the federal scale," gleefully reported the anxious Madison to the supreme Nationalist chieftain at Mount Vernon.[3]

[1] This was the point Washington had made to Randolph. It is interesting that, throughout the debate, Randolph, over and over again, used almost the exact language of Washington's letter.

[2] Elliott, iii, 23–29. Randolph's speech was apologetic for his change of heart. He was not "a candidate for popularity": he had "satisfied his conscience," etc.

[3] Madison to Washington, June 4, 1788; *Writings:* Hunt, v, 124.

"The G[overno]r exhibited a curious spectacle to view. Having refused to sign the paper [the Constitution] everybody supposed him against it," was Jefferson's comment on Randolph's change of front.[1] Washington, perfectly informed, wrote Jay in New York that "Mr. Randolph's declaration will have considerable effect with those who had hitherto been wavering."[2] Theodoric Bland wrote bitterly to Arthur Lee that, "Our chief magistrate has at length taken his party and appears to be reprobated by the honest of both sides. . . . He has openly declared for posterior amendments, or in other words, unconditional submission."[3]

All of Randolph's influence, popularity, and prestige of family were to be counted for the Constitution without previous amendment; and this was a far weightier force, in the practical business of getting votes for ratification, than oratory or argument.[4] So "the sanguine friends of the Constitution counted upon a majority of twenty . . . which number they imagine will be greatly increased."[5]

Randolph's sensational about-face saved the Constitution. Nothing that its advocates did during these seething three weeks of able discussion and skillful planning accomplished half so much to secure ratification. Washington's tremendous influence,

[1] Jefferson to Short, Sept. 20, 1788; quoting a private letter from Virginia of July 12; *Works:* Ford, v, 431.

[2] Washington to Jay, June 8, 1788; *Writings:* Ford, xi, 271.

[3] Bland to Lee, June 13, 1788; Rowland, ii, 243–44. Evidently the opposition was slow to believe that Randolph had irrevocably deserted them; for Bland's letter was not written until Randolph had made his fourth extended speech ten days later.

[4] Scott, 160.

[5] Washington to Jay, June 8, 1788; *Writings:* Ford, xi, 271.

aggressive as it was tactful, which, as Monroe truly said, "carried" the new National plan, was not so practically effective as his work in winning Randolph. For, aside from his uncloaked support, the Virginia Governor at that moment had a document under lock and key which, had even rumor of it got abroad, surely would have doomed the Constitution, ended the debate abruptly, and resulted in another Federal Convention to deal anew with the Articles of Confederation.

By now the Anti-Constitutionalists, or Republicans as they had already begun to call themselves, also were acting in concert throughout the country. Their tactics were cumbersome and tardy compared with the prompt celerity of the well-managed Constitutionalists; but they were just as earnest and determined. The Society of the Federal Republicans had been formed in New York to defeat the proposed National Government and to call a second Federal Convention. It opened correspondence in most of the States and had agents and officers in many of them.

New York was overwhelmingly against the Constitution, and her Governor, George Clinton, was the most stubborn and resourceful of its foes. On December 27, 1787, Governor Randolph, under the formal direction of Virginia's Legislature, had sent the Governors of the other States a copy of the act providing for Virginia's Convention, which included the clause for conferring with her sister Commonwealths upon the calling of a new Federal Convention. The one to Clinton of New York was delayed in the mails for exactly two months and eleven days, just long enough to prevent New York's Legislature from acting on it.[1]

After pondering over it for a month, the New York leader of the Anti-Constitutionalist forces wrote Governor Randolph, more than three weeks before the Virginia Convention assembled, the now famous letter stating that Clinton was sure that the New York Convention, to be held June 17, "will, with great cordiality, hold a communication with any sister State on the important subject [a new Federal Convention] and especially with one so respectable in point of importance, ability, and patriotism as Virginia"; and Clinton assumed that the Virginia Convention would "commence the measures for holding such communications." [2]

When Clinton thus wrote to Randolph, he supposed, of course, that the Virginia Governor was against the Constitution. Had the New York Executive known that Randolph had been proselyted by the Constitutionalists, Clinton would have written to Henry, or Mason, or taken some other means of getting his letter before the Virginia Convention. Randolph kept all knowledge of Clinton's fatal communication from everybody excepting his Executive Council. He did not make it public until after the long, hard struggle was ended; when, for the first time, too late to be of any effect, he laid the

[1] From this delay Randolph's enemies have charged that his letter to Clinton was not posted in time. Much as Randolph had to answer for, this charge is unjust. Letters between Richmond and New York sometimes were two or three months on the way. (See *supra*, chap. VII.)

[2] Clinton to Randolph, May 8, 1788; Conway, 110–12.

New York communication before the Virginia Legislature which assembled just as the Convention was adjourning.[1]

Weighty as were the arguments and brilliant the oratory that made the Virginia debate one of the noblest displays of intellect and emotion which the world ever has seen, yet nothing can be plainer than that other practices on both sides of that immortal struggle were more decisive of the result than the amazing forensic duel that took place on the floor of the Convention hall.

When one reflects that although the weight of fact and reason was decisively in favor of the Constitutionalists; that their forces were better organized and more ably led; that they had on the ground to help them the most astute politicians from other States as well as from Virginia; that Washington aggressively supported them with all his incalculable moral influence; that, if the new National Government were established, this herculean man surely would be President with all the practical power of that office, of which patronage was not the least — when one considers that, notwithstanding all of these and many other crushing advantages possessed by the Constitutionalists, their majority, when the test vote finally came, was only eight out of a total vote of one hundred and sixty-eight; when one takes into account the fact that, to make up even this slender majority, one or two members violated their instructions and several others voted

[1] Clinton to Randolph, May 8, 1788; Conway, 110–12; Henry, ii, 363; Rowland, ii, 276–79; and see *infra*, chap. XII.

against the known will of their constituents, it becomes plain how vitally necessary to their cause was the Constitutionalists' capture of the Virginia Governor.[1]

The opponents of the proposed National Government never forgave him nor was his reputation ever entirely reëstablished. Mason thereafter scathingly referred to Randolph as "young A[rno]ld." [2]

Answering Randolph, Mason went to the heart of the subject. "Whether the Constitution be good or bad," said he, "it is a national government and no longer a Confederation . . . that the new plan provides for." The power of direct taxation alone "is

[1] Randolph's change was ascribed to improper motives. Mason was almost offensive in his insinuations during the debate and Henry openly so, as will appear. Randolph's last words to the Convention were explanatory and defensive.

Washington made Randolph his first Attorney-General and he exercised great power for a time. "The Government is now solely directed by Randolph," complained Jefferson. (Conway, 140.) While Washington certainly did not appoint Randolph as a reward for his conduct in the struggle over the Constitution, it is a reasonable inference that he would not have been made a member of the Cabinet if he had not abandoned his opposition, supported the Constitution, and suppressed Clinton's letter.

Virginia had the head of the Cabinet in Jefferson as Secretary of State; Washington himself was from Virginia; and since there were numerous men from other States as well as or better equipped than Randolph for the Attorney-Generalship, his selection for that place is, at least, noteworthy. It gave Virginia the Presidency and two members of a Cabinet which numbered only four in all.

When the Attorney-Generalship was tendered to Randolph, he wrote to Madison bitterly resenting "the load of calumny which would be poured upon" him if he should accept. "For," writes Randolph, "it has been insinuated . . . that my espousal of the Constitution had alienated even its friends from me, who would not elect me to the house of representatives. The insinuation has been carried so far as to apply it to the disposal of offices under the government." (Randolph to Madison, July 19, 1789; Conway, 127–28.)

[2] Rowland, ii, 308.

calculated to annihilate totally the state governments." It means, said Mason, individual taxation "by two different and distinct powers" which "cannot exist long together; the one will destroy the other." One National Government is not fitted for an extensive country. "Popular governments can only exist in small territories." A consolidated government "is one of the worst curses that can possibly befall a nation." Clear as this now was, when the Convention came to consider the Judiciary clause, everybody would, Mason thought, "be more convinced that this government will terminate in the annihilation of the state governments."

But here again the author of Virginia's Bill of Rights made a tactical mistake from the standpoint of the management of the fight, although it was big-hearted and statesmanlike in itself. "If," said he, "such amendments be introduced as shall exclude danger. . . I shall most heartily make the greatest concessions . . . to obtain . . . conciliation and unanimity." [1] No grindstone, this, to sharpen activity — no hammer and anvil, this, to shape and harden an unorganized opposition into a single fighting blade, wielded to bring victory or even to force honorable compromise. The suggestion of conciliation before the first skirmish was over was not the way to arouse the blood of combat in the loose, undisciplined ranks of the opposition.

Swift as any hawk, the Constitutionalists pounced upon Mason's error, but they seized it gently as a dove. "It would give me great pleasure," cooed

[1] Elliott, iii, 29–34.

Madison, "to concur with my honorable colleague in any conciliatory plan." But the hour was now late, and he would postpone further remarks for the time being.[1]

So the Convention adjourned and the day ended with the Constitutionalists in high spirits.[2] Madison wrote to Washington that "Henry & Mason made a lame figure & appeared to take different and awkward ground. The Federalists [Constitutionalists][3] are a good deal elated by the existing prospect." Nevertheless, the timid Madison fluttered with fear. "I dare not," wrote he, "speak with certainty as to the decision. Kentucky has been extremely tainted and is supposed to be generally adverse, and every possible piece of address is going on privately to work on the local interests & prejudices of that & other quarters."[4]

The next day the building of the New Academy, where the Convention met, was packed with an eager throng. Everybody expected Madison to engage both Henry and Mason as he had intimated that he would do. But once more the excellent management of the Constitutionalists was displayed. Madison, personally, was not popular,[5] he was physically unimpressive, and strong only in his superb intellect. The time to discharge the artillery of that powerful

[1] Elliott, iii, 34–35. [2] Grigsby, i, 99.

[3] Those who supported the Constitution were called "Federalists" and its opponents "Anti-Federalists"; but, for sake of clearness, the terms "Constitutionalists" and "Anti-Constitutionalists" are employed in these chapters.

[4] Madison to Washington, June 4, 1788; *Writings:* Hunt, v, footnote to 123–24.

[5] Grigsby, i, footnote to 46.

mind had not yet come. Madison was not the man for this particular moment. But Pendleton was, and so was "Light-Horse Harry" Lee. The Constitutionalists combined the ermine and the sword. Virginia's most venerated jurist and her most dashing soldier were ordered to the front. In them there was an appeal to much that the Old Dominion still reverenced and loved, in spite of the "levelling spirit" manifest there as well as in Massachusetts and other States. So when all eyes were turned on Madison's seat, they beheld it vacant. Madison had stayed away. Had he been present, he could not have avoided speaking.

Dramatic, indeed, appeared the white-haired, crippled jurist, as, struggling to his feet, he finally stood upon his crutches and faced the Convention. He had been unused to public debate for many years, and was thought to be so infirm that no one expected him to do more than make or decide points of order and give his vote. Yet there the feeble old man stood to answer the resistless Henry and the learned Mason. His ancient friend and brother justice, Wythe, leaned forward from his chair to catch the tones of the beloved voice. Tears rolled down the cheeks of some of the oldest members who for decades had been Pendleton's friends.[1] The Constitutionalists had set the stage to catch the

[1] Grigsby, i, 101–02. Scenes of a similar character occurred several times in both Senate and House between 1900 and 1911, when one of our elder statesmen, who plainly was nearing the end of life, rose to speak. More than one notable contest, during that decade, was decided by the sympathetic votes of aged friends who answered the call of long years of affection.

emotions which they affected to despise, with the very character whose strength was in that pure reasoning on which they pretended solely to rely.

Without wasting a word, Pendleton came to the point. Henry, he said, had declared that all was well before "this Federal system was thought of." Was that accurate? In a few short sentences he showed that it was not. There was, said Pendleton, "no quarrel between government and liberty; the former is shield and protector of the latter. The war is between government and licentiousness, faction, turbulence, and other violations of the rules of society to preserve liberty." Why are the words "We, the people," improper? "Who but the people have a right to form government? . . . What have the state governments to do with it?" Had the Federal Convention exceeded its powers? No. Because those powers were "to propose, not to determine."

"Suppose," asked the venerable Pendleton, "the paper on your table [the Constitution] dropped from one of the planets; the people found it, and sent us here to consider whether it was proper for their adoption; must we not obey them?" Of course. "Then the question must be between this government and the Confederation," which "is no government at all." The Confederation did not carry us through the war; "common danger and the spirit of America" did that. The cry "United we stand — divided we fall," which "echoed and reëchoed through America — from Congress to the drunken carpenter" — saved us in that dark hour. And Pendleton clearly, briefly, solidly, answered every objection which Mason and Henry had made. Nothing could have been more practically effective than his close. He was of no party, Pendleton avowed; and his "age and situation" proved that nothing but the general good influenced him.[1]

The smouldering fires in Henry's blood now burned fiercely. This was the same Pendleton who had fought Henry in his immortal resolution on the Stamp Act in 1765 and in every other of those epochal battles for liberty and human rights which Henry had led and won.[2] But the Constitutionalists gave the old war horse no chance to charge upon his lifelong opponent. A young man, thirty-two years of age, rose, and, standing within a few feet of the chair, was recognized. Six feet tall, beautiful of face, with the resounding and fearless voice of a warrior, Henry Lee looked the part which reputation assigned him. Descended from one of the oldest and most honorable families in the colony, a graduate of Princeton College, one of the most daring, picturesque, and attractive officers of the Revolution, in which by sheer gallantry and military genius he had become commander of a famous cavalry command, the gallant Lee was a perfect contrast to the venerable Pendleton.[3]

Lee paid tribute to Henry's shining talents; but, said he, "I trust that he [Henry] is come to judge, and not to alarm." Henry had praised Washington; yet Washington was for the Constitution. What was there wrong with the expression "We, the

[1] Elliott, iii, 35–41.
[2] See *infra*, chap. III; also Grigsby, i, 105–06. [3] *Ib.*, 106–09.

people," since upon the people "it is to operate, if adopted"? Like every Constitutionalist speaker, Lee painted in somber and forbidding colors the condition of the country, "all owing to the imbecility of the Confederation."[1]

At last Henry secured the floor. At once he struck the major note of the opposition. "The question turns," said he, "on that poor little thing — the expression, 'We, the *people;* instead of the *states.*'" It was an "alarming transition . . . a revolution[2] as radical as that which separated us from Great Britain. . . . Sovereignty of the states . . . rights of conscience, trial by jury, liberty of the press, . . . all pretensions of human rights and privileges" were imperiled if not lost by the change.

It *was* the "despised" Confederation that had carried us through the war. Think well, he urged, before you part with it. "Revolutions like this have happened in almost every country in Europe." The new Government may prevent "licentiousness," but also "it will oppress and ruin the people," thundered their champion. The Constitution was clear when it spoke of "sedition," but fatally vague when it spoke of "privileges." Where, asked Henry, were the dangers the Constitutionalists conjured up? Purely imaginary! If any arose, he depended on "the American spirit" to defend us.

[1] Elliott, iii, 41–43.

[2] Elliott, iii, 44. The word "revolution" is printed "resolution" in Elliott's *Debates.* This is a good example of the inaccuracy of Elliott's reprint of Robertson's stenographic report. In Robertson's *Debates,* published in 1805, the word is correctly printed "revolution." I have cited Elliott only because it is accessible. Even Robertson's report is admittedly meager and unsatisfactory; all the more, therefore, is it to be regretted that Elliott's reprint should be so inaccurate.

The method of amendment provided in the Constitution, exclaimed Henry, was a mockery — it shut the door on amendment. "A contemptible minority can prevent the good of the majority." "A standing army" will "execute the execrable commands of tyranny," shouted Henry. And who, he asked, will punish them? "Will your mace-bearer be a match for a disciplined regiment?" If the Constitution is adopted, "it will be because we like a great splendid" government. "The ropes and chains of consolidation" were "about to convert this country into a powerful and mighty empire." The Constitution's so-called checks and balances, sneered Henry, were "rope-dancing, chain-rattling, ridiculous . . . contrivances."

The Constitutionalists talked of danger if the Confederation was continued; yet, under it, declared Henry, "peace and security, ease and content" were now the real lot of all. Why, then, attempt "to terrify us into an adoption of this new form of government? . . . Who knows the dangers this new system may produce? They are out of sight of the common people; they cannot foresee latent consequences." It was the operation of the proposed National Government "on the middling and lower classes of people" that Henry feared. "This government" [the Constitution], cried he, "is not a Virginian but an American government."

Throughout Henry's speech, in which he voiced, as he never failed to do, the thought of the masses, a National Government is held up as a foreign power — even one so restricted as the literal words of the

Constitution outlined. Had the Constitutionalists acknowledged those Nationalist opinions which, in later years, were to fall from the lips of a young member of the Convention and become the law of the land, the defeat of the Constitution would have been certain, prompt, and overwhelming.

In the Constitution's chief executive, Henry saw "a great and mighty President" with "the powers of a King . . . to be supported in extravagant magnificence." The National Government's tax-gatherers would "ruin you with impunity," he warned his fellow members and the people they represented. Did not Virginia's own "state sheriffs, those unfeeling blood-suckers," even "under the watchful eye of our legislature commit the most horrid and barbarous ravages on our people? . . . Lands have been sold," asserted he, "for 5 shillings which were worth one hundred pounds." What, then, would happen to the people "if their master had been at Philadelphia or New York?" asked Henry. "These harpies may search at any time your houses and most secret recesses." Its friends talked about the beauty of the Constitution, but to Henry its features were "horribly frightful. Among other deformities, it has an awful squinting; it squints toward monarchy."

The President, "your American chief," can make himself absolute, dramatically exclaimed the great orator. "If ever he violates the laws . . . he will come at the head of his army to carry everything before him; or he will give bail, or do what Mr. Chief Justice will order him." But will he submit to punishment? Rather, he will "make one bold push for the

American throne," prophesied Henry. "We shall have a king; the army will salute him monarch: your militia will leave you, and assist in making him king and fight against you."[1] It would be infinitely better, he avowed, to have a government like Great Britain with "King, Lords, and Commons, than a government so replete with such insupportable evils" as the Constitution contained.

Henry spoke of the danger of the power of Congress over elections, and the treaty-making power. A majority of the people were against the Constitution, he said, and even "the adopting states have already heart-burnings and animosity and repent their precipitate hurry. . . . Pennsylvania has been tricked into" ratification. "If other states who have adopted it have not been tricked, still they were too much hurried.[2] . . . I have not said the one hundred thousandth part of what I have on my mind and wish to impart" — with these words of warning to the Constitutionalists, Henry closed by apologizing for the time he had taken. He admitted that he had spoken out of order, but trusted that the Convention would hear him again.[3]

Studying this attack and defense of master swordsmen, following the tactical maneuvers of America's ablest politicians, a partisan on one side, yet personally friendly with members of the other, John

[1] At this point the reporter, unable to follow Henry's speech, notes that he "strongly and pathetically expatiated on the probability of the President's enslaving America and the horrid consequences that must result." (Elliott, iii, 60.)

[2] Henry had not heard of the Constitutionalists' bargain with Hancock in Massachusetts.

[3] Elliott, iii, 43–64.

Marshall was waiting for the call that should bring him into the battle and, by the method which he employed throughout his life, preparing to respond when the Constitutionalist managers should give the word. He was listening to the arguments on both sides, analyzing them, and, by that process of absorption with which he was so peculiarly and curiously gifted, mastering the subjects under discussion. Also, although casual, humorous, and apparently indifferent, he nevertheless was busy, we may be sure, with his winning ways among his fellow members.

Patrick Henry's effort was one of the two or three speeches made during the three weeks of debate which actually may have had an effect upon votes.[1] The Constitutionalists feared that Henry would take the floor next morning to follow up his success and deepen the profound impression he had made. To prevent this and to break the force of Henry's onslaught, they put forward Governor Randolph, who was quickly recognized by the chair. Madison and Nicholas were held in reserve.[2]

But in vain did Randolph employ his powers of oratory, argument, and persuasion in the great speech beginning "I am a child of the Revolution," with which he attempted to answer Henry. There is no peace; "the tempest growls over you. . . . Jus-

[1] General Posey, a Revolutionary officer, who was for the Constitution, afterwards said that Henry's speech made him believe that the Constitution would destroy liberty. Another intelligent man who heard Henry's speech said that when the great orator pictured the President at the head of the army, he felt his own wrists for the shackles, and that his place in the gallery suddenly seemed like a dungeon. (Grigsby, i, 118–19.)

[2] Grigsby, i, 121.

tice is suffocated," he said; legal proceedings to collect debts are "obscured by legislative mists." As an illustration of justice, consider the case of Josiah Philips, executed without trial or witness, on a bill of attainder passed without debate on the mere report of a member of the Legislature: "*This made the deepest impression on my heart and I cannot contemplate it without horror.*" [1] As to "the American spirit" expressed through the militia being competent to the defense of the State, Randolph asked: "Did ever militia defend a country?"

Randolph's speech was exhaustive and reached the heights of real eloquence. It all came to this, he said, Union or Dissolution, thus again repeating the argument Washington had urged in his letter to Randolph. "Let that glorious pride which once defied the British thunder, reanimate you again," he cried dramatically.[2] But his fervor, popularity, and influence were not enough.

[1] Elliott, iii, 64–86. In the debate, much was made of this famous case. Yet Philips was not executed under the provisions of the law Randolph referred to. When arrested, he was indicted, tried, and convicted in the General Court; and he was hanged by sentence of the court, December 4, 1778.

Although, at that time, Randolph was Attorney-General of Virginia and actually prosecuted the case; and although Henry was Governor and ordered the arrest of Philips (Henry, i, 611–13), yet, ten years later, both had forgotten the facts, and Randolph charged, and Henry in reply admitted, that Philips had been executed under the bill of attainder without trial. (Jefferson to Wirt, Oct. 14, 1814; *Works:* Ford, xi, 407.) The bill of attainder was drawn by Jefferson. It appears in *ib.*, ii, 330–36.

Marshall, when he came to speak later in the debate, made the same mistake. No more striking illustration exists of how public men, in the hurry and pressure of large affairs, forget the most important events, even when they themselves were principal actors in them.

[2] Again, Randolph's speech was marred by the note of personal

Although the time had not properly come for the great logician of the Constitution to expound it, the situation now precipitated the psychological hour for him to strike. The chair recognized a slender, short-statured man of thirty-seven, wearing a handsome costume of blue and buff with doubled straight collar and white ruffles on breast and at wrists. His hair, combed forward to conceal baldness, was powdered and fell behind in the long beribboned queue of fashion. He was so small that he could not be seen by all the members; and his voice was so weak that only rarely could he be heard throughout the hall.[1] Such was James Madison as he stood, hat in hand and his notes in his hat, and began the first of those powerful speeches, the strength of which, in spite of poor reporting, has projected itself through more than a hundred years.

At first he spoke so low that even the reporter could not catch what he said.[2] He would not, remarked Madison, attempt to impress anybody by "ardent professions of zeal for the public welfare." Men should be judged by deeds and not by words. The real point was whether the Constitution would be a good thing or a bad thing for the country. Henry had mentioned the dangers concealed in the Constitution; let him specify and prove them. One

explanation that pervaded it. "The rectitude of my intentions"; "ambition and popularity are no objects with me"; "I expect, in the course of a year, to retire to that private station which I most sincerely and cordially prefer to all others," — such expressions gave to his otherwise aggressive and very able appeal a defensive tone.

1 Grigsby, i, 130. Madison's apparel at this Convention was as ornate as his opinions were, in his opponents' eyes, "aristocratic."

2 Elliott, iii, 86. See entire speech, *ib.*, 86–96.

by one he caught and crushed Henry's points in the jaws of merciless logic.

What, for the gentle Madison, was a bold blow at the opposition shows how even he was angered. "The inflammatory violence wherewith it [the Constitution] was opposed by designing, illiberal, and unthinking minds, begins to subside. I will not enumerate the causes from which, in my conception, the heart-burnings of a majority of its opposers have originated." His argument was unanswerable as a matter of pure reason and large statesmanship, but it made little headway and had only slight if any influence. "I am not so sanguine," reported Washington's nephew to the General at Mount Vernon, "as to . . . flatter myself that he made many converts." [1]

The third gun of the powerful battery which the Constitutionalists had arranged to batter down the results of Henry's speech was now brought into action. George Nicholas again took the floor. He was surprised that Mason's resolution to debate the Constitution clause by clause had not been followed. But it had not been, and therefore he must speak at large. While Nicholas advanced nothing new, his address was a masterpiece of compact reasoning. [2]

Age and middle age had spoken for the Constitution; voices from the bench and the camp, from the

[1] Bushrod Washington to Washington, June 6, 1788; *Writings:* Sparks, ix, 378. But Madison gave Henry an opening through which that veteran orator drove like a troop of horse, as far as practical and momentary effect was concerned. Madison described the new government as partly National and partly Federal. (Elliott, iii, 94; and see Henry's use of this, *ib.*, 171; also *infra.*)

[2] Elliott, iii, 97–103.

bar and the seats of the mighty, had pleaded for it; and now the Constitutionalists appealed to the very young men of the Convention through one of the most attractive of their number. The week must not close with Henry's visions of desolation uppermost in the minds of the members. On Saturday morning the chair recognized Francis Corbin of Middlesex. He was twenty-eight years old and of a family which had lived in Virginia from the early part of the seventeenth century. He had been educated in England at the University of Cambridge, studied law at the Inner Temple, was a trained lawyer, and a polished man of the world.

Corbin made one of the best speeches of the whole debate. On the nonpayment of our debts to foreign nations he was particularly strong. "What!" said he, "borrow money to discharge interest on what was borrowed? . . . Such a plan would destroy the richest country on earth." As to a Republican Government not being fitted for an extensive country, he asked, "How small must a country be to suit the genius of Republicanism?" The power of taxation was the "lungs of the Constitution." His defense of a standing army was novel and ingenious. The speech was tactful in the deference paid to older men, and so captivating in the pride it must have aroused in the younger members that it justified the shrewdness of the Constitutionalist generals in putting forward this youthful and charming figure.[1]

Of course Henry could not follow a mere boy. He cleverly asked that Governor Randolph should

[1] Elliott, iii, 104–14.

finish, as the latter had promised to do.[1] Randolph could not avoid responding; and his speech, while very able, was nevertheless an attempt to explode powder already burned.[2] Madison saw this, and getting the eye of the chair delivered the second of those intellectual broadsides, which, together with his other mental efforts during the Constitutional period, mark him as almost the first, if not indeed the very first, mind of his time.[3] The philosophy and method of taxation, the history and reason of government, the whole range of the vast subject were discussed,[4] or rather begun; for Madison did not finish, and took up the subject four days later. His effort so exhausted him physically that he was ill for three days.[5]

Thus fortune favored Henry. The day, Saturday, was not yet spent. After all, he could leave the last impression on the members and spectators, could apply fresh color to the picture he wished his hearers to have before their eyes until the next week renewed the conflict. And he could retain the floor so as to open again when Monday came. The art of Henry in this speech was supreme. He began by stating the substance of Thomas Paine's terrific sentence about government being, at best, "a neces-

[1] Elliott, iii, 114. [2] *Ib.*, 114–28.

[3] Madison was equaled only by Hamilton in sheer intellectuality, but he was inferior to that colossus in courage and constructive genius.

[4] *Ib.*, 128–37.

[5] Madison to Hamilton, June 9, 1788; Hamilton MSS., Lib. Cong. Madison's four famous speeches in this Convention, are properly parts of one comprehensive exposition. (See Madison's own notes for the third of these speeches in *Writings:* Hunt, v, 148.) Mr. Hunt also prints accurately Robertson's report of the speeches themselves in that volume. Thev cannot be summarized here, but should be read in full.

sary evil"; and aroused anew that repugnance to any sturdy rule which was a general feeling in the breasts of the masses.

Both the Confederation and the proposed Constitution were "evils," asserted Henry, and the only question was which was the less. Randolph and Madison incautiously had referred to maxims. Henry seized the word with infinite skill. "It is impiously irritating the avenging hand of Heaven . . . to desert those maxims which alone can preserve liberty," he thundered. They were lowly maxims, to be sure, "poor little, humble republican maxims"; but "humble as they are" they alone could make a nation safe or formidable. He rang the changes on the catchwords of liberty.

Then Henry spoke of Randolph's change of front. The Constitution "was once execrated" by Randolph. "It seems to me very strange and unaccountable that that which was the object of his execration should now receive his encomiums. Something extraordinary must have operated so great a change in his opinion." Randolph had said that it was too late to oppose the "New Plan"; but, answered Henry, "I can never believe that it is too late to save all that is precious." Henry denied the woeful state of the country which the Constitutionalist speakers had pictured. The "imaginary dangers" conjured by them were to intimidate the people; but, cried Henry, "fear is the passion of slaves." The execution of Josiah Philips under the bill of attainder was justifiable. Philips had been a "fugitive murderer and an outlaw" leader of "an infamous banditti," perpetrator of "the most cruel and shocking barbarities . . . an enemy to human nature." [1]

It was not true, declared Henry, that the people were discontented under the Confederation — at least the common people were not; and it was the common people for whom he spoke. But, of course, sneered that consummate actor, "the middling and lower ranks of people have not those illuminated ideas" which the "well-born" are so happily possessed of; "they [the common people] cannot so readily perceive latent objects." It was only the "illuminated imaginations" and the "microscopic eyes of modern statesmen" that could see defects where there were none.

Henry hinted with great adroitness at the probable loss of the Mississippi, which was the sorest point with the members from Kentucky; and, having injected the poison, passed on to let it do its work against the time when he would strike with all his force. Then he appealed to state pride. "When I call this the most mighty state in the Union, do I not speak the truth? Does not Virginia surpass every state?" Of course! There was no danger, then, that Virginia would be left out of the Union, as the Constitutionalists had hinted might happen if Virginia rejected the Constitution; the other States would be glad to have her on her own terms.

Henry went over a variety of subjects and then returned to his favorite idea of the National Government as something foreign. Picking up a careless word of Randolph, who had spoken of the people

[1] See *supra*, footnote to 393.

as a "herd," Henry said that perhaps the words "We, the people," were used to recommend it to the masses, "to those who are likened to a *herd;* and by the operation of this blessed system are to be transformed from respectable, independent citizens, to abject, dependent subjects or slaves."[1] Finally, when he felt that he had his hearers once more under his spell, Henry, exclaiming that a Bill of Rights was vital, asked for adjournment, which was taken, the great orator still holding the floor.

[1] Elliott, iii, 137–50.

CHAPTER XI

THE SUPREME DEBATE

There will undoubtedly be a greater weight of abilities against the adoption in this convention than in any other state. (Washington.)

What are the objects of the National Government? To protect the United States and to promote the general welfare. (Marshall, in his first debate.)

Now appeared the practical political managers from other States. From Saturday afternoon until Monday morning there was great activity in both camps. The politicians of each side met in secret conference to plan the operations of the coming week and to devise ways and means of getting votes. For the Constitutionalists, Gouverneur Morris was on the ground from New York;[1] Robert Morris and probably James Wilson, both from Philadelphia, had been in Virginia at the time of the elections and the former remained for the Convention.[2] During the second week the Philadelphia financier writes Gates from Richmond, lamenting "the depre-

[1] "I am to acknowledge yours of the 19th of May, which reached me a few days since." (Gouverneur Morris from Richmond, June 13, 1788, to Hamilton in New York; Hamilton MSS., Lib. Cong.)

[2] Robert Morris to Horatio Gates, Richmond, June 12, 1788; MS., N.Y. Pub. Lib. "James [Wilson] the Caladonian, Leut. Gen. of the myrmidons of power, under Robert [Morris] the cofferer, who with his aid-de-camp, *Gouvero* [Gouverneur] the cunning man, has taken the field in Virginia." (*Centinel*, no. 10, Jan. 12, 1788; reprinted in McMaster and Stone, 631.)

Robert Morris was in Richmond, March 21, 1788. (Morris to *Independent Gazetteer* on that date; *ib.*, 787, denying the charge that paper had made against him. See *supra*, chap. x.) He was in Richmond in May and paid John Marshall four pounds, four shillings as a "retainer." (Account Book, May 2, 1788.) He had heavy business interests in Virginia; see Braxton *vs.* Willing, Morris & Co. (4 Call, 288). Marshall was his lawyer.

dations on my purse," but "inclined to think the Constitution will be adopted by Virginia." [1]

For the opposition, Oswald, publisher of the "Independent Gazetteer," came on from Philadelphia and arrived in Richmond at the close of the first week's debate. He at once went into secret conference with Henry, Mason, and the other Anti-Constitutionalist leaders. Madison reports to Hamilton that "Oswald of Phil[a] came here on Saturday; and he has closet interviews with the leaders of the opposition." [2] By the same mail Grayson advises the general Anti-Constitutionalist headquarters in New York that he is "sorry . . . that our affairs in the convention are suspended by a hair." Randolph's conduct "has not injured us," writes Grayson, thus proving how poorly the Anti-Constitutionalists estimated the real situation. But they were practical enough to know that "there are seven or eight dubious characters whose opinions are not known" and upon whose decisions the fate of the Constitution "will ultimately depend." Grayson cautions Lamb not to let this get into the newspapers.[3]

Just what was devised and decided by the leaders of both sides in these behind-the-doors meetings and

[1] Morris to Gates, June 12, 1788, *supra*. Morris's remark about depredations on his purse may or may not refer to the work of the Convention. He was always talking in this vein about his expenses; he had lost money in his Virginia business ventures; and, having his family with him, may, for that reason, have found his Southern trip expensive. My own belief is that no money was used to get votes; for Henry, Mason, and Grayson surely would have heard of and, if so, denounced such an attempt.

[2] Madison to Hamilton, June 9, 1788; Hamilton MSS., Lib. Cong.

[3] Grayson to Lamb, June 9, 1788; quoted in Leake: *Lamb*, 311

what methods were used outside the Convention hall to influence votes, there is no means of learning exactly; though "the opposition" committee seems to have been occupied chiefly in drawing amendments.[1] But the frequent references, particularly of the Constitutionalist speakers on the floor, to improper conduct of their adversaries "out of doors" show that both sides were using every means known to the politics of the day to secure support. In the debate itself Henry certainly was making headway.[2]

On Monday, Henry and Mason made a dramatic entrance into the Convention hall. Walking arm in arm from their quarters in "The Swan,"[3] they stopped on the steps at the doors of the New Academy and conferred earnestly for some minutes; so great was the throng that the two Anti-Constitutionalist chieftains made their way to their seats with great difficulty.[4] When Henry rose to go on with his speech, the plan decided on during Sunday quickly was revealed. The great prize for which both sides now were fighting was the votes from Kentucky.[5] Henry held up before them the near forfeiture to the Spanish of our right to navigate the

[1] Grayson to Lamb, June 9, 1788; quoted in Leake: *Lamb*, 311.

[2] Grigsby, i, 149–50.

[3] The new tavern at Richmond — competitor of Formicola's inn.

[4] Grigsby, i, 151.

[5] Kentucky had fourteen members. On the final vote, the Constitution was ratified by a majority of only 10 out of 168 members present and voting. At the opening of the Convention, Grayson said that "the district of Kentucke is with us, and if we can get all of the four Counties, which lye on the Ohio between the Pennsylv^a. line and Big Sandy Creek, the day is our own." (Grayson to Dane, June 4, 1788; Dane MSS., Lib. Cong.) The Constitutionalists finally succeeded in getting four of these Kentucky votes.

Mississippi.[1] This, he said, was the work of seven Northern States; but under the Confederation they had been thwarted in their fell purpose by six Southern States; and the Mississippi still remained our own. But if the Constitution was adopted, what would happen? The Senate would be controlled by those same Northern States that had nearly succeeded in surrendering the great waterway and the West and South would surely be deprived of that invaluable commercial outlet. He asked the members of Congress who were in the Convention to tell the facts about the Mississippi business. Jefferson, he avowed, had counseled Virginia to "reject this government." [2]

Henry answered the Constitutionalists' prophecy of foreign war, ridiculed danger from the Indians, proved that the Constitution would not pay Virginia's debts; and, in characteristic fashion, ranged at large over the field. The Constitution, he asserted, would "operate like an ambuscade . . . destroy the state governments . . . swallow the liberties of the people without" warning. "How are our debts to be discharged unless taxes are increased?" asked he; and demonstrated that under the Constitution taxes surely would be made heavier. Time and again he warned the Convention against the loss of liberty: "When the deprivation of our liberty was attempted, what did . . . the genius of Virginia tell us? '*Sell all and purchase liberty!*' . . . Repub-

[1] The Jay-Gardoqui agreement.

[2] Jefferson to Donald, Feb. 7, 1788; Jefferson's *Writings:* Washington, ii, 355; and see Monroe to Jefferson, July 12, 1788; *Writings:* Hamilton, i, 186-87.

lican maxims, . . . and the genius of Virginia landed you safe on the shore of freedom."

Once more he praised the British form of government — an oversight which a hawk-eyed young member of the Convention, John Marshall, was soon to use against him. Henry painted in darkest colors the secrecy of the Federal Convention. "*Look at us — hear our transactions!* — if this had been the language of the Federal Convention," there would have been no Constitution, he asserted, and with entire accuracy. Yet, the Constitution itself authorized Congress to keep its proceedings as secret as those of the Constitution's makers had been kept: "The transactions of Congress," said Henry, "may be concealed a century from the public."[1]

Seizing Madison's description of the new Government as partly National and partly Federal, Henry brought to bear all his power of satire. He was "amused" at Madison's "treatise of political anatomy. . . . In the brain it is national; the stamina are federal; some limbs are federal, others national." Absurd! The truth was, said Henry, that the Constitution provided for "a great consolidation of government." Why not abolish Virginia's Legislature and be done with it? This National Government would do what it liked with Virginia.

As to the plan of ratifying first and amending afterwards, Henry declared himself "at a loss what to say. You agree to bind yourselves hand and foot — for the sake of what? Of being unbound. You go

[1] Elliott, iii, 170–71. The reporter noted that "Mr. Henry in a very animated manner expatiated on the evil and pernicious tendency of keeping secret the common proceedings of government." (*Ib.*, 170.)

into a dungeon — for what? To get out. . . . My anxiety and fears are great lest America by the adoption of this system [the Constitution], should be cast into a fathomless bottom."

Tradition has it that during this speech Henry, having frozen his hearers' blood by a terrific description of lost "liberty," with one of his sudden turns set both Convention and spectators into roars of laughter by remarking with a grimace, and as an aside, "why, *they'll free your niggers*."[1] And then, with one of those lightning changes of genius, which Henry alone could make, he solemnly exclaimed, "I look on that paper [the Constitution] as the most fatal plan that could possibly be conceived to enslave a free people."[2]

Lee, in reply, spoke of the lobbying going on outside the Convention. "Much is said by gentlemen out of doors," exclaimed Lee; "they ought to urge all their objections here." He taunted Henry, who had praised the militia, with not having been himself a soldier. "I saw what the honorable gentleman did not see," cried Lee, "our men fight with the troops of that King whom he so much admires."[3]

When the hot-blooded young soldier had finished his aggressive speech, Randolph could no longer restrain himself. Henry's bold challenge of Randolph's change of front had cut that proud and sen-

[1] Grigsby, i, footnote to 157. [2] Elliott, iii, 150–76.

[3] Lee, while pretending to praise the militia, really condemned it severely; and cited the militia's panic and flight at Guilford Court-House, which lost the battle to the Americans. "Had the line been supported that day," said he, "Cornwallis, instead of surrendering at Yorktown, would have laid down his arms at Guilford." (Elliott, iii, 178.)

sitive nature to the heart. "I disdain," thundered he, "his aspersions and his insinuations." They were "warranted by no principle of parliamentary decency, nor compatible with the least shadow of friendship; and if our friendship must fall, *let it fall, like Lucifer, never to rise again!*" It was not to answer Henry that he spoke, snarled Randolph, "but to satisfy this respectable audience." Randolph then explained his conduct, reading part of the letter [1] that had caused all the trouble, and dramatically throwing the letter on the clerk's table, cried "that it might lie there for *the inspection of the curious and malicious*." [2] Randolph spoke for the remainder of the day and consumed most of the next forenoon.[3]

No soldier had yet spoken for the Anti-Constitutionalists; and it perhaps was Lee's fling at Henry that now called a Revolutionary officer to his feet against the Constitution. A tall, stiff, raw-boned young man of thirty years arose. Poorly educated, slow in his mental processes,[4] James Monroe made a long, dull, and cloudy speech, finally declaring of the Constitution, "I think it a dangerous government"; and asking "why . . . this haste — this wild precipitation?" Long as Monroe's speech was, he reminded the Convention that he had "not yet

[1] Randolph's letter explaining why he had refused to sign the Constitution.

[2] This was the only quarrel of the Convention which threatened serious results. A duel was narrowly averted. Colonel William Cabell, as Henry's friend, called on Randolph that night; but matters were arranged and the tense situation relieved when it was learned, next morning, that no duel would take place. (Grigsby, i, 162–65.)

[3] Elliott, iii, 187–207.

[4] Grigsby, i, 167–68.

said all that I wish upon the subject" and that he would return to the charge later on.[1]

Monroe did not help or hurt either side except, perhaps, by showing the members that all the Revolutionary veterans were not for the Constitution. Neither members nor spectators paid much attention to him, though this was no reflection on Monroe, for the Convention did not listen with patience to many speakers except Henry. When Henry spoke, every member was in his seat and the galleries were packed. But only the most picturesque of the other speakers could hold the audience for longer than half an hour; generally members walked about and the spectators were absent except when Henry took the floor.[2]

As usual, the Constitutionalists were ready with their counter-stroke. Wythe in the chair recognized a tall, ungainly young man of thirty-two. He was badly dressed in a loose, summer costume, and his blazing black eyes and unkempt raven hair made him look more like a poet or an artist than a lawyer or statesman.[3] He had bought a new coat the day the Convention met; but it was a most inexpensive addition to his raiment, for it cost but one pound, Virginia currency, then greatly depreciated.[4] He

[1] Elliott, iii, 207–22.

[2] "When any other member spoke, the members of the audience would, in half an hour, be going out or moving from their seats." (Winston to Wirt, quoted in Henry, ii, 347.) Henry spoke every day of the twenty-two days' debate, except five; and often spoke several times a day. (*Ib.*, 350.)

[3] Grigsby, i, 176.

[4] Marshall's Account Book. The entry is: "[June] 2 Paid for coat for self 1." Two months earlier Marshall paid "for Nankin for breeches for self 1.16." (*Ib.*, April 1, 1788.) Yet about the same time he spent one pound, nine shillings at a "barbecue."

probably was the best liked of all the members of the Convention. Sociable to extreme good-fellowship, "his habits," says Grigsby, "were convivial almost to excess";[1] and it is more than likely that, considering the times, these habits in his intimate social intercourse with his fellow members helped to get more votes than his arguments on the floor, of which he now was to make the first.[2] His four years' record as a soldier was as bright and clean as that of any man from any State who had fought under Washington.

So when John Marshall began to speak, he was listened to with the ears of affection; and any point the opposition had made by the fact that Monroe the soldier had spoken against the Constitution was turned by Marshall's appearance even before he had uttered a word. The young lawyer was also accounted an "orator" at this time,[3] a fact which added to the interest of his fellow members in his speech.

The question, Marshall said, was "whether democracy or despotism be most eligible."[4] He was sure that the framers and supporters of the Constitution "intend the establishment and security of the former"; they are "firm friends of the liberty and

[1] Grigsby, i, 176.

[2] Marshall had provided for entertaining during the Convention. His Account Book shows the following entry on May 8, 1788: "Paid McDonald for wine 20" (pounds); and "bottles 9/" (shillings). This was the largest quantity of wine Marshall had purchased up to that time.

[3] Marshall's reputation for "eloquence" grew, as we shall see, until his monumental work on the Supreme Bench overshadowed his fame as a public speaker.

[4] Elliott, iii, 222.

the rights of mankind." That was why they were for the Constitution. "We, sir, idolize democracy." The Constitution was, said he, the "best means of protecting liberty." The opposition had praised monarchy, but, deftly avowed Marshall, "We prefer this system to any monarchy"; for it provides for "a well regulated democracy."

He agreed with Henry that maxims should be observed; they were especially "essential to a democracy." But, "what are the . . . maxims of democracy? . . . A strict observance of justice and public faith, and a steady adherence to virtue. These, Sir, are the principles of a good government,"[1] declared the young Richmond Constitutionalist.

"No mischief, no misfortune, ought to deter us from a strict observance of justice and public faith," cried Marshall. "Would to Heaven," he exclaimed, "that these principles had been observed under the present government [the Confederation]." He was thinking now of his experience in the Legislature and appealing to the honesty of the Convention. If the principles of justice and good faith had been observed, continued he, "the friends of liberty would not be so willing now to part with it [the Confederation]."

Could Virginians themselves boast that their own Government was based on justice? "Can we pretend to the enjoyment of political freedom or security,

[1] Marshall's idea was that government should be honest and efficient; a government by the people, whether good or bad, as a method of popular self-development and progress did not appeal to him as much as excellence in government.

when we are told that a man has been, by an act of Assembly, struck out of existence without a trial by jury, without examination, without being confronted with his accusers and witnesses, without the benefits of the law of the land?"[1] Skillfully he turned against Henry the latter's excuse for the execution of Philips, and dramatically asked: "Where is our safety, when we are told that this act was justifiable because the person was not a Socrates? . . . Shall it be a maxim that a man shall be deprived of his life without the benefit of the law?"

As to the navigation of the Mississippi, he asked: "How shall we retain it? By retaining that weak government which has hitherto kept it from us?" No, exclaimed Marshall, but by a Government with "the power of retaining it." Such a Government, he pointed out, was that proposed in the Constitution. Here again the Constitutionalist managers displayed their skill. Marshall was the best man they could have chosen to appeal to the Kentucky members on the Mississippi question. His father, mother, and his family were now living in Kentucky, and his relative, Humphrey Marshall, was a member of the Convention from that district.[2] Marshall himself was the legislative agent of the District of Kentucky in Richmond. The development of the West became a vital purpose with John Marshall, strengthening with the years; and

[1] Marshall here referred to the case of Josiah Philips, and fell into the same error as had Randolph, Henry, and others. (See *supra*, 393, footnote 1.)

[2] Humphrey Marshall, i, 254. Humphrey Marshall finally voted for the Constitution, against the wishes of his constituents. (Scott, 135–38.)

this was a real force in the growth of his views on Nationality.[1]

Henry's own argument, that amendments could not be had after adoption, proved, said Marshall, that they could not be had before. In all the States, particularly in Virginia, there were, he charged, "many who are decided enemies of the Union." These were inspired by "local interests," their object being "disunion." They would not propose amendments that were similar or that all could agree upon. When the Federal Convention met, said Marshall, "we had no idea then of any particular system. The formation of the most perfect plan was our object and wish"; and, "it was imagined" that the States would with pleasure accept that Convention's work. But "consider the violence of opinions, the prejudices and animosities which have been since imbibed"; and how greatly they "operate against mutual concessions."

Marshall reiterated that what the Constitutionalists were fighting for was "a well-regulated democracy." Could the people themselves make treaties, enact laws, or administer the Government? Of course not. They must do such things through agents. And, inquired he, how could these agents act for the people if they did not have power to do so? That the people's agents might abuse power was no argument against giving it, for "the power of doing good is inseparable from that of doing some evil." If power were not given because it might be misused, "you can have no government."

[1] See vol. III of this work.

Thus Marshall stated that principle which he was to magnify from the Supreme Bench years later.

"Happy that country," exclaimed the young orator, "which can avail itself of the misfortunes of others . . . without fatal experience!" Marshall cited Holland. The woes of that country were caused, said he, by "the want of proper powers in the government, the consequent deranged and relaxed administration, the violence of contending parties" — in short, by such a government, or rather absence of government, as America then had under the Confederation. If Holland had had such a government as the Constitution proposed, she would not be in her present sorry plight. Marshall was amused at Henry's "high-colored eulogium on such a government."

There was no analogy, argued he, between "the British government and the colonies, and the relation between Congress and the states. We *were not* represented in Parliament. Here [under the Constitution] we are represented." So the arguments against British taxation "do not hold against the exercise of taxation by Congress." The power of taxation by Congress to which Henry objected was "essentially necessary; for without it there will be no efficiency in the government." That requisitions on the States could not be depended on had been demonstrated by experience, he declared; the power of direct taxation was, therefore, necessary to the very existence of the National Government.

"The possibility of its being abused is urged as an

argument against its expediency"; but, said Marshall, such arguments would prevent all government and result in anarchy. "All delegated powers are liable to be abused." The question was, whether the taxing power was "necessary to perform the objects of the Constitution? . . . What are the objects of national government? To protect the United States, and to promote the general welfare. Protection, in time of war, is one of its principal objects. Until mankind shall cease to have ambition and avarice, wars will arise."

Experience had shown, said Marshall, that one State could not protect the people or promote general welfare. "By the national government only" could these things be done; "shall we refuse to give it power to do them?" He scorned the assertion "that we need not be afraid of war. Look at history," he exclaimed, "look at the great volume of human nature. They will foretell you that a defenseless country cannot be secure. The nature of men forbids us to conclude that we are in no danger from war. The passions of men stimulate them to avail themselves of the weakness of others. The powers of Europe are jealous of us. It is our interest to watch their conduct and guard against them. They must be pleased with our disunion. If we invite them by our weakness to attack us, will they not do it? If we add debility to our present situation, a partition of America may take place."

The power of National taxation, therefore, was necessary, Marshall asserted. "There must be men and money to protect us. How are armies to be raised? Must we not have money for that purpose?" If so, "it is, then, necessary to give the government that power in time of peace, which the necessity of war will render indispensable, or else we shall be attacked unprepared." History, human nature, and "our own particular experience, will confirm this truth." If danger should come upon us without power to meet it, we might resort to a dictatorship; we once were on the point of doing that very thing, said he — and even Henry and Mason did not question this appeal of Marshall to the common knowledge of all members of the Convention.

"Were those who are now friends to this Constitution less active in the defense of liberty, on that trying occasion, than those who oppose it?" scathingly asked Marshall. "We may now . . . frame a plan that will enable us to repel attacks, and render a recurrence to dangerous expedients unnecessary. If we be prepared to defend ourselves, there will be little inducement to attack us. But if we defer giving the necessary power to the general government till the moment of danger arrives, we shall give it then, and with an *unsparing hand.*"

It was not true, asserted Marshall, that the Confederation carried us through the Revolution; "had not the enthusiasm of liberty inspired us with unanimity, that system would never have carried us through it." The war would have been won much sooner "had that government been possessed of due energy." The weakness of the Confederation and the conduct of the States prolonged the war. Only "the extreme readiness of the people to make their utmost exertions to ward off solely the pressing danger, supplied the place of requisitions." But when this danger was over, the requisition plan was no longer effective. "A bare sense of duty," said he, "is too feeble to induce men to comply with obligations."

It was plain, then, Marshall pointed out, that "the government must have the sinews of war some other way." That way was by direct taxation which would supply "the necessities of government . . . in a peaceable manner"; whereas "requisitions cannot be rendered efficient without a civil war."

What good would it do for Congress merely to remonstrate with the States, as Henry had proposed, if we were at war with foreign enemies? There was no danger that Congress, under the Constitution, would not lay taxes justly, asserted Marshall; for if members of Congress laid unjust taxes, the people would not reëlect them. Under the Constitution, they were chosen by the same voters who elected members of the State Legislature. These voters, said he, "have nothing to direct them in the choice but their own good." Men thus elected would not abuse their power because that would "militate against their own interest. . . . To procure their reelection, it will be necessary for them to confer with the people at large, and convince them that the taxes laid are for their own good."

Henry had asked whether the adoption of the Constitution "would pay our debts." "It will compel the states to pay their quotas," answered Marshall. "Without this, Virginia will be unable to pay. Unless all the states pay, she cannot. . . . Economy and industry are essential to our happiness"; but the Confederation "takes away the incitements to industry, by rendering property insecure and unprotected." The Constitution, on the contrary, "will promote and encourage industry."

The statement of the Anti-Constitutionalists that the extent of the country was too great for a strong National Government was untrue, argued Marshall. Also, said he, this objection was from writers who criticized those governments "where representation did not exist." But, under the Constitution, representation would exist.

Answering Henry's objection, that there were no effective checks in the Constitution, Marshall inquired, "What has become of his enthusiastic eulogium on the American spirit?" There, declared Marshall, was the real check and control. "In this country, there is no exclusive personal stock of interest. The interest of the community is blended and inseparably connected with that of the individual. When he promotes his own, he promotes that of the community. When we consult the common good, we consult our own." In such considerations were found the greatest security from an improper exercise of power.

"Is not liberty secure with us, where the people hold all powers in their own hands, and delegate them cautiously, for short periods, to their servants, who are accountable for the smallest mal-administration? . . . We are threatened with the loss of our liberties by the possible abuse of power, notwithstanding the maxim that those who give may take away. It is the people that give power, and can take it back. What shall restrain them? They are the masters who give it, and of whom their servants hold it."

Returning to the subject of amendments, "what," asked Marshall, "shall restrain you from amending it, if, in trying it, amendments shall be found necessary. . . . When experience shall show us any inconvenience, we can then correct it. . . . If it be necessary to change government, let us change that government which has been found to be defective." The Constitution as it stood filled the great objects which everybody desired — "union, safety against foreign enemies, and protection against faction [party] — against what has been the destruction of all republics."

He turned Henry's unhappy praise of the British Constitution into a weapon of deadly attack upon the opposition. The proposed Constitution, said Marshall, was far better than the British. "I ask you if your House of Representatives would be better than it is, if a hundredth part of the people were to elect a majority of them? If your senators were for life, would they be more agreeable to you? If your President were not accountable to you for his conduct, — if it were a constitutional maxim, that he could do no wrong, — would you be safer than you are now? If you can answer, Yes, to these questions, then adopt the British constitution. If not, then, good as that government may be, this [Constitution] is better."

Referring to "the confederacies of ancient and

modern times" he said that "they warn us to shun their calamities, and place in our government those necessary powers, the want of which destroyed them." The ocean does not protect us from war; "Sir," exclaimed Marshall, "the sea makes them neighbors to us. . . . What dangers may we not apprehend to our commerce! Does not our naval weakness invite an attack on our commerce?" Henry had said "that our present exigencies are greater than they will ever be again." But, asked he, "Who can penetrate into futurity?"

Henry's objection that the National Government, under the Constitution, would "call forth the virtue and talents of America," to the disadvantage of the States, was, Marshall said, the best guarantee that the National Government would be wisely conducted. "Will our most virtuous and able citizens wantonly attempt to destroy the liberty of the people? Will the most virtuous act the most wickedly?" On the contrary, "the virtue and talents of the members of the general government will tend to the security instead of the destruction of our liberty. . . . The power of direct taxation is essential to the existence of the general government"; if not, the Constitution was unnecessary; "for it imports not what system we have, unless it have the power of protecting us in time of war." [1]

This address to the Virginia Convention is of historic interest as John Marshall's first recorded utterance on the Constitution of which he was to become the greatest interpreter. Also, it is the first report

[1] See entire speech in Elliott, iii, 223–36.

of Marshall's debating. The speech is not, solely on its merits, remarkable. It does not equal the logic of Madison, the eloquence of Randolph or Lee, or the brilliancy of Corbin. It lacks that close sequence of reasoning which was Marshall's peculiar excellence. In provoking fashion he breaks from one subject when it has been only partly discussed and later returns to it. It is rhetorical also and gives free rein to what was then styled "Marshall's eloquence."

The warp and woof of Marshall's address was woven from his military experience; he forged iron arguments from the materials of his own soldier life. Two thirds of his remarks were about the necessity of providing against war. But the speech is notable as showing, in their infancy, those views of government which, in the shaggy strength of their maturity, were to be so influential on American destiny.[1] It also measures the growth of those ideas of government which the camp, the march, and the battlefield had planted in his mind and heart. The practical and immediate effect of the speech, which was what the Constitutionalists, and perhaps Marshall himself, cared most about, was to strengthen the soldier vote for the Constitution and to cause the Kentucky members to suspend judgment on the Mississippi question.

For the Anti-Constitutionalists there now arose a big-statured old man "elegantly arrayed in a rich suit of blue and buff, a long queue tied with a black

[1] Some of the sentences used in this unprepared speech are similar to those found in the greatest of his opinions as Chief Justice. (See vol. III of this work.)

ribbon dangling from his full locks of snow, and his long black boots encroaching on his knees."[1] His ancestors had been Virginians even before the infant colony had a House of Burgesses. When Benjamin Harrison now spoke he represented the aristocracy of the Old Dominion, and he launched all his influence against the Constitution. For some reason he was laboring "under high excitement," and was almost inaudible. He lauded the character of the Virginia Legislature, of which he had been a member. The Constitution, insisted Harrison, "would operate an infringement of the rights and liberties of the people."[2]

George Nicholas answered at length and with characteristic ability and learning.[3] But his speech was quite unnecessary, for what Harrison had said amounted to nothing. On the morning of the ninth day of the Convention Madison continued his masterful argument, two sections of which he already had delivered.[4] He went out of his way to praise Marshall, who, said Madison, had "entered into the subject with a great deal of ability."[5]

Mason, replying on taxation, said that under the Constitution there were "some land holders in this state who will have to pay twenty times as much [taxes] as will be paid for all the land on which Philadelphia stands." A National excise tax, he declared, "will carry the exciseman to every farmer's house, who distills a little brandy where he may search and ransack as he pleases." And what men, asked

[1] Grigsby, i, 183–85. [2] Elliott, iii, 236. [3] *Ib.*, 236–47.
[4] *Ib.*, 247–62. [5] *Ib.*, 254.

Mason, would be in Congress from Virginia? Most of them would be "chosen . . . from the higher order of the people — from the great, the wealthy — the *well-born* — the *well-born*, Mr. Chairman, that aristocratic idol — that flattering idea — that *exotic* plant which has been lately imported from the ports of Great Britain, and planted in the luxurious soil of this country."

It is significant to find the "well-born," wealthy, learned, and cultivated Mason taking this tone. It shows that the common people's dislike of a National Government was so intense that even George Mason pandered to it. It was the fears, prejudices, and passions of the multitude upon which the enemies of the Constitution chiefly depended; and when Mason stooped to appeal to them, the sense of class distinction must have been extreme. His statement also reveals the economic line of cleavage between the friends and foes of the Constitution.

It was in this speech that Mason made his scathing "cat and Tory" comparison. He knew those who were for the Constitution, "their connections, their conduct, their political principles, and a number of other circumstances. There are a great many wise and good men among them"; but when he looked around and observed "who are the warmest and most zealous friends to this new government," it made him "think of the story of the cat transformed to a fine lady: forgetting her transformation and happening to see a rat, she could not restrain herself, but sprang upon it out of the chair." [1]

[1] This caustic reference was to the members of the Convention who

Mason denounced Randolph for the latter's apostasy. "I know," said Mason, "that he once saw as great danger in it as I do. What has happened since this to alter his opinion?" Of course, the Confederation was defective and reform needed; but the Constitution was no reform. Without previous amendments, "we never can accede to it. Our duty to God and to our posterity forbids it," [1] declared the venerable author of Virginia's Bill of Rights and the Constitution of the State.

Henry Lee answered with fire and spirit, first rebuking "the irregular and disorderly manner" in which the opposition had carried on the debate. As to the cat story, Mason ought to know "that ridicule is not the test of truth. Does he imagine that he who can raise the loudest laugh is the soundest reasoner?" And Mason's "insinuations" about the "well-born" being elected to Congress were "unwarrantable." He hoped that "we shall hear no more of such groundless aspersions." Lee's speech is valuable only as showing the rising spirit of anger which was beginning to appear even in Virginia's well-conducted, parliamentary, and courteous debate.[2]

The Anti-Constitutionalists were now bringing all their guns into action. The second Revolutionary soldier to speak for the opposition now arose. William Grayson was almost as attractive a military

had been Tories. (Grigsby, i, 193; Elliott, iii, 269; also Rowland, ii, 240.) As we have seen most of the Tories and Revolutionary soldiers were united for the Constitution. These former enemies were brought together by a common desire for a strong National Government.

[1] Elliott, iii, 262–72.

[2] *Ib.*, 272–73.

figure as Henry Lee himself. He had been educated at Oxford, had studied law in the Inner Temple; and his style of speech was the polished result of practice in the English political clubs, in Congress, and at the bar.[1] There were few men in America with more richly stored or better trained minds. He was a precise Latinist and a caustic wit. When, during the debate, some of the Constitutionalist speakers used Latin phrases with a wrong pronunciation, Grayson, *sotto voce*, would correct them. Once he remarked, loud enough to be heard by the other members whom he set roaring with laughter, that he was not surprised that men who were about to vote away the liberties of a living people should take such liberties with a dead language.

Grayson now brought into action the heaviest battery the Anti-Constitutionalists had in reserve. He did not blame Virginia's delegates to the Federal Convention, said Grayson suavely. It was unfortunate "that they did not do more for the general good of America"; but "I do not criminate or suspect the principles on which they acted." Of course, the Confederation had defects; but these were "inseparable from the nature of such [Republican]

[1] Grigsby, i, 194–205. William Grayson was one of the strongest men in Virginia. He became Virginia's first Senator under the Constitution. (See *infra*, vol. II, chap. II.) He filled and satisfied the public eye of his day as a soldier, scholar, and statesman. And yet he has dropped out of history almost completely. He is one of those rare personalities whom the whims of time and events have so obscured that they are to be seen but dimly through the mists. His character and mind can be measured but vaguely by fragments buried in neglected pages. William Grayson's talents, work, and vanished fame remind one of the fine ability, and all but forgotten career of Sir James Mackintosh.

governments." The Constitutionalists had conjured up "phantoms and ideal dangers to lead us into measures which will . . . be the ruin of our country." He argued that we were in no danger from our default in paying foreign loans; for most European nations were friendly. "Loans from nations are not like loans from private men. Nations lend money . . . to one another from views of national interest. France was willing to pluck the fairest feather out of the British crown. This was her hope in aiding us"—a truth evident to every man in the Convention. Such loans were habitually delayed,—for instance, "the money which the Dutch borrowed of Henry IV is not yet paid"; these same Dutch "passed Queen Elizabeth's loan at a very considerable discount," and they "made their own terms with that contemptible monarch," James I.

The people had no idea, asserted Grayson, that the Federal Convention would do more than to give the National Government power to levy a five per cent tariff, but since then "horrors have been greatly magnified." He ridiculed Randolph's prophecy of war and calamity. According to Randolph, "we shall be ruined and disunited forever, unless we adopt this Constitution. Pennsylvania and Maryland are to fall upon us from the north, like the Goths and Vandals of old; the Algerines, whose flat-sided vessels never came farther than Madeira, are to fill the Chesapeake with mighty fleets, and to attack us on our front; the Indians are to invade us with numerous armies on our rear, in order to convert our cleared lands into hunting-grounds; and the Carolinians, from the South (mounted on alligators, I presume), are to come and destroy our cornfields, and eat up our little children! These, sir, are the mighty dangers which await us if we reject [the Constitution] — dangers which are merely imaginary, and ludicrous in the extreme!"

At bottom, thought Grayson, the controversy was between two opinions — "the one that mankind can only be governed by force; the other that they are capable" of governing themselves. Under the second theory, which Grayson favored, all that was necessary was to "give congress the regulation of commerce" and to "infuse new strength and spirit into the state governments."

This, he remarked, was the proper course to pursue and to maintain "till the American character be marked with some certain features. We are yet too young to know what we are fit for." If this was not to be done and we must have a government by force, then Grayson "would have a President for life, choosing his successor at the same time; a Senate for life, with the powers of the House of Lords; and a triennial House of Representatives, with the powers of the House of Commons in England."[1] Consider the Judiciary. Suppose a man seized at the same time under processes from Federal and State Courts: "Would they divide the man in two, as Solomon directed the child to be divided who was claimed by two women?"

Evidently Grayson was making a strong impres-

[1] Elliott, iii, 279.

sion as the day grew to a close, for Monroe, seconded by Henry, moved that the Convention adjourn that Grayson might go on next day; and Madison, plainly nervous, "insisted on going through the business regularly, according to the resolution of the house." Grayson consumed most of the next forenoon, displaying great learning, but sometimes drawing the most grotesque conclusions. For example, he said that Congress might grant such privileges that "the whole commerce of the United States may be exclusively carried on by merchants residing within the seat of government [now the District of Columbia] and those places of arms which may be purchased of the state legislature." The Constitution did not give equality of representation; for "the members of Delaware will assist in laying a tax on our slaves, of which they will pay no part whatever." In general, Grayson's conclusion was that "we have asked for bread and they have given us a stone."[1]

Pendleton answered. Henry's treatment of Randolph's unhappy reference to the people as a "herd" seems to have had some effect; for Pendleton regretted its use and tried to explain it away. Henry and he differed "at the threshold" on government. "I think government necessary to protect liberty. . . . Licentiousness" was "the natural offspring of liberty"; and "therefore, all free governments should endeavor to suppress it, or else it will ultimately overthrow that liberty of which it is the result." Henry "professes himself an advocate for the middling and lower classes of men, I profess to be a

[1] Elliott, iii, 273–93 (especial passage, 280).

friend to the equal liberty of all men, from the palace to the cottage."

The appeal to class hatred, said Pendleton, had been made by the opposition exclusively; the Constitutionalists knew no distinction among men except that of good and bad men. Why did the opposition make "the distinction of *well-born* from others? . . . Whether a man be great or small, he is equally dear to me." He wished "for a regular government in order to secure and protect . . . honest citizens . . . the industrious farmer and planter." The purpose of the proposed National Government was to cherish and protect industry and property. Pendleton spoke at great length, but frequently his voice was so feeble that he could not be understood or reported.[1]

Madison followed with the fourth section of what might properly be called his treatise on government. Henry replied, striking again the master chord of the people's fears — that of a National Government as something alien. "The tyranny of Philadelphia may be like the tyranny of George III." That the Constitution must be amended "re-echoed from every part of the continent"; but that could not be done "if we ratify unconditionally." Henry remade his old points with his consummate art.

He mentioned a new subject, however, of such high practical importance that it is astonishing that he had not advanced it at the beginning and driven it home persistently. "There are," he said, "thousands and thousands of contracts, whereof equity

[1] Elliott, iii, 293–305.

forbids an exact literal performance. . . . Pass that government [the Constitution] and you will be bound hand and foot. . . . An immense quantity of depreciated Continental paper money . . . is in the hands of individuals to this day. The holders of this money may call for the nominal value, if this government be adopted. This State may be compelled to pay her proportion of that currency, pound for pound. Pass this government and you will be carried to the federal court . . . and you will be compelled to pay, shilling for shilling."

Returning to this point later on, Henry said: "Some of the states owe a great deal on account of paper money; others very little. Some of the Northern States have collected and barrelled up paper money. Virginia has sent thither her cash long ago. There is little or none of the Continental paper money retained in this State. Is it not their business to appreciate this money? Yes, and it will be your business to prevent it. But there will be a majority [in Congress] against you and you will be obliged to pay your share of this money, in its nominal value." [1]

Referring to Pendleton's assertion that the State Court had declared void legislative acts which violated the State Constitution, Henry exclaimed:

[1] Elliott, iii, 319–22; and see chap. II, vol. II, of this work. Although this, like other economic phases of the contest, was of immediate, practical and serious concern to the people, Henry touched upon it only twice thereafter and each time but briefly; and Mason mentioned it only once. This fact is another proof of the small place which this grave part of the economic problem occupied in the minds of the foes of the Constitution, in comparison with that of "liberty" as endangered by a strong National Government.

"Yes, sir, our judges opposed the acts of the legisature. We have this landmark to guide us. They had the fortitude to declare that they were the judiciary and would oppose unconstitutional acts. Are you sure your federal judiciary will act thus? Is that judiciary as well constructed, and as independent of the other branches, as our state judiciary? Where are your landmarks in this government? I will be bold to say you cannot find any in it. I take it as the highest encomium on this country [Virginia] that the acts of the legislature, if unconstitutional, are liable to be opposed by the judiciary."[1]

As usual, Henry ended with a fearsome picture and prophecy, this time of the danger to and destruction of Southern interests at the hands of the Northern majority. This, said he, "is a picture so horrid, so wretched, so dreadful, that I need no longer dwell upon it"; and he "dreaded the most iniquitous speculation and stock-jobbing, from the operation of such a system" as the Constitution provided.[2] Madison replied — the first spontaneous part he had taken in the debate.[3]

The next morning the opposition centered their fire on the Mississippi question. Henry again demanded that the members of the Convention who had been in Congress should tell what had been done.[4] The members of Congress — Lee, Monroe,

[1] Elliott, iii, 325. At this time the fears of the Anti-Constitutionalists were principally that the powers given the National Government would "swallow up" the State Governments; and it was not until long afterward that objection was made to the right and power of the National Supreme Court to declare a law of Congress unconstitutional. (See vol. III of this work.)

[2] *Ib.*, 313–28. [3] *Ib.*, 328–32. [4] *Ib.*, 332–33.

Grayson, and Madison — then gave their versions of the Jay-Gardoqui transaction.[1]

The Constitutionalists rightly felt that "the whole scene has been conjured by Henry to affect the ruin of the new Constitution,"[2] and that seasoned gladiator now confirmed their fears. He astutely threw the blame on Madison and answered the charge of the Constitutionalists that "we [the opposition] are scuffling for Kentucky votes and attending to local circumstances." With all of his address and power, Henry bore down upon the Mississippi question. Thus he appealed for Kentucky votes: "Shall we appear to care less for their interests than for that of distant people [the Spaniards]?"

At Henry's word a vision rose before all eyes of the great American valley sustaining "a mighty population," farms, villages, towns, cities, colleges, churches, happiness, prosperity; and "the Mississippi covered with ships laden with foreign and domestic wealth" — a vision of a splendid West "the strength, the pride, and the flower of the Confederacy." And then quickly succeeded on the screen the picture of the deserted settlers, the West a wilderness, the Father of Waters flowing idly to the sea, unused by commerce, unadorned by the argosies of trade. Such, said he, would be the Mississippi under the Constitution "controlled by those who had no interest in its welfare."[3]

At last the Constitutionalists were stunned. For a while no one spoke. Pendleton, "his right hand

[1] Elliott, iii, 333–51.

[2] Grigsby, i, 230 and 243.

[3] *Ib.*, 245; Elliott, iii, 251–56. This, the real vote-getting part of Henry's speech, is not reported by Robertson.

grasping his crutch, sat silent and amazed."[1] Nicholas, the dauntless, was first to recover himself, and repeated Marshall's argument on the Mississippi question. Evidently the opposition had lobbied effectively with the Kentucky members on that sore point; for, exclaimed Nicholas, "we have been alarmed about the loss of the Mississippi, in and *out* of doors."[2]

The Constitutionalists strove mightily to break the force of Henry's *coup* on the Kentucky delegates. He had "seen so many attempts made," exclaimed Randolph, "and so many wrong inducements offered to influence the delegation from Kentucky," that he must speak his mind about it.[3] Corbin called the Mississippi trick "reprehensible." And well might the Constitutionalists tremble; for in spite of all they could do, ten out of fourteen of the Kentucky delegates voted against ratifying the Constitution.

That night Pendleton fell ill and John Tyler, "one of the staunchest opponents of the new Constitution," was elected Vice-President.[4] The Mississippi question was dropped for the moment; the Constitutionalists rallied and carried Corbin's motion to debate the new Government clause by clause in accordance with the original resolution. Several sections of the first article were read and debated, Henry, Mason, and Grayson for the opposition; Madison bearing the burden of the debate for the Constitutionalists.

The rich man and the poor, the State Govern-

[1] Grigsby, i, 245.
[2] Elliott, iii, 356.
[3] *Ib.*, 361–65.
[4] Grigsby, i, 248.

ment a thing of the "people" and the National Government something apart from the "people," were woven throughout the Anti-Constitutionalists' assaults. "Where," exclaimed Henry, "are the purse and the sword of Virginia? They must go to Congress. What has become of your country? The Virginian government is but a name. . . . We are to be consolidated." [1]

The second week's debate closed with the advantage on the side of the opposition. Gouverneur Morris, the New York Constitutionalist, who, still on the ground, was watching the fight in Richmond and undoubtedly advising the Virginia Constitutionalists, reported to Hamilton in New York that "matters are not going so well in this State as the Friends of America could wish." The Anti-Constitutionalists had been making headway, not only through Henry's tremendous oratory, but also by other means; and the Constitutionalists acknowledged that their own arguments in debate were having little or no effect.

"If, indeed, the Debates in Convention were alone attended to," wrote Gouverneur Morris, "a contrary Inference would be drawn for altho Mr. Henry is most warm and powerful in Declamation being perfectly Master of 'Action Utterrance and Power of Speech to stir Men's Blood' yet the Weight of Argument is so strong on the Side of Truth as wholly to destroy even on weak Minds the Effects of his Eloquence But there are as you well know certain dark Modes of operating on the Minds of Members which

[1] Elliott, iii, 366–410.

like contagious Diseases are only known by their Effects on the Frame and unfortunately our moral like our phisical Doctors are often mistaken in their Judgment from Diagnostics Be of good Chear. My Religion steps in where my Understanding falters and I feel Faith as I loose Confidence. Things will yet go right but when and how I dare not predicate. So much for this dull Subject."[1]

"We have conjectured for some days," Madison advised Hamilton, "that the policy is to spin out the Session in order to receive overtures from your [New York's] Convention: or if that cannot be, to weary the members into a adjournment without taking any decision. It [is] presumed at the same time that they do not despair of carrying the point of previous amendments which is preferable game. The parties continue to be nearly balanced. If we have a majority at all, it does not exceed three or four. If we lose it Kentucke will be the cause; they are generally if not unanimously against us."[2]

On the back of Madison's letter, Henry Lee wrote one of his own to the New York Constitutionalist chieftain. "We possess as yet," said Lee, "in defiance of great exertions a majority, but very small indeed. A correspondence has certainly been opened thro a Mr. O.[swald] of Philad[a] from the Malcontents of B. & N. Y. to us — it has its operation, but I believe we are still safe, unless the question of adjournment should be introduced, & love of home may

[1] Gouverneur Morris from Richmond to Hamilton in New York, June 13, 1788; Hamilton MSS., Lib. Cong.

[2] Madison to Hamilton, June 16, 1788; Hamilton MSS., Lib. Cong.

induce some of our friends to abandon their principles."[1]

"The business is in the most ticklish state that can be imagined," Madison informed Washington; "the majority will certainly be very small on whatever side it may finally lie; and I dare not encourage much expectation that it will be on the favorable side. Oswald of Philad[a] has been here with letters for the anti-Federal leaders from N. York and probably Philad[a] He Staid a very short time here during which he was occasionally closeted with H——y M—s—n &c."[2]

On Monday the Anti-Constitutionalists were first in the field. They were by now displaying improved tactics. Henry opened on the dangers of a standing army. "If Congress shall say that the general welfare requires it, they may keep armies continually on foot. . . . They may billet them on the people at pleasure." This is "a most dangerous power! Its principles are despotic."[3] Madison followed,[4] and Mason, Corbin, and Grayson also spoke,[5] the latter asserting that, under the Constitution, the States could not "command the militia" unless by implication.

[1] Lee to Hamilton; Hamilton MSS., Lib. Cong. The first paragraph of Lee's letter to Hamilton shows that the latter was helping his friend financially; for Lee wrote, "God bless you & your efforts to save me from the manifold purse misfortunes which have & continue to oppress me, whenever I attempt to aid human nature. You will do what you think best, & whatever you do I will confirm — Hazard has acted the part of a decided rascal, & if I fail in my right, I may not in personal revenge." (*Ib.*)

[2] Madison to Washington, June 13, 1788; *Writings:* Hunt, v, 179 and footnote.

[3] Elliott, iii, 410–12. [4] *Ib.*, 412–15. [5] *Ib.*, 415–18.

Here Marshall again took part in the debate.[1] He asked whether Grayson was serious in stating that the Constitution left no power in the States over the militia unless by implication. Under the Constitution, State and National Governments "each derived its powers from the people, and each was to act according to the powers given it." Were "powers not given retained by implication?" asked Marshall. Was "this power [over the militia] not retained by the states, as they had not given it away?"

It is true, he admitted, that "Congress may call forth the militia" for National purposes — "as to suppress insurrections and repel invasions"; but the power given the States by the people "is not taken away, for the Constitution does not say so." The power of Congress over the ten miles square where the National Capital was to be located is "exclusive . . . because it is expressed [in the Constitution] to be exclusive." Marshall contended that any power given Congress which before was in the States remained in both unless the Constitution said otherwise or unless there was incompatibility in its exercise. So the States would have the same control over the militia as formerly. "When invaded or in imminent danger they [the States] can engage in war."

Grayson had said, declared Marshall, that if the National Government disciplined the militia, "they will form an aristocratic government, unsafe and unfit to be trusted." Grayson interrupted Marshall in an unsuccessful attempt to squirm out of the posi-

[1] Elliott, iii, 419–20.

tion in which the latter had placed him. He had only said that in its military features the Constitution "was so constructed as to form a great aristocratic body."

Marshall retorted that "as the government was drawn from the people, the feelings and interests of the people would be attended to"; and, therefore, there would be no military aristocracy. "When the government is drawn from the people and depending on the people for its continuance, oppressive measures will not be attempted," argued Marshall, "as they will certainly draw on their authors the resentment of those on whom they depend." No! cried he: "On this government, thus depending on ourselves for its existence, I will rest my safety."

Again Marshall expressed his military experience and instincts. If war should come "what government is able to protect you?" he asked. "Will any state depend on its own exertions?" No! If the National Government is not given the power "state will fall after state and be a sacrifice to the want of power in the general government." Uttering the motto of American Nationalism, which, long years afterward, he declared to have been the ruling maxim of his entire life, Marshall cried, "*United we are strong, divided we fall.*" If the National militia cannot "draw the militia of one state to another . . . every state must depend upon itself. . . . It requires a superintending power, . . . to call forth the resources of all to protect all."

Replying to Grayson's assertion that "a general regulation [of the militia] may be made to inflict punishments," Marshall asked whether Grayson imagined that a militia law would be "incapable of being changed?" Grayson's idea "supposes that men renounce their own interests." And "if Congress neglect our militia, we can arm them ourselves. Cannot Virginia import arms . . . [and] put them into the hands of her militia men?" Marshall summed up with the statement that the States derived no powers from the Constitution "but retained them, though not acknowledged in any part of it." [1]

Marshall's speech must have been better than anything indicated in the stenographer's report; for the resourceful Grayson was moved to answer it at once [2] and even Henry felt called upon to reply to it.[3] Henry was very fond of Marshall; and this affection of the mature statesman for the rising young lawyer saved the latter in a furious political contest ten years afterwards.[4] The debate was continued by Madison, Mason, Nicholas, Lee, Pendleton, and finally ended in a desultory conversation,[5] but nothing important or notable was said in this phase of the debate. One statement, however, coming as it did from Mason, flashes a side-light on the prevailing feeling that the proposed National Government was something apart from the people. Mason saw the most frightful dangers from the unlimited power of Congress over the ten miles square provided for the National Capital.

[1] Elliott, iii, 419–21. [2] *Ib.*, 421–22. [3] *Ib.*, 422–24.

[4] Henry turned the tide in Marshall's favor in the latter's hard fight for Congress in 1798. (*Infra*, vol. II, chap. x.)

[5] Elliott, iii, 434.

"This ten miles square," cried Mason, "may set at defiance the laws of the surrounding states, and may, like the custom of the superstitious days of our ancestors, become the sanctuary of the blackest crimes. Here the Federal Courts are to sit. . . . What sort of a jury shall we have within the ten miles square?" asked Mason, and himself answered, "The immediate creatures of the government. What chance will poor men get? . . . If an attempt should be made to establish tyranny over the people, here are ten miles square where the greatest offender may meet protection. If any of the officers or creatures [of the National Government] should attempt to oppress the people or should actually perpetrate the blackest deed, he has nothing to do but to get into the ten miles square." [1]

The debate then turned upon amending the Constitution by a Bill of Rights, the Constitutionalists asserting that such an amendment was not necessary, and the opposition that it was absolutely essen-

[1] Elliott, iii, 431. Throughout the entire debate Henry often sounded his loudest alarms on the supreme power of Congress over the ten miles square where the National Capital was to be located; and, indeed, this seems to have been one of the chief sources of popular apprehension. The fact that the people at large looked upon the proposed National Government as something foreign, something akin to the British rule which had been overthrown, stares the student in the face wherever he turns among the records of the Constitutional period. It is so important that it cannot too often be repeated.

Patrick Henry, of course, who was the supreme popular orator of our history and who drew his strength from his perfect knowledge of the public mind and heart, might have been expected to make appeals based on this general fear. But when such men as George Mason and William Grayson, who belonged to Virginia's highest classes and who were carefully educated men of conservative temper, did the same thing, we see how deep and strong was the general feeling against any central National power.

tial. The question was "whether rights not given up were reserved?" Henry, as usual, was vivid. He thought that, without a Bill of Rights, "excisemen may come in multitudes . . . go into your cellars and rooms, and search, and ransack, and measure, everything you eat, drink, and wear." And the common law! The Constitution did not guarantee its preservation. "Congress may introduce the practice of the civil law, in preference to that of the common law; . . . the practice of . . . torturing, to extort a confession of the crime. . . . We are then lost and undone."[1]

The slavery question next got attention, Mason, Madison, Tyler, Henry, and Nicholas continuing the discussion.[2] Under the first clause of the tenth section of article one, Henry again brought up the payment of the Continental debt. "He asked gentlemen who had been high in authority, whether there were not some state speculations on this matter. He had been informed that some states had acquired vast quantities of that money, which they would be able to recover in its nominal value of the other states." Mason said "that he had been informed that some states had speculated most enormously in this matter. Many individuals had speculated so as to make great fortunes on the ruin of their fellow-citizens." Madison in reply assured the Convention that the Constitution itself placed the whole subject exactly where it was under the Confederation; therefore, said he, it is "immaterial who holds those great quantities of paper money, . . . or at what value

[1] Elliott, iii, 447–49. [2] *Ib.*, 452–57.

they acquired it." [1] To this extent only was the point raised which became most vital when the National Government was established and under way.[2]

Madison's point, said Mason, was good as far as it went; but, under the Confederation, Congress could discharge the Continental money "at its depreciated value," which had gone down "to a thousand for one." But under the Constitution "we must pay it shilling for shilling or at least at the rate of one for forty"; which would take "the last particle of our property. . . . We may be taxed for centuries, to give advantage to a few particular states in the Union and a number of rapacious speculators." Henry then turned Madison's point that "the new Constitution would place us in the same situation with the old"; for Henry saw "clearly" that "this paper money must be discharged shilling for shilling." [3] Then Henry brought up the scarecrow of the British debts, which had more to do with the opposition to the Constitution in Virginia [4] than any other specific subject, excepting, perhaps, the threatened loss of the Mississippi and the supreme objection

[1] Elliott, iii, 473.

[2] It is exceedingly strange that in the debates on the Constitution in the various State Conventions, so little, comparatively, was made of the debt and the speculations in it. The preciousness of "liberty" and the danger of "monarchy," the security of the former through State sovereignty and the peril of the latter through National Government, received far more attention than did the economic problem.

[3] Elliott, 472–74. And see vol. II, chap. II, of this work.

[4] "The recovery of the British debts can no longer be postponed and there now seems to be a moral certainty that your patrimony will all go to satisfy the unjust debt from your papa to the Hanburys." (Tucker to his stepsons, June 29, 1788, quoted in Conway, 106; and see comment, *ib.*)

that a National Government would destroy the States and endanger "liberty."

The opposition had now come to the point where they were fighting the separate provisions of the Constitution one by one. When the first section of the second article, concerning the Executive Department, was reached, the opposition felt themselves on safe ground. The Constitution here sapped the "great fundamental principle of responsibility in republicanism," according to Mason.[1] Grayson wanted to know how the President would be punished if he abused his power. "Will you call him before the Senate? They are his counsellors and partners in crime."[2]

The treaty-making power, the command of the army, the method of electing the President, the failure of the Constitution to provide for his rotation in office, all were, to the alarmed Anti-Constitutionalists, the chains and shackles of certain and inevitable despotism. The simple fears of the unlettered men who sullenly had fought the Constitution in the Massachusetts Convention were stated and urged throughout the great debate in Virginia by some of her ablest and most learned sons. Madison was at his best in his exposition of the treaty-making power. But if the debate on the Executive Department had any effect whatever in getting votes for or against the Constitution, the advantage was with the enemies of the proposed new Government.

Grayson wrote to Dane: "I think we got a Vote by debating the powers of the President. This, you will

[1] Elliott, iii, 484. [2] *Ib.*, 491.

observe, is confidential." But this was cold comfort, for, he added, "our affairs . . . are in the most ticklish situation. We have got ten out of thirteen of the Kentucke members but we wanted the whole: & I don't know that we have got one yet of the four upper counties: this is an important point & which both sides are contending for by every means in their power. I believe it is absolutely certain that we have got 80 votes on our side which are inflexible & that eight persons are fluctuating & undecided." [1]

[1] Grayson to Dane, June 18, 1788; Dane MSS., Lib. Cong. This shows the loose management of the Anti-Constitutionalist politicians: for Kentucky had fourteen votes in the Convention, instead of thirteen, as Grayson declared; and so uncertain was the outcome that to omit a single vote in calculating the strength of the contending forces was unpardonable in one who was, and was accounted to be, a leader.

CHAPTER XII

THE STRATEGY OF VICTORY

Washington's influence carried this government [Virginia's ratification of the Constitution]. (Monroe to Jefferson, July 12, 1788.)

If I shall be in the minority, I shall have those painful sensations which arise from a conviction of *being overpowered in a good cause*. Yet I will be a peaceable citizen. (Henry, in his last debate.)

Now came the real tug-of-war. The debate on the Judiciary was the climax of the fight. And here John Marshall was given the place of chief combatant. The opposition felt that again they might influence one or two delegates by mere debate, and they prepared to attack with all their might. "Tomorrow the Judiciary comes on when we [Anti-Constitutionalists] shall exert our whole force. It is expected we shall get two Votes if the point is conducted in an able & masterly manner," Grayson advised the opposition headquarters in New York.[1]

The Judiciary was, indeed, the weakest part of the Constitutionalists' battle line. The large amount of the British debts; the feeling, which Virginia's legislation against the payment of them had fostered, that the day would be far distant and perhaps would never come when those debts would have to be paid; the provision of the Constitution concerning the making of treaties, which were to be the supreme law of the land; the certainty that the Treaty of Peace would be covered by the new fundamental law; the fear that another treaty would be negotiated governing the British obligations more specifically, if

[1] Grayson to Dane, June 18, 1788; Dane MSS., Lib. Cong.

the Constitution were adopted; the fact that such a treaty and all other National laws would be enforced by National Courts — all these and many other germane considerations, such as land grants and confused titles, were focused on the fears of the planters.

The creditor class were equally anxious and alarmed. "If the new Constitution should not be adopted or something similar, we are of the opinion that such is the interest and influence of Debtors in our State that every thing . . . will be at Risk" was the opinion of the legal representatives in Virginia of the Collins mercantile house.[1]

Great quantities of land granted under the Royal Government by Great Britain, but which the State had confiscated, had been bought and settled by thousands of men whose families now lived upon this land; and these settlers felt that, in some way, their titles would be in danger if they were dragged before a National Court.[2]

The Constitutionalists did not underestimate their peril, and at no point during the three weeks' debate did they prepare for battle with greater care. They returned to their original tactics and delivered the first blow. Pendleton, of course, was the ideal man to lead the Constitutionalist attack. And never in his whole life did that extraordinary man make a more convincing argument.[3] Mason tried his best to

[1] Logan and Story to Stephen Collins, Petersburg, Nov. 2, 1787; Collins MSS., Lib. Cong.

[2] See Grigsby, i, 278–79, for an able and sympathetic account from the point of view of the settler and debtor.

[3] *Ib.*, 280–84; Elliott, iii, 517–21.

answer Pendleton, although he admitted that the Judiciary "lies out of my line." Still he was clear, in his own mind, that the National Judiciary was "so constructed as to destroy the dearest rights of the community," and thought it would "destroy the state governments, whatever may have been the intention."

While Mason spoke with uncertainty, it was in this brief speech that this eminent Virginian uncovered the hidden thought and purpose of many of the Constitutionalists; and uttered an unconscious prophecy which it was the destiny of John Marshall to realize. "There are," said Mason, "many gentlemen in the United States who think it right that we should have one great, national, consolidated government, and that it was better to bring it about slowly and imperceptibly rather than all at once. This is no reflection on any man, for I mean none. To those who think that one national, consolidated government is best for America, this extensive judicial authority will be agreeable"; and he further declared, "I know from my own knowledge many worthy gentlemen" of this opinion. Madison demanded of Mason "an unequivocal explanation." Mason exonerated Madison, personally, and admitted that "neither did I ever hear any of the delegates from this state advocate it." Thus did the extreme courtesy of the Virginia debate cause the opposition to yield one of its most effective weapons.[1]

[1] Elliott, iii, 522; Grigsby, i, 284. So overwhelming was the popular feeling against a strong National Government that, if the Anti-Constitutionalists had concentrated their attack upon this secret purpose of the leading Constitutionalists to make it such by easy stages,

But Mason made the most out of the Constitution's proposed Judiciary establishment. Take it at its best, said he: "Even suppose the poor man should be able to obtain judgment in the inferior court, for the greatest injury, what justice can he get on appeal? Can he go four or five hundred miles? Can he stand the expense attending it?" [1] As to the jurisdiction of National Courts in controversies between citizens of different States, "Can we not trust our state courts with a decision of these?" asked Mason. "What!" cried he, "carry me a thousand miles from home — from my family and business — to where, perhaps, it will be impossible for me to prove that I paid" the money sued for.

"Is not a jury excluded absolutely?" by the Constitution, asked Mason. And even if a jury be possible in National Courts, still, under the Constitution, where is there any right to challenge jurors? "If I be tried in the Federal Court for a crime which may effect my life, have I a right of challenging or excepting to the jury?" This omission was a serious and immediate peril to great numbers of Virginians, said he. "I dread the ruin that will be wrought on thirty thousand of our people [deriving their titles through Fairfax] with respect to disputed lands. I am personally endangered as an inhabitant of the Northern Neck." Under the Constitution "the people of that part will be obliged . . . to pay the quit rent of their lands." This was to Mason, "a most serious alarm. . . ."

it is more than probable that the Constitution would have been defeated.

[1] Elliott, iii, 524.

"Lord Fairfax's title was clear and undisputed," he continued. The State had "taxed his lands as private property"; but "after his death" Virginia, in 1782, "sequestered the quit rents due at his death, in the hands of his debtors. The following year" they were restored to his executor. Then came the Treaty of Peace providing against "further confiscation"; but, "after this, an act of Assembly passed, confiscating his [Fairfax's] whole property."

So, concluded Mason, "as Lord Fairfax's title was indisputably good, and as treaties [under the Constitution] are to be the supreme law of the land, will not his representatives be able to recover all in the federal court? How will gentlemen like to pay an additional tax on lands in the Northern Neck?" Yet that was what they would be compelled to do if the Constitution were adopted. Thus they would be "doubly taxed." "Were I going to my grave, I would appeal to Heaven that I think it [this] true," fervently avowed the snowy-haired Mason.

Thus Mason made one of the cleverest appeals of the whole debate to the personal and pecuniary interests of a considerable number of the people and to several members of the Convention. In this artful and somewhat demagogic argument he called attention to the lands involved in other extensive land grants. As we have seen, John Marshall was then personally interested in the Fairfax title,[1] and he was soon to possess it; in after years, it was to develop one of the great legal contests of history; and

[1] His own and his father's lands in Fauquier County were derived through the Fairfax title.

the court over which Marshall was to preside was to settle it definitively.

Although not a lawyer,[1] Madison now made an argument which was one of the distinguished intellectual performances of the Convention. But he did not comprehend the sweep of the National Judiciary's power. "It is not in the power of individuals," said Madison, "to call any state into court." It may be that this statement influenced John Marshall, who soon followed, to repeat it.[2]

But it was Henry who gave the subject of the Judiciary that thrill, anticipation of which filled every seat on the floor and packed the galleries. "Mournful," to Henry, were the recollections which the debate already had produced. "The purse is gone; the sword is gone," and now the scales of Justice are to be given away. Even the trial by jury is to be abandoned. Henry spoke long and effectively; and, extravagant as most of his statements were, his penetrating mind was sometimes more nearly right in its forecast than even that of Madison.

As he closed, the daring of the Patrick Henry of 1765 and 1775 displayed itself. "Shall Americans give up that [jury trial] which nothing could induce the English people to relinquish?" he exclaimed. "The idea is abhorrent to my mind. There was a time when we should have spurned at it. . . . Old as I am, it is probable I may yet have the appellation of *rebel*. . . . As this government [Constitution]

[1] Grigsby, i, 290.
[2] Elliott, iii, 530–39. For Marshall's repetition see *ib.*, 551–62.

stands, I despise and abhor it," cried the unrivaled orator of the people.[1]

Up now rose John Marshall, whom the Constitutionalist leaders had agreed upon for the critical task of defending the Judiciary article. Marshall, as we have seen, had begun the practice of law in Richmond only five years before; and during much of this period his time and attention had been taken by his duties as a delegate in the Legislature. Yet his intellectual strength, the power of his personality, his likableness, and all the qualities of his mind and character had so impressed every one that, by common consent, he was the man for the hour and the work at hand. And Marshall had carefully prepared his speech.[2]

The Judiciary provided by the Constitution was, said Marshall "a great improvement on that system from which we are now departing. Here [in the Constitution] are tribunals appointed for *the decision of controversies* which were before either not at all, or improperly, provided for. That many benefits will result from this to the members of the collective society, every one confesses." The National Judiciary deserved the support of all unless it was "defectively organized and so constructed as to injure, instead of accommodate, the convenience of the people."

After the "fair and able" discussion by its supporters, Marshall supposed that its opponents "would be convinced of the impropriety of some of their objections. But," he lamented, "they still continue the same opposition." And what was their

[1] Elliott, iii, 539–46. [2] Grigsby, i, 297.

complaint? This: That National Courts would not be as fair and impartial as State Courts.

But why not? asked Marshall. Was it because of their tenure of office or the method of choosing them? "What is it that makes us trust our [State] judges? Their independence in office and manner of appointment."[1] But, under the Constitution, are not National judges "chosen with as much wisdom as the judges of the state governments? Are they not equally, if not more independent? If so," will they not be equally fair and impartial? "If there be as much wisdom and knowledge in the United States as in a particular state," will they "not be equally exercised in the selection of [National] judges?" Such were the questions which Marshall poured upon the Anti-Constitutionalists.

The kernel of the objection to National Courts was, declared Marshall, "a belief that there will not be a fair trial had in those courts." But it was plain, he argued, that "we are as secure there as anywhere else. What mischief results from some causes being tried there [in the National Courts]?" Independent judges "wisely appointed . . . will never countenance an unfair trial." Assuming this to be true "what are the subjects of the jurisdiction" of National Courts? To Mason's objection that Congress could create any number of inferior courts it might deem necessary, Marshall replied that he had supposed that those who feared Congress would say that "*no* inferior courts" would be established, "but that we

[1] Virginia judges were, at this period, appointed by the General Assembly. (Constitution, 1776.)

should be dragged to the centre of the Union." On the contrary, the greater the number of these inferior courts, the less danger "of being dragged to the centre of the United States."

Mason's point, that the jurisdiction of National Courts would extend to all cases, was absurd, argued Marshall. For "has the government of the United States power to make laws on every subject? . . . laws affecting the mode of transferring property, or contracts, or claims, between citizens of the same state? Can" Congress "go beyond the delegated powers?" Certainly not. Here Marshall stated the doctrine which, fifteen years later, he was to announce from the Supreme Bench:—

"If," he asserted, "they [Congress] were to make a law not warranted by any of the powers enumerated, it would be considered by the [National] judges as an infringement of the Constitution which they are to guard. They would not consider such a law as coming under their jurisdiction. *They would declare it void*. . . . To what quarter will you look for protection from an infringement of the Constitution, if you will not give the power to the judiciary? There is no other body that can afford such a protection."

The National Courts would not supplant the State tribunals. The Constitution did not "exclude state courts" from those cases which they now possess. "They have concurrent jurisdiction with the Federal courts in those cases in which the latter have cognizance," expounded the nascent jurist. "Are not controversies respecting lands claimed under the grants of different states the only controversies between citizens of the same state which the Federal Judiciary can take [exclusive] cognizance of?"

The work of the National Courts would make the State Courts more efficient because it would relieve them of a mass of business of which they were not able to dispose. "Does not every gentleman know that the causes in our [State] courts are more numerous than they can decide?" asked Marshall. "Look at the dockets," he exclaimed. "You will find them crowded with suits which the life of man will not see determined.[1] If some of these suits be carried to other courts, will it be wrong? They will still have business enough."

How vain and fanciful, argued Marshall, the contention that National judges would screen "officers of the [National] government from merited punishment." Does anybody really believe that "the Federal sheriff will go into a poor man's house and beat him or abuse his family and the Federal court will protect him," as Mason and Henry had said would be the case? Even if a law should be passed authorizing "such great insults to the people . . . it would be void," declared Marshall. Thus he stated for the second time the doctrine which he was, from the Supreme Bench, to put beyond controversy.

Why, asked Marshall, "discriminate [in the Con-

[1] "There are upwards of 4,000 suits now entered on the docket in the General Court; and the number is continually increasing. Where this will end the Lord only knows — should an Act pass to extend the term of the Courts sitting — it is thought that the number of Executors [executions] that would issue . . . would be too heavy for our government to bear and that such a rapid transfer of Property would altogether stop the movement of our Machine." (Logan and Story, to Stephen Collins, Petersburg, Nov. 2, 1787; Collins MSS., Lib. Cong.)

stitution] between . . . chancery, admiralty and the common law" as the Anti-Constitutionalists insisted upon doing? "Why not leave it to Congress? They . . . would not wantonly infringe your rights." If they did, they would "render themselves hateful to the people at large." Therefore, "something may be left to the legislature [Congress] freely chosen by ourselves from among ourselves, who are to share the burdens imposed upon the community and who can be changed at our pleasure. Where power may be trusted and there is no motive to abuse it, it . . . is as well to leave it undetermined as to fix it in the Constitution."

These sentences had prophecy in them. Indeed, they were to be repeated almost without change by the same man that now uttered them in debate, when he should ascend to the ultimate place of official interpretation of our fundamental law. While Hamilton's immortal state papers profoundly impressed Marshall, as we shall see, they were not, as many have supposed, the source of his convictions. In the Virginia Constitutional Convention of 1788 Marshall stated in debate the elements of most of his immortal Nationalist opinions.

But there was one exception. As to "disputes between *a state and the citizens of another state*," Marshall hoped "that no gentleman will think that a state will be called at the bar of a Federal court. . . . It is not rational to suppose that the Sovereign power should be dragged before a court. The intent is to enable states to recover claims of individuals residing in other states." If there were partiality in this — "if an individual cannot . . . obtain judgment against a state, though he may be sued by a state" — it was a difficulty which could "not be avoided"; let the claimant apply to the State Legislature for relief.

The objection to suits in the National Courts between citizens of different States went "too far," contended Marshall. Such actions "may not in general be absolutely necessary," but surely in some such cases "the citizen . . . ought to be able to recur to this [National] tribunal." What harm could it do? "Will he get more than justice there? What has he to get? Justice! Shall we object to this because the citizen of another state can obtain justice without applying to our state courts?" Indeed, "it may be necessary" in causes affected by "the laws and regulations of commerce" and "in cases of debt and some other controversies." . . . "In claims for land it is not necessary — but it is not dangerous."

These suits between citizens of different States "will be instituted in the state where the defendant resides, and nowhere else," expounded the youthful interpreter of the Constitution; and the case "will be determined by the laws of the state where the contract was made. According to those laws, and those only, can it be decided." That was no "novelty," but "a principle" long recognized in the jurisprudence of Virginia. "The laws which governed the contract at its formation, govern it in its decision." National Courts, in such controversies, would "preserve the peace of the Union," because if courts of different States should not give justice between citizens of those States, the result would be "disputes between the states." Also the jurisdiction of National Courts in "controversies between a state and a foreign state . . . will be the means of preventing disputes with foreign nations"; for since "the previous consent of the parties is necessary . . . each party will acquiesce."

As to "the exclusion of trial by jury, in this case," Marshall asked, "Does the word *court* only mean the judges? Does not the determination of the jury necessarily lead to the judgment of the court? Is there anything" in the Constitution "which gives the [National] judges exclusive jurisdiction of matters of fact? What is the object of a jury trial? To inform the court of the facts." If "a court has cognizance of facts," it certainly "can make inquiry by a jury," dryly observed Marshall.

He ridiculed Mason's and Henry's statement that juries, in the ten miles square which was to be the seat of the National Government, would be "mere tools of parties with which he would not trust his person or property." "What!" exclaimed Marshall, "Will no one stay there but the tools and officers of the government? . . . Will there not be independent merchants and respectable gentlemen of fortune . . . worthy farmers and mechanics" in the National Capital just as there were in Richmond? And "will the officers of the government become improper to be on a jury? What is it to the government whether this man or that man succeeds? It is all one thing."

As to jury trial not being guaranteed by the

National Constitution in civil cases, neither did Virginia's Constitution, said Marshall, "direct trials by jury"; and the provision was "merely recommendatory" concerning jury trials in the Bill of Rights, which, as everybody knew, was no part of the State Constitution. "Have you a jury trial when a judgment is obtained on a replevin bond or by default?" Or "when a motion is made by the Commonwealth against an individual . . . or by one joint obligor against another, to recover sums paid as security." Of course not! "Yet they are all civil cases. . . . The Legislature of Virginia does not give a trial by jury where it is not necessary, but gives it wherever it is thought expedient." And Congress would do the same, he reassured the Convention.

Mason's objection, that the right to challenge jurors was not guaranteed in the Constitution, was trivial, said Marshall. Did Virginia's Constitution make such a guaranty? Did the British Constitution do so by any express provision? Was jury challenge secured by Magna Charta? Or by the Bill of Rights? [1] Every Virginian knew that they were not. "This privilege is founded in their [English people's] laws," Marshall reminded the Convention. So why insert it in the American Constitution?

Thus the inhabitants of the Northern Neck or anybody else were not in danger on that score. Neither were they placed in jeopardy in any other way by the Constitution. Here Marshall made a curious argument. Mason, he said, had "acknowl-

[1] This form of argument by asking questions to which the answers must needs be favorable to his contention was peculiarly characteristic of Marshall.

edged that there was no complete title[1] [in Fairfax]. . . . Was he [Mason] not satisfied that the right of the legal representatives of the proprietor [to collect quitrents] did not exist at the time he mentioned [the date of the Treaty of Peace]? If so, it cannot exist now," declared Marshall. "I trust those who come from that quarter [the Northern Neck] will not be intimidated on this account in voting on this question" he pleaded; for let them remember that there was "a law passed in 1782 [sequestration of quitrents] which secured this."

Let the "many poor men" who Mason had said might "be harassed by the representatives of Lord Fairfax" rest assured on that point; for "if he [Fairfax] has no right," they could not be disturbed. "If he has this right [to collect quitrents] and comes to Virginia, what laws will his claims be determined by?" By Virginia's laws. "By what tribunals will they be determined? By our state courts."[2] So the "poor man" who was "unjustly prosecuted" would "be abundantly protected and satisfied by the temper of his neighbors."[3]

[1] The reporter makes Mason assert the reverse.

[2] It is hard to see how Marshall arrived at this conclusion. But for the fact that Marshall prepared this speech, one would think the reporter erred.

[3] See Marshall's argument in Hite *vs.* Fairfax, chap. v, *supra;* and see vol. III of this work.

Randolph made the clearest statement of the whole debate on the Fairfax question: —

"Lord Fairfax . . . died during the war. In the year 1782, an act passed sequestering all quitrents, then due, in the hands of the persons holding the lands, until the right of descent should be known, and the General Assembly should make final provision therein. This act directed all quitrents, thereafter becoming due, to be paid into the public treasury; so that, with respect to his descendants, this act con-

The truth was, said Marshall, that justice would be done in all cases by both National and State Courts. Laws would not be "tyrannically executed" as the opposition feared; the "independency of your judges" would prevent that. "If," he argued, "a law be exercised tyrannically in Virginia, to whom can you trust? To your Judiciary! What security have you for justice? Their independence! Will it not be so in the Federal court?"

Like other objections to the power of Congress and the conduct of National Courts, the criticism that men might be punished for their political opinions was, declared Marshall, groundless and absurd; for, "the good opinion of the people at large must be consulted by their representatives — otherwise mischiefs would be produced which would shake the government to its foundations." Of course, then, he contended, neither Congress nor the courts would abuse their power. The charge that "unjust claims will be made, and the defendant had better pay them than go to the Supreme Court" was unthinkable. Would anybody incur great expense to oppress another? "What will he gain by an unjust demand?

fiscated the quitrents. In the year 1783, an act passed restoring to the legal representative of the proprietor the quitrents due to him at the time of his death. But in the year 1785 another act passed, by which the inhabitants of the Northern Neck are exonerated and discharged from paying composition and quitrents to the commonwealth." But Randolph then asserted that: "This last act has completely confiscated this property. It is repugnant to no part of the treaty, with respect to the quitrents confiscated by the act of 1782." So, continued he, "I ask the Convention of the free people of Virginia if there can be honesty in rejecting the government because justice is to be done by it? I beg the honourable gentleman to lay the objection to his heart." (Elliott, iii, 574–75.)

Does a claim establish a right? He must bring his witnesses to prove his claim"; otherwise "the expenses must fall on him." Will he take the chances that the injured man will not appear and defend the unjust suit? "Those who know human nature, black as it is," sarcastically observed Marshall, "must know that mankind are too attached to their own interest to run such a risk."

"The Federal Government," exclaimed Marshall, "has no other motive, and has every reason for doing right which the members of our state legislature have. Will a man on the eastern shore be sent to be tried in Kentucky, or a man from Kentucky be brought to the eastern shore to have his trial? A government, by doing this, would destroy itself."[1]

This, in effect, was John Marshall's exposition of the second section of article three of the Constitution. Although Grigsby, whose accuracy on such details is not questioned, says that the speech was prepared, Robertson's report would not indicate that such was the case. The address is wanting in that close-knit continuity of reasoning and in that neatness of thought and expression which were Marshall's peculiar excellence. Like his first debate in the Convention, his speech on the Judiciary is disjointed. A subject is half treated in one part of his remarks and resumed in another.[2] But he makes his

[1] Elliott, iii, 551-62.

[2] In summarizing Marshall's speech, it is necessary to collect his arguments on any given point, and present them consecutively. In Robertson's (Elliott) report Marshall scatters his points in distracting fashion.

principal points with clearness and power. His argument is based on the independence of the courts as the best guaranty against unjust decisions; the responsibility of Congress to the people as the strongest safeguard against oppressive laws; and the similarity of Virginia's Constitution and Courts to the National Constitution and Courts as proof of the security, fairness, and justice of the National Judiciary.

Marshall's effort really closed the case for the Constitution on the Judiciary. That night Madison wrote to Hamilton that "a great effort is making" against the Judiciary. "The retrospection to cases antecedent to the Constitution, such as British debts and an apprehended revival of Fairfax — Indiana, Vandalia, &c., claims are also brought into view in all the terrific colours which imagination can give them. . . . Delay & an adjournment will be tried if the adverse party find their numbers inferior. . . . At present it is calculated that we still retain a majority of 3 or 4; and if we can weather the storm ag^{st}." the Judiciary, "I shall hold the danger to be pretty well over. There is nevertheless a very disagreeable uncertainty in the case; and the more so as there is a possibility that our present strength may be miscalculated." [1]

Marshall's speech alarmed the opposition, and Grayson used all his learning, wit, and cleverness in an attempt to break its force. Randolph replied. Thus the second week closed. Neither side was certain of the exact number of votes it had, though every member was observed with the politician's

[1] Madison to Hamilton, June 20, 1788; Hamilton MSS., Lib. Cong.

anxiety and care.[1] The Constitutionalists had the greater confidence. Madison wrote his father that "The calculations on different sides do not accord; . . . I think however, the friends of the Constitution are most confident of superiority. . . . It is not probable that many proselytes will be made on either side." [2]

On Sunday Madison made his weekly report to Hamilton: "The Judiciary Department has been on the anvil for several days; and I presume will still be a further subject of disquisition. The attacks on it have apparently made less impression than was feared. But they may be secretly felt by particular interests that would not make the acknowledgment, and w^d. chuse to ground their vote ag^st. the Constitution on other motives." [3]

The Anti-Constitutionalists were becoming desperate. If they could not amend the Constitution as a condition of ratifying it, their game now was either an adjournment or a delay until the Legislature, scheduled to meet on the following Monday and known to be, in the main, opposed to the Constitution, should afford them relief.

If these expedients should fail, there was open talk of secession.[4] The Constitutionalists arranged for the utmost dispatch and planned to "withhold, by a studied fairness in every step on the side of the

[1] The members of the Convention were carefully watched and each side made, every night, a minute estimate of its votes.

[2] Madison to his father, June 20, 1788; *Writings:* Hunt, v, footnote to 216.

[3] Madison to Hamilton, June 22, 1788; Hamilton MSS., Lib. Cong

[4] *Ib.*

Constitution, every pretext for rash experiments." They hoped to avoid previous amendment by proposing "to preface the ratification with some plain & general matters that cannot effect the validity of the" Constitution. They felt that "these expedients are rendered prudent by the nice balance of members, and the scruples entertained by some who are in general well affected." But whether these devices "will secure us a majority," wrote Madison, "I dare not positively to declare."

So small was their expected majority likely to be, that the Constitutionalists felt that "ordinary casualties . . . may vary the result." They were exceedingly alarmed over the coming to town of the members of the Legislature who "as individuals . . . may have some influence and as coming immediately from the people at large they can give any colour they please to the popular sentiments at this moment, and may in that mode throw a bias on the representatives of the people in Convention." [1]

From the adjournment on Saturday until the Convention again assembled on the following Monday, June 23, the opposition decided that something more must be done to counteract Marshall's exposition of the Judiciary article. For this purpose their leader and strongest men took the floor. The shorthand reporter was not present on this day, but the printer of the debates took notes.[2]

Nothing so well shows the esteem in which Marshall's ability was held as Patrick Henry's compli-

[1] Madison to Hamilton, June 22, 1788; Hamilton MSS., Lib. Cong.
[2] Elliott, iii, 576.

ment to his young associate. "I have," said Henry, "the highest veneration and respect for the honorable gentleman, and I have experienced his candor on all occasions"; but "in this instance" Henry felt that Marshall was mistaken. "It is not on that paper before you we have to rely. . . . It is on those who may be appointed under it. It will be an empire of men, and not of laws."

Marshall interrupted Henry to explain that the latter had not clearly understood him as to the trial by jury. Henry responded that "the gentleman's candor, sir, as I informed you before, I have the highest opinion of, and am happy to find he has so far explained what he meant; but, sir, has he mended the matter?" Then Henry enlarged upon what he thought was the Constitution's sacrifice of rights of trial by jury. What would become of this, that, and the other? What would be the end of this contract and that? And "what is to become of the *purchases of the Indians?* — those unhappy nations who . . . by being made drunk, have given a thousand, nay I might say, ten thousand acres, for the trifling sum of sixpence!" And what of those who owed the British debts? — they will "be ruined by being dragged into Federal courts and the liberty and happiness of our citizens gone, never again to be recovered." [1]

The Constitutionalists had anticipated that Henry would touch on his hobby, the Indians; and they were ready with an answer far more effective on the votes of the members than any argument, however weighty. Hardly had Henry closed when a giant old

[1] Elliott, iii, 577–80.

man got upon his feet. For more than thirty years this bluff and ancient veteran had been a soldier. Since 1755 he had been one of the boldest and ablest of Virginia's famous Indian fighters and often had commanded the Virginia rangers that defended the frontier from the savages. His utter fearlessness and tremendous physical strength had made him the terror of the red man, and his name was a household word throughout Virginia as a bulwark against the savages. Throughout the Revolution he had borne himself as a hero. So when Colonel Adam Stephen spoke, his words were sword-thrusts.[1]

Henry, growled Stephen, "means to frighten us by his bugbears of hobgoblins, his sale of lands to pay taxes, Indian purchases and other horrors that I think I know as much about as he does." Colonel Stephen then described the Indian country, the Indian tribes, and Indian trade. He also knew "of several rich mines of gold and silver in the western country" which would pay the taxes Henry was so worried about. "If the gentleman [Henry] does not like this government, let him go and live among the Indians. I know of several nations that live very happily; and I can furnish him with a vocabulary of their language." [2]

Nothing can be plainer than that this personal assault on Henry was prearranged; for George Nich-

[1] Grigsby, i, 300. See Washington's letters to Stephen during the year of Marshall's birth, when Stephen, under Washington, was fighting the French and Indians. (*Writings:* Ford, i, 227, 322, 332, 360; also *Proceedings*, Council of War, Oct. 30, 1756; *ib.*, 364–71; in which Colonel Adam Stephen was presiding officer.)

[2] Elliott, iii, 580.

olas followed it up with what came near being an open insult. Answering Henry's insinuation about Indian lands being fraudulently purchased, Nicholas retorted, looking directly at Henry, "there are gentlemen who have come by large possessions that it is not easy to account for." This was taken as a reflection on some of Henry's land speculations. The latter felt the sting; for "here Mr. Henry interfered and hoped the honorable gentleman meant nothing personal." Nicholas snapped back, "I mean what I say, sir."

The extremes to which the opposition went in lobbying with members and the nature of their conversation are shown by an acid sentence of Nicholas in this speech. He referred to "an observation I have heard out of doors; which was that, because the New England men wore black stockings and plush breeches, there can be no union with them."

Henry was instantly on his feet when Nicholas finished. He thought the Convention floor "an improper place" to make "personal insinuations, or to wound my private reputation. . . . As to land matters, I can tell how I came by what I have . . . I hold what I hold in right, and in a just manner." Henry was most courteous and dignified in this discussion, disclaiming any intention to offend any one. Nicholas responded that he "meant no personality . . . nor . . . any resentment." But, said he, "If such conduct meets the contempt of that gentleman [Henry] I can only assure him it meets with an equal degree of contempt from me."

Here the President of the Convention interfered

and "hoped the gentlemen would not be personal; that they would proceed to investigate the subject calmly, and in a peaceable manner." Thereupon Nicholas admitted that he had not referred to Henry when he first spoke, but to "those who had taken up large tracts of land in the western country"; Nicholas had not, however, explained this before because he felt that Henry had said some things that one gentleman ought not to say to another. Thus ended the second of the only two instances in Virginia's long and masterful debate which approached a personal quarrel or displayed even the smallest discourtesy.[1]

The debate now drew swiftly to a close. Excitement ran high. The Anti-Constitutionalists, tense and desperate, threatened forcible opposition to the proposed National Government if it should be established. Mason "dreaded popular resistance" to the Constitution and was "emphatic" in his fears of "*the dreadful effects* . . . should the people resist." Gentlemen should pause before deciding "a question which involved such awful consequences." This so aroused Lee that he could "no longer suppress" his "utterance." Much as he liked and admired Mason, Lee asked him "if he has not pursued the very means to bring into action the horrors which he deprecates?"

"Such speeches within these walls, from a character so venerable and estimable," declared Lee, "easily progress into overt acts, among the less thinking and the vicious." Lee implored that the "God of heaven avert from my country the dreadful

[1] Elliott, iii, 581–82.

curse!" But, he thundered, "if the madness of some and the vice of others" should arouse popular resistance to the Constitution, the friends of that instrument "will meet the afflicting call"; and he plainly intimated that any uprising of the people against the proposed National Government would be met with arms.[1] The guns of Sumter were being forged.

On the night of June 23, the Constitutionalists decided to deliver their final assault. They knew that it must be a decisive one. The time had arrived for the meeting of the Legislature which was hostile to the Constitution;[2] and if the friends of the proposed new Government were to win at all, they must win quickly. A careful poll had shown them that straight-out ratification without amendment of some kind was impossible. So they followed the plan of the Massachusetts Constitutionalists and determined to offer amendments themselves — but amendments merely by way of recommendation and subsequent to ratification, instead of previous amendments as a condition of ratification. The venerable Wythe was chosen to carry out the programme. On Tuesday morning, June 24, Pendleton called to the chair Thomas Mathews, one of the best parliamentarians in the Convention, a stanch Constitutionalist, a veteran of the Revolution, and a popular man.

[1] Elliott, iii, 585–86.

[2] "Virginia is the only instance among the ratifying states in which the Politics of the Legislature are at variance with the sense of the people, expressed by their Representatives in Convention." (Madison to Washington, Nov. 5, 1788; *Writings:* Hunt, v, 302.)

Instantly Mathews recognized Wythe; for Henry was ready with his amendments, and, had an Anti-Constitutionalist been in the chair, would have been able to offer them before Wythe could move for ratification. Wythe, pale and fatigued, was so agitated that at first he could not speak plainly.[1] After reviewing the whole subject, he said that to insist on previous amendments might dissolve the Union, whereas all necessary amendments could easily be had after ratification. Wythe then moved the Constitutionalists' resolution for ratification.

In a towering rage, Henry rose for what, outside of the courtroom, was the last great speech of his life.[2] He felt that he had been unjustly forestalled and that the battle against the Constitution was failing because of the stern and unfair tactics of his foes.[3] The Constitutionalists admitted, said Henry, that the Constitution was "capitally defective"; yet they proposed to ratify it without first remedying its conceded faults. This was so absurd that he was "sure the gentleman [Wythe] meant nothing but to amuse the committee. I know his candor," said Henry. "His proposal is an idea dreadful to me. . . . The great body of yeomanry are in decided opposition" to the Constitution.

Henry declared that of his own personal knowledge "nine tenths of the people" in "nineteen coun-

[1] Grigsby, i, 307.

[2] The two amazing speeches which Henry made that day should be taken together. While both were inspired by what happened on the floor, yet they are in reality one. The reports give no idea of the tremendous effect which those who heard Henry tell us these speeches had.

[3] Grigsby, i, 307–08.

ties adjacent to each other" were against the proposed new National Government. The Constitutionalists' plan of "subsequent amendments will not do for men of this cast." And how do the people feel even in the States that had ratified it? Look at Pennsylvania! Only ten thousand out of seventy thousand of her people were represented in the Pennsylvania Convention.

If the Constitution was ratified without previous amendments, Henry declared that he would "have nothing to do with it." He offered the Bill of Rights and amendments which he himself had drawn, proposing to refer them to the other States "for their consideration, previous to its [Constitution's] ratification."[1] Henry then turned upon the Constitutionalists their own point by declaring that it was their plan of ratification without previous amendments which would endanger the Union.[2] Randolph followed briefly and Dawson at great length. Madison for the Constitutionalists, and Grayson for the opposition, exerted themselves to the utmost. Nature aided Henry when he closed the day in an appeal such as only the supremely gifted can make.

"I see," cried Henry, in rapt exaltation, "the awful immensity of the dangers with which it [the Constitution] is pregnant. I see it. I feel it. I see beings of a higher order anxious concerning our decision. When I see beyond the horizon that bounds

[1] Henry's amendments were practically the same as those which the Convention finally adopted as recommendations subsequent to ratification instead of previous amendment on which ratification was conditioned.

[2] Elliott, iii, 587–96.

human eyes, and look at the final consummation of all human things, and see those intelligent beings which inhabit the ethereal mansions reviewing the political decisions and revolutions which, in the progress of time, will happen in America, and the consequent happiness or misery of mankind, I am led to believe that much of the account, on one side or the other, will depend on what we now decide. Our own happiness alone is not affected by the event. All nations are interested in the determination. We have it in our power to secure the happiness of one half of the human race. Its adoption may involve the misery of the other hemisphere."[1]

In the midst of this trance-like spell which the master conjurer had thrown over his hearers, a terrible storm suddenly arose. Darkness fell upon the full light of day. Lightnings flashed and crashing thunders shook the Convention hall. With the inspiration of genius this unrivaled actor made the tempest seem a part of his own denunciation. The scene became insupportable. Members rushed from their seats.[2] As Henry closed, the tempest died away.

The spectators returned, the members recovered their composure, and the session was resumed.[3] Nicholas coldly moved that the question be put at

[1] Elliott, iii, 625. This extract is badly mangled. The reporter confesses that he could take only a little of Henry's peroration. Elliott's reprint of Robertson's reports gives scarcely a suggestion of its dramatic appeal. We are indebted to Grigsby's patient work in collecting from eye and ear witnesses first-hand accounts, for a reasonably accurate description of the scene.

[2] Grigsby, i, 316–17; also Wirt, 313; Henry, ii, 370–71; and Conway, 113.

[3] Grigsby, i, 316–17.

nine o'clock on the following morning. Clay and Ronald opposed, the latter declaring that without such amendments "as will secure the happiness of the people" he would "though much against his inclination vote against this Constitution."

Anxious and prolonged were the conferences of the Constitutionalist managers that night. The Legislature had convened. It was now or never for the friends of the Constitution. The delay of a single day might lose them the contest. That night and the next morning they brought to bear every ounce of their strength. The Convention met for its final session on the historic 25th of June, with the Constitutionalists in gravest apprehension. They were not sure that Henry would not carry out his threat to leave the hall; and they pictured to themselves the dreaded spectacle of that popular leader walking out at the head of the enraged opposition.[1]

Into the hands of the burly Nicholas the Constitutionalists wisely gave command. The moment the Convention was called to order, the chair recognized Nicholas, who acted instantly with his characteristically icy and merciless decision. "The friends of the Constitution," said Nicholas, "wish to take up no more time, the matter being now fully discussed. They are convinced that further time will answer no end but to serve the cause of those who wish to destroy the Constitution. We wish it to be ratified and such amendments as may be thought necessary to be subsequently considered by a committee in order to be recommended to Congress."

[1] Grigsby, i, 317.

Where, he defiantly asked, did the opposition get authority to say that the Constitutionalists would not insist upon amendments after they had secured ratification of the Constitution? They really wished for Wythe's amendments;[1] and would "agree to any others which" would "not destroy the spirit of the Constitution." Nicholas moved the reading of Wythe's resolution in order that a vote might be taken upon it.[2]

Tyler moved the reading of Henry's proposed amendments and Bill of Rights. Benjamin Harrison protested against the Constitutionalists' plan. He was for previous amendment, and thought Wythe's "measure of adoption to be unwarrantable, precipitate, and dangerously impolitic." Madison reassured those who were fearful that the Constitutionalists, if they won on ratification, would not further urge the amendments Wythe had offered; the Constitutionalists then closed, as they had begun, with admirable strategy.

James Innes was Attorney-General. His duties had kept him frequently from the Convention. He was well educated, extremely popular, and had been one of the most gifted and gallant officers that Virginia had sent to the front during the Revolution. Physically he was a colossus, the largest man in that State of giants. Such was the popular and imposing champion which the Constitutionalists had so well

[1] Very few of the Constitutionalists wanted any amendments; and Madison sorrowfully offered in Congress the following year those that were reluctantly adopted. See vol. II, chap. II, of this work.

[2] Elliott, iii, 627.

chosen to utter their parting word.[1] And Innes did his utmost in the hardest of situations; for if he took too much time, he would endanger his own cause; if he did not make a deep impression, he would fail in the purpose for which he was put forward.[2]

Men who heard Innes testify that "he spoke like one inspired." [3] For the opposition the learned and accomplished Tyler closed the general debate. It was time wasted on both sides. But that nothing might be left undone, the Constitutionalists now brought into action a rough, forthright member from the Valley. Zachariah Johnson spoke for "those who live in large, remote, back counties." He dwelt, he said, "among the poor people." The most that he could claim for himself was "to be of the middle rank." He had "a numerous offspring" and he was willing to trust their future to the Constitution.[4]

Henry could not restrain himself; but he would better not have spoken, for he admitted defeat. The anxious Constitutionalists must have breathed a sigh of relief when Henry said that he would not leave the hall. Though "*overpowered in a good cause*, yet I will be a peaceable citizen." All he would try to do would be "to remove the defects of that system [the Constitution] in a constitutional way." And so, declared the scarred veteran as he yielded his sword to the victors, he would "patiently wait in expectation of seeing that government changed, so as to be compatible with the safety, liberty, and happiness, of the people."

[1] Grigsby, i, 323–29.
[2] *Ib.*, 328.
[3] *Ib.*, 332.
[4] Elliott, iii, 644–49.

Wythe's resolution of ratification now came to a vote. No more carefully worded paper for the purposes it was intended to accomplish ever was laid before a deliberative body. It reassured those who feared the Constitution, in language which went far to grant most of their demands; and while the resolve called for ratification, yet, "in order to relieve the apprehensions of those who may be solicitous for amendments," it provided that all necessary amendments be *recommended* to Congress. Thus did the Constitutionalists, who had exhausted all the resources of management, debate, and personal persuasion, now find it necessary to resort to the most delicate tact.

The opposition moved to substitute for the ratification resolution one of their own, which declared "that previous to the ratification . . . a declaration of rights . . . together with amendments . . . should be referred by this Convention to the other states . . . for their consideration." On this, the first test vote of the struggle, the Constitutionalists won by the slender majority of 8 out of a total of 168. On the main question which followed, the Anti-Constitutionalists lost but one vote and the Constitution escaped defeat by a majority of only 10.

To secure ratification, eight members of the Convention voted against the wishes of their constituents,[1] and two ignored their instructions.[2] Grayson openly but respectfully stated on the floor that the

[1] Henry, ii, 377. "At least ten members voted, either in disobedience of positive instructions of their constituents, or in defiance of their well known opinions." (Grigsby, i, 41.)

[2] Scott, 235–38.

vote was the result of Washington's influence. "I think," said he, "that, were it not for one great character in America, so many men would not be for this government." [1] Followers of their old commander as the members from the Valley were, the fear of the Indians had quite as much to do with getting their support for a stronger National Government as had the weight of Washington's influence.[2]

Randolph "humbly supplicated one parting word" before the last vote was taken. It was a word of excuse and self-justification. His vote, he said, would be "ascribed by malice to motives unknown to his breast." He would "ask the mercy of God for every other act of his life," but for this he requested only Heaven's justice. He still objected to the Constitution, but the ratification of it by eight States had now "reduced our deliberations to the single question of *Union* or no *Union*." [3] So closed the greatest debate ever held over the Constitution and one of the ablest parliamentary contests of history.

A committee was appointed to report "a form of ratification pursuant to the first resolution"; and another was selected "to prepare and report such amendments as by them shall be deemed neces-

[1] Elliott, iii, 616. Madison frankly admitted that only the prominence of the framers of the Constitution secured even a consideration of it by many of its warmest friends, much less by the people. "Had the Constitution been framed and recommended by an obscure individual," wrote Madison, "instead of a body possessing public respect and confidence, there cannot be a doubt, that, although it would have stood in the identical words, it would have commanded little attention from those who now admire its wisdom." (Madison to Randolph, Jan. 10, 1788; *Writings:* Hunt, v, 81.)

[2] Grigsby, i, footnote to 110.

[3] Elliott, iii, 652.

sary."[1] Marshall was chosen as a member of both these important committees.

The lengths to which the Constitutionalists were driven in order to secure ratification are measured by the amendments they were forced to bring in. These numbered twenty, in addition to a Bill of Rights, which also had twenty articles. The ten amendments afterwards made to the Constitution were hardly a shadow of those recommended by the Virginia Convention of 1788.

That body actually proposed that National excise or direct tax laws should not operate in any State, in case the State itself should collect its quota under State laws and through State officials; that two thirds of both houses of Congress, present, should be necessary to pass navigation laws or laws regulating commerce; that no army or regular troops should be "raised or kept up in time of peace" without the consent of two thirds of both houses, present; that the power of Congress over the seat of the National Government should be confined to police and administrative regulation. The Judiciary amendment would have imprisoned the Supreme Court within limits so narrow as to render that tribunal almost powerless and would have absolutely prevented the establishment of inferior National Courts, except those of Admiralty.[2] Yet only on such terms could ratification be secured even by the small and uncertain majority that finally voted for it.

On June 25, Clinton's suppressed letter to Randolph was laid before the House of Delegates which

[1] Elliott, iii, 653–63. [2] *Ib.*, 659–61.

had just convened.[1] Mason was so furious that he drew up resolutions for an investigation of Randolph's conduct.[2] But the deed was done, anger was unavailing, and the resolutions never were offered.[3]

So frail was the Constitutionalist strength that if the news of the New Hampshire ratification had not reached Virginia, it is more than probable that Jefferson's advice would have been followed and that the Old Dominion would have held back until all the amendments desired by the opposition had been made a part of the fundamental law;[4] and the Constitution would have been a far different and infinitely weaker instrument than it is.

Burning with wrath, the Anti-Constitutionalists held a meeting on the night of the day of the vote for ratification, to consider measures for resisting the new National Government. The character of Patrick Henry never shone with greater luster than when he took the chair at this determined gathering of furious men. He had done his best against the Constitution, said Henry, but he had done it in the "*proper place*"; the question was settled now and he advised his colleagues that "as true and faithful republicans, they had all better go home!"[5] Well might Washington write that only "conciliatory con-

[1] Clinton's letter was not read, however, because all the members of the Legislature had gone to hear Henry's last great speech. (Conway, 112.)

[2] Conway, 114; Henry, ii, 363.

[3] For Mason's resolutions and a careful review of the incident, see Rowland, ii, 274–80.

[4] Henry, ii, 377.

[5] *Southern Literary Messenger*, i, 332; also quoted in Rowland, ii, 274.

duct" got the Constitution through;[1] well might he declare that "it is nearly impossible for anybody who has not been on the spot (from any description) to conceive what the delicacy and danger of our situation have been."[2]

And Marshall had been on the spot. Marshall had seen it all. Marshall had been a part of it all. From the first careful election programme of the Constitutionalists, the young Richmond lawyer had been in every meeting where the plans of the managers were laid and the order of battle arranged. No man in all the country knew better than he, the hair's breadth by which the ordinance of our National Government escaped strangulation at its very birth. No one in America better understood how carefully and yet how boldly Nationalism must be advanced if it were to grow stronger or even to survive.

It was plain to Marshall that the formal adoption of the Constitution did not end the battle. That conflict, indeed, was only beginning. The fight over ratification had been but the first phase of the struggle. We are now to behold the next stages of that great contest, each as dramatic as it was vital; and we shall observe how Marshall bore himself on every field of this mighty civil strife, note his development and mark his progress toward that supreme station for which events prepared him. We are to witness his efforts to uphold the National Government, not only with argument and

[1] Washington to Pinckney, June 28, 1788; *Writings:* Ford, xi, 285.
[2] Washington to Jefferson, Aug. 31, 1788; *ib.*, 321.

political activity, but also with a readiness to draw the sword and employ military force. We shall look upon the mad scenes resulting in America from the terrific and bloody convulsion in Europe and measure the lasting effect the French Revolution produced upon the statesmen and people of the United States. In short, we are to survey a strange swirl of forces, economic and emotional, throwing to the surface now one "issue" and now another, all of them centering in the sovereign question of Nationalism or States' Rights.

END OF VOLUME I

APPENDIX

APPENDIX

I

WILL OF THOMAS MARSHALL, "CARPENTER"

In the Name of God Amen! I, Thomas Marshall of the County of Westmoreland of Washington Parish, Carpenter, being very weak but of perfect memory thanks be to God for it doth ordain this my last will and testament in manner and form following, first I give and bequeath my soul into the hands of my blessed Creator & Redeemer hoping through meritts of my blessed Saviour to receive full pardon and remission of all my sins and my body to the Earth to be decently bur-yed according to the discretion of my Executrix which hereafter shall be named. Imps. I make and ordain my well beloved wife Martha Marshall to be my full and whole Executrix — Item, I will that my estate shall remain in the hands of my wife as long as she remain single but in case she marrys then she is to have her lawful part & the rest to be taken out of her hands equally to be divided among my children — Item, I will that if my wife marry, that David Brown Senr. and Jno. Brown to be guardians over my children and to take the estate in their hands bringing it to appraisement giving in good security to what it is valued and to pay my children their dues as they shall come to age. Item — I will that Elizabeth Rosser is to have a heifer delivered by my wife called White-Belly to be delivered as soon as I am deceast — Item, I will that my son William Marshall shall have my plantation as soon as he comes to age to him and his heirs forever, but in case that my son William die before he comes to age or die without issue then my plantation is to fall to the next heir apparent at law.

Thomas Marshall (Seal)

Test Edw: Taylor, John Hearford,
John Taylor.

WESTMORLD: SS. { At a Court held for the said County the 31st day of May 1704.

The last will and testament of Thomas Marshall within written was proved by the oaths of John Oxford and John Taylor two of the witnesses thereto subscribed and a Probat thereof granted to Martha Marshall his relict and Executrix therein named.

Test
IA: WESTCOMB Cler. Com. Ped.

Record aty: sexto die Juny:
1704. Pr.
Eundm Clerum.

A Copy. Teste:
ALBERT STUART, Clerk.
By:
F. F. CHANDLER, Deputy Clerk.

[A Copy. Will of Thomas Marshall. Recorded in the Clerk's Office of the Circuit Court of Westmoreland County, in Deed and Will Book no. 3 at page 232 *et seq.*]

II

WILL OF JOHN MARSHALL "OF THE FOREST"

THE LAST will and testament of John Marshall being very sick and weak but of perfect mind and memory is as followeth.

First of all I give and recommend my soul to God that gave it and my Body to the ground to be buried in a Christian like and Discent manner at the Discretion of my Executors hereafter mentioned? Item I give and bequeath unto my beloved daughter Sarah Lovell one negro girl named Rachel now in possession of Robert Lovell. Item I give and bequeath unto my beloved daughter Ann Smith one negro boy named Danniel now in possession of Augustine Smith. Item I give and bequeath unto my beloved daughter Lize Smith one negro boy named Will now in possession of John Smith. Item I give and bequeath unto my well beloved wife Elizabeth Marshall one negro fellow named Joe and one negro woman named Cate and one negro woman named pen after Delivering the first child next born of her Body unto my son John until which time she shall remain in the possession of my wife Likewise I leave my Corn and meat to remain unappraised for the use of my wife and children also I give and bequeath unto my wife one Gray mair named beauty and side saddle also six hogs also I leave her the use of my land During her widowhood, and afterwards to fall to my son Thomas Marshall and his heirs forever. Item I leave my Tobacco to pay my Debts and if any be over for the clothing of my small children. Item I give and bequeath unto my well Beloved son Thomas Marshall one negro woman named hanno and one negroe child named Jacob? Item I give and bequeathe unto my well beloved son John Marshall one negroe fellow named George and one negroe child named Nan. Item. I give and bequeathe unto my beloved son Wm. Marshall one negro woman named Sall and one negro boy named Hanable to remain in the possession of his mother until he come to the age of twenty years. Item I give and Bequeath unto my Beloved son Abraham Marshall one negro boy named Jim and one negroe girl named bett to remain in the possession of his mother until he come to the age of twenty years. Item I give and Bequeath unto my Beloved daughter Mary Marshall one negro girl named Cate and negro boy Gus to remain in possession of her mother until she come to the age of Eighteen years or until marriage. Item, I give and Bequeath unto my beloved Daughter Peggy Marshall one negro boy named Joshua and one negro girl named Liz to remain in possession of her mother until she come to the age of Eighteen or until marriage! Item. I leave my personal Estate Except the legacies abovementioned to be equally Divided Between my wife and six children last above mentioned. Item I constitute and appoint my wife and my two sons Thos. Marshall and John Marshall Executors of this my last will & testament In witness hereof I have hereunto set my hand and fixed my seal this first day of April One thousand seven hundred and fifty two.

Interlined before assigned.

BENJAMIN RALLINS
WILLIAM HOUSTON
AUGUSTINE SMITH } JOHN MARSHALL (Seal)

WESTMORLAND SCT. { At a Court held for the said County the 26th day of May 1752.

This Last will and testament of John Marshall decd. was presented into Court by Eliza. his relict and Thomas Marshall two of his Executors therein named who made oath thereto and being proved by the oaths of Benja. Rallings and Augustine Smith two of the witnesses thereto is admitted to record, and upon the motion of the said Eliza. & Thos. and their performing what the Law in such cases require Certificate is granted them for obtaining a probate thereof in due form.

Test

GEORGE LEE C. C. C. W.

Recorded the 22d. day of June 1752.

Per

G. L. C. C. W. C.

A Copy. Teste:

FRANK STUART, Clerk of the Circuit Court of Westmoreland County, State of Virginia.

[A copy. John Marshall's Will. Recorded in the Clerk's Office of Westmoreland County, State of Virginia, in Deeds and Wills, no. 11, at page 419 *et seq.*]

III

DEED OF WILLIAM MARSHALL TO JOHN MARSHALL "OF THE FOREST"

THIS INDENTURE made the 23d day of October in ye first year of ye reign of our sovereign Lord George ye 2d. by ye. grace of God of Great Brittain France & Ireland King defendr. of ye faith &c. and in ye year of our Lord God one thousand seven hundred & twenty seven, between William Marshall of ye. County of King & Queen in ye. Colony of Virginia planter of the one part & John Marshall of ye. County of Westmoreland Virginia of the other part: WITNESSETH that ye sd. William Marshall for and in consideration of ye. sum of five shillings sterling money of England to him in hand paid before ye sealing & delivery hereof ye. receipt whereof he doth hereby acknowledge & thereof & of every part thereof doth hereby acquit & discharge ye. sd John Marshall his heirs Exectrs & administrators by these presents, hath granted bargained & sold & doth hereby grant bargain & sell John Marshall his heirs Exectrs administrs & assigns all that tract or parsel of land (except ye parsel of land wch was sold out of it to Michael Hulburt) scitute lying & being in Westmoreland County in Washington parish on or near Appamattox Creek & being part of a tract of land containing 1200 acres formerly granted to Jno: Washington & Tho: Pope gents by Patent dated the 4th Septbr. 1661 & by them lost for want of seating & since granted to Collo. Nicholas Spencer by Ordr. Genll. Court dated Septbr. ye 21st 1668 & by ye said Spencer assign'd to ye. sd. Jno: Washington ye 9th of Octobr. 1669 which sd. two hundred acres was conveyed & sold to Thomas Marshall by Francis Wright & afterwards acknowledged in Court by John Wright ye. 28th day of May 1707 which sd two hundred acres of land be ye. same more or less and bounded as follows beginning at a black Oak standing in ye. southermost line of ye sd. 1200 acres & being a corner tree of a line that divideth this two hundred acres from One hundred acres of Michael Halbarts extending along ye. sd southermost lines west two hundred poles to a marked red Oak, thence north 160 poles to another marked red Oak thence east 200 poles to a black Oak of ye sd. Halberts to ye place it began, with all houses outhouses Orchards water water courses woods under woods timbers & all other things thereunto belonging with the revertion & revertions remainder & remainders rents issues & yearly profits & every part & parcell thereof. To have and to hold ye. sd. land & premises unto ye. sd John Marshall his heirs Executors Administrs & assignes from ye. day of ye date thereof for & during & untill the full end & term of six months from thence next ensuing fully to be compleat & ended to ye. end that by virtue thereof & of the statutes for transferring uses into possessions ye. sd John Marshall might be in actual possession of ye premises & might be enabled to take and accept of a grant release of the same to him ye. sd John Marshall his heires & assignes forever. In Witness whereof the parties to these present Indentures interchangeably have set —— hands & seals ye. day & year first above written.

Wm Marshall (seal)

Signd. Seald & d'd in sight & presence of —
Francis Lacon, Jane Lacon, Thomas Thompson

Westmorld. ss. } At a Court held for the sd. County the 27th day of March 1728.

William Marshall personally acknowledged this lease of land by him passed to John Marshall to be his proper act and deed, which at the instance of the sd. John Marshall is admitted to record.

Test
G. Turbervile, C. C. W.

Recorded the 29th day of March 1728.
Pr.
G. T. C C W.

A Copy. Teste:
Frank Stuart, Clerk of tne Circuit Court of Westmoreland County, State of Virginia.

[A copy. William Marshall to John Marshall. Deed. Recorded in the Clerk's Office of Westmoreland County, State of Virginia, in Deeds and Wills, no. 8–1, at page 276.]

IV
MEMORIAL OF THOMAS MARSHALL FOR MILITARY EMOLUMENTS

To the Honorable the Speaker and members of the house of Delegates, the Memorial of Thomas Marshall humbly sheweth.

That your Memorialist in Augt 1775 was appointed Major to the first minute Battalion raisd within this Commonwealth and early in October the same year enterd into actual service in which he continued during the following winter campaign. That while your memorialist commanded at the Great Bridge he was appointed Major to the 3^{d} Virginia Continental Regim^{t} he did not however retire from service but retaind his command and continued at his post till the latter end of March 1776 when the troops under his command were relieved by those of the continent rais'd in this State, by which time the 3^{d} Virginia Regim^{t} was rais'd and your Memorialist immediately called on to take command in it. That in Augt 1776 he together with the regiment to which he belonged in obedience to the orders they had rec^{d} began their march to New York, where they join'd the Grand-Army. That your Memorialist continued in hard and unremitting service from this time till the close of the campaign of 1777. That in the latter end of November 1777 your Memorialist was informed by an official letter from the then Governor, of his haveing been appointed by the General Assembly of Virginia to the command of the State regiment of Artillery; — a command he was only induced to take by a preference he ever felt for Artillery Service. That your Memorialist however retain'd his command and continued his service in the Northern Army till the end of the Campaign when the Troops were ordered into winter quarters. That your Memorialist then return'd to Virginia and about the middle of January following took command of his Regim^{t} of Artillery, which command he rataind till the 26th of February 1781 at which time, the term of enlistment of most of the soldiers of the Regim^{t} having expired, they were discharged and your Memorialist became a reduced officer. Your Memorialist conceived from the Laws existing at the time he enter'd into the particular service of this State and from the different acts respecting the State Troops which have since passd the Legislature, that he should be intitled to every emolument to which he would have had a just claim had he remaind in the Continental Service. If however only particular discriptions of State Officers are to receive such emoluments as Continental are intitled to, your Memorialist humbly presumes to hope that his haveing made three of the severest campaigns in the last war before he took command of the State Regim[t] of Artillery, his haveing rendered, as he trusts, some services as commanding officer of that Regiment, his haveing remaind in service till there was no longer a command fcr him, his having held himself in readiness to return to service, had his regiment been recruited, give him as fair a claim to military emoluments as any officer who has been in the particular service of this State. Your memorialist therefore humbly prays that your honorable house will take his services into consideration and allow him those emoluments which may be given to other State Officers whose services may not be superior to his.

T. Marshall.

A true copy
H. R. McIlwain,
State Librarian.
June 20, 1916.

[Marshalls Pet[n] Nov. 25th 1784 Referred to Propositions Props. discharged and ref[d] to whole on Bill for giving Commutation to Officers of 1st and 2d State Regiments.]

WORKS CITED IN THIS VOLUME

WORKS CITED IN THIS VOLUME

The material given in parentheses and following certain titles indicates the form in which those titles have been cited in the footnotes.

ADAMS, CHARLES FRANCIS, *editor*. *See* Adams, John. Works.

ADAMS, HENRY. The Life of Albert Gallatin. Philadelphia. 1879. (Adams: *Gallatin*.)

See also Gallatin, Albert. Writings.

ADAMS, JOHN. Works. Edited by Charles Francis Adams. 10 vols. Boston. 1856. (*Works:* Adams.)

—— Old Family Letters. Copied from the originals for Alexander Biddle. Philadelphia. 1892. (*Old Family Letters*.)

ALLEN, ETHAN. Narrative of the Capture of Ticonderoga, and his Captivity in England, written by himself. Burlington. 1854. (Ethan Allen.)

ALLEN, GARDNER WELD. A Naval History of the American Revolution. 2 vols. New York. 1913. (Allen: *Naval History of Revolution*.)

—— Our Navy and the Barbary Corsairs, Boston. 1905. (Allen: *Our Navy and the Barbary Corsairs*.)

AMBLER, CHARLES HENRY. Sectionalism in Virginia, from 1776 to 1861. Chicago. 1910. (Ambler.)

American Historical and Literary Curiosities. *See* Smith, John Jay, and Watson, John Fanning, *joint editors*.

American Historical Review. Managing editor, J. Franklin Jameson. Vols. 1–21. New York. 1896–1916. (*Amer. Hist. Rev.*)

American Journal of Education. Edited by Henry Barnard. Vols. 1–30. Hartford. 1856–80.

American Museum or Repository of Ancient and Modern Fugitive Pieces, Philadelphia. 1788. (*American Museum*.)

ANBUREY, THOMAS. Travels through the Interior Parts of America, in a Series of Letters, by An Officer. 2 vols. London. 1789. (Anburey.)

AVERY, ELROY MCKENDREE. A History of the United States and its people. 7 vols. Cleveland. 1904–10. (Avery.)

Baily, Francis. Journal of a Tour in Unsettled Parts of North America, in 1796 and 1797. London. 1856. (Baily's *Journal.*)

Bassett, John Spencer, *editor. See* Byrd, Colonel William, of Westover. Writings.

Bayard, James A. Papers, from 1796 to 1815. Edited by Elizabeth Donnan. Washington. 1915. (Volume 2 of *Annual Report of the American Historical Association* for 1913.) (*Bayard Papers:* Donnan.)

Beard, Charles A. An Economic Interpretation of the Constitution of the United States. New York. 1913. (Beard: *Econ. I. C.*)

—— Economic Origins of Jeffersonian Democracy. New York. 1915. (Beard: *Econ. O. J. D.*)

Belcher, Robert Henry. The First American Civil War. 2 vols. London. 1911. (Belcher.)

Binney, Horace. Eulogy on John Marshall, reprinted. *See* Dillon, John F.

Bolton, Charles Knowles. The Private Soldier Under Washington. New York. 1902. (Bolton.)

Boudinot, Elias. Journal of Events in the Revolution, or Historical Recollections of American Events during the Revolutionary War. Philadelphia. 1894. (Boudinot's *Journal.*)

Branch, John P. Historical Papers, issued by the Randolph-Macon College, Ashland, Virginia. Richmond. 1901. (*Branch Historical Papers.*)

Brissot de Warville, Jean Pierre. New Travels in the United States of America, performed in 1788. Dublin. 1792. (De Warville.)

Broglie, *Duc* de, *editor. See* Talleyrand, Prince de. Memoirs.

Bruce, Philip Alexander. Economic History of Virginia in the Seventeenth Century. 2 vols. New York. 1896. (Bruce: *Econ.*)

—— Institutional History of Virginia in the Seventeenth Century. 2 vols. New York. 1910. (Bruce: *Inst.*)

Burgess, John William. Political Science and Comparative Constitutional Law. 2 vols. Boston. 1890.

Burk, John Daly. The History of Virginia, from its First Settlement to the Present Day. Continued by Skelton Jones and Louis Hue Girardin. 4 vols. Richmond. 1804–16. (Burk.)

BURKE, JOHN, *and Sir* JOHN BERNARD. Peerages of England, Ireland, and Scotland, Extinct, Dormant, and in Abeyance. London. 1846. (Burke: *Extinct Peerages.*)

BURKE, *Sir* JOHN BERNARD. Dictionary of Peerage and Baronage. Edited by Ashworth P. Burke. New York. 1904. (Burke: *Peerage.*)

BURNABY, ANDREW. Travels Through North America. [Reprinted from the Third Edition of 1798.] New York. 1904. (Burnaby.)

BUTLER, MANN. A History of the Commonwealth of Kentucky. Louisville. 1834. (Butler: *History of Kentucky.*)

BYRD, *Colonel* WILLIAM, of Westover. Writings. Edited by John Spencer Bassett. New York. 1901. (Byrd's *Writings:* Bassett.)

CABOT, GEORGE. *See* Lodge, Henry Cabot. Life and Letters of George Cabot.

Calendar of Virginia State Papers and Other Manuscripts. Preserved in the Capitol at Richmond. Vols. 1–11. Richmond. 1875–1893. (*Cal. Va. St. Prs.*)

CAMPBELL, CHARLES. History of the Colony and Ancient Dominion of Virginia. Philadelphia. 1860. (Campbell.)

CARLYLE, THOMAS. History of Friedrich II of Prussia, called Frederick the Great. 6 vols. London. 1858–65. (Carlyle: *Frederick the Great.*)

CHALKLEY, LYMAN. Chronicles of the Scotch-Irish Settlement in Virginia, Extracted from the Original Court Records of Augusta County [Virginia], 1745–1800. 3 vols. Rosslyn, Virginia. 1912–13. (*Chalkley's Augusta County (Va.) Records.*)

CHANNING, EDWARD. A History of the United States. [Vols. 1–3.] New York. 1912–16. (Channing.)

CHASTELLUX, *Marquis* F. J. DE. Travels in North America in the years 1780–81–82. New York. 1828. (Chastellux.)

CHEETHAM, JAMES. Letters, From 1801 to 1806. Printed in Proceedings of the Massachusetts Historical Society, April and May, 1907.

CHRISTIAN WILLIAM ASBURY. Richmond, Her Past and Present. Richmond. 1912. (Christian.)

COLLINS, LEWIS. History of Kentucky. Enlarged by his son, Richard H. Collins. 2 vols. Covington, Kentucky, 1874. (Collins: *History of Kentucky.*)

CONWAY, MONCURE DANIEL. Omitted Chapters of History, disclosed in the Life and Papers of Edmund Randolph. New York. 1888. (Conway.)

—— *Also see* Paine, Thomas. Writings.

CRÈVECŒUR, MICHEL GUILLAUME SAINT JOHN DE. Letters from an American Farmer. By J. Hector St. John Crèvecœur. [*pseud.*] New York. 1904. (Crèvecœur.)

DANDRIDGE, DANSKE. American Prisoners of the Revolution. Richmond. 1911. (Dandridge: *American Prisoners of the Revolution.*)

DAVIS, JOHN. Travels of Four Years and a half in the United States of America. 1798–1802. London. 1803. (Davis.)

DAWSON, HENRY B. The Assault on Stony Point by General Anthony Wayne. Morrisania. 1863. (Dawson.)

DEFOE, DANIEL. Novels and Miscellaneous Works. Preface and Notes attributed to Sir Walter Scott. Moll Flanders [vol. 3.] [Bohn's British Classics.] 7 vols. London. 1854–66. (Defoe: *Moll Flanders.*)

DILLON, JOHN F., *compiler.* John Marshall, Life, Character, and Judicial Services. (Including the Classic Orations of Binney, Story, Phelps, Waite, and Rawle.) 3 vols. Chicago. 1903. (Story, in Dillon; and Binney, in Dillon.)

DODD, WILLIAM E. Statesmen of the Old South, or From Radicalism to Conservative Revolt. New York. 1911. (Dodd.)

DONNAN, ELIZABETH, *editor. See* Bayard, James A. Papers.

DOUGLAS, *Sir* ROBERT. Peerage of Scotland. Edinburgh. 1764. (Douglas: *Peerage of Scotland.*)

ECKENRODE, H. J. The Revolution in Virginia. Boston. 1916. (Eckenrode: *R. V.*)

—— Separation of Church and State in Virginia. A Study in the Development of the Revolution. Richmond. 1910. [Special Report of the Department of Archives and History of the Virginia State Library.] (Eckenrode: *S. of C. and S.*)

Eighty Years' Progress of the United States, from the Revolutionary War to the Great Rebellion. [By Eminent Literary Men.] New York. 1864. (*Eighty Years' Progress.*)

ELLIOTT, JONATHAN, *compiler.* The Debates in the Several

State Conventions of the Adoption of the Federal Constitution. 5 vols. Philadelphia. 1896. (Elliott.)

FITHIAN, PHILIP VICKERS. Journal and Letters, 1767–1774. Edited by John Rogers Williams. Princeton University Library. 1900. (Fithian.)

FLANDERS, HENRY. The Lives and Times of the Chief Justices of the Supreme Court of the United States. 2 vols. Philadelphia. 1881. (Flanders.)

FOOTE, REV. WILLIAM HENRY. Sketches of Virginia, Historical and Biographical. 2 vols. Philadelphia. 1850–55. (Foote: *Sketches of Virginia.*)

FORD, PAUL LEICESTER, *editor*. Essays on the Constitution of the United States. New York. 1892. (Ford: *Essays on the Constitution.*)

—— Pamphlets on the Constitution of the United States. New York. 1888. (Ford: *P. on C.*)

See also Jefferson, Thomas. Works.

FORD, WORTHINGTON CHAUNCEY, *editor*. *See* Jefferson, Thomas. Correspondence.

Also see Washington, George. Writings.

FRANKLIN, BENJAMIN. Writings. Edited by Albert Henry Smyth. 10 vols. New York. 1907. (*Writings:* Smyth.)

FRENEAU, PHILIP. Poems of Philip Freneau. Edited by Fred Lewis Pattee. 3 vols. Princeton. 1902–07. (Freneau.)

GALLATIN, ALBERT. Writings. Edited by Henry Adams. 3 vols. Philadelphia. 1879. (Gallatin's *Writings:* Adams.)

See also Adams, Henry. Life of Albert Gallatin.

GARLAND, HUGH A. Life of John Randolph of Roanoke. 2 vols. New York. 1851. (Garland: *Randolph.*)

GIBBS, GEORGE, *editor*. *See* Wolcott, Oliver. Memoirs of the Administrations of Washington and John Adams. (Gibbs.)

GOODRICH, SAMUEL G. Recollections of a Lifetime, or Men and Things I Have Seen. 2 vols. New York. 1856. (Goodrich.)

GOSSE, EDMUND. A History of Eighteenth Century Literature. London. 1889. (Gosse: *History of Eighteenth Century Literature.*)

GRAYDON, ALEXANDER. Memoirs of His Own Time, with Reminiscences of the Men and Events of the Revolution. Edited by John Stockton Littell. Philadelphia. 1846. (Graydon.)

Green Bag, The; an Entertaining Magazine for Lawyers. Edited by Horace W. Fuller. Vols. 1–26. Boston. 1889–1914. [After 1914 consolidated with *The Central Law Journal.*] (*Green Bag.*)

GRIGSBY, HUGH BLAIR. The History of the Virginia Federal Convention of 1788. Virginia Historical Society. Richmond. 1815. [Volume 1 is volume 9, new series. Volume 2 is volume 10, new series.] (Grigsby.)

HALSEY, FRANCIS WHITING. The Old New York Frontier. New York. 1901. (Halsey: *Old New York Frontier.*)

HAMILTON, ALEXANDER. Works. Edited by John C. Hamilton. 7 vols. New York. 1851. (*Works:* Hamilton.)

—— Works. Edited by Henry Cabot Lodge. [Federal Edition.] 12 vols. New York. 1904. (*Works:* Lodge.)

HAMILTON, JOHN C., *editor.* History of the Republic of the United States, as traced in the Writings of Alexander Hamilton and his Contemporaries. 6 vols. New York. 1857–60. (Hamilton: *History of the Republic.*)

See also Hamilton, Alexander. Works.

HAMILTON, STANISLAUS MURRAY, *editor. See* Monroe, James. Writings.

HARDING, SAMUEL BANNISTER. The Contest over the Ratification of the Federal Constitution in the State of Massachusetts. New York. 1896. (Harding.)

HART, ALBERT BUSHNELL. American History told by Contemporaries. 4 vols. New York. 1897–1901. (Hart.)

HATCH, LOUIS CLINTON. Administration of the American Revolutionary Army. New York. 1904. (Hatch.)

HAZEN, CHARLES DOWNER. Contemporary American Opinion of the French Revolution. Baltimore. 1897. (Hazen.)

HEITMAN, FRANCIS BERNARD. Historical Register of Officers of the Continental Army, during the War of the Revolution. Washington, D.C. 1893.

—— Same. Revised and Enlarged Edition. Washington. 1914. (Heitman.)

HENING, WILLIAM WALLER. *See* Virginia. Laws.

HENRY, PATRICK. Life, Correspondence, and Speeches. Edited by William Wirt Henry. 3 vols. New York. 1891. (Henry.)

See also Wirt, William. Sketches of Life and Character of Patrick Henry.

HENRY, WILLIAM WIRT, *editor*. *See* Henry, Patrick. Life, Correspondence, and Speeches.

HINSDALE, B. A. The Old Northwest. 2 vols. New York. 1891. (Hinsdale.)

Historical Magazine and Notes and Queries Concerning the Antiquities, History, and Biography of America. [1st Series.] Vols. 1–10. New York. 1857–75. (*Hist. Mag.*)

History of William and Mary College, from its foundation, 1693, to 1870. Baltimore. 1870.

HOWE, HENRY. Historical Collections of Virginia. Charleston, S.C. 1845. (Howe.)

HUDSON, FREDERIC. Journalism in the United States from 1690 to 1872. New York. 1873. (Hudson: *Journalism in the United States.*)

HUNT, GAILLARD, *editor*. *See* Madison, James. Writings.

IREDELL, JAMES. *See* McRee, Griffith J. Life and Correspondence of James Iredell.

IRVING, WASHINGTON. The Life of George Washington. 5 vols. New York. 1855. (Irving.)

JAMESON, J. FRANKLIN, *editor*. Essays in the Constitutional History of the United States, 1775–1789, by Graduates and Former Members of Johns Hopkins University. Boston. 1889. (Jameson.)

JAY, JOHN. Correspondence and Public Papers. Edited by Henry P. Johnston. 4 vols. New York. 1890. (*Jay:* Johnston.)

JEFFERSON, THOMAS. Correspondence, from originals in the collections of William K. Bixby. Edited by Worthington Chauncey Ford. Boston. 1916. (*Thomas Jefferson Correspondence:* Ford.)

—— Works. Edited by Paul Leicester Ford. Federal Edition. 12 vols. New York. 1904. (*Works:* Ford.)

—— Writings. Edited by H. A. Washington. 9 vols. Washington, D.C. 1853–54. (Jefferson's *Writings:* Washington.)
See Morse, John T. Thomas Jefferson.
And see Randall, Henry S. Life of Thomas Jefferson.
Also see Tucker, George. Life of Thomas Jefferson.

JOHNSTON, HENRY P., *editor*. *See* Jay, John. Correspondence and Public Papers.

JONES, HUGH. The Present State of Virginia. London. 1724. (Jones.)

KAPP, FRIEDRICH. Life of Major-General Von Steuben. New York. 1859. (Kapp.)

KEITH, *Sir* WILLIAM, *Bart*. The History of the British Plantations in America, Part I, containing the History of Virginia. London. 1738. (Keith: *History of Virginia.*)

KING, CHARLES R., *editor*. *See* King, Rufus. Life and Correspondence.

KING, RUFUS. Life and Correspondence. Edited by Charles R. King. 6 vols. New York. 1894. (King.)

LAMB, *General* JOHN. Memoir and Life. *See* Leake, Isaac Q.

LANG, ANDREW. History of English Literature. New York. 1912. [2d edition.] (Lang: *History of English Literature.*)

LA ROCHEFOUCAULD-LIANCOURT, FRANÇOIS ALEXANDRE FRÉDÉRIC, *Duc* DE. Travels through the United States of North America. 4 vols. London. 1800. (La Rochefoucauld.)

LEAKE, ISAAC Q. Memoir of the Life and Times of General John Lamb, an Officer of The Revolution, and his Correspondence with Washington, Clinton, Patrick Henry, and other Distinguished Men. Albany. 1850. (Leake: *Lamb.*)

LEE, EDMUND JENNINGS. Lee of Virginia. 1642–1892. Biographical and Genealogical Sketches of the Descendants of Colonel Richard Lee. Philadelphia. 1895. (Lee: *Lee of Virginia.*)

LEE, *Colonel* RICHARD. Lee of Virginia. *See* Lee, Edmund Jennings.

LODGE, HENRY CABOT. Life and Letters of George Cabot. Boston. 1878. (Lodge: *Cabot.*)

—— George Washington. 2 vols. Boston. 1889. [American Statesmen.] (Lodge: *Washington.*)

See also Hamilton, Alexander. Works.

LOSSING, BENSON J. The Pictorial Field-Book of the Revolution. 2 vols. New York. 1851. (Lossing.)

See also Washington, George. *Diary.*

LOWDERMILK, WILL H. History of Cumberland (Maryland). Washington, D.C. 1878. (Lowdermilk.)

M'CLUNG, JOHN ALEXANDER. Sketches of Western Adventure. Philadelphia. 1832. (M'Clung: *Sketches of Western Adventure.*)

McCrady, Edward. The History of South Carolina. 4 vols. New York. 1897–1902. (McCrady.)

McHenry, James. Life and Correspondence. *See* Steiner, Bernard C.

McMaster, John Bach, *and* Stone, Frederick D. Pennsylvania and the Federal Constitution. Philadelphia. 1888. (McMaster and Stone.)

McRee, Griffith, J. Life and Correspondence of James Iredell. 2 vols. New York. 1857. (McRee.)

Madison, James. Writings. Edited by Gaillard Hunt. 9 vols. New York. 1900. (*Writings:* Hunt.)

See also Rives, William C. History of Life and Times.

Magazine, The, of American History, with Notes and Queries. Vols. 1–42. New York. 1877–1913. (*Mag. Am. Hist.*)

Magazine of Western History. Cleveland, Ohio. Edited by William W. Williams. Vols. 1–14. 1885–94. (*Mag. Western Hist.*)

Marshall, Humphrey. The History of Kentucky. 2 vols. Frankfort. 1824. (Humphrey Marshall.)

Marshall, John. Autobiography. *See* Smith, John Jay *and* Watson, John Fanning, *joint editors.* American Historical and Literary Curiosities. (*Autobiography.*)

—— Same. In National Portrait Gallery of Eminent Americans. Paintings by Alonzo Chappel, and Biographical and Historical Narratives by Evert A. Duyckinck. 2 vols. New York. 1862.

—— Same, reprinted. *See* Dillon, John F.

—— Life of George Washington. [1st Edition.] 5 vols. Philadelphia. 1805. [2d Edition.] 2 vols. Philadelphia. 1840. [The 2d Edition is cited in this work unless otherwise stated in the notes.] (Marshall.)

See also Thayer, James Bradley. John Marshall.

And see Flanders, Henry. Lives of the Chief Justices.

Also see Van Santvoord, George. Sketches of the Lives of the Chief-Justices.

Mason, George. Life. *See* Rowland, Kate Mason.

Meade, *Bishop* William. Old Churches, Ministers, and Families of Virginia. 2 vols. Richmond. 1910. (Meade.)

Miner, Charles. History of Wyoming, in a series of letters, from Charles Miner, to his son, William Penn Miner, Esq. Philadelphia. 1845. (Miner: *History of Wyoming.*)

Minot, George Richards. The History of the Insurrections

in Massachusetts, in 1786, and the Rebellion consequent thereon. Boston. 1810. (Minot: *History of the Insurrections in Massachusetts.*)

MONROE, JAMES. Writings. Edited by Stanislaus Murray Hamilton. 7 vols. [Unfinished work.] New York. 1898–1903. (Monroe's *Writings:* Hamilton.)

MOORE, FRANK. Diary of the American Revolution, from Newspapers and Original Documents. 2 vols. New York. 1809. (Moore's *Diary.*)

MORDECAI, SAMUEL. Richmond in By-Gone Days, Being Reminiscences of An Old Citizen. Richmond. 1856. (Mordecai.)

MORRIS, GOUVERNEUR. Diary and Letters. Edited by Anne Cary Morris. 2 vols. London. 1889. (Morris.)

MORSE, JOHN T. Thomas Jefferson. Boston. 1795. [American Statesmen.] (Morse.)

MUNFORD, WILLIAM. *See* Virginia, Law Reports.

New Jersey Historical Society. Proceedings. Vols. 1–10. Newark. 1847–1905. (*Proc.*, N.J. Hist. Soc.)

NILES, HEZEKIAH. Centennial Offering, Republication of the Principles and Acts of the Revolution in America. New York. 1876. (Niles: *Principles and Acts of the Revolution.*)

NOTT, ELIPHALET. Memoirs. *See* Van Santvoord, C.

PAINE, THOMAS. Writings. Edited by Moncure Daniel Conway. 4 vols. New York. 1894–96. (*Writings:* Conway.)

PAXTON, WILLIAM M. The Marshall Family, or a Genealogical Chart of the Descendants of John Marshall and Elizabeth Markham. Cincinnati. 1885. (Paxton.)

PECQUET DU BELLET, LOUISE. Some Prominent Virginia Families. 4 vols. Lynchburg, Va. 1909. (Pecquet du Bellet.)

Pennsylvania Magazine of History and Biography. Published by the Historical Society of Pennsylvania. Vols. 1–40. Philadelphia. 1877–1916. (*Pa. Mag. Hist. and Biog.*)

PICKERING, OCTAVIUS. Life of Timothy Pickering, by his son and continued by Charles W. Upham. 4 vols. Boston. 1867–73. (Pickering: *Pickering.*)

PICKERING, TIMOTHY. Life. *See* Pickering, Octavius.

QUINCY, JOSIAH. Figures of the Past, from the leaves of Old Journals. Boston. 1883. (Quincy: *Figures of the Past.*)

Randall, Henry S. Life of Thomas Jefferson. 3 vols. New York. 1858. (Randall.)

Randolph, Edmund. Life and Papers. *See* Conway, Moncure Daniel.

Randolph, John. Life. *See* Garland, Hugh A.

Rives, William C. The History of the Life and Times of James Madison. 3 vols. Boston. 1859. (Rives.)

Rowland, Kate Mason. Life of George Mason. 2 vols. New York. 1892. (Rowland.)

Sargent, Winthrop. The History of an Expedition against Fort Du Quesne, in 1755, under Major-General Edward Braddock. Philadelphia. 1855. (Sargent.)

Schoepf, Johann David. Travels in the Confederation, 1783–1784. Translated and edited by Alfred J. Morrison. 2 vols. Philadelphia. 1911. (Schoepf.)

Scott, John, of Fauquier County, Va. The Lost Principle. By "Barbarossa" [*pseud.*]. Richmond. 1860. (Scott.)

Slaughter, *Rev.* Philip. A History of St. Mark's Parish, Culpepper County, Virginia. Baltimore. 1877. (Slaughter.)

—— A History of Bristol Parish, Virginia. Richmond. 1879. (Slaughter: *Bristol Parish.*)

Smith, John Jay, *and* Watson, John Fanning, *joint editors. American Historical and Literary Curiosities.* New York. 1852. (*Am. Hist. and Lit. Curiosities.*)

Smyth-Stuart, J. Ferdinand D. A Tour in the United States of America. 2 vols. London. 1784. (Smyth: *Tour of the United States.*)

Southern Literary Messenger. Vols. 1–38. New York and Washington. 1834–64.

Sparks, Jared. The Life of George Washington. Boston. 1839. [Same plates, 1842.] (Sparks.)

—— Correspondence of the American Revolution [being letters of eminent men to George Washington]. 4 vols. Boston. 1853. (*Cor. Rev.*: Sparks.)

See also Washington, George. Writings.

Stanard, Mary Newton. The Story of Bacon's Rebellion. New York. 1907. (Stanard: *Story of Bacon's Rebellion.*)

Steiner, Bernard C. The Life and Correspondence of James McHenry. Cleveland. 1907. (Steiner.)

Stephen, Leslie. Alexander Pope. New York. 1880. (Stephen: *Alexander Pope.*)

STEUBEN, FREIDRICH WILHELM AUGUST HEINRICH FERDINAND, *Baron* VON. Life. *See* Kapp, Friedrich.

STILLÉ, CHARLES J[ANEWAY]. Major-General Anthony Wayne, and the Pennsylvania Line in the Continental Army. Philadelphia. 1893. (Stillé.)

STORY, JOSEPH. Discourse on John Marshall, reprinted.
See Dillon, John F.
Also see Story, William Wirt.

STORY, WILLIAM WIRT. Life and Letters of Joseph Story. 2 vols. Boston. 1851. (Story.)

TALLEYRAND-PÉRIGORD, CHARLES MAURICE DE, *Prince* DE BÉNÉVENT. Memoirs. Edited by the Duc de Broglie. 5 vols. New York. 1891. (*Memoirs of Talleyrand:* Broglie's Ed.)

TERHUNE, MARY VIRGINIA HAWES. Some Colonial Homesteads and their Stories. By Marion Harland [*pseud.*]. 2 vols. New York. 1912. (Terhune: *Colonial Homesteads.*)

THAYER, JAMES BRADLEY. John Marshall. Boston. 1904. [Riverside Biographical Series, No. 9.] (Thayer.)

TRAILL, H. D., *editor.* Social England. A Record of the Progress of the People. By Various Writers. 7 vols. London. 1896. (Traill: *Social England.*)

TREVELYAN, *Sir* GEORGE OTTO, *Bart.* The American Revolution. 4 vols. New York. 1907. (Trevelyan.)

TUCKER, GEORGE. Life of Thomas Jefferson. 2 vols. Philadelphia. 1837. (Tucker.)

TURNER, FREDERICK JACKSON. The Old West. [Printed in Wisconsin Historical Society, *Proceedings* for 1908.] Madison, Wis. 1909. (Turner: *The Old West.*)

TYLER, LYON G. Letters and Times of the Tylers. 2 vols. Richmond. 1884. (Tyler.)

—— Williamsburg, the Old Colonial Capital. Richmond. 1907. (Tyler: *Williamsburg.*)

VAN BUREN, MARTIN. Inquiry into the Origin and Course of Political Parties in the United States. New York. 1867. (Van Buren.)

VAN SANTVOORD, C. Memoirs of Eliphalet Nott. New York. 1876. (Van Santvoord: *Memoirs of Eliphalet Nott.*)

Van Santvoord, George. Sketches of the Lives and Judicial Services of the Chief-Justices of the Supreme Court of United States. New York. 1854. (Van Santvoord.)

Virginia Historical Papers. Manuscripts now in the Virginia Historical Society Library, at Richmond. (*Va. Hist. Prs.*)

Virginia. House of Burgesses. Journal of the Virginia House of Burgesses. 1619–1776. Now in the Archives of the Virginia State Library. (Journal, H.B.)

Virginia. House of Delegates. Journal of the Virginia House of Delegates. 1776–1916. Now in the Archives of the Virginia State Library. (Journal, H.D.)

Virginia. Laws. Hening, William Waller. The Statutes at Large. Being a Collection of the Laws of Virginia from 1619 to 1808. 13 vols. New York. 1819–23. (Hening.)

Virginia. Law Reports. Call, Daniel. Reports of Cases Argued and Adjudged in the Court of Appeals of Virginia. 6 vols. Richmond. 1824–33. (Call.)

—— Munford, William. Reports of Cases Argued and Determined in the Supreme Court of Appeals, of Virginia. 15 vols. New York. 1812. (Munford).

Virginia Magazine of History and Biography. Published by the Virginia Historical Society. Vols. 1–24. Richmond. 1893–1916. (*Va. Mag. Hist. and Biog.*)

Waldo, *Surgeon* Albigence. Diary at Valley Forge from Nov. 1, 1777 to Jan. 15, 1778. [In *Historical Magazine*, vol. 5, pp. 129–34, 169–72.]

Wallace, David Duncan. The Life of Henry Laurens, with Sketch of the Life of Lieutenant-Colonel John Laurens. New York. 1915. (Wallace.)

Warville. *See* Brissot de Warville.

Washington, George. Diary from 1789 to 1791. Edited by Benson J. Lossing. New York. 1860. (Washington's *Diary:* Lossing.)

—— Writings. Edited by Worthington Chauncey Ford. 14 vols. New York. 1889–1893. (*Writings:* Ford.)

—— Writings. Edited by Jared Sparks. 12 vols. Boston. 1834–1837. (*Writings:* Sparks.)

See Irving, Washington. Life of George Washington.
And Lodge, Henry Cabot. George Washington.
Also Marshall, John. Life of George Washington.
Also see Sparks, Jared. Life of George Washington.

WASHINGTON, H. A., *editor. See* Jefferson, Thomas. Writings.

WATSON, WINSLOW C. Men and Times of the Revolution, or Memoirs of Elkanah Watson, by his son. New York. 1856. (Watson.)

WEEDON, *General* GEORGE. Valley Forge Orderly Book. New York. 1902. (Weedon.)

WELD, ISAAC. Travels Through the States of North America, and the Provinces of Upper and Lower Canada During the Years 1795, 1796, and 1797. [3d Edition.] 2 vols. London. 1800. (Weld.)

WERTENBAKER, THOMAS J. Patrician and Plebeian in Virginia, or the Origin and Development of the Social Classes of the Old Dominion. Charlottesville, Va. 1910. (*Wertenbaker: P. and P.*)

—— Virginia Under the Stuarts, 1607–1688. Princeton University. 1914. (Wertenbaker: *V. U. S.*)

WILD, EBENEZER. Diary in the Revolutionary War from 1776 to 1781. [In Massachusetts Historical Society, *Proceedings* (2d Series), vol. 6, pp. 78–160.]

WILKINSON, *General* JAMES. Memoirs of my Own Times. 3 vols. Philadelphia. 1816. (Wilkinson: *Memoirs.*)

William and Mary College Quarterly Historical Magazine. Richmond. Vols. 1–16. 1892–1908. (*W. and M. C. Q.*)

WIRT, WILLIAM. The Letters of the British Spy. [9th Edition.] Baltimore. 1831. (Wirt: *British Spy.*)

—— Sketches of the Life and Character of Patrick Henry. Philadelphia. 1818. (Wirt.)

WISE, JENNINGS CROPPER. Ye Kingdome of Accawmacke, or the Eastern Shore of Virginia, in the Seventeenth Century. Richmond. 1911. (Wise.)

WOLCOTT, OLIVER. Memoirs of the Administrations of Washington and John Adams. Edited from the papers of Oliver Wolcott, by George Gibbs. 2 vols. New York. 1846. (Gibbs.)

WOOD, WILLIAM. The Fight for Canada. Westminster, 1904. (Wood.)

THE LIFE OF JOHN MARSHALL

VOLUME II

Politician, Diplomatist, Statesman

1789–1801

CONTENTS

power — Gallatin admits it to be "unanswerable" — It defeats the Republicans — Jefferson's faint praise — the "Aurora's" amusing comment — Marshall defends the army and the policy of preparing for war — His speech the ablest on the Army Bill — His letter to Dabney describing conditions — Marshall helps draw the first Bankruptcy Law and, in the opinion of the Federalists, spoils it — Speaker Sedgwick vividly portrays Marshall as he appeared to the Federalist politicians at the close of the session.

XII. CHIEF JUSTICE OF THE UNITED STATES 485

The shattering of Adams's Cabinet — Marshall declines office of Secretary of War — Offered that of Secretary of State — Adams's difficult party situation — The feud with Hamilton — Marshall finally, and with reluctance, accepts portfolio of Secretary of State — Republican comment — Federalist politicians approve: "Marshall a state conservator" — Adams leaves Marshall in charge at Washington — Examples of his routine work — His retort to the British Minister — His strong letter to Great Britain on the British debts — Controversy with Great Britain over contraband, treatment of neutrals, and impressment — Marshall's notable letter on these subjects — His harsh language to Great Britain — Federalist disintegration begins — Republicans overwhelmingly victorious in Marshall's home district — Marshall's despondent letter to Otis: "The tide of real Americanism is on the ebb" — Federalist leaders quarrel; rank and file confused and angered — Hamilton's faction plots against Adams — Adams's inept retaliation: Hamilton and his friends "a British faction" — Republican strength increases — Jefferson's platform — The second mission to France succeeds in negotiating a treaty — Chagrin of Federalists and rejoicing of Republicans — Marshall dissatisfied but favors ratification — Hamilton's amazing personal attack on Adams — The Federalists dumbfounded, the Republicans in glee — The terrible campaign of 1800 — Marshall writes the President's address to Congress — The Republicans carry the election by a narrow margin — Tie between Jefferson and Burr — Federalists in House determine to elect Burr — Hamilton's frantic efforts against Burr: "The *Catiline* of America" — Hamilton appeals to Marshall, who favors Burr — Marshall refuses to aid Jefferson, but agrees to keep hands off — Ellsworth resigns as Chief Justice — Adams reappoints Jay, who declines — Adams then appoints Marshall, who, with hesitation, accepts — The appointment unexpected and arouses no interest — Marshall continues as Secretary of State — The dramatic contest in the House over Burr and Jefferson — Marshall accused of advising Federalists that Congress could provide for Presidency by law in case of deadlock — Federalists consider Marshall for the Presidency — Hay assails Marshall — Burr refuses Federalist proposals — The Federalist bargain with Jefferson — He is elected — The "midnight judges" — The power over the Supreme

LIST OF ABBREVIATED TITLES MOST FREQUENTLY CITED

All references here are to the List of Authorities at the end of this volume.

Am. St. Prs. *See* American State Papers.

Beard: *Econ. I. C.* *See* Beard, Charles A. Economic Interpretation of the Constitution of the United States.

Beard: *Econ. O. J. D.* *See* Beard, Charles A. Economic Origins of Jeffersonian Democracy.

Cor. Rev.: Sparks. *See* Sparks, Jared. Correspondence of the Revolution.

Cunningham Letters. *See* Adams, John. Correspondence with William Cunningham.

Letters: Ford. *See* Vans Murray, William. Letters to John Quincy Adams. Edited by Worthington Chauncey Ford.

Monroe's *Writings:* Hamilton. *See* Monroe, James. Writings. Edited by Stanislaus Murray Hamilton.

Old Family Letters. *See* Adams, John. Old Family Letters. Edited by Alexander Biddle.

Works: Adams. *See* Adams, John. Works. Edited by Charles Francis Adams.

Works: Ames. *See* Ames, Fisher. Works. Edited by Seth Ames.

Works: Ford. *See* Jefferson, Thomas. Works. Federal Edition. Edited by Paul Leicester Ford.

Works: Hamilton. *See* Hamilton, Alexander. Works. Edited by John C. Hamilton.

Works: Lodge. *See* Hamilton, Alexander. Works. Federal Edition. Edited by Henry Cabot Lodge.

Writings: Conway. *See* Paine, Thomas. Writings. Edited by Moncure Daniel Conway.

Writings: Ford. *See* Washington, George. Writings. Edited by Worthington Chauncey Ford.

Writings: Hunt. *See* Madison, James. Writings. Edited by Gaillard Hunt.

Writings, J. Q. A.: Ford. *See* Adams, John Quincy. Writings. Edited by Worthington Chauncey Ford.

Writings: Smyth. *See* Franklin, Benjamin. Writings. Edited by Albert Henry Smyth.

Writings: Sparks. *See* Washington, George. Writings. Edited by Jared Sparks.

THE LIFE OF JOHN MARSHALL

THE LIFE OF JOHN MARSHALL

CHAPTER I

INFLUENCE OF THE FRENCH REVOLUTION ON AMERICA

Were there but an Adam and an Eve left in every country, and left free, it would be better than it now is. (Jefferson.)

That malignant philosophy which can coolly and deliberately pursue, through oceans of blood, abstract systems for the attainment of some fancied untried good. (Marshall.)

The only genuine liberty consists in a mean equally distant from the despotism of an individual and a million. ("Publicola": J. Q. Adams, 1792.)

The decision of the French King, Louis XVI, on the advice of his Ministers, to weaken Great Britain by aiding the Americans in their War for Independence, while it accomplished its purpose, was fatal to himself and to the Monarchy of France. As a result, Great Britain lost America, but Louis lost his head. Had not the Bourbon Government sent troops, fleets, munitions, and money to the support of the failing and desperate American fortunes, it is probable that Washington would not have prevailed; and the fires of the French holocaust which flamed throughout the world surely would not have been lit so soon.

The success of the American patriots in their armed resistance to the rule of George III, although brought about by the aid of the French Crown, was, nevertheless, the shining and dramatic example which Frenchmen imitated in beginning that vast and elemental upheaval called the French Revolution.[1] Thus the unnatural alliance in 1778 between French Autocracy and American Liberty was one of the great and decisive events of human history.

In the same year, 1789, that the American Republic began its career under the forms of a National Government, the curtain rose in France on that tremendous drama which will forever engage the interest of mankind. And just as the American Revolution vitally influenced French opinion, so the French Revolution profoundly affected American thought; and, definitely, helped to shape those contending forces in American life that are still waging their conflict.

While the economic issue, so sharp in the adoption of the Constitution, became still keener, as will appear, after the National Government was established, it was given a higher temper in the forge of the French Revolution. American history, especially

[1] "That the principles of America opened the Bastille is not to be doubted." (Thomas Paine to Washington, May 1, 1790; *Cor. Rev.*[2]: Sparks, iv, 328.) "The principles of it [the French Revolution] were copied from America." (Paine to Citizens of the United States, Nov. 15, 1802; *Writings:* Conway, iii, 381.)

"Did not the American Revolution produce the French Revolution? And did not the French Revolution produce all the Calamities and Desolations to the human Race and the whole Globe ever since?" (Adams to Rush, Aug. 28, 1811; *Old Family Letters*, 352.)

"Many of . . . the leaders [of the French Revolution] have imbibed their principles in America, and all have been fired by our example." (Gouverneur Morris to Washington, Paris, April 29, 1789; *Cor. Rev.*: Sparks, iv, 256.)

"All the friends of freedom on this side the Atlantic are now rejoicing for an event which . . . has been accelerated by the American Revolution. . . . You have been the means of raising that spirit in Europe which . . . will . . . extinguish every remain of that barbarous servitude under which all the European nations, in a less . . . degree, have so long been subject." (Catharine M. Graham to Washington, Berks (England), Oct. 1789; *ib.*, 284; and see Cobbett, i, 97.)

of the period now under consideration, can be read correctly only by the lights that shine from that titanic smithy; can be understood only by considering the effect upon the people, the thinkers, and the statesmen of America, of the deeds done and words spoken in France during those inspiring if monstrous years.

The naturally conservative or radical temperaments of men in America were hardened by every episode of the French convulsion. The events in France, at this time, operated upon men like Hamilton on the one hand, and Jefferson on the other hand, in a fashion as deep and lasting as it was antagonistic and antipodal; and the intellectual and moral phenomena, manifested in picturesque guise among the people in America, impressed those who already were, and those who were to become, the leaders of American opinion, as much as the events of the Gallic cataclysm itself.

George Washington at the summit of his fame, and John Marshall just beginning his ascent, were alike confirmed in that non-popular tendency of thought and feeling which both avowed in the dark years between our War for Independence and the adoption of our Constitution.[1] In reviewing all the situations, not otherwise to be fully understood, that arose from the time Washington became President until Marshall took his seat as Chief Justice, we must have always before our eyes the extraordinary scenes and consider the delirious emotions which the French Revolution produced in America. It

[1] See vol. I, chap. VIII, of this work.

must be constantly borne in mind that Americans of the period now under discussion did not and could not look upon it with present-day knowledge, perspective, or calmness. What is here set down is, therefore, an attempt to portray the effects of that volcanic eruption of human forces upon the minds and hearts of those who witnessed, from across the ocean, its flames mounting to the heavens and its lava pouring over the whole earth.

Unless this portrayal is given, a blank must be left in a recital of the development of American radical and conservative sentiment and of the formation of the first of American political parties. Certainly for the purposes of the present work, an outline, at least, of the effect of the French Revolution on American thought and feeling is indispensable. Just as the careers of Marshall and Jefferson are inseparably intertwined, and as neither can be fully understood without considering the other, so the American by-products of the French Revolution must be examined if we would comprehend either of these great protagonists of hostile theories of democratic government.

At first everybody in America heartily approved the French reform movement. Marshall describes for us this unanimous approbation. "A great revolution had commenced in that country," he writes, "the first stage of which was completed by limiting the powers of the monarch, and by the establishment of a popular assembly. In no part of the globe was this revolution hailed with more joy than in America. The influence it would have on the affairs of the world was not then distinctly foreseen; and the philanthropist, without becoming a political partisan, rejoiced in the event. On this subject, therefore, but one sentiment existed."[1]

Jefferson had written from Paris, a short time before leaving for America: "A complete revolution in this [French] government, has been effected merely by the force of public opinion; . . . and this revolution has not cost a single life."[2] So little did his glowing mind then understand the forces which he had helped set in motion. A little later he advises Madison of the danger threatening the reformed French Government, but adds, reassuringly, that though "the lees . . . of the patriotic party [the French radical party] of wicked principles & desperate fortunes" led by Mirabeau who "is the chief . . . may produce a temporary confusion . . . they cannot have success ultimately. The King, the mass of the substantial people of the whole country, the army, and the influential part of the clergy, form a firm phalanx which must prevail."[3]

So, in the beginning, all American newspapers, now more numerous, were exultant. "Liberty will have another feather in her cap. . . . The ensuing winter [1789] will be the commencement of a Golden Age,"[4] was the glowing prophecy of an enthusiastic Boston journal. Those two sentences of the New

[1] Marshall, ii, 155. "The mad harangues of the [French] National Convention were all translated and circulated through the States. The enthusiasm they excited it is impossible for me to describe." (Cobbett in "Summary View"; Cobbett, i, 98.)

[2] Jefferson to Humphreys, March 18, 1789; *Works:* Ford, v, 467.

[3] Jefferson to Madison, Aug. 28, 1789; *ib.*, 490.

[4] *Boston Gazette*, Sept. 7 and Nov. 30, 1789; as quoted in Hazen; and see Hazen, 142–43.

England editor accurately stated the expectation and belief of all America.

But in France itself one American had grave misgivings as to the outcome. "The materials for a revolution in this country are very indifferent. Everybody agrees that there is an utter prostration of morals; but this general position can never convey to an American mind the degree of depravity. . . . A hundred thousand examples are required to show the extreme rottenness. . . The virtuous . . . stand forward from a background deeply and darkly shaded. . . . From such crumbling matter . . . the great edifice of freedom is to be erected here [in France]. . . . [There is] a perfect indifference to the violation of engagements. . . . Inconstancy is mingled in the blood, marrow, and very essence of this people. . . . Consistency is a phenomenon. . . . The great mass of the common people have . . . no morals but their interest. These are the creatures who, led by drunken curates, are now in the high road *à la liberté*." [1] Such was the report sent to Washington by Gouverneur Morris, the first American Minister to France under the Constitution.

Three months later Morris, writing officially, declares that "this country is . . . as near to anarchy as society can approach without dissolution." [2] And yet, a year earlier, Lafayette had lamented the

[1] Gouverneur Morris to Washington, Paris, April 29, 1789; *Cor. Rev.*: Sparks, iv, 256. Even Jefferson had doubted French capacity for self-government because of what he described as French light-mindedness. (Jefferson to Mrs. Adams, Feb. 22, 1787; *Works:* Ford, v, 263; also see vol. I, chap. VIII, of this work.)

[2] Morris to Washington, July 31, 1789; *Cor. Rev.*: Sparks, iv, 270.

French public's indifference to much needed reforms; "The people . . . have been so dull that it has made me sick" was Lafayette's doleful account of popular enthusiasm for liberty in the France of 1788.[1]

Gouverneur Morris wrote Robert Morris that a French owner of a quarry demanded damages because so many bodies had been dumped into the quarry that they "choked it up so that he could not get men to work at it." These victims, declared the American Minister, had been "the best people," killed "without form of trial, and their bodies thrown like dead dogs into the first hole that offered."[2] Gouverneur Morris's diary abounds in such entries as "[Sept. 2, 1792] the murder of the priests, . . . murder of prisoners, . . . [Sept. 3] The murdering continues all day. . . . [Sept. 4th] . . . And still the murders continue."[3]

John Marshall was now the attorney of Robert

[1] Lafayette to Washington, May 25, 1788; *Cor. Rev.*: Sparks, iv, 216. Lafayette's letters to Washington, from the beginning of the French Revolution down to his humiliating expulsion from France, constitute a thermometer of French temperature, all the more trustworthy because his letters are so naïve. For example, in March, 1790: "Our revolution is getting on as well as it can, with a nation that has swallowed liberty at once, and is still liable to mistake licentiousness for freedom." Or, in August of the same year: "I have lately lost some of my favor with the mob, and displeased the frantic lovers of licentiousness, as I am bent on establishing a legal subordination." Or, six months later: "I still am tossed about in the ocean of factions and commotions of every kind." Or, two months afterwards: "There appears a kind of phenomenon in my situation; all parties against me, and a national popularity which, in spite of every effort, has been unshakable." (Lafayette to Washington, March 17, 1790; *ib.*, 321; Aug. 28, *ib.*, 345; March 7, 1791, *ib.*, 361; May 3, 1791, *ib.*, 372.)

[2] G. Morris to R. Morris, Dec. 24, 1792; Morris, ii, 15.

[3] *Ib.*, i, 582–84.

Morris; was closely connected with him in business transactions; and, as will appear, was soon to become his relative by the marriage of Marshall's brother to the daughter of the Philadelphia financier. Gouverneur Morris, while not related to Robert Morris, was "entirely devoted" to and closely associated with him in business; and both were in perfect agreement of opinions.[1] Thus the reports of the scarlet and revolting phases of the French Revolution that came to the Virginia lawyer were carried through channels peculiarly personal and intimate.

They came, too, from an observer who was thoroughly aristocratic in temperament and conviction.[2] Little of appreciation or understanding of the basic causes and high purposes of the French Revolution appears in Gouverneur Morris's accounts and comments, while he portrays the horrible in unrelieved ghastliness.[3]

Such, then, were the direct and first-hand accounts that Marshall received; and the impression made upon him was correspondingly dark, and as lasting as it was somber. Of this, Marshall himself leaves us in no doubt. Writing more than a decade later he gives his estimate of Gouverneur Morris and of his accounts of the French Revolution.

[1] Louis Otto to De Montmorin, March 10, 1792; *Writings:* Conway, iii, 153.

[2] *Ib.*, 154–56.

[3] Morris associated with the nobility in France and accepted the aristocratic view. (*Ib.*; and see A. Esmein, Membre de l'Institut: *Gouverneur Morris, un témoin américain de la révolution française.* Paris, 1906.)

"The private correspondence of Mr. Morris with the president [and, of course, much more so with Robert Morris] exhibits a faithful picture, drawn by the hand of a master, of the shifting revolutionary scenes which with unparalleled rapidity succeeded each other in Paris. With the eye of an intelligent, and of an unimpassioned observer, he marked all passing events, and communicated them with fidelity. He did not mistake despotism for freedom, because it was sanguinary, because it was exercised by those who denominated themselves the people, or because it assumed the name of liberty. Sincerely wishing happiness and a really free government to France, he could not be blind to the obvious truth that the road to those blessings had been mistaken." [1]

Everybody in America echoed the shouts of the Parisian populace when the Bastille fell. Was it not the prison where kings thrust their subjects to perish of starvation and torture? [2] Lafayette, "as a missionary of liberty to its patriarch," hastened to present Washington with "the main key of the

[1] Marshall, ii, note xvi, p. 17.

[2] Recent investigation establishes the fact that the inmates of the Bastille generally found themselves very well off indeed. The records of this celebrated prison show that even prisoners of mean station, when incarcerated for so grave a crime as conspiracy against the King's life, had, in addition to remarkably abundant meals, an astonishing amount of extra viands and refreshments including comfortable quantities of wine, brandy, and beer. Prisoners of higher station fared still more generously, of course. (Funck-Brentano: *Legends of the Bastille*, 85–113; see also *ib.*, introduction.) It should be said, however, that the *lettres de cachet* were a chief cause of complaint, although the stories, generally exaggerated, concerning the cruel treatment of prisoners came to be the principal count of the public indictment of the Bastille.

fortress of despotism." [1] Washington responded that he accepted the key of the Bastille as "a token of the victory gained by liberty." [2] Thomas Paine wrote of his delight at having been chosen by Lafayette to "convey . . . the first ripe fruits of American principles, transplanted into Europe, to his master and patron." [3] Mutual congratulations were carried back and forth by every ship.

Soon the mob in Paris took more sanguinary action and blood flowed more freely, but not in sufficient quantity to quench American enthusiasm for the cause of liberty in France. We had had plenty of mobs ourselves and much crimson experience. Had not mobs been the precursors of our own Revolution?

The next developments of the French uprising and the appearance of the Jacobin Clubs, however, alarmed some and gave pause to all of the cautious friends of freedom in America and other countries.

Edmund Burke hysterically sounded the alarm. On account of his championship of the cause of American Independence, Burke had enjoyed much credit with all Americans who had heard of him. "In the last age," exclaimed Burke in Parliament, February 9, 1790, "we were in danger of being entangled by the example of France in the net of a relentless despotism. . . . Our present danger from

[1] Lafayette to Washington, March 17, 1790; *Cor. Rev.*: Sparks, iv, 322.

[2] Washington to Lafayette, August 11, 1790; *Writings:* Ford, xi, 493.

[3] Paine to Washington, May 1, 1790; *Cor. Rev.*: Sparks, iv, 328. Paine did not, personally, bring the key, but forwarded it from London.

the example of a people whose character knows no medium, is, with regard to government, a danger from anarchy; a danger of being led, through an admiration of successful fraud and violence, to an imitation of the excesses of an irrational, unprincipled, proscribing, confiscating, plundering, ferocious, bloody, and tyrannical democracy." [1]

Of the French declaration of human rights Burke declared: "They made and recorded a sort of *institute* and *digest* of anarchy, called the rights of man, in such a pedantic abuse of elementary principles as would have disgraced boys at school.... They systematically destroyed every hold of authority by opinion, religious or civil, on the minds of the people.[2] . . . On the scheme of this barbarous philosophy, which is the offspring of cold hearts and muddy understandings," exclaimed the great English liberal, "laws are to be supported only by their own terrours. . . . In the groves of *their* academy, at the end of every vista, you see nothing but the gallows." [3]

Burke's extravagant rhetoric, although reprinted in America, was little heeded. It would have been better if his pen had remained idle. For Burke's wild language, not yet justified by the orgy of blood

[1] Burke in the House of Commons; *Works:* Burke, i, 451–53.

[2] *Ib.*

[3] *Reflections on the Revolution in France; ib.*, i, 489. Jefferson well stated the American radical opinion of Burke: "The Revolution of France does not astonish me so much as the Revolution of Mr. Burke. . . . How mortifying that this evidence of the rottenness of his mind must oblige us now to ascribe to wicked motives those actions of his life which were the mark of virtue & patriotism." (Jefferson to Vaughan, May 11, 1791; *Works:* Ford, vi, 260.)

in which French liberty was, later, to be baptized, caused a voice to speak to which America did listen, a page to be written that America did read. Thomas Paine, whose "Common Sense" had made his name better known to all people in the United States than that of any other man of his time except Washington, Franklin, Jefferson, and Henry, was then in France. This stormy petrel of revolution seems always to have been drawn by instinct to every part of the human ocean where hurricanes were brooding.[1]

Paine answered Burke with that ferocious indictment of monarchy entitled "The Rights of Man," in which he went as far to one extreme as the English political philosopher had gone to the other; for while Paine annihilated Burke's Brahminic laudation of rank, title, and custom, he also penned a doctrine of paralysis to all government. As was the case with his "Common Sense," Paine's "Rights of Man" abounded in attractive epigrams and striking sentences which quickly caught the popular ear and were easily retained by the shallowest memory.

"The cause of the French people is that of . . . the whole world," declared Paine in the preface of his flaming essay;[2] and then, the sparks beginning to fly from his pen, he wrote: "Great part of that order which reigns among mankind is not the effect of government. . . . It existed prior to government, and would exist if the formality of government was

[1] Paine had not yet lost his immense popularity in the United States. While, later, he came to be looked upon with horror by great numbers of people, he enjoyed the regard and admiration of nearly everybody in America at the time his *Rights of Man* appeared.

[2] *Writings*: Conway, ii, 272.

abolished. . . . The instant formal government is abolished," said he, "society begins to act; . . . and common interest produces common security." And again: "The more perfect civilization is, the less occasion has it for government. . . . It is but few general laws that civilised life requires."

Holding up our own struggle for liberty as an illustration, Paine declared: "The American Revolution . . . laid open the imposition of governments"; and, using our newly formed and untried National Government as an example, he asserted with grotesque inaccuracy: "In America . . . all the parts are brought into cordial unison. There the poor are not oppressed, the rich are not privileged. . . . Their taxes are few, because their government is just." [1]

Proceeding thence to his assault upon all other established governments, especially that of England, the great iconoclast exclaimed: "It is impossible that such governments as have hitherto [1790] existed in the world, could have commenced by any other means than a violation of every principle sacred and moral."

Striking at the foundations of all permanent authority, Paine declared that "Every age and generation must be . . . free to act for itself *in all cases*. . . . The vanity and presumption of governing beyond the grave is the most ridiculous and insolent of all tyrannies." The people of yesterday have "no right . . . to bind or to control . . . the people of the present day . . . *in any shape whatever*. . . .

[1] *Writings:* Conway, ii, 406. At this very moment the sympathizers with the French Revolution in America were saying exactly the reverse.

Every generation is, and must be, competent to all the purposes which its occasions require." [1] So wrote the incomparable pamphleteer of radicalism.

Paine's essay, issued in two parts, was a torch successively applied to the inflammable emotions of the American masses. Most newspapers printed in each issue short and appealing excerpts from it. For example, the following sentence from Paine's "Rights of Man" was reproduced in the "Columbian Centinel" of Boston on June 6, 1792: "Can we possibly suppose that if government had originated in right principles and had not an interest in pursuing a wrong one, that the world could have been in the wretched and quarrelsome condition it is?" Such quotations from Paine appeared in all radical and in some conservative American publications; and they were repeated from mouth to mouth until even the backwoodsmen knew of them — and believed them.

"Our people . . . love what you write and read it with delight" ran the message which Jefferson sent across the ocean to Paine. "The printers," continued Jefferson, "season every newspaper with extracts from your last, as they did before from your first part of the *Rights of Man*. They have both served here to separate the wheat from the chaff. . . . Would you believe it possible that in this country there should be high & important characters [2] who need your lessons in republicanism & who do not heed them. It is but too true that we have a sect preaching up & pouting after an English constitu-

[1] *Writings:* Conway, ii, 278–79, 407, 408, 413, 910.

[2] Compare with Jefferson's celebrated letter to Mazzei (*infra*, chap. vii). Jefferson was now, however, in Washington's Cabinet.

tion of king, lords, & commons, & whose heads are itching for crowns, coronets & mitres. . .

"Go on then," Jefferson urged Paine, "in doing with your pen what in other times was done with the sword, . . . and be assured that it has not a more sincere votary nor you a more ardent well-wisher than . . . Thos Jefferson." [1]

And the wheat was being separated from the chaff, as Jefferson declared. Shocked not more by the increasing violence in France than by the principles which Paine announced, men of moderate mind and conservative temperament in America came to have misgivings about the French Revolution, and began to speak out against its doings and its doctrines.

A series of closely reasoned and well-written articles were printed in the "Columbian Centinel" of Boston in the summer of 1791, over the *nom de guerre* "Publicola"; and these were widely copied. They were ascribed to the pen of John Adams, but were the work of his brilliant son.[2]

[1] Jefferson to Paine, June 19, 1792; *Works:* Ford, vii, 121–22; and see Hazen, 157–60. Jefferson had, two years before, expressed precisely the views set forth in Paine's *Rights of Man.* Indeed, he stated them in even more startling terms. (See Jefferson to Madison, Sept. 6, 1789; *ib.*, vi, 1–11.)

[2] *Writings, J. Q. A.*: Ford, i, 65–110. John Quincy Adams wrote these admirable essays when he was twenty-four years old. Their logic, wit, and style suggest the writer's incomparable mother. Madison, who remarked their quality, wrote to Jefferson: "There is more of method . . . in the arguments, and much less of clumsiness & heaviness in the style, than characterizes his [John Adams's] writings." (Madison to Jefferson, July 13, 1791; *Writings:* Hunt, vi, 56.)

The sagacious industry of Mr. Worthington C. Ford has made these and all the other invaluable papers of the younger Adams accessible, in his *Writings of John Quincy Adams* now issuing.

The American edition of Paine's "Rights of Man" was headed by a letter from Secretary of State Jefferson to the printer, stating his pleasure that the essay was to be printed in this country and "that something is at length to be publickly said against the political heresies which have sprung up among us." [1] Publicola called attention to this and thus, more conspicuously, displayed Jefferson as an advocate of Paine's doctrines.[2]

All Americans had "seen with pleasure the temples of despotism levelled with the ground," wrote the keen young Boston law student.[3] There was "but one sentiment . . . — that of exultation." But what did Jefferson mean by "heresies"? asked Publicola. Was Paine's pamphlet "the canonical book of scripture?" If so, what were its doctrines? "That

[1] Jefferson to Adams, July 17, 1791; *Works:* Ford, vi, 283, and footnote; also see Jefferson to Washington, May 8, 1791; *ib.*, 255–56.

Jefferson wrote Washington and the elder Adams, trying to evade his patronage of Paine's pamphlet; but, as Mr. Ford moderately remarks, "the explanation was somewhat lame." (*Writings, J. Q. A.*: Ford, i, 65; and see Hazen, 156–57.) Later Jefferson avowed that "Mr. Paine's principles . . . were the principles of the citizens of the U. S." (Jefferson to Adams, Aug. 30, 1791; *Works:* Ford, vi, 314.) To his intimate friend, Monroe, Jefferson wrote that "Publicola, in attacking all Paine's principles, is very desirous of involving me in the same censure with the author. I certainly merit the same, for I profess the same principles." (Jefferson to Monroe, July 10, 1791; *ib.*, 280.)

Jefferson at this time was just on the threshold of his discovery of and campaign against the "deep-laid plans" of Hamilton and the Nationalists to transform the newborn Republic into a monarchy and to deliver the hard-won "liberties" of the people into the rapacious hands of "monocrats," "stockjobbers," and other "plunderers" of the public. (See next chapter.)

[2] *Writings, J. Q. A.*: Ford, i, 65–66.

[3] Although John Quincy Adams had just been admitted to the bar, he was still a student in the law office of Theophilus Parsons at the time he wrote the Publicola papers.

which a whole nation chooses to do, it has a right to do" was one of them.

Was that "principle" sound? No! avowed Publicola, for "the eternal and immutable laws of justice and of morality are paramount to all human legislation." A nation might have the power but never the right to violate these. Even majorities have no right to do as they please; if so, what security has the individual citizen? Under the unrestrained rule of the majority "the principles of liberty must still be the sport of arbitrary power, and the hideous form of despotism must lay aside the diadem and the scepter, only to assume the party-colored garments of democracy."

"The only genuine liberty consists in a mean equally distant from the despotism of an individual and of a million," asserted Publicola. "Mr. Paine seems to think it as easy for a nation to change its government as for a man to change his coat." But "the extreme difficulty which impeded the progress of its [the American Constitution's] adoption . . . exhibits the fullest evidence of what a more than Herculean task it is to unite the opinions of a free people on any system of government whatever."

The "mob" which Paine exalted as the common people, but which Publicola thought was really only the rabble of the cities, "can be brought to act in concert" only by "a frantic enthusiasm and ungovernable fury; their profound ignorance and deplorable credulity make them proper tools for any man who can inflame their passions; . . . and," warned Publicola, "as they have nothing to lose by the total dissolution of civil society, their rage may be easily directed against any victim which may be pointed out to them. . . . To set in motion this inert mass, the eccentric vivacity of a madman is infinitely better calculated than the sober coolness of phlegmatic reason."

"Where," asked Publicola, "is the power that should control them [Congress]?" if they violate the letter of the Constitution. Replying to his own question, he asserted that the real check on Congress "is the spirit of the people." [1] John Marshall had said the same thing in the Virginia Constitutional Convention; but even at that early period the Richmond attorney went further and flatly declared that the temporary "spirit of the people" was not infallible and that the Supreme Court could and would declare void an unconstitutional act of Congress — a truth which he was, unguessed at that time by himself or anybody else, to announce with conclusive power within a few years and at an hour when dissolution confronted the forming Nation.

Such is a rapid *précis* of the conservative essays written by the younger Adams. Taken together, they were a rallying cry to those who dared to brave the rising hurricane of American sympathy with the French Revolution; but they also strengthened the force of that growing storm. Multitudes of writers attacked Publicola as the advocate of "aristocracy" and "monarchy." "The papers under the signature of PUBLICOLA have called forth

[1] *Writings, J. Q. A.*: Ford, i, 65–110.

a torrent of abuse," declared the final essay of the series.

Brown's "Federal Gazette" of Philadelphia branded Publicola's doctrines as "abominable heresies"; and hoped that they would "not procure many proselytes either to *monarchy* or *aristocracy*."[1] The "Independent Chronicle" of Boston asserted that Publicola was trying to build up a "system of MONARCHY AND ARISTOCRACY . . . on the ruins both of the REPUTATION and LIBERTIES of the PEOPLE."[2] Madison reported to Jefferson that because of John Adams's reputed authorship of these unpopular letters, the supporters of the Massachusetts statesman had become "perfectly insignificant in . . . number" and that "in Boston he is . . . distinguished for his unpopularity."[3]

In such fashion the controversy began in America over the French Revolution.

But whatever the misgivings of the conservative, whatever the alarm of the timid, the overwhelming majority of Americans were for the French Revolution and its doctrines;[4] and men of the highest ability and station gave dignity to the voice of the people.

[1] *Writings, J. Q. A.*: Ford, i, footnote to 107.

"As soon as Publicola attacked Paine, swarms appeared in his defense. . . . Instantly a host of writers attacked Publicola in support of those [Paine's] principles." (Jefferson to Adams, Aug. 30, 1791; *Works*: Ford, vi, 314; and see Jefferson to Madison, July 10, 1791; *ib.*, 279.)

[2] *Writings, J. Q. A.*: Ford, i, 110.

[3] Madison to Jefferson, July 13, 1791; *Writings*; Hunt, vi, 56; and see Monroe to Jefferson, July 25, 1791; Monroe's *Writings*: Hamilton, i, 225–26.

[4] A verse of a song by French Revolutionary enthusiasts at a Boston "CIVIC FESTIVAL in commemoration of the SUCCESSES of their French

In most parts of the country politicians who sought election to public office conformed, as usual, to the popular view. It would appear that the prevailing sentiment was influential even with so strong a conservative and extreme a Nationalist as Madison, in bringing about his amazing reversal of views which occurred soon after the Constitution was adopted.[1] But those who, like Marshall, were not shaken, were made firmer in their opinions by the very strength of the ideas thus making headway among the masses.

An incident of the French Revolution almost within sight of the American coast gave to the dogma of equality a new and intimate meaning in the eyes of those who had begun to look with disfavor upon the results of Gallic radical thought. Marshall and Jefferson best set forth the opposite impressions made by this dramatic event.

"Early and bitter fruits of that malignant philosophy," writes Marshall, "which . . . can coolly

brethren in their glorious enterprise for the ESTABLISHMENT of EQUAL LIBERTY," as a newspaper describes the meeting, expresses in reserved and moderate fashion the popular feeling: —

"See the bright flame arise,
In yonder Eastern skies
Spreading in veins;
'T is pure Democracy
Setting all Nations free
Melting their chains."

At this celebration an ox with gilded horns, one bearing the French flag and the other the American; carts of bread and two or three hogsheads of rum; and other devices of fancy and provisions for good cheer were the material evidence of the radical spirit. (See *Columbian Centinel*, Jan. 26, 1793.)

[1] It is certain that Madison could not possibly have continued in public life if he had remained a conservative and a Nationalist. (See next chapter.)

and deliberately pursue, through oceans of blood, abstract systems for the attainment of some fancied untried good, were gathered in the French West Indies. . . . The revolutionists of France formed the mad and wicked project of spreading their doctrines of equality among persons [negroes and white people] between whom distinctions and prejudices exist to be subdued only by the grave. The rage excited by the pursuit of this visionary and baneful theory, after many threatening symptoms, burst forth on the 23d day of August 1791, with a fury alike destructive and general.

"In one night, a preconcerted insurrection of the blacks took place throughout the colony of St. Domingo; and the white inhabitants of the country, while sleeping in their beds, were involved in one indiscriminate massacre, from which neither age nor sex could afford an exemption. Only a few females, reserved for a fate more cruel than death, were intentionally spared; and not many were fortunate enough to escape into the fortified cities. The insurgents then assembled in vast numbers, and a bloody war commenced between them and the whites inhabiting the towns."[1]

After the African disciples of French liberty had overthrown white supremacy in St. Domingo, Jefferson wrote his daughter that he had been informed "that the Patriotic party [St. Domingo revolutionists] had taken possession of 600 aristocrats & monocrats, had sent 200 of them to France, & were sending 400 here. . . . I wish," avowed Jef-

[1] Marshall, ii, 239.

ferson, in this intimate family letter, "we could distribute our 400 [white French exiles] among the Indians, who would teach them lessons of liberty & equality." [1]

Events in France marched swiftly from one bloody climax to another still more scarlet. All were faithfully reflected in the views of the people of the United States. John Marshall records for us "the fervour of democracy" as it then appeared in our infant Republic. He repeats that, at first, every American wished success to the French reformers. But the later steps of the movement "impaired this . . . unanimity of opinion. . . . A few who had thought deeply on the science of government . . . believed that . . . the influence of the galleries over the legislature, and of mobs over the executive; . . . the tumultuous assemblages of the people and their licentious excesses . . . did not appear to be the symptoms of a healthy constitution, or of genuine freedom. . . . They doubted, and they feared for the future."

Of the body of American public opinion, however, Marshall chronicles that: "In total opposition to this sentiment was that of the public. There seems to be something infectious in the example of a powerful and enlightened nation verging towards democracy, which imposes on the human mind, and leads human reason in fetters. . . . Long settled opinions yield to the overwhelming weight of such dazzling authority. It wears the semblance of be-

[1] Jefferson to Martha Jefferson Randolph, May 26, 1793; *Works*: Ford, vii, 345.

ing the sense of mankind, breaking loose from the shackles which had been imposed by artifice, and asserting the freedom, and the dignity, of his nature."

American conservative writers, says Marshall, "were branded as the advocates of royalty, and of aristocracy. To question the duration of the present order of things [in France] was thought to evidence an attachment to unlimited monarchy, or a blind prejudice in favour of British institutions. . . . The war in which the several potentates of Europe were engaged against France, although in almost every instance declared by that power, was pronounced to be a war for the extirpation of human liberty, and for the banishment of free government from the face of the earth. The preservation of the constitution of the United States was supposed to depend on its issue; and the coalition against France was treated as a coalition against America also." [1]

Marshall states, more clearly, perhaps, than any one else, American conservative opinion of the time: "The circumstances under which the abolition of royalty was declared, the massacres which preceded it, the scenes of turbulence and violence which were acted in every part of the nation, appeared to them [American conservatives] to present an awful and doubtful state of things. . . . The idea that a republic was to be introduced and supported by force, was, to them, a paradox in politics."

Thus it was, he declares, that "the French revolution will be found to have had great influence

[1] Marshall, ii, 249-51.

on the strength of parties, and on the subsequent political transactions of the United States." [1]

As the French storm increased, its winds blew ever stronger over the responsive waters of American opinion. Jefferson, that accurate barometer of public weather, thus registers the popular feeling: "The sensations it [the French Revolution] has produced here, and the indications of them in the public papers, have shown that the form our own government was to take depended much more on the events of France than anybody had before imagined." [2] Thus both Marshall and Jefferson bear testimony as to the determining effect produced in America by the violent change of systems in France.

William Short, whom Jefferson had taken to France as his secretary, when he was the American Minister to France, and who, when Jefferson returned to the United States, remained as *chargé d'affaires*,[3] had written both officially and privately of what was going on in France and of the increasing dominance of the Jacobin Clubs.[4] Perhaps no

[1] Marshall, ii, 251–52.

[2] Jefferson to T. M. Randolph, Jan. 7, 1793; *Works:* Ford, vii, 207.

[3] Mass. Hist. Collections (7th Series), i, 138.

[4] Typical excerpts from Short's reports to Jefferson are: July 20, 1792: "Those mad & corrupted people in France who under the name of liberty have destroyed their own government [French Constitution of 1791] & disgusted all . . . men of honesty & property. . . . All the rights of humanity . . . are daily violated with impunity . . . universal anarchy prevails. . . . There is no succour . . . against mobs & factions which have assumed despotic power."

July 31: "The factions which have lately determined the system . . . for violating all the bonds of civil society . . . have disgusted all, except the *sans culottes* . . . with the present order of things . . . the most perfect & universal disorder that ever reigned in any country.

more trustworthy statement exists of the prevailing American view of the French cataclysm than that given in Jefferson's fatherly letter to his protégé: —

"The tone of your letters had for some time given me pain," wrote Jefferson, "on account of the extreme warmth with which they censured the proceedings of the Jacobins of France.[1] . . . Many guilty persons [aristocrats] fell without the forms of trial, and with them some innocent: . . . It was necessary to use the arm of the people, a machine

Those who from the beginning took part in the revolution . . . have been disgusted, by the follies, injustice, & atrocities of the Jacobins. . . . All power [is] in the hands of the most mad, wicked & atrocious assembly that ever was collected in any country."

August 15: "The Swiss guards have been massacred by the people & . . . streets literally are red with blood."

October 12: "Their [French] successes abroad are unquestionably evils for humanity. The spirit which they will propagate is so destructive of all order . . . so subversive of all ideas of justice — the system they aim at so absolutely visionary & impracticable — that their efforts can end in nothing but despotism after having bewildered the unfortunate people, whom they render free in their way, in violence & crimes, & wearied them with sacrifices of blood, which alone they consider worthy of the furies whom they worship under the names of *Liberté* & *Egalité!*"

August 24: "I sh^{d} not be at all surprized to hear of the present leaders being hung by the people. Such has been the moral of this revolution from the beginning. The people have gone farther than their leaders. . . . We may expect . . . to hear of such proceedings, under the cloak of liberty, *égalité* & patriotism as would disgrace any *chambre ardente* that has ever created in humanity shudders at the idea." (Short MSS., Lib. Cong.)

These are examples of the statements to which Jefferson's letter, quoted in the text following, was the reply. Short's most valuable letters are from The Hague, to which he had been transferred. They are all the more important, as coming from a young radical whom events in France had changed into a conservative. And Jefferson's letter is conclusive of American popular sentiment, which he seldom opposed.

[1] Almost at the same time Thomas Paine was writing to Jefferson from Paris of "the Jacobins who act without either prudence or morality." (Paine to Jefferson, April 20, 1793; *Writings:* Conway, iii, 132.)

not quite so blind as balls and bombs, but blind to a certain degree. . . .

"The liberty of the whole earth," continued Jefferson, "was depending on the issue of the contest, and was ever such a prize won with so little innocent blood? My own affections have been deeply wounded by some of the martyrs to this cause, but rather than it should have failed, I would have seen half the earth desolated.

"Were there but an Adam & an Eve left in every country, & left free, it would be better than as it now is," declared Jefferson; and "my sentiments . . . are really those of 99 in an hundred of our citizens," was that careful political observer's estimate of American public opinion. "Your temper of mind," Jefferson cautions Short, "would be extremely disrelished if known to your countrymen.

"There are in the U.S. some characters of opposite principles. . . . Excepting them, this country is entirely republican, friends to the constitution. . . . The little party above mentioned have espoused it only as a stepping stone to monarchy. . . . The successes of republicanism in France have given the coup de grace to their prospects, and I hope to their projects.

"I have developed to you faithfully the sentiments of your country," Jefferson admonishes Short, "that you may govern yourself accordingly." [1]

[1] Jefferson to Short, Jan. 3, 1793; *Works:* Ford, vii, 202–05. Short had written Jefferson that Morris, then in Paris, would inform him of French conditions. Morris had done so. For instance, he wrote officially to Jefferson, nearly four months before the latter's letter to Short quoted in the text, that: "We have had one

Jefferson's count of the public pulse was accurate. "The people of this country [Virginia] . . . are unanimous & explicit in their sympathy with the Revolution" was the weather-wise Madison's report.[1] And the fever was almost as high in other States.

When, after many executions of persons who had been "denounced" on mere suspicion of unfriendliness to the new order of things, the neck of Louis XVI was finally laid beneath the knife of the guillotine and the royal head rolled into the executioner's basket, even Thomas Paine was shocked. In a judicious letter to Danton he said: —

"I now despair of seeing the great object of European liberty accomplished" because of "the tumultuous misconduct" of "the present revolution" which "injure[s its] character . . . and discourage[s] the progress of liberty all over the world. . . . There ought to be some regulation with respect to the spirit of denunciation that now prevails."[2]

So it was that Thomas Paine, in France, came to speak privately the language which, in America, at that very hour, was considered by his disciples to be the speech of "aristocracy," "monarchy," and

week of unchecked murders, in which some thousands have perished in this city [Paris]. It began with between two and three hundred of the clergy, who would not take the oath prescribed by law. Thence these *executors of speedy justice* went to the Abbaye, where the prisoners were confined who were at Court on the 10th. Madame de Lamballe . . . was beheaded and disembowelled; the head and entrails paraded on pikes through the street, and the body dragged after them," etc., etc. (Morris to Jefferson, Sept. 10, 1792; Morris, i, 583–84.)

[1] Madison to Jefferson, June 17, 1793; *Writings:* Hunt, vi, 133.

[2] Paine to Danton, May 6, 1793; *Writings:* Conway, iii, 135–38.

"despotism"; for the red fountains which drenched the fires of even Thomas Paine's enthusiasm did not extinguish the flames his burning words had lighted among the people of the United States. Indeed Paine, himself, was attacked for regretting the execution of the King.[1]

Three months after the execution of the French King, the new Minister of the French Republic, "Citizen" Genêt, arrived upon our shores. He landed, not at Philadelphia, then our seat of government, but at Charleston, South Carolina. The youthful [2] representative of Revolutionary France was received by public officials with obsequious flattery and by the populace with a frenzy of enthusiasm almost indescribable in its intensity.

He acted on the welcome. He fitted out privateers, engaged seamen, issued letters of marque and reprisal, administered to American citizens oaths of "allegiance" to the authority then reigning in Paris. All this was done long before he presented his credentials to the American Government. His progress to our Capital was an unbroken festival of triumph. Washington's dignified restraint was interpreted as hostility, not only to Genêt, but also to "liberty." But if Washington's heart was ice, the people's heart was fire.

"We expect Mr. Genest here within a few days,"

[1] "Truth," in the *General Advertiser* (Philadelphia), May 8, 1793. "Truth" denied that Louis XVI had aided us in our Revolution and insisted that it was the French Nation that had come to our assistance. Such was the disregard of the times for even the greatest of historic facts, and facts within the personal knowledge of nine tenths of the people then living.

[2] See *Writings, J. Q. A.*: Ford, i, 151.

wrote Jefferson, just previous to the appearance of the French Minister in Philadelphia and before our ignored and offended President had even an opportunity to receive him. "It seems," Jefferson continued, "as if his arrival would furnish occasion for the *people* to testify their affections without respect to the cold caution of their government."[1]

Again Jefferson measured popular sentiment accurately. Genêt was made an idol by the people. Banquets were given in his honor and extravagant toasts were drunk to the Republic and the guillotine. Showers of fiery "poems" filled the literary air.[2] "What hugging and tugging! What addressing and caressing! What mountebanking and chanting! with liberty caps and other wretched trumpery of *sans culotte* foolery!" exclaimed a disgusted conservative.[3]

While all this was going on in America, Robespierre, as the incarnation of liberty, equality, and fraternity in France, achieved the summit of power and "The Terror" reached high tide. Marie Antoinette met the fate of her royal husband, and the executioners, overworked, could not satisfy the lust of the Parisian populace for human life. All this, however, did not extinguish American enthusiasm for French liberty.

Responding to the wishes of their subscribers, who at that period were the only support of the press, the Republican newspapers suppressed such atrocities as they could, but when concealment was impossible,

[1] Jefferson to Madison, April 28, 1793; *Works:* Ford, vii, 301.

[2] For examples of these, see Hazen, 220–45. [3] Graydon, 363.

they defended the deeds they chronicled.[1] It was a losing game to do otherwise, as one of the few journalistic supporters of the American Government discovered to his sorrow. Fenno, the editor of the "Gazette of the United States," found opposition to French revolutionary ideas, in addition to his support of Hamilton's popularly detested financial measures,[2] too much for him. The latter was load enough; but the former was the straw that broke the conservative editor's back.

"I am . . . incapacitate[d] . . . from printing another paper without the aid of a considerable loan," wrote the bankrupt newspaper opponent of French doctrines and advocate of Washington's Administration. "Since the 18th September, [1793] I have rec'd only 35¼ dollars," Fenno lamented. "Four years & an half of my life is gone for nothing; & worse (for I have a Debt of 2500 Dollars on my Shoulders), if at this crisis the hand of benevolence & *patriotism* is not extended." [3]

[1] Freneau's *National Gazette* defended the execution of the King and the excesses of the Terror. (Hazen, 256; and see Cobbett, iii, 4.) While Cobbett, an Englishman, was a fanatic against the whole democratic movement, and while his opinions are violently prejudiced, his statements of fact are generally trustworthy. "I have seen a bundle of Gazettes published all by the same man, wherein Mirabeau, Fayette, Brissot, Danton, Robespierre, and Barras, are all panegyrized and execrated in due succession." (*Ib.*, i, 116.) Cobbett did his best to turn the radical tide, but to no purpose. "Alas!" he exclaimed, "what can a straggling pamphlet . . . do against a hundred thousand volumes of miscellaneous falsehood in folio?" (*Ib.*, iii, 5.)

[2] See next chapter.

[3] Fenno to Hamilton, Nov. 9, 1793; King, i, 501–02. "The hand of benevolence & *patriotism*" was extended, it appears: "If you can . . . raise 1000 Dollars in New York, I will endeavor to raise another Thousand at Philadelphia. If this cannot be done, we must lose his [Fenno's and the *Gazette of the United States*] services

Forgotten by the majority of Americans was the assistance which the demolished French Monarchy and the decapitated French King had given the American army when, but for that assistance, our cause had been lost. The effigy of Louis XVI was guillotined by the people, many times every day in Philadelphia, on the same spot where, ten years before, as a monument of their gratitude, these same patriots had erected a triumphal arch, decorated with the royal lilies of France bearing the motto, "They exceed in glory," surmounted by a bust of Louis inscribed, "His merit makes us remember him." [1]

At a dinner in Philadelphia upon the anniversary of the French King's execution, the dead monarch was represented by a roasted pig. Its head was cut off at the table, and each guest, donning the liberty cap, shouted "tyrant" as with his knife he chopped the sundered head of the dead swine.[2] The news of the beheading of Louis's royal consort met with a like reception. "I have heard more than one young woman under the age of twenty declare," testifies Cobbett, "that they would willingly have dipped their hands in the blood of the queen of France." [3]

& he will be the Victim of his honest public spirit." (Hamilton to King, Nov. 11, 1793; King, i, 502.)

[1] Cobbett, i, footnote to 114. Curiously enough Louis XVI had believed that he was leading the French people in the reform movement. Thomas Paine, who was then in Paris, records that "The King . . . prides himself on being the head of the revolution." (Paine to Washington, May 1, 1790; *Cor. Rev.*: Sparks, iv, 328.)

[2] Cobbett, i, 113–14; and see Hazen, 258. For other accounts of the "feasts" in honor of *liberté, égalité, et fraternité*, in America, see *ib.*, 165–73.

[3] Cobbett, i, 113.

But if the host of American radicals whom Jefferson led and whose spirit he so truly interpreted were forgetful of the practical friendship of French Royalty in our hour of need, American conservatives, among whom Marshall was developing leadership, were also unmindful of the dark crimes against the people which, at an earlier period, had stained the Monarchy of France and gradually cast up the account that brought on the inevitable settlement of the Revolution. The streams of blood that flowed were waters of Lethe to both sides.

Yet to both they were draughts which produced in one an obsession of reckless unrestraint and in the other a terror of popular rule no less exaggerated.[1] Of the latter class, Marshall was, by far, the most moderate and balanced, although the tragic aspect of the convulsion in which French liberty was born, came to him in an especially direct fashion, as we have seen from the Morris correspondence already cited.

Another similar influence on Marshall was the case of Lafayette. The American partisans of the French Revolution accused this man, who had fought for

[1] For instance, the younger Adams wrote that the French Revolution had "contributed more to . . . Vandalic ignorance than whole centuries can retrieve. . . . The myrmidons of Robespierre were as ready to burn libraries as the followers of Omar; and if the principle is finally to prevail which puts the sceptre of Sovereignty in the hands of European Sans Culottes, they will soon reduce everything to the level of their own ignorance." (John Quincy Adams to his father, July 27, 1795; *Writings, J. Q. A.*: Ford, i, 389.)

And James A. Bayard wrote that: "The Barbarians who inundated the Roman Empire and broke to pieces the institutions of the civilized world, in my opinion innovated the state of things not more than the French revolution." (Bayard to Bassett, Dec. 30, 1797; *Bayard Papers:* Donnan, 47.)

us in our War for Independence, of deserting the cause of liberty because he had striven to hold the Gallic uprising within orderly bounds. When, for this, he had been driven from his native land and thrown into a foreign dungeon, Freneau thus sang the conviction of the American majority:—

> "Here, bold in arms, and firm in heart,
> He help'd to gain our cause,
> Yet could not from a tyrant part,
> But, turn'd to embrace his laws!"[1]

Lafayette's expulsion by his fellow Republicans and his imprisonment by the allied monarchs, was brought home to John Marshall in a very direct and human fashion. His brother, James M. Marshall, was sent by Washington[2] as his personal representative, to plead unofficially for Lafayette's release. Marshall tells us of the strong and tender personal friendship between Washington and Lafayette and of the former's anxiety for the latter. But, writes Marshall: "The extreme jealousy with which the persons who administered the government of France, as well as a large party in America, watched his [Washington's] deportment towards all those whom the ferocious despotism of the jacobins had exiled from their country" rendered "a formal interposition in favour of the virtuous and unfortunate victim [Lafayette] of their furious passions . . . unavailing."

Washington instructed our ministers to do all they could "unofficially" to help Lafayette, says Marshall; and "a confidential person [Marshall's brother

[1] Freneau, iii, 86. [2] Marshall, ii, 387.

James] had been sent to Berlin to solicit his discharge: but before this messenger had reached his destination, the King of Prussia had delivered over his illustrious prisoner to the Emperor of Germany."[1] Washington tried "to obtain the powerful mediation of Britain" and hoped "that the cabinet of St. James would take an interest in the case; but this hope was soon dissipated." Great Britain would do nothing to secure from her allies Lafayette's release.[2]

Thus Marshall, in an uncommonly personal way, was brought face to face with what appeared to him to be the injustice of the French revolutionists. Lafayette, under whom John Marshall had served at Brandywine and Monmouth; Lafayette, leader of the movement in France for a free government like our own; Lafayette, hated by kings and aristocrats because he loved genuine liberty, and yet exiled from his own country by his own countrymen for the same reason [3] — this picture, which was the one Marshall saw, influenced him profoundly and permanently.

Humor as well as horror contributed to the repugnance which Marshall and men of his type felt ever more strongly for what they considered to be mere popular caprice. The American passion for equality had its comic side. The public hatred of all

[1] Austria. [2] Marshall, ii, 387.

[3] "They have long considered the M[is] de lafayette as really the firmest supporter of the principles of liberty in France — & as they are for the most part no friends to these principles anywhere, they cannot conceal the pleasure they [the aristocracy at The Hague] feel at their [principles of liberty] supporters' being thus expelled from the country where he laboured to establish them." (Short to Jefferson, Aug. 24, 1792; Short MSS., Lib. Cong.)

rank did not stop with French royalty and nobility. Because of his impassioned plea in Parliament for the American cause, a statue of Lord Chatham had been erected at Charleston, South Carolina; the people now suspended it by the neck in the air until the sculptured head was severed from the body. But Chatham was dead and knew only from the spirit world of this recognition of his bold words in behalf of the American people in their hour of trial and of need. In Virginia the statue of Lord Botetourt was beheaded.[1] This nobleman was also long since deceased, guilty of no fault but an effort to help the colonists, more earnest than some other royal governors had displayed. Still, in life, he had been called a "lord"; so off with the head of his statue!

In the cities, streets were renamed. "Royal Exchange Alley" in Boston became "Equality Lane"; and "Liberty Stump" was the name now given to the base of a tree that formerly had been called "Royal." In New York, "*Queen Street* became *Pearl Street;* and *King Street*, Liberty Street."[2] The liberty cap was the popular headgear and everybody wore the French cockade. Even the children, thus decorated, marched in processions,[3] singing, in a mixture of French and English words, the meaning

[1] Cobbett, i, 112.

[2] *Ib.* When the corporation of New York City thus took all monarchy out of its streets, Noah Webster suggested that, logically, the city ought to get rid of "this vile aristocratical name New York"; and, why not, inquired he, change the name of Kings County, Queens County, and Orange County? "Nay," exclaimed the sarcastic savant, "what will become of the people named King? Alas for the liberties of such people!" (Hazen, 216.)

[3] Hazen, 218.

of which they did not in the least understand, the glories of "liberté, égalité, fraternité."

At a town meeting in Boston resolutions asking that a city charter be granted were denounced as an effort to "destroy the liberties of the people; . . . a link in the chain of aristocratic influence."[1] Titles were the especial aversion of the masses. Even before the formation of our government, the people had shown their distaste for all formalities, and especially for terms denoting official rank; and, after the Constitution was adopted, one of the first things Congress did was to decide against any form of address to the President. Adams and Lee had favored some kind of respectful designation of public officials. This all-important subject had attracted the serious thought of the people more than had the form of government, foreign policy, or even taxes.

Scarcely had Washington taken his oath of office when David Stuart warned him that "nothing could equal the ferment and disquietude occasioned by the proposition respecting titles. As it is believed to have originated from Mr. Adams and Mr. Lee, they are not only unpopular to an extreme, but highly odious. . . . It has given me much pleasure to hear every part of your conduct spoken of with high approbation, and particularly your dispensing with ceremony, occasionally walking the streets; while Adams is never seen but in his carriage and six. As trivial as this may appear," writes Stuart, "it appears to be more captivating to the generality, than matters

[1] J. Q. Adams, to T. B. Adams, Feb. 1, 1792; *Writings, J. Q. A.*: Ford, i, 111–13.

of more importance. Indeed, I believe the great herd of mankind form their judgments of characters, more from such slight occurrences, than those of greater magnitude." [1]

This early hostility to ostentation and rank now broke forth in rabid virulence. In the opinion of the people, as influenced by the French Revolution, a Governor or President ought not to be referred to as "His Excellency"; nor a minister of the gospel as "Reverend." Even "sir" or "esquire" were, plainly, "monarchical." The title "Honorable" or "His Honor," when applied to any official, even a judge, was base pandering to aristocracy. "Mr." and "Mrs." were heretical to the new religion of equality. Nothing but "citizen" [2] would do — citizen judge, citizen governor, citizen clergyman, citizen colonel, major, or general, citizen baker, shoemaker, banker, merchant, and farmer, — citizen everybody.

To address the master of ceremonies at a dinner or banquet or other public gathering as "Mr. Chairman" or "Mr. Toastmaster" was aristocratic: only "citizen chairman" or "citizen toastmaster" was the true speech of genuine liberty.[3] And the name of the *Greek* letter college fraternity, Phi Beta Kappa, was the trick of kings to ensnare our unsuspecting youth. Even "Φ.Β.Κ." was declared to be "an infringement of the natural rights of society." A college fraternity was destructive of the spirit of equality in American

[1] Stuart to Washington, July 14, 1789; *Cor. Rev.*: Sparks, iv, 265–66; and see Randolph to Madison, May 19, 1789; Conway, 124.

[2] See Hazen, 209–15. [3] *Ib.*, 213.

colleges.[1] "*Lèse-républicanisme*" was the term applied to good manners and politeness.[2]

Such were the surface and harmless evidences of the effect of the French Revolution on the great mass of American opinion. But a serious and practical result developed. Starting with the mother organization at Philadelphia, secret societies sprang up all over the Union in imitation of the Jacobin Clubs of France. Each society had its corresponding committee; and thus these organizations were welded into an unbroken chain. Their avowed purpose was to cherish the principles of human freedom and to spread the doctrine of true republicanism. But they soon became practical political agencies; and then, like their French prototype, the sowers of disorder and the instigators of insurrection.[3]

The practical activities of these organizations aroused, at last, the open wrath of Washington. They "are spreading mischief far and wide," he wrote;[4] and he declared to Randolph that "if these self-created societies cannot be discountenanced, they will destroy the government of this country."[5]

Conservative apprehensions were thus voiced by George Cabot: "We have seen . . . the . . . representatives of the people butchered, and a band of

[1] See Hazen, 215. [2] Cobbett, i, 111.

[3] For an impartial and comprehensive account of these clubs see Hazen, 188–208; also, Marshall, ii, 269 *et seq.* At first many excellent and prominent men were members; but these withdrew when the clubs fell under the control of less unselfish and high-minded persons.

[4] Washington to Thruston, Aug. 10, 1794; *Writings:* Ford, xii, 451.

[5] Washington to Randolph, Oct. 16, 1794; *ib.*, 475; and see Washington to Lee, Aug. 26, 1794; *ib.*, 455.

relentless murderers ruling in their stead with rods of iron. Will not this, or something like it, be the wretched fate of our country? . . . Is not this hostility and distrust [to just opinions and right sentiments] chiefly produced by the slanders and falsehoods which the anarchists incessantly inculcate?" [1]

Young men like John Quincy Adams of Massachusetts and John Marshall of Virginia thought that "the rabble that followed on the heels of Jack Cade could not have devised greater absurdities than" the French Revolution had inspired in America; [2] but they were greatly outnumbered by those for whom Jefferson spoke when he said that "I feel that the permanence of our own [Government] leans" on the success of the French Revolution.[3]

The American democratic societies, like their French originals, declared that theirs was the voice of "the people," and popular clamor justified the claim.[4] Everybody who dissented from the edicts of the clubs was denounced as a public robber or monarchist. "What a continual yelping and barking are our Swindlers, Aristocrats, Refugees, and British Agents making at the Constitutional Societies" which were "like a noble mastiff . . . with . . . impotent and noisy puppies at his heels," cried the indignant editor of the "Independent Chronicle" of Boston,[5] to whom the democratic societies were "guardians of liberty."

[1] Cabot to Parsons, Aug. 12, 1794; Lodge: *Cabot*, 79.

[2] J. Q. Adams to John Adams, Oct. 19, 1790; *Writings, J. Q. A*: Ford, i, 64.

[3] Jefferson to Rutledge, Aug. 29, 1791; *Works:* Ford, vi, 309.

[4] See Hazen, 203–07.

[5] September 18, 1794.

While these organizations strengthened radical opinion and fashioned American sympathizers of the French Revolution into disciplined ranks, they also solidified the conservative elements of the United States. Most viciously did the latter hate these "Jacobin Clubs," the principles they advocated, and their interference with public affairs. "They were born in sin, the impure offspring of Genêt," wrote Fisher Ames.

"They are the few against the many; the sons of darkness (for their meetings are secret) against those of the light; and above all, it is a *town* cabal, attempting to rule the *country*." [1] This testy New Englander thus expressed the extreme conservative feeling against the "insanity which is epidemic": [2] "This French mania," said Ames, "is the bane of our politics, the mortal poison that makes our peace so sickly." [3] "They have, like toads, sucked poison from the earth. They thirst for vengeance." [4] "The spirit of mischief is as active as the element of fire and as destructive." [5] Ames describes the activities of the Boston Society and the aversion of the "better classes" for it: "The club is despised here by men of right heads," he writes. "But . . . they [the members of the Club] poison every spring; they whisper lies to every gale; they are everywhere, always acting like Old Nick and his imps. . . . They will be as busy as Macbeth's witches at the election." [6]

[1] Ames to Dwight, Sept. 11, 1794; *Works:* Ames, i, 150.
[2] Cabot to King, July 25, 1795; Lodge: *Cabot,* 80.
[3] Ames to Gore, March 26, 1794; *Works:* Ames, i, 139.
[4] Ames to Minot, Feb. 20, 1793; *ib.,* 128.
[5] Ames to Gore, Jan. 28, 1794; *ib.,* 134.
[6] Ames to Dwight, Sept. 3, 1794; *ib.,* 148.

In Virginia the French Revolution and the American "Jacobins" helped to effect that change in Patrick Henry's political sentiments which his increasing wealth had begun. "If my Country," wrote Henry to Washington, "is destined in my day to encounter the horrors of anarchy, every power of mind or body which I possess will be exerted in support of the government under which I live." [1] As to France itself, Henry predicted that "anarchy will be succeeded by despotism" and Bonaparte, "Caesar-like, subvert the liberties of his country." [2]

Marshall was as much opposed to the democratic societies as was Washington, or Cabot, or Ames, but he was calmer in his opposition, although vitriolic enough. When writing even ten years later, after time had restored perspective and cooled feeling, Marshall says that these "pernicious societies" [3] were "the resolute champions of all the encroachments attempted by the agents of the French republic on the government of the United States, and the steady defamers of the views and measures of the American executive." [4] He thus describes their decline:—

"The colossean power of the [French] clubs, which had been abused to an excess that gives to faithful history the appearance of fiction, fell with that of their favourite member, and they sunk into long merited disgrace. The means by which their political influence had been maintained were wrested

[1] Henry to Washington, Oct. 16, 1795; Henry, ii, 559.
[2] *Ib.*, 576. [3] Marshall, ii, 353. [4] *Ib.*, 269.

from them; and, in a short time, their meetings were prohibited. Not more certain is it that the boldest streams must disappear, if the fountains which fed them be emptied, than was the dissolution of the democratic societies of America, when the Jacobin clubs were denounced by France. As if their destinies depended on the same thread, the political death of the former was the unerring signal for that of the latter." [1]

Such was the effect of the French Revolution on American thought at the critical period of our new Government's first trials. To measure justly the speech and conduct of men during the years we are now to review, this influence must always be borne in mind. It was woven into every great issue that arose in the United States. Generally speaking, the debtor classes and the poorer people were partisans of French revolutionary principles; and the creditor classes, the mercantile and financial interests, were the enemies of what they called "Jacobin philosophy." In a broad sense, those who opposed taxes, levied to support a strong National Government, sympathized with the French Revolution and believed in its ideas; those who advocated taxes for that purpose, abhorred that convulsion and feared its doctrines.

Those who had disliked government before the Constitution was established and who now hated National control, heard in the preachings of the French revolutionary theorists the voice of their hearts; while those who believed that government is essen-

[1] Marshall, ii, 353–54.

tial to society and absolutely indispensable to the building of the American Nation, heard in the language and saw in the deeds of the French Revolution the forces that would wreck the foundations of the state even while they were but being laid and, in the end, dissolve society itself. Thus were the ideas of Nationality and localism in America brought into sharper conflict by the mob and guillotine in France.

All the passion for irresponsible liberty which the French Revolution increased in America, as well as all the resentment aroused by the financial measures and foreign policy of the "Federal Administrations," were combined in the opposition to and attacks upon a strong National Government. Thus provincialism in the form of States' Rights was given a fresh impulse and a new vitality. Through nearly all the important legislation and diplomacy of those stirring and interpretative years ran, with ever increasing clearness, the dividing line of Nationalism as against localism.

Such are the curious turns of human history. Those whom Jefferson led profoundly believed that they were fighting for human rights; and in their view and as a practical matter at that particular time this sacred cause meant State Rights. For everything which they felt to be oppressive, unjust, and antagonistic to liberty, came from the National Government. By natural contrast in their own minds, as well as by assertions of their leaders, the State Governments were the sources of justice and the protectors of the genuine rights of man.

In the development of John Marshall as well as of his great ultimate antagonist, Thomas Jefferson, during the formative decade which we are now to consider, the influence of the French Revolution must never be forgotten. Not a circumstance of the public lives of these two men and scarcely an incident of their private experience but was shaped and colored by this vast series of human events. Bearing in mind the influence of the French Revolution on American opinion, and hence, on Marshall and Jefferson, let us examine the succeeding years in the light of this determining fact.

CHAPTER II

A VIRGINIA NATIONALIST

Lace Congress up straitly within the enumerated powers. (Jefferson.)

Construe the constitution liberally in advancement of the common good. (Hamilton.)

To organize government, to retrieve the national character, to establish a system of revenue, to create public credit, were among the duties imposed upon them. (Marshall.)

I trust in that Providence which has saved us in six troubles, yea, in seven, to rescue us again. (Washington.)

The Constitution's narrow escape from defeat in the State Conventions did not end the struggle against the National principle that pervaded it.[1] The Anti-Nationalists put forth all their strength to send to the State Legislatures and to the National House and Senate as many antagonists of the National idea as possible.[2] "Exertions will be made to engage two thirds of the legislatures in the task of regularly undermining the government" was Madison's "hint" to Hamilton.[3]

Madison cautioned Washington to the same effect, suggesting that a still more ominous part of the plan was "to get a Congress appointed in the

[1] Marshall, ii, 150–51. "The agitation had been too great to be suddenly calmed; and for the active opponents of the system [Constitution] to become suddenly its friends, or even indifferent to its fate, would have been a victory of reason over passion." (*Ib.*; and see Beard: *Econ. O. J. D.*, 85, 101, 102–07.)

[2] "The effort was made to fill the legislature with the declared enemies of the government, and thus to commit it, in its infancy, to the custody of its foes." (Marshall, ii, 151.)

[3] Madison to Hamilton, June 27, 1788; Hamilton MSS., Lib. Cong. Madison adds this cryptic sentence: "This hint may not be unworthy of your attention."

first instance that will commit suicide on their own Authority."[1] Not yet had the timorous Madison personally felt the burly hand of the sovereign people so soon to fall upon him. Not yet had he undergone that familiar reversal of principles wrought in those politicians who keep an ear to the ground. But that change was swiftly approaching. Even then the *vox populi* was filling the political heavens with a clamor not to be denied by the ambitious. The sentiment of the people required only an organizer to become formidable and finally omnipotent.

Such an artisan of public opinion was soon to appear. Indeed, the master political potter was even then about to start for America where the clay for an Anti-Nationalist Party was almost kneaded for the moulder's hands. Jefferson was preparing to leave France; and not many months later the great politician landed on his native soil and among his fellow citizens, who, however, welcomed him none too ardently.[2]

[1] Madison to Washington, June 27, 1788; *Writings:* Hunt, v, 234. Madison here refers to the project of calling a new Federal Convention for the purpose of amending the Constitution or making a new one.

Randolph was still more apprehensive. "Something is surely meditated against the new Constitution more animated, forcible, and violent than a simple application for calling a Convention." (Randolph to Madison, Oct. 23, 1788; Conway, 118.)

[2] When Jefferson left Virginia for France, his political fortunes were broken. (Eckenrode: *R. V.*, chap. viii; and Dodd, 63–64; and Ambler, 35–36.) The mission to France at the close of the American Revolution, while "an honor," was avoided rather than sought by those who were keen for career. (Dodd, 36–39.)

Seldom has any man achieved such a recovery as that of Jefferson in the period now under review. Perhaps Talleyrand's rehabilitation most nearly approaches Jefferson's achievement. From the depths of disfavor this genius of party management climbed to the heights of popularity and fame.

No one knew just where Jefferson stood on the fundamental question of the hour when, with his two daughters, he arrived in Virginia in 1789. The brilliant Virginian had uttered both Nationalist and Anti-Nationalist sentiments. "I am not of the party of the Federalists," he protested, "but I am much farther from that of the Antifederalists." Indeed, declared Jefferson, "If I could not go to heaven but with a party, I would not go there at all." [1]

His first opinions of the Constitution were, as we have seen, unfavorable. But after he had learned that the new Government was to be a fact, Jefferson wrote Washington: "I have seen with infinite pleasure our new constitution accepted." Careful study had taught him, he said, "that circumstances may arise, and probably will arise, wherein all the resources of taxation will be necessary for the safety of the state." He saw probability of war which "requires every resource of taxation & credit." He thought that "the power of making war often prevents it." [2]

Thus Jefferson could be quoted on both sides and claimed by neither or by both. But, because of his absence in France and of the reports he had received from the then extreme Nationalist, Madison, he had not yet apprehended the people's animosity to National rule. Upon his arrival in Virginia, however, he discovered that "Antifederalism is not yet dead

[1] Jefferson to Hopkinson, March 13, 1789; *Works:* Ford, v, 456.

[2] Jefferson to Washington, Paris, Dec. 4, 1788; *Works:* Ford, v, 437–38. Compare with Jefferson's statements when the fight was on against ratifying the Constitution. (See vol. I, chap. VIII; also Jefferson to Humphreys, Paris, March 18, 1789; *Works:* Ford, v, 470.)

in this country." [1] That much, indeed, was clear at first sight. The Legislature of Virginia, which met three months after her Convention had ratified the Constitution, was determined to undo that work, as Madison had foreseen.[2]

That body was militantly against the new Government as it stood. "The conflict between the powers of the general and state governments was coeval with those governments," declares Marshall. "The old line of division was still as strongly marked as ever." The enemies of National power thought that "liberty could be endangered only by encroachments upon the states; and that it was the great duty of patriotism to restrain the powers of the general government within the narrowest possible limits." On the other hand, the Nationalists, says Marshall, "sincerely believed that the real danger which threatened the republic was to be looked for in the undue ascendency of the states." [3]

Patrick Henry was supreme in the House of Delegates. Washington was vastly concerned at the prospect. He feared that the enemies of Nationalism would control the State Legislature and that

[1] Jefferson to Short, Dec. 14, 1789; *Works:* Ford, vi, 24.

[2] The Legislature which met on the heels of the Virginia Constitutional Convention hastened to adjourn in order that its members might attend to their harvesting. (Monroe to Jefferson, July 12, 1788; Monroe's *Writings:* Hamilton, i, 188.) But at its autumn session, it made up for lost time in its practical display of antagonism to the Nationalist movement.

[3] Marshall, ii, 205–26. Throughout this chapter the terms "Nationalist" and "Anti-Nationalist" are used instead of the customary terms "Federalist" and "Anti-Federalist," the latter not clearly expressing the fundamental difference between the contending political forces at that particular time.

it would respond to New York's appeal for a new Federal Constitutional Convention. He was "particularly alarmed" that the General Assembly would elect Senators "entirely anti-Federal." [1] His apprehension was justified. Hardly a week passed after the House convened until it passed resolutions, drawn by Henry,[2] to answer Clinton's letter, to ask Congress to call a new Federal Convention, and to coöperate with other States in that business.

In vain did the Nationalist members strive to soften this resolution. An amendment which went so far as to request Congress to recommend to the several States "the ratification of a bill of rights" and of the twenty amendments proposed by the Virginia Convention, was defeated by a majority of 46 out of a total vote of 124.[3] Swiftly and without mercy the triumphant opposition struck its next blow. Washington had urged Madison to stand for the Senate,[4] and the Nationalists exerted themselves to elect him. Madison wrote cleverly in his own behalf.[5] But he had no hope of success because it was "certain that a clear majority of the assembly are enemies to the Gov^{t}."[6] Madison was still the ultra-Nationalist, who, five years earlier, had wanted

[1] Carrington to Madison, Oct. 19, 1788; quoted in Henry, ii, 415.

[2] *Ib.*, 416–18.

[3] Journal, H.D. (Oct. 30, 1788), 16–17; see Grigsby, ii, 319; also see the vivid description of the debate under these resolutions in Henry, ii, 418–23.

[4] Carrington to Madison, Oct. 19, 1788; quoted in Henry, ii, 415.

[5] Madison to Randolph Oct. 17, 1788; to Pendleton, Oct. 20, 1788; *Writings:* Hunt, v, 269–79.

[6] Madison to Randolph, Nov. 2, 1788; *Writings:* Hunt, v, 296.

the National Government to have an absolute veto on *every* State law.[1]

Henry delivered "a tremendous philippic" against Madison as soon as his name was placed before the General Assembly.[2] Madison was badly beaten, and Richard Henry Lee and William Grayson were chosen as the first Senators from Virginia under the new National Government.[3] The defeated champion of the Constitution attributed Henry's attack and his own misfortune to his Nationalist principles: Henry's "enmity was levelled . . . agst the *whole system;* and the destruction of the whole system, I take to be the secret wish of his heart." [4]

In such fashion did Madison receive his first chastisement for his Nationalist views and labors. He required no further discipline of a kind so rough and humiliating; and he sought and secured election to the National House of Representatives,[5] with opinions much subdued and his whole being made pliant for the wizard who so soon was to invoke his spell over that master mind.

Though Marshall was not in the Virginia Legislature at that session, it is certain that he worked with its members for Madison's election as Senator.

[1] See vol. I of this work.

[2] Henry, ii, 427; see also Scott, 172.

[3] Journal, H.D. (Nov. 8, 1788), 32; see also Conway, 120; and Henry, ii, 427–28.

[4] Madison to Randolph, Nov. 2, 1788; *Writings:* Hunt, v, 295.

[5] Monroe became a candidate against Madison and it was "thought that he [would] . . . carry his election." (Mason to John Mason, Dec. 18, 1788; Rowland, ii, 304.) But so ardent were Madison's assurances of his modified Nationalist views that he was elected. His majority, however, was only three hundred. (Monroe to Jefferson, Feb. 15, 1789; Monroe's *Writings:* Hamilton, i, 199.)

But even Marshall's persuasiveness was unavailing. "Nothing," wrote Randolph to Madison. "is left undone which can tend to the subversion of the new government." [1]

Hard upon its defeat of Madison the Legislature adopted an ominous address to Congress. "The sooner . . . the [National] government is possessed of the confidence of the people . . . *the longer its duration*" — such was the language and spirit of Virginia's message to the lawmakers of the Nation, even before they had assembled.[2] The desperate Nationalists sought to break the force of this blow. They proposed a substitute which even suggested that the widely demanded new Federal Convention should be called by Congress if that body thought best. But all to no purpose. Their solemn [3] amendment was beaten by a majority of 22 out of a total vote of 122.[4]

Thus again was displayed that hostility to Nationalism which was to focus upon the newborn National Government every burning ray of discontent from the flames that sprang up all over the country during the constructive but riotous years that followed. Were the people taxed to pay obligations incurred in our War for Independence? — the Na-

[1] Randolph to Madison, Nov. 10, 1788; Conway, 121.

[2] Journal, H.D. (Nov. 14, 1788), 42–44. Also see *Annals*, 1st Cong., 1st Sess., 259.

[3] The Nationalist substitute is pathetic in its apprehensive tone. It closes with a prayer "that Almighty God in his goodness and wisdom will direct your councils to such measures as will establish our lasting peace and welfare and secure to our latest posterity the blessings of freedom; and that he will always have you in his holy keeping." (Journal, H.D. (Nov. 14, 1788), 43.)

[4] *Ib.*, 44.

tional Government was to blame. Was an excise laid on whiskey, "the common drink of the nation" [1] — it was the National Government which thus wrung tribute from the universal thirst. Were those who owed debts compelled, at last, to pay them? — it was the National Government which armed the creditor with power to recover his own.

Why did we not aid French Republicans against the hordes of "despotism"? Because the National Government, with its accursed Neutrality, would not let us! And who but the National Government would dare make a treaty with British Monarchy, sacrificing American rights? Speculation and corruption, parade and ostentation, — everything that could, reasonably or unreasonably, be complained of, — were, avowed the Anti-Nationalists, the wretched but legitimate offspring of Nationalism. The remedy, of course, was to weaken the power of the Nation and strengthen that of the States. Such was the course pursued by the foes of Nationalism, that we shall trace during the first three administrations of the Government of the United States.

Thus, the events that took place between 1790 and 1800, supplemented and heated by the French Revolution, developed to their full stature those antagonistic theories of which John Marshall and Thomas Jefferson were to become the chief expounders. Those events also finished the preparation of these two men for the commanding stations they were to

[1] Pennsylvania Resolutions: Gallatin's *Writings:* Adams, i, 3. This was unjust to New England, where rum was "the common drink of the nation" and played an interesting part in our tariff laws and New England trade.

occupy. The radical politician and States' Rights leader on the one hand, and the conservative politician and Nationalist jurist on the other hand, were finally settled in their opinions during these developing years, at the end of which one of them was to occupy the highest executive office and the other the highest judicial office in the Government.

It was under such circumstances that the National Government, with Washington at its head, began its uncertain career. If the Legislature of Virginia had gone so far before the infant National establishment was under way, how far might not succeeding Legislatures go? No one knew. But it was plain to all that every act of the new Administration, even with Washington at the helm, would be watched with keen and jealous eyes; and that each Nationalist turn of the wheel would meet with prompt and stern resistance in the General Assembly of the greatest of American Commonwealths. Mutiny was already aboard.

John Marshall, therefore, determined again to seek election to the House of Delegates.

Immediately upon the organization of the National Government, Washington appointed Marshall to be United States Attorney for the District of Virginia. The young lawyer's friends had suggested his name to the President, intimating that he wished the place.[1] Marshall, high in the esteem of every one, had been consulted as to appointments on the National bench,[2] and Washington gladly named

[1] Washington to Marshall, Nov. 23, 1789; MS., Lib. Cong.

[2] Randolph to Madison, July 19, 1789; Conway, 127.

him for District Attorney. But when notified of his appointment, Marshall declined the honor.

A seat in the Virginia Legislature, was, however, quite another matter. Although his work as a legislator would interfere with his profession much more than would his duties as United States Attorney, he could be of practical service to the National Government in the General Assembly of the State where, it was plain, the first battle for Nationalism must be fought.

The Virginia Nationalists, much alarmed, urged him to make the race. The most popular man in Richmond, he was the only Nationalist who could be elected by that constituency; and, if chosen, would be the ablest supporter of the Administration in the Legislature. Although the people of Henrico County were more strongly against a powerful National Government than they had been when they sent Marshall to the Constitutional Convention the previous year, they nevertheless elected him; and in 1789 Marshall once more took his seat as a member of Virginia's law-making and law-marring body.

He was at once given his old place on the two principal standing committees;[1] and on special committees to bring in various bills,[2] among them one concerning descents, a difficult subject and of particular concern to Virginians at that time.[3] As a member of the Committee of Privileges and Elections, he passed on a hotly contested election case.[4] He was made a

[1] Journal, H.D. (Oct. 20, 1789), 4. [2] *Ib.*, 7–16.

[3] *Ib.*, 16. Marshall probably drew the bill that finally passed. He carried it from the House to the Senate. (*Ib.*, 136.)

[4] *Ib.* (Oct. 28, 1790), 19–22. Whether or not a voter owned land was weighed in delicate scales. Even "treating" was examined.

member of the important special committee to report upon the whole body of laws in force in Virginia, and helped to draw the committee's report, which is comprehensive and able.[1] The following year he was appointed a member of the committee to revise the tangled laws of the Commonwealth.[2]

The irrepressible subject of paying taxes in something else than money soon came up. Marshall voted against a proposition to pay the taxes in hemp and tobacco, which was defeated by a majority of 37 out of a total vote of 139; and he voted for the resolution "that the taxes of the present year ought to be paid in specie only or in warrants equivalent thereto," which carried.[3] He was added to the committee on a notable divorce case.[4]

Marshall was, of course, appointed on the special committee to bring in a bill giving statehood to the District of Kentucky.[5] Thus he had to do with the creation of the second State to be admitted after the Constitution was adopted. A bill was passed authorizing a lottery to raise money to establish an

[1] Journal, H.D. (Oct. 28, 1790), 24–29.

[2] *Ib.*, 1st Sess. (1790), 41; and 2d Sess. (Dec. 8), 121–22. For extent of this revision see Conway, 130.

[3] Journal, H.D. (1789), 57–58.

[4] *Ib.*, 78. See report of the committee in this interesting case. (*Ib.*, 103.) The bill was passed. (*Ib.*, 141.) At that time divorces in Virginia could be had only by an act of the Legislature. Contrast the above case, where the divorce was granted for cruelty, abandonment, waste of property, etc., with that of the Mattauer case (*ib.* (1793), 112, 126), where the divorce was refused for admitted infidelity on the part of the wife who bore a child by the brother of her husband while the latter was abroad.

[5] *Ib.* (1789), 96. Kentucky was then a part of Virginia and legislation by the latter State was necessary. It is more than probable that Marshall drew this important statute, which passed. (*Ib.*, 115, 131, 141.)

academy in Marshall's home county, Fauquier.[1] He voted with the majority against the perennial Baptist petition to democratize religion;[2] and for the bill to sell lands for taxes.[3]

Marshall was appointed on the committee to bring in bills for proceeding against absent debtors;[4] on another to amend the penal code;[5] and he was made chairman of the special committee to examine the James River Company,[6] of which he was a stock-

[1] Journal, H.D. (1789), 112. At this period, lotteries were the common and favorite methods of raising money for schools, and other public institutions and enterprises. Even the maintenance of cemeteries was provided for in this way. The Journals of the House of Delegates are full of resolutions and Hening's Statutes contain many acts concerning these enterprises. (See, for example, Journal, H.D. (1787), 16–20; (1797), 39.)

[2] An uncommonly able state paper was laid before the House of Delegates at this session. It was an arraignment of the Virginia Constitution of 1776, and mercilessly exposed, without the use of direct terms, the dangerous political machine which that Constitution made inevitable; it suggested "that as harmony with the Federal Government . . . is to be desired our own Constitution ought to be compared with that of the United States and retrenched where it is repugnant"; and it finally recommended that the people instruct their representatives in the Legislature to take the steps for reform. The author of this admirable petition is unknown. (Journal, H.D. (1789), 113.)

From this previous vote for a new Constitution, it is probable that Marshall warmly supported this resolution. But the friends of the old and vicious system instantly proposed an amendment "that the foregoing statement contains principles repugnant to Republican Government and dangerous to the freedom of this country, and, therefore, ought not to meet with the approbation of this House or be recommended to the consideration of the people"; and so strong were they that the whole subject was dropped by postponement, without further contest. (Journal, H.D. (1789), 108–09.)

[3] *Ib.* (Nov. 17, 1789), 20.

[4] *Ib.* (Nov. 13, 1789), 12.

[5] *Ib.* (Nov. 16, 1789), 14.

[6] *Ib.* (Nov. 27, 1789), 49. The James River Company was formed in 1784. Washington was its first president. (Randolph to Washington, Aug. 8, 1784; Conway, 58.) Marshall's Account Book shows many payments on stock in this company.

holder. Such are examples of his routine activities in the Legislature of 1789.

The Legislature instructed the Virginia Senators in Congress "to use their utmost endeavors to procure the admission of the citizens of the United States to hear the debates of their House, whenever they are sitting in their legislative capacity." [1]

An address glowing with love, confidence, and veneration was sent to Washington.[2] Then Jefferson came to Richmond; and the Legislature appointed a committee to greet him with polite but coldly formal congratulations.[3] No one then foresaw that a few short years would turn the reverence and affection for Washington into disrespect and hostility, and the indifference toward Jefferson into fiery enthusiasm.

The first skirmish in the engagement between the friends and foes of a stronger National Government soon came on. On November 30, 1789, the House ratified the first twelve amendments to the Constitution,[4] which the new Congress had submitted to the States; but three days later it was proposed

[1] Journal, H.D. (1789), 117, 135. For many years after the Constitution was adopted the United States Senate sat behind closed doors. The Virginia Legislature continued to demand public debate in the National Senate until that reform was accomplished. (See Journal, H.D. (Oct. 25, 1791), 14; (Nov. 8, 1793), 57, etc.)

In 1789 the Nationalists were much stronger in the Legislatures of the other States than they had been in the preceding year. Only three States had answered Virginia's belated letter proposing a new Federal Convention to amend the Constitution. Disgusted and despondent, Henry quitted his seat in the House of Delegates in the latter part of November and went home in a sulk. (Henry, ii, 448–49; Conway, 131.)

[2] Journal, H.D. (1789), 17, 19, 98. [3] *Ib.*, 107–12.

[4] *Ib.*, 90–91.

that the Legislature urge Congress to reconsider the amendments recommended by Virginia which Congress had not adopted.[1] An attempt to make this resolution stronger was defeated by the deciding vote of the Speaker, Marshall voting against it.[2]

The Anti-Nationalist State Senate refused to concur in the House's ratification of the amendments proposed by Congress;[3] and Marshall was one of the committee to hold a conference with the Senate committee on the subject.

After Congress had passed the laws necessary to set the National Government in motion, Madison had reluctantly offered his summary of the volume of amendments to the Constitution recommended by the States "in order," as he said, "to quiet that anxiety which prevails in the public mind."[4] The debate is illuminating. The amendments, as agreed to, fell far short of the radical and extensive alterations which the States had asked and were understood to be palliatives to popular discontent.[5]

[1] Journal, H.D. (1789), 96. [2] *Ib.*, 102.

[3] *Ib.*, 119. The objections were that the liberty of the press, trial by jury, freedom of speech, the right of the people to assemble, consult, and "to instruct their representatives," were not guaranteed; and in general, that the amendments submitted "fall short of affording security to personal rights." (Senate Journal, December 12, 1789; MS., Va. St. Lib.)

[4] *Annals*, 1st Cong., 1st Sess., 444; and see entire debate. The amendments were offered as a measure of prudence to mollify the disaffected. (Rives, iii, 38–39.)

[5] The House agreed to seventeen amendments. But the Senate reduced these to twelve, which were submitted to the States. The first of these provided for an increase of the representation in the House; the second provided that no law "varying" the salaries of Senators or Representatives "shall take effect until an election of Representatives shall have intervened." (*Annals*, 1st Cong., 1st Sess., Appendix to ii, 2033.) The States ratified only the last ten.

Randolph in Richmond wrote that the amendments were "much approved by the *strong* federalists . . . being considered as an anodyne to the discontented. Some others . . . expect to hear, . . . that a real amelioration of the Constitution was not so much intended, as a soporific draught to the restless. I believe, indeed," declared Randolph, "that nothing — nay, not even the abolishment of direct taxation — would satisfy those who are most clamorous." [1]

The amendments were used by many, who changed from advocates to opponents of broad National powers, as a pretext for reversed views and conduct; but such as were actually adopted were not a sufficient justification for their action.[2]

The great question, however, with which the First Congress had to deal, was the vexed and vital problem of finance. It was the heart of the whole constitutional movement.[3] Without a solution of it the National Government was, at best, a doubtful experiment. The public debt was a chaos of variegated obligations, including the foreign and domestic debts contracted by the Confederation, the debts of the various States, the heavy accumulation of interest on all.[4] Public and private credit, which had risen when

(For good condensed treatment of the subject see Hildreth, iv, 112–24.) Thus the Tenth Amendment, as ratified, was the twelfth as submitted and is sometimes referred to by the latter number in the documents and correspondence of 1790–91, as in Jefferson's "Opinion on the Constitutionality of the Bank of the United States." (See *infra.*) New York, Virginia, Maryland, South Carolina, North Carolina, and Rhode Island accepted the twelve amendments as proposed. The other States rejected one or both of the first two amendments.

[1] Randolph to Madison, June 30, 1789; Conway, 126.

[2] See Beard: *Econ. O. J. D.*, 76. [3] *Ib.*, 86. [4] *Ib.*, 132–33.

the Constitution finally became an accomplished fact, was now declining with capital's frail timidity of the uncertain.

In his "First Report on the Public Credit," Hamilton showed the way out of this maddening jungle. Pay the foreign debt, said Hamilton, assume as a National obligation the debts of the States and fund them, together with those of the Confederation. All had been contracted for a common purpose in a common cause; all were "the price of liberty." Let the owners of certificates, both State and Continental, be paid in full with arrears of interest, without discrimination between original holders and those who had purchased from them. And let this be done by exchanging for the old certificates those of the new National Government bearing interest and transferable. These latter then would pass as specie;[1] the country would be supplied with a great volume of sound money, so badly needed,[2] and the debt be in the process of extinguishment.[3]

Hamilton's entire financial system was assailed with fury both in Congress and among the people. The funding plan, said its opponents, was a stock-jobbing scheme, the bank a speculator's contrivance, the National Assumption of State debts a dishonest

[1] Marshall, ii, 192.

[2] Money was exceedingly scarce. Even Washington had to borrow to travel to New York for his inauguration, and Patrick Henry could not attend the Federal Constitutional Convention for want of cash. (Conway, 132.)

[3] "First Report on the Public Credit"; *Works;* Lodge, ii, 227 *et seq.* The above analysis, while not technically precise, is sufficiently accurate to give a rough idea of Hamilton's plan. (See Marshall's analysis; Marshall, ii, 178–80.)

trick. The whole was a plot designed to array the moneyed interests in support of the National Government.[1] Assumption of State debts was a device to increase the National power and influence and to lessen still more the strength and importance of the States.[2] The speculators, who had bought the depreciated certificates of the needy, would be enriched from the substance of the whole people.

Without avail had Hamilton answered every objection in advance; the careful explanations in Congress of his financial measures went for naught; the materials for popular agitation against the National Government were too precious to be neglected by its foes.[3] "The first regular and systematic opposition

[1] This, indeed, was a portion of Hamilton's plan and he succeeded in it as he did in other parts of his broad purpose to combine as much strength as possible in support of the National Government. "The northern states and the commercial and monied people are zealously attached to . . . the new government." (Wolcott to his father, Feb. 12, 1791; Gibbs, i, 62.)

[2] This was emphatically true. From the National point of view it was the best feature of Hamilton's plan.

[3] In his old age, John Adams, Hamilton's most venomous and unforgiving enemy, while unsparing in his personal abuse, paid high tribute to the wisdom and necessity of Hamilton's financial statesmanship. "I know not," writes Adams, "how Hamilton could have done otherwise." (Adams to Rush, Aug. 23, 1805; *Old Family Letters*, 75.) "The sudden rise of public securities, after the establishment of the funding system was no misfortune to the Public but an advantage. The necessity of that system arose from the inconsistency of the People in contracting debts and then refusing to pay them." (Same to same, Jan. 25, 1806; *ib.*, 93.)

Fisher Ames thus states the different interests of the sections: "The funding system, they [Southern members of Congress] say, is in favor of the moneyed interest — oppressive to the land; that is, favorable to us [Northern people], hard on them. They pay tribute, they say, and the middle and eastern people . . . receive it. And here is the burden of the song, almost all the little [certificates of State or Continental debts] that they had and which cost them twenty shillings, for supto the principles on which the affairs of the union were administered," writes Marshall, "originated in the measures which were founded on it [the "First Report on the Public Credit"]."[1]

The Assumption of State debts was the strategic point of attack, especially for the Virginia politicians; and upon Assumption, therefore, they wisely concentrated their forces. Nor were they without plausible ground of opposition; for Virginia, having given as much to the common cause as any State and more than most of her sisters, and having suffered greatly, had by the sale of her public lands paid off more of her debt than had any of the rest of them.

It seemed, therefore, unjust to Virginians to put their State on a parity with those Commonwealths who had been less prompt. On the other hand, the certificates of debt, State and Continental, had accumulated in the North and East;[2] and these sections were determined that the debt should be assumed by the Nation.[3] So the debate in Congress was heated and prolonged, the decision doubtful. On various

plies or services, has been bought up, at a low rate, and now they pay more tax towards the interest than they received for the paper. This *tribute*, they say, is aggravating." (Ames to Minot, Nov. 30, 1791; *Works;* Ames, i, 104.)

[1] Marshall, ii, 181. The attack on Hamilton's financial plan and especially on Assumption was the beginning of the definite organization of the Republican Party. (Washington's *Diary:* Lossing, 166.)

[2] Gore to King, July 25, 1790; King, i, 392; and see McMaster, ii, 22.

[3] At one time, when it appeared that Assumption was defeated, Sedgwick of Massachusetts intimated that his section might secede. (*Annals*, 1st Cong., April 12, 1790, pp. 1577–78; and see Rives, iii, 90 *et seq.*)

amendments, sometimes one side and sometimes the other prevailed, often by a single vote.[1]

At the same time the question of the permanent location of the National Capital arose.[2] On these two subjects Congress was deadlocked. Both were disposed of finally by the famous deal between Jefferson and Hamilton, by which the latter agreed to get enough votes to establish the Capital on the Potomac and the former enough votes to pass the Assumption Bill.

Washington had made Jefferson his Secretary of State purely on merit. For similar reasons of efficiency Hamilton had been appointed Secretary of the Treasury, after Robert Morris, Washington's first choice, had declined that office.

At Jefferson's dinner table, the two Secretaries discussed the predicament and made the bargain. Thereupon, Jefferson, with all the zeal of his ardent temperament, threw himself into the contest to pass Hamilton's financial measure; and not only secured the necessary votes to make Assumption a law, but wrote letters broadcast in support of it.

"Congress has been long embarrassed," he advised Monroe, "by two of the most irritating questions that ever can be raised, . . . the funding the public debt and . . . the fixing on a more central residence. . . . Unless they can be reconciled by

[1] Marshall's statement of the debate is the best and fairest brief account of this historic conflict. (See Marshall, ii, 181–90. See entire debate in *Annals*, 1st Cong., i, ii, under caption "Public Debt.")

[2] "This despicable grog-shop contest, whether the taverns of New York or Philadelphia shall get the custom of Congress, keeps us in discord and covers us all with disgrace." (Ames to Dwight, June 11, 1790; *Works:* Ames, i, 80.)

some plan of compromise, there will be no funding bill agreed to, our credit . . . will burst and vanish and the states separate to take care every one of itself." Jefferson outlines the bargain for fixing the Capital and assuming the debts, and concludes: "If this plan of compromise does not take place, I fear one infinitely worse."[1] To John Harvie he writes: "With respect to Virginia the measure is . . . divested of . . . injustice."[2]

Jefferson delivered three Southern votes to pass the bill for Assumption of the State debts, and Hamilton got enough Northern votes to locate the National Capital permanently where it now stands.[3] Thus this vital part of Hamilton's comprehensive financial plan was squeezed through Congress by only two votes.[4] But Virginia was not appeased and remained the center of the opposition.[5]

Business at once improved. "The sudden increase of monied capital," writes Marshall, "invigorated commerce, and gave a new stimulus to agriculture."[6]

[1] Jefferson to Monroe, June 20, 1790; *Works:* Ford, vi, 78–80; and see *ib.*, 76; to Gilmer, June 27, *ib.*, 83; to Rutledge, July 4, *ib.*, 87–88; to Harvie, July 25, *ib.*, 108.

[2] *Ib.*; and see also Jefferson to Eppes, July 25, *ib.*, 106; to Randolph, March 28, *ib.*, 37; to same, April 18, *ib.*, 47; to Lee, April 26, *ib.*, 53; to Mason, June 13, *ib.*, 75; to Randolph, June 20, *ib.*, 76–77; to Monroe, June 20, *ib.*, 79; to Dumas, June 23, *ib.*, 82; to Rutledge, July 4, *ib.*, 87–88; to Dumas, July 13, *ib.*, 96. Compare these letters with Jefferson's statement, February, 1793; *ib.*, vii, 224–26; and with the "Anas," *ib.*, i, 171–78. Jefferson then declared that "I was really a stranger to the whole subject." (*Ib.*, 176.)

[3] Jefferson's statement; *Works:* Ford, vii, 224–26, and i, 175–77.

[4] Gibbs, i, 32; and see Marshall, ii, 190–91.

[5] Henry, ii, 453. But Marshall says that more votes would have changed had that been necessary to consummate the bargain. (See Marshall, ii, footnote to 191.)

[6] *Ib.*, 192.

But the "immense wealth which individuals acquired" by the instantaneous rise in the value of the certificates of debt caused popular jealousy and discontent. The debt was looked upon, not as the funding of obligations incurred in our War for Independence, but as a scheme newly hatched to strengthen the National Government by "the creation of a monied interest . . . subservient to its will." [1]

The Virginia Legislature, of which Marshall was now the foremost Nationalist member, convened soon after Assumption had become a National law. A smashing resolution, drawn by Henry,[2] was proposed, asserting that Assumption "is repugnant to the constitution of the United States, as it goes to the exercise of a power not expressly granted to the general government." [3] Marshall was active among and, indeed, led those who resisted to the uttermost the attack upon this thoroughly National measure of the National Government.

Knowing that they were outnumbered in the Legislature and that the people were against Assumption, Marshall and his fellow Nationalists in the House of Delegates employed the expedient of compromise. They proposed to amend Henry's resolution by stating that Assumption would place on Virginia a "heavy debt . . . which never can be extinguished" so long as the debt of any other State remained unpaid; that it was "inconsistent with justice"; that it would "alienate the affections of good citizens of this Commonwealth from the gov-

[1] Marshall, ii, 191–92.
[2] Henry, ii, 453–55.
[3] Journal, H.D. (1790), 35.

ernment of the United States . . . and finally tend to produce measures extremely unfavorable to the interests of the Union."[1]

Savage enough for any one, it would seem, was this amendment of the Nationalists in the Virginia Legislature; but its fangs were not sufficiently poisonous to suit the opposition. It lacked, particularly, the supreme virtue of asserting the law's unconstitutionality. So the Virginia Anti-Nationalists rejected it by a majority of 41 votes out of a total of 135.

Marshall and his determined band of Nationalists labored hard to retrieve this crushing defeat. On Henry's original resolution, they slightly increased their strength, but were again beaten by a majority of 23 out of 127 voting.[2]

Finally, the triumphant opposition reported a protest and remonstrance to Congress. This brilliant Anti-Nationalist State paper — the Magna Charta of States' Rights — sounded the first formal call to arms for the doctrine that all powers not expressly given in the Constitution were reserved to the States. It also impeached the Assumption Act as an effort "to erect and concentrate and perpetuate a large monied interest in opposition to the landed interests," which would prostrate "agriculture at the feet of commerce" or result in a "change in the present form of Federal Government, fatal to the existence of American liberty."[3]

But the unconstitutionality of Assumption was the main objection. The memorial declared that "during the whole discussion of the federal consti-

[1] Journal, H.D. (1790), 35. [2] *Ib.* [3] *Ib.*, 80–81.

tution by the convention of Virginia, your memorialists were taught to believe 'that every power not expressly granted was retained' . . . and upon this positive condition" the Constitution had been adopted. But where could anything be found in the Constitution "authorizing Congress to express terms or to assume the debts of the states?" Nowhere! Therefore, Congress had no such power.

"As the guardians, then, of the rights and interests of their constituents; as sentinels placed by them over the ministers of the Federal Government, to shield it from their encroachments," the Anti-Nationalists in the Virginia Legislature sounded the alarm.[1] It was of this jealous temper of the States that Ames so accurately wrote a year later: "The [National] government is too far off to gain the affections of the people. . . . Instead of feeling as a Nation, a State is our country. We look with indifference, often with hatred, fear, and aversion, to the other states."[2]

Marshall and his fellow Nationalists strove earnestly to extract from the memorial as much venom as possible, but were able to get only three or four lines left out;[3] and the report was adopted practically as originally drafted.[4] Thus Marshall was in

[1] Journal, H.D. (1790), 80–81; and see *Am. St. Prs., Finance*, i, 90–91. The economic distinction is here clearly drawn. Jefferson, who later made this a chief part of his attack, had not yet raised the point.

[2] Ames to Minot, Feb. 16, 1792; *Works;* Ames, i, 113.

[3] This was the sentence which declared that Hamilton's reasoning would result in "fictitious wealth through a paper medium," referring to his plan for making the transferable certificates of the National debt serve as currency.

[4] Journal, H.D. (1790), 141.

the first skirmish, after the National Government had been established, of that constitutional engagement in which, ultimately, Nationalism was to be challenged on the field of battle. Sumter and Appomattox were just below the horizon.

The remainder of Hamilton's financial plan was speedily placed upon the statute books of the Republic, though not without determined resistance which, more and more, took on a grim and ugly aspect both in Congress and throughout the country.

When Henry's resolution, on which the Virginia remonstrance was based, reached Hamilton, he instantly saw its logical result. It was, he thought, the major premise of the syllogism of National disintegration. "This," exclaimed Hamilton, of the Virginia resolution, "is the first symptom of a spirit which must either be killed or it will kill the Constitution of the United States." [1]

[1] Hamilton to Jay, Nov. 13, 1790; *Works:* Lodge, ix, 473–74. Virginia was becoming very hostile to the new Government. First, there was a report that Congress was about to emancipate the slaves. Then came the news of the Assumption of the State debts, with the presence in Virginia of speculators from other States buying up State securities; and this added gall to the bitter cup which Virginians felt the National Government was forcing them to drink. Finally the tidings that the Senate had defeated the motion for public sessions inflamed the public mind still more. (Stuart to Washington, June 2, 1790; *Writings:* Ford, xi, footnote to 482.)

Even close friends of Washington deeply deplored a "spirit so subversive of the true principles of the constitution. . . . If Mr. Henry has sufficient boldness to aim the blow at its [Constitution's] existence, which he has threatened, I think he can never meet with a more favorable opportunity if the assumption should take place." (*Ib.*)

Washington replied that Stuart's letter pained him. "The public mind in Virginia . . . seems to be more irritable, sour, and discontented than . . . it is in any other State in the Union except Massachusetts." (Washington to Stuart, June 15, 1790; *ib.*, 481–82.)

Marshall's father most inaccurately reported to Washington that

The Anti-Nationalist memorial of the Legislature of Virginia accurately expressed the sentiment of the State. John Taylor of Caroline two years later, in pamphlets of marked ability, attacked the Administration's entire financial system and its management. While he exhaustively analyzed its economic features, yet he traced all its supposed evils to the Nationalist idea. The purpose and result of Hamilton's whole plan and of the manner of its execution was, declared Taylor, to "Swallow up . . . the once sovereign . . . states. . . . Hence all assumptions and . . . the enormous loans." Thus "the state governments will become only speculative commonwealths to be read for amusement, like Harrington's *Oceana* or Moore's *Utopia*." [1]

The fight apparently over, Marshall declined to become a candidate for the Legislature in the following year. The Administration's financial plan was now enacted into law and the vital part of the National machinery thus set up and in motion. The country was responding with a degree of prosperity hitherto unknown, and, for the time, all seemed secure.[2] So Marshall did not again consent to serve

Kentucky favored the measures of the Administration; and the President, thanking him for the welcome news, asked the elder Marshall for "any information of a public or private nature . . . from your district." (Washington to Thomas Marshall, Feb., 1791; Washington's Letter Book, MS., Lib. Cong.) Kentucky was at that time in strong opposition and this continued to grow.

[1] Taylor's "An Enquiry, etc.," as quoted in Beard: *Econ. O. J. D.*, 209. (*Ib.*, chap. vii.) Taylor's pamphlet was revised by Pendleton and then sent to Madison before publication. (Monroe to Madison, May 18, 1793; Monroe's *Writings*: Hamilton, i, 254.) Taylor wanted "banks . . . demolished" and bankers "excluded from public councils." (Beard: *Econ. O. J. D.*, 209.)

[2] Marshall, ii, 192.

in the House of Delegates until 1795. But the years between these periods of his public life brought forth events which were determinative of the Nation's future. Upon the questions growing out of them, John Marshall was one of the ever-decreasing Virginia minority which stanchly upheld the policies of the National Government.

Virginia's declaration of the unconstitutionality of the Assumption Act had now thundered in Jefferson's ears. He himself was instrumental in the enactment of this law and its unconstitutionality never occurred to him [1] until Virginia spoke. But, faithful to the people's voice,[2] Jefferson was already publicly opposing, through the timid but resourceful Madison [3] and the fearless and aggressive [4] Giles, the Nationalist statesmanship of Hamilton.[5]

[1] In Jefferson's letters, already cited, not the faintest suggestion appears that he thought the law unconstitutional. Not until Patrick Henry's resolution, and the address of the Virginia Legislature to Congress based thereon, made the point that Assumption was in violation of this instrument, because the power to pass such a law was not expressly given in the Constitution, did Jefferson take his stand against implied powers.

[2] "Whether . . . right or wrong, abstractedly, more attention should be paid to the general opinion." (Jefferson to Mason, Feb. 4, 1791; *Works:* Ford, vi, 186.)

[3] Monroe had advised Madison of the hostility of Virginia to Assumption and incidentally asked for an office for his own brother-in-law. (Monroe to Madison, July 2, 1790; Monroe's *Writings:* Hamilton, i, 208; and see Monroe to Jefferson, July 3, 1790; *ib.*, 209.)

[4] Anderson, 21.

[5] Jefferson himself, a year after he helped pass the Assumption Act, had in a Cabinet paper fiercely attacked Hamilton's plan; and the latter answered in a formal statement to the President. These two documents are the ablest summaries of the opposing sides of this great controversy. (See Jefferson to President, May 23, 1792; *Works:* Ford, vi, 487–95; and Hamilton to Washington, Aug. 18, 1792; *Works:* Lodge, ii, 426–72.)

Thus it came about that when Washington asked his Cabinet's opinion upon the bill to incorporate the Bank of the United States, Jefferson promptly expressed with all his power the constitutional theory of the Virginia Legislature. The opposition had reached the point when, if no other objection could be found to any measure of the National Government, its "unconstitutionality" was urged against it. "We hear, incessantly, from the old foes of the Constitution 'this is unconstitutional and that is,' and, indeed, what is not? I scarce know a point which has not produced this cry, not excepting a motion for adjourning."[1] Jefferson now proceeded "to produce this cry" against the Bank Bill.

Hamilton's plan, said Jefferson, violated the Constitution. "To take a single step beyond the boundaries thus specially drawn around the powers of Congress [the Twelfth Amendment][2] is to take possession of a boundless field of power, no longer susceptible of any definition." Even if the bank were "convenient" to carry out any power specifically granted in the Constitution, yet it was not "*necessary*," argued Jefferson; all powers expressly given could be exercised without the bank. It was only indispensable powers that the Constitution permitted to be implied from those definitely bestowed on Congress — "convenience is not necessity."[3]

[1] Ames to Minot, March 8, 1792; *Works:* Ames, i, 114.

[2] Tenth Amendment, as ratified.

[3] "Opinion on the Constitutionality of a National Bank of the United States"; *Works:* Ford, vi, 198; and see Madison's argument against the constitutionality of the Bank Act in *Annals*, 1st Cong., Feb. 2, 1791, pp. 1944–52; Feb. 8, 2008–12; also, *Writings:* Hunt,

Hamilton answered with his argument for the doctrine of implied powers.[1] Banks, said he, are products of civilized life — all enlightened commercial nations have them. He showed the benefits and utility of banks; answered all the objections to these financial agencies; and then examined the disputed constitutionality of the bill for the incorporation of the Bank of the United States.

All the powers of the National Government were not set down in words in the Constitution and could not be. For instance, there are the "resulting powers," as over conquered territory. Nobody could deny the existence of such powers — yet they were not granted by the language of the fundamental law. As to Jefferson's argument based on the word "necessary," his contention meant, said Hamilton, that "no means are to be considered *necessary* without which the power would be *nugatory*" — which was absurd. Jefferson's reasoning would require that an implied power should be "*absolutely* or *indispensably* necessary."

But this was not the ordinary meaning of the word and it was by this usual and customary understanding of terms that the Constitution must be interpreted. If Jefferson was right, Congress could act only in "a case of extreme necessity." Such a construction of the Constitution would prevent

vi, 19–42. This argument best shows Madison's sudden and radical change from an extreme Nationalist to an advocate of the most restricted National powers.

[1] Hamilton's "Opinion as to the Constitutionality of the Bank of the United States"; *Works:* Lodge, iii, 445–93. Adams took the same view. (See Adams to Rush, Dec. 27, 1810; *Old Family Letters,* 272.)

the National Government even from erecting light-houses, piers, and other conveniences of commerce which *could* be carried on without them. These illustrations revealed the paralysis of government concealed in Jefferson's philosophy.

The true test of implied powers, Hamilton showed, was the "natural relation [of means] to the . . . lawful ends of the government." Collection of taxes, foreign and interstate trade, were, admittedly, such ends. The National power to "*regulate*" these is "*sovereign*"; and therefore "to employ all the means which will relate to their regulation to the best and greatest advantage" is permissible.

"This *general principle* is *inherent* in the very *definition* of government," declared he, "and *essential* to every step of the progress to be made by that of the United States, namely: That every power vested in a government is in its nature *sovereign* and included by *force* of the *term*, a right to employ all the *means* requisite and fairly applicable to the attainment of the *ends* of such power, and which are not precluded by restrictions and exceptions specified in the Constitution or not immoral, or not contrary to the *essential* ends of political society. . . .

"The powers of the Federal Government, as to *its objects* are sovereign"; the National Constitution, National laws, and treaties are expressly declared to be "the supreme law of the land." And he added, sarcastically: "The power which can create *the supreme law of the land* in *any case* is doubtless *sovereign* as to such case." But, said Hamilton, "it is unquestionably incident to *sove-*

reign power to erect corporations, and consequently to *that* of the United States, in *relation* to the *objects* intrusted to the management of the government."

And, finally: "The powers contained in a constitution of government . . . ought to be construed liberally in advancement of the public good. . . . The means by which natural exigencies are to be provided for, national inconveniences obviated, national prosperity promoted are of such infinite variety, extent, and complexity, that there must of necessity be great latitude of discretion in the selection and application of those means." [1]

So were stated the opposing principles of liberal and narrow interpretation of the Constitution, about which were gathering those political parties that, says Marshall, "in their long and dubious conflict . . . have shaken the United States to their centre." [2] The latter of these parties, under the name "Republican," was then being shaped into a compact organization. Its strength was increasing. The object of Republican attack was the National Government; that of Republican praise and affection was the sovereignty of the States.

"The hatred of the Jacobites towards the house of Hanover was never more deadly than that . . . borne by many of the partisans of State power towards the government of the United States," testi-

[1] "Opinion as to the Constitutionality of the Bank of the United States"; *Works:* Lodge, iii, 445–93. Washington was sorely perplexed by the controversy and was on the point of vetoing the Bank Bill. (See Rives, iii, 170–71.)

[2] Marshall, ii, 206–07.

fies Ames.[1] In the Republican view the basis of the two parties was faith as against disbelief in the ability of the people to govern themselves; the former favored the moneyed interests, the latter appealed to the masses.[2] Such was the popular doctrine preached by the opponents of the National Government; but all economic objections centered in a common assault on Nationalism.

Thus a clear dividing line was drawn separating the people into two great political divisions; and political parties, in the present-day sense of definite organizations upon fundamental and popularly recognized principles, began to emerge. Henceforth the terms "Federalist" and "Republican" mean opposing party groups, the one standing for the National and the other for the provincial idea. The various issues that arose were referred to the one or the other of these hostile conceptions of government.

In this rise of political parties the philosophy of the Constitution was negatived; for our fundamental law, unlike those of other modern democracies, was built on the non-party theory and did not contemplate party government. Its architects did not foresee parties. Indeed, for several years after the Constitution was adopted, the term "party" was used as an expression of reproach. The correspondence of the period teems with illustrations of this important fact.

For a considerable time most of the leading men

[1] Ames to Dwight, Jan. 23, 1792; *Works:* Ames, i, 110–11.
[2] "A Candid State of Parties" — *National Gazette,* Sept. 26, 1792.

of the period looked with dread upon the growing idea of political parties; and the favorite rebuke to opponents was to accuse them of being a "party" or a "faction," those designations being used interchangeably. The "Farewell Address" is a solemn warning against political parties [1] almost as much as against foreign alliances.

[1] "I was no party man myself and the first wish of my heart was, if parties did exist, to reconcile them." (Washington to Jefferson, July 6, 1796; *Writings:* Ford, xiii, 230.)

CHAPTER III

LEADING THE VIRGINIA FEDERALISTS

I think nothing better could be done than to make him [Marshall] a judge. (Jefferson to Madison, June 29, 1792.)

To doubt the holiness of the French cause was the certain road to odium and proscription. (Alexander Graydon.)

The trouble and perplexities have worn away my mind. (Washington.)

In Richmond, Marshall was growing ever stronger in his belief in Nationalism. Hamilton's immortal plea for a vital interpretation of the fundamental law of the Nation and his demonstration of the constitutionality of extensive implied powers was a clear, compact statement of what Marshall himself had been thinking. The time was coming when he would announce it in language still more lucid, expressive of a reasoning even more convincing. Upon Hamilton's constitutional doctrine John Marshall was to place the seal of finality.[1]

But Marshall did not delay until that great hour to declare his Nationalist opinions. Not only did he fight for them in the House of Delegates; but in his club at Farmicola's Tavern, on the street corners, riding the circuit, he argued for the constitutionality and wisdom of those measures of Washington's

[1] Compare Hamilton's "Opinion as to the Constitutionality of the Bank of the United States" with Marshall's opinion in McCulloch *vs.* Maryland. The student of Marshall cannot devote too much attention to Hamilton's great state papers, from the "First Report on the Public Credit" to "Camillus." It is interesting that Hamilton produced all these within five years, notwithstanding the fact that this was the busiest and most crowded period of his life.

Administration which strengthened and broadened the powers of the National Government.[1]

Although he spoke his mind, in and out of season, for a cause increasingly unpopular, Marshall, as yet, lost little favor with the people. At a time when political controversy severed friendship and interrupted social relations,[2] his personality still held sway over his associates regardless of their political convictions. Even Mason, the ultra-radical foe of broad National powers, wrote, at this heated juncture, that Marshall "is an intimate friend of mine." [3]

His winning frankness, easy manner, and warm-heartedness saved him from that dislike which his bold views otherwise would have created. "Independent principles, talents, and integrity are denounced [in Virginia] as badges of aristocracy; but if you add to these good manners and a decent appearance, his political death is decreed without the benefit of a hearing," testifies Francis Corbin.[4]

"Independent principles, talents, and integrity" Marshall possessed in fullest measure, as all admitted; but his manners were far from those which men like the modish Corbin called "good," and his appearance would not have passed muster under the critical eye of that fastidious and disgruntled young Federalist. We shall soon hear Jefferson denouncing Marshall's deportment as the artifice of a cunning

[1] Binney, in Dillon, iii, 301–02.

[2] La Rochefoucauld, iii, 73. For a man even "to be passive . . . is a satisfactory proof that he is on the wrong side." (Monroe to Jefferson, July 17, 1792; Monroe's *Writings:* Hamilton, i, 238.)

[3] George Mason to John Mason, July 12, 1791; Rowland, ii, 338.

[4] Corbin to Hamilton, March 17, 1793; as quoted in Beard: *Econ O. J. D.*, 226.

and hypocritical craft. As yet, however, Jefferson saw in Marshall only an extremely popular young man who was fast becoming the most effective supporter in Virginia of the National Government.

In the year of the Bank Act, Jefferson and Madison went on their eventful "vacation," swinging up the Hudson and through New England. During this journey Jefferson drew around Madison "the magic circle" of his compelling charm and won entirely to the extreme Republican cause [1] the invaluable aid of that superb intellect. In agreement as to common warfare upon the Nationalist measures of the Administration,[2] the two undoubtedly talked over the Virginia Federalists.[3]

Marshall's repeated successes at the polls with a constituency hostile to the young lawyer's views particularly impressed them. Might not Marshall become a candidate for Congress? If elected, here would be a skillful, dauntless, and captivating supporter of all Nationalist measures in the House of Representatives. What should be done to avert this misfortune?

[1] "Patrick Henry once said 'that he could forgive anything else in Mr. Jefferson, but his corrupting Mr. Madison.'" (Pickering to Marshall, Dec. 26, 1828; Pickering MSS., Mass. Hist. Soc.) "His [Madison's] placing himself under the pupilage of Mr. Jefferson and supporting his public deceptions, are sufficient to put him out of my book." (Pickering to Rose, March 22, 1808; *ib.*)

[2] Madison's course was irreconcilable with his earlier Nationalist stand. (See Beard: *Econ. O. J. D.*, 77; and see especially the remarkable and highly important letter of Hamilton to Carrington, May 26, 1792; *Works:* Lodge, ix, 513–35, on Madison's change, Jefferson's conduct, and the politics of the time.) Carrington was now the brother-in-law of Marshall and his most intimate friend. Their houses in Richmond almost adjoined. (See *infra*, chap. v.)

[3] See brief but excellent account of this famous journey in Gay: *Madison* (American Statesmen Series), 184–85; and *contra*, Rives, iii, 191.

Jefferson's dexterous intellect devised the idea of getting rid of Marshall, politically, by depositing him on the innocuous heights of the State bench. Better, far better, to make Marshall a Virginia judge than to permit him to become a Virginia Representative in Congress. So, upon his return, Jefferson wrote to Madison: —

"I learn that he [Hamilton] has expressed the strongest desire that Marshall should come into Congress from Richmond, declaring that there is no man in Virginia whom he wishes so much to see there; and I am told that Marshall has expressed half a mind to come. Hence I conclude that Hamilton has plyed him well with flattery & sollicitation and I think nothing better could be done than to make him a judge." [1]

Hamilton's "plying" Marshall with "flattery & solicitation" occurred only in Jefferson's teeming, but abnormally suspicious, mind. Marshall was in Virginia all this time, as his Account Book proves, while Hamilton was in New York, and no letters seem to have passed between them.[2] But Jefferson's information that his fellow Secretary wished the Nationalist Richmond attorney in Congress was probably correct. Accounts of Marshall's striking ability and of his fearless zeal in support of the Administration's measures had undoubtedly reached Hamilton, perhaps through Washington himself; and so sturdy and capable a Federalist in Congress

[1] Jefferson to Madison, June 29, 1792; *Works:* Ford, vii, 129–30.

[2] No letters have been discovered from Hamilton to Marshall or from Marshall to Hamilton dated earlier than three years after Jefferson's letter to Madison.

from Virginia would have been of great strategic value.

But Jefferson might have spared his pains to dispose of Marshall by cloistering him on the State bench. Nothing could have induced the busy lawyer to go to Congress at this period. It would have been fatal to his law practice [1] which he had built up until it was the largest in Richmond and upon the returns from which his increasing family depended for support. Six years later, Washington himself labored with Marshall for four days before he could persuade him to stand for the National House, and Marshall then yielded to his adored leader only as a matter of duty, at one of the Nation's most critical hours, when war was on the horizon.[2]

The break-up of Washington's Cabinet was now approaching. Jefferson was keeping pace with the Anti-Nationalist sentiment of the masses — drilling his followers into a sternly ordered political force. "The discipline of the [Republican] party," wrote Ames, "is as severe as the Prussian."[3] Jefferson and Madison had secured an organ in the "National Gazette," [4] edited by Freneau, whom Jefferson employed as translator in the State Department. Through this paper Jefferson attacked Hamilton without mercy. The spirited Secretary of the Treas-

[1] "The length of the last session has done me irreparable injury in my profession, as it has made an impression on the general opinion that two occupations are incompatible." (Monroe to Jefferson, June 17, 1792; Monroe's *Writings:* Hamilton, i, 230.)

[2] See *infra*, chap. x.

[3] Ames to Dwight, Jan., 1793; *Works:* Ames, i, 126–27.

[4] Rives, iii, 192–94; and see McMaster, ii, 52–53; also Hamilton to Carrington, May 26, 1792; *Works:* Lodge, ix, 513–35.

ury keenly resented the opposition of his Cabinet associate which was at once covert and open.

In vain the President pathetically begged Jefferson for harmony and peace.[1] Jefferson responded with a bitter attack on Hamilton. "I was duped," said he, "by the Secretary of the Treasury and made a tool for forwarding his schemes, not then sufficiently understood by me." [2] To somewhat, but not much, better purpose did Washington ask Hamilton for "mutual forbearances." [3] Hamilton replied with spirit, yet pledged his honor that he would "not, directly or indirectly, say or do a thing that shall endanger a feud." [4]

The immense speculation, which had unavoidably grown out of the Assumption and Funding Acts, inflamed popular resentment against the whole financial statesmanship of the Federalists.[5] More material, this, for the hands of the artificer who was fashioning the Republican Party into a capacious vessel into which the people might pour all their discontent, all their fears, all their woes and all their

[1] Washington to Jefferson, Aug. 23, 1792; *Writings:* Ford, xii, 174–75. This letter is almost tearful in its pleading.

[2] Jefferson to Washington, Sept. 9, 1792; *Works:* Ford, vii, 137 *et seq.* The quotation in the text refers to Jefferson's part in the deal fixing the site of the Capital and passing the Assumption Act. Compare with Jefferson's letters written at the time. (*Supra,* 64.) It is impossible that Jefferson was not fully advised; the whole country was aroused over Assumption, Congress debated it for weeks, it was the one subject of interest and conversation at the seat of government, and Jefferson himself so testifies in his correspondence.

[3] Washington to Hamilton, Aug. 26, 1792; *Writings:* Ford, xii, 177–78.

[4] Hamilton to Washington, Sept 9, 1792; *Works:* Lodge, vii, 306.

[5] See Marshall, ii, 191–92.

hopes. And Jefferson, with practical skill, used for that purpose whatever material he could find.

Still more potter's earth was brought to Jefferson. The National Courts were at work. Creditors were securing judgments for debts long due them. In Virginia the debtors of British merchants, who for many years had been rendered immune from payment, were brought to the bar of this "alien" tribunal. Popular feeling ran high. A resolution was introduced into the House of Delegates requesting the Virginia Senators and Representatives in Congress to "adopt such measures as will tend, not only to suspend all executions and the proceedings thereon, but prevent any future judgments to be given by the Federal Courts in favor of British creditors until" Great Britain surrendered the posts and runaway negroes.[1] Thus was the practical overthrow of the National Judiciary proposed.[2]

Nor was this all. A State had been haled before a National Court.[3] The Republicans saw in this the monster "consolidation." The Virginia Legislature passed a resolution instructing her Senators and Representatives to "unite their utmost and earliest exertions" to secure a constitutional amendment preventing a State from being sued "in any court of

[1] Journal, H.D. (Nov. 28, 1793), 101.

[2] *Ib.* The Legislature instructed Virginia's Senators and Representatives to endeavor to secure measures to "suspend the operation and completion" of the articles of the treaty of peace looking to the payment of British debts until the posts and negroes should be given up. (*Ib.*, 124–25; also see Virginia Statutes at Large, New Series, i, 285.) Referring to this Ames wrote: "Thus, murder, at last, is out." (Ames to Dwight, May 6, 1794; *Works:* Ames, i, 143–44.)

[3] Chisholm *vs.* Georgia, 2 Dallas, 419.

the United States."[1] The hostility to the National Bank took the form of a resolution against a director or stockholder of the Bank of the United States being a Senator or Representative in Congress.[2] But apparently this trod upon the toes of too many ambitious Virginians, for the word "stockholders" was stricken out.[3]

The slander that the Treasury Department had misused the public funds had been thoroughly answered;[4] but the Legislature of Virginia by a majority of 111 out of a total vote of 124, applauded her Senators and Representatives who had urged the inquiry.[5] Such was the developing temper of Republicanism as revealed by the emotionless pages of the public records; but these furnish scarcely a hint of the violence of public opinion.

Jefferson was now becoming tigerish in his assaults on the measures of the Administration. Many

[1] Journal, H.D. (1793), 92–99; also see Virginia Statutes at Large, New Series, i, 284. This was the origin of the Eleventh Amendment to the Constitution. The Legislature "Resolved, That a State cannot, under the Constitution of the United States, be made a defendant at the suit of any individual or individuals, and that the decision of the Supreme Federal Court, that a State may be placed in that situation, is incompatible with, and dangerous to the sovereignty and independence of the individual States, as the same tends to a general consolidation of these confederated republics." Virginia Senators were "instructed" to make "their utmost exertions" to secure an amendment to the Constitution regarding suits against States. The Governor was directed to send the Virginia resolution to all the other States. (Journal, H.D. (1793), 99.)

[2] *Ib.*, 125.

[3] *Ib.*; also Statutes at Large, *supra*, 284.

[4] See *Annals*, 2d Cong., 900–63.

[5] Journal, H.D. (1793), 56–57. Of Giles's methods in this attack on Hamilton the elder Wolcott wrote that it was "such a piece of baseness as would have disgraced the council of Pandemonium." (Wolcott to his son, March 25, 1793; Gibbs, i, 91.)

members of Congress had been holders of certificates which Assumption and Funding had made valuable. Most but not all of them had voted for every feature of Hamilton's financial plan.[1] Three or four were directors of the Bank, but no dishonesty existed.[2] Heavy speculation went on in Philadelphia.[3] This, said Republicans, was the fruit which Hamilton's Nationalist financial scheme gathered from the people's industry to feed to "monocrats."

"Here [Philadelphia]," wrote Jefferson, "*the unmonied farmer* . . . his cattle & corps [*sic*] are no more thought of than if they did not feed us. Script & stock are food & raiment here. . . . The credit & fate of the nation seem to hang on the desperate throws & plunges of gambling scoundrels." [4] But Jefferson comforted himself with the prophecy that

[1] Beard: *Econ. O. J. D.*, chap. vi.

[2] Professor Beard, after a careful treatment of this subject, concludes that "The charge of mere corruption must fall to the ground." (*Ib.*, 195.)

[3] "To the northward of Baltimore everybody . . . speculates, trades, and jobs in the stocks. The judge, the advocate, the physician and the minister of divine worship, are all, or almost all, more or less interested in the sale of land, in the purchase of goods, in that of bills of exchange, and in lending money at two or three per cent." (La Rochefoucauld, iv, 474.) The French traveler was also impressed with the display of riches in the Capital. "The profusion of luxury of Philadelphia, on great days, at the tables of the wealthy, in their equipages and the dresses of their wives and daughters, are . . . extreme. I have seen balls on the President's birthday where the splendor of the rooms, and the variety and richness of the dresses did not suffer, in comparison with Europe." The extravagance extended to working-men who, on Sundays, spent money with amazing lavishness. Even negro servants had balls; and negresses with wages of one dollar per week wore dresses costing sixty dollars. (*Ib.*, 107–09.)

[4] Jefferson to T. M. Randolph, March 16, 1792; *Works:* Ford, vi, 408.

"this nefarious business" would finally "tumble its authors headlong from their heights."[1]

The National law taxing whiskey particularly aroused the wrath of the multitude. Here it was at last! — a direct tax laid upon the universal drink of the people, as the razor-edged Pennsylvania resolutions declared.[2] Here it was, just as the patriotic foes of the abominable National Constitution had predicted when fighting the ratification of that "oppressive" instrument. Here was the exciseman at every man's door, just as Henry and Mason and Grayson had foretold — and few were the doors in the back counties of the States behind which the owner's private still was not simmering.[3] And why was this tribute exacted? To provide funds required by the corrupt Assumption and Funding laws, asserted the agitators.

[1] Jefferson to Short, May 18, 1792; *Works:* Ford, vi, 413; and see "A Citizen" in the *National Gazette,* May 3, 1792, for a typical Republican indictment of Funding and Assumption.

[2] Gallatin's *Writings:* Adams, i, 3.

[3] Pennsylvania alone had five thousand distilleries. (Beard: *Econ. O. J. D.,* 250.) Whiskey was used as a circulating medium. (McMaster, ii, 29.) Every contemporary traveler tells of the numerous private stills in Pennyslvania and the South. Practically all farmers, especially in the back country, had their own apparatus for making whiskey or brandy. (See chap. VII, vol. I, of this work.)

Nor was this industry confined to the lowly and the frontiersmen. Washington had a large distillery. (Washington to William Augustine Washington, Feb. 27, 1798; *Writings:* Ford, xiii, 444.)

New England's rum, on the other hand, was supplied by big distilleries; and these could include the tax in the price charged the consumer. Thus the people of Pennsylvania and the South felt the tax personally, while New Englanders were unconscious of it. Otherwise there doubtless would have been a New England "rum rebellion," as Shays's uprising and as New England's implied threat in the Assumption fight would seem to prove. (See Beard: *Econ. O. J. D.,* 250–51.)

Again it was the National Government that was to blame; in laying the whiskey tax it had invaded the rights of the States, hotly declared the Republicans. "All that powerful party," Marshall bears witness, "which attached itself to the local [State] rather than to the general [National] government . . . considered . . . a tax by Congress on any domestic manufacture as the intrusion of a foreign power into their particular concerns which excited serious apprehensions for state importance and for liberty."[1] The tariff did not affect most people, especially those in the back country, because they used few or no imported articles; but the whiskey tax did reach them, directly and personally.[2]

Should such a despotic law be obeyed? Never! It was oppressive! It was wicked! Above all, it was "unconstitutional"! But what to do! The agencies of the detested and detestable National Government were at work! To arms, then! That was the only thing left to outraged freemen about to be ravaged of their liberty![3] Thus came the physical defiance of the law in Pennsylvania; Washington's third proclamation[4] demanding obedience to the National statutes after his earnest pleas[5] to the disaffected to observe the laws; the march of the troops accompanied by Hamilton[6] against the insurgents; the

[1] Marshall, ii, 200. [2] *Ib.*, 238. [3] Graydon, 372.

[4] Sept. 25, 1794; *Writings:* Ford, xii, 467.

[5] Sept. 15, 1792; Richardson, i, 124; Aug. 7, 1794; *Writings:* Ford, xii, 445.

[6] Hamilton remained with the troops until the insurrection was suppressed and order fully established. (See Hamilton's letters to Washington, written from various points, during the expedition, from Oct. 25 to Nov. 19, 1794; *Works:* Lodge, vi, 451–60.)

forcible suppression of this first armed assault on the laws of the United States in which men had been killed, houses burned, mails pillaged — all in the name of the Constitution,[1] which the Republicans now claimed as their peculiar property.[2]

Foremost in the fight for the whiskey insurgents were the democratic societies, which, as has been seen, were the offspring of the French Jacobin Clubs. Washington finally became certain that these organizations had inspired this uprising against National law and authority. While the Whiskey Rebellion was economic in its origin, yet it was sustained by the spirit which the French Revolution had kindled in the popular heart. Indeed, when the troops sent to put down the insurrection reached Harrisburg, they found the French flag flying over the courthouse.[3]

Marshall's old comrade in the Revolution, close personal friend, and business partner,[4] Henry Lee, was now Governor of Virginia. He stood militantly with Washington and it was due to Lee's efforts that

[1] Marshall, ii, 200, 235–38, 340–48; Gibbs, i, 144–55; and see Hamilton's Report to the President, Aug. 5, 1794; *Works*: Lodge, vi, 358–88. But see Gallatin's *Writings:* Adams, i, 2–12; Beard: *Econ. O. J. D.*, 250–60. For extended account of the Whiskey Rebellion from the point of view of the insurgents, see Findley: *History of the Insurrection*, etc., and Breckenridge: *History of the Western Insurrection*.

[2] The claim now made by the Republicans that they were the only friends of the Constitution was a clever political turn. Also it is an amusing incident of our history. The Federalists were the creators of the Constitution; while the Republicans, generally speaking and with exceptions, had been ardent foes of its adoption. (See Beard: *Econ. O. J. D.*)

[3] Graydon, 374. Jefferson's party was called Republican because of its championship of the French Republic. (Ambler, 63.)

[4] In the Fairfax purchase. (See *infra*, chap. v.)

the Virginia militia responded to help suppress the Whiskey Rebellion. He was made Commander-in-Chief of all the forces that actually took the field.[1] To Lee, therefore, Washington wrote with unrestrained pen.

"I consider," said the President, "this insurrection as the first *formidable* fruit of the Democratic Societies . . . instituted by . . . *artful and designing* members [of Congress] . . . to sow the seeds of jealousy and distrust among the people of the government. . . . I see, under a display of popular and fascinating guises, the most diabolical attempts to destroy . . . the government."[2] He declared: "That they have been the fomenters of the western disturbances admits of no doubt."[3]

Never was that emphatic man more decided than now; he was sure, he said, that, unless lawlessness were overcome, republican government was at an end, "and nothing but anarchy and confusion is to be expected hereafter."[4] If "the daring and factious spirit" is not crushed, "adieu to all government in this country, except mob and club government."[5]

Such were Washington's positive and settled opinions, and they were adopted and maintained by Marshall, his faithful supporter.

And not only by argument and speech did Marshall uphold the measures of Washington's Adminis-

[1] See Hamilton's orders to General Lee; *Works:* Lodge, vi, 445–51; and see Washington to Lee, Oct. 20, 1794; *Writings:* Ford, xii, 478–80.

[2] Washington to Lee, Aug. 26, 1794; *Writings:* Ford, xii, 454–56.

[3] Washington to Jay, Nov. 1, 1794; *ib.*, 486.

[4] Washington to Thruston, Aug. 10, 1794; *ib.*, 452.

[5] Washington to Morgan, Oct. 8, 1794; *ib.*, 470. The Virginia militia were under the Command of Major-General Daniel Morgan.

tration. In 1793 he had been commissioned as Brigadier-General of Militia, and when the President's requisition came for Virginia troops to enforce the National revenue law against those who were violently resisting the execution of it, he was placed in command of one of the detachments to be raised for that purpose.[1] Although it is not established that his brigade was ordered to Pennsylvania, the probabilities are that it was and that Marshall, in command of it, was on the scene of the first armed opposition to the National Government. And it is certain that Marshall was busy and effective in the work of raising and properly equipping the troops for duty. He suggested practical plans for expediting the muster and for economizing the expenditure of the public money, and his judgment was highly valued.[2]

All the ability, experience, and zeal at the disposal of the State were necessary, for the whiskey tax was only less disliked in Virginia than in Pennsylvania, and a portion of the Commonwealth was inclined to assist rather than to suppress the insurrection.[3] Whether or not he was one of the military force that, on the ground, overawed the whiskey insurgents, it is positively established that Marshall was ready, in person, to help put down with arms all forcible opposition to the National laws and authority.

Jefferson, now the recognized commander-in-chief of the new party, was, however, heartily with the popular outbreak. He had approved Washington's

[1] General Order, June 30, 1794; *Cal. Va. St. Prs.*, vii, 202.

[2] Carrington to Lieutenant-Governor Wood, Sept. 1, 1794; *ib.*, 287.

[3] Major-General Daniel Morgan to the Governor of Virginia, Sept. 7, 1794; *ib.*, 297.

first proclamations against the whiskey producers;[1] but, nevertheless, as the anger of the people grew, it found Jefferson responsive. "The excise law is an infernal one," he cried; the rebellion against it, nothing more than "riotous" at the worst.[2]

And Jefferson wielded his verbal cat-o'-nine-tails on Washington's order to put the rebellion down by armed forces.[3] It was all "for the favorite purpose of strengthening government and increasing public debt."[4] Washington thought the Whiskey Rebellion treasonable; and Jefferson admitted that "there was . . . a meeting to consult about a separation" from the Union; but talking was not acting.[5] Thus the very point was raised which Marshall enforced in the Burr trial twelve years later, when Jefferson took exactly opposite grounds. But to take the popular view now made for Republican solidarity and strength. Criticism is ever more profitable politics than building.

All this had different effects on different public men. The Republican Party was ever growing stronger, and under Jefferson's skillful guidance, was fast becoming a seasoned political army. The sentiment of the multitude against the National Government continued to rise. But instead of weakening John Marshall's Nationalist principles, this turbulent opposition strengthened and hardened them. So did other and larger events of that period which tumultuously crowded fast upon one another's heels.

[1] Jefferson to Washington, Sept. 18, 1792; *Works:* Ford, vii, 153.
[2] Jefferson to Madison, Dec. 28, 1794; *ib.*, viii, 157. [3] *Ib.*
[4] Jefferson to Monroe, May 26, 1795; *ib.*, 177.
[5] Jefferson to Madison, Dec. 28, 1794; *ib.*, 157.

As we have seen, the horrors of the Reign of Terror in Paris did not chill the frenzied enthusiasm of the masses of Americans for France. "By a strange kind of reasoning," wrote Oliver Wolcott to his brother, "some suppose the liberties of America depend on the right of cutting throats in France." [1]

In the spring of 1793 France declared war against England. The popular heart in America was hot for France, the popular voice loud against England. The idea that the United States was an independent nation standing aloof from foreign quarrels did not enter the minds of the people. But it was Washington's one great conception. It was not to make the American people the tool of any foreign government that he had drawn his sword for their independence. It was to found a separate nation with dignity and rights equal to those of any other nation; a nation friendly to all, and allied with none [2] — this was the supreme purpose for which he had fought, toiled, and suffered. And Washington believed that only on this broad highway could the American people travel to ultimate happiness and power.[3] He determined upon a policy of absolute impartiality.

On the same day that the Minister of the new French Republic landed on American shores, Wash-

[1] Wolcott to Wolcott, Dec. 15, 1792; Gibbs, i, 85.

[2] Marshall, ii, 256; see Washington's "Farewell Address."

[3] John Adams claimed this as his particular idea. "Washington learned it from me . . . and practiced upon it." (Adams to Rush, July 7, 1805; *Old Family Letters*, 71.)

"I trust that we shall have too just a sense of our own interest to originate any cause, that may involve us in it [the European war]." (Washington to Humphreys, March 23, 1793; *Writings:* Ford, xii, 276.)

ington proclaimed Neutrality.[1] This action, which to-day all admit to have been wise and far-seeing statesmanship, then caused an outburst of popular resentment against Neutrality and the Administration that had dared to take this impartial stand. For the first time Washington was openly abused by Americans.[2]

"A great majority of the American people deemed it criminal to remain unconcerned spectators of a conflict between their ancient enemy [Great Britain] and republican France," declares Marshall. The people, he writes, thought Great Britain was waging war "with the sole purpose of imposing a monarchical government on the French people. The few who did not embrace these opinions, and they were certainly very few, were held up as objects of public detestation; and were calumniated as the tools of Britain and the satellites of despotism." [3]

The National Government was ungrateful, cried the popular voice; it was aiding the tyrants of Europe against a people struggling for freedom; it was cowardly, infamous, base. "Could any friend of his kind be neutral?" was the question on the popular tongue; of course not! unless, indeed, the miscreant who dared to be exclusively American was a monarchist at heart. "To doubt the holiness of their [the French] cause was the certain road to odium

[1] Marshall, ii, 259; and see Rules of Neutrality, *ib.*, note 13, p. 15. Washington's proclamation was drawn by Attorney-General Randolph. (Conway, 202.)

[2] Marshall, ii, 259–60. "The publications in Freneau's and Bache's papers are outrages on common decency." (Washington to Lee, July 21, 1793; *Writings:* Ford, xii, 310.)

[3] Marshall, ii, 256.

and proscription," testifies an observer.[1] The Republican press, following Paine's theory, attacked "all governments, including that of the United States, as naturally hostile to the liberty of the people," asserts Marshall.[2] Few were the friends of Neutrality outside of the trading and shipping interests.[3]

Jefferson, although still in Washington's Cabinet, spoke of "the pusillanimity of the proclamation"[4] and of "the sneaking neutrality" it set up.[5] "In every effort made by the executive to maintain the neutrality of the United States," writes Marshall,

[1] Graydon, 382.

[2] Marshall, ii, 260. "A Freeman" in the *General Advertiser* of Philadelphia stated the most moderate opinion of those who opposed Neutrality. "France," said he, "is not only warring against the despotism of monarchy but the despotism of aristocracy and it would appear rather uncommon to see men [Washington and those who agreed with him] welcoming the Ambassador of republicanism who are warring [against] their darling aristocracy. But . . . shall the officers of our government prescribe rules of conduct to freemen? Fellow citizens, view this conduct [Neutrality] well and you will discover principles lurking at bottom at variance with your liberty. Who is the superior of the people? Are we already so degenerate as to acknowledge a superior in the United States?" (*General Advertiser*, April 25, 1793.)

[3] "Our commercial and maritime people feel themselves deeply interested to prevent every act that may put our peace at hazard." (Cabot to King, Aug. 2, 1793; Lodge: *Cabot*, 74.)

The merchants and traders of Baltimore, "as participants in the general prosperity resulting from peace, and the excellent laws and constitution of the United States . . . beg leave to express the high sense they entertain of the provident wisdom and watchfulness over the concerns and peace of a happy people which you have displayed in your late proclamation declaring neutrality . . . well convinced that the true interests of America consist in a conduct, impartial, friendly, and unoffending to all the belligerent powers." (Address of the Merchants and Traders of Baltimore to George Washington, President of the United States; *General Advertiser*, Philadelphia, June 5, 1793.)

[4] Jefferson to Madison, May 19, 1793; *Works:* Ford, vii, 336.

[5] Jefferson to Monroe, May 5, 1793; *ib.*, 309.

"that great party [Republican] which denominated itself 'THE PEOPLE' could perceive only a settled hostility to France and to liberty." [1]

And, of course, Washington's proclamation of Neutrality was "unconstitutional," shouted the Republican politicians. Hamilton quickly answered. The power to deal with foreign affairs was, he said, lodged somewhere in the National Government. Where, then? Plainly not in the Legislative or Judicial branches, but in the Executive Department, which is "the *organ* of intercourse between the nation and foreign nations" and "the *interpreter* of . . . treaties in those cases in which the judiciary is not competent — that is between government and government. . . . The *executive power* of the United States is completely lodged in the President," with only those exceptions made by the Constitution, as that of declaring war. But if it is the right of Congress to declare war, "it is the duty of the Executive to preserve peace till the declaration is made." [2]

Washington's refusal to take sides in the European war was still more fuel for the Republican furnace. The bill to maintain Neutrality escaped defeat in Congress by a dangerously narrow margin: on amendments and motions in the Senate it was rescued time and again only by the deciding vote of the Vice-President.[3] In the House, resolutions were introduced which, in the perspective of history, were stupid. Public speakers searched for expressions strong enough for the popular taste; the newspapers

[1] Marshall, ii, 273.

[2] Pacificus No. 1; *Works:* Lodge, iv, 432–44.

[3] Marshall, ii, 327.

blazed with denunciation. "The artillery of the press," declares Marshall, "was played with unceasing fury on" the supporters of Neutrality; "and the democratic societies brought their whole force into operation. Language will scarcely afford terms of greater outrage, than were employed against those who sought to stem the torrent of public opinion and to moderate the rage of the moment."[1]

At the most effective hour, politically, Jefferson resigned[2] from the Cabinet, as he had declared, two years before, he intended to do.[3] He had prepared well for popular leadership. His stinging criticism of the Nationalist financial measures, his warm championship of France, his bitter hostility to Great Britain, and most of all, his advocacy of the popular view of the Constitution, secured him the favor of the people. Had he remained Secretary of State, he would have found himself in a hazardous political situation. But now, freed from restraint, he could openly lead the Republican forces which so eagerly awaited his formal command.[4]

As in the struggle for the Constitution, so now Neutrality was saved by the combined efforts of the mercantile and financial interests who dreaded the effect of the war on business and credit;[5] and by

[1] Marshall, ii, 322.

[2] Jefferson to Washington, Dec. 31, 1793; *Works:* Ford, viii, 136.

[3] Jefferson to Short, Jan. 28, 1792; *ib.*, vi, 382.

[4] Marshall, ii, 233.

[5] Generally speaking, the same classes that secured the Constitution supported all the measures of Washington's Administration. (See Beard: *Econ. O. J. D.*, 122–24.)

While the Republicans charged that Washington's Neutrality was inspired by favoritism to Great Britain, as it was certainly championed by trading and moneyed interests which dealt chiefly with British

the disinterested support of those who wished the United States to become a nation, distinct from, unconnected with, and unsubservient to any other government.

Among these latter was John Marshall, although he also held the view of the commercial classes from which most of his best clients came; and his personal loyalty to Washington strengthened his opinions. Hot as Virginia was against the Administration, Marshall was equally hot in its favor. Although he was the most prudent of men, and in Virginia silence was the part of discretion for those who approved Washington's course, Marshall would not be still. He made speeches in support of Washington's stand, wrote pamphlets, and appealed in every possible way to the solid reason and genuine Americanism of his neighbors. He had, of course, read Hamilton's great defense of Neutrality; and he asserted that sound National policy required Neutrality and that it was the duty of the President to proclaim and enforce it. Over and over again, by tongue and pen,

houses, the Federalists made the counter-charge, with equal accuracy, that the opponents of Neutrality were French partisans and encouraged by those financially interested.

The younger Adams, who was in Europe during most of this period and who carefully informed himself, writing from The Hague, declared that many Americans, some of them very important men, were "debtors to British merchants, creditors to the French government, and speculators in the French revolutionary funds, all to an immense amount," and that other Americans were heavily indebted in England. All these interests were against Neutrality and in favor of war with Great Britain — those owing British debts, because "war . . . would serve as a sponge for their debts," or at least postpone payment, and the creditors of the French securities, because French success would insure payment. (J. Q. Adams to his father, June 24, 1796; *Writings, J. Q. A.*: Ford, i, 506.)

he demonstrated the constitutional right of the Executive to institute and maintain the Nation's attitude of aloofness from foreign belligerents.[1]

Marshall rallied the friends of the Administration, not only in Richmond, but elsewhere in Virginia. "The [Administration] party in Richmond was soon set in motion," Monroe reported to Jefferson; "from what I have understood here [I] have reason to believe they mean to produce the most extensive effect they are capable of. Mr Marshall has written G. Jones [2] on the subject and the first appearances threatened the most furious attack on the French Minister [Genêt]." [3]

At last Marshall's personal popularity could no longer save him from open and public attack. The enraged Republicans assailed him in pamphlets; he was criticized in the newspapers; his character was impugned.[4] He was branded with what, in Virginia, was at that time the ultimate reproach: Marshall, said the Republicans, was the friend and follower of Alexander Hamilton, the monarchist, the financial manipulator, the father of Assumption, the inventor of the rotten Funding system, the designer of the stock-jobbing Bank of the United States, and, worst of all, the champion of a power-

[1] Story, in Dillon, iii, 350.

[2] Gabriel Jones, the ablest lawyer in the Valley, and, of course, a stanch Federalist.

[3] Monroe to Jefferson, Sept. 3, 1793; Monroe's *Writings:* Hamilton, i, 274–75. Considering the intimate personal friendship existing between Monroe and Marshall, the significance and importance of this letter cannot be overestimated.

[4] It was at this point, undoubtedly, that the slander concerning Marshall's habits was started. (See *infra*, 101–03.)

ful Nationalism and the implacable foe of the sovereignty of the States.

Spiritedly Marshall made reply. He was, indeed, a disciple of Washington's great Secretary of the Treasury, he said, and proud of it; and he gloried in his fealty to Washington, for which also he had been blamed. In short, Marshall was aggressively for the Administration and all its measures. These were right, he said, and wise and necessary. Above all, since that was the chief ground of attack, all of them, from Assumption to Neutrality, were plainly constitutional. At a public meeting at Richmond, Marshall offered resolutions which he had drawn up in support of the Administration's foreign policy, spoke in their favor, and carried the meeting for them by a heavy majority.[1]

Marshall's bold course cost him the proffer of an honor. Our strained relations with the Spaniards required an alert, able, and cool-headed representative to go to New Orleans. Jefferson[2] confided to Madison the task of finding such a man in Virginia. "My imagination has hunted thro' this whole state," Madison advised the Secretary of State in reply, "without being able to find a single character fitted for the mission to N. O. Young Marshall seems to possess some of the qualifications, but there would be objections of several sorts to

[1] The above paragraphs are based on Justice Story's account of Marshall's activities at this period, supplemented by Madison and Monroe's letters; by the well-known political history of that time; and by the untrustworthy but not negligible testimony of tradition. While difficult to reconstruct a situation from such fragments, the account given in the text is believed to be substantially accurate.

[2] See *Works:* Ford, xii, footnote to 451.

him."[1] Three months later Madison revealed one of these "several objections" to Marshall; but the principal one was his sturdy, fighting Nationalism. This "objection" was so intense that anybody who was even a close friend of Marshall was suspected and proscribed by the Republicans. The Jacobin Clubs of Paris were scarcely more intolerant than their disciples in America.

So irritated, indeed, were the Republican leaders by Marshall's political efforts in support of Neutrality and other policies of the Administration, that they began to hint at improper motives. With his brother, brother-in-law, and General Henry Lee (then Governor of Virginia) Marshall had purchased the Fairfax estate.[2] This was evidence, said the Republicans, that he was the tool of the wicked financial interests. Madison hastened to inform Jefferson.

"The circumstances which derogate from full confidence in W[ilson] N[icholas]," cautioned Madison, "are . . . his connection & intimacy with Marshall, of whose *disinterestedness* as well as understanding he has the highest opinion. It is said that Marshall, who is at the head of the great purchase from Fairfax, has lately obtained pecuniary aids from the bank [of the United States] or people connected with it. I think it certain that he must have felt, in the moment of purchase, an absolute confidence in the monied interests which will explain him to everyone that reflects in the active character he is assuming."[3]

[1] Madison to Jefferson, June 17, 1793; *Writings:* Hunt, vi, 134.

[2] See *infra*, chap. v.

[3] Madison to Jefferson, Sept. 2, 1793; *Writings:* Hunt, vi, 196.

In such fashion do the exigencies of politics generate suspicion and false witness. Marshall received no money from the Bank for the Fairfax purchase and it tied him to "the monied interests" in no way except through business sympathy. He relied for help on his brother's father-in-law, Robert Morris, who expected to raise the funds for the Fairfax purchase from loans negotiated in Europe on the security of Morris's immense real-estate holdings in America.[1] But even the once poised, charitable, and unsuspicious Madison had now acquired that state of mind which beholds in any business transaction, no matter how innocent, something furtive and sinister. His letter proves, however, that the fearless Richmond lawyer was making himself effectively felt as a practical power for Washington's Administration, to the serious discomfort of the Republican chieftains.

While Marshall was beloved by most of those who knew him and was astonishingly popular with the masses, jealousy of his ability and success had made remorseless enemies for him. It appears, indeed, that a peculiarly malicious envy had pursued him almost from the time he had gone to William and Mary College. His sister-in-law, with hot resentment, emphasizes this feature of Marshall's career. "Notwithstanding his amiable and correct conduct," writes Mrs. Carrington, "there were those who would catch at the most trifling circumstance to throw a shade over his fair fame." He had little education, said his detractors; "his talents

[1] See *infra*, chap. v. Robert Morris secured in this way all the money he was able to give his son-in-law for the Fairfax purchase.

were greatly overrated"; his habits were bad. "Tho' no man living ever had more ardent friends, yet there does not exist one who had at one time more slanderous enemies." [1]

These now assailed Marshall with all their pent-up hatred. They stopped at no charge, hesitated at no insinuation. For instance, his conviviality was magnified into reports of excesses and the tale was carried to the President. "It was cruelly insinuated to G[eorge] W[ashington]," writes Marshall's sister-in-law, "by an after great S[olo?]n that to Mr. M[arsha]lls fondness for play was added an increasing fondness for liquor." Mrs. Carrington loyally defends Marshall, testifying, from her personal knowledge, that "this S——n knew better than most others how Mr. M——ll always played for amusement and never, never for gain, and that he was, of all men, the most temperate." [2]

Considering the custom of the time [3] and the habits of the foremost men of that period,[4] Marshall's

[1] Mrs. Carrington to her sister Nancy; undated; MS. [2] *Ib.*

[3] See *supra*, vol. I, chap. VII.

[4] See, for instance, Jefferson to Short (Sept 6, 1790; *Works:* Ford, vi, 146), describing a single order of wine for Washington and one for himself; and see Chastellux's account of an evening with Jefferson: "We were conversing one evening over a bowl of punch after Mrs. Jefferson had retired. Our conversation turned on the poems of Ossian. . . . The book was sent for and placed near the bowl, where by their mutual aid the night far advanced imperceptibly upon us." (Chastellux, 229.)

Marshall's Account Book does not show any purchases of wine at all comparable with those of other contemporaries. In March, 1791, Marshall enters, "wine £60"; August, ditto, "£14–5–8"; September, 1792, "Wine £70"; in July, 1793, "Whisky 6.3.9" (pounds, shillings, and pence); in May, 1794, "Rum and brandy 6–4"; August, 1794, ditto, five shillings, sixpence; May, 1795, "Whisky £6.16"; Sept. "wine £3"; Oct., ditto, "£17.6."

sister-in-law is entirely accurate. Certainly this political slander did not impress Washington, for his confidence in Marshall grew steadily; and, as we shall presently see, he continued to tender Marshall high honors and confide to him political tasks requiring delicate judgment.

Such petty falsehoods did not disturb Marshall's composure. But he warmly resented the assault made upon him because of his friendship for Hamilton; and his anger was hot against what he felt was the sheer dishonesty of the attacks on the measures of the National Government. "I wish very much to see you," writes Marshall to Archibald Stuart at this time: "I want to observe [illegible] how much honest men you and I are [illegible] half our acquaintance. Seriously there appears to me every day to be more folly, envy, malice, and damn rascality in the world than there was the day before and I do verily begin to think that plain downright honesty and unintriguing integrity will be kicked out of doors." [1]

A picturesque incident gave to the Virginia opponents of Washington's Administration more substantial cause to hate Marshall than his pamphlets, speeches, and resolutions had afforded. At Smithfield, not far from Norfolk, the ship Unicorn was fitting out as a French privateer. The people of Isle of Wight County were almost unanimous in their sympathy with the project, and only seven or eight men could be procured to assist the United States Marshal in seizing and holding the vessel.[2] Twenty-

[1] Marshall to Stuart, March 27, 1794; MS., Va. Hist. Soc.

[2] Major George Keith Taylor to Brigadier-General Mathews, July 19, 1794; *Cal. Va. St. Prs.*, vii, 223.

five soldiers and three officers were sent from Norfolk in a revenue cutter; [1] but the Governor, considering this force insufficient to outface resistance and take the ship, dispatched Marshall, with a considerable body of militia, to Smithfield.

Evidently the affair was believed to be serious; "the Particular Orders . . . to Brigadier General Marshall" placed under his command forces of cavalry, infantry, and artillery from Richmond and another body of troops from Petersburg. The Governor assures Marshall that "the executive know that in your hands the dignity and rights of the Commonwealth will ever be safe and they are also sure that prudence, affection to our deluded fellow citizens, and marked obedience to law in the means you will be compelled to adopt, will equally characterize every step of your procedure." He is directed to "collect every information respecting this daring violation of order," and particularly "the conduct of the Lieutenant Colonel Commandant of Isle of Wight," who had disregarded his instructions.[2]

Clad in the uniform of a brigadier-general of the Virginia Militia,[3] Marshall set out for Smithfield riding at the head of the cavalry, the light infantry and

[1] Mathews to Taylor, July 20, 1794; *ib.*, 224.

[2] Governor Henry Lee "Commander-in-chief," to Marshall, July 21, 1794; MS., "War 10," Archives, Va. St. Lib.

[3] "Dark blue coat, skirts lined with buff, capes, lapels and cuffs buff, buttons yellow. Epaulets gold one on each shoulder, black cocked hat, with black cockade, black stock, boots and side arms." (Division Orders, July 4, 1794; *Cal. Va. St. Prs.*, vii, 204. But see Schoepf (ii, 43), where a uniform worn by one brigadier-general of Virginia Militia is described as consisting of "a large white hat, a blue coat, a brown waistcoat, and green breeches.")

artillery following by boat.[1] He found all thought of resistance abandoned upon his arrival. A "peaceable search" of Captain Sinclair's house revealed thirteen cannon with ball, grape-shot, and powder. Three more pieces of ordnance were stationed on the shore. Before General Marshall and his cavalry arrived, the United States Marshal had been insulted, and threatened with violence. Men had been heard loading muskets in Sinclair's house, and fifteen of these weapons, fully charged, were discovered. The house so "completely commanded the Deck of the" Unicorn "that . . . one hundred men placed in the vessel could not have protected her ten minutes from fifteen placed in the house." [2]

The State and Federal officers had previously been able to get little aid of any kind, but "since the arrival of distant militia," reports Marshall, "those of the County are as prompt as could be wished in rendering any service required of them," and he suggests that the commandant of the county, rather than the men, was responsible for the failure to act earlier. He at once sent messengers to the infantry and artillery detachment which had not yet arrived, with orders that they return to Richmond and Petersburg.[3]

Marshall "had . . . frequent conversations with individuals of the Isle of Wight" and found them much distressed at the necessity for calling distant militia "to protect from violence the laws of our

[1] Particular Orders, *supra*.

[2] Marshall to Governor of Virginia, July 23, 1794; *Cal. Va. St. Prs.*, vii, 228; and same to same, July 28, 1794; *ib.*, 234.

[3] *Ib.*

common country. . . . The commanding officers [of the county] . . . seem not to have become sufficiently impressed with the importance of maintaining the Sovereignty of the law" says Marshall, but with unwarranted optimism he believes "that a more proper mode of thinking is beginning to prevail." [1]

Thus was the Smithfield defiance of Neutrality and the National laws quelled by strong measures, taken before it had gathered dangerous headway. "I am very much indebted to Brig.-Gen'l Marshall and Major Taylor [2] for their exertions in the execution of my orders," writes Governor Lee to the Secretary of War.[3]

But the efforts of the National Government and the action of Governor Lee in Virginia to enforce obedience to National laws and observance of Neutrality, while they succeeded locally in their immediate purpose, did not modify the public temper toward the Administration. Neutrality, in particular, grew in disfavor among the people. When the congressional elections of 1794 came on, all complaints against the National Government were vivified by that burning question. As if, said the Republicans, there could be such a status as neutrality between "right and wrong," between "liberty" and "tyranny." [4]

Thus, in the campaign, the Republicans made the French cause their own. Everything that Washing-

[1] Marshall to Governor of Virginia, July 28, 1794; *Cal. Va. St. Prs.* vii, 235.

[2] George Keith Taylor; see *infra*, chaps. x and xii.

[3] Lee to the Secretary of War, July 28, 1794; *Cal. Va. St. Prs.*, vii, 234.

[4] See, for instance, Thompson's speech, *infra*, chap. vi.

ton's Administration had accomplished was wrong, said the Republicans, but Neutrality was the work of the Evil One. The same National power which had dared to issue this "edict" against American support of French "liberty" had foisted on the people Assumption, National Courts, and taxes on whiskey. This identical Nationalist crew had, said the Republicans, by Funding and National Banks, fostered, nay, created, stock-jobbing and speculation by which the few "monocrats" were made rich, while the many remained poor. Thus every Republican candidate for Congress became a knight of the flaming sword, warring upon all evil, but especially and for the moment against the dragon of Neutrality that the National Government had uncaged to help the monarchs of Europe destroy free government in France.[1] Chiefly on that question the Republicans won the National House of Representatives.

But if Neutrality lit the flames of public wrath, Washington's next act in foreign affairs was powder and oil cast upon fires already fiercely burning. Great Britain, by her war measures against France, did not spare America. She seized hundreds of American vessels trading with her enemy and even with neutrals; in order to starve France [2] she lifted cargoes from American bottoms; to man her warships she forcibly took sailors from American ships, "often leaving scarcely hands enough to navigate the vessel into port"; [3] she conducted herself as if she were not only mistress of the seas, but their sole pro-

[1] Marshall, ii, 293. [2] *Ib.*, 285. [3] *Ib.*, 285.

prietor. And the British depredations were committed in a manner harsh, brutal, and insulting.

Even Marshall was aroused and wrote to his friend Stuart: "We fear, not without reason, a war. The man does not live who wishes for peace more than I do; but the outrages committed upon us are beyond human bearing. Farewell — pray Heaven we may weather the storm." [1] If the self-contained and cautious Marshall felt a just resentment of British outrage, we may, by that measure, accurately judge of the inflamed and dangerous condition of the general sentiment.

Thus it came about that the deeply rooted hatred of the people for their former master [2] was heated to the point of reckless defiance. This was the same Monarchy, they truly said, that still kept the military and trading posts on American soil which, more than a decade before, it had, by the Treaty of Peace, solemnly promised to surrender. [3] The Government that was committing these savage outrages was the same faithless Power, declared the general voice, that had pledged compensation for the slaves its armies had carried away, but not one shilling of which had been paid.

If ever a country had good cause for war, Great Britain then furnished it to America; and, had we been prepared, it is impossible to believe that we

[1] Marshall to Stuart, March 27, 1794; MS., Va. Hist. Soc.

[2] "The idea that Great Britain was the natural enemy of America had become habitual" long before this time. (Marshall, ii, 154.)

[3] One reason for Great Britain's unlawful retention of these posts was her purpose to maintain her monopoly of the fur trade. (*Ib.*, 194. And see Beard: *Econ. O. J. D.*, 279.)

should not have taken up arms to defend our ravaged interests and vindicate our insulted honor. In Congress various methods of justifiable retaliation were urged with intense earnestness, marred by loud and extravagant declamation.[1] "The noise of debate was more deafening than a mill. . . . We sleep upon our arms," wrote a member of the National House.[2] But these bellicose measures were rejected because any one of them would have meant immediate hostilities.

For we were not prepared. War was the one thing America could not then afford. Our Government was still tottering on the unstable legs of infancy. Orderly society was only beginning and the spirit of unrest and upheaval was strong and active. In case of war, wrote Ames, expressing the conservative fears, "I dread anarchy more than great guns."[3] Our resources had been bled white by the Revolution and the desolating years that followed. We had no real army, no adequate arsenals,[4] no efficient ships of war; and the French Republic, surrounded by hostile bayonets and guns and battling for very existence, could not send us armies, fleets, munitions, and money as the French Monarchy had done.

Spain was on our south eager for more territory on the Mississippi, the mouth of which she con-

[1] Marshall, ii, 320–21; and see *Annals*, 3d Cong., 1st Sess., 1793, 274–90; also Anderson, 29; and see prior war-inviting resolves and speeches in *Annals*, 3d Cong., *supra*, 21, 30, 544 *et seq.*; also Marshall, ii, 324 *et seq.*

[2] Ames to Dwight, Dec. 12, 1794; *Works:* Ames, i, 154.

[3] Ames to Gore, March 26, 1794; *Works:* Ames, i, 140. And see Marshall, ii, 324 *et seq.*

[4] See Washington to Ball, Aug. 10, 1794; *Writings:* Ford, xii, 449.

trolled; and ready to attack us in case we came to blows with Great Britain. The latter Power was on our north, the expelled Loyalists in Canada burning with that natural resentment [1] which has never cooled; British soldiers held strategic posts within our territory; hordes of Indians, controlled and their leaders paid by Great Britain,[2] and hostile to the United States, were upon our borders anxious to avenge themselves for the defeats we had inflicted on them and their kinsmen in the savage wars incited by their British employers.[3] Worst of all, British warships covered the oceans and patrolled every mile of our shores just beyond American waters. Our coast defenses, few, poor, and feeble in their best estate, had been utterly neglected for more than ten years and every American port was at the mercy of British guns.[4]

Evidence was not wanting that Great Britain courted war.[5] She had been cold and unresponsive to every approach for a better understanding with us. She had not even sent a Minister to our Government until eight years after the Treaty of Peace had been signed.[6] She not only held our posts, but established

[1] See Van Tyne, chap. xi. [2] Marshall, ii, 286, 287. [3] *Ib.*

[4] John Quincy Adams, who was in London and who was intensely irritated by British conduct, concluded that: "A war at present with Great Britain must be total destruction to the commerce of our country; for there is no maritime power on earth that can contend with the existing naval British force." (J. Q. Adams to Sargent, The Hague, Oct. 12, 1795; *Writings, J. Q. A.*: Ford, i, 419.)

[5] "I believe the intention is to draw the United States into it [war] merely to make tools of them. . . . The conduct of the British government is so well adapted to increasing our danger of war, that I cannot but suppose they are secretly inclined to produce it." (J. Q. Adams to his father, The Hague, Sept. 12, 1795; *ib.*, 409.)

[6] Marshall, ii, 194.

a new one fifty miles south of Detroit; and her entire conduct indicated, and Washington believed, that she meant to draw a new boundary line which would give her exclusive possession of the Great Lakes.[1] She had the monopoly of the fur trade[2] and plainly meant to keep it.

Lord Dorchester, supreme representative of the British Crown in Canada, had made an ominous speech to the Indians predicting hostilities against the United States within a year and declaring that a new boundary line would then be drawn "by the warriors."[3] Rumors flew and gained volume and color in their flight. Even the poised and steady Marshall was disturbed.

"We have some letters from Philadelphia that wear a very ugly aspect," he writes Archibald Stuart. "It is said that Simcoe, the Governor of Upper Canada, has entered the territory of the United States at the head of about 500 men and has possessed himself of Presque Isle." But Marshall cannot restrain his humor, notwithstanding the gravity of the report: "As this is in Pennsylvania," he observes, "I hope the democratic society of Philadelphia will at once demolish him and if they should fail I still trust that some of our upper brothers [Virginia Republicans] will at one stride place themselves by him and prostrate his post. But seriously," continues Marshall,

[1] Marshall, ii, 337.

[2] *Ib.*, 195; and see Beard: *Econ. O. J. D.*, 279.

[3] See this speech in Rives, iii, footnote to 418–19. It is curious that Marshall, in his *Life of Washington*, makes the error of asserting that the account of Dorchester's speech was "not authentic." It is one of the very few mistakes in Marshall's careful book. (Marshall, ii, 320.)

"if this be true we must bid adieu to all hope of peace and prepare for serious war. My only hope is that it is a mere speculating story." [1]

Powerless to obtain our rights by force or to prevent their violation by being prepared to assert them with arms, Washington had no recourse but to diplomacy. At all hazards and at any cost, war must be avoided for the time being. It was one of Great Britain's critical mistakes that she consented to treat instead of forcing a conflict with us; for had she taken the latter course it is not improbable that, at the end of the war, the southern boundary of British dominion in America would have been the Ohio River, and it is not impossible that New York and New England would have fallen into her hands. At the very least, there can be little doubt that the Great Lakes and the St. Lawrence would have become exclusively British waters.[2]

Amid a confusion of counsels, Washington determined to try for a treaty of amity, commerce, and

[1] Marshall to Stuart, May 28, 1794; MS., Va. Hist. Soc.

[2] It must not be forgotten that we were not so well prepared for war in 1794 as the colonies had been in 1776, or as we were a few years after Jay was sent on his mission. And on the traditional policy of Great Britain when intending to make war on any country, see J. Q. Adams to his father, June 24, 1796; *Writings, J. Q. A.*: Ford, i, 499–500.

Also, see same to same, The Hague, June 9, 1796; *ib.*, 493, predicting dissolution of the Union in case of war with Great Britain. "I confess it made me doubly desirous to quit a country where the malevolence that is so common against America was exulting in triumph." (*Ib.*)

"The truth is that the American *Government* . . . have not upon earth more rancorous enemies, than the springs which move the machine of this Country [England] . . . Between Great Britain and the United States no *cordiality* can exist." (Same to same, London, Feb. 10, 1796; *ib.*, 477; also, March 24, 1794; *ib.*, 18, 183, 187.)

navigation with Great Britain, a decision, the outcome of which was to bring Marshall even more conspicuously into politics than he ever had been before. Indeed, the result of the President's policy, and Marshall's activity in support of it, was to become one of the important stepping-stones in the latter's career.

Chief Justice Jay was selected for the infinitely delicate task of negotiation. Even the news of such a plan was received with stinging criticism. What! Kiss the hand that smote us! It was "a degrading insult to the American people; a pusillanimous surrender of their honor; and an insidious injury to France." [1] And our envoy to carry out this shameful programme! — was it not that same Jay who once tried to barter away the Mississippi? [2]

It was bad enough to turn our backs on France; but to treat with the British Government was infamous. So spoke the voice of the people. The democratic societies were especially virulent; "Let us unite with France and stand or fall together" [3] was their heroic sentiment. But abhorrence of the mission did not blind the Republicans to the advantages of political craft. While the negotiations were in progress they said that, after all, everything would be gained that America desired, knowing that they could say afterward, as they did and with just cause, that everything had been lost.[4]

At last Jay secured from Great Britain the famous

[1] Marshall, ii, 363. [2] *American Remembrancer*, i, 9.

[3] Resolution of Wythe County (Va.) Democratic Society, quoted in Anderson, 32.

[4] Ames to Dwight, Feb. 3, 1795; *Works:* Ames, i, 166.

treaty that bears his name. It is perhaps the most humiliating compact into which America ever entered. He was expected to secure the restriction of contraband — it was enlarged; payment for the slaves — it was refused; recognition of the principle that "free ships make free goods" — it was denied; equality with France as to belligerent rights — it was not granted; opening of the West Indian trade — it was conceded upon hard and unjust conditions; payment for British spoliation of American commerce — it was promised at some future time, but even then only on the award of a commission; immediate surrender of the posts — their evacuation was agreed to, but not until a year and a half after the treaty was signed.

On the other hand, the British secured from us free navigation and trading rights on the Mississippi —never contemplated; agreement that the United States would pay all debts due from American citizens to British creditors — a claim never admitted hitherto; prohibition of any future sequestration of British debts; freedom of all American ports to British vessels, with a pledge to lay no further restrictions on British commerce — never before proposed; liberty of Indians and British subjects to pass our frontiers, trade on our soil, retain lands occupied without becoming American citizens, but privileged to become such at pleasure — an odious provision, which, formerly, had never occurred to anybody.

Thus, by the Treaty of 1794, we yielded everything and gained little not already ours. But we secured peace; we were saved from war. That supreme end was worth the sacrifice and that, alone, justified it. It more than demonstrated the wisdom of the Jay Treaty.

While the Senate was considering the bitter terms which Great Britain, with unsheathed sword, had forced upon us, Senator Stephen T. Mason of Virginia, in violation of the Senate rules, gave a copy of the treaty to the press.[1] Instantly the whole land shook with a tornado of passionate protest.[2] From one end of the country to the other, public meetings were held. Boston led off.[3] Washington was smothered with violent petitions that poured in upon him from every quarter praying, demanding, that he withhold his assent.[4] As in the struggle for the Constitution and in the violent attacks on Neutrality, so now the strongest advocates of the Jay Treaty were the

[1] Marshall, ii, 362–64. [2] *Ib.*, 366.

[3] The Boston men, it appears, had not even read the treaty, as was the case with other meetings which adopted resolutions of protest. (Marshall, ii, 365 *et seq.*) Thereupon the Boston satirists lampooned the hasty denunciators of the treaty as follows: —

> "I've never read it, but I say 't is bad.
> If it goes down, I'll bet my ears and eyes,
> It will the people all unpopularize;
> Boobies may hear it read ere they decide,
> I move it quickly be unratified."

On Dr. Jarvis's speech at Faneuil Hall against the Jay Treaty; Loring: *Hundred Boston Orators*, 232. The Republicans were equally sarcastic: "I say the treaty is a good one . . . for I do not think about it. . . . What did we choose the Senate for . . . but to think for us. . . . Let the people remember that it is their sacred right to submit and obey; and that all those who would persuade them that they have a right to think and speak on the sublime, mysterious, and to them incomprehensible affairs of government are factious Democrats and outrageous Jacobins." (Essay on Jacobinical Thinkers: *American Remembrancer*, i, 141.)

[4] See Marshall's vivid description of the popular reception of the treaty; Marshall, ii, 365–66.

commercial interests. "The common opinion among men of business of all descriptions is," declares Hamilton, "that a disagreement would greatly shock and stagnate pecuniary plans and operations in general."[1]

The printing presses belched pamphlets and lampoons, scurrilous, inflammatory, even indecent. An example of these was a Boston screed. This classic of vituperation, connecting the treaty with the financial measures of Washington's Administration, represented the Federalist leaders as servants of the Devil; Independence, after the death of his first wife, Virtue, married a foul creature, Vice, and finally himself expired in convulsions, leaving Speculation, Bribery, and Corruption as the base offspring of his second marriage.[2]

Everywhere Jay was burned in effigy. Hamilton was stoned in New York when he tried to speak to the mob; and with the blood pouring down his face went, with the few who were willing to listen to him, to the safety of a hall.[3] Even Washington's granite resolution was shaken. Only once in our history have the American people so scourged a great public servant.[4] He was no statesman, raged the Republicans; everybody knew that he had been a failure as a soldier, they said; and now, having

[1] Hamilton to King, June 20, 1795; *Works:* Lodge, x, 103.

[2] "An Emetic for Aristocrats. . . . Also a History of the Life and Death of Independence; Boston, 1795." Copies of such attacks were scattered broadcast — "Emissaries flew through the country spreading alarm and discontent." (Camillus, no. 1; *Works:* Lodge, v, 189–99.)

[3] McMaster, ii, 213–20; Gibbs, i, 207; and Hildreth, iv, 548.

[4] Present-day detraction of our public men is gentle reproof contrasted with the savagery with which Washington was, thenceforth, assailed.

trampled on the Constitution and betrayed America, let him be impeached, screamed the infuriated opposition.[1] Seldom has any measure of our Government awakened such convulsions of popular feeling as did the Jay Treaty, which, surrendering our righteous and immediate demands, yet saved our future. Marshall, watching it all, prepared to defend the popularly abhorred compact; and thus he was to become its leading defender in the South.

When, finally, Washington reluctantly approved its ratification by the Senate,[2] many of his friends deserted him.[3] "The trouble and perplexities . . . have worn away my mind," wrote the abused and distracted President.[4] Mercer County, Kentucky,

[1] Marshall, ii, 370. Of the innumerable accounts of the abuse of Washington, Weld may be cited as the most moderate. After testifying to Washington's unpopularity this acute traveler says: "It is the spirit of dissatisfaction which forms a leading trait in the character of the Americans as a people, which produces this malevolence [against Washington]; if their public affairs were regulated by a person sent from heaven, I firmly believe his acts, instead of meeting with universal approbation, would by many be considered as deceitful and flagitious." (Weld, i, 108–09.)

[2] Washington almost determined to withhold ratification. (Marshall, ii, 362.) The treaty was signed November 19, 1794; received by the President, March 7, 1795; submitted to the Senate June 8, 1795; ratified by the Senate June 24; and signed by Washington August 12, 1795. (*Ib.*, 360, 361, 368.)

[3] "Washington now defies the whole Sovereign that made him what he is —— and can unmake him again. Better his hand had been cut off when his glory was at its height before he blasted all his Laurels!" (Dr. Nathaniel Ames's Diary, Aug. 14, 1795; *Dedham* (*Mass.*) *Historical Register*, vii, 33.) Of Washington's reply to the address of the merchants and traders of Philadelphia "An Old Soldier of '76," wrote: "Has adulation . . . so bewildered his senses, that relinquishing even common decency, he tells 408 merchants and traders of Philadelphia that they are more immediately concerned than any other class of his fellow citizens?" (*American Remembrancer*, ii, 280–81.)

[4] Washington to Jay, May 8, 1796; *Writings:* Ford, xiii, 189.

denounced Senator Humphrey Marshall for voting for ratification and demanded a constitutional amendment empowering State Legislatures to recall Senators at will.[1] The Legislature of Virginia actually passed a resolution for an amendment of the National Constitution to make the House of Representatives a part of the treaty-making power.[2] The Lexington, Kentucky, resolutions branded the treaty as "shameful to the American name."[3] It was reported that at a dinner in Virginia this toast was drunk: "A speedy death to General Washington."[4] Orators exhausted invective; poets wrote in the ink of gall.[5]

Jefferson, in harmony, of course, with the public temper, was against the treaty. "So general a burst of dissatisfaction," he declared, "never before appeared against any transaction. . . . The whole body of the people . . . have taken a greater interest in this transaction than they were ever known to do in any other."[6] The Republican chieftain carefully observed the effect of the popular commotion on his own and the opposite party. "It has in my opinion completely demolished the monarchical party here[7]

[1] *American Remembrancer*, ii, 265.

[2] Journal, H.D. (1795), 54–55; and see Anderson, 43.

[3] *American Remembrancer*, ii, 269.

[4] Ames to Gore, Jan. 10, 1795; *Works:* Ames, i, 161.

[5] "This treaty in one page confines,
The sad result of base designs;
The wretched purchase here behold
Of Traitors — who their country sold.
Here, in their proper shape and mien,
Fraud, perjury, and guilt are seen."
(Freneau, iii, 133.)

[6] Jefferson to Monroe, Sept. 6, 1795; *Works:* Ford, viii, 187–88.

[7] *Ib.*

[Virginia]." Jefferson thought the treaty itself so bad that it nearly turned him against all treaties. "I am not satisfied," said he, "we should not be better without treaties with any nation. But I am satisfied we should be better without such as this."[1]

The deadliest charge against the treaty was the now familiar one of "unconstitutionality." Many urged that the President had no power to begin negotiations without the assent of the Senate;[2] and all opponents agreed that it flagrantly violated the Constitution in several respects, especially in regulating trade, to do which was the exclusive province of Congress.[3] Once more, avowed the Jeffersonians, it was the National Government which had brought upon America this disgrace. "Not one in a thousand would have resisted Great Britain . . . in the be-

[1] Jefferson to Tazewell, Sept. 13, 1795; *Works:* Ford, viii, 191. The Jay Treaty and Neutrality must be considered together, if the temper of the times is to be understood. "If our neutrality be still preserved, it will be due to the President alone," writes the younger Adams from Europe. "Nothing but his weight of character and reputation, combined with his firmness and political intrepidity could have stood against the torrent that is still tumbling with a fury that resounds even across the Atlantic. . . . If his system of administration now prevails, ten years more will place the United States among the most powerful and opulent nations on earth. . . . Now, when a powerful party at home and a mighty influence from abroad, are joining all their forces to assail his reputation, and his character I think it my duty as an American to avow my sentiments." (J. Q. Adams to Bourne, Dec. 24, 1795; *Writings, J. Q. A.*: Ford, i, 467.)

[2] Charles Pinckney's Speech; *American Remembrancer*, i, 7.

[3] Marshall, ii, 378. The Republicans insisted that the assent of the House of Representatives is necessary to the ratification of any treaty that affects commerce, requires appropriation of money, or where any act of Congress whatever may be necessary to carry a treaty into effect. (*Ib.*; and see Livingston's resolutions and debate; *Annals*, 4th Cong., 1st Sess., 1795, 426; 628.)

ginning of the Revolution" if the vile conduct of Washington had been foreseen; and it was plain, at this late day, that "either the Federal or State governments must fall" — so wrote Republican pamphleteers, so spoke Republican orators.[1]

Again Hamilton brought into action the artillery of his astounding intellect. In a series of public letters under the signature of "Camillus," he vindicated every feature of the treaty, evading nothing, conceding nothing. These papers were his last great constructive work. In numbers three, six, thirty-seven, and thirty-eight of "Camillus," he expounded the Constitution on the treaty-making power; demonstrated the exclusive right of the President to negotiate, and, with the Senate, to conclude, treaties; and proved, not only that the House should not be consulted, but that it is bound by the Constitution itself to pass all laws necessary to carry treaties into effect.[2]

Fearless, indeed, and void of political ambition were those who dared to face the tempest. "The cry against the Treaty is like that against a mad-dog," wrote Washington from Mount Vernon.[3] Particularly was this true of Virginia, where it raged un-

[1] "Priestly's Emigration," printed in Cobbett, i, 196, quoting "Agricola."

[2] "Camillus"; *Works:* Lodge, v and vi. It is impossible to give a satisfactory condensation of these monumental papers. Struck off in haste and under greatest pressure, they equal if not surpass Hamilton's "First Report on the Public Credit," his "Opinion as to the Constitutionality of the Bank of the United States," or his "Report on Manufactures." As an intellectual performance, the "Letters of Camillus" come near being Hamilton's masterpiece.

[3] Washington to Hamilton, July 29, 1795; *Writings:* Ford, xiii, 76.

governably.[1] A meeting of Richmond citizens "have outdone all that has gone before them" in the resolutions passed,[2] bitterly complained Washington. Virginians, testified Jefferson, "were never more unanimous. 4. or 5. individuals of Richmond, distinguished however, by their talents as by their devotion to all the sacred acts of the government, & the town of Alexandria constitute the whole support of that instrument [Jay Treaty] here."[3] These four or five devoted ones, said Jefferson, were "Marshall, Carrington, Harvey, Bushrod Washington, Doctor Stewart."[4] But, as we are now to see, Marshall made up in boldness and ability what the Virginia friends of the Administration lacked in numbers.

[1] The whole country was against the treaty on general grounds; but Virginia was especially hostile because of the sore question of runaway slaves and the British debts.

[2] Washington to Randolph, Aug. 4, 1795; *Writings:* Ford, xiii, footnote to 86. See Resolutions, which were comparatively mild; *American Remembrancer*, i, 133–34; and see *Richmond and Manchester Advertiser*, of July 30, and Aug. 6, 1795.

[3] Jefferson to Coxe, Sept. 10, 1795; *Works:* Ford, vii, 29.

[4] Jefferson to Monroe, Sept. 6, 1795; *ib.*, 27.

CHAPTER IV

WASHINGTON'S DEFENDER

His [Marshall's] lax, lounging manners have made him popular. (Jefferson.)

Having a high opinion of General Marshall's honor, prudence, and judgment, consult him. (Washington.)

The man [Washington] who is the source of all the misfortunes of our country is no longer possessed of the power to multiply evils on the United States. (The *Aurora* on Washington's retirement from the Presidency.)

JEFFERSON properly named Marshall as the first of Washington's friends in Virginia. For, by now, he had become the leader of the Virginia Federalists. His lucid common sense, his level poise, his steady courage, his rock-like reliability — these qualities, together with his almost uncanny influence over his constituents, had made him chief in the Virginia Federalist councils.

So high had Marshall risen in Washington's esteem and confidence that the President urged him to become a member of the Cabinet.

"The office of Attorney Genl of the United States has become vacant by the death of Will Bradford, Esq.[1] I take the earliest opportunity of asking if you will accept the appointment? The salary annexed thereto, and the prospects of lucrative practice in this city [Philadelphia] — the present seat of the Genl Government, must be as well known to you, perhaps better, than they are to me, and therefore I shall say nothing concerning them.

[1] When Jefferson resigned, Randolph succeeded him as Secretary of State, and continued in that office until driven out of public life by the famous Fauchet disclosure. William Bradford of Pennsylvania succeeded Randolph as Attorney-General.

"If your answer is in the affirmative, it will readily occur to you that no unnecessary time should be lost in repairing to this place. If, on the contrary, it should be the negative (which would give me concern) it might be as well to say nothing of this offer. But in either case, I pray you to give me an answer as promptly as you can." [1]

Marshall decided instantly; he could not possibly afford to accept a place yielding only fifteen hundred dollars annually, the salary of the Attorney-General at that period,[2] and the duties of which permitted little time for private practice which was then allowable.[3] So Marshall, in a "few minutes" declined Washington's offer in a letter which is a model of good taste.

"I had the honor of receiving a few minutes past your letter of the 26th inst.

"While the business I have undertaken to complete in Richmond,[4] forbids me to change my situation tho for one infinitely more eligible, permit me Sir to express my sincere acknowledgments for the offer your letter contains & the real pride & gratification I feel at the favorable opinion it indicates.

"I respect too highly the offices of the present government of the United States to permit it to be suspected that I have declined one of them." [5]

[1] Washington to Marshall, Aug. 26, 1795; Washington MSS., Lib. Cong.

[2] Act of 1789, *Annals*, 1st Cong., 1st Sess., Appendix, 2238.

[3] For Randolph's pathetic account of his struggles to subsist as Attorney-General, see Conway, chap. xv.

[4] The Fairfax purchase. See *infra*, chap. v.

[5] Marshall to Washington, Aug. 31, 1795; Washington MSS., Lib. Cong.

When he refused the office of Attorney-General, Washington, sorely perplexed, wrote Marshall's brother-in-law,[1] Edward Carrington, United States Marshal and Collector of Internal Revenue for the District of Virginia,[2] a letter, "the *whole*" of which "is perfectly confidential, written, perhaps, with more candor than prudence," concerning Innes or Henry for the place; but, says the President, "having a high opinion of General[3] Marshall's honor, prudence, and judgment," Carrington must consult him.[4]

The harassed President had now come to lean heavily on Marshall in Virginia affairs; indeed, it may be said that he was Washington's political agent at the State Capital. Carrington's answer is typical of his reports to the President: "The inquiry [concerning the selection of an Attorney-General] which you have been pleased to submit to Genl Marshall and myself demands & receives our most serious attention — On his [Marshall's] aid I rely for giving you accurate information."[5]

Later Carrington advises Washington that Marshall "wishes an opportunity of conversing with Col. Innes before he decides."[6] Innes was absent at Williamsburg; and although the matter was urgent, Marshall and Carrington did not write Innes, be-

[1] See *infra*, chap. v.

[2] Executive Journal, U.S. Senate, i, 81, 82. And see Washington's *Diary:* Lossing, 166. Carrington held both of these offices at the same time.

[3] Referring to Marshall's title as General of Virginia Militia. He was called "General" from that time until he became Chief Justice of the United States.

[4] Washington to Carrington, Oct. 9, 1795; *Writings:* Ford, xiii, 116.

[5] Carrington to Washington, Oct. 2, 1795; MS., Lib. Cong. [6] *Ib.*

cause, to do so, would involve a decisive offer from Washington which "Genl Marshall does not think advisable." [1]

When Washington's second letter, suggesting Patrick Henry, was received by Carrington, he "immediately consulted Gen. Marshall thereon"; and was guided by his opinion. Marshall thought that Washington's letter should be forwarded to Henry because "his nonacceptance, from domestic considerations, may be calculated on"; the offer "must tend to soften" Henry "if he has any asperities"; and the whole affair would make Henry "active on the side of Government & order." [2]

Marshall argued that, if Henry should accept, his friendship for the Administration could be counted on. But Marshall's strongest reason for trying to induce Henry to become a member of the Cabinet was, says Carrington, that "we are fully persuaded that a more deadly blow could not be given to the Faction [Republican party] in Virginia, & perhaps elsewhere, than that Gentleman's acceptance of the" Attorney-Generalship. "So much have the opposers of the Government held him [Henry] up as their oracle, even since he has ceased to respond to them, that any event demonstrating his active support to Government, could not but give the [Republican] party a severe shock." [3]

[1] Carrington to Washington, Oct. 8, 1795; MS., Lib. Cong.

[2] *Ib.*, Oct. 13, 1795; MS., Lib. Cong.

[3] *Ib.* A passage in this letter clearly shows the Federalist opinion of the young Republican Party and suggests the economic line dividing it from the Federalists. "In the present crisis Mr. H.[enry] may reasonably be calculated on as taking the side of Government, even though he may retain his old prejudices against the Constitution. He has

A week later Carrington reports that Henry's "conduct & sentiments generally both as to government & yourself [Washington] are such as we [Marshall and Carrington] calculated on . . . which assure us of his discountenancing calumny of every description & disorder,"[1] meaning that Henry was hostile to the Republicans.

In the rancorous assaults upon the Jay Treaty in Virginia, Marshall, of course, promptly took his position by Washington's side, and stoutly defended the President and even the hated compact itself. Little cared Marshall for the effect of his stand upon his popularity. Not at all did he fear or hesitate to take that stand. And high courage was required to resist the almost universal denunciation of the treaty in Virginia. Nor was this confined to the masses of the people; it was expressed also by most of the leading men in the various communities. At every meeting of protest, well-drawn and apparently convincing resolutions were adopted, and able, albeit extravagant, speeches were made against the treaty and the Administration.

Typical of these was the address of John Thompson at Petersburg, August 1, 1795.[2] With whom,

indubitably an abhorrence of Anarchy. . . . We know too that he is improving his fortune fast, which must additionally attach him to the existing Government & order, the only Guarantees of property. Add to all this, that he has no affection for the present leaders of the opposition in Virg[a]." (Carrington to Washington, Oct. 13, 1795; MS., Lib. Cong.)

[1] Carrington to Washington, Oct. 20, 1795; MS., Lib. Cong. Carrington's correspondence shows that everything was done on Marshall's judgment and that Marshall himself personally handled most of the negotiations. (See *ib.*, Oct. 28; Oct. 30, 1795.)

[2] *American Remembrancer*, i, 21 *et seq.* John Thompson was nineteen years old when he delivered this address. His extravagant

asked Thompson, was the treaty made? With the British King "who had sworn eternal enmity to republics"; that hateful monarch who was trying "to stifle the liberty of France" and "to starve thirty millions of men" by "intercepting the correspondence and plundering the commerce of neutral nations," especially that of the United States. The British, declared Thompson, sought "the destruction of our rising commerce; the annihilation of our growing navigation," and were pursuing that object "with all the . . . oppression which rapacity can practice."

Sequestration of British debts and other justifiable measures of retaliation would, said he, have stopped Great Britain's lawless practices. But the Administration preferred to treat with that malign Power; and our envoy, Jay, instead of "preserving the attitude of dignity and speaking the language of truth . . . basely apostatizing from republican principles, stooped to offer the incense of flattery to a tyrant, the scourge of his country, the foe of mankind. . . . Yes!" exclaimed the radical orator, "we hesitated to offend a proud King, who had captured our vessels, enslaved our fellow-citizens, ruined our merchants, invaded our territory and trampled on our sovereignty." In spite of these wrongs and insults, "we prostrated ourselves before him, smiled in his face, flattered, and obtained this treaty."

The treaty thus negotiated was, declared Thompson, the climax of the Funding system which had

rhetoric rather than his solid argument is quoted in the text as better illustrating the public temper and prevailing style of oratory. (See sketch of this remarkable young Virginian, *infra*, chap. x.)

"organized a great aristocracy . . . usurped the dominion of the senate . . . often preponderated in the house of representatives and which proclaims itself in servile addresses to our supreme executive, in dangerous appointments, in monstrous accumulations of debt, in violation of the constitution, in proscriptions of democrats, and, to complete the climax of political infamy, in this treaty."

Concerning the refusal to observe the principle that "free bottoms make free goods," our yielding the point rendered us, avowed Thompson, "a cowardly confederate . . . of . . . ruthless despots, who march to desolate France, to restore the altars of barbarous superstition and to extinguish the celestial light which has burst upon the human mind. O my countrymen, when you are capable of such monstrous baseness, even the patriot will invoke upon you the contempt of ages." This humiliation had been thrust upon us as a natural result of Washington's Neutrality proclamation — "a sullen neutrality between freemen and despots."

Thompson's searching, if boyish, rhetoric truly expressed the feeling in the hearts of the people; it was a frenzied sentiment with which Marshall had to contend. Notwithstanding his blazing language, Thompson analyzed the treaty with ability. In common with opponents of the treaty everywhere, he laid strongest emphasis on its unconstitutionality

[1] A favorite Republican charge was that the treaty would separate us from France and tie us to Great Britain: "A treaty which children cannot read without discovering that it tends to disunite us from our present ally, and unite us to a government which we abhor, detest and despise." ("An Old Soldier of '76"; *American Remembrancer*, ii, 281.)

and the "usurpation" by the President and Senate of the rights and powers of the House of Representatives.

But Thompson also mentioned one point that touched Marshall closely. "The ninth article," said he, "invades the rights of this commonwealth, by contemplating the case of Denny Fairfax."[1] Marshall and his brother were now the owners of this estate;[2] and the Jay Treaty confirmed all transfers of British property and authorized British subjects to grant, sell, or devise lands held in America in the same manner as if they were citizens of the United States. In Congress a few months later, Giles, who, declared Ames, "has no scruples and certainly less sense,"[3] touched lightly on this same chord.[4] So did Heath, who was from that part of Virginia lying within the Fairfax grant.[5]

Such was the public temper in Virginia, as accurately if bombastically expressed by the youthful Thompson, when the elections for the Legislature of 1795 were held. It was certain that the General Assembly would take drastic and hostile action against the treaty; and, perhaps, against Washington himself, in case the Republicans secured a majority in that body. The Federalists were in terror and justly so; for the Republicans, their strength much increased by the treaty, were aggressive and confident.

1 *American Remembrancer*, i, 27.

2 See *infra*, chap. v.

3 Ames to Gore, March 11, 1796; *Works:* Ames, i, 189.

4 *Annals*, 4th Cong., 1st Sess., 1033–34.

5 *Ib.*, 1063. See Anderson, 41–43. As one of the purchasers of the Fairfax estate, Marshall had a personal interest in the Jay Treaty, though it does not appear that this influenced him in his support of it.

The Federalist candidate in Richmond was the member of the Legislature whom the Federalists had succeeded in electing after Marshall's retirement three years before. He was Marshall's intimate friend and a stanch supporter of Washington's Administration. But it appears that in the present crisis his popularity was not sufficient to secure his election, nor his courage robust enough for the stern fight that was certain to develop in the General Assembly.

The polls were open and the voting in progress. Marshall was among the first to arrive; and he announced his choice.[1] Upon his appearance "a gentleman demanded that a poll be opened for Mr. Marshall."[2] Marshall, of course, indignantly refused; he had promised to support his friend, he avowed, and now to become a candidate was against "his wishes and feeling and honor." But Marshall promised that he would stand for the Legislature the following year.

Thereupon Marshall left the polls and went to the court-house to make an argument in a case then pending. No sooner had he departed than a poll was opened for him in spite of his objections;[3] he was elected; and in the evening was told of the undesired honor with which the freeholders of Richmond had crowned him.

[1] The voting was *viva voce*. See *infra*, chap. x.

[2] Undoubtedly this gentleman was one of the perturbed Federalist managers.

[3] *North American Review*, xxvi, 22. While this story seems improbable, no evidence has appeared which throws doubt upon it. At any rate, it serves to illustrate Marshall's astonishing popularity.

Washington was apprehensive of the newly elected Legislature. He anxiously questioned Carrington "as to the temper of our Assembly." The latter reported that he did not "expect an extravagant conduct during the session."[1] He thought that "the spirit of dissatisfaction is considerably abated abroad" (throughout Virginia and away from Richmond), because recent attempts to hold county and district meetings "for the avowed purpose of condemning the Administration & the Treaty" had been "abortive." It seemed to him, however, that "there is a very general impression unfavorable to the Treaty, owing to the greater industry of those who revile, over the supporters of it."[2]

Still, Carrington was not sure about the Legislature itself; for, as he said, "it has every year for several past been observable, that, at meeting [of the Legislature] but few hot heads were to be seen, while the great body were rational; but in the course of the session it has seldom happened otherwise than

[1] Carrington's reports to Washington were often absurd in their optimistic inaccuracy. They are typical of those which faithful office-holding politicians habitually make to the appointing power. For instance, Carrington told Washington in 1791 that, after traveling all over Virginia as United States Marshal and Collector of Internal Revenue, he was sure the people were content with Assumption and the whiskey tax (Washington's *Diary:* Lossing, footnote to 166), when, as a matter of fact, the State was boiling with opposition to those very measures.

[2] The mingling, in the Republican mind, of the Jay Treaty, Neutrality, unfriendliness to France, and the Federalist Party is illustrated in a toast at a dinner in Lexington, Virginia, to Senator Brown, who had voted against the treaty: "The French Republic — May every power or party who would attempt to throw any obstacle in the way of its independence or happiness receive the reward due to corruption." (*Richmond and Manchester Advertiser*, Oct. 15, 1795.)

that the spirit of party has been communicated so as to infect a majority. In the present instance I verily believe a question put on this day [the first day of the session] for making the Treaty a subject of consideration would be negatived — yet sundry members are here who will attempt every injury to both the Administration & the Treaty. The party will want ability in their leaders. . . . General Lee, C. Lee, Gen[l] Marshall & Mr. Andrews will act with ability on the defensive." [1]

Three days later the buoyant official advised the President that the Republicans doubted their own strength and, at worst, would delay their attack "in order that, as usual, a heat may be generated." Marshall was still busy searching for a properly qualified person to appoint to the unfilled vacancy in the office of Attorney-General; and Carrington tells Washington that "Gen[l] Marshall and myself have had a private consultation" on that subject and had decided to recommend Judge Blain. But, he adds, "The suggestion rests entirely with Gen[l] M[arshall] & myself & will there expire, should you, for any consideration, forbear to adopt it." His real message of joy, however, was the happy frame of mind of the Legislature. [2]

Alas for this prophecy of optimism! The Legislature had not been in session a week before the anti-Administration Banquo's ghost showed its grim visage. The Republicans offered a resolution approving the vote of Virginia Senators against the

[1] Carrington to Washington, Nov. 10, 1795; MS., Lib. Cong.
[2] *Ib.*, Nov. 13, 1795; MS.; Lib. Cong.

Jay Treaty. For three days the debate raged. Marshall led the Federalist forces. "The support of the Treaty has fallen altogether on Gen[l] Marshall and Mr. Chas. Lee," Carrington reports to Washington.[2]

Among the many objections to the treaty the principal one, as we have seen, was that it violated the Constitution. The treaty regulated commerce; the Constitution gave that power to Congress, which included the House of Representatives; yet the House had not been consulted. The treaty involved naturalization, the punishment of piracies, the laying of imposts and the expenditure of money — all of these subjects were expressly placed under the control of Congress and one of them[3] (the raising and expending of public money) must originate in the House; yet that popular branch of the Government had been ignored. The treaty provided for a quasi-judicial commission to settle the question of the British debts; yet "all the power of the Federal government with respect to debts is given [Congress] by a concise article of the Constitution. . . . What article of the Constitution authorizes President and Senate to establish a judiciary colossus which is to stand with one foot on America and the other on Britain, and drag the reluctant governments of those countries to the altar of justice?"[4]

[1] The resolution "was warmly agitated three whole days." (Randolph to Jefferson, Nov. 22, 1795; *Works:* Ford, viii, footnote to 197.)

[2] Carrington to Washington, Nov. 20, 1795; MS., Lib. Cong.

[3] See debates; *Annals*, 4th Cong., 1st Sess., 423–1291; also see Petersburg Resolutions; *American Remembrancer*, i, 102–07.

[4] Thompson's address, Aug. 1, 1795, at Petersburg; *ib.*, 21 *et seq.*

Thus the question was raised whether a commercial treaty, or an international compact requiring an appropriation of money, or, indeed, any treaty whatever in the execution of which any action of any kind on the part of the House of Representatives was necessary, could be made without the concurrence of the House as well as the Senate. On this, the only vital and enduring question involved, Marshall's views were clear and unshakable.

The defense of the constitutional power of the President and Senate to make treaties was placed solely on Marshall's shoulders. The Federalists considered his argument a conclusive demonstration. Carrington wrote Washington that "on the point of constitutionality many conversions were acknowledged." [1] He was mistaken; the Republicans were not impressed. On the contrary, they thought that the treaty "was much less ably defended than opposed." [2]

The Republicans had been very much alarmed over Marshall and especially feared the effect of one clever move. "John Marshall," wrote Jefferson's son-in-law from Richmond to the Republican commander in Monticello, "it was once apprehended would make a great number of converts by an argument which cannot be considered in any other light than an uncandid artifice. To prevent what would be a virtual censure of the President's conduct he maintained *that the treaty in all its commercial parts*

[1] Carrington to Washington, Nov. 20, 1795; MS., Lib. Cong.

[2] Randolph to Jefferson, Nov. 22, 1795; *Works:* Ford, viii, footnote to 197.

was still under the power of the H.[ouse] *of R.*[epresentatives]." [1]

Marshall, indeed, did make the most of this point. It was better, said he, and "more in the spirit of the constitution" for the National House to refuse support after ratification than to have a treaty "stifled in embryo" by the House passing upon it before ratification. "He compared the relation of the Executive and the Legislative department to that between the states and the Congress under the old confederation. The old Congress might have given up the right of laying discriminating duties in favor of any nation by treaty; it would never have thought of taking beforehand the assent of each state thereto. Yet, no one would have pretended to deny the power of the states to lay such [discriminating duties]." [2]

Such is an unfriendly report of this part of Marshall's effort which, wrote Jefferson's informant, "is all that is original in his argument. The sophisms of Camillus, & the nice distinctions of the Examiner made up the rest." [3] Marshall's position was that a "treaty is as completely a valid and obligatory contract when negotiated by the President and ratified by him, with the assent and advice of the Senate, as if sanctioned by the House of Representatives also, under a constitution requiring such sanction"; and he admitted only that the powers of the House in

[1] Randolph to Jefferson, Nov. 22, 1795; *Works:* Ford, viii, footnote to 197.

[2] *Ib.*

[3] *Ib.* See Hamilton's dissertation on the treaty-making power in numbers 36, 37, 38, of his "Camillus"; *Works:* Lodge, vi, 160–97.

reference to a treaty were limited to granting or refusing appropriations to carry it into effect.[1]

But as a matter of practical tactics to get votes, Marshall appears to have put this in the form of an assertion — no matter what treaty the President and Senate made, the House held the whip hand, he argued, and in the end, could do what it liked; why then unnecessarily affront and humiliate Washington by applauding the Virginia Senators for their vote against the treaty? This turn of Marshall's, thought the Republicans, "was brought forward for the purpose of gaining over the unwary & wavering. It has never been admitted by the writers in favor of the treaty to the northward."[2]

But neither Marshall's unanswerable argument on the treaty-making power, nor his cleverness in holding up the National House of Representatives as the final arbiter, availed anything. The Federalists offered an amendment affirming that the President and Senate "have a right to make" a treaty; that discussion of a treaty in a State Legislature, "except as to its constitutionality," was unnecessary; and that the Legislature could not give "any mature opinion upon the conduct of the Senators from Virginia . . . without a full investigation of the treaty." They were defeated by a majority of 46 out of a total of 150 members present and voting; John Marshall voting for the amendment.[3] On the main resolution proposed by the Republicans the

[1] Marshall to Hamilton, April 25, 1796; *Works:* Hamilton, vi, 109.

[2] Randolph to Jefferson, Nov. 22, 1795; *Works:* Ford, viii, 198.

[3] Journal, H.D. (Nov. 20, 1795), 27–28.

Federalists lost two votes and were crushed by a majority of two to one; Marshall, of course, voting with the minority.[1]

Carrington hastily reported to Washington that though "the discussion has been an able one on the side of the Treaty," yet, "such was the apprehension that a vote in its favor would be unpopular, that argument was lost"; and that, notwithstanding many members were convinced by Marshall's constitutional argument, "obligations of expediency" held them in line against the Administration. The sanguine Carrington assured the President, however, that "during the discussion there has been preserved a decided respect for & confidence in you."[2]

But alas again for the expectations of sanguinity! The Republican resolution was, as Jefferson's son-in-law had reported to the Republican headquarters at Monticello, "a virtual censure of the President's conduct." This was the situation at the close of the day's debate. Realizing it, as the night wore on, Washington's friends determined to relieve the President of this implied rebuke by the Legislature of his own State. The Republicans had carried their point; and surely, thought Washington's supporters, the Legislature of Virginia would not openly affront the greatest of all Americans, the pride of the State, and the President of the Nation.

Infatuated imagination! The next morning the friends of the Administration offered a resolution

[1] Journal, H.D. (Nov. 20, 1795), 28.

[2] Carrington to Washington, Nov. 20, 1795; MS., Lib. Cong.

that Washington's "motives" in approving the treaty met "the entire approbation of this House"; and that Washington, "for his great abilities, *wisdom* and integrity merits and possesses the undiminished confidence of his country." The resolution came near passing. But some lynx-eyed Republican discovered in the nick of time the word "*wisdom*."[1] That would never do. The Republicans, therefore, offered an amendment "that this House do entertain the highest sense of the integrity and patriotism of the President of the United States; and that while they approve of the vote of the Senators of this State" on the treaty, "they in no wise censure the motives which influenced him in his [Washington's] conduct thereupon."[2]

The word "wisdom" was carefully left out. Marshall, Lee, and the other Federalists struggled hard to defeat this obnoxious amendment; but the Republicans overwhelmed them by a majority of 33 out of a total of 145 voting, Marshall, of course, casting his vote against it.[3]

In worse plight than ever, Washington's friends moved to amend the Republican amendment by resolving: "That the President of the United States, for his great abilities, *wisdom*, and integrity, merits

[1] The italics are mine. "The word 'wisdom' in expressing the confidence of the House in the P.[resident] was so artfully introduced that if the fraudulent design had not been detected in time the vote of the House, as to its effect upon the P. would have been entirely done away. . . . A resolution so worded as to acquit the P. of all evil intention, but at the same time silently censuring his error, was passed by a majority of 33." (Letter of Jefferson's son-in-law, enclosed by Jefferson to Madison; *Works:* Ford, viii, footnote to 198.)

[2] Journal, H.D. (Nov. 21, 1795), 29. [3] *Ib.*

and possesses the undiminished confidence of this House." But even this, which omitted all reference to the treaty and merely expressed confidence in Washington's "abilities, wisdom, and integrity," was beaten by a majority of 20 out of a total of 138 voting.[1]

As soon as Jefferson got word of Marshall's support of Washington's Administration in the Legislature, he poured out his dislike which had long been distilling: —

"Though Marshall will be able to embarras [*sic*] the republican party in the assembly a good deal," wrote Jefferson to Madison, "yet upon the whole his having gone into it will be of service. He has been, hitherto, able to do more mischief acting under the mask of Republicanism than he will be able to do after throwing it plainly off. His lax lounging manners have made him popular with the bulk of the people of Richmond; & a profound hypocrisy, with many thinking men of our country. But having come forth in the plenitude of his English principles the latter will see that it is high time to make him known."[2]

Such was Jefferson's inability to brook any opposition, and his readiness to ascribe improper motives to any one having views different from his own. So far from Marshall's having cloaked his opinions, he had been and was imprudently outspoken in avowing them. Frankness was as much a part of Marshall's mental make-up as his "lax, lounging manners"

[1] Journal, H.D. (Nov. 21, 1795), 29.

[2] Jefferson to Madison, Nov. 26, 1795; *Works:* Ford, viii, 197–98.

were a part of his physical characteristics. Of all the men of the period, not one was cleaner of hypocrisy than he. From Patrick Henry in his early life onward to his associates on the bench at the end of his days the testimony as to Marshall's open-mindedness is uniform and unbroken.

With the possible exception of Giles and Roane, Jefferson appears to have been the only man who even so much as hinted at hypocrisy in Marshall. Although strongly opposing his views and suggesting the influence of supposed business connections, Madison had supreme confidence in Marshall's integrity of mind and character. So had Monroe. Even Jefferson's most panegyrical biographer declares Marshall to have been "an earnest and sincere man."[1]

The House of Delegates having refused to approve Washington, even indirectly, the matter went to the State Senate. There for a week Washington's friends fought hard and made a slight gain. The Senate struck out the House resolution and inserted instead: "The General Assembly entertain the highest sense of the integrity, patriotism and wisdom of the President of the United States, and in approving the vote of the Senators of the State in the Congress of the United States, relative to the treaty with Great Britain, they in no wise mean to censure the motives which influenced him in his conduct thereupon." To this the House agreed, although by a slender majority, Marshall, of course, voting for the Senate amendment.[2]

[1] Randall, ii, 36. [2] Journal, H.D. (1795), 72.

During this session Marshall was, as usual, on the principal standing committees and did his accustomed share of general legislative work. He was made chairman of a special committee to bring in a bill "authorizing one or more branches of the bank of the United States in this commonwealth"; [1] and later presented the bill,[2] which finally passed, December 8, 1795, though not without resistance, 38 votes being cast against it.[3]

But the Republicans had not yet finished with the Jay Treaty or with its author. On December 12, 1795, they offered a resolution instructing Virginia's Senators and Representatives in Congress to attempt to secure amendments to the Constitution providing that: "Treaties containing stipulations upon the subject of powers vested in Congress shall be approved by the House of Representatives"; that "a tribunal other than the Senate be instituted for trying impeachments"; that "Senators shall be chosen for three years"; and that "U.S. Judges shall hold no other appointments." [4]

The Federalists moved to postpone this resolution until the following year "and print and distribute proposed amendments for the consideration of the people"; but they were beaten by a majority of 11 out of a total vote of 129, Marshall voting for the resolution. The instruction to secure these radical constitutional changes then passed the House by a majority of 56 out of a total vote of 120, Marshall voting against it.[5]

[1] Journal, H.D. (1795), 50. [2] *Ib.*, 53.
[3] *Ib.*, 79. [4] *Ib.*, 90. [5] *Ib.*, 91–92.

Marshall's brother-in-law, United States Marshal Carrington, had a hard time explaining to Washington his previous enthusiasm. He writes: "The active powers of the [Republican] party . . . unveiled themselves, & carried in the House some points very extraordinary indeed, manifesting disrespect towards you." But, he continues, when the Virginia Senate reversed the House, "the zealots of Anarchy were backward to act . . . while the friends of Order were satisfied to let it [the Virginia Senate amendment] remain for farther effects of reflection"; and later succeeded in carrying it.

"The fever has raged, come to its crisis, and is abating." Proof of this, argued Carrington, was the failure of the Republicans to get signatures to "some seditious petitions [against the Jay Treaty] which was sent in vast numbers from Philadelphia" and which "were at first patronized with great zeal by many of our distinguished anarchists; but . . . very few copies will be sent to Congress fully signed." [1]

Never was appointive officer so oblivious of facts in his reports to his superior, as was Carrington. Before adjournment on December 12, 1795, the Legislature adopted part of the resolution which had been offered in the morning: "No treaty containing any stipulation upon the subject of powers vested in Congress by the eighth section of the first article [of the Constitution] shall become the Supreme law of the land until it shall have been approved in those particulars by a majority in the House of

[1] Carrington to Washington, Dec. 6, 1795; MS., Lib. Cong.

Representatives; and that the President, before he shall ratify *any* treaty, shall submit the same to the House of Representatives." [1]

Carrington ignored or failed to understand this amazing resolution of the Legislature of Virginia; for nearly three months later he again sought to solace Washington by encouraging reports. "The public mind in Virginia was never more tranquil than at present. The fever of the late session of our assembly, had not been communicated to the Country. . . . The people do not approve of the violent and petulant measures of the Assembly, because, in several instances, public meetings have declared a decided disapprobation." In fact, wrote Carrington, Virginia's "hostility to the treaty has been exaggerated." Proof "of the mass of the people being less violent than was asserted" would be discovered "in the failure of our Zealots in getting their signatures to certain printed papers, sent through the Country almost by Horse loads, as copies of a petition to Congress on the subject of the Treaty." [2] But a few short months would show how rose-colored were the spectacles which Mr. Carrington wore when he wrote this reassuring letter.

The ratification of the British treaty; the rage against England; and the devotion to France which already had made the Republican a French party; the resentment of the tri-color Republic toward the American Government — all forged a new and desperate menace. It was, indeed, Scylla or Charybdis,

[1] Journal, H.D. (Dec. 12, 1795), 91–92.

[2] Carrington to Washington, Feb. 24, 1796; MS., Lib. Cong.

as Washington had foreseen, and bluntly stated, that confronted the National Government. War with France now seemed the rock on which events were driving the hard-pressed Administration — war for France or war from France.

The partisan and simple-minded Monroe had been recalled from his diplomatic post at Paris. The French mission, which at the close of our Revolution was not a place of serious moment,[1] now became critically — vitally — important. Level must be the head and stout the heart of him who should be sent to deal with that sensitive, proud, and now violent country. Lee thus advises the President: "No person would be better fitted than John Marshall to go to France for supplying the place of our minister; but it is scarcely short of absolute certainty that he would not accept any such office."[2]

But Washington's letter was already on the way, asking Marshall to undertake this delicate task: —

"In confidence I inform you," wrote Washington to Marshall, "that it has become indispensably necessary to recall our minister at Paris & to send one in his place, who will explain faithfully the views of this government & ascertain those of France.

"Nothing would be more pleasing to me than that you should be this organ, if it were only for a temporary absence of a few months; but it being feared that even this could not be made to comport with your present pursuits, I have in order that as little delay as possible may be incurred put the enclosed

[1] Dodd, 39.
[2] Lee to Washington, July 7, 1796; *Writings:* Sparks, xi, 487.

letter [to Charles Cotesworth Pinckney] under cover to be forwarded to its address, if you decline the present offer or to be returned to me if you accept it. Your own correct knowledge of circumstances renders details unnecessary." [1]

Marshall at once declined this now high distinction and weighty service, as he had already refused the United States district attorneyship and a place in Washington's Cabinet. Without a moment's delay, he wrote the President:—

"I will not attempt to express those sensations which your letter of the 8th instant has increased. Was it possible for me in the present crisis of my affairs to leave the United States, such is my conviction of the importance of that duty which you would confide to me, &, pardon me if I add, of the fidelity with which I shoud attempt to perform it, that I woud certainly forego any consideration not decisive with respect to my future fortunes, & woud surmount that just diffidence I have entertain[d] of myself, to make one effort to convey truly & faithfully to the government of France those sentiments which I have ever believed to be entertained by that of the United States.

"I have forwarded your letter to Mr. Pinckney. The recall of our minister at Paris has been conjectured while its probable necessity has been regretted by those who love more than all others, our own country. I will certainly do myself the honor of waiting on you at Mt. Vernon." [2]

[1] Washington to Marshall, July 8, 1796; Washington MSS., Lib. Cong.

[2] Marshall to Washington, July 11, 1796; *ib.*

Washington, although anticipating Marshall's refusal of the French mission, promptly answered: "I . . . regret that present circumstances should deprive our Country of the services, which, I am confident, your going to France would have rendered it"; and Washington asks Marshall's opinion on the proper person to appoint to the office of Surveyor-General.[1]

The President's letter, offering the French post to Pinckney, was lost in the mails; and the President wrote Marshall about it, because it also enclosed a note "containing three bank bills for one hundred dollars each for the sufferers by fire in Charlestown."[2] In answer, Marshall indulged in a flash of humor, even at Washington's expense. "Your letter to General Pinckney was delivered by myself to the post master on the night on which I received it and was, as he says, immediately forwarded by him. Its loss is the more remarkable, as it could not have been opened from a hope that it contained bank notes." He also expressed his gratification "that a gentleman of General Pinckney's character will represent our government at the court of France."[3]

The office of Secretary of State now became vacant, under circumstances apparently forbidding. The interception of Fauchet's[4] famous dispatch number 10[5] had been fatal to Randolph. The French

[1] Washington to Marshall, July 15, 1796; Washington's Private Letter Book; MS., Lib. Cong.

[2] Washington to Marshall, Oct. 10, 1796; *ib.*

[3] Marshall to Washington, Oct. 12, 1796; Washington MSS., Lib. Cong.

[4] Genêt's successor as French Minister to the United States.

[5] *Interesting State Papers*, 48 *et seq.*

Minister, in this communication to his Government, portrays a frightful state of corrupt public thinking in America; ascribes this to the measures of Washington's Administration; avows that a revolution is imminent; declares that powerful men, "all having without doubt" Randolph at their head, are balancing to decide on their party; asserts that Randolph approached him with suggestions for money; and concludes: —

"Thus with some thousands of dollars the [French] republic could have decided on civil war or on peace [in America]! Thus the consciences of the pretended patriots of America have already their prices! . . . What will be the old age of this [American] government, if it is thus early decrepid!" [1]

The discovery of this dispatch of the French Minister destroyed Randolph politically. Washington immediately forced his resignation.[2]

The President had great difficulty in finding a suitable successor to the deposed Secretary of State. He tendered the office to five men, all of whom declined.[3] "What am I to do for a Secretary of State?" he asks Hamilton; and after recounting his fruitless efforts to fill that office the President adds that "Mr. Marshall, of Virginia, has declined the office of Attorney General, and I am pretty certain, would accept of

[1] *Interesting State Papers*, 55.

[2] For able defense of Randolph see Conway, chap. xxiii; but *contra*, see Gibbs, i, chap. ix.

[3] Patterson of New Jersey, Johnson of Maryland, C. C. Pinckney of South Carolina, Patrick Henry of Virginia, and Rufus King of New York. (Washington to Hamilton, Oct. 29, 1795; *Writings:* Ford, xiii, 129–30.) King declined because of the abuse heaped upon public officers. (Hamilton to Washington, Nov. 5, 1795; *ib.*, footnote to 130.)

no other."[1] It is thus made clear that Washington would have made Marshall the head of his Cabinet in 1795 but for the certainty that his Virginia champion would refuse the place, as he had declined other posts of honor and power.

Hardly had the Virginia Legislature adjourned when the conflict over the treaty was renewed in Congress. The Republicans had captured the House of Representatives and were full of fight. They worked the mechanism of public meetings and petitions to its utmost. On March 7 the House plunged into a swirl of debate over the British treaty; time and again it seemed as though the House would strangle the compact by withholding appropriations to make it effective.[2] If the treaty was to be saved, all possible pressure must be brought to bear on Congress. So the Federalists took a leaf out of the book of Republican tactics, and got up meetings wherever they could to petition Congress to grant the necessary money.

In Virginia, as elsewhere, the merchants were the principal force in arranging these meetings.[3] As we have seen, the business and financial interests had from the first been the stanchest supporters of Washington's Administration. "The commercial and monied people are zealously attached to" and support the Government, wrote Wolcott in 1791.[4] And now Hamilton advised King that "men of busi-

[1] Washington to Hamilton, Oct. 29, 1795; *Writings:* Ford, xiii, 131.

[2] For debate see *Annals*, 4th Cong., 1st Sess., 423–1291.

[3] Carrington to Washington, May 9, 1796; MS., Lib. Cong.

[4] Oliver Wolcott to his father, Feb. 12, 1791; Gibbs, i, 62.

ness of all descriptions" thought the defeat of the treaty "would greatly shock and stagnate pecuniary plans and operations in general." [1] Indeed, the one virtue of the treaty, aside from its greatest purpose, that of avoiding war, was that it prevented the collapse of credit and the wreck of Hamilton's financial system.

Washington, with the deceptive hopefulness of responsibility, had, even when it seemed that the people were as one man against the treaty, "doubted much whether the great body of the yeomanry have formed any opinions on the subject." [2] The Federalist meetings were designed to show that the "yeomanry," having been "educated," had at last made up its mind in favor of Washington's policy.

Marshall and Carrington arranged for the Richmond gathering. "The disorganizing machinations of a faction [Republicans]," reported the busy United States Marshal, "are no longer left to be nourished and inculcated on the minds of the credulous by clamorous demagogues, while the great mass of citizens, viewing these, as evils at a distance, remain inactive. . . . All who are attached to peace and order, . . . will now come forward and speak for themselves. . . . A meeting of the people of this city will take place on Monday next" to petition the National House of Representatives to support the treaty. So Carrington advised the President; and the same thing, said he, was to be done "exten-

[1] Hamilton to King, June 20, 1795; *Works:* Lodge, x, 103.
[2] Washington to Knox, Sept. 20, 1795; *Writings:* Ford, xiii, 105–06.

sively" by "public meetings and Petitions throughout Virginia."[1]

Washington was expecting great results from the Richmond demonstration. "It would give me and . . . every friend to order and good government throughout the United States very great satisfaction," he wrote to encourage the Virginia Federalists; "more so than similar sentiments from any other State in the Union; for people living at a distance from it [Virginia] know not how to believe it possible" that the Virginia Legislature and her Senators and Representatives in Congress should speak and act as they had done.[2] "It is," philosophized Washington, "on *great* occasions *only* and after time has been given for cool and deliberate reflection that the *real* voice of the people can be known. The present . . . is one of those great occasions, than which none more important has occurred, or probably may occur again to call forth their decision."[3]

By such inspiration and management the historic Federalist gathering was brought about at Richmond on April 25, 1796, where the "Marshall eloquence" was to do its utmost to convert a riotously hostile sentiment into approval of this famous treaty and of the Administration which was responsible for it. All day the meeting lasted. Marshall put forth his whole strength. At last a "decided majority" adopted a favorable resolution drawn by

[1] Carrington to the President, April 22, 1796; *Writings:* Ford, xiii, footnote to 185.

[2] Washington to Carrington, May 1, 1796; *ib.*, 185.

[3] *Ib.*, 186.

an "original opponent" of the treaty. Thus were sweetened the bitter resolutions adopted by these same freeholders of Richmond some months before, which had so angered Washington.

The accounts of this all-day public discussion are as opposite as were the prejudices and interests of the narrators. Justice Story tells us that Marshall's speech was "masterly," the majority for the resolution "flattering," and the assemblage itself made up of the "same citizens" who formerly had "denounced" the treaty.[1] But there was present at the meeting an onlooker who gives a different version. Randolph, who, in disgrace, was then sweating venom from every pore, thus reports to Madison at the end of the hard-fought day: —

"Between 3 & 400 persons were present; a large proportion of whom were British merchants, some of whom pay for the British purchases of horses — their clerks — officers, who have held posts under the President at his will, — stockholders — expectants of office — and many without the shadow of a freehold.[2] Notwithstanding this, the numbers on the republican side, tho' inferior, were inferior in a small degree only; and it is believed on good grounds that the majority of free-holders were on the side of the house of representatives [against the treaty].

"Campbell[3] and Marshall the principal combatants [word illegible] as you know without being

[1] Story, in Dillon, iii, 352.

[2] Senator Stephen Thompson Mason wrote privately to Tazewell that the Fairfax purchasers and British merchants were the only friends of the treaty in Virginia. (Anderson, 42.)

[3] Alexander Campbell. (See *infra*, chap. v.)

told. Marshall's argument was inconsistent, and shifting; concluding every third sentence with the horrors of war. Campbell spoke elegantly and forcibly; and threw ridicule and absurdity upon his antagonist with success. Mr. Clofton [Clopton, member of Congress from Richmond] will receive two papers; one signed by the treaty men, many of whom he will know to have neither interest nor feeling in common with the citizens of Virginia, and to have been transplanted hither from England or Caledonia since the war, interspersed pretty considerably with fugitive tories who have returned under the amnesty of peace.

"The notice, which I sent you the other day," he goes on to say, "spoke of instructions and a petition; but Marshall, suspecting that he would be outnumbered by freeholders, and conscious that none should instruct those who elect, quitted the idea of instruction, and betook himself to a petition, in which he said all the inhabitants of Richmond, though not freeholders, might join. Upon which Campbell gave notice, that it would be published that he (Marshall) declined hazarding the question on the true sense of the country. Very few of the people [freeholders] of the county were present; but three-fourths of those who were present voted with Campbell. Dr. Foushee was extremely active and influential." [1]

Marshall, on the contrary, painted in rich colors his picture of this town-hall contest. He thus reports

[1] Randolph to Madison, Richmond, April 25, 1796; Conway, 362. Only freeholders could vote.

to Hamilton: "I had been informed of the temper of the House of Representatives and we [Richmond Federalists] had promptly taken such measures as appeared to us fitted to the occasion. We could not venture an expression of the public mind under the violent prejudices with which it has been impressed, so long as a hope remained, that the House of Representatives might ultimately consult the interest or honor of the nation. . . . But now, when all hope of this has vanished, it was deemed advisable to make the experiment, however hazardous it might be.

"A meeting was called," continues Marshall, "which was more numerous than I have ever seen at this place; and after a very ardent and zealous discussion which consumed the day, a decided majority declared in favor of a resolution that the wellfare and honor of the nation required us to give full effect to the treaty negotiated with Britain. This resolution, with a petition drawn by an original opponent of the treaty, will be forwarded by the next post to Congress." [1]

The resolution which Marshall's speech caused an "original opponent" [2] of the treaty to draw was "that the Peace, Happiness, & Wellfare, not less than the National Honor of the United States, depend in a great degree upon giving, with good faith, Full effect to the Treaty lately negotiated with Great Britain." The same newspaper that printed this resolution, in another account of the meeting

[1] Marshall to Hamilton, April 25, 1796; *Works:* Hamilton, vi, 109.
[2] Author unknown.

"which was held at the instance of some friends of the British Treaty," says that "in opposition to that resolution a vast number of the meeting" subscribed to counter-declarations which "are now circulated throughout this City and the county of Henrico for the subscription of all those who" are opposed to the treaty.[1] Even the exultant Carrington reported "that the enemies of the Treaty or rather of the Government, are putting in practice every part and effort to obtain subscriptions to a counteracting paper."

Carrington denounced the unfavorable newspaper account as "a most absolute falsehood." He tells Washington that the opposition resolution "was not even listened [to] in the meeting." But still he is very apprehensive — he beholds the politician's customary "crisis" and strives to make the people see it: "There never was a crisis at which the activity of the Friends of Government was more urgently called for — some of us here have endeavored to make this impression in different parts of the Country."[2] The newspaper reported that the Federalists had induced "school boys & apprentices" to sign the petition in favor of the treaty; Carrington adds a postscript stating that this was, "I believe, a little incorrect."

Marshall foresaw that the Republicans would make this accusation and hastened to anticipate it by advancing the same charge against his opponents. The Republicans, says Marshall, secured the signa-

[1] *Richmond and Manchester Advertiser*, April 27, 1796.
[2] Carrington to the President, April 27, 1796; MS., Lib. Cong.

tures to their petition not only "of many respectable persons but of still a greater number of mere boys. . . . Altho' some caution has been used by us in excluding those who might not be considered as authorized to vote," yet, Marshall advises King, "they [Republicans] will not fail to charge us with having collected a number of names belonging to foreigners and to persons having no property in the place. The charge is as far untrue," asserts Marshall, "as has perhaps ever happened on any occasion of the sort. We could, by resorting to that measure, have doubled our list of petitioners." And he adds that "the ruling party [Republican] of Virginia are extremely irritated at the vote of to-day, and will spare no exertion to obtain a majority in other counties. Even here they will affect to have the greater number of freeholders."[1]

It was in this wise that petitions favorable to the Jay Treaty and to Washington were procured in the President's own State. It was thus that the remainder of the country was assured that the Administration was not without support among the people of Virginia. Unsuspected and wholly unforeseen was the influence on Marshall's future which his ardent championship of this despised treaty was to exercise.

The Federalists were wise to follow the Republican practice of petition to Congress; for, "nothing . . . but the torrent of petitions and remonstrances . . . would have produced a division (fifty-one to forty-

[1] Marshall to King, April 25, 1796; King, ii, 45–46.

eight) in favor of the appropriation." [1] So great was the joy of the commercial classes that in Philadelphia, the financial heart of the country, a holiday was celebrated when the House voted the money.[2]

Marshall's activity, skill, courage, ability, and determination in the Legislature and before the people at this critical hour lifted him higher than ever, not only in the regard of Washington, but in the opinion of the Federalist leaders throughout the country.[3] They were casting about for a successor to Washington who could be most easily elected. The Hamiltonian Federalists were already distrustful of Adams for the presidency, and, even then, were warily searching for some other candidate. Why not Patrick Henry? Great changes had occurred in the old patriot's mind and manner of thinking. He was now a man of wealth and had come to lean strongly toward the Government. His friendship for Washington, Marshall, and other Virginia Federalists had grown; while for Jefferson and other Virginia Republicans it had turned to dislike. Still, with Henry's lifelong record, the Federalists could not be sure of him.

To Marshall's cautious hands the Federalist leaders committed the delicate business of sounding Henry. King of New York had written Marshall on the subject. "Having never been in habits of correspondence with Mr. H.[enry]," replies Marshall,

[1] Washington to Thomas Pinckney, May 22, 1796; *Writings:* Ford, xiii, 208.

[2] Robert Morris to James M. Marshall, May 1, 1796; Morris's Private Letter Book; MS., Lib. Cong.

[3] Story, in Dillon, iii, 350.

"I cou'd not by letter ask from him a decision on the proposition I was requested to make him without giving him at the same time a full statement of the whole conversation & of the persons with whom that conversation was held." Marshall did not think this wise, for "I am not positively certain what course that Gentleman might take. The proposition might not only have been rejected but mentioned publickly to others in such manner as to have become an unpleasant circumstance."

A prudent man was Marshall. He thought that Lee, who "corresponds familiarly with Mr. H. & is in the habit of proposing offices to him," was the man to do the work; and he asked Lee "to sound Mr. H. as from himself or in such manner as might in any event be perfectly safe." Lee did so, but got no answer. However, writes Marshall, "Mr. H.[enry] will be in Richmond on the 22[d] of May. I can then sound him myself & if I find him (as I suspect I shall) totally unwilling to engage in the contest, I can stop where prudence may direct. I trust it will not then be too late to bring forward to public view Mr. H. or any other gentleman who may be thought of in his stead. Shou'd anything occur to render it improper to have any communication with M[r] H. on this subject, or shou'd you wish the communication to take any particular shape you will be so obliging as to drop me a line concerning it."[1]

[1] Marshall to King, April 19, 1796; Hamilton MSS., Lib. Cong. Hamilton, it seems, had also asked Marshall to make overtures to Patrick Henry for the Presidency. (King, ii, footnote to 46.) But no correspondence between Hamilton and Marshall upon this subject has been discovered. Marshall's correspondence about Henry was with King.

Marshall finally saw Henry and at once wrote the New York lieutenant of Hamilton the result of the interview. "Mr. Henry has at length been sounded on the subject you communicated to my charge," Marshall advises King. "Gen! Lee and myself have each conversed with him on it, tho' without informing him particularly of the persons who authorized the communication. He is unwilling to embark in the business. His unwillingness, I think, proceeds from an apprehension of the difficulties to be encountered by those who shall fill high Executive offices." [1]

The autumn of 1796 was at hand. Washington's second term was closing in Republican cloudbursts and downpours of abuse of him. He was, said the Republicans, an aristocrat, a "monocrat," a miser, an oppressor of the many for the enrichment of the few. Nay, more! Washington was a thief, even a murderer, charged the Republicans. His personal habits were low and base, said these champions of purity.[2] Washington had not even been true to the cause of the Revolution, they declared; and to prove this, an ancient slander, supported by forged letters alleged to have been written by Washington during the war, was revived.[3]

Marshall, outraged and insulted by these assaults on the great American, the friend of his father and himself and the commander of the patriots who had,

[1] Marshall to King, May 24, 1796; King, ii, 48.

[2] For an accurate description of the unparalleled abuse of Washington, see McMaster, ii, 249–50, 289–91, 302–06.

[3] Marshall, ii, 391–92. Also see Washington to Pickering, March 3, 1797; *Writings:* Ford, xiii, 378–80; and to Gordon, Oct. 15; *ib.*, 427.

by arms, won liberty and independence for the very men who were now befouling Washington's name, earnestly defended the President. Although his law practice and private business called for all his strength and time, Marshall, in order to serve the President more effectively, again stood for the Legislature, and again he was elected.

In the Virginia House of Delegates, Marshall and the other friends of Washington took the initiative. On November 17, 1796, they carried a motion for an address to the President, declaratory of Virginia's "gratitude for the services of their most excellent fellow citizen"; who "has so wisely and prosperously administrated the national concerns."[1] But how should the address be worded? The Republicans controlled the committee to which the resolution was referred. Two days later that body reported a cold and formal collection of sentences as Virginia's address to Washington upon his leaving, apparently forever, the service of America. Even Lee, who headed the committee, could not secure a declaration that Washington was or had been wise.

This stiff "address" to Washington, reported by the committee, left out the word "wisdom." Commendation of Washington's conduct of the Government was carefully omitted. Should his friends submit to this? No! Better to be beaten in a manly contest. Marshall and the other supporters of the President resolved to try for a warmer expression. On December 10, they introduced a substitute declaring that, if Washington had not declined, the

[1] Journal, H.D. (1796), 46–47; MS. Archives, Va. St. Lib.

people would have reëlected him; that his whole life had been "strongly marked by wisdom, valor, and patriotism"; that "posterity to the most remote generations and the friends of true and genuine liberty and of the rights of man throughout the world, and in all succeeding ages, will unite" in acclaiming "that you have never ceased to deserve well of your country"; that Washington's "valor and wisdom . . . had essentially contributed to establish and maintain the happiness and prosperity of the nation." [1]

But the Republicans would have none of it. After an acrid debate and in spite of personal appeals made to the members of the House, the substitute was defeated by a majority of three votes. John Marshall was the busiest and most persistent of Washington's friends, and of course voted for the substitute,[2] which, almost certainly, he drew. Cold as was the original address which the Federalists had failed to amend, the Republicans now made it still more frigid. They would not admit that Washington deserved well of the whole country. They moved to strike out the word "country" and in lieu thereof insert "native state." [3]

Many years afterward Marshall told Justice Story his recollection of this bitter fight: "In the session of 1796 . . . which," said Marshall, "called forth all

[1] Journal, H.D. (1796), 153; MS. Archives, Va. St. Lib. [2] *Ib.*

[3] *Ib.* This amendment is historically important for another reason. It is the first time that the Virginia Legislature refers to that Commonwealth as a "State" in contra-distinction to the country. Although the Journal shows that this important motion was passed, the manuscript draft of the resolution signed by the presiding officer of both Houses does not show the change. (MS. Archives, Va. St. Lib.)

the strength and violence of party, some Federalist moved a resolution expressing the high confidence of the House in the virtue, patriotism, and wisdom of the President of the United States. A motion was made to strike out the word *wisdom*. In the debate the whole course of the Administration was reviewed, and the whole talent of each party was brought into action. Will it be believed that the word was retained by a very small majority? A very small majority in the legislature of Virginia acknowledged the wisdom of General Washington!" [1]

Dazed for a moment, the Federalists did not resist. But, their courage quickly returning, they moved a brief amendment of twenty words declaring that Washington's life had been "strongly marked by wisdom, in the cabinet, by valor, in the field, and by the purest patriotism in both." Futile effort! The Republicans would not yield. By a majority of nine votes [2] they flatly declined to declare that Washington had been wise in council, brave in battle, or patriotic in either; and the original address, which, by these repeated refusals to endorse either Washington's sagacity, patriotism, or even courage, had now been made a dagger of ice, was sent to Washington as the final comment of his native

[1] Story, in Dillon, iii, 355. Marshall's account was inaccurate, as we have seen. His memory was confused as to the vote in the two contests (*supra*), a very natural thing after the lapse of twenty years. In the first contest the House of Delegates voted overwhelmingly against including the word "wisdom" in the resolutions; and on the Senate amendment restored it by a dangerously small majority. On the second contest in 1796, when Marshall declares that Washington's friends won "by a very small majority," they were actually defeated.

[2] Journal, H.D., 153–90.

State upon his lifetime of unbearable suffering and incalculable service to the Nation.

Arctic as was this sentiment of the Virginia Republicans for Washington, it was tropical compared with the feeling of the Republican Party toward the old hero as he retired from the Presidency. On Monday, March 5, 1797, the day after Washington's second term expired, the principal Republican newspaper of America thus expressed the popular sentiment: —

"'Lord, now lettest thou thy servant depart in peace, for mine eyes have seen thy salvation,' was the pious ejaculation of a man who beheld a flood of happiness rushing in upon mankind. . . .

"If ever there was a time that would license the reiteration of the exclamation, that time is now arrived, for the man [Washington] who is the source of all the misfortunes of our country, is this day reduced to a level with his fellow citizens, and is no longer possessed of power to multiply evils upon the United States.

"If ever there was a period for rejoicing this is the moment — every heart, in unison with the freedom and happiness of the people ought to beat high with exultation, that the name of Washington from this day ceases to give a currency to political iniquity, and to legalize corruption. . . .

"A new æra is now opening upon us, an æra which promises much to the people; for public measures must now stand upon their own merits, and nefarious projects can no longer be supported by a name.

"When a retrospect is taken of the Washingtonian

administration for eight years, it is a subject of the greatest astonishment, that a single individual should have cankered the principles of republicanism in an enlightened people, just emerged from the gulph of despotism, and should have carried his designs against the public liberty so far as to have put in jeopardy its very existence.

"Such however are the facts, and with these staring us in the face, this day ought to be a JUBILEE in the United States." [1]

Such was Washington's greeting from a great body of his fellow citizens when he resumed his private station among them after almost twenty years of labor for them in both war and peace. Here rational imagination must supply what record does not reveal. What must Marshall have thought? Was this the fruit of such sacrifice for the people's welfare as no other man in America and few in any land throughout all history had ever made — this rebuke of Washington — Washington, who had been the soul as well as the sword of the Revolution; Washington, who alone had saved the land from anarchy; Washington, whose level sense, far-seeing vision, and mighty character had so guided the newborn Government that the American people had taken their

[1] *Aurora*, Monday, March 5, 1797. This paper, expressing Republican hatred of Washington, had long been assailing him. For instance, on October 24, 1795, a correspondent, in the course of a scandalous attack upon the President, said: "The consecrated ermine of Presidential chastity seems too foul for time itself to bleach." (See Cobbett, i, 411; and *ib.*, 444, where the *Aurora* is represented as having said that "Washington has the ostentation of an eastern bashaw.") From August to September the *Aurora* had accused Washington of peculation. (See "Calm Observer" in *Aurora*, Oct. 23 to Nov. 5, 1795.)

place as a separate and independent Nation? Could any but this question have been asked by Marshall?

He was not the only man to whom such reflections came. Patrick Henry thus expressed his feelings: "I see with concern our old commander-in-chief most abusively treated — nor are his long and great services remembered. . . . If he, whose character as our leader during the whole war, was above all praise, is so roughly handled in his old age, what may be expected by men of the common standard of character?" [1]

And Jefferson! Had he not become the voice of the majority?

Great as he was, restrained as he had arduously schooled himself to be, Washington personally resented the brutal assaults upon his character with something of the fury of his unbridled youth: "I had no conception that parties would or even could go to the length I have been witness to; nor did I believe, until lately, that it was within the bounds of probability — hardly within those of possibility — that . . . every act of my administration would be tortured and the grossest and most insidious misrepresentations of them be made . . . and that too in such exaggerated and indecent terms as could scarcely be applied to a Nero — a notorious defaulter — or even to a common pickpocket." [2]

[1] Henry to his daughter, Aug. 20, 1796; Henry, ii, 569–70. Henry was now an enemy of Jefferson and his dislike was heartily reciprocated.

[2] Washington to Jefferson, July 6, 1796; *Writings:* Ford, xiii, 230–31. This letter is in answer to a letter from Jefferson denying responsibility for the publication of a Cabinet paper in the *Aurora.* (Jefferson to Washington, June 19, 1796; *Works:* Ford, viii, 245; and

Here, then, once more, we clearly trace the development of that antipathy between Marshall and Jefferson, the seeds of which were sown in those desolating years from 1776 to 1780, and in the not less trying period from the close of the Revolution to the end of Washington's Administration. Thus does circumstance mould opinion and career far more than abstract thinking; and emotion quite as much as reason shape systems of government. The personal feud between Marshall and Jefferson, growing through the years and nourished by events, gave force and speed to their progress along highways which, starting at the same point, gradually diverged and finally ran in opposite directions.

see Marshall, ii, 390–91.) Even in Congress Washington did not escape. In the debate over the last address of the National Legislature to the President, Giles of Virginia declared that Washington had been "neither wise nor firm." He did not think "so much of the President." He "wished him to retire . . . the government of the United States could go on very well without him." (*Annals*, 4th Cong., 2d Sess. (Dec. 14, 1796), 1614–18.) On the three roll-calls and passage of the address Giles voted against Washington. (*Ib.*, 1666–68.) So did Andrew Jackson, a new member from Tennessee. (*Ib.*)

The unpopularity of Washington's Administration led to the hostile policy of Bache's paper, largely as a matter of business. This provident editor became fiercely "Republican" because, as he explained to his relative, Temple Franklin, in England, he "could not [otherwise] maintain his family," and "he had determined to adopt a bold experiment and to come out openly against the Administration. He thought the public temper would bear it." (Marshall to Pickering, Feb. 28, 1811, relating the statement of Temple Franklin to James M. Marshall while in England in 1793.)

CHAPTER V

THE MAN AND THE LAWYER

Tall, meagre, emaciated, his muscles relaxed, his joints loosely connected, his head small, his complexion swarthy, his countenance expressing great good humor and hilarity. (William Wirt.)

Mr. Marshall can hardly be regarded as a learned lawyer. (Gustavus Schmidt.)

His head is one of the best organized of any I have known. (Rufus King.)

ON a pleasant summer morning when the cherries were ripe, a tall, ungainly man in early middle life sauntered along a Richmond street. His long legs were encased in knee breeches, stockings, and shoes of the period; and about his gaunt, bony frame hung a roundabout or short linen jacket. Plainly, he had paid little attention to his attire. He was bareheaded and his unkempt hair was tied behind in a queue. He carried his hat under his arm, and it was full of cherries which the owner was eating as he sauntered idly along.[1] Mr. Epps's hotel (The Eagle) faced the street along which this negligently appareled person was making his leisurely way. He greeted the landlord as he approached, cracked a joke in passing, and rambled on in his unhurried walk.

At the inn was an old gentleman from the country who had come to Richmond where a lawsuit, to which he was a party, was to be tried. The venerable litigant had a hundred dollars to pay to the lawyer who should conduct the case, a very large fee for those

[1] *Southern Literary Messenger*, 1836, ii, 181–91; also see Howe, 266.

days. Who was the best lawyer in Richmond, asked he of his host? "The man who just passed us, John Marshall by name," said the tavern-keeper. But the countryman would have none of Marshall. His appearance did not fill the old man's idea of a practitioner before the courts. He wanted, for his hundred dollars, a lawyer who looked like a lawyer. He would go to the court-room itself and there ask for further recommendation. But again he was told by the clerk of the court to retain Marshall, who, meanwhile, had ambled into the court-room.

But no! This searcher for a legal champion would use his own judgment. Soon a venerable, dignified person, solemn of face, with black coat and powdered wig, entered the room. At once the planter retained him. The client remained in the court-room, it appears, to listen to the lawyers in the other cases that were ahead of his own. Thus he heard the pompous advocate whom he had chosen; and then, in astonishment, listened to Marshall.

The attorney of impressive appearance turned out to be so inferior to the eccentric-looking advocate that the planter went to Marshall, frankly told him the circumstances, and apologized. Explaining that he had but five dollars left, the troubled old farmer asked Marshall whether he would conduct his case for that amount. With a kindly jest about the power of a black coat and a powdered wig, Marshall good-naturedly accepted.[1]

[1] *Southern Literary Messenger*, ii, 181–91; also Howe, 266. Apparently the older lawyer had been paid the one hundred dollars, for prepayment was customary in Virginia at the time. (See La Rochefoucauld, iii, 76.) This tale, fairly well authenticated, is so character-

This not too highly colored story is justified by all reports of Marshall that have come down to us. It is some such picture that we must keep before us as we follow this astonishing man in the henceforth easy and giant, albeit accidental, strides of his great career. John Marshall, after he had become the leading lawyer of Virginia, and, indeed, throughout his life, was the simple, unaffected man whom the tale describes. Perhaps consciousness of his own strength contributed to his disregard of personal appearance and contempt for studied manners. For Marshall knew that he carried heavier guns than other men. "No one," says Story, who knew him long and intimately, "ever possessed a more entire sense of his own extraordinary talents . . . than he."[1]

Marshall's most careful contemporary observer, William Wirt, tells us that Marshall was "in his person, tall, meagre, emaciated; his muscles relaxed and his joints so loosely connected, as not only to disqualify him, apparently, for any vigorous exertion of body, but to destroy everything like elegance and harmony in his air and movements.

"Indeed, in his whole appearance, and demeanour; dress, attitudes, gesture; sitting, standing, or walking; he is as far removed from the idolized graces of lord Chesterfield, as any other gentleman on earth.

"To continue the portrait; his head and face are small in proportion to his height; his complexion swarthy; the muscles of his face being relaxed; . . .

istic of Marshall that it is important. It visualizes the man as he really was. (See Jefferson's reference, in his letter to Madison, to Marshall's "lax, lounging manners," *supra*, 139.)

[1] Story, in Dillon, iii, 363.

his countenance has a faithful expression of great good humour and hilarity; while his black eyes — that unerring index — possess an irradiating spirit which proclaims the imperial powers of the mind that sits enthroned within. . . .

"His voice is dry, and hard; his attitude, in his most effective orations, often extremely awkward; as it was not unusual for him to stand with his left foot in advance, while all his gesture proceeded from his right arm, and consisted merely in a vehement, perpendicular swing of it from about the elevation of his head to the bar, behind which he was accustomed to stand." [1]

During all the years of clamorous happenings, from the great Virginia Convention of 1788 down to the beginning of Adams's Administration and in the midst of his own active part in the strenuous politics of the time, Marshall practiced his profession, although intermittently. However, during the critical three weeks of plot and plan, debate and oratory in the famous month of June, 1788, he managed to do some "law business": while Virginia's Constitutional Convention was in session, he received twenty fees, most of them of one and two pounds and the largest from "Col? W. Miles Cary 6.4." He drew a deed for his fellow member of the Convention, James Madison, while the Convention was in session, for which he charged his colleague one pound and four shillings.

But there was no time for card-playing during this notable month and no whist or backgammon en-

[1] Wirt: *The British Spy,* 110–12.

tries appear in Marshall's Account Book. Earlier in the year we find such social expenses as "Card table 5.10 Cards 8/ paper 2/–6" and "expenses and loss at billiards at dif[t] times 3" (pounds). In September, 1788, occurs the first entry for professional literature, "Law books 20/–1"; but a more important book purchase was that of "Mazai's book sur les etats unis [1] 18" (shillings), an entry which shows that some of Marshall's family could read French.[2]

Marshall's law practice during this pivotal year was fairly profitable. He thus sums up his earnings and outlay, "Rec[d] in the year 1788 1169.05; and expended in year 1788, 515–13–7" which left Marshall more than 653 pounds or about $1960 Virginia currency clear profit for the year.[3]

The following year (1789) he did a little better, his net profit being a trifle over seven hundred pounds, or about $2130 Virginia currency. In 1790 he earned a few shillings more than 1427 pounds and had about $2400 Virginia currency remaining, after paying all expenses. In 1791 he did not do so well, yet he cleared over $2200 Virginia currency. In 1792 his earnings fell off a good deal, yet he earned more than he expended, over 402 pounds (a little more than $1200 Virginia currency).

In 1793 Marshall was slightly more successful, but

[1] Mazzei's *Recherches sur les États-Unis,* published in this year (1788) in four volumes.

[2] Marshall himself could not read French at this time. (See *infra,* chap. VI.)

[3] In this chapter of Marshall's receipts and expenditures all items are from his Account Book, described in vol. I, chap. V, of this work.

his expenses also increased, and he ended this year with a trifle less than 400 pounds clear profit. He makes no summary in 1794, but his Account Book shows that he no more than held his own. This business barometer does not register beyond the end of 1795,[1] and there is no further evidence than the general understanding current in Richmond as to the amount of his earnings after this date. La Rochefoucauld reported in 1797 that "Mr. Marshall does not, from his practice, derive above four or five thousand dollars per annum and not even that sum every year."[2] We may take this as a trustworthy estimate of Marshall's income; for the noble French traveler and student was thorough in his inquiries and took great pains to verify his statements.

In 1789 Marshall bought the tract of land amounting to an entire city "square" of two acres,[3] on which, four years later, he built the comfortable brick residence where he lived, while in Richmond, during the remainder of his life. This house still stands (1916) and is in excellent repair. It contains nine rooms, most of them commodious, and one of them of generous dimensions where Marshall gave the "lawyer dinners" which, later, became so celebrated. This structure was one of a number of the important houses of Richmond.[4] Near by were the residences of Colonel Edward Carrington, Daniel Call, an ex-

[1] Marshall's third child, Mary, was born Sept. 17, of this year.

[2] La Rochefoucauld, iii, 75–76.

[3] Records, Henrico County, Virginia, Deed Book, iii, 74.

[4] In 1911 the City Council of Richmond presented this house to the Association for the Preservation of Virginia Antiquities, which now owns and occupies it.

cellent lawyer, and George Fisher, a wealthy merchant; these men had married the three sisters of Marshall's wife. The house of Jacquelin Ambler was also one of this cluster of dwellings. So that Marshall was in daily association with four men to whom he was related by marriage, a not negligible circumstance; for every one of them was a strong and successful man, and all of them were, like Marshall, pronounced Federalists. Their views and tastes were the same, they mutually aided and supported one another; and Marshall was, of course, the favorite of this unusual family group.

In the same locality lived the Leighs, Wickhams, Ronalds, and others, who, with those just mentioned, formed the intellectual and social aristocracy of the little city.[1] Richmond grew rapidly during the first two decades that Marshall lived there. From the village of a few hundred people abiding in small wooden houses, in 1783, the Capital became, in 1795, a vigorous town of six thousand inhabitants, dwelling mostly in attractive brick residences.[2] This architectural transformation was occasioned by a fire which, in 1787, destroyed most of the buildings in Richmond.[3] Business kept pace with the growth of the city, wealth gradually and healthfully accumulated, and the comforts of life appeared. Marshall steadily wove his activities into those of the developing Virginia metropolis and his prosperity increased in moderate and normal fashion.

[1] Mordecai, 63–70; and *ib.*, chap. vii.

[2] La Rochefoucauld, iii, 63. Negroes made up one third of the population.

[3] *Ib.*, 64; also Christian, 30.

In his personal business affairs Marshall showed a childlike faith in human nature which sometimes worked to his disadvantage. For instance, in 1790 he bought a considerable tract of land in Buckingham County, which was heavily encumbered by a deed of trust to secure "a debt of a former owner" of the land to Caron de Beaumarchais.[1] Marshall knew of this mortgage "at the time of the purchase, but he felt no concern . . . because" the seller verbally "promised to pay the debt and relieve the land from the incumbrance."

So he made the payments through a series of years, in spite of the fact that Beaumarchais's mortgage remained unsatisfied, that Marshall urged its discharge, and, finally, that disputes concerning it arose. Perhaps the fact that he was the attorney of the Frenchman in important litigation quieted apprehension. Beaumarchais having died, his agent, unable to collect the debt, was about to sell the land under the trust deed, unless Marshall would pay the obligation it secured. Thus, thirteen years after this improvident transaction, Marshall was forced to take the absurd tangle into a court of equity.[2]

But he was as careful of matters entrusted to him by others as this land transaction would suggest

[1] This celebrated French playwright and adventurer is soon to appear again at a dramatic moment of Marshall's life. (See *infra*, chaps. VI to VIII.)

[2] Marshall's bill in equity in the "High Court of Chancery sitting in Richmond," January 1, 1803; Chamberlin MSS., Boston Public Library. Marshall, then Chief Justice, personally drew this bill. After the Fairfax transaction, he seems to have left to his brother and partner, James M. Marshall, the practical handling of his business affairs.

that he was negligent of his own affairs. Especially was he in demand, it would seem, when an enterprise was to be launched which required public confidence for its success. For instance, the subscribers to a fire insurance company appointed him on the committee to examine the proposed plan of business and to petition the Legislature for a charter,[1] which was granted under the name of the "Mutual Assurance Society of Virginia." [2] Thus Marshall was a founder of one of the oldest American fire insurance companies.[3] Again, when in 1792 the "Bank of Virginia," a State institution, was organized,[4] Marshall was named as one of the committee to receive and approve subscriptions for stock.[5]

No man could have been more watchful than was Marshall of the welfare of members of his family. At one of the most troubled moments of his life, when greatly distressed by combined business and political complications,[6] he notes a love affair of his sister and, unasked, carefully reviews the eligibility of her suitor. Writing to his brother James on business and politics, he says: —

"I understand that my sister Jane, while here [Richmond], was addressed by Major Taylor and that his addresses were encouraged by her. I am not by any means certain of the fact nor did I suspect

1 Memorial of William F. Ast and others; MS. Archives, Va. St. Lib.

2 Christian, 46.

3 This company is still doing business in Richmond.

4 Christian, 46.

5 The enterprise appears not to have filled the public with investing enthusiasm and no subscriptions to it were received.

6 See *infra*, chap. x.

it until we had separated the night preceding her departure and consequently I could have no conversation with her concerning it.

"I believe that tho' Major Taylor was attach'd to her, it would probably have had no serious result if Jane had not manifested some partiality for him. This affair embarrasses me a good deal. Major Taylor is a young gentleman of talents and integrity for whom I profess and feel a real friendship. There is no person with whom I should be better pleased if there were not other considerations which ought not to be overlook'd. Mr. Taylor possesses but little if any fortune, he is encumbered with a family, and does not like his profession. Of course he will be as eminent in his profession as his talents entitle him to be. These are facts unknown to my sister but which ought to be known to her.

"Had I conjectured that Mr. Taylor was contemplated in the character of a lover I shou'd certainly have made to her all proper communications. I regret that it was concealed from me. I have a sincere and real affection and esteem for Major Taylor but I think it right in affairs of this sort that the real situation of the parties should be mutually understood. Present me affectionately to my sister." [1]

[1] Marshall to James M. Marshall, April 3, 1799; MS. This was the only one of Marshall's sisters then unmarried. She was twenty years of age at this time and married Major George Keith Taylor within a few months. He was a man of unusual ability and high character and became very successful in his profession. In 1801 he was appointed by President Adams, United States Judge for a Virginia district. (See *infra*, chap. XII.) The union of Mr. Taylor and Jane Marshall turned out to be very happy indeed. (Paxton, 77.)

Compare this letter of Marshall with that of Washington to his niece,

From the beginning of his residence in Richmond, Marshall had been an active member of the Masonic Order. He had become a Free Mason while in the Revolutionary army,[1] which abounded in camp lodges. It was due to his efforts as City Recorder of Richmond that a lottery was successfully conducted to raise funds for the building of a Masonic hall in the State Capital in 1785.[2] The following year Marshall was appointed Deputy Grand Master. In 1792 he presided over the Grand Lodge as Grand Master *pro tempore;* and the next year he was chosen as the head of the order in Virginia. He was reëlected as Grand Master in 1794; and presided over the meetings of the Grand Lodge held during 1793 until 1795 inclusive. During the latter year the Masonic hall in Manchester was begun and he assisted in the ceremonies attending the laying of the corner-stone, which bore this inscription: "This stone was laid by the Worshipful Archibald Campbell, Master of the Manchester Lodge of free & accepted Masons Assisted by & in the presence of the Most Worshipful John Marshall Grand Master of Masons to Virginia."[3]

Upon the expiration of his second term in this office, the Grand Lodge "Resolved, that the Grand Lodge are truly sensible of the great attention of our late Grand Master, John Marshall, to the duties of Masonry, and that they entertain an high sense

in which he gives extensive advice on the subject of love and marriage. (Washington to Eleanor Parke Custis, Jan. 16, 1795; *Writings:* Ford, xiii, 29–32.)

[1] Marshall to Everett, July 22, 1833.

[2] Christian, 28.

[3] *Richmond and Manchester Advertiser*, Sept. 24, 1795.

of the wisdom displayed by him in the discharge of the duties of his office; and as a token of their entire approbation of his conduct do direct the Grand Treasurer to procure and present him with an elegant Past Master's jewel." [1]

From 1790 until his election to Congress, nine years later,[2] Marshall argued one hundred and thirteen cases decided by the Court of Appeals of Virginia. Notwithstanding his almost continuous political activity, he appeared, during this time, in practically every important cause heard and determined by the supreme tribunal of the State. Whenever there was more than one attorney for the client who retained Marshall, the latter almost invariably was reserved to make the closing argument. His absorbing mind took in everything said or suggested by counsel who preceded him; and his logic easily marshaled the strongest arguments to support his position and crushed or threw aside as unimportant those advanced against him.

Marshall preferred to close rather than open an argument. He wished to hear all that other counsel might have to say before he spoke himself; for, as has appeared, he was but slightly equipped with legal learning [3] and he informed himself from the knowledge displayed by his adversaries. Even after he had become Chief Justice of the Supreme Court of the United States and throughout his long and epochal occupancy of that high place, Marshall

[1] *Proceedings* of the M. W. Grand Lodge of Ancient York Masons of the State of Virginia, from 1778 to 1822, by John Dove, i, 144; see also 121, 139.

[2] See *infra*, chap. x.

[3] See vol. I, chap. v, of this work.

showed this same peculiarity which was so prominent in his practice at the bar.

Every contemporary student of Marshall's method and equipment notes the meagerness of his learning in the law. "Everyone has heard of the gigantick abilities of John Marshall; as a most able and profound reasoner he deserves all the praise which has been lavished upon him," writes Francis Walker Gilmer, in his keen and brilliant contemporary analysis of Marshall. "His mind is not very richly stored with knowledge," he continues, "but it is so creative, so well organized by nature, or disciplined by early education, and constant habits of systematick thinking, that he embraces every subject with the clearness and facility of one prepared by previous study to comprehend and explain it." [1]

Gustavus Schmidt, who was a competent critic of legal attainments and whose study of Marshall as a lawyer was painstaking and thorough, bears witness to Marshall's scanty acquirements. "Mr. Marshall," says Schmidt, "can hardly be regarded as a learned lawyer. . . . His acquaintance with the Roman jurisprudence as well as with the laws of foreign countries was not very extensive. He was what is called a common law lawyer in the best & noblest acceptation of that term."

Mr. Schmidt attempts to excuse Marshall's want of those legal weapons which knowledge of the books supply.

"He was educated for the bar," writes Schmidt, "at a period when digests, abridgments & all the

[1] Gilmer, 23–24.

numerous facilities, which now smooth the path of the law student were almost unknown & when you often sought in vain in the Reporters which usually wore the imposing form of folios, even for an index of the decisions & when marginal notes of the points determined in a case was a luxury not to be either looked for or expected.

"At this period when the principles of the Common Law had to be studied in the black-letter pages of Coke upon Littleton, a work equally remarkable for quaintness of expression, profundity of research and the absence of all method in the arrangements of its very valuable materials; when the rules of pleading had to be looked for in Chief Justice Saunders's Reports, while the doctrinal parts of the jurisprudence, based almost exclusively on the precedents had to be sought after in the reports of Dyer, Plowden, Coke, Popham. . . . it was . . . no easy task to become an able lawyer & it required no common share of industry and perseverance to amass sufficient knowledge of the law to make even a decent appearance in the forum."[1]

It would not be strange, therefore, if Marshall did cite very few authorities in the scores of cases argued by him. But it seems certain that he would not have relied upon the "learning of the law" in any event; for at a later period, when precedents were more abundant and accessible, he still ignored them. Even in these early years other counsel exhibited the results of much research; but not so Marshall. In most of his arguments, as reported in volumes one,

[1] Gustavus Schmidt, in *Louisiana Law Journal* (1841), 81–82.

two, and four of Call's Virginia Reports and in volumes one and two of Washington's Virginia Reports,[1] he depended on no authority whatever. Frequently when the arguments of his associates and of opposing counsel show that they had explored the whole field of legal learning on the subject in hand, Marshall referred to no precedent.[2] The strongest feature of his argument was his statement of the case.

The multitude of cases which Marshall argued before the General Court of Appeals and before the High Court of Chancery at Richmond covered every possible subject of litigation at that time. He lost almost as frequently as he won. Out of one hundred and twenty-one cases reported, Marshall was on the winning side sixty-two times and on the losing side fifty times. In two cases he was partly successful and partly unsuccessful, and in seven it is impossible to tell from the reports what the outcome was.

Once Marshall appeared for clients whose cause was so weak that the court decided against him on his own argument, refusing to hear opposing counsel.[3] He was extremely frank and honest with the

[1] For a list of cases argued by Marshall and reported in Call and Washington, with title of case, date, volume, and page, see Appendix I.

[2] A good illustration of a brilliant display of legal learning by associate and opposing counsel, and Marshall's distaste for authorities when he could do without them, is the curious and interesting case of Coleman *vs.* Dick and Pat, decided in 1793, and reported in 1 Washington, 233. Wickham for appellant and Campbell for appellee cited ancient laws and treaties as far back as 1662. Marshall cited no authority whatever.

[3] See Stevens *vs.* Taliaferro, Adm'r, 1 Washington, 155, Spring Term, 1793.

court, and on one occasion went so far as to say that the opposing counsel was in the right and himself in the wrong.[1] "My own opinion," he admitted to the court in this case, "is that the law is correctly stated by Mr. Ronald [the opposing counsel], but the point has been otherwise determined in the General Court." Marshall, of course, lost.[2]

Nearly all the cases in which Marshall was engaged concerned property rights. Only three or four of the controversies in which he took part involved criminal law. A considerable part of the litigation in which he was employed was intricate and involved; and in this class of cases his lucid and orderly mind made him the intellectual master of the contending lawyers. Marshall's ability to extract from the confusion of the most involved question its vital elements and to state those elements in simple terms was helpful to the court, and frankly appreciated by the judges.

Few letters of Marshall to his fellow lawyers written during this period are extant. Most of these are very brief and confined strictly to the particular cases which he had been retained by his associate attorneys throughout Virginia to conduct before the Court of Appeals. Occasionally, however, his humor breaks forth.

"I cannot appear for Donaghoe," writes Marshall to a country member of the bar who lived in the Valley over the mountains. "I do not decline his business from any objection to his *bank*. To that I should like very well to have free access & wou'd certainly

[1] Johnson *vs.* Bourn, 1 Washington, 187, Spring Term, 1793. [2] *Ib.*

discount *from* it as largely as he wou'd permit, but I am already fixed by Rankin & as those who are once in the bank do not I am told readily get out again I despair of being ever able to touch the guineas of Donaghoe.

"Shall we never see you again in Richmond? I was very much rejoiced when I heard that you were happily married but if that amounts to a ne exeat which is to confine you entirely to your side of the mountain, I shall be selfish enough to regret your good fortune & almost wish you had found some little crooked rib among the fish and oysters which would once a year drag you into this part of our terraqueous globe.

"You have forgotten I believe the solemn compact we made to take a journey to Philadelphia together this winter and superintend for a while the proceedings of Congress."[1]

Again, writing to Stuart concerning a libel suit, Marshall says: "Whether the truth of the libel may be justified or not is a perfectly unsettled question. If in that respect the law here varies from the law of England it must be because such is the will of their Honors for I know of no legislative act to vary it. It will however be right to appeal was it only to secure a compromise."[2]

Marshall's sociableness and love of play made him the leader of the Barbecue Club, consisting of thirty of the most agreeable of the prominent men in Richmond. Membership in this club was eagerly

[1] Marshall to Archibald Stuart, March 27, 1794; MS., Va. Hist. Soc.
[2] *Ib.*, May 28, 1794.

sought and difficult to secure, two negatives being sufficient to reject a candidate. Meetings were held each Saturday, in pleasant weather, at "the springs" on the farm of Mr. Buchanan, the Episcopal clergyman. There a generous meal was served and games played, quoits being the favorite sport. One such occasion of which there is a trustworthy account shows the humor, the wit, and the good-fellowship of Marshall.

He welcomed the invited guests, Messrs. Blair and Buchanan, the famous "Two Parsons" of Richmond, and then announced that a fine of a basket of champagne, imposed on two members for talking politics at a previous meeting of the club, had been paid and that the wine was at hand. It was drunk from tumblers and the Presbyterian minister joked about the danger of those who "drank from tumblers *on* the table becoming tumblers *under* the table." Marshall challenged "Parson" Blair to a game of quoits, each selecting four partners. His quoits were big, rough, heavy iron affairs that nobody else could throw, those of the other players being smaller and of polished brass. Marshall rang the meg and Blair threw his quoit directly over that of his opponent. Loud were the cries of applause and a great controversy arose as to which player had won. The decision was left to the club with the understanding that when the question was determined they should "crack another bottle of champagne."

Marshall argued his own case with great solemnity and elaboration. The one first ringing the meg must be deemed the winner, unless his adversary knocked off the first quoit and put his own in its place. This required perfection, which Blair did not possess. Blair claimed to have won by being on top of Marshall; but suppose he tried to reach heaven "by riding on my back," asked Marshall. "I fear that from my many backslidings and deficiencies, he may be badly disappointed." Blair's method was like playing leap frog, said he. And did anybody play backgammon in that way? Also there was the ancient legal maxim, "*Cujus est solum, ejus est usque ad cœlum*": being "the first occupant his right extended from the ground up to the vault of heaven and no one had a right to become a squatter on his back." If Blair had any claim "he must obtain a writ of ejectment or drive him [Marshall] from his position *vi et armis*." Marshall then cited the boys' game of marbles and, by analogy, proved that he had won and should be given the verdict of the club.

Wickham argued at length that the judgment of the club should be that "where two adversary quoits are on the same meg, neither is victorious." Marshall's quoit was so big and heavy that no ordinary quoit could move it and "no rule requires an impossibility." As to Marshall's insinuation that Blair was trying to reach "Elysium by mounting on his back," it was plain to the club that such was not the parson's intention, but that he meant only to get a more elevated view of earthly things. Also Blair, by "riding on that pinnacle," will be apt to arrive in time at the upper round of the ladder of fame. The legal maxim cited by Marshall was really against his claim, since the ground belonged to Mr. Buchanan and Marshall was as much of a "squatter" as Blair was. "The first squatter was no better than the second." And why did Marshall talk of ejecting him by force of arms? Everybody knew that "parsons are men of peace and do not vanquish their antagonists *vi et armis.* We do not deserve to prolong this riding on Mr. Marshall's back; he is too much of a *Rosinante* to make the ride agreeable." The club declined to consider seriously Marshall's comparison of the manly game of quoits with the boys' game of marbles, for had not one of the clergymen present preached a sermon on "marvel not"? There was no analogy to quoits in Marshall's citation of leap frog nor of backgammon; and Wickham closed, amid the cheers of the club, by pointing out the difference between quoits and leap frog.

The club voted with impressive gravity, taking care to make the vote as even as possible and finally determined that the disputed throw was a draw. The game was resumed and Marshall won.[1]

Such were Marshall's diversions when an attorney at Richmond. His "lawyer dinners" at his house,[2] his card playing at Farmicola's tavern, his quoit-throwing and pleasant foolery at the Barbecue Club, and other similar amusements which served to take his mind from the grave problems on which, at other times, it was constantly working, were continued, as we shall see, and with increasing zest, after he became the world's leading jurist-statesman of his time. But neither as lawyer nor judge did these wholesome frivolities interfere with his serious work.

[1] Munford, 326–38.

[2] See vol. III of this work.

Marshall's first case of nation-wide interest, in which his argument gave him fame among lawyers throughout the country, was the historic controversy over the British debts. When Congress enacted the Judiciary Law of 1789 and the National Courts were established, British creditors at once began action to recover their long overdue debts. During the Revolution, other States as well as Virginia had passed laws confiscating the debts which their citizens owed British subjects and sequestering British property.

Under these laws, debtors could cancel their obligations in several ways. The Treaty of Peace between the United States and Great Britain provided, among other things, that "It is agreed that creditors on either side shall meet with no legal impediments to the recovery of the full value in sterling money of all bona fide debts heretofore contracted." The Constitution provided that "All treaties made, or which shall be made, under the authority of the United States, shall be the supreme law of the land; and the judges in every State shall be bound thereby, anything in the Constitution or laws of any State to the contrary notwithstanding,"[1] and that "The judicial power shall extend to all cases in law and equity arising under this Constitution, the laws of the United States, and treaties made, or which shall be made, under their authority; to all cases . . . between a State, or the citizens thereof, and foreign States citizens, or subjects."[2]

Thus the case of Ware, Administrator, *vs.* Hylton

[1] Constitution of the United States, article vi.

[2] *Ib.*, article iii, section 2.

et al., which involved the validity of a State law in conflict with a treaty, attracted the attention of the whole country when finally it reached the Supreme Court. The question in that celebrated controversy was whether a State law, suspending the collection of a debt due to a subject of Great Britain, was valid as against the treaty which provided that no "legal impediment" should prevent the recovery of the obligation.

Ware *vs.* Hylton was a test case; and its decision involved immense sums of money. Large numbers of creditors who had sought to cancel their debts under the confiscation laws were vitally interested. Marshall, in this case, made the notable argument that carried his reputation as a lawyer beyond Virginia and won for him the admiration of the ablest men at the bar, regardless of their opinion of the merits of the controversy.

It is an example of "the irony of fate" that in this historic legal contest Marshall supported the theory which he had opposed throughout his public career thus far, and to demolish which his entire after life was given. More remarkable still, his efforts for his clients were opposed to his own interests; for, had he succeeded for those who employed him, he would have wrecked the only considerable business transaction in which he ever engaged.[1] He was employed by the debtors to uphold those laws of Virginia which sequestered British property and prevented the collection of the British debts; and he put forth all his power in this behalf.

[1] The Fairfax deal; see *infra*, 203 *et seq.*

Three such cases were pending in Virginia; and these were heard twice by the National Court in Richmond as a consolidated cause, the real issue being the same in all. The second hearing was during the May Term of 1793 before Chief Justice Jay, Justice Iredell of the Supreme Court, and Judge Griffin of the United States District Court. The attorneys for the British creditors were William Ronald, John Baker, John Stark, and John Wickham. For the defendants were Alexander Campbell, James Innes, Patrick Henry, and John Marshall. Thus we see Marshall, when thirty-six years of age, after ten years of practice at the Richmond bar, interrupted as those years were by politics and legislative activities, one of the group of lawyers who, for power, brilliancy, and learning, were unsurpassed in America.

The argument at the Richmond hearing was a brilliant display of eloquence, reasoning, and erudition, and, among lawyers, its repute has reached even to the present day. Counsel on both sides exerted every ounce of their strength. When Patrick Henry had finished his appeal, Justice Iredell was so overcome that he cried, "Gracious God! He is an orator indeed!"[1] The Countess of Huntingdon, who was then in Richmond and heard the arguments of all the attorneys, declared: "If every one had spoken in Westminster Hall, they would have been honored with a peerage."[2]

In his formal opinion, Justice Iredell thus expressed his admiration: "The cause has been spoken to, at the bar, with a degree of ability equal to any

[1] Henry, ii, 475. [2] Howe, 221–22.

occasion. . . . I shall as long as I live, remember with pleasure and respect the arguments which I have heard on this case: they have discovered an ingenuity, a depth of investigation, and a power of reasoning fully equal to anything I have ever witnessed. . . . Fatigue has given way under its influence; the heart has been warmed, while the understanding has been instructed." [1]

Marshall's argument before the District Court of Richmond must have impressed his debtor clients more than that of any other of their distinguished counsel, with the single exception of Alexander Campbell; for when, on appeal to the Supreme Court of the United States, the case came on for hearing in 1796, we find that only Marshall and Campbell appeared for the debtors.

It is unfortunate that Marshall's argument before the Supreme Court at Philadelphia is very poorly reported. But inadequate as the report is, it still reveals the peculiar clearness and the compact and simple reasoning which made up the whole of Marshall's method, whether in legal arguments, political speeches, diplomatic letters, or judicial opinions.

Marshall argued that the Virginia law barred the recovery of the debts regardless of the treaty. "It has been conceded," said he, "that independent

[1] 3 Dallas, 256–57, and footnote. In his opinion Justice Iredell decided for the debtors. When the Supreme Court of the United States, of which he was a member, reversed him in Philadelphia, the following year, Justice Iredell, pursuant to a practice then existing, and on the advice of his brother justices, placed his original opinion on record along with those of Justices Chase, Paterson, Wilson, and Cushing, each of whom delivered separate opinions in favor of the British creditors.

nations have, in general, the right to confiscation; and that Virginia, at the time of passing her law, was an independent nation." A State engaged in war has the powers of war, "and confiscation is one of those powers, weakening the party against whom it is employed and strengthening the party that employs it." Nations have equal powers; and, from July 4, 1776, America was as independent a nation as Great Britain. What would have happened if Great Britain had been victorious? "Sequestration, confiscation, and proscription would have followed in the train of that event," asserted Marshall.

Why, then, he asked, "should the confiscation of British property be deemed less just in the event of an American triumph?" Property and its disposition is not a natural right, but the "creature of civil society, and subject in all respects to the disposition and control of civil institutions." Even if "an individual has not the power of extinguishing his debts," still "the community to which he belongs . . . may . . . upon principles of public policy, prevent his creditors from recovering them." The ownership and control of property "is the offspring of the social state; not the incident of a state of nature. But the Revolution did not reduce the inhabitants of America to a state of nature; and if it did, the plaintiff's claim would be at an end." Virginia was within her rights when she confiscated these debts.

As an independent nation Virginia could do as she liked, declared Marshall. Legally, then, at the time of the Treaty of Peace in 1783, "the defendant owed nothing to the plaintiff." Did the treaty revive the debt thus extinguished? No: For the treaty provides "that creditors on either side shall meet with no lawful impediment to the recovery" of their debts. Who are the creditors? "There cannot be a creditor where there is not a debt; and the British debts were extinguished by the act of confiscation," which was entirely legal.

Plainly, then, argued Marshall, the treaty "must be construed with reference to those creditors" whose debts had not been extinguished by the sequestration laws. There were cases of such debts and it was to these only that the treaty applied. The Virginia law must have been known to the commissioners who made the treaty; and it was unthinkable that they should attempt to repeal those laws in the treaty without using plain words to that effect.

Such is an outline of Marshall's argument, as inaccurately and defectively reported.[1]

Cold and dry as it appears in the reporter's notes, Marshall's address to the Supreme Court made a tremendous impression on all who heard it. When he left the court-room, he was followed by admiring crowds. The ablest public men at the Capital were watching Marshall narrowly and these particularly were captivated by his argument. "His head is one of the best organized of any one that I have known," writes the keenly observant King, a year later, in giving to Pinckney his estimate of Marshall. "This I say from general Reputation, and more satisfactorily from an Argument that I heard him de-

[1] For Marshall's argument in the British Debts case before the Supreme Court, see 3 Dallas, 199–285.

liver before the fed'l Court at Philadelphia." [1] King's judgment of Marshall's intellectual strength was that generally held.

Marshall's speech had a more enduring effect on those who listened to it than any other address he ever made, excepting that on the Jonathan Robins case.[2] Twenty-four years afterwards William Wirt, then at the summit of his brilliant career, advising Francis Gilmer upon the art of oratory, recalled Marshall's argument in the British Debts case as an example for Gilmer to follow. Wirt thus contrasts Marshall's method with that of Campbell on the same occasion: —

"Campbell played off all his Apollonian airs; but they were lost. Marshall spoke, as he always does, to the judgment merely and for the simple purpose of convincing. Marshall was justly pronounced one of the greatest men of the country; he was followed by crowds, looked upon, and courted with every evidence of admiration and respect for the great powers of his mind. Campbell was neglected and slighted, and came home in disgust.

"Marshall's maxim seems always to have been, 'aim exclusively *at Strength:*' and from his eminent success, I say, if I had my life to go over again, I would practice on his maxim with the most rigorous severity, until the character of my mind was established." [3]

[1] King to Pinckney, Oct. 17, 1797; King, ii, 234–35. King refers to the British Debts case, the only one in which Marshall had made an argument before the Supreme Court up to this time.

[2] See *infra*, chap. XI.

[3] Kennedy, ii, 76. Mr. Wirt remembered the argument well; but twenty-four years having elapsed, he had forgotten the case in which

In another letter to Gilmer, Wirt again urges his son-in-law to imitate Marshall's style. In his early career Wirt had suffered in his own arguments from too much adornment which detracted from the real solidity and careful learning of his efforts at the bar. And when, finally, in his old age he had, through his own mistakes, learned the value of simplicity in statement and clear logic in argument, he counseled young Gilmer accordingly.

"In your arguments at the bar," he writes, "*let argument strongly predominate*. Sacrifice your flowers. . . . Avoid as you would the gates of death, the reputation for floridity. . . . Imitate . . . Marshall's simple process of reasoning." [1]

Following the advice of his distinguished brother-in-law, Gilmer studied Marshall with the hungry zeal of ambitious youth. Thus it is that to Francis Gilmer we owe what is perhaps the truest analysis, made by a personal observer, of Marshall's method as advocate and orator.

"So perfect is his analysis," records Gilmer, "that he extracts the whole matter, the kernel of the inquiry, unbroken, undivided, clean and entire. In this process, such is the instinctive neatness and precision of his mind that no superfluous thought, or even word, ever presents itself and still

it was made. He says that it was the Carriage Tax case and that Hamilton was one of the attorneys. But it was the British Debts case and Hamilton's name does not appear in the records.

[1] Kennedy, ii, 66. Francis W. Gilmer was then the most brilliant young lawyer in Virginia. His health became too frail for the hard work of the law; and his early death was universally mourned as the going out of the brightest light among the young men of the Old Dominion.

he says everything that seems appropriate to the subject.

"This perfect exemption from any unnecessary encumbrance of matter or ornament, is in some degree the effect of an aversion for the labour of thinking. So great a mind, perhaps, like large bodies in the physical world, is with difficulty set in motion. That this is the case with Mr. Marshall's is manifest, from his mode of entering on an argument both in conversation and in publick debate.

"It is difficult to rouse his faculties; he begins with reluctance, hesitation, and vacancy of eye; presently his articulation becomes less broken, his eye more fixed, until finally, his voice is full, clear, and rapid, his manner bold, and his whole face lighted up, with the mingled fires of genius and passion; and he pours forth the unbroken stream of eloquence, in a current deep, majestick, smooth, and strong.

"He reminds one of some great bird, which flounders and flounces on the earth for a while before it acquires the impetus to sustain its soaring flight.

"The characteristick of his eloquence is an irresistible cogency, and a luminous simplicity in the order of his reasoning. His arguments are remarkable for their separate and independent strength, and for the solid, compact, impenetrable order in which they are arrayed.

"He certainly possesses in an eminent degree the power which had been ascribed to him, of mastering the most complicated subjects with facility, and when moving with his full momentum, even without the appearance of resistance."

Comparing Marshall and Randolph, Gilmer says: —

"The powers of these two gentlemen are strikingly contrasted by nature. In Mr. Marshall's speeches, all is reasoning; in Mr. Randolph's everything is declamation. The former scarcely uses a figure; the latter hardly an abstraction. One is awkward; the other graceful.

"One is indifferent as to his words, and slovenly in his pronunciation; the other adapts his phrases to the sense with poetick felicity; his voice to the sound with musical exactness.

"There is no breach in the train of Mr. Marshall's thoughts; little connection between Mr. Randolph's. Each has his separate excellence, but either is far from being a finished orator." [1]

Another invaluable first-hand analysis of Marshall's style and manner of argument is that of William Wirt, himself, in the vivacious descriptions of "The British Spy": —

"He possesses one original, and, almost supernatural faculty, the faculty of developing a subject by a single glance of his mind, and detecting at once, the very point on which every controversy depends. No matter what the question; though ten times more knotty than 'the gnarled oak,' the lightning of heaven is not more rapid nor more resistless, than his astonishing penetration.

"Nor does the exercise of it seem to cost him an effort. On the contrary, it is as easy as vision. I am persuaded that his eye does not fly over a landscape and take in its various objects with more prompti-

[1] Gilmer, 23–24.

tude and facility, than his mind embraces and analyses the most complex subject.

"Possessing while at the bar this intellectual elevation, which enabled him to look down and comprehend the whole ground at once, he determined immediately and without difficulty, on which side the question might be most advantageously approached and assailed.

"In a bad cause his art consisted in laying his premises so remotely from the point directly in debate, or else in terms so general and so spacious, that the hearer, seeing no consequence which could be drawn from them, was just as willing to admit them as not; but his premises once admitted, the demonstration, however distant, followed as certainly, as cogently, as inevitably, as any demonstration in Euclid."[1]

Marshall's supremacy, now unchallenged, at the Virginia bar was noted by foreign observers. La Rochefoucauld testifies to this in his exhaustive volumes of travel: —

"Mr. J. Marshall, conspicuously eminent as a professor of the law, is beyond all doubt one of those who rank highest in the public opinion at Richmond. He is what is termed a federalist, and perhaps somewhat warm in support of his opinions, but never exceeding the bounds of propriety, which a man of his goodness and prudence and knowledge is incapable of transgressing.

"He may be considered as a distinguished character in the United States. His political enemies

[1] Wirt: *The British Spy*, 112–13.

allow him to possess great talents but accuse him of ambition. I know not whether the charge be well or ill grounded, or whether that ambition might ever be able to impel him to a dereliction of his principles — a conduct of which I am inclined to disbelieve the possibility on his part.

"He has already refused several employments under the general government, preferring the income derived from his professional labours (which is more than sufficient for his moderate system of economy), together with a life of tranquil ease in the midst of his family and in his native town.

"Even by his friends he is taxed with some little propensity to indolence; but even if this reproach were well founded, he nevertheless displays great superiority in his profession when he applies his mind to business." [1]

When Jefferson foresaw Marshall's permanent transfer to public life he advised James Monroe to practice law in Richmond because "the business is very profitable; [2] . . . and an opening of great importance must be made by the retirement of Marshall." [3]

[1] La Rochefoucauld, iii, 120. Doubtless La Rochefoucauld would have arrived at the above conclusion in any event, since his estimate of Marshall is borne out by every contemporary observer; but it is worthy of note that the Frenchman while in Richmond spent much of his time in Marshall's company. (*Ib.*, 119.)

[2] *Ib.*, 75. "The profession of a lawyer is . . . one of the most profitable. . . . In Virginia the lawyers usually take care to insist on payment before they proceed in a suit; and this custom is justified by the general disposition of the inhabitants to pay as little and as seldom as possible."

[3] Jefferson to Monroe, Feb. 8, 1798; *Works:* Ford, viii, 365. Marshall was in France at the time. (See *infra*, chaps. VI to VIII inclusive.)

Marshall's solid and brilliant performance in the British Debts case before the Supreme Court at Philadelphia did much more than advance him in his profession. It also focused upon him the keen scrutiny of the politicians and statesmen who at that time were in attendance upon Congress in the Quaker City. Particularly did the strength and personality of the Virginia advocate impress the Federalist leaders.

These vigilant men had learned of Marshall's daring championship of the Jay Treaty in hostile Virginia. And although in the case of Ware *vs.* Hylton, Marshall was doing his utmost as a lawyer before the Supreme Court to defeat the collection of the British debts, yet his courageous advocacy of the Jay Treaty outweighed, in their judgment, his professional labors in behalf of the clients who had employed him.

The Federalist leaders were in sore need of Southern support; and when Marshall was in Philadelphia on the British Debts case, they were prompt and unsparing in their efforts to bind this strong and able man to them by personal ties. Marshall himself unwittingly testifies to this. "I then [during this professional visit to Philadelphia] became acquainted," he relates, "with Mr. Cabot, Mr. Ames, Mr. Dexter, and Mr. Sedgwick of Massachusetts, Mr. Wadsworth of Connecticut, and Mr. King of New York. I was delighted with these gentlemen. The particular subject (the British Treaty) which introduced me to their notice was at that time so interesting, and a Virginian who supported, with any sort of reputation, the measures of the government, was such a *rara avis*, that I was received by them all with a degree of kindness which I had not anticipated. I was particularly intimate with Mr. Ames, and could scarcely gain credit with him when I assured him that the appropriations [to effectuate the treaty] would be seriously opposed in Congress." [1]

As we shall presently see, Marshall became associated with Robert Morris in the one great business undertaking of the former's life. Early in this transaction when, for Marshall, the skies were still clear of financial clouds, he appears to have made a small purchase of bank stock and ventured modestly into the commercial field. "I have received your letter of 18 ulto," Morris writes Marshall, "& am negotiating for Bank Stock to answer your demand." [2]

And again: "I did not succeed in the purchase of the Bank Stock mentioned in my letter of the 3^d^ Ulto to you and as Mr Richard tells me in his letter of the 4 Inst that you want the money for the Stock, you may if you please draw upon me for $7000 giving me as much time in the sight as you can, and I will most certainly pay your drafts as they become due. The Brokers shall fix the price of the Stock at the market price at the time I pay the money & I will then state the Am^t^ including Dividends & remit you the Balance but if you prefer having the Stock

[1] Story, in Dillon, iii, 354. Ware *vs.* Hylton was argued Feb. 6, 8, 9, 10, 11, and 12. The fight against the bill to carry out the Jay Treaty did not begin in the National House of Representatives until March 7, 1796.

[2] Morris to Marshall, May 3, 1796; Morris's Private Letter Book; MS., Lib. Cong. The stock referred to in this correspondence is probably that of the Bank of the United States.

I will buy it on receiving your Answer to this, cost what it may." [1]

Soon afterward, Morris sent Marshall the promised shares of stock, apparently to enable him to return shares to some person in Richmond from whom he had borrowed them.

"You will receive herewith enclosed the Certificates for four shares of Bank Stock of the United States placed in your name to enable you to return the four shares to the Gentlemen of whom you borrowed them, this I thought better than remitting the money lest some difficulty should arise about price of shares. Two other shares in the name of Mr Geo Pickett is also enclosed herewith and I will go on buying and remitting others untill the number of Ten are completed for him which shall be done before the time limited in your letter of the 12^h Ins^t The dividends shall also be remitted speedily." [2]

Again Washington desired Marshall to fill an important public office, this time a place on the joint commission, provided for in the Jay Treaty, to settle the British claims. These, as we have seen, had been for many years a source of grave trouble between the two countries. Their satisfactory adjustment would mean, not only the final settlement of this serious controversy, but the removal of an ever-present cause of war.[3] But since Marshall had re-

[1] Morris to Marshall, June 16, 1796; Morris's Private Letter Book; MS., Lib. Cong.

[2] Morris to Marshall, Aug. 24, 1796; *ib.*

[3] The commission failed and war was narrowly averted by the payment of a lump sum to Great Britain. It is one of the curious turns of

fused appointment to three offices tendered him by Washington, the President did not now communicate with him directly, but inquired of Charles Lee, Attorney-General of Virginia, whether Marshall might be prevailed upon to accept this weighty and delicate business.

"I have very little doubt," replied Lee, "that Mr. John Marshall would not act as a Commissioner under the Treaty with Great Britain, for deciding on the claims of creditors. I have been long acquainted with his private affairs, and I think it almost impossible for him to undertake that office. If he would, I know not any objection that subsists against him.

"First, he is not a debtor.[1] Secondly, he cannot be benefitted or injured by any decision of the Commissioners. Thirdly, his being employed as counsel, in suits of that kind, furnishes no reasonable objection; nor do I know of any opinions that he has published, or professes, that might, with a view of impartiality, make him liable to be objected to.

"Mr. Marshall is at the head of his profession in Virginia, enjoying every convenience and comfort; in the midst of his friends and the relations of his wife at Richmond; in a practice of his profession that annually produces about five thousand dollars on an average; with a young and increasing family; and under a degree of necessity to continue his pro-

history that Marshall, as Secretary of State, made the proposition that finally concluded the matter and that Jefferson consummated the transaction. (See *infra*, chap. XII.)

[1] Lee means a debtor under the commission. Marshall was a debtor to Fairfax. (See *infra*.)

fession, for the purpose of complying with contracts not yet performed." [1]

The "contracts" which Marshall had to fulfill concerned the one important financial adventure of his life. It was this, and not, as some suppose, the condition of his invalid wife, to which Marshall vaguely referred in his letter to Washington declining appointment as Attorney-General and as Minister to France.

The two decades following the establishment of the National Government under the Constitution were years of enormous land speculation. Hardly a prominent man of the period failed to secure large tracts of real estate, which could be had at absurdly low prices, and to hold the lands for the natural advance which increasing population would bring. The greatest of these investors was Robert Morris, the financier of the Revolution, the second richest man of the time,[2] and the leading business man of the country.

[1] Lee to Washington, March 20, 1796; *Cor. Rev.*: Sparks, iv, 481–82.

[2] William Bingham of Philadelphia was reputed to be "the richest man of his time." (Watson: *Annals of Philadelphia* i. 414.) Chastellux estimates Morris's wealth at the close of the Revolution at 8,000,000 francs. (Chastellux, 107.) He increased his fortune many fold from the close of the war to 1796.

The operations of Robert Morris in land were almost without limit. For instance, one of the smaller items of his purchases was 199,480 acres in Burke County, North Carolina. (Robert Morris to James M. Marshall, Sept. 24, 1795; Morris's Private Letter Book; MS., Lib. Cong.)

Another example of Morris's scattered and detached deals was his purchase of a million acres "lying on the western counties of Virginia . . . purchased of William Cary Nicholas. . . . I do not consider one shilling sterling as one fourth the real value of the lands. . . . If, therefore," writes Morris to James M. Marshall, "a little over £5000 Stg. could be made on this security it would be better than selling especially at 12^{d} per acre." (Robert Morris to James M. Marshall, Oct. 10, 1795; *ib.*)

Morris owned at one time or another nearly all of the western half

John Marshall had long been the attorney in Virginia for Robert Morris, who frequently visited that State, sometimes taking his family with him. In all probability, it was upon some such journey that James M. Marshall, the brother of John Marshall, met and became engaged to Hester Morris, daughter of the great speculator, whom he married on April 19, 1795.[1] James M. Marshall — nine years younger than his brother — possessed ability almost equal to John Marshall and wider and more varied accomplishments.[2]

It is likely that the Pennsylvania financier, before the marriage, suggested to the Marshall brothers the purchase of what remained of the Fairfax estate in the Northern Neck, embracing over one hundred and sixty thousand acres of the best land in Virginia.[3] At any rate, sometime during 1793 or 1794 John

of New York State. (See Oberholtzer, 301 *et seq.*) "You knew of Mr. Robert Morris's purchase . . of one million, three hundred thousand acres of land of the State of Massachusetts, at five pence per acre. It is said he has sold one million two hundred thousand acres of these in Europe." (Jefferson to Washington, March 27, 1791; *Cor. Rev.*: Sparks, iv, 365.)

Patrick Henry acquired considerable holdings which helped to make him, toward the end of his life, a wealthy man. Washington, who had a keen eye for land values, became the owner of immense quantities of real estate. In 1788 he already possessed two hundred thousand acres. (De Warville, 243.)

[1] Oberholtzer, 266 *et seq.* Hester Morris, at the time of her marriage to John Marshall's brother, was the second greatest heiress in America.

[2] Grigsby, i, footnote to 150.

[3] Deed of Lieutenant-General Phillip Martin (the Fairfax heir who made the final conveyance) to Rawleigh Colston, John Marshall, and James M. Marshall; Records at Large, Fauquier County (Virginia) Circuit Court, 200 *et seq.* At the time of the contract of purchase, however, the Fairfax estate was supposed to be very much larger than the quantity of land conveyed in this deed. It was considerably reduced before the Marshalls finally secured the title.

Marshall, his brother, James M. Marshall, his brother-in-law, Rawleigh Colston, and General Henry Lee contracted for the purchase of this valuable holding.[1] In January of that year James M. Marshall sailed for England to close the bargain.[2] The money to buy the Fairfax lands was to be advanced by Robert Morris, who, partly for this purpose, sent James M. Marshall to Europe to negotiate [3] loans, immediately after his marriage to Hester Morris.

At Amsterdam "some Capitalists proposed to supply on very hard terms a Sum more than Sufficient to pay Mr. Fairfax," writes Morris, and James M. Marshall "has my authority to apply the first Monies he receives on my acco[t] to that Payment."[4] By the end of 1796 Morris's over-speculations had gravely impaired his fortune. The old financier writes pathetically to James M. Marshall: "I am struggling hard, very hard, indeed to regain my Position." He tells his son-in-law that if a loan cannot be obtained on his other real estate he "expects these Washington Lotts will be the most

[1] Lee is mentioned in all contemporary references to this transaction as one of the Marshall syndicate, but his name does not appear in the Morris correspondence nor in the deed of the Fairfax heir to the Marshall brothers and Colston.

[2] J[s] Marshall to —— [Edmund Randolph] Jan. 21, 1794; MS. Archives Department of State. Marshall speaks of dispatches which he is carrying to Pinckney, then American Minister to Great Britain. This letter is incorrectly indexed in the Archives as from John Marshall. It is signed "J[s] Marshall" and is in the handwriting of James M. Marshall. John Marshall was in Richmond all this year, as his Account Book shows.

[3] Morris to John Marshall, Nov. 21, 1795; and Aug. 24, 1796; Morris's Private Letter Book; MS., Lib. Cong.

[4] Morris to Colston, Nov. 11, 1796; *ib.*

certain of any Property to raise Money on"; and that "[I] will have a number of them Placed under your Controul."[1]

The loan failed, for the time being, but, writes Morris to John Marshall, "Mr. Hottenguer[2] who first put the thing in motion says it will come on again" and succeed; "if so, your brother will, of course, be ready for Mr. Fairfax." Morris is trying, he says, to raise money from other sources lest that should fail. "I am here distressed exceedingly in money matters," continues the harried and aging speculator "as indeed every body here are but I will immediately make such exertions as are in my power to place funds with your brother and I cannot but hope that his and my exertions will produce the needful in proper time to prevent mischief."[3]

A month later Morris again writes John Marshall that he is "extremely anxious & fearing that it [the

[1] Robert Morris to James M. Marshall, Dec. 3, 1796; Morris's Private Letter Book; MS., Lib. Cong. By the expression "Washington Lotts" Morris refers to his immense real estate speculations on the site of the proposed National Capital. Morris bought more lots in the newly laid out 'Federal City" than all other purchasers put together. Seven thousand two hundred and thirty-four lots stood in his name when the site of Washington was still a primeval forest. (Oberholtzer, 308–12.) Some of these he afterwards transferred to the Marshall brothers, undoubtedly to make good his engagement to furnish the money for the Fairfax deal, which his failure prevented him from advancing entirely in cash. (For account of Morris's real estate transactions in Washington see La Rochefoucauld, iii, 622–26.)

[2] This Hottenguer soon appears again in John Marshall's life as one of Talleyrand's agents who made the corrupt proposals to Marshall, Pinckney, and Gerry, the American Commissioners to France in the famous X.Y.Z. transaction of 1797–98. (See *infra*, chaps. VI to VIII.)

[3] Robert Morris to John Marshall, Dec. 30, 1796; Morris's Private Letter Book; MS., Lib. Cong.

Amsterdam loan] may fall through I am trying to obtain a loan here for the purposes of your Brother in London. This," says the now desperate financier, "is extremely difficult, for those who have money or credit in Europe seem to dread every thing that is American." He assures John Marshall that he will do his utmost. "My anxiety . . . [to make good the Fairfax purchase] is beyond what I can express." Alexander Baring "could supply the money . . . but he parries me. He intends soon for the Southward I will introduce him to you." [1]

The title to the Fairfax estate had been the subject of controversy for many years. Conflicting grants, overlapping boundaries, sequestration laws, the two treaties with Great Britain, were some of the elements that produced confusion and uncertainty in the public mind and especially in the minds of those holding lands within the grant. The only real and threatening clouds upon the title to the lands purchased by the Marshall syndicate, however, were the confiscatory laws passed during the Revolution [2] which the Treaty of Peace and the Jay Treaty nullified.[3] There were also questions growing out of grants made by the colonial authorities between 1730 and 1736, but these were not weighty.

The case of Hunter *vs.* Fairfax, Devisee, involving these questions, was pending in the Supreme Court of the United States. John Marshall went to Phila-

[1] Morris to John Marshall, Jan. 23, 1797; Morris's Private Letter Book; MS., Lib. Cong.

[2] Hening, ix, chap. ix, 377 *et seq.*; also *ib.*, x, chap. xiv, 66 *et seq.*; xi, chap. xliv, 75–76; xi, chap. xlv, 176 *et seq.*; xi, chap. xlvii, 81 *et seq.*; xi, chap. xxx, 349 *et seq.*

[3] Such effect of these treaties was not yet conceded, however.

delphia and tried to get the cause advanced and decided. He was sadly disappointed at his failure and so wrote his brother. "Your Brother has been here," writes Morris to his son-in-law, "as you will see by a letter from him forwarded by this conveyance. He could not get your case brought forward in the Supreme Court of the U. S. at which he was much dissatisfied & I am much concerned thereat, fearing that real disadvantage will result to your concern thereby." [1]

The case came on for hearing in regular course during the fall term. Hunter, on the death of his attorney, Alexander Campbell, prayed the Court, by letter, for a continuance, which was granted over the protest of the Fairfax attorneys of record, Lee and Ingersoll of Philadelphia, who argued that "from the nature of the cause, delay would be worse for the defendant in error [the Fairfax heir] than a decision adverse to his claim." The Attorney-General stated that the issue before the Court was "whether . . . the defendant in error being an alien can take and hold the lands by devise. And it will be contended that his title is completely protected by the treaty of peace." Mr. Justice Chase remarked: "I recollect that . . . a decision in favor of such a devisee's title was given by a court in Maryland. It is a matter, however, of great moment and ought to be deliberately and finally settled." [2] The Marshalls, of course, stood in the shoes of the Fairfax devisee; had the Supreme Court decided against the Fairfax title,

[1] Morris to James M. Marshall, March 4, 1796; Morris's Private Letter Book; MS., Lib. Cong.

[2] Hunter *vs.* Fairfax, Devisee, 3 Dallas, 303, and footnote.

their contract of purchase would have been nullified and, while they would not have secured the estate, they would have been relieved of the Fairfax indebtedness. It was, then, a very grave matter to the Marshalls, in common with all others deriving their titles from Fairfax, that the question be settled quickly and permanently.

A year or two before this purchase by the Marshalls of what remained of the Fairfax estate, more than two hundred settlers, occupying other parts of it, petitioned the Legislature of Virginia to quiet their titles.[1] Acting on these petitions and influenced, perhaps, by the controversy over the sequestration laws which the Marshall purchase renewed, the Legislature in 1796 passed a resolution proposing to compromise the dispute by the State's relinquishing "all claim to any lands specifically appropriated by . . . Lord Fairfax to his own use either by deed or actual survey . . . if the devises of Lord Fairfax, or those claiming under them, will relinquish all claims to lands . . . which were waste and unappropriated at the time of the death of Lord Fairfax." [2]

Acting for the purchasing syndicate, John Marshall, in a letter to the Speaker of the House, accepted this legislative offer of settlement upon the condition that "an act passes during this session confirming . . . the title of those claiming under Mr. Fairfax the lands specifically appropriated and

[1] Originals in Archives of Virginia State Library. Most of the petitions were by Germans, many of their signatures being in German script. They set forth their sufferings and hardships, their good faith, loss of papers, death of witnesses, etc.

[2] Laws of Virginia, Revised Code (1819), i, 352.

reserved by the late Thomas Lord Fairfax or his ancestors for his or their use." [1]

When advised of what everybody then supposed to be the definitive settlement of this vexed controversy, Robert Morris wrote John Marshall that "altho' you were obliged to give up a part of your claim yet it was probably better to do that than to hold a contest with such an opponent [State of Virginia]. I will give notice to Mr. Jas. Marshall of this compromise." [2] John Marshall, now sure of the title, and more anxious than ever to consummate the deal by paying the Fairfax heir, hastened to Philadelphia to see Morris about the money.

"Your Brother John Marshall Esqr. is now in this City," writes Robert Morris to his son-in-law, "and his principal business I believe is to see how you are provided with Money to pay Lord Fairfax.

[1] Laws of Virginia, Revised Code (1819), i, 352. Marshall's letter accepting the proposal of compromise is as follows: —

"RICHMOND, November 24th, 1796.

"SIR, being one of the purchasers of the lands of Mr. Fairfax, and authorized to act for them all, I have considered the resolution of the General Assembly on the petitions of sundry inhabitants of the counties of Hampshire, Hardy, and Shenandoah, and have determined to accede to the proposition it contains.

"So soon as the conveyance shall be transmitted to me from Mr. Fairfax, deeds extinguishing his title to the waste and unappropriated lands in the Northern Neck shall be executed, provided an act passes during this session, confirming, on the execution of such deeds, the title of those claiming under Mr. Fairfax the lands specifically appropriated and reserved by the late Thomas Lord Fairfax, or his ancestors, for his or their use.

"I remain Sir, with much respect and esteem,

"Your obedient servant, JOHN MARSHALL.

"The Honorable, the Speaker of the House of Delegates."

(Laws of Virginia.)

[2] Morris to John Marshall, Dec. 30, 1796; Morris's Private Letter Book; MS., Lib. Cong.

. . . I am so sensible of the necessity there is for your being prepared for Lord Fairfax's payment that there is nothing within my power that I would not do to enable you to meet it." [1]

The members of the Marshall syndicate pressed their Philadelphia backer unremittingly, it appears, for a few days later he answers what seems to have been a petulant letter from Colston assuring that partner in the Fairfax transaction that he is doing his utmost to "raise the money to enable Mr. James Marshall to meet the Payments for your Purchase at least so far as it is incumbent on me to supply the means. . . . From the time named by John Marshall Esqre when here, I feel perfect Confidence, because I will furnish him before that period with such Resources & aid as I think cannot fail." [2]

Finally Marshall's brother negotiated the loan, an achievement which Morris found "very pleasing, as it enables you to take the first steps with Lord Fairfax for securing your bargain." [3] Nearly forty thousand dollars of this loan was thus applied. In his book of accounts with Morris, James M. Marshall enters: "Jany 25 '97 To £7700 paid the Revd Denny Fairfax and credited in your [Morris's] account with me 7700" (English pounds sterling).[4]

[1] Morris to James M. Marshall, Feb. 10, 1797; Morris's Private Letter Book; MS., Lib. Cong. Morris adds that "I mortgaged to Col^o^ Hamilton 100,000 acres of Genesee Lands to secure payment of $75,000 to Mr. Church in five years. This land is worth at this moment in Cash two Dollars pr Acre."

[2] Morris to Colston, Feb. 25, 1797; *ib.*

[3] Morris to James M. Marshall, April 27, 1797; *ib.*

[4] MS. The entry was made in Amsterdam and Morris learned of the loan three months afterwards.

The total amount which the Marshalls had agreed to pay for the remnant of the Fairfax estate was "fourteen thousand pounds British money." [1] When Robert Morris became bankrupt, payment of the remainder of the Fairfax indebtedness fell on the shoulders of Marshall and his brother.

This financial burden caused Marshall to break his rule of declining office and to accept appointment as one of our envoys to France at the time of Robert Morris's failure and imprisonment for debt; for from that public employment of less than one year, Marshall, as we shall see, received in the sorely needed cash, over and above his expenses, three times the amount of his annual earnings at the bar.[2] "Mr. John Marshall has said here," relates Jefferson after Marshall's return, "that had he not been appointed minister [envoy] to France, he was desperate in his affairs and must have sold his estate [the Fairfax purchase] & that immediately. That that appointment was the greatest God-send that could ever have befallen a man."[3] Jefferson adds: "I have this from J. Brown and S. T. Mason [Senator Mason]." [4]

[1] Records at Large in Clerk's Office of Circuit Court of Fauquier County, Virginia, 200 *et seq.* The deed was not filed until 1806, at which time, undoubtedly, the Marshalls made their last payment.

[2] See *infra*, chap. VIII. It was probably this obligation too, that induced Marshall, a few years later, to undertake the heavy task of writing the *Life of Washington*, quite as much as his passionate devotion to that greatest of Americans. (See vol. III of this work.)

[3] "Anas," March 21, 1800; *Works:* Ford, I, 355.

[4] *Ib.* Misleading as Jefferson's "Anas" is, his information in this matter was indisputably accurate.

So it was that Marshall accepted a place on the mission to France[1] when it was offered to him by

[1] See *infra*, chap. VI. A short time before the place on the French mission was tendered Marshall, his father in Kentucky resigned the office of Supervisor of Revenue for the District of Ohio. In his letter of resignation Thomas Marshall gives a résumé of his experiences as an official under Washington's Administrations. Since this is one of the only two existing letters of Marshall's father on political subjects, and because it may have turned Adams's mind to John Marshall, it is worthy of reproduction: —

SIR,

Having determined to resign my Commission as Supervisor of the Revenue for the district of Ohio, on the 30th day of June next, which terminates the present fiscal year, I have thought it right to give this timely notice to you as President of the United States, in whom the nomination and appointment of my successor is vested; in order that you may in the meantime select some fit person to fill the office. You will therefore be pleased to consider me as out of office on the first day of July ensuing.

It may possibly be a subject of enquiry, why, after holding the office during the most critical & troublesome times, I should now resign it, when I am no longer insulted, and abused, for endeavoring to execute the Laws of my Country — when those Laws appear to be, more than formerly, respected — and when the probability is, that in future they may be carried into effect with but little difficulty?

In truth this very change, among other considerations, furnishes a reason for the decision I have made. For having once engaged in the business of revenue I presently found myself of sufficient importance with the enemies of the Government here to be made an object of their particular malevolence — and while this was the case, I was determined not to be driven from my post.

At this time, advanced in years and declining in health, I find myself unfit for the cares, and active duties of the office; and therefore cheerfully resign a situation, which I at first accepted and afterwards held, more from an attachment to the Government, than from any pecuniary consideration, to be filled by some more active officer, as still more conducive to the public service.

To the late President I had the honor of being known, and combined, with respect and veneration for his public character, the more social and ardent affections of the man, and of the friend.

You Sir I have not the honor to know personally, but you have filled too many important stations in the service of your country; & fame has been too busy with your name to permit me to remain ignorant of

Adams, who "by a miracle," as Hamilton said, had been elected President.[1]

your character; for which in all its public relations permit me to say, I feel the most entire respect and esteem: Nor is it to me among the smallest motives for my rejoicing that you are the President; and of my attachment to your administration to know that you have ever been on terms of friendship with the late President — that you have approved his administration, — and that you propose to yourself his conduct as an example for your imitation.

On this occasion I may say without vanity that I have formerly and not infrequently, given ample testimony of my attachment to Republican Government, to the peace, liberty and happiness of my country and that it is not now to be supposed that I have changed my principles — or can esteem those who possess different ones.

And altho' I am too old [Thomas Marshall was nearly sixty-five years of age when he wrote this letter] and infirm for active services, (for which I pray our country may not feel a call) yet my voice shall ever be excited in opposition to foreign influence, (from whence the greatest danger seems to threaten, as well as against internal foes) and in support of a manly, firm, and independent, exercise of those constitutional rights, which belong to the President, and Government of the United States. And, *even opinions*, have their effect.

I am Sir with the most
entire respect and esteem
Your very humble Servt,
T. MARSHALL.

JOHN ADAMS, ESQ.
President of the
United States.

(Thomas Marshall to Adams, April 28, 1797; MS., Dept. of State.)

[1] See *infra*, chaps. XI and XII.

CHAPTER VI

ENVOY TO FRANCE

My dearest life, continue to write to me, as my heart clings with delight only to what comes from you. (Marshall to his wife.)

He is a plain man, very sensible and cautious. (Adams.)

Our poor insulted country has not before it the most flattering prospects. (Marshall at Antwerp.)

"PHILADELPHIA July 2nd 1797.

"MY DEAREST POLLY

"I am here after a passage up the bay from Baltimore . . . I dined on saturday in private with the President whom I found a sensible plain candid good tempered man & was consequently much pleased with him. I am not certain when I shall sail. . . . So you . . . my dearest life continue to write to me as your letters will follow me should I be gone before their arrival & as my heart clings with real pleasure & delight only to what comes from you. I was on friday evening at the faux hall of Philadelphia. . . . The amusements were walking, sitting, punch ice cream etc Music & conversation. . . . Thus my dearest Polly do I when not engaged in the very serious business which employs a large portion of my time endeavor by a-[muse]ments to preserve a mind at ease & [keep] it from brooding too much over my much loved & absent wife. By all that is dear on earth, I entreat you to do the same, for separation will not I trust be long & letters do everything to draw its sting I am my dearest life your affectionate

"J MARSHALL." [1]

[1] Marshall to his wife, July 2, 1797; MS.

So wrote John Marshall at the first stage of his journey upon that critical diplomatic mission which was to prove the most dramatic in our history and which was to be the turning-point in Marshall's life. From the time when Mary Ambler became his bride in 1783, Marshall had never been farther away from his Richmond home than Philadelphia, to which city he had made three flying visits in 1796, one to argue the British Debts case, the other two to see Robert Morris on the Fairfax deal and to hasten the decision of the Supreme Court in that controversy.

But now Marshall was to cross the ocean as one of the American envoys to "the terrible Republic" whose "power and vengeance" everybody dreaded.[1] He was to go to that now arrogant Paris whose streets were resounding with the shouts of French victories. It was the first and the last trans-Atlantic voyage Marshall ever undertook; and although he was to sail into a murky horizon to grapple with vast difficulties and unknown dangers, yet the mind of the home-loving Virginian dwelt more on his Richmond fireside than on the duties and hazards before him.

Three days after his arrival at Philadelphia, impressionable as a boy, he again writes to his wife: "My dearest Polly I have been extremely chagrined at not having yet received a letter from you. I hope you are well as I hear nothing indicating the contrary but you know not how solicitous how anxiously solicitous I am to hear it from yourself. Write me that

[1] Sedgwick to King, June 24, 1797; King, ii, 192.

you are well & in good spirits & I shall set out on my voyage with a lightened heart . . . you will hear from me more than once before my departure."

The Virginia envoy was much courted at Philadelphia before he sailed. "I dined yesterday," Marshall tells his wife, "in a very large company of Senators & members of the house of representatives who met to celebrate the 4th of July. The company was really a most respectable one & I experienced from them the most flattering attention. I have much reason to be satisfied & pleased with the manner in which I am received here." But flattery did not soothe Marshall — "Something is wanting to make me happy," he tells his "dearest Polly." "Had I my dearest wife with me I should be delighted indeed." [1]

Washington had sent letters in Marshall's care to acquaintances in France commending him to their attention and good offices; and the retired President wrote Marshall himself a letter of hearty good wishes. "Receive sir," replies Marshall, "my warm & grateful acknowledgments for the polite &, allow me to add, friendly wishes which you express concerning myself as well as for the honor of being mentioned in your letters." [2]

A less composed man, totally unpracticed as Marshall was in diplomatic usages, when embarking on an adventure involving war or peace, would have occupied himself constantly in preparing for the vast business before him. Not so Marshall. While waiting

[1] Marshall to his wife, July 5, 1797; MS.
[2] Marshall to Washington, July 7, 1797; MS., Lib. Cong.

for his ship, he indulged his love of the theater. Again he tells his wife how much he misses her. "I cannot avoid writing to you because while doing so I seem to myself to be in some distant degree enjoying your company. I was last night at the play & saw the celebrated Mrs. Mary in the character of Juliet. She performs that part to admiration indeed but I really do not think Mrs. Westig is far her inferior in it. I saw," gossips Marshall, "Mrs. Heyward there. I have paid that lady one visit to one of the most delightful & romantic spots on the river Schuylkil. . . . She expressed much pleasure to see me & has pressed me very much to repeat my visit. I hope I shall not have time to do so."

Marshall is already bored with the social life of Philadelphia. "I am beyond expression impatient to set out on the embassy," he informs his wife. "The life I lead here does not suit me I am weary of it I dine out every day & am now engaged longer I hope than I shall stay. This disipated life does not long suit my temper. I like it very well for a day or two but I begin to require a frugal repast with good cold water" — There was too much wine, it would seem, at Philadelphia to suit Marshall.

"I would give a great deal to dine with you to day on a piece of cold meat with our boys beside us to see Little Mary running backwards & forwards over the floor playing the sweet little tricks she [is] full of. . . . I wish to Heaven the time which must intervene before I can repass these delightful scenes was now terminated & that we were looking back on our separation instead of seeing it before us. Farewell my dearest Polly. Make yourself happy & you will bless your ever affectionate

"J. MARSHALL."[1]

If Marshall was pleased with Adams, the President was equally impressed with his Virginia envoy to France. "He [Marshall] is a plain man very sensible, cautious, guarded, and learned in the law of nations.[2] I think you will be pleased with him,"[3] Adams writes Gerry, who was to be Marshall's associate and whose capacity for the task even his intimate personal friend, the President, already distrusted. Hamilton was also in Philadelphia at the time[4]—a circumstance which may or may not have been significant. It was, however, the first time, so far as definite evidence attests, that these men had met since they had been comrades and fellow officers in the Revolution.

The "Aurora," the leading Republican newspaper, was mildly sarcastic over Marshall's ignorance of the French language and general lack of equipment for his diplomatic task. "Mr. Marshall, one of our extra envoys to France, will be eminently qualified for the mission by the time he reaches that country," says the "Aurora." Some official of great legal learning was coaching Marshall, it seems, and advised him to read certain monarchical books on the old France and on the fate of the ancient republics.

[1] Marshall to his wife, July 11, 1797; MS.

[2] This, of course, was untrue, at that time. Marshall probably listened with polite interest to Adams, who was a master of the subject, and agreed with him. Thus Adams was impressed, as is the way of human nature.

[3] Adams to Gerry, July 17, 1797; *Works:* Adams, viii, 549.

[4] *Aurora*, July 17, 1797.

The "Aurora" asks "whether some history of France since the overthrow of the Monarchy would not have been more instructive to Mr. Marshall. The Envoy, however," continues the "Aurora," "approved the choice of his sagacious friend, but very shrewdly observed 'that he must first purchase Chambaud's grammar, English and French.' We understand that he is a very apt scholar, and no doubt, during the passage, he will be able to acquire enough of the French jargon for all the purposes of the embassy." [1]

Having received thirty-five hundred dollars for his expenses,[2] Marshall set sail on the brig Grace for Amsterdam where Charles Cotesworth Pinckney, the expelled American Minister to France and head of the mission, awaited him. As the land faded, Marshall wrote, like any love-sick youth, another letter to his wife which he sent back by the pilot.

"The land is just escaping from my view," writes Marshall to his "dearest Polly"; "the pilot is about to leave us & I hasten from the deck into the cabin once more to give myself the sweet indulgence of writing to you. . . . There has been so little wind that we are not yet entirely out of the bay. It is so wide however that the land has the appearance of a light blue cloud on the surface of the water & we shall very soon lose it entirely."

Marshall assures his wife that his "cabin is neat & clean. My berth a commodious one in which I

[1] *Aurora*, July 19, 1797. For documents given envoys by the Government, see *Am. St. Prs.*, *For. Rel.*, Class I, ii, 153.

[2] Marshall to Secretary of State, July 10, 1797; Memorandum by Pickering; Pickering MSS., in *Proc.*, Mass. Hist. Soc., xxi, 177.

have my own bed & sheets of which I have a plenty so that I lodge as conveniently as I could do in any place whatever & I find I sleep very soundly altho on water." He is careful to say that he has plenty of creature comforts. "We have for the voyage, the greatest plenty of salt provisions live stock & poultry & as we lay in our own liquors I have taken care to provide myself with a plenty of excellent porter wine & brandy. The Captain is one of the most obliging men in the world & the vessel is said by every body to be a very fine one."

There were passengers, too, who suited Marshall's sociable disposition and who were "well disposed to make the voyage agreeable. . . . I have then my dearest Polly every prospect before me of a passage such as I could wish in every respect but one . . . fear of a lengthy passage. We have met in the bay several vessels. One from Liverpool had been at sea nine weeks, & the others from other places had been proportionately long. . . . I shall be extremely impatient to hear from you & our dear children."

Marshall tells his wife how to direct her letters to him, "some . . . by the way of London to the care of Rufus King esquire our Minister there, some by the way of Amsterdam or the Hague to the care of William Vanns [*sic*] Murr[a]y esquire our Minister at the Hague & perhaps some directed to me as Envoy extraordinary of the United States to the French Republic at Paris.

"Do not I entreat you omit to write. Some of your letters may miscarry but some will reach me & my heart can feel till my return no pleasure comparable to what will be given it by a line from you telling me that all remains well. Farewell my dearest wife. Your happiness will ever be the first prayer of your unceasingly affectionate

"J Marshall."[1]

So fared forth John Marshall upon the adventure which was to open the door to that historic career that lay just beyond it; and force him, against his will and his life's plans, to pass through it. But for this French mission, it is certain that Marshall's life would have been devoted to his law practice and his private affairs. He now was sailing to meet the ablest and most cunning diplomatic mind in the contemporary world whose talents, however, were as yet known to but few; and to face the most venal and ruthless governing body of any which then directed the affairs of the nations of Europe. Unguessed and unexpected by the kindly, naïve, and inexperienced Richmond lawyer were the scenes about to unroll before him; and the manner of his meeting the emergencies so soon to confront him was the passing of the great divide in his destiny.

Even had the French rulers been perfectly honest and simple men, the American envoys would have had no easy task. For American-French affairs were sadly tangled and involved. Gouverneur Morris, our first Minister to France under the Constitution, had made himself unwelcome to the French Revolutionists; and to placate the authorities then reigning in Paris, Washington had recalled Morris and appointed

[1] Marshall to his wife, "The Bay of Delaware," July 20, 1797: MS.

Monroe in his place "after several attempts had failed to obtain a more eligible character." [1]

Monroe, a partisan of the Revolutionists, had begun his mission with theatrical blunders; and these he continued until his recall,[2] when he climaxed his imprudent conduct by his attack on Washington.[3] During most of his mission Monroe was under the influence of Thomas Paine,[4] who had then become the venomous enemy of Washington.

Monroe had refused to receive from his fellow Minister to England, John Jay, "confidential informal statements" as to the British treaty which Jay prudently had sent him by word of mouth only. When the Jay Treaty itself arrived, Monroe

[1] Washington's remarks on Monroe's "View"; *Writings:* Ford, xiii, 452.

[2] See McMaster, ii, 257–59, 319, 370. But Monroe, although shallow, was well meaning; and he had good excuse for over-enthusiasm; for his instructions were: "Let it be seen that in case of a war with any nation on earth, we shall consider France as our first and natural ally." (*Am. St. Prs., For. Rel.*, Class I, ii, 669.)

[3] "View of the Conduct of the Executive of the United States, etc.," by James Monroe (Philadelphia, Bache, Publisher, 1797). This pamphlet is printed in full in Monroe's *Writings:* Hamilton, iii, as an Appendix.

Washington did not deign to notice Monroe's attack publicly; but on the margin of Monroe's book answered every point. Extracts from Monroe's "View" and Washington's comments thereon are given in Washington's *Writings:* Ford, xiii, 452–90.

Jefferson not only approved but commended Monroe's attack on Washington. (See Jefferson to Monroe, Oct. 25, 1797; *Works:* Ford, viii, 344–46.) It is more than probable that he helped circulate it. (Jefferson to Eppes, Dec. 21, 1797; *ib.*, 347; and to Madison, Feb. 8, 1798; *ib.*, 362; see also Jefferson to Monroe, Dec. 27; *ib.*, 350. "Your book was later coming than was to have been wished: however it works irresistibly. It would have been very gratifying to you to hear the unqualified eulogies . . . by all who are not hostile to it from principle.")

[4] Ticknor, ii, 113.

publicly denounced the treaty as "shameful,"[1] a grave indiscretion in the diplomatic representative of the Government that had negotiated the offending compact.

Finally Monroe was recalled and Washington, after having offered the French mission to John Marshall, appointed Charles Cotesworth Pinckney of South Carolina as his successor. The French Revolutionary authorities had bitterly resented the Jay compact, accused the American Government of violating its treaty with France, denounced the United States for ingratitude, and abused it for undue friendship to Great Britain.

In all this the French Directory had been and still was backed up by the Republicans in the United States, who, long before this, had become a distinctly French party. Thomas Paine understated the case when he described "the Republican party in the United States" as "that party which is the sincere ally of France."[2]

The French Republic was showing its resentment by encouraging a piratical warfare by French privateers upon American commerce. Indeed, vessels of the French Government joined in these depredations. In this way, it thought to frighten the United States into taking the armed side of France against Great Britain. The French Republic was emulating the recent outrages of that Power; and, except that

[1] For a condensed but accurate and impartial statement of Monroe's conduct while Minister, see Gilman: *James Monroe* (American Statesmen Series), 36–73.

[2] Paine to editors of the *Bien-Informé*, Sept. 27, 1797; *Writings:* Conway, iii, 368–69.

the French did not impress Americans into their service, as the British had done, their Government was furnishing to America the same cause for war that Great Britain had so brutally afforded.

In less than a year and a half before Marshall sailed from Philadelphia, more than three hundred and forty American vessels had been taken by French privateers.[1] Over fifty-five million dollars' worth of American property had been destroyed or confiscated under the decrees of the Directory.[2] American seamen, captured on the high seas, had been beaten and imprisoned. The officers and crew of a French armed brig tortured Captain Walker, of the American ship Cincinnatus, four hours by thumbscrews.[3]

When Monroe learned that Pinckney had been appointed to succeed him, he began a course of insinuations to his French friends against his successor; branded Pinckney as an "aristocrat"; and thus sowed the seeds for the insulting treatment the latter received upon his appearance at the French Capital.[4] Upon Pinckney's arrival, the French Directory refused to receive him, threatened him with arrest by the Paris police, and finally ordered the new American Minister out of the territory of the Republic.[5]

To emphasize this affront, the Directory made a great ado over the departure of Monroe, who re-

[1] *Am. St. Prs., For. Rel.*, ii, 55–63.

[2] See condensed summary of the American case in instructions to Pinckney, Marshall, and Gerry; *ib.*, 153–57.

[3] *Ib.*, 64; and for numerous other examples see *ib.*, 28–64.

[4] Ticknor, ii, 113.

[5] Pinckney to Secretary of State, Amsterdam, Feb. 18, 1797; *Am. St. Prs., For. Rel.*, vii, 10.

sponded with a characteristic address. To this speech Barras, then President of the Directory, replied in a harangue insulting to the American Government; it was, indeed, an open appeal to the American people to repudiate their own Administration,[1] of the same character as, and no less offensive than, the verbal performances of Genêt.

And still the outrages of French privateers on American ships continued with increasing fury.[2] The news of Pinckney's treatment and the speech of Barras reached America after Adams's inauguration. The President promptly called Congress into a special session and delivered to the National Legislature an address in which Adams appears at his best.

The "refusal [by the Directory] . . . to receive him [Pinckney] until we had acceded to their demands without discussion and without investigation, is to treat us neither as allies nor as friends, nor as a sovereign state," said the President; who continued: —

"The speech of the President [Barras] discloses sentiments more alarming than the refusal of a minister [Pinckney], because more dangerous to our independence and union. . . .

"It evinces a disposition to separate the people of the United States from the government, to persuade them that they have different affections, principles and interests from those of their fellow citizens whom they themselves have chosen to manage their com-

[1] See Barras's speech in *Am. St. Prs., For. Rel.*, ii, 12.

[2] See Allen: *Naval War with France*, 31–33.

mon concerns and thus to produce divisions fatal to our peace.

"Such attempts ought to be repelled with a decision which shall convince France and the world that we are not a degraded people, humiliated under a colonial spirit of fear and sense of inferiority, fitted to be the miserable instruments of foreign influence, and regardless of national honor, character, and interest.

"I should have been happy to have thrown a veil over these transactions if it had been possible to conceal them; but they have passed on the great theatre of the world, in the face of all Europe and America, and with such circumstances of publicity and solemnity that they cannot be disguised and will not soon be forgotten. They have inflicted a wound in the American breast. It is my sincere desire, however, that it may be healed."

Nevertheless, so anxious was President Adams for peace that he informed Congress: "I shall institute a fresh attempt at negotiation. . . . If we have committed errors, and these can be demonstrated, we shall be willing to correct them; if we have done injuries, we shall be willing on conviction to redress them; and equal measures of justice we have a right to expect from France and every other nation." [1]

Adams took this wise action against the judgment of the Federalist leaders,[2] who thought that, since the outrages upon American commerce had been

[1] Adams, Message to Congress, May 16, 1797; Richardson, i, 235–36; also, *Works:* Adams, ix, 111–18.

[2] Gibbs, ii, 171–72.

committed by France and the formal insult to our Minister had been perpetrated by France, the advances should come from the offending Government. Technically, they were right; practically, they were wrong. Adams's action was sound as well as noble statesmanship.

Thus came about the extraordinary mission, of which Marshall was a member, to adjust our differences with the French Republic. The President had taken great care in selecting the envoys. He had considered Hamilton, Jefferson, and Madison,[1] for this delicate and fateful business; but the two latter, for reasons of practical politics, would not serve, and without one of them, Hamilton's appointment was impossible. Pinckney, waiting at Amsterdam, was, of course, to head the commission. Finally Adams's choice fell on John Marshall of Virginia and Francis Dana, Chief Justice of the Supreme Court of Massachusetts; and these nominations were confirmed by the Senate.[2]

But Dana declined,[3] and, against the unanimous advice of his Cabinet,[4] Adams then nominated Elbridge Gerry, who, though a Republican, had, on account of their personal relations, voted for Adams for President, apologizing, however, most humbly to Jefferson for having done so.[5]

No appointment could have better pleased that unrivaled politician. Gerry was in general agree-

[1] Hamilton proposed Jefferson or Madison. (Hamilton to Pickering, March 22, 1797; Lodge: *Cabot*, 101.)

[2] *Works:* Adams, ix, 111–18. [3] *Ib.*

[4] Gibbs, i, 467, 469, and footnote to 530–31.

[5] Austin: *Gerry*, ii, 134–35.

ment with Jefferson and was, temperamentally, an easy instrument for craft to play upon. When Gerry hesitated to accept, Jefferson wrote his "dear friend" that "it was with infinite joy to me that you were yesterday announced to the Senate" as one of the envoys; and he pleaded with Gerry to undertake the mission.[1]

The leaders of the President's party in Congress greatly deplored the selection of Gerry. "No appointment could . . . have been more injudicious," declared Sedgwick.[2] "If, sir, it was a desirable thing to distract the mission, a fitter person could not, perhaps, be found. It is ten to one against his agreeing with his colleagues," the Secretary of War advised the President.[3] Indeed, Adams himself was uneasy about Gerry, and in a prophetic letter sought to forestall the very indiscretions which the latter afterwards committed.

"There is the utmost necessity for harmony, complaisance, and condescension among the three envoys, and unanimity is of great importance," the President cautioned Gerry. "It is," said Adams, "my sincere desire that an accommodation may take place; but our national faith, and the honor of our government, cannot be sacrificed. You have known enough of the unpleasant effects of disunion among ministers to convince you of the necessity of avoiding it, like a rock or quicksand. . . It is prob-

[1] Jefferson to Gerry, June 21, 1797; *Works:* Ford, viii, 314. This letter flattered Gerry's vanity and nullified Adams's prudent advice to him given a few days later. (See *infra.*)

[2] Sedgwick to King, June 24, 1797; King, ii, 193.

[3] McHenry to Adams, in Cabinet meeting, 1797; Steiner, 224.

able there will be manœuvres practiced to excite jealousies among you." [1]

Forty-eight days after Marshall took ship at Philadelphia, he arrived at The Hague.[2] The long voyage had been enlivened by the sight of many vessels and the boarding of Marshall's ship three times by British men-of-war.

"Until our arrival in Holland," Marshall writes Washington, "we saw only British & neutral vessels. This added to the blockade of the dutch fleet in the Texel, of the french fleet in Brest & of the spanish fleet in Cadiz, manifests the entire dominion which one nation [Great Britain] at present possesses over the seas.

"By the ships of war which met us we were three times visited & the conduct of those who came on board was such as wou'd proceed from general orders to pursue a system calculated to conciliate America.

"Whether this be occasion'd by a sense of justice & the obligations of good faith, or solely by the hope that the perfect contrast which it exhibits to the conduct of France may excite keener sensations

[1] Adams to Gerry, July 8, 1797; *Works:* Adams, viii, 547–48. Nine days later the President again admonishes Gerry. While expressing confidence in him, the President tells Gerry that "Some have expressed . . . fears of an unaccommodating disposition [in Gerry] and others of an obstinacy that will risk great things to secure small ones.

"Some have observed that there is, at present, a happy and perfect harmony among all our ministers abroad, and have expressed apprehension that your appointment might occasion an interruption of it." (Adams to Gerry, July 17, 1797; *ib.*, 549.)

[2] Marshall took the commission and instructions of John Quincy Adams as the American Minister to Prussia (*Writings, J. Q. A.*: Ford, ii, footnote to 216), to which post the younger Adams had been appointed by Washington because of his brilliant "Publicola" essays.

at that conduct, its effects on our commerce is the same." [1]

It was a momentous hour in French history when the Virginian landed on European soil. The French elections of 1797 had given to the conservatives a majority in the National Assembly, and the Directory was in danger. The day after Marshall reached the Dutch Capital, the troops sent by Bonaparte, that young eagle, his pinions already spread for his imperial flight, achieved the revolution of the 18th Fructidor (4th of September); gave the ballot-shaken Directory the support of bayonets; made it, in the end, the jealous but trembling tool of the youthful conqueror; and armed it with a power through which it nullified the French elections and cast into prison or drove into exile all who came under its displeasure or suspicion.

With Lodi, Arcola, and other laurels upon his brow, the Corsican already had begun his astonishing career as dictator of terms to Europe. The native Government of the Netherlands had been replaced by one modeled on the French system; and the Batavian Republic, erected by French arms, had become the vassal and the tool of Revolutionary France.

Three days after his arrival at The Hague, Marshall writes his wife of the safe ending of his voyage and how "very much pleased" he is with Pinckney, whom he "immediately saw." They were waiting "anxiously" for Gerry, Marshall tells her. "We

[1] Marshall, to Washington, The Hague, Sept. 15, 1797; Washington MSS., Lib. Cong. See citations *ib.*, *infra*. (Sparks MSS., *Proc. Mass. Hist. Soc.*, lxvi; also *Amer. Hist. Rev.*, ii, no. 2, Jan., 1797.)

shall wait a week or ten days longer & shall then proceed on our journey [to Paris]. You cannot conceive (yes you can conceive) how these delays perplex & mortify me. I fear I cannot return until the spring & that fear excites very much uneasiness & even regret at my having ever consented to cross the Atlantic. I wish extremely to hear from you & to know your situation. My mind clings so to Richmond that scarcely a night passes in which during the hours of sleep I have not some interesting conversation with you or concerning you."

Marshall tells his "dearest Polly" about the appearance of The Hague, its walks, buildings, and "a very extensive wood adjoining the city which extends to the sea," and which is "the pride & boast of the place." "The society at the Hague is probably very difficult, to an American it certainly is, & I have no inclination to attempt to enter into it. While the differences with France subsist the political characters of this place are probably unwilling to be found frequently in company with our countrymen. It might give umbrage to France." Pinckney had with him his wife and daughter, "who," writes Marshall, "appears to be about 12 or 13 years of age. Mrs. Pinckney informs me that only one girl of her age has visited her since the residence of the family at the Hague.[1] In fact we seem to have no communication but with Americans, or those who are employed by America or who have property in our country."

[1] Pinckney and his family had been living in Holland for almost seven months. (Pinckney to Pickering, Feb. 8, 1797; *Am. St. Prs., For. Rel.*, ii, 10.)

While at The Hague, Marshall yields, as usual, to his love for the theater, although he cannot understand a word of the play. "Near my lodgings is a theatre in which a french company performs three times a week," he tells his wife. "I have been frequently to the play & tho' I do not understand the language I am very much amused at it. The whole company is considered as having a great deal of merit but there is a Madame de Gazor who is considered as one of the first performers in Paris who bears the palm in the estimation of every person."

Marshall narrates to his wife the result of the *coup d'état* of September 4. "The Directory," he writes, "with the aid of the soldiery have just put in arrest the most able & leading members of the legislature who were considered as moderate men & friends of peace. Some conjecture that this event will so abridge our negotiations as probably to occasion my return to America this fall. A speedy return is my most ardent wish but to have my return expedited by the means I have spoken of is a circumstance so calamitous that I deprecate it as the greatest of evils. Remember me affectionately to our friends & kiss for me our dear little Mary. Tell the boys how much I expect from them & how anxious I am to see them as well as their beloved mother. I am my dearest Polly unalterably your

"J MARSHALL." [1]

[1] Marshall to his wife, The Hague, Sept. 9, 1797, MS. Marshall's brother had been in The Hague July 30, but had gone to Berlin. Vans Murray to J. Q. Adams, July 30, 1797; *Letters:* Ford, 358. Apparently the brothers did not meet, notwithstanding the critical state of the Fairfax contract.

The theaters and other attractions of The Hague left Marshall plenty of time, however, for serious and careful investigations. The result of these he details to Washington. The following letter shows not only Marshall's state of mind just before starting for Paris, but also the effect of European conditions upon him and how strongly they already were confirming Marshall's tendency of thought so firmly established by every event of his life since our War for Independence: —

"Tho' the face of the country [Holland] still exhibits a degree of wealth & population perhaps unequal'd in any other part of Europe, its decline is visible. The great city of Amsterdam is in a state of blockade. More than two thirds of its shipping lie unemploy'd in port. Other seaports suffer tho' not in so great a degree. In the meantime the requisitions made [by the French] upon them [the Dutch] are enormous. . . .

"It is supposed that France has by various means drawn from Holland about 60,000,000 of dollars. This has been paid, in addition to the national expenditures, by a population of less than 2,000,000. . . . Not even peace can place Holland in her former situation. Antwerp will draw from Amsterdam a large portion of that commerce which is the great source of its wealth; for Antwerp possesses, in the existing state of things, advantages which not even weight of capital can entirely surmount."

Marshall then gives Washington a clear and striking account of the political happenings among the Dutch under French domination: —

"The political divisions of this country & its uncertainty concerning its future destiny must also have their operation. . . .

"A constitution which I have not read, but which is stated to me to have contain'd all the great fundamentals of a representative government, & which has been prepar'd with infinite labor, & has experienc'd an uncommon length of discussion was rejected in the primary assemblies by a majority of nearly five to one of those who voted. . . .

"The substitute wish'd for by its opponents is a legislature with a single branch having power only to initiate laws which are to derive their force from the sanction of the primary assemblies. I do not know how they wou'd organize it. . . . It is remarkable that the very men who have rejected the form of government propos'd to them have reëlected a great majority of the persons who prepar'd it & will probably make from it no essential departure. . . . It is worthy of notice that more than two thirds of those entitled to suffrage including perhaps more than four fifths of the property of the nation & who wish'd, as I am told, the adoption of the constitution, withheld their votes. . . .

"Many were restrain'd by an unwillingness to take the oath required before a vote could be receiv'd; many, disgusted with the present state of things, have come to the unwise determination of revenging themselves on those whom they charge with having occasion'd it by taking no part whatever in the politics of their country, & many seem to be indifferent to every consideration not immediately connected with their particular employments."

Holland's example made the deepest impression on Marshall's mind. What he saw and heard fortified his already firm purpose not to permit America, if he could help it, to become the subordinate or ally of any foreign power. The concept of the American people as a separate and independent Nation unattached to, unsupported by, and unafraid of any other country, which was growing rapidly to be the passion of Marshall's life, was given fresh force by the humiliation and distress of the Dutch under French control.

"The political opinions which have produc'd the rejection of the constitution," Marshall reasons in his report to Washington, "& which, as it wou'd seem, can only be entertain'd by intemperate & ill inform'd minds unaccustom'd to a union of the theory & practice of liberty, must be associated with a general system which if brought into action will produce the same excesses here which have been so justly deplor'd in France.

"The same materials exist tho' not in so great a degree. They have their clubs, they have a numerous poor & they have enormous wealth in the hands of a minority of the nation."

Marshall interviewed Dutch citizens, in his casual, indolent, and charming way; and he thus relates to Washington the sum of one such conversation: —

"On my remarking this to a very rich & intelligent merchant of Amsterdam & observing that if one class of men withdrew itself from public duties

& offices it wou'd immediately be succeeded by another which wou'd acquire a degree of power & influence that might be exercis'd to the destruction of those who had retir'd from society, he replied that the remark was just, but that they relied on France for a protection from those evils which she had herself experienc'd. That France wou'd continue to require great supplies from Holland & knew its situation too well to permit it to become the prey of anarchy.

"That Holland was an artificial country acquired by persevering industry & which cou'd only be preserv'd by wealth & order. That confusion & anarchy wou'd banish a large portion of that wealth, wou'd dry up its sources & wou'd entirely disable them from giving France that pecuniary aid she so much needed. That under this impression very many who tho' friends to the revolution, saw with infinite mortification french troops garrison the towns of Holland, wou'd now see their departure with equal regret.

"Thus, they willingly relinquish national independence for individual safety. What a lesson to those who wou'd admit foreign influence into the United States!"

Marshall then narrates the events in France which followed the *coup d'état* of September 4. While this account is drawn from rumors and newspapers and therefore contains a few errors, it is remarkable on the whole for its general accuracy. No condensation can do justice to Marshall's review of this period of French history in the making. It is of first importance, also, as disclosing his opinions of the Government he was so soon to encounter and his convictions that unrestrained liberty must result in despotism.

"You have observed the storm which has been long gathering in Paris," continues Marshall. "The thunderbolt has at length been launch'd at the heads of the leading members of the legislature & has, it is greatly to be fear'd, involv'd in one common ruin with them, the constitution & liberties of their country. . . . Complete & impartial details concerning it will not easily be obtained as the press is no longer free. The journalists who had ventur'd to censure the proceedings of a majority of the directory are seiz'd, & against about forty of them a sentence of transportation is pronounced.

"The press is plac'd under the superintendence of a police appointed by & dependent on the executive. It is supposed that all private letters have been seiz'd for inspection.

"From some Paris papers it appears, that on the first alarm, several members of the legislature attempted to assemble in their proper halls which they found clos'd & guarded by an arm'd force. Sixty or seventy assembled at another place & began to remonstrate against the violence offer'd to their body, but fear soon dispersed them.

"To destroy the possibility of a rallying point the municipal administrations of Paris & the central administration of the seine were immediately suspended & forbidden by an arrêté of the directoire, to assemble themselves together.

"Many of the administrators of the departments through France elected by the people, had been previously remov'd & their places filled by persons chosen by the directory. . . .

"The fragment of the legislature convok'd by the directory at L'Odéon & L' école de santé, hasten'd to repeal the law for organizing the national guards, & authoriz'd the directory to introduce into Paris as many troops as shou'd be judg'd necessary. The same day the liberty of the press was abolish'd by a line, property taken away by another & personal security destroy'd by a sentence of transportation against men unheard & untried.

"All this," sarcastically remarks Marshall, "is still the triumph of liberty & of the constitution."

Although admitting his lack of official information, Marshall "briefly" observes that: "Since the election of the new third, there were found in both branches of the legislature a majority in favor of moderate measures & apparently, wishing sincerely for peace. They have manifested a disposition which threaten'd a condemnation of the conduct of the directory towards America, a scrutiny into the transactions of Italy, particularly those respecting Venice & Genoa, an enquiry into the disposition of public money & such a regular arrangement of the finances as wou'd prevent in future those dilapidations which are suspected to have grown out of their disorder. They [French conservatives] have sought too by their laws to ameliorate the situation of those whom terror had driven out of France, & of those priests who had committed no offense."

Marshall thus details to Washington the excuse of the French radicals for their severe treatment of the conservatives: —

"The cry of a conspiracy to reëstablish royalism was immediately rais'd against them [conservatives]. An envoy was dispatched to the Army of Italy to sound its disposition. It was represented that the legislature was hostile to the armies, that it withheld their pay & subsistence, that by its opposition to the directory it encourag'd Austria & Britain to reject the terms of peace which were offer'd by France & which but for that opposition wou'd have been accepted, & finally that it had engag'd in a conspiracy for the destruction of the constitution & the republic & for the restoration of royalty.

"At a feast given to the armies of Italy to commemorate their fellow soldiers who had fallen in that country the Generals address'd to them their complaints, plainly spoke of marching to Paris to support the directory against the councils & received from them addresses manifesting the willingness of the soldiers to follow them.

"The armies also addressed the directory & each other, & addresses were dispatched to different departments. The directory answer'd them by the stronge[st] criminations of the legislature. Similar proceedings were had in the army of the interior commanded by Gen[l] Hoche. Detachments were mov'd within the limits prohibited by the constitution, some of which declar'd they were marching to Paris 'to bring the legislature to reason.'"

Here follows Marshall's story of what then happened, according to the accounts which were given him at The Hague: —

"Alarm'd at these movements the council of five hundred call'd on the directory for an account of them. The movement of the troops within the constitutional circle was attributed to accident & the discontents of the army to the faults committed by the legislature who were plainly criminated as conspirators against the army & the republic.

"This message was taken up by Tronçon in the council of antients & by Thibideau in the council of five hundred. I hope you have seen their speeches. They are able, & seem to me entirely exculpated the legislature.

"In the mean time the directory employed itself in the removal of the administrators of many of the departments & cantons & replacing those whom the people had elected by others in whom it cou'd confide, and in the removal generally of such officers both civil & military as cou'd not be trusted to make room for others on whom it cou'd rely.

"The legislature on its part, pass'd several laws to enforce the constitutional restrictions on the armies & endeavored to organize the national guards. On this latter subject especially Pichegru, great & virtuous I believe in the cabinet as in the field, was indefatigable. We understand that the day before the law for their organization wou'd have been carried into execution the decisive blow was struck."

Marshall now relates, argumentatively, the facts as he heard them in the Dutch Capital; and in doing so, reveals his personal sentiments and prejudices: —

"To support the general charge of conspiracy in favor of royalty I know of no particular facts alledged against the arrested Members except Pichegru & two or three others. . . . Pichegru is made in the first moment of conversation to unbosom himself entirely to a perfect stranger who had only told him that he came from the Prince of Conde & cou'd not exhibit a single line of testimonial of any sort to prove that he had ever seen that Prince or that he was not a spy employ'd by some of the enemies of the General.

"This story is repel'd by Pichegru's character which has never before been defil'd. Great as were the means he possess'd of personal aggrandizement he retir'd clean handed from the army without adding a shilling to his private fortune. It is repel'd by his resigning the supreme command, by his numerous victories subsequent to the alleged treason, by its own extreme absurdity & by the fear which his accusers show of bringing him to trial according to the constitution even before a tribunal they can influence & overawe, or of even permitting him to be heard before the prostrate body which is still term'd the legislature & which in defiance of the constitution has pronounc'd judgment on him.

"Yet this improbable & unsupported tale seems to be receiv'd as an established truth by those who the day before [his] fall bow'd to him as an idol. I am mortified as a man to learn that even his old army which conquer'd under him, which ador'd him, which partook of his fame & had heretofore not join'd their brethren in accusing the legislature, now unite in bestowing on him the heaviest execrations & do not hesitate to pronounce him a traitor of the deepest die."

Irrespective of the real merits of the controversy, Marshall tells Washington that he is convinced that constitutional liberty is dead or dying in France: —

"Whether this conspiracy be real or not," he says, "the wounds inflicted on the constitution by the three directors seem to me to be mortal. In opposition to the express regulations of the constitution the armies have deliberated, the result of their deliberations addressed to the directory has been favorably received & the legislature since the revolution has superadded its thanks.

"Troops have been marched within those limits which by the constitution they are forbidden to enter but on the request of the legislature. The directory is forbidden to arrest a member of the legislature unless in the very commission of a criminal act & then he can only be tried by the high court, on which occasion forms calculated to protect his person from violence or the prejudice of the moment are carefully prescrib'd.

"Yet it has seized, by a military force, about fifty leading members not taken in a criminal act & has not pursued a single step mark'd out by the constitution. The councils can inflict no penalty on their own members other than reprimand, arrest for eight & imprisonment for three days. Yet they have banished to such places as the directory shall chuse a large portion of their body without the poor formality of hearing a defense.

"The legislature shall not exercise any judiciary power or pass any retrospective law. Yet it has pronounc'd this heavy judgment on others as well as its own members & has taken from individuals property which the law has vested in them."

Marshall is already bitter against the Directory because of its violation of the French Constitution, and tells Washington: —

"The members of the directory are personally secur'd by the same rules with those of the legislature. Yet three directors have depriv'd two of their places, the legislature has then banished them without a hearing & has proceeded to fill up the alledg'd vacancies. Merlin late minister of justice & François de Neufchatel have been elected.

"The constitution forbids the house of any man to be entered in the night. The orders of the constituted authorities can only be executed in the day. Yet many of the members were seiz'd in their beds.

"Indeed, sir, the constitution has been violated in so many instances that it wou'd require a pamphlet to detail them. The detail wou'd be unnecessary for the great principle seems to be introduc'd that the government is to be administered according to the will of the nation."

Marshall now indulges in his characteristic eloquence and peculiar method of argument: —

"Necessity, the never to be worn out apology for violence, is alledg'd — but cou'd that necessity go further than to secure the persons of the conspirators? Did it extend to the banishment of the printers & to the slavery of the press? If such a necessity did exist it was created by the disposition of the people at large & it is a truth which requires no demonstration that if a republican form of government cannot be administered by the general will, it cannot be administered against that will by an army."

Nevertheless, hope for constitutional liberty in France lingers in his heart in spite of this melancholy recital.

"After all, the result may not be what is apprehended. France possesses such enormous power, such internal energy, such a vast population that she may possibly spare another million & preserve or reacquire her liberty. Or, the form of the government being preserved, the independence of the legislature may be gradually recover'd.

"With their form of government or resolutions we have certainly no right to intermeddle, but my regrets at the present state of things are increased by an apprehension that the rights of our country will not be deem'd so sacred under the existing system as they wou'd have been had the legislature preserved its legitimate authority." [1]

Washington's reply, which probably reached Marshall some time after the latter's historic letter to Talleyrand in January, 1798,[2] is informing. He "prays for a continuance" of such letters and hopes he will be able to congratulate Marshall "on the favorable conclusion of your embassy. . . . To predict the contrary might be as unjust as it is im-

[1] Marshall to Washington, The Hague, Sept. 15, 1797; *Amer. Hist. Rev.*, ii, no. 2, Jan., 1897; and MS., Lib. Cong.

[2] See *infra*, next chapter.

politic, and therefore," says Washington, "mum — on that topic. Be the issue what it may," he is sure "that nothing which justice, sound reasoning, and fair representation would require will be wanting to render it just and honorable." If so, and the mission fails, "then the eyes of all who are not willfully blind . . . . will be fully opened." The Directory will have a rude awakening, if they expect the Republicans to support France against America in the "dernier ressort. . . . For the mass of our citizens require no more than to understand a question to decide it properly; and an adverse conclusion of the negotiation will effect this." Washington plainly indicates that he wishes Marshall to read his letter between the lines when he says: "I shall dwell very little on European politics . . . because this letter may pass through many hands." [1]

Gerry not arriving by September 18, Marshall and Pinckney set out for Paris, "proceeding slowly in the hope of being overtaken" by their tardy associate. From Antwerp Marshall writes Charles Lee, then Attorney-General, correcting some unimportant statements in his letter to Washington, which, when written, were "considered as certainly true," but which "subsequent accounts contradict." [2] Downheartedly he says: —

[1] Washington to Marshall, Dec. 4, 1797; *Writings:* Ford, xiii, 432–34.

[2] To justify the violence of the 18th Fructidor, the Directory asserted that the French elections, in which a majority of conservatives and anti-revolutionists were returned and General Pichegru chosen President of the French Legislature, were parts of a royal conspiracy to destroy liberty and again place a king upon the throne of France. In these elections the French liberals, who were not in the army, did not

"Our insulted injured country has not before it the most flattering prospects. There is no circumstance calculated to flatter us with the hope that our negotiations will terminate as they ought to do. . . . We understand that all is now quiet in France, the small show of resistance against which Napoleon march'd is said to have dispersed on hearing of his movement."

He then describes the celebration in Antwerp of the birth of the new French régime: —

"To-day being the anniversary of the foundation of the Republic, was celebrated with great pomp by the military at this place. Very few indeed of the

vote; while all conservatives, who wished above all things for a stable and orderly government of law and for peace with other countries, flocked to the polls.

Among the latter, of course, were the few Royalists who still remained in France. Such, at least, was the view Marshall took of this episode. To understand Marshall's subsequent career, too much weight cannot be given this fact and, indeed, all the startling events in France during the six historic months of Marshall's stay in Paris.

But Marshall did not take into account the vital fact that the French soldiers had no chance to vote at this election. They were scattered far and wide — in Italy, Germany, and elsewhere. Yet these very men were the soul of the Revolutionary cause. And the private soldiers were more enraged by the result of the French elections than their generals — even than General Augereau, who was tigerish in his wrath.

They felt that, while they were fighting on the battlefield, they had been betrayed at the ballot box. To the soldiers of France the revolution of the 18th Fructidor was the overthrow of their enemies in their own country. The army felt that it had answered with loyal bayonets a conspiracy of treasonable ballots. It now seems probable that the soldiers and officers of the French armies were right in this view.

Pinckney was absurdly accused of interfering in the elections in behalf of the "Royalist Conspiracy." (Vans Murray to J. Q. Adams, April 3, 1798; *Letters:* Ford, 391.) Such a thing, of course, was perfectly impossible.

inhabitants attended the celebration. Everything in Antwerp wears the appearance of consternation and affright.

"Since the late revolution a proclamation has been published forbidding any priest to officiate who has not taken the oath prescribed by a late order. No priest at Antwerp has taken it & yesterday commenced the suspension of their worship.

"All the external marks of their religion too with which their streets abound are to be taken down. The distress of the people at the calamity is almost as great as if the town was to be given up to pillage."[1]

Five days after leaving Antwerp, Marshall and Pinckney arrived in the French Capital. The Paris of that time was still very much the Paris of Richelieu, except for some large buildings and other improvements begun by Louis XIV. The French metropolis was in no sense a modern city and bore little resemblance to the Paris of the present day. Not until some years afterward did Napoleon as Emperor begin the changes which later, under Napoleon III, transformed it into the most beautiful city in the world. Most of its ancient interest, as well as its mediæval discomforts, were in existence when Marshall and Pinckney reached their destination.

The Government was, in the American view, incredibly corrupt, and the lack of integrity among the rulers was felt even among the people. "The venal-

[1] Marshall to Lee, Antwerp, Sept. 22, 1797; MS., New York Pub. Lib.

ity is such," wrote Gouverneur Morris, in 1793, "that if there be no traitor it is because the enemy has not common sense." [1] And again: "The . . . administration is occupied in acquiring wealth." [2] Honesty was unknown, and, indeed, abhorrent, to most of the governing officials; and the moral sense of the citizens themselves had been stupefied by the great sums of money which Bonaparte extracted from conquered cities and countries and sent to the treasury at Paris. Time and again the Republic was saved from bankruptcy by the spoils of conquest; and long before the American envoys set foot in Paris the popular as well as the official mind had come to expect the receipt of money from any source or by any means.

The bribery of ministers of state and of members of the Directory was a matter of course; [3] and weaker countries paid cash for treaties with the arrogant Government and purchased peace with a price. During this very year Portugal was forced to advance a heavy bribe to Talleyrand and the Directory before the latter would consent to negotiate concerning a treaty; and, as a secret part of the compact, Portugal was required to make a heavy loan to France. It was, indeed, a part of this very Portuguese money with which the troops were

[1] Gouverneur Morris to Washington, Feb., 1793; Morris, ii, 37. While Morris was an aristocrat, thoroughly hostile to democracy and without sympathy with or understanding of the French Revolution, his statements of facts have proved to be generally accurate. (See Lyman: *Diplomacy of the United States*, i, 352, on corruption of the Directory.)

[2] Morris to Pinckney, Aug. 13, 1797; Morris, ii, 51.

[3] Loliée: *Talleyrand and His Times*, 170–71.

brought to Paris for the September revolution of 1797.[1]

Marshall and Pinckney at once notified the French Foreign Office of their presence, but delayed presenting their letters of credence until Gerry should join them before proceeding to business. A week passed; and Marshall records in his diary that every day the waiting envoys were besieged by "Americans whose vessels had been captured & condemned. By appeals & other dilatory means the money had been kept out of the hands of the captors & they were now waiting on expenses in the hope that our [the envoys'] negotiations might relieve them."[2] A device, this, the real meaning of which was to be made plain when the hour should come to bring it to bear on the American envoys.

Such was the official and public atmosphere in which Marshall and Pinckney found themselves on their mission to adjust, with honor, the differences between France and America: a network of unofficial and secret agents was all about them; and at its center was the master spider, Talleyrand. The unfrocked priest had been made Foreign Minister under the Directory in the same month and almost the day that Marshall embarked at Philadelphia for Paris. It largely was through the efforts and influence of Madame de Staël[3] that this prince of intriguers was

[1] King to Secretary of State, Dispatch no. 54, Nov. 18, 1897; King, ii, 243.

[2] Marshall's Journal, official copy, Pickering Papers, Mass. Hist. Soc., 1.

[3] Loliée: *Talleyrand and His Times*, 147; and Blennerhassett: *Talleyrand*, ii, 256–57.

able to place his feet upon this first solid step of his amazing career.

Talleyrand's genius was then unknown to the world, and even the Directory at that time had no inkling of his uncanny craft. To be sure, his previous life had been varied and dramatic and every page of it stamped with ability; but in the tremendous and flaming events of that tragic period he had not attracted wide attention. Now, at last, Talleyrand had his opportunity.

Among other incidents of his life had been his exile to America. For nearly two years and a half he had lived in the United States, traveling hither and yon through the forming Nation. Washington as President had refused to receive the expelled Frenchman, who never forgave the slight. In his journey from State to State he had formed a poor opinion of the American people. "If," he wrote, "I have to stay here another year I shall die." [1]

The incongruities of what still was pioneer life, the illimitable forests, the confusion and strife of opinion, the absence of National spirit and general purpose, caused Talleyrand to look with contempt upon the wilderness Republic. But most of all, this future master spirit of European diplomacy was impressed with what seemed to him the sordid, money-grubbing character of the American people. Nowhere did he find a spark of that idealism which had achieved our independence; and he concluded that gold was the American god.[2]

[1] Talleyrand to Mme. de Staël, quoted in McCabe: *Talleyrand*, 137.
[2] *Memoirs of Talleyrand:* Broglie's ed., i, 179–82; also see McCabe's

Fauchet's disclosures [1] had caused official Paris to measure the American character by the same yardstick that Talleyrand applied to us, when, on leaving our shores, he said: "The United States merit no more consideration than Genoa or Genève."[2]

The French Foreign Minister was not fairly established when the American affair came before him. Not only was money his own pressing need, but to pander to the avarice of his master Barras and the other corrupt members of the Directory was his surest method of strengthening his, as yet, uncertain official position. Such were Talleyrand's mind, views, and station, when, three days after Gerry's belated arrival, the newly installed Minister received the American envoys informally at his house, "where his office was held." By a curious freak of fate, they found him closeted with the Portuguese Minister from whom the very conditions had been exacted which Talleyrand so soon was to attempt to extort from the Americans.

It was a striking group — Talleyrand, tall and thin of body, with pallid, shrunken cheeks and slumberous eyes, shambling forward with a limp, as,

summary in his *Talleyrand*, 136–38. Talleyrand was greatly impressed by the statement of a New Jersey farmer, who wished to see Bingham rather than President Washington because he had heard that Bingham was "so wealthy. . . . Throughout America I met with a similar love of money," says Talleyrand. (*Memoirs of Talleyrand:* Broglie's ed., i, 180.) In this estimate of American character during that period, Talleyrand did not differ from other travelers, nor, indeed, from the opinion of most Americans who expressed themselves upon this subject. (See vol. I, chaps. VII, and VIII, of this work.)

[1] Talleyrand as quoted in Pickering to King, Nov. 7, 1798; *Pickering:* Pickering, ii, 429.

[2] *Am. St. Prs., For. Rel.*, ii, 158.

with halting speech,[1] he coldly greeted his diplomatic visitors; Gerry, small, erect, perfectly attired, the owl-like solemnity of his face made still heavier by his long nose and enormous wig; Pinckney, handsome, well-dressed, clear-eyed, of open countenance;[2] and Marshall, tall, lean, loose-jointed, carelessly appareled, with only his brilliant eyes to hint at the alert mind and dominant personality of the man.

Talleyrand measured his adversaries instantly. Gerry he had known in America and he weighed with just balance the qualities of the Massachusetts envoy; Pinckney he also had observed and feared nothing from the blunt, outspoken, and transparently honest but not in the least subtle or far-seeing South Carolinian; the ill-appearing Virginian, of whom he had never heard, Talleyrand counted as a cipher. It was here that this keen and cynical student of human nature blundered.

Marshall and Talleyrand were almost of an age,[3] the Frenchman being only a few months older than his Virginia antagonist. The powers of neither were known to the other, as, indeed, they were at that time unguessed generally by the mass of the people, even of their own countries.

A month after Talleyrand became the head of French Foreign Affairs, Rufus King, then our Min-

[1] *Memoirs of Talleyrand:* Stewarton, ii, 10.

[2] Pinckney was the only one of the envoys who could speak French. He had received a finished education in England at Westminster and Oxford and afterward had studied in France at the Royal Military College at Caen.

[3] Marshall and Talleyrand were forty-two years of age, Pinckney fifty-one, and Gerry fifty-three.

ister at London, as soon as he had heard of the appointment of the American envoys, wrote Talleyrand a conciliatory letter congratulating the French diplomat upon his appointment. King and Talleyrand had often met both in England and America.

"We have been accustomed," writes King, "to converse on every subject with the greatest freedom"; then, assuming the frankness of friendship, King tries to pave the way for Marshall, Pinckney, and Gerry, without mentioning the latter, however. "From the moment I heard that you had been named to the Department of Foreign Affairs," King assures Talleyrand, "I have felt a satisfactory Confidence that the Cause of the increasing Misunderstanding between us would cease, and that the overtures mediated by our Government would not fail to restore Harmony and Friendship between the two Countries."[1]

King might have saved his ink. Talleyrand did not answer the letter; it is doubtful whether he even read it. At any rate, King's somewhat amateurish effort to beguile the French Foreign Minister by empty words utterly failed of its purpose.

The Americans received cold comfort from Talleyrand; he was busy, he said, on a report on Franco-American affairs asked for by the Directory; when he had presented it to his superiors he would, he said, let the Americans know "what steps were to follow." Talleyrand saw to it, however, that the envoys received "cards of hospitality" which had been

[1] King to Talleyrand, London, Aug. 3, 1797; King, ii, 206–08.

denied to Pinckney. These saved the Americans at least from offensive attentions from the police.[1]

Three days later, a Mr. Church, an American-born French citizen, accompanied by his son, called on Gerry, but found Marshall, who was alone. From Thomas Paine, Church had learned of plans of the Directory concerning neutrals which, he assured Marshall, "would be extremely advantageous to the United States." "Do not urge your mission now," suggested Church — the present was "a most unfavorable moment." Haste meant that "all would probably be lost." What were these measures of the Directory? asked Marshall. Church was not at liberty to disclose them, he said; but the envoys' "true policy was to wait for events."

That night came a letter from the author of "Common Sense." "This letter," Marshall records, "made very different impressions on us. I thought it an insult which ought to be received with that coldness which would forbid the repetition of it. Mr. Gerry was of a contrary opinion." Marshall insisted that the Directory knew of Paine's letter and would learn of the envoys' answer, and that Pinckney, Gerry, and himself must act only as they knew the American Government would approve. It was wrong, said he, and imprudent to lead the Directory to expect anything else from the envoys; and Paine's "aspersions on our government"

[1] *Am. St. Prs., For. Rel.*, ii, 158; Marshall's Journal, Official Copy; MS., Mass. Hist. Soc., 2. The envoys' dispatches to the Secretary of State were prepared by Marshall, largely, from his Journal. Citations will be from the dispatches except when not including matter set out exclusively in Marshall's Journal.

should be resented.[1] So began the break between Marshall and Gerry, which, considering the characters of the two men, was inevitable.

Next, Talleyrand's confidential secretary confided to Major Mountflorence, of the American Consulate, that the Directory would require explanations of President Adams's speech to Congress, by which they were exasperated. The Directory would not receive the envoys, he said, until the negotiations were over; but that persons would be appointed "to treat with" the Americans, and that these agents would report to Talleyrand, who would have "charge of the negotiations."[2] Mountflorence, of course, so advised the envoys.

Thus the curtain rose upon the melodrama now to be enacted — an episode without a parallel in the history of American diplomacy. To understand what follows, we must remember that the envoys were governed by careful, lengthy, and detailed instructions to the effect that "no blame or censure be directly, or indirectly, imputed to the United States"; that in order not to "wound her [France] feelings or to excite her resentment" the negotiations were to be on the principles of the British Treaty; "that no engagement be made inconsistent with . . . any prior treaty"; that "no restraint on our lawful commerce with any other nation be admitted"; that nothing be done "incompatible with the complete sovereignty and independence of the United States in matters of policy, commerce, and government";

[1] Marshall's Journal, Oct. 11, 2–4.

[2] *Am. St. Prs., For. Rel.*, ii, 8–11, and 158. Fulwar Skipwith was consul; but Mountflorence was connected with the office.

and "*that no aid be stipulated in favor of France during the present war.*" [1]

We are now to witness the acts in that strange play, known to American history as the X. Y. Z. Mission, as theatrical a spectacle as any ever prepared for the stage. Indeed, the episode differs from a performance behind the footlights chiefly in that in this curious arrangement the explanation comes after the acting is over. When the dispatches to the American Government, which Marshall now is to write, were transmitted to Congress, diplomatic prudence caused the names of leading characters to be indicated only by certain letters of the alphabet. Thus, this determining phase of our diplomatic history is known to the present day as "The X. Y. Z Affair."

[1] *Am. St. Prs., For. Rel.*, ii, 157. Italics are mine.

CHAPTER VII

FACING TALLEYRAND

Society is divided into two classes; the shearers and the shorn. We should always be with the former against the latter. (Talleyrand.)

To lend money to a belligerent power is to relinquish our neutrality. (Marshall.)

Diplomatically Marshall and his associates found themselves marooned. Many and long were their discussions of the situation. "We have had several conversations on the extraordinary silence of the Government concerning our reception," writes Marshall in his Journal. "The plunder of our commerce sustains no abatements, the condemnations of our vessels are press'd with ardor . . . our reception is postponed in a manner most unusual & contemptuous.

"I urge repeatedly that we ought, in a respectful communication to the Minister [Talleyrand] . . . to pray for a suspension of all further proceedings against American vessels until the further order of the Directory. . . .

"We have already permitted much time to pass away, we could not be charged with precipitation, & I am willing to wait two or three days longer but not more. . . . The existing state of things is to France the most beneficial & the most desirable, but to America it is ruinous. I therefore urge that in a few days we shall lay this interesting subject before the Minister." [1]

[1] Marshall's Journal, Oct. 15, 4–5.

Marshall tells us that Gerry again opposed action, holding that for the envoys to act would "irritate the [French] Government." The Directory "might take umbrage." [1] Besides, declared Gerry, France was in a quandary what to do and "any movement on our part" would relieve her and put the blame on the envoys. "But," records Marshall, "in the address I propose I would say nothing which could give umbrage, & if, as is to be feared, France is determined to be offended, she may quarrel with our answer to any proposition she may make or even with our silence." Pinckney agreed with Marshall; but they yielded to Gerry in order to "preserve unanimity." [2]

Tidings soon arrived of the crushing defeat of the Dutch fleet by the British; and on the heels of this came reports that the Directory were ready to negotiate with the Americans.[3] Next morning, and four days after the mysterious intimations to the Ameri-

[1] Paris made an impression on the envoys as different as their temperaments. Vans Murray records the effect on Gerry, who had written to his friends in Boston of "how handsomely they [the envoys] were received in Paris and how hopeful he is of settlement! ! !"

"Good God — he has mistaken the lamps of Paris for an illumination on his arrival," writes our alarmed Minister at The Hague, "and the salutations of fisherwomen for a procession of chaste matrons hailing the great Pacificator! . . . His foible is to mistake things of common worldly politeness for deference to his rank of which he rarely loses the idea. . . . Gerry is no more fit to enter the labyrinth of Paris as a town — alone — than an innocent is, much less formed to play a game with the political genius of that city . . . without some very steady friend at his elbow. . . . Of all men in America he is . . . the least qualify'd to play a part in Paris, either among the men or the women — he is too virtuous for the last — too little acquainted with the world and himself for the first." (Vans Murray to J. Q. Adams, April 13, 1798; *Letters:* Ford, 394.)

[2] Marshall's Journal, 5.

[3] *Ib.*, Oct. 17, 6.

can envoys from Talleyrand through his confidential secretary, a Parisian business man called on Pinckney and told him that a Mr. Hottenguer,[1] "a native of Switzerland who had been in America," [2] and "a gentleman of considerable credit and reputation," would call on Pinckney. Pinckney had met Hottenguer on a former occasion, probably at The Hague. That evening this cosmopolitan agent of financiers and foreign offices paid the expected visit. After a while Hottenguer "whispered . . . that he had a message from Talleyrand." Into the next room went Pinckney and his caller. There Hottenguer told Pinckney that the Directory were "exceedingly irritated" at President Adams's speech and that "they should be softened."

Indeed, the envoys would not be received, said Hottenguer, unless the mellowing process were applied to the wounded and angry Directory. He was perfectly plain as to the method of soothing that sore and sensitive body — "money" for the pockets of its members and the Foreign Minister which would be "at the disposal of M. Talleyrand." Also a loan must be made to France. Becoming still more explicit, Hottenguer stated the exact amount of financial salve which must be applied in the first step of the healing treatment required from our envoys — a small bribe of one million two hundred thousand livres [about fifty thousand pounds sterling, or two hundred and fifty thousand dollars].

[1] Probably the same Hottenguer who had helped Marshall's brother negotiate the Fairfax loan in Amsterdam. (*Supra*, chap. IV.)

[2] Marshall's Journal, Oct. 17, 6.

"It was absolutely required," reports Marshall, "that we should . . . pay the debts due by contract from France to our citizens . . . pay for the spoliations committed on our commerce . . . & make a considerable loan. . . . Besides this, added Mr. Hottenguer, there must be something for the pocket . . . for the private use of the Directoire & Minister under the form of satisfying claims which," says Marshall, "did not in fact exist."[1]

Pinckney reported to his colleagues. Again the envoys divided as to the course to pursue. "I was decidedly of opinion," runs Marshall's chronicle, "& so expressed myself, that such a proposition could not be made by a nation from whom any treaty, short of the absolute surrender of the independence of the United States was to be expected, but that if there was a possibility of accommodation, to give any countenance whatever to such a proposition would be certainly to destroy that possibility because it would induce France to demand from us terms to which it was impossible for us to accede. I therefore," continues Marshall, "thought we ought, so soon as we could obtain the whole information, to treat the terms as inadmissible and without taking any notice of them to make some remonstrance to the minister on our situation & on that of our countrymen." Pinckney agreed with Marshall; Gerry dissented and declared that "the whole negotiation . . . would be entirely broken off if such an answer was given as I [Marshall] had hinted & there would be a war between the two

[1] *Am. St. Prs., For. Rel.*, ii, 158; Marshall's Journal, 6–7.

nations." At last it was decided to get Hottenguer's proposition in writing.[1]

When Pinckney so informed Hottenguer, the latter announced that he had not dealt "immediately with Talleyrand but through another gentleman in whom Talleyrand had great confidence." Hottenguer had no objection, however, to writing out his "suggestions," which he did the next evening.[2] The following morning he advised the envoys that a Mr. Bellamy, "the confidential friend of M. Talleyrand," would call and explain matters in person. Decidedly, the fog was thickening. The envoys debated among themselves as to what should be done.

"I again urg'd the necessity of breaking off this indirect mode of procedure," testifies Marshall; but "Mr. Gerry reprobated precipitation, insisted on further explanations as we could not completely understand the scope & object of the propositions & conceiv'd that we ought not abruptly object to them." Marshall and Pinckney thought "that they [Talleyrand's demands] were beyond our powers & . . . amounted to a surrender of the independence of our country." [3] But Gerry had his way and the weaving of the spider's web went on.

Two hours after candlelight that evening Hottenguer and Bellamy entered Marshall's room where the three Americans were waiting for them; and Bellamy was introduced as "the confidential friend of M. Talleyrand," of whom Hottenguer had told

[1] Marshall's Journal, 7–8. [2] *Am. St. Prs., For. Rel.*, ii, 158.
[3] Marshall's Journal, Oct. 20, 8–9.

the envoys. Bellamy was, says Marshall, "a genevan now residing in Hamburg but in Paris on a visit." [1] He went straight to the point. Talleyrand, he confided to the envoys, was "a friend of America . . . the kindness and civilities he had personally received in America" had touched his heart; and he was burning to "repay these kindnesses." But what could this anxious friend of America do when the cruel Directory were so outraged at the American President's address to Congress that they would neither receive the envoys nor authorize "Talleyrand to have any communications with" them.

Bellamy pointed out that under these circumstances Talleyrand could not, of course, communicate directly with the envoys; but "had authorized" him to deal with them "and to promise" that the French Foreign Minister would do his best to get the Directory to receive the Americans if the latter agreed to Talleyrand's terms. Nevertheless, Bellamy "stated explicitly and repeatedly that he was clothed with no authority" — he was not a diplomat, he said, but only the trusted friend of Talleyrand. He then pointed out the passages from Adams's address [2] which had so exasperated the French rulers and stated what the envoys must do to make headway.

The American envoys, asserted Bellamy, must make "a formal disavowal in writing . . . that . . . the speech of the Citizen President," Barras, was "not offensive" to America; must offer "reparation" for President Adams's address; must affirm

[1] Marshall's Journal, Oct. 20, 8–9.

[2] *Supra*, 226.

that the decree of the Directory,[1] which Adams had denounced, was not "contrary to the treaty of 1778"; must state "in writing" the depredations on American trade "by the English and French privateers," and must make "a formal declaration" that Adams in his speech to Congress had not referred to the French Government or its agents: if all this were done "the French Republic is disposed to renew their old-time relations with America" by a new treaty which should place France "with respect to the United States exactly on the same footing as they [the United States] should be with England." But, said Bellamy, there must be a secret article of this new treaty providing for a loan from America to France.[2]

Impossible as these terms were, the whole business must be preceded by a bribe. "I will not disguise from you," said Bellamy, "that this situation being met, the essential part of the treaty remains to be adjusted. . . . *You must pay money —you must pay a great deal of money*." Little was said about the two hundred and fifty thousand dollars bribe; "that," declare the envoys' dispatches to the American Secretary of State, "being completely understood on all sides to be required for the officers of the government, and, therefore, needing no further explanation." When all these conditions were complied with, said Bellamy, "M. Talleyrand trusted that, by his influence with the Directory, he could prevail

[1] Directing the capture of enemy goods on American ships, thus nullifying the declaration in the Franco-American Treaty that "free bottoms make free goods."

[2] *Am. St. Prs., For. Rel.*, ii, 159.

on the government to receive" the Americans. For two hours the talk ran on. Before Talleyrand's agents left, the anxiously hospitable Gerry invited them to breakfast the next morning.

Into consultation once more went the envoys. "I pressed strongly," writes Marshall in his Journal, "the necessity of declaring that the propositions were totally inadmissible" and that "it was derogatory from the honor and wounded the real interests of our country to permit ourselves, while unacknowledg'd, to carry on this clandestine negotiation with persons who produced no evidence of being authoriz'd by the Directoire or the Minister to treat with us. Mr. Gerry was quite of a contrary opinion & the old beaten ground about precipitation &c. was trodden once again. Gen'l Pinckney advocated decidedly the same opinions with myself & we determined that the next morning should positively put an end to these conferences." [1]

"On our retiring," continues Marshall's narrative, "Mr. Gerry began to propose further delays & that we shou'd inform them [Talleyrand's go-betweens] that we wou'd take their propositions into consideration — I improperly interrupted him & declared that I wou'd not consent to any proposition of the sort, that the subject was already considered & that so far as my voice wou'd go I wou'd not permit it to be supposed longer that we cou'd deliberate on such propositions as were made to us."

Pinckney agreed with Marshall; but, for harmony's sake, Marshall finally said that he would

[1] Marshall's Journal, Oct. 20, 10. *Am. St. Prs., For. Rel.*, ii, 159.

return to America to "consult our government" on this express condition only — "that France should previously and immediately suspend all depredations upon American commerce." For once, Gerry assented and a letter was written accordingly.[1]

Hottenguer was prompt in his engagement to breakfast with Gerry the next morning; but Bellamy did not come till ten o'clock, explaining that he had been closeted with Talleyrand. Bellamy was much depressed; the Directory, he declared, would not receive the envoys until the latter had disavowed President Adams's speech, *unless* they "could find the means to change their [the Directory's] determination in this particular." What were such "means?" asked the envoys. "I am not authorized to state them," said Bellamy. "You must search for them and propose them yourselves."

Still, Bellamy, merely as an individual, was willing to suggest such "means." It was money, he explained. The "Directory were jealous of their own honor and the honor of the nation"; they demanded the same treatment formerly accorded to the King; and their "honor must be maintained in the manner required" unless "the envoys substituted . . . something perhaps more valuable, and that was money." [2]

It was all so simple, according to Bellamy. All that the envoys had to do was to buy thirty-two million florins of Dutch inscriptions at twenty shillings to the pound. "It was certain," he assured

1 Marshall's Journal, Oct. 21, 10–11.
2 *Am. St. Prs., For. Rel.*, ii, 159–60.

the Americans, "that after a time the Dutch Government would repay . . . the money, so that America would ultimately lose nothing" and everybody would be happy. But even if the envoys made the loan in this way, the bribe of two hundred and fifty thousand dollars must be paid in addition. Thereupon the envoys handed him the letter which Marshall had prepared the night before, which stated that they had no power to make a loan, but could send one of their number to America for consultation and instruction.

Bellamy was "disappointed" and at once modified his language. Why did the envoys treat the money proposition as coming from the Directory? It was only his own personal suggestion. Then "what has led to our present conversation?" asked the envoys. Pinckney recalled Hottenguer's first visit and the latter confirmed Pinckney's account.

Upon the envoys stating the differences between France and America, to settle which was the purpose of their mission, and gently resenting the demands made upon them, Bellamy became excited. The envoys' conduct was not to be borne, he exclaimed; let them beware of the resentment of France. They "could not help it," answered the envoys — the Directory must look after France; the envoys must look after the United States.

Bellamy was "in despair." What a provincial view these Americans took of a diplomatic negotiation! They must broaden their horizon. They must acquire worldly wisdom. They must remember "the respect which the Directory required"; they must realize that that august body "would exact as much as was paid to the ancient kings." The envoys would not be received without it; that was flat, Bellamy informed them; and "he seemed to shudder at the consequences."

Marshall and Pinckney simply would not see the point. But Gerry was a man of the world who could understand European diplomacy. Marshall declared that the envoys were there to adjust international differences. If, however, France "would make war," then, said they: "We regret the unavoidable necessity of defending ourselves." [1]

For a little while Talleyrand's leeches dropped away from the perplexed Americans. Marshall reported to Washington French conditions as he had observed them up to that time. He confirms to the former President the American report that French agriculture had been improved "in the course of the present war": —

"In that part of the country through which I have passed the evidences of plenty abound. The whole earth appears to be in cultivation & the harvests of the present year appear to be as productive as the fields which yield them are extensive.

"I am informed that every part of the country exhibits the same aspect. If this be the fact, there will probably remain, notwithstanding the demands of the armies, a surplus of provisions."

Marshall briefly but clearly analyzes the economic and commercial outcome of the war: —

"Manufactures have declined in the same ratio

[1] *Am. St. Prs., For. Rel.*, ii, 159–60.

that the cultivation of the soil has increas'd. War has been made upon the great manufacturing towns & they are in a considerable degree destroy'd. With manufactures France does not supply herself fully from her internal resources.

"Those of Britain flow in upon her notwithstanding the most severe prohibitory laws. The port of Rotterdam is purposely left open by the English & their goods are imported by the Dutch under Prussian and other neutral colors. They are smuggled in great quantities into France.

"Peace, then, will find this [French] nation entirely competent to the full supply of her colonies with provisions and needing manufactures to be imported for her own consumption. . . . France can take from America tobacco & raw cotton she can supply us with wines, brandies & silks."

Marshall then makes a searching commentary on French politics.

"The existing political state of France is connected with certain internal & powerfully operating causes by which it has been & will continue to be greatly influenc'd. Not the least of these is the tenure by which property is held.

"In the course of the revolution it is believed that more than half the land of France has become national.[1] Of this a very considerable proportion has been sold at a low rate.

"It is true that much of it belonged to those who have fallen under the Guillotine or who have been termed emigrants. Among the emigrants are many

[1] By "national" lands, Marshall refers to the confiscated estates.

whose attachment to their country has never been shaken; & what is remarkable, among them are many who were never out of France. The law upon this subject is worthy of attention.

"Any two persons, no matter what their reputation, may, to some authority, I believe the municipality of the district, write & subscribe against any person whatever a charge, that such person is an emigrant, on receipt of which the person so charg'd is without further investigation inscribed on the list of emigrants.

"If the person so inscribed be afterwards apprehended while his name remains on the list, the trial, as I understand, is, not of the fact of emigration, but of the identity of the persons, & if this identity be established, he is instantly fusiller'd[shot]. The law is either rightly executed or permitted to be relax'd, as the occasion or the temper of the times may direct.

"During intervals of humanity some disposition has been manifested to permit the return of those who have never offended, who have been banished by a terror which the government itself has reprobated, & to permit in case of arrestation, an investigation of the fact of emigration as well as of the identity of the person accus'd.

"There is too a great deal of property which has been sold as national but which in truth was never so, & which may be reclaimed by the original proprietors.

"In this state the acquirers of national property are of course extremely suspicious. They form a vast proportion of the population of France. They are not only important in consequence of their numbers, but in consequence of their vigor, their activity & that unity of interest which produces a unity of effort among them.

"The armies too have been promised a milliard. This promise rests upon the national property for its performance. The effect of these circumstances cannot escape your observation. Classes of citizens are to be disfranchised against the next election."

Marshall and Pinckney, at this early stage of Talleyrand's financial-diplomatic intrigue, were so disgusted that they were on the point of "returning to America immediately." The continuance of French depredations on the high seas caused Marshall to write to Washington as follows: —

"The captures of our vessels seem to be only limited by the ability to capture. That ability is increasing, as the government has let out to hardy adventurers the national frigates. Among those who plunder us, who are most active in this infamous business, & most loud in vociferating criminations equally absurd and untrue, are some unprincipled apostates who were born in America.

"These sea rovers by a variety of means seem to have acquired great influence in the government.

"This influence will be exerted to prevent an accommodation between the United States & France and to prevent any regulations which may intercept the passage of the spoils they have made on our commerce, to their pockets. The government I believe is too well disposed to promote their views. At present it seems to me to be radically hostile to our country.

"I cou'd wish to form a contrary opinion, but to do so I must shut my eyes on every object which presents itself to them & fabricate in my own mind non-existing things, to be substituted for realities, & to form the basis of my creed.

"Might I be permitted to hazard an opinion it wou'd be the Atlantic only can save us, & that no consideration will be sufficiently powerful to check the extremities to which the temper of this government will carry it, but an apprehension that we may be thrown into the arms of Britain."

Although the Treaty of Campo Formio had been signed on the 17th of October, Paris had not yet heard of it. This treaty marked Bonaparte as the most constructive diplomat, as well as the foremost captain, of the age, for such he had already proved himself to be. A week later, when Marshall wrote the above letter to Washington (October 24, 1797), he reported that "The negotiations with the Emperor of Austria are said not to have been absolutely broken off. Yesterday it was said that peace with him was certain. Several couriers have arrived lately from Buonaparte & the national debt rose yesterday from seven to ten livres in the hundred. Whether this is founded on a real expectation of peace with Austria or is the mere work of stock jobbers is not for me to decide."

But three days afterward (October 27) the news reached Paris; and Marshall adds this postscript: "The definitive peace is made with the Emperor.

You will have seen the conditions. Venice has experienced the fate of Poland. England is threatened with an invasion." [1]

The thunders of cannon announcing Bonaparte's success were still rolling through Paris when Talleyrand's plotters again descended upon the American envoys. Bellamy came and, Pinckney and Gerry being at the opera, saw Marshall alone. The triumph of Bonaparte was his theme. The victorious general was now ready to invade England, announced Bellamy; but "concerning America not a syllable was said." [2]

Already Talleyrand, sensitive as any hawk to coming changes in the political weather, had begun to insinuate himself into the confidence of the future conqueror of Europe, whose diplomatic right arm he so soon was to become. The next morning the thrifty Hottenguer again visits the envoys. Bonaparte's success in the negotiations of Campo Formio, which sealed the victories of the French arms, has alarmed Hottenguer, he declares, for the success of the American mission.

Why, he asks, have the Americans made no proposition to the Directory? That haughty body "were becoming impatient and would take a decided course in regard to America" if the envoys "could not soften them," exclaims Talleyrand's solicitous messenger. Surely the envoys can see that Bonaparte's treaty with Austria has changed everything,

[1] Marshall to Washington, Paris, Oct. 24 (postscript, 27th), 1797; *Amer. Hist. Rev.*, Jan., 1897, ii, 301–03; also, Washington MSS., Lib. Cong.; or Sparks MSS., Mass. Hist. Soc.

[2] Marshall's Journal, Oct. 26, 12.

and that therefore the envoys themselves must change accordingly.

Exhibiting great emotion, Hottenguer asserts that the Directory have determined "that all nations should aid them [the French], or be considered and treated as enemies." Think, he cries, of the "power and violence of France." Think of the present danger the envoys are in. Think of the wisdom of "softening the Directory." But he hints that "the Directory might be made more friendly." Gain time! Gain time! Give the bribe, and gain time! the wily agent advises the Americans. Otherwise, France may declare war against America.

That would be most unfortunate, answer the envoys, but assert that the present American "situation was more ruinous than a declared war could be"; for now American "commerce was floundering unprotected." In case of war "America would protect herself."

"You do not speak to the point," Hottenguer passionately cries out; "it is money; it is expected that you will offer money."

"We have given an answer to that demand," the envoys reply.

"No," exclaims Hottenguer, "you have not! What is your answer?"

"It is no," shouts Pinckney; "no; not a sixpence!"

The persistent Hottenguer does not desist. He tells the envoys that they do not know the kind of men they are dealing with. The Directory, he insists, disregard the justice of American claims; care nothing even for the French colonies; "consider themselves as perfectly invulnerable" from the United States. Money is the only thing that will interest such terrible men. The Americans, parrying, ask whether, even if they give money, Talleyrand will furnish proofs that it will produce results. Hottenguer evades the question. A long discussion ensues.

Pay the bribe, again and again urges the irritated but tenacious go-between. Does not your Government "know that nothing is to be obtained here without money?"

"Our Government had not even suspected such a state of things," declare the amazed Americans.

"Well," answers Hottenguer, "there is not an American in Paris who could not have given that information. . . . Hamburgh and other states of Europe were obliged to buy peace . . . nothing could resist" the power of France; let the envoys think of "the danger of a breach with her."[1]

Thus far Pinckney mostly had spoken for the envoys. Marshall now took up the American case. Few utterances ever made by him more clearly reveal the mettle of the man; and none better show his conception of the American Nation's rights, dignity, and station among the Governments of the world.

"I told him [Hottenguer]," writes Marshall, "that . . . no nation estimated her [France's] power more highly than America or wished more to be on amicable terms with her, but that one object was still dearer to us than the friendship of France which was our national independence. That America had taken a neutral station. She had a right to take it. No

[1] *Am. St. Prs., For. Rel.*, ii, 161–62.

nation had a right to force us out of it. That to lend . . . money to a belligerent power abounding in every thing requisite for war but money was to relinquish our neutrality and take part in the war. To lend this money under the lash & coercion of France was to relinquish the government of ourselves & to submit to a foreign government imposed on us by force," Marshall declared. "That we would make at least one manly struggle before we thus surrendered our national independence.

"Our case was different from that of the minor nations of Europe," he explained. "They were unable to maintain their independence & did not expect to do so. America was a great, & so far as concerned her self-defense, a powerful nation. She was able to maintain her independence & must deserve to lose it if she permitted it to be wrested from her. France & Britain have been at war for near fifty years of the last hundred & might probably be at war for fifty years of the century to come."

Marshall asserted that "America has no motives which could induce her to involve herself in those wars and that if she now preserved her neutrality & her independence it was most probable that she would not in future be afraid as she had been for four years past — but if she now surrendered her rights of self government to France or permitted them to be taken from her she could not expect to recover them or to remain neutral in any future war." [1]

[1] Marshall's Journal, Oct. 27, 16–17. This statement of the American case by Marshall is given in the dispatches, which Marshall prepared as coming from the envoys generally. (See *Am. St. Prs., For. Rel.*, ii, 161–62.)

For two hours Talleyrand's emissary pleads, threatens, bullies, argues, expostulates. Finally, he departs to consult with his fellow conspirator, or to see Talleyrand, the master of both. Thus ran the opening dialogue between the French bribe procurers and the American envoys. Day after day, week after week, the plot ran on like a play upon the stage. "A Mr. Hauteval whose fortune lay in the island of St. Domingo" called on Gerry and revealed how pained Talleyrand was that the envoys had not visited him. Again came Hauteval, whom Marshall judged to be the only one of the agents "solicitous of preserving peace."

Thus far the envoys had met with the same request, that they "call upon Talleyrand at private hours." Marshall and Pinckney said that, "having been treated in a manner extremely disrespectful" to their country, they could not visit the Minister of Foreign Affairs "in the existing state of things . . . unless he should expressly signify his wish" to see them "& would appoint a time & place." But, says Marshall, "Mr. Gerry having known Mr. Talleyrand in Boston considered it a piece of personal respect to wait on him & said that he would do so." [1]

Hottenguer again calls to explain how anxious Talleyrand was to serve the envoys. Make "one more effort," he urges, "to enable him to do so." Bonaparte's daring plan for the invasion of England was under way and Hottenguer makes the most of this. "The power and haughtiness of France," the inevitable destruction of England, the terrible cor-

[1] Marshall's Journal, Oct. 23, 11–12.

sequences to America, are revealed to the Americans. "Pay by way of fees" the two hundred and fifty thousand dollar bribe, and the Directory would allow the envoys to stay in Paris; Talleyrand would then even consent to receive them while one of them went to America for instructions.[1]

Why hesitate? It was the usual thing; the Portuguese Minister had been dealt with in similar fashion, argues Hottenguer. The envoys counter by asking whether American vessels will meanwhile be restored to their owners. They will not, was the answer. Will the Directory stop further outrages on American commerce, ask the envoys? Of course not, exclaims Hottenguer. We do "not so much regard a little money as [you] said," declare the envoys, "although we should hazard ourselves by giving it but we see only evidences of the most extreme hostility to us." Thereupon they go into a long and useless explanation of the American case.

Gerry's visit to his "old friend" Talleyrand was fruitless; the Foreign Minister would not receive him.[2] Gerry persisted, nevertheless, and finally found the French diplomat at home. Talleyrand demanded the loan, and held a new decree of the Directory before Gerry, but proposed to withhold it for a week so that the Americans could think it over. Gerry hastened to his colleagues with the news. Marshall and Pinckney told Hauteval to inform Talleyrand "that unless there is a hope that the Directory itself might be prevailed upon by reason to

[1] *Am. St. Prs., For. Rel.*, ii, 163; Marshall's Journal, Oct. 29, 21–22.
[2] Marshall's Journal, Oct. 23, 12.

alter its arrêté, we do not wish to suspend it for an instant." [1]

The next evening, when Marshall and Pinckney were away from their quarters, Bellamy and Hottenguer called on Gerry, who again invited them to breakfast. This time Bellamy disclosed the fact that Talleyrand was now intimately connected with Bonaparte and the army in Italy. Let Gerry ponder over that! "The fate of Venice was one which might befall the United States," exclaimed Talleyrand's mouthpiece; and let Gerry not permit Marshall and Pinckney to deceive themselves by expecting help from England — France could and would attend to England, invade her, break her, force her to peace. Where then would America be? Thus for an hour Bellamy and Hottenguer worked on Gerry.[2]

Far as Talleyrand's agents had gone in trying to force the envoys to offer a bribe of a quarter of a million dollars, to the Foreign Minister and Directory, they now went still further. The door of the chamber of horrors was now opened wide to the stubborn Americans. Personal violence was intimated; war was threatened. But Marshall and Pinckney refused to be frightened.

The Directory, Talleyrand, and their emissaries, however, had not employed their strongest resource. "Perhaps you believe," said Bellamy to the envoys, "that in returning and exposing to your countrymen the unreasonableness of the demands of this government, you will unite them in their resistance to those

[1] Marshall's Journal, Oct. 28, 18–19.
[2] *Am. St. Prs., For. Rel.*, ii, 163.

demands. You are mistaken; you ought to know that the diplomatic skill of France and the means she possesses in your country are sufficient to enable her, with the French party in America,[1] to throw the blame which will attend the rupture of the negotiations on the federalists, as you term yourselves, but on the British party as France terms you. And you may assure yourselves that this will be done."[2]

Thus it was out at last. This was the hidden card that Talleyrand had been keeping back. And it was a trump. Talleyrand managed to have it played again by a fairer hand before the game was over. Yes, surely; here was something to give the obstinate Marshall pause. For the envoys knew it to be true. There was a French party in America, and there could be little doubt that it was constantly growing stronger.[3] Genêt's reception had made that plain. The outbursts throughout America of enthusiasm for France had shown it. The popular passion exhibited, when the Jay Treaty was made public, had proved it. Adams's narrow escape from defeat had demonstrated the strength of French sympathy in America.

[1] "Infinite pains have been taken there [in France] to spread universally the idea that there are, in America, only two parties, the one entirely devoted to France and the other to England." (J. Q. Adams to his father, The Hague, July 2, 1797; *Writings, J. Q. A.*: Ford, ii, 181.)

[2] Marshall's Journal, Oct. 30, 25–26; *Am. St. Prs., For. Rel.*, 164.

[3] "The French were extremely desirous of seeing Mr. Jefferson President; . . . they exerted themselves to the utmost in favor of his election [in 1796]; . . . they made a great point of his success." (Harper to his Constituents, Jan. 5, 1797; *Bayard Papers:* Donnan, 25: and see *supra*, chaps. I, II, III, and IV, of this volume.)

A far more dangerous circumstance, as well known to Talleyrand as it was to the envoys, made the matter still more serious — the democratic societies, which, as we have seen, had been organized in great numbers throughout the United States had pushed the French propaganda with zeal, system, and ability; and were, to America, what the Jacobin Clubs had been to France before their bloody excesses. They had already incited armed resistance to the Government of the United States.[1] Thorough information of the state of things in the young country across the ocean had emboldened Barras, upon taking leave of Monroe, to make a direct appeal to the American people in disregard of their own Government, and, indeed, almost openly against it. The threat, by Talleyrand's agents, of the force which France could exert in America, was thoroughly understood by the envoys. For, as we have seen, there was a French party in America — "a party," as Washington declared, "determined to advocate French measures under *all* circumstances." [2] It was common knowledge among all the representatives of the American Government in Europe that the French Directory depended upon the Republican Party in this country. "They reckon . . . upon many friends and partisans among us," wrote the American Minister in London to the American Minister at The Hague.[3]

The Directory even had its particular agents in the United States to inflame the American people

[1] See *supra*, chap. III, 86 *et seq.*
[2] Washington to King, June 25, 1797; King, II, 194.
[3] King to Murray, March 31, 1798; *ib.*, 294.

against their own Government if it did not yield to French demands. Weeks before the President, in 1797, had called Congress in special session on French affairs, "the active and incessant manœuvres of French agents in" America made William Smith think that any favorable action of France "will drive the great mass of knaves & fools back into her [France's] arms," notwithstanding her piracies upon our ships.[1]

On November 1 the envoys again decided to "hold no more indirect intercourse with" Talleyrand or the Directory. Marshall and Pinckney told Hottenguer that they thought it "degrading our country to carry on further such an indirect intercourse"; and that they "would receive no propositions" except from persons having "acknowledged authority." After much parrying, Hottenguer again unparked the batteries of the French party in America.

He told Marshall and Pinckney that "intelligence had been received from the United States, that if Colonel Burr and Mr. Madison had constituted the Mission, the difference between the two nations would have been accommodated before this time." Talleyrand was even preparing to send a memorial to America, threatened Hottenguer, complaining that the envoys were "unfriendly to an accommodation with France."

The insulted envoys hotly answered that Talleyrand's "correspondents in America took a good deal on themselves when they undertook to say how the Directory would have received Colonel Burr and

[1] Smith to King, Philadelphia, April 3, 1797; King, ii, 165.

Mr. Madison"; and they defied Talleyrand to send a memorial to the United States.[1]

Disgusted with these indirect and furtive methods, Marshall insisted on writing Talleyrand on the subject that the envoys had been sent to France to settle. "I had been for some time extremely solicitous" that such a letter should be sent, says Marshall. "It appears to me that for three envoys extraordinary to be kept in Paris thirty days without being received can only be designed to degrade & humiliate their country & to postpone a consideration of its just & reasonable complaints till future events in which it ought not to be implicated shall have determined France in her conduct towards it. Mr. Gerry had been of a contrary opinion & we had yielded to him but this evening he consented that the letter should be prepared." [2]

Nevertheless Gerry again objected.[3] At last the Paris newspapers took a hand. "It was now in the power of the Administration [Directory]," says Marshall, "to circulate by means of an enslaved press precisely those opinions which are agreeable to itself & no printer dares to publish an examination of them."

"With this tremendous engine at its will, it [the Directory] almost absolutely controls public opinion on every subject which does not immediately affect the interior of the nation. With respect to its designs against America it experiences not so much difficulty as . . . would have been experienced had not

[1] *Am. St. Prs., For. Rel.*, ii, 163–64.
[2] Marshall's Journal, Nov. 4, 31. [3] *Ib.*, 31.

our own countrymen labored to persuade them that our Government was under a British influence." [1]

On November 3, Marshall writes Charles Lee: "When I clos'd my last letter I did not expect to address you again from this place. I calculated on being by this time on my return to the United States. . . . My own opinion is that France wishes to retain America in her present situation until her negotiation with Britain, which it is believed is about to recommence, shall have been terminated, and a present absolute rupture with America might encourage England to continue the war and peace with England . . . will put us more in her [France's] power. . . . Our situation is more intricate and difficult than you can believe. . . . The demand for money has been again repeated. The last address to us . . . concluded . . . that the French party in America would throw all the blame of a rupture on the federalists. . . . We were warned of the fate of Venice. All these conversations are preparing for a public letter but the delay and the necessity of writing only in cypher prevents our sending it by this occasion. . . . I wish you could . . . address the Minister concerning our reception. We despair of doing anything. . . . Mr. Putnam an American citizen has been arrested and sent to jail under the pretext of his cheating frenchmen. . . . This . . . is a mere pretext. It is considered as ominous toward Americans generally. He like most of them is a creditor of the [French] government." [2]

[1] Marshall's Journal, Nov. 8, 33.

[2] Marshall to Lee, Nov. 3, 1797; MS., Lib. Cong. Lee was Attorney-General. Marshall's letter was in cipher.

Finally the envoys sent Talleyrand the formal request, written by Marshall,[1] that the Directory receive them. Talleyrand ignored it. Ten more days went by. When might they expect an answer? inquired the envoys. Talleyrand parried and delayed. "We are not yet received," wrote the envoys to Secretary of State Pickering, "and the condemnation of our vessels . . . is unremittingly continued. Frequent and urgent attempts have been made to inveigle us again into negotiations with persons not officially authorized, of which the obtaining of money is the basis; but we have persisted in declining to have any further communication relative to diplomatic business with persons of that description." [2]

Anxious as Marshall was about the business of his mission, which now rapidly was becoming an intellectual duel between Talleyrand and himself, he was far more concerned as to the health of his wife, from whom he had heard nothing since leaving America. Marshall writes her a letter full of apprehension, but lightens it with a vague account of the amusements, distractions, and dissipations of the French Capital.

"I have not, since my departure from the United States," Marshall tells his wife, "received a single letter from you or from any one of my friends in America. Judge what anxiety I must feel concerning you. I do not permit myself for a moment to suspect that you are in any degree to blame for this. I am sure you have written often to me but unhappily for

[1] Marshall to Lee, Nov. 7, 8, 9, 10, and 11; MS., Lib. Cong.
[2] *Am. St. Prs., For. Rel.*, ii, 166.

me your letters have not found me. I fear they will not. They have been thrown over board or intercepted. Such is the fate of the greater number of the letters addressed by Americans to their friends in France, such I fear will be the fate of all that may be address'd to me.

"In my last letter I informed you that I counted on being at home in March. I then expected to have been able to leave this country by christmas at furthest & such is my impatience to see you & my dear children that I had determined to risk a winter passage." He asks his wife to request Mr. Wickham to see that one of Marshall's law cases "may ly till my return. I think nothing will prevent my being at the chancery term in May.

"Oh God," cries Marshall, "how much time & how much happiness have I thrown away! Paris presents one incessant round of amusement & dissipation but very little I believe even for its inhabitants of that society which interests the heart. Every day you may see something new magnificent & beautiful, every night you may see a spectacle which astonishes & enchants the imagination. The most lively fancy aided by the strongest description cannot equal the reality of the opera. All that you can conceive & a great deal more than you can conceive in the line of amusement is to be found in this gay metropolis but I suspect it would not be easy to find a friend.

"I would not live in Paris," Marshall tells his "dearest Polly" "[if I could] . . . be among the wealthiest of its citizens. I have changed my lodging much for the better. I liv'd till within a few days in a house where I kept my own apartments perfectly in the style of a miserable old bachelor without any mixture of female society. I now have rooms in the house of a very accomplished a very sensible & I believe a very amiable Lady whose temper, very contrary to the general character of her country women, is domestic & who generally sits with us two or three hours in the afternoon.

"This renders my situation less unpleasant than it has been but nothing can make it eligible. Let me see you once more & I . . . can venture to assert that no consideration would induce me ever again to consent to place the Atlantic between us. Adieu my dearest Polly. Preserve your health & be happy as possible till the return of him who is ever yours." [1]

The American Minister in London was following anxiously the fortunes of our envoys in Paris, and gave them frequent information and sound advice. Upon learning of their experiences, King writes that "I will not allow myself yet to despair of your success, though my apprehensions are greater than my hopes." King enclosed his Dispatch number 52 to the American Secretary of State, which tells of the Portuguese Treaty and the decline of Spain's power in Paris. [2]

In reply, Pinckney writes King, on December 14, that the Directory "are undoubtedly hostile to our Government, and are determined, if possible, to

[1] Marshall to his wife, Paris, Nov. 27, 1797; MS.

[2] King to Pinckney, Marshall, and Gerry, Nov. 15, 1797; enclosing Dispatch no. 52 to Pinckney; King, II, 240–41. See *ib.*, 245; and Dec. 9, 1797; *ib.*, 247.

effectuate a change in our administration, and to oblige our present President [Adams] to resign," and further adds that the French authorities contemplate expelling from France "every American who could not prove" that he was for France and against America.

"Attempts," he continues, "are made to divide the Envoys and with that view some civilities are shown to Mr. G.[erry] and none to the two others [Marshall and Pinckney]. . .. The American Jacobins here pay him [Gerry] great Court."[1] The little New Englander already was yielding to the seductions of Talleyrand, and was also responsive to the flattery of a group of unpatriotic Americans in Paris who were buttering their own bread by playing into the hands of the Directory and the French Foreign Office.

Marshall now beheld a stage of what he believed was the natural development of unregulated democracy. Dramatic events convinced him that he was witnessing the growth of license into absolutism. Early in December Bonaparte arrived in Paris. Swiftly the Conqueror had come from Rastadt, traveling through France *incognito*, after one of his lightning-flash speeches to his soldiers reminding them of "the Kings whom you have vanquished, the people upon whom you have conferred liberty." The young general's name was on every tongue.

Paris was on fire to see and worship the hero. But Bonaparte kept aloof from the populace. He made himself the child of mystery. The future Emperor of

[1] Pinckney to King, Paris, Dec. 14, 1797; King, ii, 259–60.

the French, clad in the garments of a plain citizen, slipped unnoticed through the crowds. He would meet nobody but scholars and savants of world renown. These he courted; but he took care that this fact was known to the people. In this course he continued until the stage was set and the cue for his entrance given.

Finally the people's yearning to behold and pay homage to their soldier-statesman becomes a passion not to be denied. The envious but servile Directory yield, and on December 10, 1797, a splendid festival in Bonaparte's honor is held at the Luxembourg. The scene flames with color: captured battle-flags as decorations; the members of the Directory appareled as Roman Consuls; foreign ministers in their diplomatic costumes; officers in their uniforms; women brilliantly attired in the height of fashion.[1] At last the victorious general appears on the arm of Talleyrand, the latter gorgeously clad in the dress of his high office; but Bonaparte, short, slender, and delicate, wearing the plainest clothes of the simplest citizen.

Upon this superb play-acting John Marshall looked with placid wonder. Here, then, thought this Virginian, who had himself fought for liberty on many a battlefield, were the first fruits of French revolutionary republicanism. Marshall beheld no

[1] Talleyrand, who gave the fête, wrote: "I spared no trouble to make it brilliant and attractive; although in this I experienced some difficulty on account of the vulgarity of the directors' wives who, of course, enjoyed precedence over all other ladies." (*Memoirs of Talleyrand:* Broglie's ed., i, 197; also see Sloane: *Life of Napoleon,* ii, 20; and Lanfrey: *Life of Napoleon,* i, 254–57.)

devotion here to equal laws which should shield all men, but only adoration of the sword-wielder who was strong enough to rule all men. In the fragile, eagle-faced little warrior,[1] Marshall already saw the man on horseback advancing out of the future; and in the thunders of applause he already heard the sound of marching armies, the roar of shotted guns, the huzzas of charging squadrons.

All this was something that Jefferson had not seen. Jefferson's sojourn in France had been at the time when the French Revolution was just sprouting; and he foresaw only that beautiful idealism into which the glorious dreamers of the time fondly imagined the Revolution would flower.

But Marshall was in Paris after the guillotine had done its work; when corruption sat in the highest places of government; and when military glory in the name of liberty had become the deity of the people. So where Jefferson expected that the roses of peace would bloom, Marshall saw clusters of bayonets, as the fruitage of the French Revolution.

[1] "At first sight he [Bonaparte] seemed . . . to have a charming face, so much do the halo of victory, fine eyes, a pale and almost consumptive look, become a young hero." (*Memoirs of Talleyrand*: Broglie's ed., i, 196.)

CHAPTER VIII

THE AMERICAN MEMORIAL

Separated far from Europe, we mean not to mingle in her quarrels. (Marshall.)

A fraudulent neutrality is no neutrality at all. (Marshall.)

We have a very considerable party in America who are strongly in our interest. (Madame de Villette.)

Four days after the festival of triumph to Bonaparte, Talleyrand's agents resumed their work. The sordid scenes were repeated, but their monotony was broken. Now the lady of the plot appeared upon the scene. In the long, vexed, and fruitless days of their stay in Paris, the American envoys, it seems, were not without the solace and diversion of the society of the French Capital.

Among the attractive feminine acquaintances they made, one was undoubtedly an agent of the French Foreign Office. Madame de Villette was one of the most engaging women in the French Capital.[1] Cultivated, brilliant, and altogether charming, she made herself particularly agreeable to the American envoys. She and Marshall became especially good

[1] *Am. St. Prs., For. Rel.*, ii, 167. This lady was "understood to be Madame de Villette, the celebrated Belle and Bonne of Voltaire." (Lyman: *Diplomacy of the United States*, ii, footnote to 336.) Lyman says that "as to the lady an intimation is given that that part of the affair was not much to the credit of the Americans." (And see Austin: *Gerry*, ii, footnote to 202.) Madame de Villette was the widow of a Royalist colonel. Her brother, an officer in the King's service, was killed while defending Marie Antoinette. Robespierre proscribed Madame de Villette and she was one of a group confined in prison awaiting the guillotine, of whom only a few escaped. (*Ib.*)

friends; but Madame de Villette ventured no diplomatic suggestions to him, notwithstanding his easy good nature. She was far too good a judge of character to commit that indiscretion. So was Talleyrand, who by this time had begun to appreciate Marshall's qualities. But Pinckney, hearty, handsome man of the world, but without Marshall's penetration and adroitness, was another matter. Gerry the intriguers could already count upon; and only one other member of the commission was necessary to their ends. Perhaps Pinckney might be won over by this captivating Frenchwoman. On some occasion Madame de Villette approached him: —

"Why will you not lend us money?" said she to Pinckney. "If you were to make us a loan, all matters will be adjusted. When you were contending for your Revolution we lent you money." Pinckney pointed out the differences — that America had *requested* a loan of France, and France now *demanded* a loan of America. "Oh, no," said she. "We do not make a demand; we think it more delicate that the offer should come from you; but M. Talleyrand has mentioned to me (who am surely not in his confidence) the necessity of your making us a loan, and I know that he has mentioned it to two or three others; and that you have been informed of it; and I will assure you that, if you remain here six months longer, you will not advance a single step further in your negotiations without a loan."

If that is so, bluntly answered Pinckney, the envoys might as well leave at once. "Why," exclaimed Talleyrand's fair agent, "that might possibly lead to a rupture, which you had better avoid; for we have a very considerable party in America who are strongly in our interest."[1]

The fox-like Talleyrand had scented another hole by which he might get at his elusive quarry. "Every man has his price" was his doctrine; and his experience hitherto had proved it sound. He found that the brilliant Paris adventurer, Beaumarchais, had a lawsuit against the State of Virginia. Beaumarchais had won this suit in the lower court and it was now pending on appeal. John Marshall was his attorney.[2] Here, then, thought Talleyrand, was the way to reach this unknown quantity in his problem.

On December 17, Marshall, happening into Gerry's

[1] *Am. St. Prs., For. Rel.*, ii, 167.

[2] Beaumarchais was one of the most picturesque figures of that theatrical period. He is generally known to-day only as the author of the operas, *The Barber of Seville* and the *Marriage of Figaro.* His suit was to recover a debt for supplies furnished the Americans during the Revolution. Silas Deane, for our Government, made the original contract with Beaumarchais. In addition to the contest before the courts, in which Marshall was Beaumarchais's attorney, the matter was before Congress three times during the claimant's life and, through his heirs, twice after his death. In 1835 the case was settled for 800,000 francs, which was nearly 2,500,000 francs less than Alexander Hamilton, in an investigation, ordered by Congress, found to be due the Frenchman; and 3,500,000 livres less than Silas Deane reported that America owed Beaumarchais.

Arthur Lee, Beaumarchais's enemy, to whom Congress in 1787 left the adjustment, had declared that the Frenchman owed the United States two million francs. This prejudiced report was the cause of almost a half-century of dispute, and of gross injustice. (See Loménie: *Beaumarchais et son temps;* also, Channing, iii, 283, and references in the footnote; and Perkins: *France in the American Revolution.* Also see Henry to Beaumarchais, Jan. 8, 1785; Henry, iii, 264, in which Henry says: "I therefore feel myself gratified in seeing, as I think, ground for hope that yourself, and those worthy and suffering of ours in your nation, who in so friendly a manner advanced their money and goods when we were in want, will be satisfied that nothing has been omitted which lay in our power towards paying them.")

apartment, found Bellamy there. Beaumarchais had given a dinner to Marshall and his fellow envoys, from which Bellamy had been kept by a toothache. The envoys had returned Beaumarchais's courtesy; and he had retired from this dinner "much indisposed." [1] Since then Marshall had not seen his client. Bellamy casually remarked that he had not known, until within a short time, that Marshall was the attorney for Beaumarchais, who, he said, had very high regard for his Virginia attorney.

Marshall, his lawyer's instincts at once aroused, told Bellamy that Beaumarchais's case was of very great magnitude and that he was deeply interested in it. Whereupon, in a low tone, spoken aside for his ear only, Bellamy told Marshall that, in case the latter won the suit, Beaumarchais would "sacrifice £50,000 Sterling of it as the private gratification" demanded by the Directory and Talleyrand, "so that the gratification might be made without any actual loss to the American government." Marshall rejected this offer and informed Pinckney of it.[2]

Marshall's character is revealed by the entry he promptly made in his Journal. "Having been originally the Counsel of Mr. de Beaumarchais, I had determined & so I informed Genl. Pinckney, that I would not by my voice establish any argument in his favor, but that I would positively oppose any admission of the claim of any French citizen if not accompanied with the admission of claims of the American

[1] Marshall's Journal, ii, Dec. 17, 36.

[2] *Am. St. Prs., For. Rel.*, ii, 167; Marshall's Journal, Dec. 17, 36–37.

citizens to property captured and condemned for want of a Rôle d'équipage."[1]

Bellamy then urged upon Gerry his plan of the Marshall-Beaumarchais arrangement. Talleyrand had been entertaining Gerry privately, and the flattered New Englander again wished to call on the French Minister, "to return the civility" by inviting Talleyrand to dinner.[2] To Talleyrand, then, went Gerry in company with Bellamy and asked the Foreign Minister to dine with him. Then Gerry tediously reviewed the situation, concluding in a manner that must have amused the bored Talleyrand: He would rather see the envoys depart for some city in another nation, said Gerry, until the Directory would receive them, than to stay in Paris under the circumstances.

Gerry was sure that the French diplomat was alarmed by this stern threat. "M. Talleyrand appeared to be uneasy at this declaration," he told his colleagues. Still, Talleyrand avoided "saying a word on it"; but he did say that Bellamy's representations "might always be relied on." Talleyrand declared that he would go further; he would himself write out his propositions. This he proceeded to do, held the writing before Gerry's eyes and then burned it; after this performance Talleyrand said he would dine with Gerry "the decade [ten days] after the present."[3]

[1] Marshall's Journal, Dec. 17, 38. The "*Rôle d'équipage*" was a form of ship's papers required by the French Government which it was practically impossible for American masters to furnish; yet, without it, their vessels were liable to capture by French ships under one of the many offensive decrees of the French Government.

[2] Marshall's Journal, Dec. 17, 38. [3] *Am. St. Prs., For. Rel.*, ii, 168.

Meanwhile, however, Gerry dined with the Foreign Minister. It was not a merry function. Aside from his guest of honor, the French Minister also had at his board Hottenguer, Bellamy, and Hauteval. Gerry could not speak French and Hauteval acted as translator. It must have been a pallid feast; the brilliant, witty, accomplished Talleyrand, man of the world, *bon vivant*, and lover of gayety; the solemn, dull, and rigid Gerry; the three trained French agents, one of them, as interpreter, the only means of general communication.[1] On rising from the table, Hottenguer at once brought up the question of the bribe. Would the envoys now give it? Had they the money ready? Gerry answered no![2]

Talleyrand, by now the mouthpiece of the rising Bonaparte, had proposed terms of peace to Great Britain; "the price was a Bribe of a Million Sterling to be divided among Directors, Ministers, and others. Talleyrand's Department was to share one hundred thousand Pounds Sterling." The British Government declined.[3]

King in London hastens to inform his American diplomatic associates in Paris of this offer, and cautions the envoys to act in concert. To Pinckney, King writes in cipher his anxiety about Gerry, whose integrity King had hoped would "overcome a miserable vanity and a few little defects of character . . .

[1] This account in the dispatches is puzzling, for Talleyrand spoke English perfectly.

[2] *Am. St. Prs., For. Rel.*, ii, 230.

[3] King to Secretary of State (in cipher) London, Dec. 23, 1797; King, ii, 261. King to Pinckney, Marshall, and Gerry, Dec. 23, 1797; *ib.*, 263.

which I now fear have been discovered by those who will be assiduous to turn them to mischief."

From the same source Pinckney is warned: "You must not appear to suspect what you may really know; . . . you must . . . save him [Gerry] and, in doing so, prevent the Division that would grow out of a Schism in your Commission." Gerry will be all right, thinks King, "unless Pride shall be put in opposition to Duty, or Jealousy shall mislead a mind neither ingenuous nor well organized, but habitually suspicious, and, when assailed by personal vanity, inflexible." [1]

Pinckney informs King of the situation in Paris on December 27, declaring "that we ought to request our Passports and no longer exhibit to the World the unprecedented Spectacle of three Envoys Extraordinary from a free and independent nation, in vain soliciting to be heard." [2]

Marshall now insists that the American case be formally stated to the French Government. Gerry at last agrees.[3] Marshall, of course, prepares this vastly important state paper. For two weeks he works over the first half of this historic document. "At my request Genl. Pinckney & Mr. Gerry met in my room & I read to them the first part of a letter to the Minister of Exterior Relations which consisted of a justification of the American Government," [4] he relates in his Journal.

Over the last half of the American case, Marshall

[1] King to Pinckney (in cipher) London, Dec. 24, 1797; King, ii, 263–64.

[2] Pinckney to King, Dec. 27, 1797; King, ii, 266–67.

[3] Marshall's Journal, Dec. 18, 1797, 38. [4] *Ib.*, Jan. 2, 1798, 39.

spends seven days. "The Second part of the letter to the Minister of Exterior Relations, comprehending the claims of the United States upon France, being also prepared, I read it to Genl Pinckney & Mr. Gerry." Both sections of Marshall's letter to Talleyrand were submitted to his colleagues for suggestions.[1]

It was hard work to get Gerry to examine and sign the memorial. "I had so repeatedly pressed Mr. Gerry," notes Marshall, "on the subject of our letter prepared for the Minister of Exterior Relations & manifested such solicitude for its being so completed as to enable us to send it, that I had obviously offended. Today I have urged that subject and for the last time." [2] Two days later Marshall chronicles that "Mr. Gerry finished the examination of our letter to the Minister of Exterior Relations." [3] A week later the letter, translated and signed, is delivered to Talleyrand.[4]

Upon this memorial were based future and successful American negotiations,[5] and the statement by Marshall remains to this day one of the ablest state papers ever produced by American diplomacy.

Marshall reminds Talleyrand of the frequent and open expressions of America's regard for France, given "with all the ardor and sincerity of youth." These, he says, were considered in America "as evidencing a mutual friendship, to be as durable as the republics themselves." Unhappily the scene changed, says Marshall, and "America looks around in vain

[1] Marshall's Journal, Jan. 2 and 10, 39.

[2] *Ib.*, Jan. 22, 40. [3] *Ib.*, 40. [4] *Ib.*, Jan. 31.

[5] The Ellsworth mission. (See *infra*, chap. XII.)

for the ally or the friend." He pictures the contrast in the language and conduct of the French Government with what had passed before, and says that the French charge of American partiality toward Great Britain is unfounded.

Marshall then reviews the international situation and makes it so plain that America could not take part in the European wars, that even Talleyrand was never able to answer the argument. "When that war [began] which has been waged with such unparalleled fury," he writes, "which in its vast vicissitudes of fortune has alternately threatened the very existence of the conflicting parties, but which, in its progress, has surrounded France with splendor, and added still more to her glory than to her territory," America found herself at peace with all the belligerent Powers; she was connected with some of them by treaties of amity and commerce, and with France by a treaty of alliance.

But these treaties, Marshall points out, did not require America to take part in this war. "Being bound by no duty to enter into the war, the Government of the United States conceived itself bound by duties, the most sacred, to abstain from it." Upon the ground that man, even in different degrees of social development, is still the natural friend of man, "the state of peace, though unstipulated by treaty," was the only course America could take. "The laws of nature" enjoined this, Marshall announces; and in some cases "solemn and existing engagements . . . require a religious observance" of it.[1]

[1] *Am. St. Prs., For. Rel.*, ii, 169.

Such was the moral ground upon which Marshall built his argument, and he strengthened it by practical considerations. "The great nations of Europe," he writes, "either impelled by ambition or by existing or supposed political interests, peculiar to themselves, have consumed more than a third of the present century in wars." The causes that produced this state of things "cannot be supposed to have been entirely extinguished, and humanity can scarcely indulge the hope that the temper or condition of man is so altered as to exempt the next century from the ills of the past. Strong fortifications, powerful navies, immense armies, the accumulated wealth of ages, and a full population, enable the nations of Europe to support those wars." [1]

Problems of this character, Marshall explains, must be solved by European countries, not by the United States. For, "encircled by no dangerous Powers, they [the Americans] neither fear, nor are jealous of their neighbors," says Marshall, "and are not, on that account, obliged to arm for their own safety." He declares that America, separated from Europe "by a vast and friendly ocean," has "no motive for a voluntary war," but "the most powerful reasons to avoid it." [2]

America's great and undefended commerce, made necessary by her then economic conditions, would be, Marshall contends, the "immediate and certain victim" of engaging in European wars; and he then demonstrates the disastrous results to America of departing from her policy of Neutrality.

[1] *Am. St. Prs., For. Rel.*, ii, 169–70. [2] *Ib.*, 170.

The immense and varied resources of the United States can only be used for self-defense, reasons the Virginia lawyer. "Neither the genius of the nation, nor the state of its own finances admit of calling its citizens from the plough but to defend their own liberty and their own firesides."

He then points out that, in addition to the moral wrong and material disaster of America's taking part in France's wars, such a course means the launching into the almost boundless ocean of European politics. It implies "contracting habits of national conduct and forming close political connections which must have compromitted the future peace of the nation, and have involved it in all the future quarrels of Europe."

Marshall then describes the "long train of armies, debts, and taxes, checking the growth, diminishing happiness, and perhaps endangering the liberty of the United States, which must have followed." And all this for what? Not to fulfill America's treaties; "not to promote her own views, her own objects, her own happiness, her own safety; but to move as a satellite around some other greater planet, whose laws she must of necessity obey." [1]

"It was believed," he declares, "that France would derive more benefit from the Neutrality of America than from her becoming a party in the war." Neutrality determined upon, he insists that "increased motives of honor and of duty commanded its faithful observance. . . . A fraudulent neutrality is no neutrality at all. . . . A . . . nation which would

[1] *Am. St. Prs., For. Rel.*, ii, 170.

be admitted to its privileges, should also perform the duties it enjoins."

If the American Government, occupying a neutral position, had granted "favors unstipulated by treaty, to one of the belligerent Powers which it refused to another, it could no longer have claimed the immunities of a situation of which the obligations were forgotten; it would have become a party to the war as certainly as if war had been openly and formally declared, and it would have added to the madness of wantonly engaging in such a hazardous conflict, the dishonor of insincere and fraudulent conduct; it would have attained, circuitously, an object which it could not plainly avow or directly pursue, and would have tricked the people of the United States into a war which it would not venture openly to declare."

Then follows this keen thrust which Talleyrand could not evade: "It was a matter of real delight to the government and people of America," suavely writes Marshall, "to be informed that France did not wish to interrupt the peace they [the American people] enjoyed."

Marshall then makes a sudden and sharp attack memorable in the records of diplomatic dueling. He calls attention to the astounding conduct of the French Minister on American soil immediately after the American Government had proclaimed its Neutrality to the world and had notified American citizens of the duties which that Neutrality enjoined. In polite phrase he reminds Talleyrand of Genêt's assumption of "the functions of the government to which he was deputed, . . . although he was not even acknowledged as a minister or had reached the authority which should inspect his credentials."

But, notwithstanding this, says Marshall, "the American Government resolved to see in him [Genêt] only the representative of a republic to which it was sincerely attached" and "gave him the same warm and cordial reception which he had experienced from its citizens without a single exception from Charleston to Philadelphia."

Two paragraphs follow of fulsome praise of France, which would seem to have been written by Gerry, who insisted on revising the memorial.[1] But in swift contrast Marshall again throws on the screen the indefensible performances of the French Minister in America and the tolerance with which the American Government treated them. "In what manner would France have treated any foreign minister, who should have dared to so conduct himself toward this republic? . . . In what manner would the American Government have treated him [Genêt] had he been the representative of any other nation than France?"

No informed man can doubt the answer to these questions, says Marshall. "From the Minister of France alone could this extraordinary conduct be borne with temper." But "to have continued to bear it without perceiving its extreme impropriety would have been to have merited the contempt" of the world and of France herself. "The Government of the United States did feel it," declares Marshall, but did not attribute Genêt's misconduct to the French Nation. On the contrary, the American Government

[1] Marshall's Journal, 39; also see Austin: *Gerry*, ii, chap. VI.

"distinguished strongly between the [French] Government and its Minister," and complained "in the language of a friend afflicted but not irritated." Genêt's recall "was received with universal joy" in America, "as a confirmation that his . . . conduct was attributable only to himself"; and "not even the publication of his private instructions could persuade the American Government to ascribe any part of it to this [French] republic." [1]

Marshall further points out "the exertions of the United States to pay up the arrearages" of their debt to France; America's "disinterested and liberal advances to the sufferers of St. Domingo . . . whose recommendation was that they were Frenchmen and unfortunate"; and other acts of good-will of the American Government toward the French Republic.

He then makes a characteristically clear and convincing argument upon the points at issue between France and America. France complained that one article of the Jay Treaty provided that in case of war the property of an enemy might be taken by either out of the ships of the other; whereas, by the Treaty of 1778 between France and America, neither party should take out of the vessels of the other the goods of its enemy. France contended that this was a discrimination against her in favor of Great Britain. Marshall shows that this provision in the Jay Treaty was merely the statement of the existing law of nations, and that therefore the Jay Treaty gave no new rights to Great Britain.

Marshall reminds Talleyrand that any two na-

[1] *Am. St. Prs., For. Rel.*, ii, 170–71.

tions by treaty have the power to alter, as to their mutual intercourse, the usages prescribed by international law; that, accordingly, France and America had so changed, as between themselves, the law of nations respecting enemy's goods in neutral bottoms. He cites the ordinance of France herself in 1744 and her long continued practice under it; and he answers so overwhelmingly the suggestion that the law of nations had not been changed by the rules laid down by the "Armed Neutrality" of the Northern Powers of Europe in the war existing at the time of that confederation, that the resourceful Talleyrand made no pretense of answering it.

The stipulation in the Franco-American Treaty of "protecting the goods of the enemy of either party in the vessels of the other, and in turn surrendering its own goods found in the vessels of the enemy," extended, Marshall insists, to no other nation except to France and America; and contends that this could be changed only by further specific agreements between those two nations.

Marshall wishes "that the principle that neutral bottoms shall make neutral goods" were universally established, and declares that that principle "is perhaps felt by no nation on earth more strongly than by the United States." On this point he is emphatic, and reiterates that "no nation is more deeply interested in its establishment" than America. "It is an object they [the United States] have kept in view, and which, if not forced by violence to abandon it, they will pursue in such manner as their own judgment may dictate as being best calculated to attain it."

"But," he says, "the wish to establish a principle is essentially different from a determination that it is already established. . . . However solicitous America might be to pursue all proper means, tending to obtain for this principle the assent of any or all of the maritime Powers of Europe, she never conceived the idea of attaining that consent by force." [1] "The United States will only arm to defend their own rights," declares Marshall; "neither their policy nor their interests permit them to arm, in order to compel a surrender of the rights of others."

He then gives the history of the Jay Treaty, and points out that Jay's particular instructions not to preserve peace with Great Britain, "nor to receive compensations for injuries sustained, nor security against their future commission, at the expense of the smallest of its [America's] engagements to France," [2] were incorporated in the treaty itself, in the clause providing that "nothing in this treaty shall, however, be construed or operate contrary to former and existing public treaties with other sovereignties or states." [3] So careful, in fact, was America to meet the views of France that "previous to its ratification" the treaty was submitted to the French Minister to the United States, who did not even comment on the article relating to enemy's goods in neutral bottoms, but objected only to that enlarging the list of contraband; [4] and the American Government went to extreme lengths to meet the views of

[1] *Am. St. Prs., For. Rel.*, ii, 172.
[2] *Ib.*, 173. [3] *Ib.* [4] *Ib.*

the French Minister, who finally appeared to be satisfied.

The articles of contraband enumerated in the Jay Treaty, to which the French Government objected, says Marshall, were contraband by the laws of nations and so admitted by France herself in her treaties with other countries.[1]

Answering the charge that in the treaty the United States had agreed that more articles should be contraband than she had in compacts with other Powers, Marshall explains that "the United States, desirous of liberating commerce, have invariably seized every opportunity which presented itself to diminish or remove the shackles imposed on that of neutrals. In pursuance of this policy, they have on no occasion hesitated to reduce the list of contraband, as between themselves and any nation consenting to such reduction. Their preëxisting treaties have been with nations as willing as themselves to change this old rule." But these treaties leave other governments, who do not accept the American policy, "to the law which would have governed had such particular stipulation never been made" — that is, to the law of nations.

Great Britain declined to accept this American view of the freedom of the seas; and, therefore, America was forced to leave that nation where it had found her on the subject of contraband and freedom of ocean-going commerce. Thus, contends Marshall, the Jay Treaty "has not added to the catalog of contraband a single article . . . ceded no

[1] *Am. St. Prs., For. Rel.*, ii, 175.

privilege . . . granted no right," nor changed, in the most minute circumstance, the preëxisting situation of the United States in relation either to France or to Great Britain. Notwithstanding these truths, "the Government of the United States has hastened to assure its former friend [France], that, if the stipulations between them are found oppressive in practice, it is ready to offer up those stipulations a willing sacrifice at the shrine of friendship." [1]

Stating the general purposes of the United States, Marshall strikes at the efforts of France to compel America to do what France wishes and in the manner that France wishes, instead of doing what American interests require and in the manner America thinks wisest.

The American people, he asserts, "must judge exclusively for themselves how far they will or ought to go in their efforts to acquire new rights or establish new principles. When they surrender this privilege, they cease to be independent, and they will no longer deserve to be free. They will have surrendered into other hands the most sacred of deposits — the right of self-government; and instead of approbation, they will merit the contempt of the world." [2]

Marshall states the economic and business reasons why the United States, of all countries, must depend upon commerce and the consequent necessity for the Jay Treaty. He tartly informs Talleyrand that in doing so the American Government was "transacting a business exclusively its own." Marshall denies the insinuation that the negotiations of the

[1] *Am. St. Prs., For. Rel.*, ii, 175. [2] *Ib.*, 176.

Jay Treaty had been unusually secret, but sarcastically observes that "it is not usual for nations about to enter into negotiations to proclaim to others the various objects to which those negotiations may possibly be directed. Such is not, nor has it ever been, the principle of France." To suppose that America owed such a duty to France, "is to imply a dependence to which no Government ought willingly to submit." [1]

Marshall then sets forth specifically the American complaints against the French Government, [2] and puts in parallel columns the words of the Jay Treaty to which the French objected, and the rules which the French Directory pretended were justified by that treaty. So strong is Marshall's summing up of the case in these portions of the American memorial that it is hard for the present-day reader to see how even the French Directory of that lawless time could have dared to attempt to withstand it, much less to refuse further negotiations.

Drawing to a conclusion, Marshall permits a lofty sarcasm to lighten his weighty argument. "America has accustomed herself," he observes, "to perceive in France only the ally and the friend. Consulting the feelings of her own bosom, she [America] has believed that between republics an elevated and refined friendship could exist, and that free nations were capable of maintaining for each other a real and permanent affection. If this pleasing theory, erected with so much care, and viewed with so much delight, has been impaired by experience, yet the hope con-

[1] *Am. St. Prs., For. Rel.*, ii, 177. [2] *Ib.*, 178.

tinues to be cherished that this circumstance does not necessarily involve the opposite extreme." [1]

Then, for a moment, Marshall indulges his eloquence: "So intertwined with every ligament of her heart have been the cords of affection which bound her to France, that only repeated and continued acts of hostility can tear them asunder." [2]

Finally he tells Talleyrand that the American envoys, "searching only for the means of effecting the objects of their mission, have permitted no personal considerations to influence their conduct, but have waited, under circumstances beyond measure embarrassing and unpleasant, with that respect which the American Government has so uniformly paid to that of France, for permission to lay before you, citizen Minister, these important communications with which they have been charged." But, "if no such hope" remains, "they [the envoys] have only to pray that their return to their own country may be facilitated." [3]

But Marshall's extraordinary power of statement and logic availed nothing with Talleyrand and the Directory. "I consider Marshall, whom I have heard speak on a great subject,[4] as one of the most powerful reasoners I ever met with either in public or in print," writes William Vans Murray from The Hague, commenting on the task of the envoys. "Reasoning in such cases will have a fine effect in America, but to depend upon it in Europe is really to place Quixote with Ginés de Passamonte and among

[1] *Am. St. Prs.*, *For. Rel.*, ii, 181. [2] *Ib.*, 181–82. [3] *Ib.*, 182.
[4] British Debts cases. (See vol. I, chap. v.)

the men of the world whom he reasoned with, and so sublimely, on their way to the galleys. They answer him, with you know stones and blows, though the Knight is an *armed* as well as an eloquent Knight." [1]

The events which had made Marshall and Pinckney more resolute in demanding respectful treatment had made Gerry more pliant to French influence. "Mr. Gerry is to see Mr. Talleyrand the day after to-morrow. Three appointments have been made by that gentleman," Marshall notes in his Journal, "each of which Mr. Gerry has attended and each of which Mr. Talleyrand has failed to attend; nor has any apology for these disappointments been thought necessary." [2] Once more Gerry waits on Talleyrand, who remains invisible.[3] And now again Beaumarchais appears. The Directory issues more and harsher decrees against American commerce. Marshall's patience becomes finite. "I prepared to-day a letter to the Minister remonstrating against the decree, . . . subjecting to confiscation all neutral vessels having on board any article coming out of England or its possessions." The letter closes by "requesting our passports." [4]

Marshall's memorial of the American case remained unread. One of Talleyrand's many secretaries asked Gerry "what it contained? (for they could not take the trouble to read it) and he added

[1] Murray to J. Q. Adams, Feb. 20, 1798, *Letters:* Ford, 379. Murray thought Marshall's statement of the American case "unanswerable" and "proudly independent." (*Ib.*, 395.) Contrast Murray's opinion of Marshall with his description of Gerry, *supra*, chap. VII, 258, and footnote.

[2] Marshall's Journal, Jan. 31, 1798, 40.

[3] *Ib.*, Feb. 2. [4] *Ib.*, Feb. 2, 41.

that such long letters were not to the taste of the French Government who liked a short address coming straight to the point." [1] Gerry, who at last saw Talleyrand, "informed me [Marshall] that communications & propositions had been made to him by that Gentleman, which he [Gerry] was not at liberty to impart to Genl Pinckney or myself." Upon the outcome of his secret conferences with Talleyrand, said Gerry, "probably depended peace or war." [2]

Gerry's "communication necessarily gives birth to some very serious reflections," Marshall confides to his Journal. He recalls the attempts to frighten the envoys "from our first arrival" — the threats of "a variety of ills . . . among others with being ordered immediately to quit France," none of them carried out; "the most haughty & hostile conduct . . . towards us & our country and yet . . . an unwillingness . . . to profess the war which is in fact made upon us." [3]

A French agent, sent by the French Consul-General in America, just arrived in Paris, "has probably brought with him," Marshall concludes, "accurate details of the state of parties in America. . . . I should think that if the French Government continues its hostility and does not relax some little in its hauteur its party in the United States will no longer support it. I suspect that some intelligence of this complexion has been received . . . whether she [France] will be content to leave us our Independence if she can neither cajole or frighten us

[1] Marshall's Journal, Feb. 3, 42.
[2] *Ib.*, Feb. 4, 42. [3] *Ib.*. 42–43, 46.

out of it or will even endeavor to tear it from us by open war there can be no doubt of her policy in one respect — she will still keep up and cherish, if it be possible, . . . her party in the United States." Whatever course France takes, Marshall thinks will be "with a view to this her primary object."

Therefore, reasons Marshall, Talleyrand will maneuver to throw the blame on Pinckney and himself if the mission fails, and to give Gerry the credit if it succeeds. "I am led irresistibly by this train of thought to the opinion that the communication made to Mr. Gerry in secret is a proposition to furnish passports to General Pinckney and myself and to retain him for the purpose of negotiating the differences between the two Republics." This would give the advantage to the French party in any event.

"I am firmly persuaded of his [Talleyrand's] unwillingness to dismiss us while the war with England continues in its present uncertain state. He believed that Genl Pinckney and myself are both determined to remain no longer unless we can be accredited." Gerry had told Marshall that he felt the same way; "but," says Marshall, "I am persuaded the Minister [Talleyrand] does not think so. He would on this account as well as on another which has been the base of all propositions for an accommodation [the loan and the bribe] be well pleased to retain only one minister and to chuse that one [Gerry]." [1]

Marshall and Pinckney decided to let Gerry go his own gait. "We shall both be happy if, by remaining

[1] Marshall's Journal, Feb. 4, 42–45.

without us, Mr. Gerry can negotiate a treaty which shall preserve the peace without sacrificing the independence of our country. We will most readily offer up all personal considerations as a sacrifice to appease the haughtiness of this Republic." [1]

Marshall gave Gerry the letter on the decree and passport question "and pressed his immediate attention to it." But Gerry was too excited by his secret conferences with Talleyrand to heed it. Time and again Gerry, bursting with importance, was closeted with the Foreign Minister, hinting to his colleagues that he held peace or war in his hand. Marshall bluntly told him that Talleyrand's plan now was "only to prevent our taking decisive measures until the affairs of Europe shall enable France to take them. I have pressed him [Gerry] on the subject of the letter concerning the Decree but he has not yet read it." [2]

Talleyrand and Gerry's "private intercourse still continues," writes Marshall on February 10. "Last night after our return from the Theatre Mr. Gerry told me, just as we were separating to retire each to his own apartment, that he had had in the course of the day a very extraordinary conversation with" a clerk of Talleyrand. It was, of course, secret. Marshall did not want to hear it. Gerry said he could tell his colleagues that it was on the subject of money. Then, at last, Marshall's restraint gave way momentarily and his anger, for an instant, blazed. Money proposals were useless; Talleyrand was playing with the Americans, he declared. "Mr. Gerry was

[1] Marshall's Journal, Feb. 5, 45–46. [2] *Ib.*, Feb. 6 and 7, 46.

a little warm and the conversation was rather unpleasant. A solicitude to preserve harmony restrained me from saying all I thought."[1]

Money, money, money! Nothing else would do! Gerry, by now, was for paying it. No answer yet comes to the American memorial delivered to Talleyrand nearly three weeks before. Marshall packs his belongings, in readiness to depart. An unnamed person[2] calls on him and again presses for money; France is prevailing everywhere; the envoys had better yield; why resist the inevitable, with a thousand leagues of ocean between them and home? Marshall answers blandly but crushingly.

Again Talleyrand's clerk sees Gerry. The three Americans that night talk long and heatedly. Marshall opposes any money arrangement; Gerry urges it "very decidedly"; while Pinckney agrees with Marshall. Gerry argues long about the horrors of war, the expense, the risk. Marshall presents the justice of the American cause. Gerry reproaches Marshall with being too suspicious. Marshall patiently explains, as to a child, the real situation. Gerry again charges Marshall and Pinckney with undue suspicion. Marshall retorts that Gerry "could not answer the argument but by misstating it." The evening closes, sour and chill.[3]

The next night the envoys once more endlessly

[1] Marshall's Journal, Feb. 10, 47–48.

[2] Undoubtedly Beaumarchais. Marshall left his client's name blank in his Journal, but Pickering, on the authority of Pinckney, in the official copy, inserted Beaumarchais's name in later dates of the Journal.

[3] Marshall's Journal, Feb. 26, 52–60.

debate their course. Marshall finally proposes that they shall demand a personal meeting with Talleyrand on the real object of the mission. Gerry stubbornly dissents and finally yields, but indulges in long and childish discussion as to what should be said to Talleyrand, confusing the situation with every word.[1] Talleyrand fixes March 2 for the interview.

The following day Marshall accidentally discovers Gerry closeted with Talleyrand's clerk, who came to ask the New Englander to attend Talleyrand "in a particular conversation." Gerry goes, but reports that nothing important occurred. Then it comes out that Talleyrand had proposed to get rid of Marshall and Pinckney and keep Gerry. Gerry admits it. Thus Marshall's forecast made three weeks earlier[2] is proved to have been correct.

At last, for the first time in five months, the three envoys meet Talleyrand face to face. Pinckney opens and Talleyrand answers. Gerry suggests a method of making the loan, to which Talleyrand gives qualified assent. The interview seems at an end. Then Marshall comes forward and states the American case. There is much parrying for an hour.[3]

The envoys again confer. Gerry urges that their instructions permit them to meet Talleyrand's demands. He goes to Marshall's room to convince the granite-like Virginian, who would not yield. "I told him," writes Marshall, "that my judgment was not

[1] Marshall's Journal, Feb. 27, 61–67.
[2] *Ib.*, Feb. 28, 67–68. See *supra*, 312.
[3] *Am. St. Prs., For. Rel.*, ii, 186–87; Marshall's Journal, March 2, 68–72.

more perfectly convinced that the floor was wood or that I stood on my feet and not on my head than that our instructions would not permit us to make the loan required." [1] Let Gerry or Marshall or both together return to America and get new instructions if a loan must be made.

Two days later, another long and absurd discussion with Gerry occurs. Before the envoys go to see Talleyrand the next day, Gerry proposes to Marshall that, with reference to President Adams's speech, the envoys should declare, in any treaty made, "that the complaints of the two governments had been founded in mistake." Marshall hotly retorts: "With my view of things, I should tell an absolute lye if I should say that our complaints were founded in mistake. He [Gerry] replied hastily and with warmth that he wished to God, I would propose something which was accommodating: that I would propose nothing myself and objected to every thing which he proposed. I observed that it was not worth while to talk in that manner: that it was calculated to wound but not to do good: that I had proposed every thing which in my opinion was calculated to accommodate differences on just and reasonable grounds. He said that . . . to talk about justice was saying nothing: that I should involve our country in a war and should bring it about in such a manner, as to divide the people among themselves. I felt a momentary irritation, which I afterwards regretted, and told Mr. Gerry that I was not accustomed to such language and did

[1] Marshall's Journal, March 3, 74.

not permit myself to use it with respect to him or his opinions."

Nevertheless, Marshall, with characteristic patience, once more begins to detail his reasons. Gerry interrupts — Marshall "might think of him [Gerry] as I [he] pleased." Marshall answers moderately. Gerry softens and "the conversation thus ended."[1]

Immediately after the bout between Marshall and Gerry the envoys saw Talleyrand for a third time. Marshall was dominant at this interview, his personality being, apparently, stronger even than his words. These were strong enough — they were, bluntly, that the envoys could not and would not accept Talleyrand's proposals.

A week later Marshall's client, Beaumarchais, called on his American attorney with the alarming news that "the effects of all Americans in France were to be Sequestered." Pay the Government money and avoid this fell event, was Beaumarchais's advice; he would see Talleyrand and call again. "Mr. Beaumarchais called on me late last evening," chronicles Marshall. "He had just parted from the Minister. He informed me that he had been told confidentially . . . that the Directory were determined to give passports to General Pinckney and myself but to retain Mr. Gerry." But Talleyrand would hold the order back for "a few days to give us time to make propositions conforming to the views of the Government," which "if not made Mr. Talleyrand would be compelled to execute the order."

[1] Marshall's Journal, March 6, 79–81.

"I told him," writes Marshall, "that if the proposition . . . was a loan it was perfectly unnecessary to keep it [the order] up [back] a single day: that the subject had been considered for five months" and that the envoys would not change; "that for myself, if it were impossible to effect the objects of our mission, I did not wish to stay another day in France and would as cheerfully depart the next day as at any other time." [1]

Beaumarchais argued and appealed. Of course, France's demand was not just — Talleyrand did not say it was; but "a compliance would be useful to our country [America]." "France," said Beaumarchais, "thought herself sufficiently powerful to give the law to the world and exacted from all around her money to enable her to finish successfully her war against England."

Finally, Beaumarchais, finding Marshall flint, "hinted" that the envoys themselves should propose which one of them should remain in France, Gerry being the choice of Talleyrand. Marshall countered. If two were to return for instructions, the envoys would decide that for themselves. If France was to choose, Marshall would have nothing to do with it.

"General Pinckney and myself and especially me," said Marshall, "were considered as being sold to the English." Beaumarchais admitted "that our positive refusal to comply with the demands of France was attributed principally to me who was considered as entirely English. . . . I felt some little

[1] Marshall's Journal, 82–88; *Am. St. Prs., For. Rel.*, ii, 187–88.

resentment and answered that the French Government thought no such thing; that neither the government nor any man in France thought me English: but they knew I was not French: they knew I would not sacrifice my duty and the interest of my country to any nation on earth, and therefore I was not a proper man to stay, and was branded with the epithet of being English: that the government knew very well I loved my own country exclusively, and it was impossible to suppose any man who loved America, fool enough to wish to engage her in a war with France if that war was avoidable."

Thus Marshall asserted his purely American attitude. It was a daring thing to do, considering the temper of the times and the place where he then was. Even in America, at that period, any one who was exclusively American and, therefore, neutral, as between the European belligerents, was denounced as being British at heart. Only by favoring France could abuse be avoided. And to assert Neutrality in the French Capital was, of course, even more dangerous than to take this American stand in the United States.

But Beaumarchais persisted and proposed to take passage with his attorney to America; not on a public mission, of course (though he had hinted at wishing to "reconcile" the two governments), but merely "to testify," writes Marshall, "to the moderation of my conduct and to the solicitude I had uniformly expressed to prevent a rupture with France."

Beaumarchais "hinted very plainly," continues Marshall, "at what he had before observed that means would be employed to irritate the people of the United States against me and that those means would be successful. I told him that I was much obliged to him but that I relied entirely on my conduct itself for its justification and that I felt no sort of apprehension for consequences, as they regarded me personally; that in public life considerations of that sort never had and never would in any degree influence me. We parted with a request, on his part, that, whatever might arise, we would preserve the most perfect temper, and with my assuring him of my persuasion that our conduct would always manifest the firmness of men who were determined, and never the violence of passionate men."

"I have been particular," concludes Marshall, "in stating this conversation, because I have no doubt of its having been held at the instance of the Minister [Talleyrand] and that it will be faithfully reported to him. I mentioned to-day to Mr. Gerry that the Government wished to detain him and send away General Pinckney and myself. He said he would not stay; but I find I shall not succeed in my efforts to procure a Serious demand of passports for Mr. Gerry and myself." [1]

During his efforts to keep Gerry from dangerously compromising the American case, and while waiting for Talleyrand to reply to his memorial, Marshall again writes to Washington a letter giving a survey of the war-riven and intricate European situation. He tells Washington that, "before this reaches you it will be known universally in

[1] Marshall's Journal, March 13, 87–93.

America[1] that scarcely a hope remains of" honorable adjustment of differences between France and America; that the envoys have not been and will not be "recognized" without "acceding to the demands of France . . . for money — to be used in the prosecution of the present war"; that according to "reports," when the Directory makes certain that the envoys "will not add a loan to the mass of American property already in the hands of this [French] government, they will be ordered out of France and a nominal [formally declared] as well as actual war will be commenc'd against the United States."[2]

Marshall goes on to say that his "own opinion has always been that this depends on the state of war with England"; the French are absorbed in their expected attack on Great Britain; "and it is perhaps justly believed that on this issue is stak'd the independence of Europe and America." He informs Washington of "the immense preparations for an invasion" of England; the "numerous and veteran army lining the coast"; the current statement that if "50,000 men can be" landed "no force in England will be able to resist them"; the belief that "a formidable and organized party exists in Britain, ready, so soon as a landing shall be effected, to rise and demand a reform"; the supposition that England then "will be in . . . the situation of the bata-

[1] This would seem to indicate that Marshall knew that his famous dispatches were to be published.

[2] France was already making "actual war" upon America; the threat of formally declaring war, therefore, had no terror for Marshall.

vian and cisalpine republics and that its wealth, its commerce, and its fleets will be at the disposition of this [French] government."

But, he continues, "this expedition is not without its hazards. An army which, arriving safe, would sink England, may itself be . . . sunk in the channel. . . . The effect of such a disaster on a nation already tir'd of the war and groaning under . . . enormous taxation" and, intimates Marshall, none too warm toward the "existing arrangements . . . might be extremely serious to those who hold the reins of government" in France. Many intelligent people therefore think, he says, that the "formidable military preparations" for the invasion of England "cover and favor secret negotiations for peace." This view Marshall himself entertains.

He then briefly informs Washington of Bonaparte's arrangement with Austria and Prussia which will "take from England, the hope of once more arming" those countries "in her favor," "influence the secret [French] negotiations with England," and greatly affect "Swisserland." Marshall then gives an extended account of the doings and purposes of the French in Switzerland, and refers to revolutionary activities in Sardinia, Naples, and Spain.

But notwithstanding the obstacles in its way, he concludes that "the existing [French] government . . . needs only money to enable it to effect all its objects. A numerous brave and well disciplined army seems to be devoted to it. The most military and the most powerful nation on earth [the French] is entirely at its disposal.[1] Spain, Italy, and Holland, with the Hanseatic towns, obey its mandates."

But, says he, it is hard to "procure funds to work this vast machine. Credit being annihilated . . . the enormous contributions made by foreign nations," together with the revenue from imposts, are not enough to meet the expenses; and, therefore, "France is overwhelmed with taxes. The proprietor complains that his estate yields him nothing. Real property pays in taxes nearly a third of its produce and is greatly reduc'd in its price."[2]

While Marshall was thus engaged in studying French conditions and writing his long and careful report to Washington, Talleyrand was in no hurry to reply to the American memorial. Indeed, he did not answer until March 18, 1798, more than six weeks after receiving it. The French statement reached Marshall and Pinckney by Gerry's hands, two days after its date. "Mr. Gerry brought in, just before dinner, a letter from the Minister of exterior relations," writes Marshall, "purporting to be an answer to our long memorial criminating in strong terms our government and ourselves, and proposing that two of us should go home leaving for the negotiation the person most acceptable to France. The person is not named but no question is entertained that Mr. Gerry is alluded to. I read the letter and gave it again to Mr. Gerry."[3]

[1] Here Marshall contradicts his own statement that the French Nation was tired of the war, groaning under taxation, and not "universally" satisfied with the Government.

[2] Marshall to Washington, Paris, March 8, 1798; *Amer. Hist. Rev.*, Jan., 1897, ii, 303; also MS., Lib. Cong.

[3] Marshall's Journal, March 20, 93.

The next day the three envoys together read Talleyrand's letter. Gerry protests that he had told the French Foreign Minister that he would not accept Talleyrand's proposal to stay, "That," sarcastically writes Marshall, "is probably the very reason why it was made." Talleyrand's clerk calls on Gerry the next morning, suggesting light and innocent duties if he would remain. No, theatrically exclaims Gerry, I "would sooner be thrown into the Seine." [1] But Gerry remained.

It is impossible, without reading Talleyrand's answer in full, to get an idea of the weak shiftiness to which that remarkable man was driven in his reply to Marshall. It was, as Pinckney said, "weak in argument, but irritating and insulting in style." [2] The great diplomat complains that the Americans have "claimed the right to take cognizance of the validity of prizes carried into the ports of the United States by French cruisers"; that the American Government permitted "any vessels to put into the ports of the United States after having captured the property of ships belonging to French citizens"; that "a French corvette had anchored at Philadelphia and was seized by the Americans"; and that the Jay Treaty was hostile to France.

But his chief complaint was with regard to the American newspapers which, said Talleyrand, "have since the treaty redoubled the invectives and calumnies against the [French] republic, and against her

[1] Marshall's Journal, March 22, 95.

[2] Murray to J. Q. Adams, April 3, 1798, quoting Pinckney; *Letters*: Ford, 391.

principles, her magistrates, and her envoys";[1] and of the fact that the American Government might have, but did not, repress "pamphlets openly paid for by the Minister of Great Britain" which contained "insults and calumnies." So far from the American Government stopping all this, snarls Talleyrand, it encouraged "this scandal in its public acts" and, through its President, had denounced the French Directory as endeavoring to propagate anarchy and division within the United States.

Talleyrand then openly insults Marshall and Pinckney by stating that it was to prevent the restoration of friendship that the American Government had sent "to the French republic persons whose opinions and connections are too well known to hope from them dispositions sincerely conciliatory." Appealing directly to the French party in the United States, he declares that he "does not hesitate to believe that the American nation, like the French nation, sees this state of affairs with regret, and does not consider its consequences without sorrow. He apprehends that the American people will not commit a mistake concerning the prejudices with which it has been desired to inspire them against an allied people, nor concerning the engagements which it seems to be wished to make them contract to the detriment of an alliance, which so powerfully contributed to place them in the rank of nations, and to support them in it; and that they

[1] The exact reverse was true. Up to this time American newspapers, with few exceptions, were hot for France. Only a very few papers, like Fenno's *Gazette of the United States*, could possibly be considered as unfriendly to France at this point. (See *supra*, chap. I.)

will see in these new combinations the only dangers their prosperity and importance can incur." [1]

Finally, with cynical effrontery, Talleyrand actually proposes that Gerry alone shall conduct the negotiations. "Notwithstanding the kind of prejudice which has been entertained with respect to them [the envoys], the Executive Directory is disposed to treat with that one of the three, whose opinions, presumed to be more impartial, promise, in the course of explanations, more of that reciprocal confidence which is indispensable." [2]

Who should answer Talleyrand? Marshall, of course. "It was agreed . . . that I should . . . prepare an answer . . . in which I should state that no one of the ministers could consent to remain on a business committed to all three." [3] In the discussion leading to this decision, "I," writes Marshall, "was perfectly silent." Again Dutrimond, a clerk of Talleyrand's, calls on Gerry, but sees Marshall instead, Gerry being absent.

Dutrimond's advice to Marshall is to leave France. The truth is, he declares, that his chief must order the envoys out of France "in three days at farthest." But spare them Gerry; let him remain — all this in polite terms and with plausible argument. "I told him," relates Marshall, "that personally nothing could be more desirable to me than to return immediately to the United States."

Then go on your own initiative, urges Talleyrand's clerk. Marshall grows evasive; for he wishes the

[1] *Am. St. Prs., For. Rel.*, ii, 190–91. [2] *Ib.*, 191.
[3] Marshall's Journal, March 22, 95.

Directory to order his departure. A long talk ensues. Dutrimond leaves and Gerry returns. Marshall relates what had passed. "To prevent war I will stay," exclaims Gerry. "I made no observation on this," dryly observes Marshall in his Journal.[1]

Beaumarchais again tries his luck with Marshall, who replies that he will go home by "the direct passage to America" if he can get safe-conduct, "tho' I had private business of very considerable consequence in England."[2] Otherwise, declares Marshall, "I should embark immediately for England." That would never do, exclaims Beaumarchais; it would enrage the Directory and subject Marshall to attacks at home. Marshall remarks that he prefers to sail direct, although he knows "that the captains of privateers had received orders to cruise for us . . . and take us to the West Indies."[3]

Beaumarchais sees Talleyrand and reports that the Foreign Minister is horrified at the thought of Marshall's returning by way of England; it would "irritate this government" and delay "an accommodation"; it would blast Marshall's reputation; the Directory "would immediately publish . . . that I was gone to England to receive the wages I had earned by breaking off the treaty with France," Marshall records of the representations made to him.

"I am entitled to safe conduct," cries Marshall; and "the calumny threatened against myself is too contemptible to be credited for a moment by those

[1] Marshall's Journal, March 22, 95–97. [2] The Fairfax purchase.
[3] Marshall's Journal, March 23, 99.

who would utter it." I "despise" it, exclaims the insulted Virginian.[1] Thus back and forth went this fantastic dance of corrupt diplomacy and cautious but defiant honesty.

At the long last, the interminable Gerry finished his review of Marshall's reply to Talleyrand and made a lengthy and unctuous speech to his colleagues on the righteousness of his own motives. Pinckney, intolerably bored and disgusted, told Gerry what he thought of him. The New Englander peevishly charged Marshall and Pinckney with concealing their motives.

"It is false, sir," shouted Pinckney. Gerry, he said, was the one who had concealed from his colleagues, not only his purposes, but his clandestine appointments with Talleyrand. Pinckney rode Gerry hard, "and insisted in plain terms on the duplicity which had been practiced [by Gerry] upon us both." The latter ridiculously explained, evaded, and, in general, acted according to the expectation of those who warned Adams against his appointment. Finally, however, Marshall's reply was signed by all three and sent to Talleyrand.[2]

The calmness, dignity, and conclusiveness of Marshall's rejoinder can be appreciated only by reading the entire document. Marshall begins his final statement of the American case and refutation of the French claims by declaring what he had stated before, that the American envoys "are ready to consider and to compensate the injury, if the American Government has given just cause of complaint to

[1] Marshall's Journal, March 29, 99–100. [2] *Ib.*, April 3, 102–07

that of France"; and points out that the negotiations which the American envoys had sought fruitlessly for six months, if taken up even now, would "demonstrate the sincerity of this declaration." [1] This offer Marshall repeats again and again.

Before taking up Talleyrand's complaints in detail, he states that if the envoys cannot convince Talleyrand that the American Government is not in the wrong on a single point Talleyrand mentions, the envoys will prove their good faith; and thus, with an offer to compensate France for any wrong, "a base for an accommodation" is established. Every grievance Talleyrand had made is then answered minutely and at great length. History, reason, evidence, march through these pages like infantry, cavalry, and artillery going to battle. Marshall's paper was irresistible. Talleyrand never escaped from it.

In the course of it there is a passage peculiarly applicable to the present day. Answering Talleyrand's complaints about newspapers, Marshall says: —

"The genius of the Constitution, and the opinions of the people of the United States, cannot be overruled by those who administer the Government. Among those principles deemed sacred in America, . . . there is no one . . . more deeply impressed on the public mind, than the liberty of the press. That this liberty is often carried to excess, that it has sometimes degenerated into licentiousness, is seen and lamented; but the remedy has not been discovered. Perhaps it is an evil inseparable from the good with

[1] *Am. St. Prs., For. Rel.*, ii, 191.

which it is allied; perhaps it is a shoot which cannot be stripped from the stalk, without wounding vitally the plant from which it is torn."

At any rate, declares Marshall, there is, in America, no redress for "the calumnies and invectives" of the press except "legal prosecution in courts which are alike open to all who consider themselves as injured. Without doubt this abuse of a valuable privilege is [a] matter of peculiar regret when it is extended to the Government of a foreign nation." It never is so extended "with the approbation of the Government of the United States." But, he goes on to say, this is unavoidable "especially on points respecting the rights and interests of America, . . . in a nation where public measures are the results of public opinion."

This practice of unrestricted criticism was not directed toward France alone, Marshall assures Talleyrand; "it has been lavished still more profusely on its [France's] enemies and has even been bestowed, with an unsparing hand, on the Federal [American] Government itself. Nothing can be more notorious than the calumnies and invectives with which the wisest measures and most virtuous characters of the United States have been pursued and traduced [by American newspapers]." It is plain, therefore, that the American Government cannot influence the American press, the excesses of which are, declares Marshall, "a calamity incident to the nature of liberty."

He reminds Talleyrand that "the same complaint might be urged on the part of the United States.

You must well know what degrading and unworthy calumnies against their Government, its principles, and its officers, have been published to the world by French journalists and in French pamphlets." Yet America had not complained of "these calumnies, atrocious as they are. . . . Had not other causes, infinitely more serious and weighty, interrupted the harmony of the two republics, it would still have remained unimpaired and the mission of the undersigned would never have been rendered necessary."[1]

Marshall again briefly sums up in broad outline the injuries which the then French Government had inflicted upon Americans and American property, and finally declares: "It requires no assurance to convince, that every real American must wish sincerely to extricate his country from the ills it suffers, and from the greater ills with which it is threatened; but all who love liberty must admit that it does not exist in a nation which cannot exercise the right of maintaining its neutrality."

Referring to Talleyrand's desire that Gerry remain and conduct the negotiations, Marshall remarks that the request "is not accompanied by any assurances of receding from those demands of money heretofore made the consideration on which alone the cessation of hostility on American commerce could be obtained." No one of the three American envoys had power to act alone, he maintains. In spite of neglect and insult Marshall still hopes that negotiations may begin; but if that is impossible, he asks for passports and safe-conduct.

[1] *Am. St. Prs., For. Rel.*, ii, 196.

Marshall made his final preparations for sailing, in order, he says, "that I might be in readiness to depart so soon as the will of the government should be signified to me." He was so hurried, he declares, that "I could not even lay in a moderate stock of wine or send my foul linen to be washed."[1] The now inescapable Beaumarchais saw Marshall again and told him that Talleyrand said that "I [Marshall] was no foreign minister; that I was to be considered as a private American citizen, to obtain my passport in the manner pursued by all others through the Consul . . . I must give my name, stature, age, complexion, &c., to our Consul."

Marshall answered with much heat. Beaumarchais conferred with Talleyrand, taking Marshall's side. Talleyrand was obdurate and said that "he was mistaken in me [Marshall]; that I prevented all negotiation and that so soon as I was gone the negotiation would be carried on; that in America I belonged to the English faction, which universally hated and opposed the French faction; that all I sought for was to produce a rupture in such a manner as to throw the whole blame on France." Marshall replied that Talleyrand "endeavored to make our situation more unpleasant than his orders required, in order to gratify his personal feelings," and he flatly refused to leave until ordered to go.[2]

Finally Marshall and Pinckney received their

[1] This would seem to dispose of the story that Marshall brought home enough "very fine" Madeira to serve his own use, supply weddings, and still leave a quantity in existence three quarters of a century after his return. (*Green Bag*, viii, 486.)

[2] Marshall's Journal, April 10 and 11, 1798, 107–14.

passports. Pinckney, whose daughter was ill and could leave France at that time only at the risk of her life, had serious difficulty in getting permission to stay in the south of France. On April 24, Marshall sailed for home. It is characteristic of the man that, notwithstanding his humiliating experiences and the failure of the mission, he was neither sour nor depressed. He had made many personal friends in Paris; and on taking ship at Bordeaux he does not forget to send them greetings, singling out Madame de Villette for a gay message of farewell. "Present me to my friends in Paris," he writes the American Consul-General at the French Capital, "& have the goodness to say to Madam Vilette in my name & in the handsomest manner, every thing which respectful friendship can dictate. When you have done that You will have rendered not quite half justice to my sentiments." [1]

Gerry, to whom Pinckney and Marshall did not even bid farewell,[2] remained in Paris, "extremely miserable." [3] Infinitely disgusted, Pinckney writes King that Gerry, "as I suspected, is resolved to remain here," notwithstanding Pinckney's "warm remonstrances with him on the bad consequences . . . of such conduct and on the impropriety of" his secret "correspondence with Talleyrand under injunction not to communicate it to his colleagues." Pinckney says: "I have made great sacrifices of my feelings to preserve union; but in vain. I never met

[1] Marshall to Skipwith, Bordeaux, April 21, 1798; MS., Pa. Hist. Soc.

[2] Murray to J. Q. Adams, April 24, 1798; *Letters:* Ford, 399.

[3] Same to same, May 18, 1798; *ib.*, 407.

with a man of less candour and so much duplicity as Mr. Gerry. General Marshall is a man of extensive ability, of manly candour, and an honest heart." [1]

[1] Pinckney to King, Paris, April 4, 1798, enclosed in a letter to Secretary of State, April 16, 1798; Pickering MSS., Mass. Hist. Soc.

CHAPTER IX

THE TRIUMPHANT RETURN

The present crisis is the most awful since the days of Vandalism. (Robert Troup.)

Millions for defense but not one cent for tribute. (Toast at banquet to Marshall.)

We shall remain free if we do not deserve to be slaves. (Marshall to citizens of Richmond.)

What a wicked use has been made of the X. Y. Z. dish cooked up by Marshall. (Jefferson.)

WHILE Talleyrand's drama of shame was enacting in Paris, things were going badly for the American Government at home. The French party in America, with whose wrath Talleyrand's male and female agents had threatened our envoys, was quite as powerful and aggressive against President Adams as the French Foreign Office had been told that it was.[1]

Notwithstanding the hazard and delay of ocean travel,[2] Talleyrand managed to communicate at least once with his sympathizers in America, whom he told that the envoys' "pretensions are high, that possibly no arrangement may take place, but that there will be no declaration of war by France." [3]

Jefferson was alert for news from Paris. "We have still not a word from our Envoys. This long silence (if they have been silent) proves things are not going on very roughly. If they have not been silent,

[1] See summary in McMaster, ii, 374.

[2] Six copies of the dispatches of the American envoys to the Secretary of State were sent by as many ships, so that at least one of them might reach its destination.

[3] Jefferson to Madison, Jan. 25, 1798; *Works:* Ford, viii, 259.

it proves their information, if made public, would check the disposition to arm."[1] He had not yet received the letter written him March 17, by his agent, Skipwith. This letter is abusive of the Administration of Washington as well as of that of Adams. Marshall was "one of the declaiming apostles of Jay's Treaty"; he and Pinckney courted the enemies of the Revolutionary Government; and Gerry's "paralytic mind" was "too weak" to accomplish anything.[2]

The envoys' first dispatches, sent from Paris October 22, 1797, reached Philadelphia on the night of March 4, 1798.[3] These documents told of the corrupt French demands and machinations. The next morning President Adams informed Congress of their arrival.[4] Two weeks later came the President's startling message to Congress declaring that the envoys could not succeed "on terms compatible with the safety, the honor, or the essential interests of the nation" and "exhorting" Congress to prepare for war.[5]

The Republicans were dazed. White hot with anger, Jefferson writes Madison that the President's "insane message . . . has had great effect. Exultation on the one side & a certainty of victory; while

[1] Jefferson to Madison, Feb. 15, 1798; *Works:* Ford, viii, 368.

[2] Skipwith to Jefferson, Paris, March 17, 1798; Gibbs, ii, 160.

[3] *Am. St. Prs., For. Rel.*, ii, 152, 157, 159, 161, 166.

[4] *Ib.* The President at this time communicated only the first dispatch, which was not in cipher. It merely stated that there was no hope that the envoys would be received and that a new decree directed the capture of all neutral ships carrying any British goods whatever. (*Ib.*, 157.)

[5] *Ib.*, 152; Richardson, i, 264; and *Works:* Adams, ix, 156.

the other [Republican] is petrified with astonishment."[1] The same day he tells Monroe that the President's "almost insane message" had alarmed the merchants and strengthened the Administration; but he did not despair, for the first move of the Republicans "will be a call for papers [the envoys' dispatches].[2] In Congress the battle raged furiously; "the question of war & peace depends now on a toss of cross & pile,"[3] was Jefferson's nervous opinion.

But the country itself still continued French in feeling; the Republicans were gaining headway even in Massachusetts and Connecticut; Jefferson expected the fall elections to increase the Republican strength in the House; petitions against war measures were pouring into Congress from every section; the Republican strategy was to gain time. Jefferson thought that "the present period, . . . of two or three weeks, is the most eventful ever known since that of 1775."[4]

The Republicans, who controlled the House of Representatives, demanded that the dispatches be made public: they were sure that these papers would not justify Adams's grave message. If the President should refuse to send Congress the papers it would demonstrate, said the "Aurora," that he "suspects the popularity of his conduct if exposed to public view. . . . If he thinks he has done right, why should he be afraid of letting his measures be known?" Let

[1] Jefferson to Madison, March 21, 1798; *Works:* Ford, viii, 386.
[2] Jefferson to Monroe, March 21, 1798; *ib.*, 388–89.
[3] Jefferson to Madison, March 29, 1798; *ib.*, 392.
[4] Jefferson to Pendleton, April 2, 1798; *ib.*, 394–97.

the representatives of the people see "*the whole* of the papers . . . a *partial* communication would be worse than none." [1]

Adams hesitated to reveal the contents of the dispatches because of "a regard for the *personal safety* of the Commissioners and an apprehension of the effect of a disclosure upon our future diplomatic intercourse." [2] High Federalist business men, to whom an intimation of the contents of the dispatches had been given, urged their publication. "We wish much for the papers if they can with propriety be made public" was Mason's reply to Otis. "The Jacobins want them. And in the name of God let them be gratified; it is not the first time they have wished for the means of their destruction." [3]

Both Federalists who were advised and Republicans who were still in the dark now were gratified in their wish to see the incessantly discussed and mysterious message from the envoys. The effect on the partisan maneuvering was as radical and amusing as it is illuminative of partisan sincerity. When, on April 3, the President transmitted to Congress the dispatches thus far received, the Republicans instantly altered their tactics. The dispatches did not show that the negotiations were at an end, said the "Aurora"; it was wrong, therefore, to publish them — such a course might mean war. Their publication was a Federalist trick to discredit the Republican Party; and anyway Talleyrand was

[1] *Aurora*, April 3, 1798.

[2] Otis to Mason, March 22, 1798; Morison, i, 90.

[3] Jonathan Mason to Otis, March 30, 1798; *ib.*, 93. And see the valuable New England Federalist correspondence of the time in *ib.*

a monarchist, the friend of Hamilton and King. So raged and protested the Republican organ.[1]

Troup thus reports the change: The Republicans, he says, "were very clamorous for the publication [of the dispatches] until they became acquainted with the intelligence communicated. From that moment they opposed publication, and finally they carried a majority against the measure. The Senate finding this to be the case instantly directed publication."[2] The President then transmitted to Congress the second dispatch which had been sent from Paris two weeks after the first. This contained Marshall's superb memorial to Talleyrand. It was another blow to Republican hopes.

The dispatches told the whole story, simply yet with dramatic art. The names of Hottenguer, Bellamy, and Hauteval were represented by the letters X, Y, and Z,[3] which at once gave to this picturesque episode the popular name that history has adopted. The effect upon public opinion was instantaneous and terrific.[4] The first result, of course, was felt in Congress. Vice-President Jefferson now thought it his "duty to be silent."[5] In the House the Republi-

[1] *Aurora*, April 7, 1798. A week later, under the caption, "The Catastrophe," the *Aurora* began the publication of a series of ably written articles excusing the conduct of the French officials and condemning that of Marshall and Pinckney.

[2] Troup to King, June 3, 1798; King, ii, 329. Ten thousand copies of the dispatches were ordered printed and distributed at public expense. Eighteen hundred were sent to Virginia alone. (Pickering to Marshall, July 24, 1798; Pickering MSS., Mass. Hist. Soc.) This was the beginning of the printing and distributing of public documents by the National Government. (Hildreth, ii, 217.)

[3] Pickering's statement, April 3, 1798; *Am. St. Prs.*, ii, 157.

[4] Jefferson to Madison, April 5, 1798: *Works:* Ford, viii, 398. [5] *Ib.*

cans were "thunderstruck."[1] Many of their boldest leaders left for home; others went over openly to the Federalists.[2] Marshall's disclosures "produced such a shock on the republican mind, as has never been seen since our independence," declared Jefferson.[3] He implored Madison to write for the public an analysis of the dispatches from the Republican point of view.[4]

After recovering from his "shock" Jefferson tried to make light of the revelations; the envoys had "been assailed by swindlers," he said, "but that the Directory knew anything of it is neither proved nor probable." Adams was to blame for the unhappy outcome of the mission, declared Jefferson; his "speech is in truth the only obstacle to negotiation."[5] Promptly taking his cue from his master, Madison asserted that the publication of the dispatches served "more to inflame than to inform the country." He did not think Talleyrand guilty — his "conduct is scarcely credible. I do not allude to its depravity, which, however heinous, is not without example. Its unparalleled stupidity is what fills me with astonishment."[6]

The hot-blooded Washington exploded with anger. He thought "the measure of infamy was filled" by the "profligacy . . . and corruption" of the French

[1] Pickering to Jay, April 9, 1798; *Jay:* Johnston, iv, 236.

[2] Jefferson to Madison, April 26, 1798; *Works:* Ford, viii, 411. Among the Republicans who deserted their posts Jefferson names Giles, Nicholas, and Clopton.

[3] Jefferson to Madison, April 6, 1798; *ib.*, 403.

[4] *Ib.*, April 12, 1798; *ib.*, 404.

[5] Jefferson to Carr, April 12, 1798; *Works:* Ford, viii, 405–06.

[6] Madison to Jefferson, April 15, 1798; *Writings:* Hunt, vi, 315.

Directory; the dispatches ought "to open the eyes of the blindest," but would not "change . . . the *leaders* of the opposition unless there shou'd appear a manifest desertion of the followers."[1] Washington believed the French Government "capable [of] any thing bad" and denounced its "outrageous conduct . . . toward the United States"; but he was even more wrathful at the "inimitable conduct of its partisans [in America] who aid and abet their measures." He concluded that the Directory would modify their defiant attitude when they found "the spirit and policy of this country rising with resistance and that they have falsely calculated upon support from a large part of the people thereof."[2]

Then was heard the voice of the country. "The effects of the publication [of the dispatches] . . . on the people . . . has been prodigious. . . . The leaders of the opposition . . . were astonished & confounded at the profligacy of their beloved friends the French."[3] In New England, relates Ames, "the Jacobins [Republicans] were confounded, and the trimmers dropt off from the party, like windfalls from an apple tree in September."[4] Among all classes were observed "the most magical effects"; so "irresistible has been the current of public opinion . . . that . . . it has broken down the opposition in Congress."[5] Jefferson mournfully informed Madison that "the spirit kindled up in the towns is wonder-

[1] Washington to Pickering, April 16, 1798; *Writings:* Ford, xiii, 495.
[2] Washington to Hamilton, May 27, 1798; *ib.*, xiv, 6–7.
[3] Sedgwick to King, May 1, 1798; King, ii, 319.
[4] Ames to Gore, Dec. 18, 1798; *Works:* Ames, i, 245–46.
[5] Troup to King, June 3, 1798; King, ii, 329.

ful. . . . Addresses . . . are pouring in offering life & fortune."[1] Long afterwards he records that the French disclosures "carried over from us a great body of the people, real republicans & honest men, under virtuous motives."[2] In New England, especially, the cry was for "open and deadly war with France."[3] From Boston Jonathan Mason wrote Otis that "war for a time we must have and our fears . . . are that . . . you [Congress] will rise without a proper *climax*. . . . We pray that decisive orders may be given and that accursed Treaty [with France] may be annulled. . . . The time is now passed, when we should fear giving offense. . . . The yeomanry are not only united but spirited."[4]

Public meetings were held everywhere and "addresses from all bodies and descriptions of men" poured "like a torrent on the President and both Houses of Congress."[5] The blood of Federalism was boiling. "We consider the present crisis as the most awful since the days of Vandalism," declared the ardent Troup.[6] "Yankee Doodle," "Stony Point," "The President's March," supplanted in popular favor "Ça ira" and the "Marseillaise," which had been the songs Americans best loved to sing.

[1] Jefferson to Madison, May 3, 1797, *Works:* Ford, viii, 413.

[2] Jefferson to Monroe, March 7, 1801; *ib.*, ix, 203.

[3] Higginson to Pickering, June 26, 1798; Pickering MSS., Mass. Hist. Soc.

[4] Jonathan Mason to Otis, May 28, 1798; Morison, i, 95–96.

[5] Troup to King, June 3, 1798; King, ii, 329.

[6] *Ib.*, 330; and see letters of Bingham, Lawrence, and Cabot to King, *ib.*, 331–34. From the newspapers of the time, McMaster has drawn a brilliant picture of the thrilling and dramatic scenes which all over the United States marked the change in the temper of the people. (McMaster, ii, 376 *et seq.*)

The black cockade, worn by patriots during the Revolutionary War, suddenly took the place of the French cockade which until the X. Y. Z. disclosures had decorated the hats of the majority in American cities. The outburst of patriotism produced many songs, among others Joseph Hopkinson's "Hail Columbia!" ("The President's March"), which, from its first presentation in Philadelphia, caught the popular ear. This song is of historic importance, in that it expresses lyrically the first distinctively National consciousness that had appeared among Americans. Everywhere its stirring words were sung. In cities and towns the young men formed American clubs after the fashion of the democratic societies of the French party.

> "Hail, Columbia! happy land!
> Hail, ye heroes! heaven-born band!
> Who fought and bled in Freedom's cause,"—

sang these young patriots, and "Hail, Columbia!" chanted the young women of the land.[1] On every hilltop the fires of patriotism were signaling devotion and loyalty to the American Government.

Then came Marshall. Unannounced and unlooked for, his ship, the Alexander Hamilton, had sailed into New York Harbor after a voyage of fifty-three days from Bordeaux.[2] No one knew of his coming. "General Marshall arrived here on Sunday last. His arrival was unexpected and his stay with us was very short. I have no other apology to make,"

[1] "Hail Columbia exacts not less reverence in America than the Marseillaise Hymn in France and Rule Britannia in England." (Davis, 128.)

[2] Norfolk (Va.) *Herald*, June 25, 1798.

writes Troup, "for our not giving him a public demonstration of our love and esteem."[1] Marshall hurried on to Philadelphia. Already the great memorial to Talleyrand and the brilliantly written dispatches were ascribed to his pen, and the belief had become universal that the Virginian had proved to be the strong and resourceful man of the mission.

On June 18, 1798, he entered the Capital, through which, twenty years before, almost to a day, he had marched as a patriot soldier on the way to Monmouth from Valley Forge. Never before had any American, excepting only Washington, been received with such demonstration.[2] Fleets of carriages filled with members of Congress and prominent citizens, and crowds of people on horseback and on foot, went forth to meet him.

"The concourse of citizens . . . was immense." Three corps of cavalry "in full uniform" gave a warlike color to the procession which formed behind Marshall's carriage six miles out from Philadelphia. "The occasion cannot be mentioned on which so prompt and general a muster of the cavalry ever before took place." When the city was reached, the church bells rang, cannon thundered, and amid "the shouts of the exulting multitudes" Marshall was "escorted through the principal streets to the city Tavern." The leading Federalist newspaper, the "Gazette of the United States," records that, "even in the Northern Liberties,[3] where the demons

[1] Troup to King, June 23, 1798; King, II, 349.

[2] Even Franklin's welcome on his first return from diplomatic service in England did not equal the Marshall demonstration.

[3] A strenuously Republican environ of Philadelphia.

of anarchy and confusion are attempting to organize treason and death, repeated shouts of applause were given as the cavalcade approached and passed along." [1] The next morning O'Ellers Tavern was thronged with Senators and Representatives and "a numerous concourse of respectable citizens" who came to congratulate Marshall.[2]

The "Aurora" confirms this description of its Federalist rival; but adds bitterly: "What an occasion for rejoicing! Mr. Marshall was sent to France for the *ostensible* purpose, at least, of effecting an amicable accommodation of differences. He returns without having accomplished that object, and on his return the Tories rejoice. This certainly looks as if they did not wish him to succeed. . . . Many pensive and melancholy countenances gave the glare of parade a gloom much more suited to the occasion, and more in unison with the feelings of Americans. Well may they despond: For tho' the patriotic Gerry may succeed in settling the differences between the two countries — it is too certain that his efforts can be of no avail when the late conduct of our administration, and the unprecedented intemperance of our chief executive magistrate is known in Europe." [3]

Jefferson watched Marshall's home-coming with keen anxiety. "We heard of the arrival of Marshall at New York," he writes, "and I concluded to stay & see whether that circumstance would produce any

[1] *Gazette of the United States*, June 20, 1798; see also Claypoole's *American Daily Advertiser*, Wednesday, June 20, 1798.

[2] *Gazette of the United States*, June 21, 1798.

[3] *Aurora*, June 21, 1798; and see *ib.*, June 20.

new projects. No doubt he there received more than hints from Hamilton as to the tone required to be assumed. . . . Yet I apprehend he is not hot enough for his friends."

With much chagrin he then describes what happened when Marshall reached Philadelphia: "M. was received here with the utmost éclat. The Secretary of State & many carriages, with all the city cavalry, went to Frankfort to meet him, and on his arrival here in the evening, the bells rung till late in the night, & immense crowds were collected to see & make part of the shew, which was circuitously paraded through the streets before he was set down at the city tavern." But, says Jefferson, "all this was to secure him [Marshall] to their [the Administration's] views, that he might say nothing which would expose the game they have been playing.[1] Since his arrival I can hear nothing directly from him."

Swallowing his dislike for the moment, Jefferson called on Marshall while the latter was absent from the tavern. "Thomas Jefferson presents his compliments to General Marshall" ran the card he left. "He had the honor of calling at his lodgings twice this morning, but was so ^un^lucky as to find that he was out on both occasions. He wished to have expressed in person his regret that a pre-engagement for to-day which could not be dispensed with, would prevent him the satisfaction of dining in company with General Marshall, and therefore begs leave to place here the expressions of that respect

[1] Jefferson to Madison, June 21, 1798; *Works:* Ford, viii, 439–40.

which in company with his fellow citizens he bears him." [1]

Many years afterwards Marshall referred to the adding of the syllable "un" to the word "lucky" as one time, at least, when Jefferson came near telling the truth.[2] To this note Marshall returned a reply as frigidly polite as Jefferson's: —

"J. Marshall begs leave to accompany his respectful compliments to Mr. Jefferson with assurances of the regret he feels at being absent when Mr. Jefferson did him the honor to call on him.

"J. Marshall is extremely sensible to the obliging expressions contained in Mr. Jefferson's polite billet of yesterday. He sets out to-morrow for Winchester & would with pleasure charge himself with any commands of Mr. Jefferson to that part of Virginia." [3]

Having made his report to the President and Secretary of State, Marshall prepared to start for Virginia. But he was not to leave without the highest compliment that the Administration could, at that time, pay him. So gratified were the President, Cabinet, and Federalist leaders in Congress with Marshall's conduct in the X. Y. Z. mission, and so high their opinion of his ability, that Adams tendered him the appointment to the place on the Supreme Bench,[4] made vacant by the death of Justice Wilson. Marshall promptly declined. After applying to the Fairfax indebtedness all the money which he

[1] General Marshall at O'Eller's Hotel, June 23, 1798; Jefferson MSS., Lib. Cong.

[2] *Green Bag*, viii, 482–83.

[3] Marshall to Jefferson; Jefferson MSS., Lib. Cong.

[4] Pickering to Marshall, Sept. 20, 1798; Pickering MSS., Mass. Hist. Soc.

might receive as compensation for his services in the French mission, there would still remain a heavy balance of obligation; and Marshall must devote all his time and strength to business.

On the night before his departure, the members of Congress gave the hero of the hour the historic dinner at the city's principal tavern, "as an evidence of their affection for his person and their gratified approbation of the patriotic firmness with which he sustained the dignity of his country during his important mission." One hundred and twenty enthusiastic men sat at the banquet table.

The Speaker of the National House, the members of the Cabinet, the Justices of the Supreme Court, the Speaker of the Pennsylvania State Senate, the field officers of the army, the Right Reverend Bishops Carroll and White, "and other distinguished public characters attended." Toasts "were drank with unbounded plaudits" and "many of them were encored with enthusiasm." High rose the spirit of Federalism at O'Eller's Tavern in Philadelphia that night; loud rang Federalist cheers; copiously flowed Federalist wine.

"Millions for Defense but not a cent for Tribute!" was the crowning toast of that jubilant evening. It expressed the spirit of the gathering; out over the streets of Philadelphia rolled the huzzas that greeted it. But its unknown author[1] "builded bet-

[1] This sentiment has been ascribed to General C. C. Pinckney, Marshall's colleague on the X. Y. Z. mission. But it was first used at the Philadelphia banquet to Marshall. Pinckney's nearest approach to it was his loud, and wrathful, "No! not a sixpence!" when Hottenguer made one of his incessant demands for money. (See *supra*, 273.)

ter than he knew." He did more than flatter Marshall and bring the enthusiastic banqueters, wildly shouting, to their feet: he uttered the sentiment of the Nation. "Millions for Defense but not a cent for Tribute" is one of the few historic expressions in which Federalism spoke in the voice of America. Thus the Marshall banquet in Philadelphia, June 18, 1798, produced that slogan of defiant patriotism which is one of the slowly accumulating American maxims that have lived.

After Marshall retired from the banquet hall, the assemblage drank a final toast to "The man whom his country delights to Honor." [1]

[1] Claypoole's *American Daily Advertiser*, Wednesday, June 20, 1798; Pa. Hist. Soc. The toasts drank at this dinner to Marshall illustrate the popular spirit at that particular moment. They also furnish good examples of the vocabulary of Federalism at the period of its revival and only two years before its annihilation by Jefferson's new party: —

" 1. The United States — 'free, sovereign & independent.'

" 2. The people and the Government — 'one and indivisible.'

" 3. The President — 'some other hand must be found to sign the ignominious deed' that would surrender the sovereignty of his Country.

" 4. General Washington — 'His name a rampart & the Knowledge that he lives a bulwark against mean and secret enemies of his Country's Peace.'

" 5. General Pinckney. ''T is not in mortals to command success: He has done more — deserved it.'

" 6. The Officers & Soldiers of the American Army. 'May glory be their Theme, Victory their Companion, & Gratitude & Love their Rewards.'

" 7. The Navy of the United States. 'May its infant efforts, like those of Hercules, be the Presage of its future Greatness.'

" 8. The Militia. 'May they never cease to combine the Valor of the Soldier with the Virtues of the Citizen.'

" 9. The Gallant Youth of America. 'May they disdain to hold as Tenants at Will, the Independence inherited from their ancestors.'

"10. The Heroes who fell in the Revolutionary War. 'May their memory never be dishonored by a surrender of the Freedom purchased with their Blood.'

Marshall was smothered with addresses, congratulations, and every variety of attention from public bodies and civic and military organizations. A committee from the Grand Jury of Gloucester County, New Jersey, presented the returned envoy a laudatory address. His answer, while dignified, was somewhat stilted, perhaps a trifle pompous. The Grand Jury compliment was, said Marshall, "a sweet reward" for his "exertions." The envoys wished, above all things, for peace, but felt "that not even peace was to be purchased at the price of national independence." [1]

The officers of a militia brigade delivered to Marshall a eulogy in which the war note was clear and dominant. Marshall answered that, desirable as peace is, it "ought not to have been bought by dishonor and national degradation"; and that the resort to the sword, for which the militia officers declared themselves ready, made Marshall "feel with an elevated pride the dignity and grandeur of the American character." [2]

"11. The American Eagle. 'May it regard with disdain the crowing of the Gallic cock.'
"12. Union & Valour — infallible Antidotes against diplomatic skill.
"13. Millions for Defense but not a cent for Tribute.
"14. The first duties of a good citizen — Reverence for the Laws and Respect for the Magistracy.
"15. Agriculture & Commerce — A Dissolution of whose partnership will be the Bankruptcy of both.
"16. The Constitution — 'Esto Perpetua.'
"After General Marshall Retired: —
"General Marshall — The man whom his country delights to Honor." (*Ib.*, June 25, 1798.)

[1] Claypoole's *American Daily Advertiser*, Monday, June 25, 1798; and *Gazette of the United States*, Saturday, June 23, 1798.

[2] *Ib.*, June 25, 1798; and June 23, 1798.

The day before Marshall's departure from Philadelphia the President, addressing Congress, said: "I congratulate you on the arrival of General Marshall . . . at a place of safety where he is justly held in honor. . . . The negotiation may be considered at an end. *I will never send another Minister to France without assurances that he will be received, respected, and honored as the representative of a great, free, powerful, and independent nation.*"[1] Bold and defiant words expressive of the popular sentiment of the hour; but words which were to be recalled later by the enemies of Adams, to his embarrassment and to the injury of his party.[2]

"Having heard that Mrs. Marshall is in Winchester I shall immediately set out for that place,"[3] Marshall writes Washington. His departure from the Capital was as spectacular as his arrival. He "was escorted by detachments of cavalry," says the "Aurora." "Certainly nothing less was due considering the distinguished services which he has rendered by his mission — he has acquired some knowledge of the French language,"[4] sneers that partisan newspaper in good Republican fashion. When Marshall approached Lancaster he was met by companies of "cavalry and uniformed militia" which escorted him into the town, where he was "welcomed by the discharges of artillery and the ringing of bells."[5]

[1] Adams to Congress, June 21, 1798; *Works:* Adams, ix, 158; and Richardson, i, 266. Italics are mine.

[2] *Infra*, chap. XII.

[3] Marshall to Washington, June 22, 1798; MS., Lib. Cong.

[4] *Aurora*, June 30, 1798.

[5] *Gazette of the United States*, June 28, 1797.

His journey throughout Pennsylvania and Virginia, repeating scenes of his welcome at Philadelphia and Lancaster, ended at Richmond. There, among his old neighbors and friends, the demonstrations reached their climax. A long procession of citizens went out to meet him. Again rang the cheers, again the bells pealed, again the cannon thundered. And here, to his townsmen and friends, Marshall, for the first time, publicly opened his heart and told, with emotion, what had befallen in France. In this brief speech the Nationalist and fighting spirit, which appears in all his utterances throughout his entire life, flashes like a sword in battle.

Marshall cannot express his "emotions of joy" which his return to Richmond has aroused; nor "paint the sentiments of affection and gratitude towards" his old neighbors. Nobody, he assures his hearers, could appreciate his feelings who had not undergone similar experiences.

The envoys, far from their country with no news from their Government, were in constant anxiety, says Marshall. He tells of their trials, of how they had discharged their duty, of his exultation over the spirit America was now displaying. "I rejoice that I was not mistaken in the opinion I had formed of my countrymen. I rejoice to find, though they know how to estimate, and therefore seek to avoid the horrors and dangers of war, yet they know also how to value the blessings of liberty and national independence. Peace would be purchased at too high a price by bending beneath a foreign yoke" and such a peace would be but brief; for "the nation thus submitting would be soon involved in the quarrels of its master. . . . We shall remain free if we do not deserve to be slaves."

Marshall compares the governments of France and America. To one who, like himself, is so accustomed to real liberty that he "almost considers it as the indispensable companion of man, a view of [French] despotism," though "borrowing the garb usurping the name of freedom," teaches "the solid safety and real security" existing in America. The loss of these "would poison . . . every other joy." Without them "freemen would turn with loathing and disgust from every other comfort of life." To preserve them, "all . . . difficulties ought to be encountered."

Stand by "the government of your choice," urges Marshall; its officials are from the people, "subject in common with others to the laws they make," and must soon return to the popular body "whose destiny involves their own and in whose ruin they must participate." This is always a good rule, but "it is peculiarly so in a moment of peril like the present" when "want of confidence in our government . . . furnishes . . . a foreign real enemy [France] those weapons which have so often been so successfully used." [1]

The Mayor, Recorder, Aldermen, and Common Council of Richmond presented Marshall with an address of extravagant praise. "If reason and argument . . . if integrity, candor, and the pure spirit of conciliation" had met like qualities in France, "smiling peace would have returned along with you." But if Marshall had not brought peace, he

[1] *Columbian Centinel*, Boston, Sept. 22, 1798.

had warned America against a government "whose touch is death." Perhaps he had even preserved "our excellent constitution and . . . our well earned liberties." In answer Marshall said that he reciprocated the "joy" of his "fellow citizens, neighbors, and ancient friends" upon his return; that they were right in thinking honorable peace with France was impossible; and warned them against "the countless dangers which lurk beneath foreign attachments."[1]

Marshall had become a national hero. Known before this time, outside of his own State, chiefly to the eminent lawyers of America, his name now became a household word in the remotest log cabins of Kentucky and Tennessee, as well as in the residences of Boston and New York. "Saving General Washington, I believe the President, Pinckney, and Marshall are the most popular characters now in our country," Troup reported to King in London.[2]

For the moment, only one small cloud appeared upon the horizon of Marshall's popularity; but a vicious flash blazed from it. Marshall went to Fredericksburg on business and attended the little theater at that place. The band of the local artillery company furnished the music. A Philadelphia Federalist, who happened to be present, ordered them to play "The President's March" ("Hail, Columbia!"). Instantly the audience was in an uproar. So violent did they become that "a considerable riot took place." Marshall was openly insulted. Nor did their hostility subside with Marshall's departure.

[1] Norfolk (Va.) *Herald*, Aug. 30, 1798.

[2] Troup to King, Nov. 16, 1798; King, ii, 465; and see same to same, July 10, 1798; *ib.*, 363.

"The inhabitants of Fredericksburg waited," in anxious expectation, for an especially hated Federalist Congressman, Harper of South Carolina, to pass through the town on his way home, with the intention of treating him even more roughly.[1]

With this ominous exception, the public demonstrations for Marshall were warmly favorable. His strength with the people was greater than ever. By the members of the Federal Party he was fairly idolized. This, the first formal party organization in our history, was, as we have seen, in sorry case even under Washington. The assaults of the Republicans, directed by Jefferson's genius for party management, had all but wrecked the Federalists. That great party general had out-maneuvered his adversaries at every point and the President's party was already nearing the breakers.

The conduct of the French mission and the publication of Marshall's dispatches and letters to Talleyrand saved the situation for the moment. Those whom Jefferson's consummate skill had won over to the Republican Party returned by thousands to their former party allegiance.[2]

Congress acted with belated decision. Our treaty with France was abrogated; non-intercourse laws passed; a provisional army created; the Navy Department established; arsenals provided; the building of warships directed. For a season our National machinery was permitted to work with vigor and effectiveness.

[1] Carey's *United States Recorder*, Aug. 16, 1798.
[2] McMaster, ii, 380–85; Hildreth, v, 203 *et seq.*

The voices that were wont to declaim the glories of French democracy were temporarily silent. The people, who but yesterday frantically cheered the "liberté, égalité, fraternité" of Robespierre and Danton, now howled with wrath at mention of republican France. The pulpit became a tribune of military appeal and ministers of the gospel preached sermons against American "Jacobins."[1] Federalist orators had their turn at assailing "despotism" with rhetoric and defending "liberty" with eloquence; but the French Government was now the international villain whom they attacked.

"The struggle between Liberty and Despotism, Government and Anarchy, Religion and Atheism, has been gloriously decided. . . . France has been foiled, and America is free. The elastick veil of Gallick perfidy has been rent, . . . the severing blow has been struck." Our abrogation of the treaty with France was "the completion of our Liberties, the acme of our Independence . . . and . . . emancipated us from the oppressive friendship of an ambitious, malignant, treacherous ally." That act evidenced "our nation's manhood"; our Government was now "an Hercules, who, no longer amused with the coral and bells of 'liberty and equality' . . . no longer willing to trifle at the *distaff* of a 'Lady Negociator,' boldly invested himself in the *toga virilis*."[2] Such was the language of the public platform; and private expressions of most men were even less restrained.

[1] McMaster, ii, 380–85.

[2] "Oration of Robert Treat Paine to Young Men of Boston," July 17, 1799; in *Works of Robert Treat Paine*, ed. 1812, 301 *et seq.*

Denouncing "the Domineering Spirit and boundless ambition of a nation whose Turpitude has set *all objections*, divine & human, at naught,"[1] Washington accepted the appointment as Commander-in-Chief of the newly raised army. "Huzza! Huzza! Huzza! How transporting the fact! The great, the good, the aged WASHINGTON has said 'I am ready again to go with my fellow citizens to the field of battle in defense of the Liberty & Independence of my Country,'" ran a newspaper announcement, typically voicing the popular heart.[2]

To Marshall's brother James, who had offered his services as an aide-de-camp, Washington wrote that the French "(although *I* conceive them capable of *anything* that is unjust or dishonorable)" will not "attempt a serious invasion of this country" when they learn of "the preparation which [we] are making to receive them." They have "made calculations on false ground" in supposing that Americans would not "support Independence and the Government of their country *at every hazard*." Nevertheless, "the highest possible obligation rests upon the country to be prepared for the event as the most effective means to avert the evil."[3] Military preparations were active and conspicuous: On July 4, New York City "resembles a camp rather than a commercial port," testifies Troup.[4]

[1] Washington to Murray, Aug. 10, 1798; *Writings:* Ford, xiv, 72.

[2] Norfolk (Va.) *Herald*, July 10, 1798.

[3] Washington to Jas. Marshall, July 18, 1798; MS., N.Y. Pub. Lib. And see Washington to Murray, Aug. 10, 1798; *Writings:* Ford, xiv, 71. "I . . . hope that . . . when the Despots of France find how much they . . . have been deceived by their partisans *among us*, . . . that an appeal to arms . . . will be . . . unnecessary." (*Ib.*)

[4] Troup to King, July 10, 1798; King, ii, 362.

The people for the moment believed, with Marshall and Washington, that we were on the brink of war; had they known what Jefferson knew, their apprehension would have been still keener. Reporting from Paris, the French partisan Skipwith tells Jefferson that, from motives of "commercial advantage and aggrandisement" as well as of "vengeance," France will probably fall upon America. "Yes sir, the moment is come that I see the fortunes, nay, independence, of my country at hazard, and in the hands of the most gigantic nation on earth. . . . Already, the language of planting new colonies upon the . . . Mississippi is the language of Frenchmen here."[1] Skipwith blames this predicament upon Adams's character, speech, and action and upon Marshall's and Pinckney's conduct in Paris;[2] and advises Jefferson that "war may be prevented, and our country saved" by "modifying or breaking" the Jay Treaty and lending money to France.[3]

Jefferson was frantic with disappointment and anger. Not only did he see the Republican Party, which he had built up with such patience and skill, going to pieces before his very eyes; but the prospect of his election to the Presidency as the successor of Adams, which until then appeared to be inviting, now jeopardized if not made hopeless. With his almost uncanny understanding of men, Jefferson laid all this to Marshall; and, from the moment of his fellow Virginian's arrival from France, this captain of the popular cause began that open and malignant

[1] Skipwith to Jefferson, March 17, 1798; Gibbs, ii, 158.
[2] *Supra*, chap. VIII.
[3] Skipwith to Jefferson, March 17, 1798; Gibbs, ii, 158.

warfare upon Marshall which ended only with Jefferson's last breath.

At once he set out to repair the havoc which Marshall's work had wrought in his party. This task was made the harder because of the very tactics which Jefferson had employed to increase the Republican strength. For, until now, he had utilized so thoroughly the deep and widespread French sentiment in America as his immediate party weapon, and made so emphatic the French issue as a policy of party tactics, that, in comparison, all other issues, except the central one of States' Rights, were secondary in the public mind at this particular time.

The French propaganda had gone farther than Jefferson, perhaps, intended it to go. "They [the French] have been led to believe by their agents and Partisans amongst *us*," testifies Washington, "that we are a divided people, that the latter are opposed to their own Government."[1] At any rate, it is certain that a direct connection, between members of what the French politicians felt themselves justified in calling "the French party" in America and the manipulators of French public opinion, existed and was made use of. This is shown by the effect in France of Jefferson's famous letter to Mazzei of April 24, 1796.[2] It is proved by the amazing fact that Talleyrand's answer to the memorial of the envoys was published in the Jeffersonian organ, the "Aurora," before Adams had transmitted that document to Congress, if not indeed before the President himself

[1] Washington to Adams, July 4, 1798; *Writings:* Ford, xiv, 15–19.
[2] See *infra*, chap. XII.

had received from our envoys Talleyrand's reply to Marshall's statement of the American case.[1]

Jefferson took the only step possible to a party leader. He sought to minimize the effect of the disclosures revealed in Marshall's dispatches. Writing to Peter Carr, April 12, 1798, Jefferson said: "You will perceive that they [the envoys] have been assailed by swindlers, whether with or without the participation of Talleyrand is not very apparent. . . . That the Directory knew anything of it is neither proved nor probable." [2] On June 8, 1798, Jefferson wrote to Archibald Stuart: "It seems fairly presumable that the douceur of 50,000 Guineas mentioned in the former dispatches was merely from X. and Y. as not a word is ever said by Talleyrand to our envoys nor by them to him on the subject." [3] Thus Jefferson's political desperation caused him to deny facts which were of record, for the dispatches show, not only that Talleyrand had full knowledge of the disgraceful transaction, but also that he originated and directed it.

The efforts of the Republicans to sneer away the envoys' disclosures awakened Washington's bitter sarcasm. The Republicans were " thunder-stricken . . . on the publication of the dispatches from our envoys," writes he, "but the contents of these dispatches are now resolved by them into harmless chit-chat — mere trifles — less than was or ought to have been expected from the misconduct of the Adminis-

[1] See Marshall (1st ed.), v, footnote to 743; Hildreth, v, 218 also McMaster, ii, 390.

[2] Jefferson to Carr, April 12, 1798; *Works:* Ford, viii, 405.

[3] Jefferson to Stuart, June 8, 1798; *ib.*, 436.

tration of this country, and that it is better to submit to such chastisement than to hazard greater evils by shewing futile resentment." [1]

Jefferson made no headway, however, in his attempts to discredit the X. Y. Z. revelations. Had the Federalists stopped with establishing the Navy Department and providing for an army, with Washington at its head; had they been content to build ships and to take other proper measures for the National defense, Adams's Administration would have been saved, the Federalist Party kept alive for at least four years more, the Republican Party delayed in its recovery and Jefferson's election to the Presidency made impossible. Here again Fate worked, through the blindness of those whose day had passed, the doom of Federalism. The Federalists enacted the Alien and Sedition Laws and thus hastened their own downfall.

Even after this legislation had given him a new, real, and irresistible "issue," Jefferson still assailed the conduct of Marshall and Pinckney; he was resolved that not a single Republican vote should be lost. Months later he reviews the effect of the X. Y. Z. disclosures. When the envoys were appointed, he asserts, many "suspected . . . from what was understood of their [Marshall's and Pinckney's] dispositions," that the mission would not only fail, but "widen the breach and provoke our citizens to consent to a war with" France "& union with England." While the envoys were in Paris the Adminis-

[1] Washington to McHenry, May, 1798; *Writings:* Ford, xiii, footnote to 495.

tration's hostile attitude toward France alarmed the people; "meetings were held . . . in opposition to war"; and the "example was spreading like a wildfire."

Then "most critically for the government [Administration]," says Jefferson, "the dispatches . . . prepared by . . . Marshall, with a view to their being made public, dropped into their laps. It was truly a God-send to them & they made the most of it. Many thousands of copies were printed & dispersed gratis, at the public expense; & the zealots for war co-operated so heartily, that there were instances of single individuals who printed & dispersed 10. or 12,000 copies at their own expense. The odiousness of the corruption supposed in those papers excited a general & high indignation among the people."

Thus, declares Jefferson, the people, "unexperienced in such maneuvers," did not see that the whole affair was the work of "private swindlers" unauthorized by "the French government of whose participation there was neither proof nor probability." So "the people . . . gave a loose [tongue] to" their anger and declared "their honest preference of war to dishonor. The fever was long & successfully kept up and . . . war measures as ardently crowded." [1]

Jefferson's deep political sagacity did not underestimate the revolution in the thought and feelings of the masses produced by the outcome of the French mission; and he understood, to a nicety, the gigantic task which must be performed to reassemble and solidify the shattered Republican

[1] Jefferson to Gerry, Jan. 26, 1799; *Works:* Ford, ix, 21–22.

ranks. For public sentiment was, for the time being, decidedly warlike. "We will pay tribute to no nation; . . . We shall water our soil with our blood . . . before we yield," [1] was Troup's accurate if bombastic statement of the popular feeling.

When the first ship with American newspapers containing the X. Y. Z. dispatches reached London, they were at once "circulated throughout Europe," [2] and "produced everywhere much sensation favorable to the United States and hostile to France." [3] The intimates of Talleyrand and the Directory were "disappointed and chagrined. . . . Nothing can exceed the rage of the apostate Americans, who have so long misrepresented and disgraced their country at Paris." [4] From the first these self-expatriated Americans had flattered Gerry and sent swarms of letters to America about the good intentions of the Directory.[5]

American diplomatic representatives abroad were concerned over Gerry's whimsical character and conduct. "Gerry is yet in Paris! . . I . . . fear . . . that man's more than infantine weakness. Of it you cannot have an idea, unless you had seen him here [The Hague] and at Paris. Erase all the two lines above; it is true, but it is cruel. If they get hold of him they will convert him into an innocent baby-engine against the government." [6]

[1] Troup to King, July 10, 1798; King, ii, 363.

[2] King to Hamilton, London, July 14, 1798; *ib.*, 365.

[3] Smith to Wolcott, Lisbon, Aug. 14, postscript Aug. 17, 1798; Gibbs, ii, 120.

[4] King to Troup, July 31, 1798; King, ii, 377.

[5] King to Pickering, July 19, 1798; *ib.*, 370.

[6] Murray to J. Q. Adams, June 8, 1787; *Letters:* Ford, 416.

And now Gerry, with whom Talleyrand had been amusing himself and whose conceit had been fed by American partisans of France in Paris, found himself in sorry case. Talleyrand, with cynical audacity, in which one finds much grim humor, peremptorily demands that Gerry tell him the names of the mysterious "X., Y., and Z." With comic self-abasement, the New Englander actually writes Talleyrand the names of the latter's own agents whom Gerry had met in Talleyrand's presence and who the French Minister personally had informed Gerry were dependable men.

The Federalists made the most of Gerry's remaining in Paris. Marshall told them that Gerry had "suffered himself to be wheedled in Paris."[1] "I . . . rejoice that I voted against his appointment,"[2] declared Sedgwick. Cabot denounced Gerry's "course" as "the most dangerous that cou'd have been taken."[3] Higginson asserted that "those of us who knew him [Gerry] regretted his appointment and expected mischief from it; but he has conducted himself worse than we had anticipated."[4] The American Minister to Great Britain, bitterly humiliated, wrote to Hamilton that Gerry's "answer to Talleyrand's demands of the names of X, Y, and Z, place him in a more degraded light than I ever believed it possible that he or any other American citizen could be exhibited."[5] And Thomas Pinckney

[1] Troup to King, July 10, 1798; King, ii, 363.

[2] Sedgwick to King, July 1, 1798; *ib.*, 353.

[3] Cabot to King, July 2, 1798; *ib.*, 353.

[4] Higginson to Wolcott, Sept. 11, 1798; Gibbs, ii, 107.

[5] King to Hamilton, London, July 14, 1798; King, ii, 365.

feared "that to want of [Gerry's] judgment . . . may be added qualities of a more criminal nature." [1]

Such sentiments, testifies Pickering, were common to all "the public men whom I had heard speak of Mr. G."; Pinckney, Gerry's colleague, tells his brother that he "never met with a man *so destitute of candour and so full of deceit as Mr. Gerry*," and that this opinion was shared by Marshall.[2] Troup wrote: "We have seen and read with the greatest contempt the correspondence between Talleyrand and Mr. Gerry relative to Messrs. X. Y. and Z. . . . I can say nothing honorable to [of] him [Gerry]. De mortuis nil nisi bonum is a maxim as applicable to him as if he was in his grave." [3] Washington gave his opinion with unwonted mildness: "Nothing can excuse his [Gerry's] *secret* negotiations . . . I fear . . . that *vanity* which may have led him into the mistake — & consciousness of being *duped* by the *Diplomatic skill* of our good and magnanimous Allies are too powerful for a weak mind to overcome." [4]

Marshall was on tenter-hooks for fear that Gerry would not leave France before the Directory got wind "of the present temper" of the American people, and would hint to Gerry "insidious propositions . . . not with real pacific views but for the purpose of dividing the people of this country and

[1] Thomas Pinckney to King, July 18, 1798; King, ii, 369.

[2] Pickering to King, Sept. 15, 1798, quoting Pinckney; *ib.*, 414. Italics are Pinckney's.

[3] Troup to King, Oct. 2, 1798; *ib.*, 432–33.

[4] Washington to Pickering, Oct. 26, 1798; *Writings:* Ford, xiv, 121.

separating them from their government."[1] The peppery Secretary of State grew more and more intolerant of Gerry. He tells Marshall that "Gerry's correspondence with Talleyrand about W.[2] X. Y. and Z: . . . is the finishing stroke to his conduct in France, by which he has dishonoured and injured his country and sealed his own indelible disgrace."[3]

Marshall was disgusted with the Gerry-Talleyrand correspondence about the names of "X. Y. Z.," and wrote Pickering of Gerry's dinner to Talleyrand at which Hottenguer, Bellamy, and Hauteval were present and of their corrupt proposition to Gerry in Talleyrand's presence.[4] Pickering urged Marshall to write "a short history of the mission of the envoys extraordinary," and asked permission to show Marshall's journal to President Adams.[5]

Marshall is "unwilling," he says, "that my hasty journal, which I had never even read over until I received it from you, should be shown to him. This unwillingness proceeds from a repugnance to give him the vexation which I am persuaded it would give him." Nevertheless, Adams did read Marshall's Journal, it appears; for Cabot believed that "the reading of Marshall's journal has compelled the

[1] Marshall to Pickering, Aug. 11, 1798; Pickering MSS., Mass. Hist. Soc.

[2] Beaumarchais.

[3] Pickering to Marshall, Sept. 4, 1798; Pickering MSS., Mass. Hist. Soc.

[4] Marshall to Secretary of State, Sept. 15, 1798; *ib.*

[5] Pickering to Marshall, Oct. 19, 1798; *ib.*

P[resident] to . . . acquiesce in the unqualified condemnation of Gerry." [1]

On his return to America, Gerry writes a turgid letter defending himself and exculpating Talleyrand and the Directory. The Secretary of State sends Gerry's letter to Marshall, declaring that Gerry "ought to be impeached." [2] It "astonishes me," replies Marshall; and while he wishes to avoid altercation, he thinks "it is proper for me to notice this letter," and encloses a communication to Gerry, together with a "certificate," stating the facts of Gerry's now notorious dinner to Talleyrand. [3]

Marshall is especially anxious to avoid any personal controversy at the particular moment; for, as will presently appear, he is again running for office. He tells Pickering that the Virginia Republicans are "perfectly prepared" to use Gerry in any way "which can be applied to their purposes"; and are ready "to receive him into their bosoms or to drop him entirely as he may be French or American." He is so exasperated, however, that he contemplates publishing the whole truth about Gerry, but adds: "I have been restrained from doing so by my having as a punishment for some unknown sins, consented to be nam'd a candidate for the ensuing election to Congress." [4]

Finding himself so violently attacked in the press, Marshall says: "To protect myself from the vexation of these newspaper altercations . . . I wish if it be

[1] Cabot to King, April 26, 1798; King, iii, 9.
[2] Pickering to Marshall, Nov. 5, 1798; Pickering MSS.
[3] Marshall to Pickering, Nov. 12, 1798; *ib.*
[4] See next chapter.

possible to avoid appearing in print myself." Also he makes the excuse that the courts are in session, and that "my absence has plac'd my business in such a situation as scarcely to leave a moment which I can command for other purposes."[1]

A week later Marshall is very anxious as to what course Gerry intends to take, for, writes Marshall, publications to mollify public opinion toward France and to irritate it against England "and to diminish the repugnance to pay money to the French republic are appearing every day."[2]

The indefatigable Republican chieftain had been busily inspiring attacks upon the conduct of the mission and particularly upon Marshall. "You know what a wicked use has been made of the . . . X. Y. Z. dish cooked up by Marshall, where the swindlers are made to appear as the French government," wrote Jefferson to Pendleton. "Art and industry combined have certainly wrought out of this business a wonderful effect on the people." But "now that Gerry comes out clearing the French government of that turpitude, . . . the people will be disposed to suspect they have been duped."

Because Marshall's dispatches "are too voluminous for them [the people] and beyond their reach" Jefferson begs Pendleton to write a pamphlet "recapitulating the whole story . . . short, simple & levelled to every capacity." It must be "so concise as omitting nothing material, yet may be printed

[1] Marshall to Pickering, Oct. 15, 1798; Pickering MSS., Mass. Hist. Soc.

[2] Marshall to Pickering, Oct. 22, 1798; *ib.*, Mass. Hist. Soc., xxiii, 251.

in handbills." Jefferson proposes to "print & disperse 10. or 20,000 copies"[1] free of postage under the franks of Republican Congressmen.

Pickering having referred scathingly to the Gerry-Talleyrand dinner, Gerry writes the President, to deny Marshall's account of that function. Marshall replies in a personal letter to Gerry, which, considering Marshall's placid and unresentful nature, is a very whiplash of rebuke; it closes, however, with the hope that Gerry "will think justly of this subject and will thereby save us both the pain of an altercation I do so wish to avoid."[2]

A few months later Marshall, while even more fixed than ever in his contempt for Gerry, is mellower in expressing it. "I am grieved rather than surprised at Mr. Gerry's letter," he writes.[3] So ended the only incident in Marshall's life where he ever wrote severely of any man. Although the unfriendliness between Jefferson and himself grew through the years into unrelenting hatred on both sides, Marshall did not express the intensity of his feeling. While his courage, physical and moral, was perfect, he had no stomach for verbal encounters. He could fight to the death with arms or arguments; but personal warfare by tongue or pen was beyond or beneath him. Marshall simply could not scold or browbeat. He was incapable of participating in a brawl.

Soon after reaching Richmond, the domestic

[1] Jefferson to Pendleton, Jan. 29, 1799; *Works:* Ford, ix, 27–28.

[2] Marshall to Pickering, November 12, 1798; Pickering MSS., Mass. Hist. Soc.

[3] Marshall to Secretary of State, Feb. 19, 1799; *ib.*

Marshall again shines out sunnily in a letter to his wife at Winchester, over the Blue Ridge. He tells his "dearest Polly" that although a week has passed he has "scarcely had time to look into any business yet, there are so many persons calling every hour to see me. . . . The hot and disagreeable ride" to Richmond had been too much for him, but "if I could only learn that you were entirely restored I should be happy. Your Mama & friends are in good health & your Mama is as cheerful as usual except when some particular conversation discomposes her.

"Your sweet little Mary is one of the most fascinating little creatures I ever beheld. She has improved very much since I saw her & I cannot help agreeing that she is a substitute for her lovely sister. She talks in a way not easily to be understood tho she comprehends very well everything that is said to her & is the most coquettish little prude & the most prudish little coquet I ever saw. I wish she was with you as I think she would entertain you more than all the rest of your children put together.

"Poor little John[1] is cutting teeth & of course is sick. He appeared to know me as soon as he saw me. He would not come to me, but he kept his eyes fixed on me as on a person he had some imperfect recollection of. I expect he has been taught to look at the picture & had some confused idea of a likeness. He is small & weakly but by no means an ugly child. If as I hope we have the happiness to raise him I

[1] **Marshall's fourth child, born January 15, 1798, during Marshall's absence in France.**

trust he will do as well as the rest. Poor little fellow, the present hot weather is hard on him cutting teeth, but great care is taken of him & I hope he will do well.

"I hear nothing from you my dearest Polly but I will cherish the hope that you are getting better & will indulge myself with expecting the happiness of seeing you in october quite yourself. Remember my love to give me this pleasure you have only to take the cold bath, to use a great deal of exercise, to sleep tranquilly & to stay in cheerful company. I am sure you will do everything which can contribute to give you back to yourself & me. This hot weather must be very distressing to you — it is to everybody — but it will soon be colder. Let me know in time everything relative to your coming down. Farewell my dearest Polly. I am your ever affectionate

"J. MARSHALL."[1]

On taking up his private business, Marshall found himself hard-pressed for money. Payments for the Fairfax estate were overdue and he had no other resources with which to meet them but the money due him upon his French mission. "The disarrangement," he writes to the Secretary of

[1] Marshall to his wife, Richmond, Aug. 18, 1798; MS. Mrs. Marshall remained in Winchester, where her husband had hurried to see her after leaving Philadelphia. Her nervous malady had grown much worse during Marshall's absence. Mrs. Carrington had been "more than usual occupied with my poor sister Marshall . . . who fell into a deep melancholy. Her husband, who might by his usual tenderness (had he been here) have dissipated this frightful gloom, was long detained in France. . . . The malady increased." (Mrs. Carrington to Miss C[airns], 1800; Carrington MSS)

State, "produc'd by my absence and the dispersion of my family oblige me to make either sales which I do not wish or to delay payments of money which I ought not to delay, unless I can receive from the treasury. This state of things obliges me to apply to you and to ask whether you can furnish me either with an order from the Secretary of the Treasury on Colo. Carrington or with your request to him to advance money to me. The one or the other will be sufficient." [1]

Pickering writes Marshall that Carrington can safely advance him the needed cash. "I will lose no time to place the balance in your hands," [2] says Pickering, upon the receipt of Marshall's statement of his account with the Government.

The total amount paid Marshall for his eleven months' absence upon the French mission was $19,963.97,[3] which, allowing five thousand dollars for his expenses — a generous estimate — was considerably more than three times as much as Marshall's annual income from his law practice. It was an immense sum, considering the compensation of public officials at that period — not much less than the annual salaries of the President and his entire Cabinet; more than the total amount annu-

[1] Marshall to Pickering, August 11, 1798; Pickering MSS., Mass. Hist. Soc., xxiii, 33.

[2] Pickering to Marshall, Sept. 4, 1798; *ib.*

[3] Archives, State Department. Thirty-five hundred dollars was placed at Marshall's disposal when he sailed for France, five hundred dollars in specie and the remainder by letter of credit on governments and European bankers. (Marshall to Secretary of State, July 10, 1797; Pickering MSS. Also Archives, State Department.) He drew two thousand dollars more when he arrived at Philadelphia on his return (June 23; *ib.*), and $14,463.97 on Oct. 13 (*ib.*).

ally paid to the justices of the Supreme Court. Thus, for the time being, the Fairfax estate was saved.

It was still necessary, however, if he, his brother, and brother-in-law, were to discharge the remaining payments, that Marshall should give himself to the business of making money — to work much harder than ever he had done before and than his natural inclinations prompted. Therefore, no more of unremunerative public life for him — no more waste of time in the Legislature. There never could, of course, come another such "God-send," to use Marshall's phrase as reported by Jefferson,[1] as the French mission; and few public offices, National or State, yielded so much as he could make in the practice of his profession. Thus financial necessity and his own desire settled Marshall in the resolve, which he believed nothing ever could shake, to give the remainder of his days to his personal and private business. But Fate had her own plans for John Marshall and again overruled what he believed to be his fixed and unalterable purpose.

[1] The "Anas"; *Works:* Ford, i, 355.

CHAPTER X

CANDIDATE FOR CONGRESS

Of the three envoys, the conduct of General Marshall alone has been entirely satisfactory. (Adams.)

In heart and sentiment, as well as by birth and interest, I am an American. We should make no political connection with any nation on earth. (Marshall to constituents.)

Tell Marshall I love him because he felt and acted as a Republican and an American. (Patrick Henry.)

In the congressional campaign of 1798–99, the Federalists of the Richmond District were without a strong candidate. The one they had put up lacked that personal popularity which then counted for as much in political contests as the issues involved. Upon Marshall's return from France and his enthusiastic reception, ending with the Richmond demonstration, the Federalist managers pressed Marshall to take the place of the candidate then running, who, indeed, was anxious to withdraw in his favor. But the returned envoy refused, urged the Federalist then standing to continue his candidacy, and pledged that he would do all in his power to secure his election.

Finally Washington asked Marshall to come to see him. "I received an invitation from General Washington," writes Marshall in his account of this important event, "to accompany his nephew . . . on a visit to Mount Vernon." [1]

[1] Marshall to Paulding, April 4, 1835; *Lippincott's Magazine* (1868), ii, 624–25.

When Bushrod Washington wrote that Marshall accepted the invitation, the General was extremely gratified. "I learnt with much pleasure . . . of General Marshall's intention to make me a visit," he writes his nephew. "I wish it of all things; and it is from the ardent desire I have to see him that I have not delayed a moment to express it. . . . The crisis is most important. . . . The temper of the people in this state . . . is so violent and outrageous that I wish to converse with General Marshall and yourself on the elections which must soon come." [1] Washington says that when his visitors arrive the matter of the fictitious Langhorne letter will also be taken up "and we will let General Marshall into the whole business and advise with him thereon." [2]

To Mount Vernon, therefore, Marshall and his

[1] Washington to Bushrod Washington, Aug. 27, 1798; *Writings:* Ford, xiv, 75.

[2] *Ib.* In September, 1797, when Marshall was absent on the X. Y. Z. mission, Washington received a letter from one "John Langhorne" of Albemarle County. Worded with skillful cunning, it was designed to draw from the retired President imprudent expressions that could be used against him and the Federalists. It praised him, denounced his detractors, and begged him to disregard their assaults. (Langhorne to Washington, Sept. 25, 1797; *Writings:* Sparks, xi, 501.) Washington answered vaguely. (Washington to Langhorne, Oct. 15, 1797; *Writings:* Ford, xiii, 428–30.) John Nicholas discovered that the Langhorne letter had been posted at Charlottesville; that no person of that name lived in the vicinity; and that Washington's answer was called for at the Charlottesville post-office (where Jefferson posted and received letters) by a person closely connected with the master of Monticello. It was suspected, therefore, that Jefferson was the author of the fictitious letter. The mystery caused Washington much worry and has never been cleared up. (See Washington to Nicholas, Nov. 30, 1797; *ib.*, footnote to 429–30; to Bushrod Washington, March 8, 1798; *ib.*, 448; to Nicholas, March 8, 1798; *ib.*, 449–50.) It is not known what advice Marshall gave Washington when the latter asked for his opinion; but from his lifelong conduct in such matters and his strong repugnance to personal disputes, it is probable that Marshall advised that the matter be dropped.

companion journeyed on horseback. For convenience in traveling, they had put their clothing in the same pair of saddle-bags. They arrived in a heavy rain and were "drenched to the skin." Unlocking the saddle-bags, the first article they took out was a black bottle of whiskey. With great hilarity each charged this to be the property of the other. Then came a thick twist of tobacco, some corn bread, and finally the worn apparel of wagoners; at some tavern on the way their saddle-bags had become exchanged for those of drivers. The rough clothes were grotesque misfits; and when, clad in these, his guests presented themselves, Washington, roaring with laughter, expressed his sympathy for the wagoners when they, in turn, discovered the exchange they had made with the lawyers.[1] In such fashion began the conference that ended in John Marshall's candidacy for Congress in the vital campaign of 1798–99.

This was the first time, so far as is known, that Marshall had visited Washington at his Potomac home. No other guest except Washington's nephew seems to have been present at this conference, so decisive of Marshall's future. The time was September, 1798, and the conversations were held on the broad piazza,[2] looking out upon the river, with the new Capitol almost within sight. There, for "four or five days," his old commander used all his influence to induce Marshall to become the Federalist candidate.

"General Washington urged the importance of the crisis," writes Marshall in describing the cir-

[1] Paulding: *Washington*, ii, 191–92. [2] Marshall to Paulding, *supra*.

cumstance; "every man," insisted Washington, "who could contribute to the success of sound opinions was required by the most sacred duty to offer his services to the public." Marshall doubted his "ability to do any good. I told him that I had made large pecuniary engagements which required close attention to my profession and which would distress me should the emoluments derived from it be abandoned."

Marshall told of his promise to the Federalist candidate who was then making his campaign for election. Washington declared that this candidate still would withdraw in Marshall's favor; but Marshall remained unshaken. Finally Washington gave his own conduct as an example. Marshall thus describes the final appeal which his old leader made to him: "He had withdrawn from office with a declaration of his determination never again, under any circumstances, to enter public life. No man could be more sincere in making that declaration, nor could any man feel stronger motives for adhering to it. No man could make a stronger sacrifice than he did in breaking a resolution, thus publicly made, and which he had believed to be unalterable. Yet I saw him," continues Marshall, "in opposition to his public declaration, in opposition to his private feelings, consenting, under a sense of duty, to surrender the sweets of retirement, and again to enter the most arduous and perilous station which an individual could fill. My resolution yielded to this representation." [1]

[1] Marshall to Paulding, *supra.* This letter was in answer to one from Paulding asking Marshall for the facts as to Washington's part in inducing Marshall to run for Congress.

There is a tradition that, at one point in the conference, Marshall, becoming offended by Washington's insistence, which, runs the story, took the form of a peremptory and angrily expressed command, determined to leave so early in the morning that his host would have no opportunity to press the matter further; but, Washington noting Marshall's irritation and anticipating his purpose, was on the piazza when his departing guest appeared at dawn, and there made the final appeal which won Marshall's reluctant consent.

Marshall felt that he was making a heavy personal sacrifice; it meant to him the possible loss of the Fairfax estate. As we have seen, he had just declined appointment to the Supreme Bench [1] for this very reason, and this place later was given to Bushrod Washington, largely on Marshall's advice.[2] Adams had been reluctant to give Marshall up as one of the Associate Justices of the Supreme Court; "General Marshall or Bushrod Washington will succeed Judge Wilson," wrote the President to his Secretary of State [3] nearly three months after the first tender of the place to Marshall in Philadelphia. Later on the President again returned to Marshall.

"I still think that General Marshall ought to be preferred," he wrote. "Of the three envoys, the conduct of Marshall alone has been entirely satisfactory, and ought to be marked by the most decided approbation of the public. He has raised the

[1] Pickering to Marshall, Sept. 20, 1798; Pickering MSS., Mass. Hist. Soc.

[2] *Ib.*

[3] Adams to Pickering, Sept. 14, 1798; *Works:* Adams, viii, 595.

American people in their own esteem, and, if the influence of truth and justice, reason and argument is not lost in Europe, he has raised the consideration of the United States in that quarter of the world. . . . If Mr. Marshall should decline, I should next think of Mr. [Bushrod] Washington."[1]

Washington's appeal to Marshall's patriotism and sense of duty, however, outbalanced the weighty financial reasons which decided him against becoming an Associate Justice of the Supreme Court. Thus, against his desire, he found himself once more in the hurly-burly of partisan politics. But this time the fight which he was forced to lead was to be desperate, indeed.

The moment Marshall announced his candidacy he became the center of Republican attack in Virginia. The virulence of the campaign against him was so great that it has become a tradition; and while scarcely any of the personal assaults, which appeared in print, are extant, they are known to have been ruthless, and utterly unrestrained both as to the charges made and the language used in making them.

In his scurrilous review of Adams's Administration, which Adams properly denounced as "a Mass of Lyes from the first page to the last,"[2] John Wood repeats the substance of some of the attacks which, undoubtedly, were launched against Marshall in this bitter political conflict. "John Marshall," says Wood, "was an improper character in several

[1] Adams to Pickering, Sept. 26, 1798; *Works:* Adams, viii, 597.
[2] Adams to Rush, June 25, 1807; *Old Family Letters*, 152.

respects; his principles of aristocracy were well known. Talleyrand, when in America, knew that this man was regarded as a royalist and not as a republican, and that he was abhorred by most honest characters."[1]

The abuse must have been very harsh and unjust; for Marshall, who seldom gave way to resentment, complained to Pickering with uncharacteristic temper. "The whole malignancy of Anti-federalism," he writes, "not only in the district, where it unfortunately is but too abundant, but throughout the State, has become uncommonly active and considers itself as peculiarly interested in the reëlection of the old member [Clopton].

"The Jacobin presses, which abound with us and only circulate within the State, teem with publications of which the object is to poison still further the public opinion and which are level'd particularly at me. Anything written by me on the subject of French affairs wou'd be ascrib'd to me, whether it appear'd with or without my signature and wou'd whet and sharpen up the sting of every abusive scribbler who had vanity enough to think himself a writer because he cou'd bestow personal abuse and cou'd say things as malignant as they are ill founded."[2]

[1] Wood, 260. Wood's book was "suppressed" by Aaron Burr, who bought the plates and printer's rights. It consists of dull attacks on prominent Federalists. Jefferson's friends charged that Burr suppressed it because of his friendship for the Federalist leaders. (See Cheetham's letters to Jefferson, Dec. 29, 1801, Jan. 30, 1802, *Proceedings*, Mass. Hist. Soc. (April and May, 1907) 51–58.) Soon afterward Jefferson began his warfare on Burr.

[2] Marshall to Pickering, Oct. 15, 1798; Pickering MSS., Mass

The publication of the American envoys' dispatches from France, which had put new life into the Federalist Party, had also armed that decaying organization with enough strength to enact the most imprudent measures that its infatuated leaders ever devised. During June and July, 1798, they had succeeded in driving through Congress the famous Alien and Sedition Laws.[1]

The Alien Act authorized the President to order out of the country all aliens whom he thought "dangerous" or "suspected" of any "treasonable or secret machination against the government" on pain of imprisonment not to exceed three years and of being forever afterwards incapacitated from becoming citizens of the United States. But if the alien could prove to the satisfaction of the President that he was not dangerous, a presidential "license" might be granted, permitting the alien to remain in the United States as long as the President saw fit and in such place as he might designate. If any expelled alien returned without permission he was to be imprisoned as long as the President thought "the public safety may require."

The Sedition Act provided penalties for the crime of unlawful combination and conspiracy against the Government;[2] a fine not exceeding two thousand dollars and imprisonment not exceeding two years

Hist. Soc. This campaign was unusually acrimonious everywhere. "This Electioneering is worse than the Devil." (Smith to Bayard, Aug. 2, 1798; *Bayard Papers:* Donnan, 69.)

[1] See Statutes at Large, 566, 570, 577, for Alien Acts of June 18, June 25, and July 6, and *ib.*, 196, for Sedition Law of July 14, 1798.

[2] This section was not made a campaign issue by the Republicans.

for any person who should write, print, publish, or speak anything "false, scandalous and malicious" against the Government, either House of Congress, or the President "with intent to defame" the Government, Congress, or the President, or "to bring them or either of them into contempt or disrepute; or to excite against them or either or any of them the hatred of the good people of the United States, or to stir up sedition within the United States."

When Jefferson first heard of this proposed stupid legislation, he did not object to it, even in his intimate letters to his lieutenant Madison.[1] Later, however, he became the most ferocious of its assailants. Hamilton, on the other hand, saw the danger in the Sedition Bill the moment a copy reached him: "There are provisions in this bill . . . highly exceptionable," he wrote. "I hope sincerely the thing may not be hurried through. Let us not establish a tyranny. Energy is a very different thing from violence."[2] When Madison got the first inkling of the Alien Bill, he wrote to Jefferson that it "is a monster that must forever disgrace its parents."[3]

As soon as the country learned what the Alien and Sedition Laws contained, the reaction against the Federalist Party began. In vain did the Federalists plead to the people, as they had urged in the debate in Congress, that these laws were justified by events; in vain did they point out the presence in America of

[1] Jefferson to Madison, May 10, 1798; *Works:* Ford, viii, 417; and to Monroe, May 21, 1798; *ib.*, 423. Jefferson's first harsh word was to Madison, June 7, 1798; *ib.*, 434.

[2] Hamilton to Wolcott, June 29, 1798; *Works:* Lodge, x, 295.

[3] Madison to Jefferson, May 20, 1798; *Writings:* Hunt, vi, 320.

large numbers of foreigners who were active and bitter against the American Government; in vain did they read to citizens the abuse published in newspapers against the Administration and cite the fact that the editors of these libelous sheets were aliens.[1]

The popular heart and instinct were against these crowning blunders of Federalism. Although the patriotic wave started by Marshall's return and the X. Y. Z. disclosures was still running strong, a more powerful counter-current was rising. "Liberty of the press," "freedom of speech," "trial by jury" at once became the watchwords and war-cries of Republicanism. On the hustings, in the newspapers, at the taverns, the Alien and Sedition Laws were denounced as unconstitutional — they were null and void — no man, much less any State, should obey or respect them.

The Alien Law, said its opponents, merged the Judicial and the Executive Departments, which the Constitution guaranteed should be separate and distinct; the Sedition Act denied freedom of speech, with which the Constitution expressly forbade Congress to interfere; both struck at the very heart of liberty — so went the Republican argument and appeal.[2]

In addition to their solid objections, the Republicans made delirious prophecies. The Alien and Sedition Laws were, they asserted, the beginning of mon-

[1] For the Federalists' justification of the Alien and Sedition Laws see Gibbs, ii, 78 *et seq.*

[2] As a matter of fact, the anger of Republican leaders was chiefly caused by their belief that the Alien and Sedition Laws were aimed at the Republican Party as such, and this, indeed, was true.

archy, the foundation of absolutism. The fervid Jefferson indulged, to his heart's content, in these grotesque predictions: "The alien & sedition laws are working hard," declared the great Republican. Indeed, he thought them only "an experiment on the American mind to see how far it will bear an avowed violation of the constitution. If this goes down, we shall immediately see attempted another act of Congress declaring that the President shall continue in office during life, reserving to another occasion the transfer of the succession to his heirs, and the establishment of the Senate for life. . . . That these things are in contemplation, I have no doubt; nor can I be confident of their failure, after the dupery of which our countrymen have shewn themselves susceptible." [1]

Washington was almost as extravagant on the other side. When an opponent of the Alien and Sedition Acts asked him for his opinion of them, he advised his questioner to read the opposing arguments "and consider to what lengths a certain description of men in our country have already driven and seem resolved further to drive matters" and then decide whether these laws are not necessary, against those "who acknowledge no allegiance to this country, and in many instances are sent among us . . . for the express purpose of poisoning the minds of our people, — and to sow dissensions among them, in order to alienate their affections from the government of their choice, thereby endeavoring to dissolve the Union." [2]

[1] Jefferson to S. T. Mason, Oct. 11, 1798; *Works:* Ford, viii, 450.

[2] Washington to Spotswood, Nov. 22, 1798; *Writings:* Ford, xiv, 121–22.

Washington thought that the ferocious Republican attack on the Alien and Sedition Laws was but a cunning maneuver of politicians, and this, indeed, for the moment at least, seems to have been the case. "The Alien and Sedition Laws are now the desiderata of the Opposition. . . . But any thing else would have done, — and something there will always be, for them to torture; and to disturb the public mind with their unfounded and ill favored forebodings" was his pessimistic judgment.[1]

He sent "to General Marshall Judge Addison's charge to the grand juries of the county courts of the Fifth Circuit of the State of Pennsylvania. . . . This charge is on the liberty of speech and of the press and is a justification of the sedition and alien laws. But," wrote Washington, "I do not believe that . . . it . . . or . . . any other writing will produce the least change in the conduct of the leaders of the opposition to the measures of the general government. They have points to carry from which no reasoning, no consistency of conduct, no absurdity can divert them. If, however, such writings should produce conviction in the mind of those who have hitherto placed faith in their assertions, it will be a fortunate event for this country." [2]

[1] Washington to Murray, Dec. 26, 1798; *Writings:* Ford, xiv, 132.

[2] Washington to Bushrod Washington, Dec. 31, 1798; *ib.*, 135–36. Judge Addison's charge was an able if intemperate interpretation of the Sedition Law. The Republican newspapers assailed and ridiculed this very effectively in the presidential campaign of 1800. "Alexander Addison has published in a volume a number of his *charges* to juries — and *precious* charges they are — brimstone and saltpetre, assifœtida and train oil." (*Aurora*, Dec. 6, 1800. See Chief Justice Ellsworth's comments upon Judge Addison's charge in Flanders, ii, 193.)

Marshall had spoken in the same vein soon after his arrival at Richmond. "The people . . . are pretty right as it respects France," he reports to the Secretary of State. The Republican criticisms of the X. Y. Z. mission "make so little impression that I believe France will be given up and the attack upon the government will be supported by the alien and sedition laws. I am extremely sorry to observe that here they are more successful and that these two laws, especially the sedition bill, are viewed by a great many well meaning men, as unwarranted by the constitution.

"I am entirely persuaded that with many the hate of Government of our country is implacable and that if these bills did not exist the same clamor would be made by them on some other account, but," truthfully and judicially writes Marshall, "there are also many who are guided by very different motives, and who tho' less noisy in their complaints are seriously uneasy on this subject." [1]

The Republicans pressed Marshall particularly hard on the Alien and Sedition Laws, but he found a way to answer. Within a few days after he had become the Federalist candidate, an anonymous writer, signing himself "Freeholder," published in the Richmond newspapers an open letter to Marshall asking him whether he was for the Constitution; whether the welfare of America depended on a foreign alliance; whether a closer connection with Great Britain was desirable; whether the Administration's

[1] Marshall to Pickering, Aug. 11, 1798; Pickering MSS., Mass. Hist. Soc.

conduct toward France was wise; and, above all, whether Marshall was "an advocate of the alien and sedition bills or in the event of your election will you use your influence to obtain a repeal of these laws?"

In printing Marshall's answers to "Freeholder," the "Times and Virginia Advertiser" of Alexandria remarked: "Mr. John Marshall has offered as a candidate for a representative in the next Congress. He has already begun his electioneering campaign. The following are answers to some queries proposed to him. Whether the queries were propounded with a view of discovering his real sentiments, or whether they were published by one of his friends to serve electioneering purposes, is immaterial: — The principles Mr. Marshall professes to possess are such as influence the conduct of every real American." [1]

A week later Marshall published his answers. "Every citizen," says he, "has a right to know the political sentiments of a candidate"; and besides, the candidate wishes everybody to know his "real principles" and not "attribute" to him "those with which active calumny has . . . aspersed" him. In this spirit Marshall answers that "in heart and sentiment, as well as by birth and interest," he is "an American; attached to the . . . Constitution . . . which will preserve us if we support it firmly."

He is, he asserts, against any alliance, "offensive or defensive," with Great Britain or "any closer connection with that nation than already exists. . . .

[1] Oct. 11, 1798. The questions of "Freeholder" were, undoubtedly, written with Marshall's knowledge. Indeed a careful study of them leads one to suspect that he wrote or suggested them himself.

No man in existence is more decidedly opposed to such an alliance or more fully convinced of the evils that would result from it." Marshall declares that he is for American neutrality in foreign wars; and cites his memorial to Talleyrand as stating his views on this subject.

"The whole of my politics respecting foreign nations, are reducible to this single position: . . . Commercial intercourse with all, but political ties with none . . . buy as cheap and sell as dear as possible . . . never connect ourselves politically with any nation whatever."

He disclaims the right to speak for the Administration, but believes it to have the same principles. It France, while at war with Great Britain, should also make war on America, "it would be madness and folly" not to secure the "aid of the British fleets to prevent our being invaded"; but, not even for that, would he "make such a sacrifice as . . . we should make by forming a permanent political connection with . . . any nation on earth."

Marshall says that he believes the Administration's policy as regards France to have been correct, and necessary to the maintenance "of the neutrality and independence of our country." Peace with France was not possible "without sacrificing those great objects," for "the primary object of France is . . . dominion over others." The French accomplish this purpose by "immense armies on their part and divisions among . . . those whom they wish to subdue."

Marshall declares that he is "not an advocate of

the Alien and Sedition Bills," and, had he been in Congress, "certainly would have opposed them," although he does not "think them fraught with all those mischiefs ascribed to them." But he thinks them "useless . . . calculated to create unnecessary discontents and jealousies"; and that, too, "at a time when our very existence as a nation may depend on our union."

He believes that those detested laws "would never have been enacted" if they had been opposed on these principles by a man not suspected of intending to destroy the government or being hostile to it." The effort to repeal them "will be made before he can become a member of Congress"; if it fails and is renewed after he takes his seat, he "will obey the voice of his constituents." He thinks, however, it will be unwise to revive the Alien and Sedition Acts which are, by their own terms, about to expire; and Marshall pledges that he will "indisputably oppose their revival." [1]

Upon Marshall as their favorite candidate for Congress, the eyes of the Federalist leaders in other States were focused. They were particularly anxious and uncertain as to his stand on the Alien and Sedition Laws; for he seems to have privately expressed, while in Philadelphia on his return from France, a mild disapproval of the wisdom and political expe-

[1] The *Times and Virginia Advertiser*, Alexandria, Virginia, October 11, 1798. This paper, however, does not give "Freeholder's" questions. The *Columbian Centinel*, Boston, October 20, 1798, prints both questions and answers, but makes several errors in the latter. The correct version is given in Appendix III, *infra*, where "Freeholder's" questions and Marshall's answers appear in full.

diency of this absurd legislation. His answers to "Freeholder" were therefore published everywhere. When the New England Federalists read them in the "Columbian Centinel" of Saturday, October 20, most of them were as hot against Marshall as were the rabid Virginia Republicans.

Ames whetted his rhetoric to razor edge and slashed without mercy. He describes Republican dismay when Marshall's dispatches were published: "The wretches [Republicans] looked round, like Milton's devils when first recovering from the stunning force of their fall from Heaven, to see what new ground they could take." They chose, says Ames, "the alien and sedition bills, and the land tax" with which to arouse discontent and revive their party. So "the implacable foes of the Constitution — foes before it was made, while it was making, and since — became full of tender fears lest it should be violated by the alien and sedition laws."

The Federalists, complained Ames, "are forever hazarding the cause by heedless and rash concessions. John Marshall, with all his honors in blossom and bearing fruit, answers some newspaper queries unfavorably to these laws. . . . No correct man, — no incorrect man, even, — whose affections and feelings are wedded to the government, would give his name to the base opposers of the law. . . . This he has done. Excuses may palliate, — future zeal in the cause may partially atone, — but his character is done for. . . . Like a man who in battle receives an ounce ball in his body — it may heal, it lies too deep to be extracted. . . . There let it lie. False Federalists, or such as act wrong from false fears, should be dealt hardly by, if I were Jupiter Tonans. . . . The moderates [like Marshall] are the meanest of cowards, the falsest of hypocrites."[1] Theodore Sedgwick declared that Marshall's "mysterious & unpardonable" conduct had aided "french villainy" and that he had "degraded himself by a mean & paltry electioneering trick."[2]

At first, the Republicans praised Marshall's stand; and this made the New England Federalists frantic. Cabot, alone, defended Marshall in the press, although not over his own name and only as a matter of party tactics. He procured some one to write to the "Columbian Centinel" under the name of "A Yankee Freeholder." This contributor tried to explain away Marshall's offense.

"General Marshall is a citizen too eminent for his talents, his virtues and his public services, to merit so severe a punishment as to [receive the] applause of disorganizers [Republicans]." He should be saved from the "admiration of the *seditious*" — that much was due to Marshall's "spirit, firmness and eloquence" in the contest with "the Despots of *France.*" As "drowning men would catch at straws" so "the eagle-eyed and disheartened sons of faction" had "with forlorn and desperate . . . avidity . . . seized on" Marshall's answers to "Freeholder."

And no wonder; for "even *good men* have stood

[1] Ames to Gore, Dec. 18, 1798; *Works:* Ames, i, 245–47.

[2] Sedgwick to Pickering, Oct. 23, 1798; Pickering MSS., Mass. Hist. Soc.

appalled, at observing a man whom they so highly venerate soliciting votes at the expense of principles which they deem sacred and inviolable." "Yankee Freeholder" therefore proposes "to vindicate General MARSHALL."

Marshall was the only Richmond Federalist who could be elected; he "patriotically" had consented to run only because of "the situation and danger of his country at this moment." Therefore "it was absolutely necessary to take all the ordinary steps" to succeed. This "may appear extraordinary . . . to those who are only acquainted with the delicacy of *New England* elections where *personal* solicitation is the Death-warrant to success"; but it was "not only pardonable but necessary . . . in the Southern States."

"Yankee Freeholder" reminded his readers that "Calumny had assailed General MARSHALL, in common with other men of merit." Virginia newspapers had "slandered him"; politicians had called him "*Aristocrat*, *Tory*, and *British Agent.* All this abuse . . . would infallibly have rendered him popular in *New-England*" — but not so in "*Virginia,*" where there were "too many ignorant, ill-informed and inflamed minds."

Therefore, "it became necessary that General MARSHALL should explicitly exhibit his political creed." After all, his answers to "Freeholder" were not so bad — he did not assail the constitutionality of the Alien and Sedition Laws. "If Gen. MARSHALL thought them unconstitutional or dangerous to liberty, would he" be content merely to say they were unnecessary? "Would a man of General MARSHALL's force of reasoning, simply denominate *laws useless*," if he thought them unconstitutional? "No — the idea is too absurd to be indulged. . . . Time and General MARSHALL's conduct will hereafter prove that I am not mistaken in my opinion of his sentiments." [1]

Cabot's strategy had little effect on New England, which appeared to dislike Virginia with a curious intolerance. The Essex County politician, nevertheless, stood by his guns; and six months later thus reassures King: "I am ready to join you as well as Ames in reprobating the publication of Marshall's sentiments on the Sedition & Alien Acts, but I still *adhere* to my first opinion that Marshall ought not to be attacked in the Newspapers, nor too severely condemned anywhere, because Marshall has not yet learned his whole lesson, but has a mind & disposition which can hardly fail to make him presently an accomplished (political) Scholar & a very useful man.

"Some allowance too should be made," contends Cabot, "for the influence of the Atmosphere of Virginia which doubtless makes every one who breathes it visionary &, upon the subject of Free Govt., incredibly credulous; but it is certain that Marshall at Phila. would become a most powerful auxiliary to the cause of order & good Govt., & *therefore* we ought not to diminish his fame which wou'd ultimately be a loss to ourselves." [2]

[1] *Columbian Centinel* (Boston), Oct. 24, 1798.
[2] Cabot to King, April 26, 1799; King, iii, 9.

The experienced practical politician, Sedgwick, correctly judged that "Freeholder's" questions to Marshall and Marshall's answers were an "electioneering trick." But Pickering stoutly defended Marshall upon this charge. "I have not met with one good federalist, who does not regret his answers to the Freeholder; but I am sorry that it should be imagined to be an 'electioneering trick.' . . . General Marshall is incapable of doing a dishonorable act." Only Marshall's patriotism had induced him to accept the French mission, said the Secretary of State.[1] Nothing but "the urging of friends . . . overcame his reluctance to come to Congress. . . . A man of untainted honor," had informed Pickering that "Marshall is a *Sterling fellow*." [2]

The Federalists' complaints of him continued to be so strong and widespread, however, that they even reached our legations in Europe: "I too have lamented that John Marshall, after such a mission particularly, should lend himself thus against a law which the French Jacobinism in the United States had forced government to adopt. M[arshall] *before*, was not, that we ever heard of, one of us." [3]

Toward the end of October Marshall gives his private opinion of the Virginia Republicans and their real motives, and foretells the Virginia Resolutions. "The real french party of this country

[1] This was not true. The Fairfax embarrassment, alone, caused Marshall to go to France in 1797.

[2] Pickering to Sedgwick, Nov. 6, 1798; Pickering MSS., Mass. Hist. Soc.

[3] Murray to J. Q. Adams, March 22, 1799; *Letters:* Ford, 530. Murray had been a member of Congress and a minor Federalist politician. By "us" he means the extreme Federalist politicians.

again begins to show itself," he writes. "There are very many indeed in this part of Virginia who speak of our own government as an enemy infinitely more formidable and infinitely more to be guarded against than the French Directory. Immense efforts are made to induce the legislature of the state which will meet in Dec'r to take some violent measure which may be attended with serious consequences. I am not sure that these efforts will entirely fail. It requires to be in this part of Virginia to know the degree of irritation which has been excited and the probable extent of the views of those who excite it."[1]

The most decent of the attacks on Marshall were contained in a series of open letters first published in the "Aurora"[2] and signed "Curtius."

"You have long been regarded," writes Curtius, "as the leader of that party in this State" which has tried "by audacious efforts to erect a monarchy or aristocracy upon the ruins of our free constitution. The energy of your mind and the violence of your zeal have exalted you to this bad eminence." If you had "employed your talents in defense of the people . . . your history would have been read in a nation's eyes."

"The publication of your dispatches and the happy exercise of diplomatic skill has produced a momentary delusion and infatuation in which an opposition to the administration is confounded with hostility to the government and treason to the country. . . . The execrations and yells against French

[1] Marshall to Pickering, Oct. 22, 1798; Pickering MSS., Mass. Hist. Soc.

[2] Adams: *Gallatin*, 212.

cruelty and French ambition, are incessantly kept up by the hirelings of Great Britain and the enemies of liberty."

But, he cries, "the vengeance of an oppressed and insulted people is almost as terrible as the wrath of Heaven"; and, like a true partisan, Curtius predicts that this is about to fall on Marshall. Why, he asks, is Marshall so vague on the constitutionality of the Alien and Sedition Laws?[1] "Notwithstanding the magnitude . . . of your talents, you are ridiculously awkward in the arts of dissimulation and hypocrisy. . . . It is painful to attack . . . a man whose talents are splendid and whose private character is amiable"; but "sacred duties . . . to the cause of truth and liberty require it." Alas for Marshall! "You have lost forever," Curtius assures him, "the affection of a nation and the applause of a world. In vain will you pursue the thorny and rugged path that leads to fame."[2]

But while "monarchist," "aristocrat," "British

[1] "Freeholder" had not asked Marshall what he thought of the constitutionality of these laws.

[2] Thompson: *The Letters of Curtius.* John Thompson of Petersburg was one of the most brilliant young men that even Virginia ever produced. See Adams: *Gallatin*, 212, 227. There is an interesting resemblance between the uncommon talents and fate of young John Thompson and those of Francis Walker Gilmer. Both were remarkably intellectual and learned; the characters of both were clean, fine, and high. Both were uncommonly handsome men. Neither of them had a strong physical constitution; and both died at a very early age. Had John Thompson and Francis Walker Gilmer lived, their names would have been added to that wonderful list of men that the Virginia of that period gave to the country.

The intellectual brilliancy and power, and the lofty character of Thompson and Gilmer, their feeble physical basis and their early passing seem like the last effort of that epochal human impulse which produced Henry, Madison, Mason, Jefferson, Marshall, and Washington.

agent," "enemy of free speech," "destroyer of trial by jury" were among the more moderate epithets that filled the air from Republican lips; and "anarchist," "Frenchman," "traitor," "foe of law and order," "hater of government" were the milder of the counter-blasts from the Federalists, all this was too general, scattered, and ineffective to suit the leader of the Republican Party. Jefferson saw that the growing popular rage against the Alien and Sedition Laws must be gathered into one or two concentrated thunderbolts and thus hurled at the heads of the already quaking Federalists.

How to do it was the question to which Jefferson searched for an answer. It came from the bravest, most consistent, most unselfish, as well as one of the very ablest of Republicans, John Taylor "of Caroline," Virginia. In a letter to Jefferson concerning the Alien and Sedition Laws, this eminent and disinterested radical suggested that "*the right of the State governments to expound the constitution* might possibly be made the basis of a movement towards its amendment. If this is insufficient the people in state conventions are incontrovertibly the contracting parties and, possessing the infringing rights, may proceed by orderly steps to attain the object." [1]

So was planted in Jefferson's mind the philosophy of secession. In that fertile and receptive soil it grew with magic rapidity and bore fatal fruit. Within two months after he received Taylor's letter, Jefferson wrote the historic resolutions which produced a situ-

[1] Taylor to Jefferson, June 25, 1798; as quoted in *Branch Historical Papers*, ii, 225. See entire letter, *ib.*, 271–76.

ation that, a few years afterward, called forth Marshall's first great constitutional opinion, and, not many decades later, gave the battle-cry that rallied heroic thousands to armed resistance to the National Government.[1] On October 5, 1798, Nicholas writes Jefferson that he has delivered to "Mr. John Breckenridge a copy of the resolutions that you sent me."[2] They were passed by the Legislature of Kentucky on November 14, 1798; and the tremendous conflict between Nationality and States' Rights, which for so long had been preparing, at last was formally begun.[3] Jefferson's "Kentucky Resolutions" declared that parts of the Alien and Sedition Laws were "altogether void and of no effect."[4] Thus a State

[1] For an excellent treatment of the Kentucky and Virginia Resolutions see Von Holst: *Constitutional History of the United States*, i, chap. iv.

[2] Nicholas to Jefferson, Oct. 5, 1798; quoted by Channing in "Kentucky Resolutions of 1798"; *Amer. Hist. Rev.*, xx, no. 2, Jan., 1915, 333–36.

[3] Writing nearly a quarter of a century later, Jefferson states that Nicholas, Breckenridge, and he conferred on the matter; that his draft of the "Kentucky Resolutions" was the result of this conference; and that he "strictly required" their "solemn assurance" that no one else should know that he was their author. (Jefferson to Breckenridge, Dec. 11, 1821; *Works:* Ford, viii, 459–60.)

Although this letter of Jefferson is positive and, in its particulars, detailed and specific, Professor Channing has demonstrated that Jefferson's memory was at fault; that no such conference took place; and that Jefferson sent the resolutions to Nicholas, who placed them in the hands of Breckenridge for introduction in the Kentucky Legislature; and that Breckenridge and Nicholas both thought that the former should not even see Jefferson, lest the real authorship of the resolutions be detected. (See "The Kentucky Resolutions": Channing, in *Amer. Hist. Rev.*, xx, no. 2, Jan., 1915, 333–36.)

[4] See Jefferson's "Rough Draught" and "Fair Copy" of the Kentucky Resolutions; and the resolutions as the Kentucky Legislature passed them on Nov. 10, 1798; *Works:* Ford, viii, 458–79. See examination of Marshall's opinion in Marbury *vs.* Madison, vol. III of this work.

asserted the "right" of any or all States to annul and overthrow a National law.

As soon as Kentucky had acted, Jefferson thus writes Madison: "I enclose you a copy of the draught of the Kentucky resolves. I think we should distinctly affirm all the important principles they contain so as to hold that ground in future, and leave the matter in such a train as that we may not be committed absolutely to push the matter to extremities, & yet may be free to push as far as events will render prudent." [1]

Madison accordingly drew the resolutions adopted by the Legislature of Virginia, December 21, 1798. While declaring the Alien and Sedition Laws unconstitutional, the Virginia Resolutions merely appealed to the other States to "co-operate with this state in maintaining unimpaired the authority, rights, and liberties reserved to the states respectively or to the people." [2]

The Legislature promptly adopted them and would gladly have approved far stronger ones. "The leaders . . . were determined upon the overthrow of the General Government; and if no other measure would effect it, that they would risk it upon the chance of war. . . . Some of them talked of 'seceding from the Union.'" [3] Iredell writes his wife: "The General Assembly of Virginia are pursuing steps which directly lead to a civil war; but there is a respectable minority struggling in defense of

[1] Jefferson to Madison, Nov. 17, 1798; *Works:* Ford, viii, 457.

[2] *Writings:* Hunt, vi, 326–31.

[3] Davie to Iredell, June 17, 1799; quoting from a Virginia informant — very probably Marshall; McRee, ii. 577.

the General Government, and the Government itself is fully prepared for anything they can do, resolved, if necessary, to meet force with force." [1] Marshall declared that he "never saw such intemperance as existed in the V[irginia] Assembly." [2]

Following their defiant adoption of Madison's resolutions, the Republican majority of the Legislature issued a campaign pamphlet, also written by Madison,[3] under the form of an address to the people. The "guardians of State Sovereignty would be perfidious if they did not warn" the people "of encroachments which . . . may" result in "usurped power"; the State Governments would be "precipitated into impotency and contempt" in case they yielded to such National laws as the Alien and Sedition Acts; if like "infractions of the Federal Compact" were repeated "until the people arose . . . in the majesty of their strength," it was certain that "the way for a revolution would be prepared."

The Federalist pleas "to disregard usurpation until foreign danger shall have passed" was "an artifice which may be forever used," because those who wished National power extended "can ever create national embarrassments to soothe the people to sleep whilst that power is swelling, silently, secretly and fatally."

Such was the Sedition Act which "commits the sacrilege of arresting reason; . . . punishes without trial; . . . bestows on the President despotic powers

[1] Iredell to Mrs. Iredell; Jan. 24, 1799; McRee, ii, 543.

[2] Murray to J. Q. Adams, April 1, 1799; quoting Marshall to Sykes, Dec. 18, 1798; *Letters:* Ford, 534.

[3] *Writings:* Hunt, vi, 332–40.

. . . which was never expected by the early friends of the Constitution." But now "Federal authority is deduced by implication" by which "the states will be stript of every right reserved." Such "tremendous pretensions . . . inflict a death wound on the Sovereignty of the States." Thus wrote the same Madison who had declared that nothing short of a veto by the National Government on "any and every act of the states" would suffice. There was, said Madison's campaign document, no "specified power" in the National Government "embracing a right against freedom of the press" — that was a "constitutional" prerogative of the States.

"Calumny" could be redressed in the State courts; but "usurpation can only be controuled by the act of society [revolution]." Here Madison quotes *verbatim* and in italics from Marshall's second letter to Talleyrand in defense of the liberty of the press, without, however, giving Marshall credit for the language or argument.[1] Madison's argument is characteristically clear and compact, but abounds in striking phrases that suggest Jefferson.[2]

This "Address" of the Virginia Legislature was aimed primarily at Marshall, who was by far the most important Federalist candidate for Congress in the entire State. It was circulated at public expense and Marshall's friends could not possibly get his views before the people so authoritatively or so widely. But they did their best, for it was plain that

[1] For Marshall's defense of the liberty of the press, quoted by Madison, see *supra*, chap. VIII.

[2] Address of the General Assembly to the People of the Commonwealth of Virginia, Journal, H.D. (Dec., 1798), 88–90.

Madison's Jeffersonized appeal, so uncharacteristic of that former Nationalist, must be answered. Marshall wrote the reply [1] of the minority of the Legislature, who could not "remain silent under the unprecedented" attack of Madison. "Reluctantly," then, they "presented the present crisis plainly before" the people.

"For . . . national independence . . . the people of united America" changed a government by the British King for that of the Constitution. "The will of the majority produced, ratified, and conducts" this constitutional government. It was not perfect, of course; but "the best rule for freemen . . . in the opinion of our ancestors, was . . . that . . . of obedience to laws enacted by a majority of" the people's representatives.

Two other principles "promised immortality" to this fundamental idea: power of amendment and frequency of elections. "Under a Constitution thus formed, the prosperity of America" had become "great and unexampled." The people "bemoaned foreign war" when it "broke out"; but "they did not possess even a remote influence in its termination." The true American policy, therefore, was in the "avoiding of the existing carnage and the continuance of our existing happiness." It was for this reason that Washington, after considering everything, had proclaimed American Neutrality. Yet Genêt had "appealed" to the people "with acrimony" against the Government. This was resented

[1] Sedgwick to Hamilton, Feb. 7, 1799; *Works:* Hamilton, vi, 392–93; and to King, March 20, 1799; King, ii, 581. And Murray to J. Q. Adams, April 5, 1799; *Letters:* Ford, 536.

"for a while only" and "the fire was rekindled as occasion afforded fuel."

Also, Great Britain's "unjustifiable conduct . . . rekindled our ardor for hostility and revenge." But Washington, averse to war, "made his last effort to avert its miseries." So came the Jay Treaty by which "peace was preserved with honor."

Marshall then reviews the outbursts against the Jay Treaty and their subsidence. France "taught by the bickerings of ourselves . . . reëchoed American reproaches with French views and French objects"; as a result "our commerce became a prey to French cruisers; our citizens were captured" and British outrages were repeated by the French, our "former friend . . . thereby committing suicide on our national and individual happiness."

Emulating Washington, Adams had twice striven for "honorable" adjustment. This was met by "an increase of insolence and affront." Thus America had "to choose between submission . . . and . . . independence. What American," asks Marshall, "could hesitate in the option?" And, "the choice being made, self-preservation commanded preparations for self-defense . . . — the fleet, . . . an army, a provision for the removal of dangerous aliens and the punishment of seditious citizens." Yet such measures "are charged with the atrocious design of creating a monarchy . . . and violating the constitution." Marshall argues that military preparation is our only security.

"Upon so solemn an occasion what curses would be adequate," asks Marshall, "to the supineness of our government, if militia were the only resort for safety, against the invasion of a veteran army, flushed with repeated victories, strong in the skill of its officers, and led by distinguished officers?" He then continues with the familiar arguments for military equipment.

Then comes his attack on the Virginia Resolutions. Had the criticisms of the Alien and Sedition Laws "been confined to ordinary peaceable and constitutional efforts to repeal them," no objection would have been made to such a course; but when "general hostility to our government" and "proceedings which may sap the foundations of our union" are resorted to, "duty" requires this appeal to the people.

Marshall next defends the constitutionality of these acts. "Powers necessary for the attainment of all objects which are general in their nature, which interest all America" and "can only be obtained by the coöperation of the whole . . . would be naturally vested in the government of the whole." It is obvious, he argues, that States must attend to local subjects and the Nation to general affairs.

The power to protect "the nation from the intrigues and conspiracies of dangerous aliens; . . . to secure the union from their wicked machinations, . . . which is essential to the common good," belongs to the National Government in the hands of which "is the force of the nation and the general power of protection from hostilities of every kind." Marshall then makes an extended argument in support of his Nationalist theory. Occasionally he employs almost the exact language which, years afterwards, appears in those constitutional opinions from the Supreme Bench that have given him his lasting fame. The doctrine of implied powers is expounded with all of his peculiar force and clearness, but with some overabundance of verbiage. In no writing or spoken word, before he became Chief Justice of the United States, did Marshall so extensively state his constitutional views as in this unknown paper.[1]

The House of Delegates, by a vote of 92 against 52,[2] refused to publish the address of the minority along with that of the majority. Thereupon the Federalists printed and circulated it as a campaign document. It was so admired by the supporters of the Administration in Philadelphia that, according to the untrustworthy Callender, ten thousand copies were printed in the Capital and widely distributed.[3]

Marshall's authorship of this paper was not popularly known; and it produced little effect. Its tedious length, lighted only by occasional flashes of eloquence, invited Republican ridicule and derision. It contained, said Callender, "such quantities of words . . . that you turn absolutely tired"; it abounded in "barren tautology"; some sentences were nothing more than mere "assemblages of syllables"; and "the hypocritical canting that so strongly marks it corresponds very well with the dispatches of X. Y. and Z." [4]

Marshall's careful but over-elaborate paper was

[1] Address of the Minority: Journal, H.D. (Dec., 1798), 88–90. Also printed as a pamphlet. Richmond, 1798.

[2] Journal, H.D. (1799), 90.

[3] Callender: *Prospect Before Us*, 91.

[4] *Ib.*, 112 *et seq.*

not, therefore, generally read. But the leading Federalists throughout the country were greatly pleased. The address was, said Sedgwick, "a masterly performance for which we are indebted to the pen of General Marshall, who has, by it, in some measure atoned for his pitiful electioneering epistle." [1]

When Murray, at The Hague, read the address, he concluded that Marshall was its author: "He may have been weak enough to declare *against* those laws that *might* be against the *policy* or necessity, etc., etc., etc., yet sustain their constitutionality. . . . I *hope* J. Marshall did write the Address." [2]

The Republican appeal, unlike that of Marshall, was brief, simple, and replete with glowing catchwords that warmed the popular heart and fell easily from the lips of the multitude. And the Republican spirit was running high. The Virginia Legislature provided for an armory in Richmond to resist "encroachments" of the National Government.[3] Memorials poured into the National Capital.[4] By February "the tables of congress were loaded with petitions against" the unpopular Federalist legislation.[5]

Marshall's opinion of the motives of the Republican leaders, of the uncertainty of the campaign, of the real purpose of the Virginia Resolutions, is frankly set forth in his letter to Washington acknowl-

[1] Sedgwick to King, March 20, 1799; King, ii, 581.

[2] Murray to J. Q. Adams, April 5, 1799; *Letters:* Ford, 536.

[3] Mordecai, 202; also Sedgwick to King, Nov. 15, 1799; King, iii, 147–48.

[4] Jefferson to Pendleton, Feb. 14, 1799; *Works:* Ford, ix, 46; and to Madison, Jan. 30, 1799; *ib.*, 31.

[5] Jefferson to Bishop James Madison, Feb. 27, 1799; *ib.*, 62.

edging the receipt of Judge Addison's charge: "No argument," wrote Marshall, "can moderate the leaders of the opposition. . . . However I may regret the passage of one of the acts complained of [Sedition Law] I am firmly persuaded that the tempest has not been raised by them. Its cause lies much deeper and is not easily to be removed. Had they [Alien and Sedition Laws] never been passed, other measures would have been selected. An act operating on the press in any manner, affords to its opposers arguments which so captivate the public ear, which so mislead the public mind that the efforts of reason" are unavailing.

Marshall tells Washington that "the debates were long and animated" upon the Virginia Resolutions "which were substantiated by a majority of twenty-nine." He says that "sentiments were declared and . . . views were developed of a very serious and alarming extent. . . . There are men who will hold power by any means rather than not hold it; and who would prefer a dissolution of the union to a continuance of an administration not of their own party. They will risk all ills . . . rather than permit that happiness which is dispensed by other hands than their own."

He is not sure, he says, of being elected; but adds, perhaps sarcastically, that "whatever the issue . . . may be I shall neither reproach myself, nor those at whose instance I have become a candidate, for the step I have taken. The exertions against me by" men in Virginia "and even from other states" are more "active and malignant than personal considerations would excite. If I fail," concludes Marshall, "I shall regret the failure more" because it will show "a temper hostile to our government . . . than of" his own "personal mortification." [1]

The Federalists were convinced that these extreme Republican tactics were the beginning of a serious effort to destroy the National Government. "The late attempt of Virginia and Kentucky," wrote Hamilton, "to unite the State Legislatures in a direct resistance to certain laws of the Union can be considered in no other light than as an attempt to change the government"; and he notes the "hostile declarations" of the Virginia Legislature; its "actual preparation of the means of supporting them by force"; its "measures to put their militia on a more efficient footing"; its "preparing considerable arsenals and magazines"; and its "laying new taxes on its citizens" for these purposes.[2]

To Sedgwick, Hamilton wrote of the "tendency of the doctrine advanced by Virginia and Kentucky to destroy the Constitution of the United States," and urged that the whole subject be referred to a special committee of Congress which should deal with the Virginia and Kentucky Resolutions and justify the laws at which they were aimed. "No pains or expense," he insisted, "should be spared to disseminate this report. . . . A little pamphlet containing it should find its way into every house in Virginia." [3]

[1] Marshall to Washington, Jan. 8, 1799; Washington MSS., Lib. Cong.

[2] Hamilton to Dayton, 1799; *Works:* Lodge, x, 330. The day of the month is not given, but it certainly was early in January. Mr. Lodge places it before a letter to Lafayette, dated Jan. 6, 1799.

[3] Hamilton to Sedgwick, Feb. 2, 1799; *Works:* Lodge, x, 340–42.

Thus the congressional campaign of 1798–99 drew to a close. Marshall neglected none of those personal and familiar campaign devices which the American electorate of that time loved so well. His enemies declared that he carried these to the extreme; at a rally in Hanover County he "threw billets into the bonfires and danced around them with his constituents"; [1] he assured the voters that "his sentiments were the same as those of Mr. Clopton [the Republican candidate]"; he "spent several thousands of dollars upon barbecues." [2]

These charges of the besotted Callender,[3] written from his cell in the jail at Richmond, are, of course, entirely untrue, except the story of dancing about the bonfire. Marshall's answers to "Freeholder" dispose of the second; his pressing need of money for the Fairfax purchase shows that he could have afforded no money for campaign purposes; and, indeed, this charge was so preposterous that even the reckless Callender concludes it to be unworthy of belief.

From the desperate nature of the struggle and the temper and political habit of the times, one might expect far harder things to have been said. Indeed, as the violence of the contest mounted to its climax, worse things were charged or intimated by word of mouth than were then put into type. Again it is the political hack, John Wood, who gives us a hint of the baseness of the slanders that were circulated; he

[1] This was probably true; it is thoroughly characteristic and fits in perfectly with his well-authenticated conduct after he became Chief Justice. (See vol. III of this work.)

[2] Callender: *Prospect Before Us*, 90 *et seq.*

[3] See Hildreth, v, 104, 210, 214, 340, 453–55.

describes a scandal in which Marshall and Pinckney were alleged to have been involved while in Paris, the unhappy fate of a woman, her desperate voyage to America, her persecution and sad ending.[1]

Marshall was profoundly disgusted by the methods employed to defeat him. Writing to his brother a short time before election day he briefly refers to the Republican assaults in stronger language than is to be found in any other letter ever written by him: —

"The fate of my election is extremely uncertain. The means us'd to defeat it are despicable in the extreme and yet they succeed. Nothing I believe more debases or pollutes the human mind than faction [party]." [2]

The Republicans everywhere grew more confident as the day of voting drew near. Neutrality, the Alien and Sedition Laws, the expense of the provisional army, the popular fear and hatred of a permanent military force, the high taxes, together with the reckless charges and slanders against the Federalists and the perfect discipline exacted of the Republicans by Jefferson — all were rapidly overcoming the patriotic fervor aroused by the X. Y. Z. disclosures. "The tide is evidently turning . . . from Marshall's

[1] Wood, 261–62. This canard is an example of the methods employed in political contests when American democracy was in its infancy.

[2] Marshall to his brother James M., April 3, 1799; MS. Marshall uses the word "faction" in the sense in which it was then employed. "Faction" and "party" were at that time used interchangeably; and both words were terms of reproach. (See *supra*, chap. II.) If stated in the vernacular of the present day, this doleful opinion of Marshall would read: "Nothing, I believe, more debases or pollutes the human mind than partisan politics."

romance" was the Republican commander's conclusion as the end of the campaign approached.[1]

For the first time Marshall's personal popularity was insufficient to assure victory. But the animosity of the Republicans caused them to make a false move which saved him at the very last. They circulated the report that Patrick Henry, the arch-enemy of "aristocrats," was against Marshall because the latter was one of this abhorred class. Marshall's friend, Archibald Blair, Clerk of the Executive Council, wrote Henry of this Republican campaign story.

Instantly both the fighter and the politician in Henry were roused; and the old warrior, from his retirement at Red Hill, wrote an extraordinary letter, full of affection for Marshall and burning with indignation at the Republican leaders. The Virginia Resolutions meant the "dissolution" of the Nation, wrote Henry; if that was not the purpose of the Republicans "they have none and act *ex tempore*." As to France, "her conduct has made it to the interest of the great family of mankind to wish the downfall of her present government." For the French Republic threatened to "destroy the great pillars of all government and social life — I mean virtue, morality, and religion," which "alone . . . is the armour . . . that renders us invincible." Also, said Henry, "infidelity, in its broad sense, under the name of philosophy, is fast spreading . . . under the patronage of French manners and principles."

Henry makes "these prefatory remarks" to

[1] Jefferson to Pendleton, April 22, 1799; *Works:* Ford, ix, 64–65.

"point out the kind of character amongst our countrymen most estimable in my [his] eyes." The ground thus prepared, Henry discharges all his guns against Marshall's enemies. "General Marshall and his colleagues exhibited the American character as respectable. France, in the period of her most triumphant fortune, beheld them as unappalled. Her threats left them as she found them. . . .

"Can it be thought that with these sentiments I should utter anything tending to prejudice General Marshall's election? Very far from it indeed. Independently of the high gratification I felt from his public ministry, he ever stood high in my esteem as a private citizen. His temper and disposition were always pleasant, his talents and integrity unquestioned.

"These things are sufficient to place that gentleman far above any competitor in the district for congress. But when you add the particular information and insight which he has gained, and is able to communicate to our public councils, it is really astonishing, that even blindness itself should hesitate in the choice. . . .

"Tell Marshall I love him, because he felt and acted as a republican, as an American. The story of the Scotch merchants and old torys voting for him is too stale, childish, and foolish, and is a French *finesse;* an appeal to prejudice, not reason and good sense. . . . I really should give him my vote for Congress, preferably to any citizen in the state at this juncture, one only excepted [Washington]." [1]

[1] Henry to Blair, Jan. 8, 1799; Henry, ii, 591–94.

Henry's letter saved Marshall. Not only was the congressional district full of Henry's political followers, but it contained large numbers of his close personal friends. His letter was passed from hand to hand among these and, by election day, was almost worn out by constant use.[1]

But the Federalist newspapers gave Henry no credit for turning the tide; according to these partisan sheets it was the "anarchistic" action of the Kentucky and Virginia Legislatures that elected Marshall. Quoting from a letter of Bushrod Washington, who had no more political acumen than a turtle, a Federalist newspaper declared: "We hear that General Marshall's election is placed beyond all doubt. I was firmly convinced that the violent measures of our Legislature (which were certainly intended to influence the election) would favor the pretensions of the Federal candidates by disclosing the views of the opposite party." [2]

Late in April the election was held. A witness of that event in Richmond tells of the incidents of the voting which were stirring even for that period of turbulent politics. A long, broad table or bench was placed on the Court-House Green, and upon it the local magistrates, acting as election judges, took their seats, their clerks before them. By the side of the judges sat the two candidates for Congress; and when an elector declared his preference for either, the favored one rose, bowing, and thanked his supporter.

[1] Henry to Blair, Jan. 8, 1799; Henry, ii, 595.

[2] *Virginia Herald* (Fredericksburg), March 5, 1799.

Nobody but freeholders could then exercise the suffrage in Virginia.[1] Any one owning one hundred acres of land or more in any county could vote, and this landowner could declare his choice in every county in which he possessed the necessary real estate. The voter did not cast a printed or written ballot, but merely stated, in the presence of the two candidates, the election officials, and the assembled gathering, the name of the candidate of his preference. There was no specified form for this announcement.[2]

"I vote for John Marshall."

"Thank you, sir," said the lank, easy-mannered Federalist candidate.

"Hurrah for Marshall!" shouted the compact band of Federalists.

"And I vote for Clopton," cried another freeholder.

"May you live a thousand years, my friend," said Marshall's competitor.

"Three cheers for Clopton!" roared the crowd of Republican enthusiasts.

Both Republican and Federalist leaders had seen to it that nothing was left undone which might bring victory to their respective candidates. The two political parties had been carefully "drilled to move together in a body." Each party had a business committee which attended to every practical detail

[1] This was true in most of the States at that period.

[2] This method of electing public officials was continued until the Civil War. (See John S. Wise's description of a congressional election in Virginia in 1855; Wise: *The End of An Era*, 55–56. And see Professor Schouler's treatment of this subject in his "Evolution of the American Voter"; *Amer. Hist. Rev.*, ii, 665–74.)

of the election. Not a voter was overlooked. "Sick men were taken in their beds to the polls; the halt, the lame, and the blind were hunted up and every mode of conveyance was mustered into service." Time and again the vote was a tie. No sooner did one freeholder announce his preference for Marshall than another gave his suffrage to Clopton.

"A barrel of whisky with the head knocked in," free for everybody, stood beneath a tree; and "the majority took it straight," runs a narrative of a witness of the scene. So hot became the contest that fist-fights were frequent. During the afternoon, knock-down and drag-out affrays became so general that the county justices had hard work to quell the raging partisans. Throughout the day the shouting and huzzaing rose in volume as the whiskey sank in the barrel. At times the uproar was "perfectly deafening; men were shaking fists at each other, rolling up their sleeves, cursing and swearing. . . . Some became wild with agitation." When a tie was broken by a new voter shouting that he was for Marshall or for Clopton, insults were hurled at his devoted head.

"You, sir, ought to have your mouth smashed," cried an enraged Republican when Thomas Rutherford voted for Marshall; and smashing of mouths, blacking of eyes, and breaking of heads there were in plenty. "The crowd rolled to and fro like a surging wave." [1] Never before and seldom, if ever,

[1] This account of election day in the Marshall-Clopton contest is from Munford, 208–10. For another fairly accurate but mild description of a congressional election in Virginia at this period, see Mary Johnston's novel, *Lewis Rand*, chap. iv.

since, in the history of Virginia, was any election so fiercely contested. When this "democratic" struggle was over, it was found that Marshall had been elected by the slender majority of 108.[1]

Washington was overjoyed at the Federalist success. He had ridden ten miles to vote for General Lee, who was elected;[2] but he took a special delight in Marshall's victory. He hastened to write his political protégé: "With infinite pleasure I received the news of your Election. For the honor of the District I wish the majority had been greater; but let us be content, and hope, as the tide is turning, the current will soon run strong in your favor."[3]

Toward the end of the campaign, for the purpose of throwing into the contest Washington's personal influence, Marshall's enthusiastic friends had published the fact of Marshall's refusal to accept the various offices which had been tendered him by Washington. They had drawn a long bow, though very slightly, and stated positively that Marshall could have been Secretary of State.[4] Marshall hastened to apologize:—

"Few of the unpleasant occurrences" of the campaign "have given me more real chagrin than this. To make a parade of proffered offices is a vanity which I trust I do not possess; but to boast of one never in my power would argue a littleness of mind

[1] Henry, ii, 598. [2] Randall, ii, 495.

[3] Washington to Marshall, May 5, 1799; *Writings:* Ford, xiv, 180.

[4] As a matter of fact, they were not far wrong. Marshall almost certainly would have been made Secretary of State if Washington had believed that he would accept the portfolio. (See *supra*, 147.) The assertion that the place actually had been offered to Marshall seems to have been the only error in this campaign story.

at which I ought to blush." Marshall tells Washington that the person who published the report "never received it directly or indirectly from me." If he had known "that such a publication was designed" he "would certainly have suppressed it." It was inspired "unquestionably . . . by a wish to serve me," says Marshall, "and by resentment at the various malignant calumnies which have been so profusely bestowed on me." [1]

Washington quickly reassured Marshall: "I am sorry to find that the publication you allude to should have given you a moment's disquietude. I can assure you it made no impression on my mind, of the tendency apprehended by you." [2]

As soon as all the election returns were in, Marshall reported to Washington that the defeat of two of the Federalist candidates for Congress was unexpected and "has reduced us to eight in the legislature of the Union"; that the Republicans maintained their "majority in the house of Delegates," which "means an antifederal senator and governor," and that "the baneful influence of a legislature hostile perhaps to the Union — or if not so — to all its measures will be kept up." [3]

Marshall's campaign attracted the attention of the whole country, and the news of his success deeply interested both Federalists and Republicans. Pickering, after writing King of the Federalist success in New York City, declared that "the other domestic

[1] Marshall to Washington, May 1, 1799; *Writings*: Ford, xiv, footnote to 180–81; also Flanders, ii, 389.

[2] Washington to Marshall, May 5, 1799; *Writings*: Ford, xiv, 180.

[3] Marshall to Washington, May 16, 1799; Washington MSS., Lib. Cong.

intelligence, still more important, is, that Genl. Marshall is elected a member of Congress for his district." [1]

Speaker Sedgwick also informed King of Marshall's election. "General Marshall you know is a member of the House of Representatives. His talents, his character and the situation he has been in, will combine to give him an influence, which will be further aided by the scene which he immediately represents. He may and probably will give a tone to the federal politics South of the Susquehannah. I well know the respect he entertains for you and for your opinions." [2]

But the Federalist leaders were none too sure of their Virginia congressional recruit. He was entirely too independent to suit the party organization. His campaign statement on the Alien and Sedition Laws angered and troubled them when it was made; and, now that Marshall was elected, his opinion on this, to the Federalists, vital subject, his admitted power of mind and character, and his weighty influence over the Southern wing of the Federalists caused serious apprehension among the party's Northern leaders. Sedgwick advises King to write Marshall on the subject of party regularity.

"I have brought this subject to your mind, that you may decide on the propriety of a communication of your sentiments to him, which you may do in season to be useful. Should he, which, indeed, I do not expect, conform his political conduct generally, to

[1] Pickering to King, May 4, 1799; King, iii, 13.

[2] Sedgwick to King, July 26, 1799; King, iii, 69.

what seems indicated by his public declaration relative to the alien & sedition acts, it would have been better that his insignificant predecessor should have been reëlected. There never has been an instance where the commencement of a political career was so important as is that of General Marshall."[1]

Apprehension and uncertainty as to Marshall's course in the House was in the minds of even the Federalist leaders who were out of the country. The American Minister at The Hague was as much troubled about Marshall as were the Federalist politicians at home: "If M[arshall]'s silly declaration on the *inexpediency* of the Sedition law does not entangle him he may be very useful."[2] But Murray was uneasy: "Marshall, I fear, comes in on middle ground, and when a man plays the amiable in a body like that [House of Representatives] he cannot be counted [on], but he will vote generally right. I was amiable the first session! It cannot last."[3]

Jefferson, of course, was much depressed by the Federalist congressional victories, which he felt "are extremely to be regretted." He was especially irritated by Marshall's election: It "marks a taint in that part of the State which I had not expected." He was venomous toward Henry for having helped Marshall: "His [Henry's] apostacy, must be unaccountable to those who do not know all the recesses of his heart."[4]

[1] Sedgwick to King, July 26, 1799; King, iii, 69.

[2] Murray to J. Q. Adams, June 25, 1799; *Letters:* Ford, 566.

[3] Murray to J. Q. Adams, July 1, 1799; *ib.*, 568.

[4] Jefferson to Stuart, May 14, 1799; *Works:* Ford, ix, 67.

A week later, however, Jefferson decided that the Federalist success did not mean a permanent Republican reverse. Spoils and corruption, he concluded, were the real cause of the Federalist gain. "The Virginia congressional elections have astonished every one," he informs Tench Coxe. "This result has proceeded from accidental combinations of circumstances, & not from an unfavorable change of sentiment. . . . We are not incorruptible; on the contrary, corruption is making sensible tho' silent progress. Offices are as acceptable here as elsewhere, & whenever a man has cast a longing on them, a rottenness begins in his conduct." [1]

Jefferson, with settled and burning hatred, now puts his branding-iron on Henry: "As to the effect of his name among the people, I have found it crumble like a dried leaf the moment they become satisfied of his apostacy." [2]

During the weeks which immediately followed his election, Marshall was busy reporting to Washington on the best men to be appointed as officers in the provisional army; and his letters to the Commander-in-Chief show a wide and careful acquaintance with Virginians of military training, and a delicate judgment of their qualities.[3]

By now the hated Sedition Law was justifying the political hydrophobia which it had excited among the Republicans.[4] All over the country men

[1] Jefferson to Coxe, May 21, 1799; *Works:* Ford, ix, 69–70. [2] *Ib.*, 70.

[3] For instances of these military letters, see Marshall to Washington, June 12, 1799; Washington MSS., Lib. Cong.

[4] See Morison, i, 156–57; also Hudson: *Journalism in the United States*, 160. Party newspapers and speakers to-day make state-

were being indicted and convicted for wholly justifiable political criticisms, — some of them trivial and even amusing, — as well as for false and slanderous attacks on public officers. President Adams himself had begun to urge these prosecutions. He was particularly bitter against the "Aurora," the Republican organ, which, according to Adams, contained an "uninterrupted stream of slander on the American government."[1] He thought that the editor ought to be expelled from the country.[2]

All this was more fuel to the Republican furnace. Wicked and outrageous as were some of these prosecutions, they were not so extravagant as the horrors which Republican politicans declared that the Sedition Laws would bring to every fireside.

During the summer after his election Marshall visited his father in Kentucky. Thomas Marshall was ill, and his son's toilsome journey was solely for the purpose of comforting him; but Jefferson could see in it nothing but a political mission. He writes to Wilson Cary Nicholas to prepare an answer to the States that had opposed the Kentucky and Virginia Resolutions; but, says Jefferson, "As to the preparing anything [myself] I must decline it, to avoid suspicions (which were pretty strong in some quarters on the last occasion) [the Kentucky Resolu-

ments, as a matter of course, in every political campaign much more violent than those for which editors and citizens were fined and imprisoned in 1799–1800. (See *ib.*, 315; and see summary from the Republican point of view of these prosecutions in Randall, ii, 416–20.)

[1] Adams to Pickering, July 24, 1799; *Works*: Adams, ix, 3.

[2] Adams to Pickering, Aug. 1, 1799; *ib.*, 5; and same to same, Aug. 3, 1799; *ib.*, 7.

tions]. . . . The visit of the apostle Marshall [1] to Kentucky, excite[s] anxiety. However, we doubt not that his poisons will be effectually counterworked." [2]

Jefferson's suspicions were groundless. Marshall did not even sound public opinion on the subject. On his return to Richmond he writes the Secretary of State, who was the most active politician of Adams's Cabinet, and to whom Marshall freely opened his mind on politics, that "a visit to an aged & rever'd Father" prevented an earlier answer to a letter from Pickering; and, although Marshall has much to say, not one word is written of the Kentucky and Virginia Resolutions. He is obsessed with the French question and of the advantage the French "party in America" may secure by the impression that France was not really hostile. "This will enable her [France's] party in America to attack from very advantageous ground the government of the United States." [3]

Now came the public circumstance that made the schism in the Federalist Party an open and remorseless feud. The President's militant declaration, that he would "never send another minister to France without assurances that he will [would] be received, respected, and honored as the represent-

[1] Professor Washington, in his edition of Jefferson's *Writings*, leaves a blank after "apostle." Mr. Ford correctly prints Marshall's name as it is written in Jefferson's original manuscript copy of the letter.

[2] Jefferson to Wilson Cary Nicholas, Sept. 5, 1799; *Works:* Ford, ix, 79–81.

[3] Marshall to Pickering, Aug. 25, 1799; Pickering MSS., Mass. Hist. Soc. Marshall had not yet grasped the deadly significance of Jefferson's States' Rights and Nullification maneuver.

ative of a great, free, powerful, and independent people,"[1] was perfectly attuned to the warlike spirit of the hour. The country rang with approval. The Federalist politicians were exultant.

Thereupon the resourceful Talleyrand wrote the Secretary of the French Legation at The Hague to intimate to Murray, the American Minister, that the French Directory would now receive a minister from the United States.[2] Murray hastened the news to Adams.[3] It was a frail assurance, indirect, irregular, unacknowledged to the world; and from men who had insulted us and who would not hesitate to repudiate Murray's statement if their purposes so required. Yet the President grasped by the forelock this possibility for peace, and, against the emphatic protest of his Cabinet, suddenly sent a second commission to try again for that adjustment which Marshall and his associates had failed to secure. It was the wisest and most unpopular act of Adams's troubled Administration.

The leading Federalist politicians were enraged. Indeed, "the whole [Federalist] party were prodigiously alarmed."[4] They thought it a national humiliation. What! said they, kiss the hand that had slapped our face! "The new embassy . . . disgusts most men here," reported Ames from New

[1] *Supra.*

[2] Talleyrand to Pichon, Aug. 28, and Sept. 28; *Am. St. Prs.*, ii, 241–42; Murray to Adams, Appendix of *Works:* Adams, viii. For familiar account of Pichon's conferences with Murray, see Murray's letters to J. Q. Adams, then U.S. Minister to Berlin, in *Letters:* Ford, 445, 473, 475–76; and to Pickering, *ib.*, 464.

[3] "Murray, I guess, wanted to make himself a greater man than he is by going to France," was Gallatin's shrewd opinion. Gallatin to his wife, March 1, 1799; Adams: *Gallatin*, 227–28.

[4] *Ib.*

England.[1] Cabot confirmed Ames's doleful message — "Surprise, indignation, grief, & disgust followed each other in swift succession in the breasts of the true friends of our country," he advised King.[2]

The Federalist leaders really wanted war with France, most of them as a matter of patriotism; some, undoubtedly, because war would insure party success in the approaching presidential election. Upon his return Marshall had prophesied formal declaration of hostilities from the Republic of France, when news of the dispatches reached Europe; and the war Federalists were sorely disappointed at the failure of his prediction. "Genl. Marshall unfortunately held the decided opinion that France would DECLARE war when the Dispatches should appear; and T. Sewell with other good men were so strongly impressed with the advantage of such a declaration by them that they could not be persuaded to relinquish the belief in it — I was astonished that they should have attributed to the French such miserable policy." So wrote the able and balanced Cabot.[3] That France refused to adopt "such miserable policy" as Marshall had expected was sufficiently exasperating to the war Federalists; but to meet that country three fourths of the way on the road to peace was intolerable.

"The end [peace] being a bad one all means are unwise and indefensible" was the ultra-Federalist belief.[4] Adams's second mission was, they said,

[1] Ames to Dwight, Feb. 27, 1799; *Works:* Ames, i, 252.
[2] Cabot to King, March 10, 1799; King, ii, 551.
[3] Cabot to King, Feb. 16, 1799; *ib.*, 543.
[4] Ames to Pickering, March 12, 1799; *Works:* Ames, i, 253.

party surrender to the Republicans; it was "a policy that threatens . . . to revive the Jacobin faction in our bosom."[1] Federalist members of Congress threatened to resign. "I have sacrificed as much as most men . . . to support this Govt. and root out Democracy, & French principles, but . . . I feel it to be lost and worse . . . I can & will resign if all must be given up to France," cried the enraged Tracy.[2]

These "enemies of government" had said all along that things could be arranged with France; that the X. Y. Z. disclosures were merely a Federalist plot; and that the army was a wicked and needless expense. What answer could the Federalists make to these Republican charges now? Adams's new French mission, the Federalist chieftains declared, was "a measure to *make* dangers, and to nullify resources; to make the navy without object; the army an object of popular terror."[3]

And the presidential election was coming on! To hold the situation just as it was might mean Federalist victory. Suppose events did develop a formal declaration of war with France? That would make Federalist success more certain. The country would not turn out a party in charge of the Government when cannon were roaring. Even more important, an open and avowed conflict with the "bloody Republic" would, reasoned the Federalist leaders, check the miasmic growth of French revolutionary ideas among the people.

[1] Ames to Pickering, Oct. 19, 1799; *ib.*, 257.
[2] Uriah Tracy to McHenry, Sept. 2, 1799; Steiner, 417.
[3] Ames to Pickering, Nov. 5, 1799; *Works:* Ames, i, 260–61.

In short, a declaration of war with France would do everything which the Federalists wished and hoped for. "Peace [with France] . . . is not desired as it should not be" [1] was their opinion of the statesmanship demanded by the times. And now Adams, without one word to the men who reluctantly had made him President,[2] had not only prevented a rupture which would have accomplished every Federalist purpose, but had delivered his party into the hands of the "Jacobins." He had robbed the Federalists of their supreme campaign "issue." "Peace with France, they think an evil and holding out the hope of it another, as it tends to chill the public fervor"; [3] and the "public fervor" surely needed no further reduction of temperature, for Federalist health.

If Adams did not wish for a formal declaration of war, at least he might have let things alone. But now! "Government will be weakened by the friends it loses and betrayed by those it will gain. It will lose . . . the friendship of the sense, and worth, and property of the United States, and get in exchange the prejudice, vice, and bankruptcy of the nation," [4] wrote Ames to Pickering. "In Resistance alone there is safety," [5] was Cabot's

[1] Ames to Pickering, March 12, 1799; *Works:* Ames, i, 254.

[2] "Men of principal influence in the Federal party . . . began to entertain serious doubts about his [Adams's] fitness for the station, yet . . . they thought it better to indulge their hopes than to listen to their fears, [and] . . . determined to support Mr. Adams for the Chief Magistracy." ("Public Conduct, etc., John Adams"; Hamilton: *Works:* Lodge, vii, 318.)

[3] Ames to Dwight, Feb. 27, 1799; *Works:* Ames, i, 252.

[4] Ames to Pickering, Nov. 5, 1799; *ib.*, 260.

[5] Cabot to King, March 10, 1799; King, ii, 552.

opinion. "The Jacobin influence is rising, and has been ever since the mission to France was determined on; . . . if a Treaty be made with France their [Republican] ascendancy will be sure"; [1] and, after that, the deluge.

The Federalist leaders felt that, even without a declaration of hostilities by Congress, they might make shift to win the approaching election. For on the sea we already were waging war on France, while formally at peace with her. Our newborn navy was taking French privateers, defeating French men-of-war, and retaliating with pike, cutlass, and broadside for the piratical French outrages upon American commerce.[2] As things stood, it was certain that this would continue until after the election, and with each glorious victory of a Truxton or a Hull, National pride and popular enthusiasm would mount higher and grow stronger. So the Federalist politicians thought that "the only negotiation compatible with our honor or our safety is that begun by Truxton in the capture of the L'Insurgente." [3]

Priceless campaign ammunition was this for the Federalist political guns. Early in the year the bilious but keen-eyed watchman on the ramparts of New England Federalism had noted the appearance of "a little patriotism, and the capture of the *Insurgente* cherishes it." [4] And now Adams's second

[1] Higginson to Pickering, April 16, 1800; Pickering MSS., Mass. Hist. Soc., printed in *An. Rept.*, Amer. Hist. Assn., 1896, i, 836.

[2] For an excellent summary of this important episode in our history see Allen: *Our Naval War with France.*

[3] Pickering to King, March 6, 1799; King, ii, 548–49.

[4] Ames to Pickering, March 12, 1799; *Works:* Ames, i, 254.

mission might spoil everything. "The Jacobins will rise in consequence of this blunder," [1] was the doleful prophecy. Indeed, it was already in fulfillment even with the utterance: "Already the Jacobins raise their disgraced heads from the mire of contempt!" [2] The "country gentlemen" were the hands as the business interests were the brain and heart of the Federalist Party; "the President destroyed their influence, and . . . left them prostrate before their vindictive adversaries." [3]

The Republicans were overjoyed. Adams had reversed himself, eaten his own words, confessed the hypocrisy of the "infamous X. Y. Z. plot." "This renders their [Federalists'] efforts for war desperate, & silences all further denials of the sincerity of the French government," gleefully wrote Jefferson.[4]

Marshall alone of the commanding Federalists, approved Adams's action. "I presume it will afford you satisfaction to know that a measure which excited so much agitation here, has met the approbation of so good a judge as Mr. Marshall," Lee reported to the President.[5] Marshall's support cheered the harried Chief Executive. "Esteeming very highly the opinion and character of your friend General Marshall, I thank you for inclosing his letter," responded Adams.[6]

[1] Ames to Dwight, Oct. 20, 1799; *ib.*, 259.
[2] Ames to Pickering, Oct. 19, 1799; *ib.*, 257.
[3] Wolcott to Ames, Aug. 10, 1800; Gibbs, ii, 403.
[4] Jefferson to Pendleton, Feb. 19, 1799; *Works:* Ford, ix, 54.
[5] Lee to Adams, March 14, 1799; *Works:* Adams, viii, 628.
[6] Adams to Lee, March 29, 1799; *ib.*, 629.

The President had done still worse. Auctioneer John Fries, a militia captain, had headed an armed mob in resistance to the National officers who were levying the National direct tax on the houses and lands of the farmers of eastern Pennsylvania. He had been finally taken prisoner, tried, and convicted of sedition and treason, and sentenced to death. Against the unanimous written advice of his Cabinet, formally tendered,[1] the President pardoned the "traitor" and "his fellow criminals."[2] And this clemency was granted at the plea of McKean, the arch-"Jacobin" of Pennsylvania,[3] without even consulting the judges of the courts in which they were twice tried and convicted.[4]

What was this, asked the Federalist leaders in dazed and angry amazement! Paralyze the arm of the law! Unloose the fingers of outraged authority from the guilty throat which Justice had clutched! What was to become of "law and order" when the Nation's head thus sanctioned resistance to both?[5] In his charge to the Federal Grand Jury, April 11, 1799, Justice Iredell declared that if "traitors" are not punished "anarchy will ride triumphant and all lovers of order, decency, truth & justice will be trampled under foot."[6]

[1] Cabinet to President, Sept. 7, 1799; *Works:* Adams, ix, 21–23; and same to same, May 20, 1799; *ib.*, 59–60.

[2] Adams to Lee, May 21, 1800; *ib.*, 60. For account of Fries's Rebellion see McMaster, ii, 435–39. Also Hildreth, v, 313.

[3] Pickering to Cabot, June 15, 1800; Lodge: *Cabot*, 275.

[4] "Public Conduct, etc., John Adams"; Hamilton: *Works:* Lodge, vii, 351–55; and see Gibbs, ii, 360–62.

[5] See Hamilton's arraignment of the Fries pardon in "Public Conduct, etc., John Adams"; *Works:* Lodge, vii, 351–55.

[6] McRee, ii, 551.

How, now, could the Federalists repel Republican assaults on this direct tax? How, now, could they reply to the Republican attacks upon the army to support which the tax was provided! In pardoning Fries, Adams had admitted everything which the hated Jefferson had said against both tax and army.[1] If Adams was right in pardoning Fries, then Washington was wrong in suppressing the Whiskey Rebellion. The whole Federalist system was abandoned.[2] The very roots of the Federalist philosophy of government and administration were torn from their none too firm hold upon the scanty soil which Federalist statesmen had laboriously gathered for their nourishment. And why had Adams done this?

[1] "The Aurora, in analyzing the reasons upon which Fries, Hainy, and Getman have been pardoned brings the President forward as, by this act, condemning: 1. The tax law which gave rise to the insurrection; 2. The conduct of the officers appointed to collect the tax; 3. The marshal; 4. The witnesses on the part of the United States; 5. The juries who tried the prisoners; 6. The court, both in their personal conduct and in their judicial decisions. In short, every individual who has had any part in passing the law — in endeavoring to execute it, or in bringing to just punishment those who have treasonably violated it." (*Gazette of the United States*, reviewing bitterly the comment of the Republican organ on Adams's pardon of Fries.)

[2] Many Federalists regretted that Fries was not executed by court-martial. "I suppose military execution was impracticable, but if some executions are not had, of the most notorious offenders — I shall regret the events of lenity in '94 & '99 — as giving a fatal stroke to Government. . . . Undue mercy to villains, is cruelty to all the good & virtuous. Our people in this State are perfectly astonished, that cost must continually be incurred for insurrections in Pennsylvania for which they say they are taxed & yet no punishment is inflicted on the offenders. I am fatigued & mortified that our Govt. which is weak at best, would withhold any of its strength when all its energies should be doubled." (Uriah Tracy to McHenry, on Fries, May 6, 1799; Steiner, 436.) And "I am in fear that something will occur to release that fellow from merited Death." (Same to same, May 20, 1790; *ib.*)

Because, said the Federalist politicians, it was popular in Pennsylvania;[1] that was the President's motive — the same that moved him to send the new mission to France.[2]

Bending under heavy burdens of state, harassed by the politicians, Adams was enduring a private pain sharper than his public cares. His wife, the incomparable Abigail, was in Massachusetts and seriously ill. The President had left her to meet his Cabinet and dispatch the second mission to France. That done, he hastened back to the bedside of his sick wife. But the politicians made no allowances. Adams's absence "from the seat of government . . . is a source of much disgust," chronicles the ardent Troup. "It . . . has the air of an abdication."[3] A month later he records that the President "still continues at Braintree,[4] and the government, like Pope's wounded snake, drags its slow length along."[5]

Such was the condition of the country and the state of political parties when Marshall took his seat in Congress. For the Federalists, the House was a very "cave of the winds," with confusion, uncertainty, suspicion, anger, and all the disintegrating passions blowing this way and that. But the Republicans were a compact, disciplined, determined body full of spirit and purpose.

[1] "Public Conduct, etc., John Adams"; Hamilton: *Works:* Lodge, vii, 351–55.
[2] Ames to Pickering, Nov. 23, 1799; *Works:* Ames, i, 270.
[3] Troup to King, May 6, 1799; King, iii, 14.
[4] Adams's home, now Quincy, Massachusetts.
[5] Troup to King, June 5, 1799; King, iii, 34.

CHAPTER XI

INDEPENDENCE IN CONGRESS

The Constitution is not designed to secure the rights of the people of Europe or Asia or to direct proceedings against criminals throughout the universe. (Marshall.)

The whole world is in arms and no rights are respected but those that are maintained by force. (Marshall.)

Marshall is disposed to express great respect for the sovereign people and to quote their expressions as evidence of truth. (Theodore Sedgwick.)

"I HAVE been much in Company with General Marshall since we arrived in this City. He possesses great powers and has much dexterity in the application of them. He is highly & deservedly respected by the friends of Government [Federalists] from the South. In short, we can do nothing without him. I believe his intentions are perfectly honorable, & yet I do believe he would have been a more decided man had his education been on the other side of the Delaware, and he the immediate representative of that country."[1]

So wrote the Speaker of the House of Representatives after three weeks of association with the Virginia member whom he had been carefully studying. After another month of Federalist scrutiny, Cabot agreed with Speaker Sedgwick as to Marshall's qualities.

"In Congress, you see Genl. M.[arshall] is a leader. He is I think a virtuous & certainly an able man; but you see in him the faults of a Virginian. He thinks too much of that State, & he expects the

[1] Sedgwick to King, Dec. 29, 1799; King, iii, 163.

world will be governed according to the Rules of Logic. I have seen such men often become excellent legislators after experience has cured their errors. I hope it will prove so with Genl. M.[arshall], who seems calculated to act a great part." [1]

The first session of the Sixth Congress convened in Philadelphia on December 2, 1799. Marshall was appointed a member of the joint committee of the Senate and the House to wait upon the President and inform him that Congress was in session.[2]

The next day Adams delivered his speech to the Senators and Representatives. The subject which for the moment now inflamed the minds of the members of the President's party was Adams's second French mission. Marshall, of all men, had most reason to resent any new attempt to try once more where he had failed, and to endeavor again to deal with the men who had insulted America and spun about our representatives a network of corrupt intrigue. But if Marshall felt any personal humiliation, he put it beneath his feet and, as we have seen, approved the Ellsworth mission. "The southern federalists have of course been induced [by Marshall] to vindicate the mission, as a sincere, honest, and politic measure," wrote Wolcott to Ames.[3]

Who should prepare the answer of the House to the President's speech? Who best could perform the difficult task of framing a respectful reply which would support the President and yet not offend the rebellious Federalists in Congress? Marshall was

[1] Cabot to King, Jan. 20, 1800; *ib.*, 184.
[2] *Annals*, 6th Cong., 1st Sess., 187.
[3] Wolcott to Ames, Dec. 29, 1799; Gibbs, ii, 314.

selected for this delicate work. "Mr. Marshall, from the committee appointed to draught an Address in answer to the Speech of the President of the United States . . . reported same." [1] Although written in admirable temper, Marshall's address failed to please; the result was pallid.

"Considering the state of the House, it was necessary and proper that the answer to the speech should be prepared by Mr. Marshall," testifies Wolcott. "He has had a hard task to perform, and you have seen how it has been executed. The object was to unite all opinions, at least of the federalists; it was of course necessary to appear to approve the mission, and yet to express the approbation in such terms as when critically analyzed would amount to no approbation at all. No one individual was really satisfied; all were unwilling to encounter the danger and heat which a debate would produce and the address passed with silent dissent; the President doubtless understood the intention, and in his response has expressed his sense of the dubious compliment in terms inimitably obscure." [2] Levin Powell, a Federalist Representative from Virginia, wrote to his brother: "There were members on both sides that disliked that part of it [Marshall's address] where he spoke of the Mission to France." [3]

The mingled depression, excitement, and resentment among Marshall's colleagues must have been

[1] *Annals*, 6th Cong. 1st Sess., 194. The speech as reported passed with little debate.

[2] Wolcott to Ames, Dec. 29, 1799; Gibbs, ii, 314. And see McMaster, ii, 452.

[3] Levin Powell to Major Burr Powell, Dec. 11, 1799; *Branch Historical Papers*, ii, 232.

great indeed to have caused them thus to look upon his first performance in the House; for the address, which, even now, is good reading, is a strong and forthright utterance. While, with polite agreement, gliding over the controverted question of the mission, Marshall's speech is particularly virile when dealing with domestic politics. In coupling Fries's Pennsylvania insurrection with the Kentucky and Virginia Resolutions Marshall displayed as clever political dexterity as even Jefferson himself.

The address enumerates the many things for which Americans ought to thank "the benevolent Deity," and laments "that any portion of the people . . . should permit themselves, amid such numerous blessings, to *be seduced* by . . . *designing men* into an open resistance to the laws of the United States. . . . Under a Constitution where the public burdens can only be imposed by the people themselves, for their own benefit, and to promote their own objects, a hope might well have been indulged that the general interest would have been too well understood, and the general welfare too highly prized, to have produced in any of our citizens a disposition to hazard so much felicity, by the criminal effort of a part, to oppose with lawless violence the will of the whole." [1]

While it augured well that the courts and militia coöperated with "the military force of the nation" in "restoring order and submission to the laws," still, this only showed the necessity of Adams's "recommendation" that "the judiciary system"

[1] *Annals*, 6th Cong., 1st Sess., 194.

should be extended. As to the new French mission, the address "approves the pacific and humane policy" which met, by the appointment of new envoys, "the first indications on the part of the French Republic" of willingness to negotiate; and "offers up fervent prayers to the Supreme Ruler of the Universe for the success of their embassy."

Marshall declares "the present period critical and momentous. The important changes which are occurring, the new and great events which are every hour preparing . . . the spirit of war . . . prevalent in almost every nation . . . demonstrate" the need of providing "means of self-defense." To neglect this duty from "love of ease or other considerations" would be "criminal and fatal carelessness." No one could tell how the new mission would terminate: "It depends not on America alone. The most pacific temper will not ensure peace." Preparation for "national defense . . . is an . . . obvious duty. Experience the parent of wisdom . . . has established the truth . . . that . . . nothing short of the power of repelling aggression will" save us from "war or national degradation." [1]

Gregg of Pennsylvania moved to strike out the italicized words in Marshall's address to the President, but after a short debate the motion was defeated without roll-call.[2]

Wolcott gives us a clear analysis of the political situation and of Marshall's place and power in it at this particular moment: "The federal party is composed of the old members who were generally re-

[1] *Annals*, 6th Cong., 1st Sess., 194–97. [2] *Ib.*, 194.

elected in the northern, with new members from the southern states. New York has sent an anti-federal majority; Pennsylvania has done the same; opposition principles are gaining ground in New Jersey and Maryland, and in the present Congress, the votes of these states will be fluctuating and undecided."

Nothing shows more clearly the intimate gossip of the time than the similarity of Wolcott's and Cabot's language in describing Marshall. "A number of distinguished men," continues Wolcott, "appear from the southward, who are not pledged by any act to support the system of the last Congress; these men will pay great respect to the opinions of General Marshall; he is doubtless a man of virtue and distinguished talents, but he will think much of the State of Virginia, and is too much disposed to govern the world according to rules of logic; he will read and expound the constitution as if it were a penal statute, and will sometimes be embarrassed with doubts of which his friends will not perceive the importance."[1]

Marshall headed the committee to inquire of the President when he would receive the address of the House, and on December 10, "Mr. Speaker, attended by the members present, proceeded to the President's house, to present him their Address in answer to his Speech."[2] A doleful procession the hostile, despondent, and irritated Representatives made as they trudged along Philadelphia's streets to greet the equally hostile and exasperated Chief Magistrate.

[1] Wolcott to Ames, Dec. 29, 1799; Gibbs, ii, 314.
[2] *Annals*, 6th Cong., 1st Sess., 198.

Presidential politics was much more on the minds of the members of Congress than was the legislation needed by the country. Most of the measures and practically all the debates of this remarkable session were shaped and colored by the approaching contest between the Federalists and Republicans and, personally, between Jefferson and Adams. Without bearing this fact in mind the proceedings of this session cannot be correctly understood. A mere reading of the maze of resolutions, motions, and debates printed in the "Annals" leaves one bewildered. The principal topic of conversation was, of course, the impending presidential election. Hamilton's faction of extreme Federalists had been dissatisfied with Adams from the beginning. Marshall writes his brother "in confidence" of the plots these busy politicians were concocting.

"I can tell you in confidence," writes Marshall, "that the situation of our affairs with respect to domestic quiet is much more critical than I had conjectured. The eastern people are very much dissatisfied with the President on account of the late [second] Mission to France. They are strongly disposed to desert him & push some other candidate. King or Ellsworth with one of the Pinckneys — most probably the General, are thought of.

"If they are deter'd from doing this by the fear that the attempt might elect Jefferson I think it not improbable that they will vote generally for Adams & Pinckney so as to give the latter gentleman the best chance if he gets the Southern vote to be President.

"Perhaps this ill humor may evaporate before

the election comes on — but at present it wears a very serious aspect. This circumstance is rendered the more unpleasant by the state of our finances. The impost received this year has been less productive than usual & it will be impossible to continue the present armament without another loan. Had the impost produced the sum to which it was calculated, a loan would have been unavoidable.

"This difficulty ought to have been foreseen when it was determined to execute the law for raising the army. It is now conceiv'd that we cannot at the present stage of our negotiation with France change the defensive position we have taken without much hazard.

"In addition to this many influential characters not only contend that the army ought not now to be disbanded but that it ought to be continued so long as the war in Europe shall last. I am apprehensive that our people would receive with very ill temper a system which should keep up an army of observation at the expense of the annual addition of five millions to our debt. The effect of it wou'd most probably be that the hands which hold the reins wou'd be entirely chang'd. You perceive the perplexities attending our situation.

"In addition to this there are such different views with respect to the future, such a rancorous malignity of temper among the democrats,[1] such [an ap]-

[1] The Federalists called the Republicans "Democrats," "Jacobins," etc., as terms of contempt. The Republicans bitterly resented the appellation. The word "Democrat" was not adopted as the formal name of a political party until the nomination for the Presidency of Andrew Jackson, who had been Jefferson's determined enemy.

parent disposition — (if the Aurora be the index of the [mind of] those who support it) to propel us to a war with B[ritain] & to enfold us within the embrace of Fran[ce], [s]uch a detestation & fear of France among others [that I] look forward with more apprehension than I have ever done to the future political events of our country." [1]

On December 18 a rumor of the death of Washington reached the Capital. Marshall notified the House. His grief was so profound that even the dry and unemotional words of the formal congressional reports express it. "Mr. Marshall," says the "Annals" of Congress, "in a voice that bespoke the anguish of his mind, and a countenance expressive of the deepest regret, rose, and delivered himself as follows: —

"Mr. Speaker: Information has just been received, that our illustrious fellow-citizen, the Commander-in-Chief of the American Army, and the late President of the United States, is no more!

"Though this distressing intelligence is not certain, there is too much reason to believe its truth. After receiving information of this national calamity, so heavy and so afflicting, the House of Representatives can be but ill fitted for public business. I move, therefore, they adjourn." [2]

The next day the news was confirmed, and Marshall thus addressed the House: —

"Mr. Speaker: The melancholy event which was

[1] Marshall to James M. Marshall, Philadelphia, Dec. 16, 1799; MS.

[2] *Annals*, 6th Cong., 1st Sess., 203.

yesterday announced with doubt, has been rendered but too certain.

"Our WASHINGTON is no more! The Hero, the Sage, and the Patriot of America — the man on whom in times of danger every eye was turned and all hopes were placed — lives now only in his own great actions, and in the hearts of an affectionate and afflicted people.

"If, sir, it has even not been usual openly to testify respect for the memory of those whom Heaven had selected as its instrument for dispensing good to men, yet such has been the uncommon worth, and such the extraordinary incidents, which have marked the life of him whose loss we all deplore, that the American Nation,[1] impelled by the same feelings, would call with one voice for a public manifestation of that sorrow which is so deep and so universal.

"More than any other individual, and as much as to one individual was possible, has he contributed to found this our wide-spread empire,[2] and to give to the Western World its independence and its freedom.

"Having effected the great object for which he was placed at the head of our armies, we have seen him converting the sword into the plough-share, and voluntarily sinking the soldier in the citizen.

"When the debility of our federal system had become manifest, and the bonds which connected

[1] Marshall appears to have been the first to use the expression "the American Nation."

[2] The word "empire" as describing the United States was employed by all public men of the time. Washington and Jefferson frequently spoke of "our empire."

the parts of this vast continent were dissolving, we have seen him the Chief of those patriots who formed for us a Constitution, which, by preserving the Union, will, I trust, substantiate and perpetuate those blessings our Revolution had promised to bestow.

"In obedience to the general voice of his country, calling on him to preside over a great people, we have seen him once more quit the retirement he loved, and in a season more stormy and tempestuous than war itself, with calm and wise determination, pursue the true interests of the Nation, and contribute, more than any other could contribute, to the establishment of that system of policy which will, I trust, yet preserve our peace, our honor and our independence.

"Having been twice unanimously chosen the Chief Magistrate of a free people, we see him, at a time when his re-election with the universal suffrage could not have been doubted, affording to the world a rare instance of moderation, by withdrawing from his high station to the peaceful walks of private life. However the public confidence may change, and the public affections fluctuate with respect to others, yet with respect to him they have in war and in peace, in public and in private life, been as steady as his own firm mind, and as constant as his own exalted virtues.

"Let us, then, Mr. Speaker, pay the last tribute of respect and affection to our departed friend — let the Grand Council of the Nation display those sentiments which the Nation feels. For this purpose

I hold in my hand some resolutions which I will take the liberty to offer to the House." [1]

The resolutions offered by Marshall declared that: —

"The House of Representatives of the United States, having received intelligence of the death of their highly valued fellow-citizen, GEORGE WASHINGTON, General of the Armies of the United States, and sharing the universal grief this distressing event must produce, *unanimously resolve:* —

"1. That this House will wait on the President of the United States, in condolence of this national calamity.

"2. That the Speaker's chair be shrouded with black, and that the members and officers of the House wear mourning during the session.

"3. That a joint committee of both Houses be appointed to report measures suitable to the occasion, and expressive of the profound sorrow with which Congress is penetrated on the loss of a citizen, first in war, first in peace, and first in the hearts of his countrymen." [2]

Thus it came about that the designation of Washington as "First in war, first in peace, and first in the hearts of his countrymen" was attributed to Marshall. But Marshall's colleague, Henry Lee, was the author of these words. Marshall's refusal to allow history to give him the credit for this famous description is characteristic. He might easily have accepted that honor. Indeed, he found it difficult to make the public believe that he did not originate

[1] *Annals*, 6th Cong., 1st. Sess., 203–04. [2] *Ib.*, 204.

this celebrated phraseology. He presented the resolutions; they stand on the record in Marshall's name; and, for a long time, the world insisted on ascribing them to him.

In a last effort to make history place the laurels on General Lee, where they belong, Marshall, three years before his death, wrote the exact facts: —

"As the stage passed through Philadelphia," says Marshall, "some passenger mentioned to a friend he saw in the street the death of General Washington. The report flew to the hall of Congress, and I was asked to move an adjournment. I did so.

"General Lee was not at the time in the House. On receiving the intelligence which he did on the first arrival of the stage, he retired to his room and prepared the resolutions which were adopted with the intention of offering them himself.

"But the House of Representatives had voted on my motion, and it was expected by all that I on the next day announce the lamentable event and propose resolutions adapted to the occasion.

"General Lee immediately called on me and showed me his resolutions. He said it had now become improper for him to offer them, and wished me to take them. As I had not written anything myself and was pleased with his resolutions which I entirely approved, I told him I would offer them the next day when I should state to the House of Representatives the confirmation of the melancholy intelligence received the preceding day. I did so.

"You will see the fact stated in a note to the preface of the Life of Washington on p. [441] v. [2] and again in a note to the 5th vol. p. 765. Whenever the subject has been mentioned in my presence," Marshall adds in a postscript, "I have invariably stated that the resolution was drawn by General Lee and have referred to these notes in the Life of Washington." [1]

During the first session Marshall was incessantly active, although his work was done with such ease that he gave to his colleagues the impression of indolence. Few questions came before the House on which he did not take the floor; and none, apparently, about which he did not freely speak his mind in private conversation. The interminable roll-calls of the first session show that Marshall failed to vote only six times.[2] His name is prominent throughout the records of the session. For example, the Republicans moved to amend the army laws so that enlistments should not exempt non-commissioned officers and privates from imprisonment for debt. Marshall spoke against the motion, which was defeated.[3] He was appointed chairman of a special committee to bring in a bill for removing military forces from election places and "preventing their interference in elections." Marshall drew this measure, reported

[1] Marshall to Charles W. Hannan, of Baltimore, Md., March 29, 1832; MS., N.Y. Pub. Lib.; also Marshall, ii, 441.

[2] These were: On the bill to enable the President to borrow money for the public (*Annals*, 6th Cong., 1st Sess., 632); a bill for the relief of Rhode Island College (*ib.*, 643); a salt duty bill (*ib.*, 667); a motion to postpone the bill concerning the payment of admirals (*ib.*, 678); a bill on the slave trade (*ib.*, 699–700); a bill for the additional taxation of sugar (*ib.*, 705).

[3] *Ib.*, 521–22.

it to the House, where it passed, only to be defeated in the Senate.[1]

Early in the session Marshall was appointed chairman of the committee to report upon the cession by Connecticut to the United States of that priceless domain known as the Western Reserve. He presented the committee report recommending the acceptance of the lands and introduced the bill setting out the terms upon which they could be taken over.[2] After much debate, which Marshall led, Gallatin fighting by his side, the bill was passed by a heavy majority.[3]

Marshall's vote against abrogating the power of the Governor of the Territory of the Mississippi to prorogue the Legislature;[4] his vote for the resolution that the impertinence of a couple of young officers to John Randolph at the theater did not call "for the interposition of this House," on the ground of a breach of its privileges;[5] his vote against that part of the Marine Corps Bill which provided that any officer, on the testimony of two

[1] *Annals*, 6th Cong., 1st Sess., *House*, 522–23, 527, 626; *Senate*, 151.

[2] *Ib.*, 633–34.

[3] *Ib.*, 662. See *ib.*, Appendix II, 495, 496. Thus Marshall was the author of the law under which the great "Western Reserve" was secured to the United States. The bill was strenuously resisted on the ground that Connecticut had no right or title to this extensive and valuable territory.

[4] *Ib.*, 532. On this vote the *Aurora* said: "When we hear such characters as General Lee calling it *innovation* and *speculation* to withhold from the Executive magistrate the dangerous and unrepublican power of *proroguing* and dissolving a legislature at his pleasure, what must be the course of our reflections? When we see men like General Marshall voting for such a principle in a Government of a portion of the American people is there no cause for alarm?" (*Aurora*, March 20, 1800.)

[5] *Annals*, 6th Cong., 1st Sess., 504–06.

witnesses, should be cashiered and incapacitated forever from military service for refusing to help arrest any member of the service who, while on shore, offended against the person or property of any citizen,[1] are fair examples of the level good sense with which Marshall invariably voted.

On the Marine Corps Bill a debate arose so suddenly and sharply that the reporter could not record it. Marshall's part in this encounter reveals his military bent of mind, the influence of his army experience, and his readiness in controversy, no less than his unemotional sanity and his disdain of popular favor if it could be secured only by sacrificing sound judgment. Marshall strenuously objected to subjecting the Marine Corps officers to trial by jury in the civil courts; he insisted that courts-martial were the only tribunals that could properly pass on their offenses. Thereupon, young John Randolph of Roanoke, whose pose at this particular time was extravagant hostility to everything military, promptly attacked him. The incident is thus described by one who witnessed the encounter "which was incidentally and unexpectedly started and as suddenly and warmly debated": —

"Your representative, Mr. Marshall, was the principal advocate for *letting the power remain with courts martial and for withholding it from the courts of law.* In the course of the debate there was some warmth and personality between him and Mr. Randolph, in consequence of the latter charging the former with adopting opinions, and using argu-

[1] *Annals*, 6th Cong., 1st Sess., 623–24.

ments, which went to sap the mode of trial by jury.

"Mr. Marshall, with leave, rose a third time, and exerted himself to repel and invalidate the deductions of Mr. Randolph, who also obtained permission, and defended the inference he had drawn, by stating that Mr. Marshall, in the affair of Robbins,[1] had strenuously argued against the jurisdiction of the American courts, and had contended that it was altogether an *Executive* business; that in the present instance he strongly contended that the business ought not to be left with the civil tribunals, but that it ought to be transferred to military tribunals, and thus the trial by jury would be lessened and frittered away, and insensibly sapped, at one time by transferring the power to the Executive, and at another to the military departments; and in other ways, as occasions might present themselves. The debate happened so unexpectedly that the shorthand man did not take it down, although its manner, its matter, and its tendency, made it more deserving of preservation, than most that have taken place during the session."[2]

Marshall's leadership in the fight of the Virginia Revolutionary officers for land grants from the National Government, strongly resisted by Gallatin and other Republican leaders, illustrates his unfailing support of his old comrades. Notwith-

[1] See *infra*, 458 *et seq.*

[2] "Copy of a letter from a gentleman in Philadelphia, to his friend in Richmond, dated 13th March, 1800," printed in *Virginia Gazette and Petersburg Intelligencer*, April 1, 1800.

standing the Republican opposition, he was victorious by a vote of more than two to one.[1]

But Marshall voted to rebuke a petition of "free men of color" to revive the slave-trade laws, the fugitive from justice laws, and to take "such measures as shall in due course" free the slaves.[2] The debate over this resolution is important, not only as explaining the vote of Marshall, who came from Virginia and was himself a slaveholder, as were Washington and Jefferson, but also as showing the mind of the country on slavery at that particular time.

Marshall's colleague, General Lee, said that the petition "contained sentiments . . . highly improper . . . to encourage."[3] John Rutledge of South Carolina exclaimed: "They now tell the House these people are in slavery — I thank God they are! if they were not, dreadful would be the consequences. . . . Some of the states would never have adopted the Federal form of government if it had not been secured to them that Congress never would legislate on the subject of slavery."[4]

Harrison Gray Otis of Massachusetts was much disgusted by the resolution, whose signers "were incapable of writing their names or of reading the petitions"; he "thought those who did not possess that species of property [slaves] had better leave the regulation of it to those who were cursed with it." John Brown of Rhode Island "considered [slaves] as much personal property as a farm or a ship. . . .

[1] *Annals*, 6th Cong., 1st Sess., 668–69.
[2] *Ib.*, 229. [3] *Ib.*, 231. [4] *Ib.*, 230–32.

We want money; we want a navy; we ought therefore to use the means to obtain it. . . . Why should we see Great Britain getting all the slave trade to themselves; why may not our country be enriched by that lucrative traffic?"[1] Gabriel Christie of Maryland hoped the petition would "go under the table instead of upon it."[2] Mr. Jones of Georgia thought that the slaves "have been immensely benefited by coming amongst us."[3]

Finally, after two days of debate, in which the cause of freedom for the blacks was almost unsupported, Samuel Goode of Virginia moved: "That the parts of the said petition which invite Congress to legislate upon subjects from which the General Government is precluded by the Constitution have a tendency to create disquiet and jealousy, and ought therefore to receive the pointed disapprobation of this House."[4] On this motion, every member but one, including John Marshall, voted aye. George Thacher, a Congregationalist preacher from Massachusetts, alone voted nay.[5] Such, in general, and in spite of numerous humanitarian efforts against slavery, was American sentiment on that subject at the dawn of the nineteenth century.[6]

Five subjects of critical and historic importance came before the session: the Federalists' Disputed Elections Bill; the Republican attack on the pro-

[1] *Annals*, 6th Cong., 1st Sess., 233. [2] *Ib.*, 234.
[3] *Ib.*, 235. [4] *Ib.*, 240. [5] *Ib.*, 245.
[6] Concerning a similar effort in 1790, Washington wrote: "The memorial of the Quakers (and a very *malapropos* one it was) has at length been put to sleep, and will scarcely awake before the year 1808." (Washington to Stuart, March 28, 1790; *Writings:* Ford, xi, 474.)

visional army raised for the probable emergency of war with France; the Republican attack on the Executive power in the Jonathan Robins case; the Republican onslaught upon the Alien and Sedition Laws; and the National Bankruptcy Bill. In each of these Marshall took a leading and determining part.

Early in the session (January 23) the Republicans brought up the vexed question of the Sedition Law. A resolution to repeal the obnoxious section of this measure was presented on January 29, and after a hot debate was adopted by the close vote of 50 to 48. Marshall voted for the repeal and against his own party.[1] Had he voted with his party, the Republican attack would have failed. But no pressure of party regularity could influence Marshall against his convictions, no crack of the party whip could frighten him.

Considering the white heat of partisan feeling at the time, and especially on the subject of the Alien and Sedition Laws; considering, too, the fact that these offensive acts were Administration measures; and taking into account the prominence as a Federalist leader which Marshall had now achieved, his vote against the reprobated section of the Sedition Law was a supreme act of independence of political ties and party discipline. He had been and still was the only Federalist to disapprove, openly, the Alien and Sedition Laws.[2] "To make a little saving for our friend Marshall's address," Chief Justice Ells-

[1] *Annals*, 6th Cong., 1st Sess., Resolution and debate, ii, 404–19.
[2] Bassett, 260.

worth sarcastically suggested that, in case of the repeal of the Sedition Law, "the preamble . . . should read thus: 'Whereas the increasing danger and depravity of the present time require that the law against seditious practices *should be restored to its full rigor*, therefore,' etc." [1]

From the point of view of its probable effect on Marshall's political fortunes, his vote appeared to spell his destruction, for it practically left him outside of either party. He abhorred the doctrine of State Sovereignty which Jefferson now was making the rallying-point of the Republican Party; he believed, quite as fervently as had Washington himself, that the principle of Nationality alone could save the Republic. So Marshall could have no hopes of any possible future political advancement through the Republican Party.

On the other hand, his vote against his own party on its principal measure killed Marshall's future as a Federalist in the opinion of all the politicians of his time, both Federal and Republican.[2] And we may be certain that Marshall saw this even more clearly than did the politicians, just as he saw most things more clearly than most men.

But if Marshall's vote on the Sedition Law was an act of insubordination, his action on the Disputed Elections Bill was nothing short of party treason. This next to the last great blunder of the Federalists was in reality a high-handed attempt to control the coming presidential election, regardless of the

[1] Ellsworth to Pickering, Dec. 12, 1798; Flanders, ii, 193.

[2] Adams: *Gallatin*, 211. And see Federalist attacks on Marshall's answers to "Freeholder," *supra*.

votes of the people. It was aimed particularly at the anticipated Republican presidential majority in Pennsylvania which had just elected a Republican Governor over the Federalist candidate.

On January 3, Senator Ross of Pennsylvania, the defeated Federalist candidate for Governor of that State, offered a resolution that a committee should be appointed to consider a law "for deciding disputed elections of President and Vice-President . . . and . . the legality or illegality of the votes given for those officers in the different states." In a brief but pointed debate, the Republicans insisted that such a law would be unconstitutional.

The Federalist position was that, since the Constitution left open the manner of passing upon votes, Congress had the power to regulate that subject and ought to provide some method to meet anticipated emergencies. Suppose, said Senator Ross, that "persons should claim to be Electors who had never been *properly* appointed [elected], should their vote be received? Suppose they should vote for a person to be President who had not the age required by the Constitution or who had not been long enough a citizen of the United States or for two persons who were both citizens of the same State? . . . What situation would the country be in if such a case was to happen?"[1]

So lively was the interest and high the excitement that Marshall did not go to Richmond when his fifth child was born on February 13, 1800.[2] He spoke in

[1] *Annals*, 6th Cong., 1st Sess., 29.

[2] James Keith Marshall.

the House February 12, and was appointed on an important committee February 13.[1]

On February 14, the bill was reported to the Senate. Five days later the Republican organ, the "Aurora," made shift to get a copy of the measure,[2] and printed it in full with a bold but justifiable attack upon it and the method of its origin.[3] On March 28, the bill passed the Senate by a strict party vote.[4] It provided that a "Grand Committee," consisting of six Senators and six Representatives elected by ballot and the Chief Justice of the Supreme Court, should take charge of the certificates of electoral votes immediately after they had been opened and read in the presence of Congress.

This Grand Committee was to be given power to send for papers and persons and, in secret session, to consider and *determine* all questions concerning the election. Had bribery been employed, had force been used, had threats or intimidation, persuasion or cajolery polluted the voters? — the Grand Committee was to decide these questions; it was to declare what electoral votes should be counted; it was to throw out electoral votes which it thought to be tainted or improper; and the report of this Grand Committee was to be final and conclusive. In short,

[1] *Annals*, 6th Cong., 1st Sess., 520, 522.

[2] At this period the Senate still sat behind closed doors and its proceedings were secret.

[3] *Annals*, 6th Cong., 1st Sess., 105. This led to one of the most notably dramatic conflicts between the Senate and the press which has occurred during our history. For the prosecution of William Duane, editor of the *Aurora*, see *ib.*, 105, 113–19, 123–24. It was made a campaign issue, the Republicans charging that it was a Federalist plot against the freedom of the press. (See *Aurora*, March 13 and 17, 1800.)

[4] *Ib.*, 146.

it was to settle absolutely the Presidency; from its decree there was to be no appeal.[1]

On March 31, this bill reached the House. While no action was taken on it for more than two weeks, it was almost the sole topic of conversation among the members. In these cloak-room talks, Marshall, to the intense disgust and anger of the Federalist leaders, was outspoken against this attempt to seize the Presidency under the forms of a National law.

Two weeks later Marshall expressed his opinion on the floor. He thought that "some salutary mode" to guard against election frauds and to settle disputed presidential contests should be adopted; but he did not think that the Senate should appoint the chairman of the Grand Committee, and he objected especially to the finality of its authority.[2] He moved that these portions of the bill be stricken out and offered a substitute.[3]

Opposed as he was to the measure as it came from the Senate, he nevertheless was against its indefinite postponement and so voted.[4] His objections were to the autocratic and definitive power of the Grand Committee; with this cut from the measure, he was in favor of a joint committee of the House and Senate to examine into alleged election frauds and illegalities. The Senate bill was referred to a special committee of the House,[5] which reported a measure in accordance with Marshall's

[1] For a review of this astonishing bill, see McMaster, ii, 462–63, and Schouler, i, 475.

[2] *Annals*, 6th Cong., 1st Sess., 670.

[3] Marshall's substitute does not appear in the *Annals*.

[4] *Annals*, 6th Cong., 1st Sess., 674.

[5] *Ib.*, 678.

views.[1] After much debate and several roll-calls, the bill, as modified by Marshall, passed the House.[2]

Marshall's reconstruction of the Senate's Disputed Elections Bill killed that measure. It no longer served the purpose of the Federalist presidential conspiracy. By a strict party vote, the Senate disagreed with the House amendments;[3] and on the day before adjournment, the bill was finally disposed of by postponement.[4]

Thus did Marshall destroy the careful plans for his party's further control of the National Government, and increase the probability of the defeat of his friend, John Adams, and of the election of his enemy, Thomas Jefferson. Had not Marshall interfered, it seems certain that the Disputed Elections Bill would have become a law. If it had been enacted, Jefferson's election would have been impossible. Once again, as we shall see, Marshall is to save the political life of his great and remorseless antagonist.

Yet Jefferson had no words of praise for Marshall. He merely remarks that "the bill . . . has undergone much revolution. Marshall made a dexterous manœuver; he declares against the constitutionality of the Senate's bill, and proposes that the right of decision of their grand committee should be controllable by the *concurrent* vote of the two houses of congress; but to stand good if not rejected by a concurrent vote. You will readily estimate the amount of this sort of controul." [5]

[1] *Annals*, 6th Cong., 1st Sess., 691–92. [2] *Ib.*, 687–710.
[3] *Ib.*, 179. [4] *Ib.*, 182.
[5] Jefferson to Livingston, April 30, 1800; *Works*: Ford, ix, 132.

The party leaders labored hard and long with Marshall while the Disputed Elections Bill was before the House. Speaker Sedgwick thus describes the Federalist plot and the paralyzing effect of Marshall's private conversations with his fellow members: "Looking forward to the ensuing election," writes the disgusted Speaker, "it was deemed indispensable to prescribe a mode for canvassing the votes, provided there should be a dispute. There being no law in the state [Pennsylvania], the governor had declined, and the jacobins [Republicans] propagated the report . . . that he would return their votes. A bill was brought into the Senate & passed, wisely & effectually providing against the evil, by the constitution of a committee with ultimate powers of decision.

"Mr. Marshall in the first place called in question the constitutional powers of the legislature to delegate such authority to a Committee. On this question I had a long conversation with him, & he finally confessed himself (for there is not a more candid man on earth) to be convinced.

"He then resorted to another ground of opposition. He said the people having authorized the members to decide, personally, all disputes relative to those elections, altho' the power was not indelegable, yet he thought, in its nature, it was too delicate to be delegated, until experience had demonstrated that great inconveniences would attend its exercise by the Legislature; altho' he had no doubt such would be the result of the attempt.

"This objection is so attenuated and unsubstantial as to be hardly perceivable by a mind so merely practical as mine. He finally was convinced that it was so and abandoned it.

"In the mean time, however, he had dwelt so much, in conversation, on these subjects that he had dissipated our majority, and it never could again be compacted. The consequence was that the bill was lost." [1]

Marshall's most notable performance while in Congress was his effort in the celebrated Jonathan Robins case — "a speech," declares that capable and cautious critic, Henry Adams, "that still stands without a parallel in our Congressional debates." [2] In 1797 the crew of the British ship Hermione mutinied, murdered their officers, took the ship to a Spanish port, and sold it. One of the murderers was Thomas Nash, a British subject. Two years later, Nash turned up at Charleston, South Carolina, as the member of a crew of an American schooner.

On the request of the British Consul, Nash was seized and held in jail under the twenty-seventh article of the Jay Treaty. Nash swore that he was not a British subject, but an American citizen, Jonathan Robins, born in Danbury, Connecticut, and impressed by a British man-of-war. On overwhelming evidence, uncontradicted except by Nash, that the accused man was a British subject and a murderer, President Adams requested Judge Bee, of the United States District Court of South Carolina, to

[1] Sedgwick to King, May 11, 1800; King, iii, 237–38.
[2] Adams: *Gallatin*, 232.

deliver Nash to the British Consul pursuant to the article of the treaty requiring the delivery.[1]

Here was, indeed, a campaign issue. The land rang with Republican denunciation of the President. What servile truckling to Great Britain! Nay, more, what a crime against the Constitution! Think of it! An innocent American citizen delivered over to British cruelty. Where now were our free institutions? When President Adams thus surrendered the Connecticut "Yankee," Robins, he not only prostituted patriotism, showed himself a tool of British tyranny, but also usurped the functions of the courts and struck a fatal blow at the Constitution. So shouted Republican orators and with immense popular effect.

The fires kindled by the Alien and Sedition Laws did not heat to greater fervency the public imagination. Here was a case personal and concrete, flaming with color, full of human appeal. Jefferson took quick party advantage of the incident. "I think," wrote he, "no circumstance since the establishment of our government has affected the popular mind more. I learn that in Pennsylvania it had a great effect. I have no doubt the piece you inclosed will run through all the republican papers, & carry the question home to every man's mind." [2]

"It is enough to call a man an *Irishman*, to make it *no murder* to pervert the law of nations and to degrade national honor and character. . . . Look at what has been done in the case of *Jonathan*

[1] United States *vs*. Nash *alias* Robins, Bee's *Reports*, 266.

[2] Jefferson to Charles Pinckney, Oct. 29, 1799; *Works:* Ford, ix, 87.

Robbins," [*sic*] exclaimed the "Aurora." "A British lieutenant who never saw him until he was prisoner at Charleston swears his name is Thomas Nash." So "The man is hanged!" [1]

For the purposes of the coming presidential campaign, therefore, the Robins affair was made the principal subject of Republican congressional attack on the Administration. On February 4, the House requested the President to transmit all the papers in the case. He complied immediately.[2] The official documents proved beyond a doubt that the executed sailor had not been an American citizen, but a subject of the British King and that he had committed murder while on board a British vessel on the high seas.

The selectmen of Danbury, Connecticut, certified that no such person as Jonathan Robins nor any family of the name of Robins ever had lived in that town. So did the town clerk. On the contrary, a British naval officer, who knew Nash well, identified him.[3]

Bayard, for the Federalists, took the aggressive and offered a resolution to the effect that the President's conduct in the Robins case "was conformable to the duty of the Government and to . . . the 27th article of the Treaty . . . with Great Britain." [4]

Forced to abandon their public charge that the Administration had surrendered an innocent Ameri-

[1] *Aurora*, Feb. 12, 1800. [2] *Annals*, 6th Cong., 1st Sess., 511.

[3] *Ib.*, 515–18. Nash himself confessed before his execution that he was a British subject as claimed by the British authorities and as shown by the books of the ship Hermione.

[4] *Ib.*, 526.

can citizen to British cruelty,[1] the Republicans based their formal assault in Congress upon the ground that the President had disobeyed the laws, disregarded the Constitution, and taken upon himself the discharge of duties and functions which belonged exclusively to the courts. They contended that, even if Nash were guilty, even if he were not an American citizen, he should, nevertheless, have been tried by a jury and sentenced by a court.

On February 20, Livingston of New York offered the Republican resolutions to this effect. Not only was the President's conduct in this serious business a "dangerous interference of the Executive with judicial decisions," declared the resolution, but the action of the court in granting the President's request was "a sacrifice of the Constitutional independence of the judicial power and exposes the administration thereof to suspicion and reproach." [2]

The House decided to consider the Livingston resolutions rather than those offered by Bayard, the Federalists to a man supporting this method of meeting the Republicans on the ground which the latter, themselves, had chosen. Thus the question of constitutional power in the execution of treaties came squarely before the House, and the great debate was on.[3] For two weeks this notable discussion continued. The first day was frittered away on questions of order.

The next day the Republicans sought for delay[4]

[1] The Republicans, however, still continued to urge this falsehood before the people and it was generally believed to be true.

[2] *Annals*, 6th Congress, 1st Sess., 532–33.

[3] *Ib.*, 541–47. [4] *Ib.*, 548.

— there were not sufficient facts before the House, they said, to justify that body in passing upon so grave a question. The third day the Republicans proposed that the House should request the President to secure and transmit the proceedings before the South Carolina Federal Court on the ground that the House could not determine the matter until it had the court proceedings.[1]

Marshall's patience was exhausted. He thought this procrastinating maneuver a Republican trick to keep the whole matter open until after the coming presidential campaign,[2] and he spoke his mind sharply to the House.

"Let gentlemen recollect the nature of the case," exclaimed Marshall; "the President of the United States is charged by this House with having violated the Constitution and laws of his country, by having committed an act of dangerous interference with a judicial decision — he is so charged by a member of this House. Gentlemen were well aware how much the public safety and happiness depended on a well or a misplaced confidence in the Executive.

"Was it reasonable or right," he asked, "to receive this charge — to receive in part the evidence in support of it — to receive so much evidence as almost every gentleman declared himself satisfied with, and to leave the charge unexamined, hanging over the head of the President of the United States . . . how long it was impossible to say, but certainly long enough to work a very bad effect? To him it

[1] *Annals*, 6th Cong., 1st Sess., 558.

[2] This, in fact, was the case.

seemed of all things the most unreasonable and unjust; and the mischief resulting therefrom must be very great indeed."

The House ought to consider the evidence it already had; if, on such examination, it appeared that more was needed, the matter could then be postponed. And, in any event, why ask the President to send for the court proceedings? The House had as much power to procure the papers as the President had. "Was he [the President] to be a *menial* to the House in a business wherein himself was seriously charged?"[1]

Marshall was aroused. To his brother he thus denounces the tactics of the Republicans: "Every stratagem seems to be used to give to this business an undue impression. On the motion to send for the evidence from the records of South Carolina altho' it was stated & prov'd that this would amount to an abandonment of the enquiry during the present session & to an abandonment under circumstances which would impress the public mind with the opinion that we really believed Mr. Livingston's resolutions maintainable; & that the record could furnish no satisfaction since it could not contain the parol testimony offered to the Judge & further that it could not be material to the President but only to the reputation of the Judge what the amount of the testimony was, yet the debate took a turn as if we were precipitating a decision without enquiry & without evidence."[2]

[1] *Annals*, 6th Cong., 1st Sess., 565.
[2] Marshall to James M. Marshall, Feb. 28, 1800; MS.

This Republican resolution was defeated. So was another by Gallatin asking for the papers in the case of William Brigstock, which the Republicans claimed was similar to that of Jonathan Robins. Finally the main question came on. For two hours Gallatin made an ingenious argument in support of the Livingston resolutions.[1]

The next day, March 7, Marshall took the floor and made the decisive speech which put a period to this partisan controversy. He had carefully revised his argument,[2] and it is to this prevision, so unlike Marshall's usual methods, that we owe the perfection of the reporter's excellent transcript of his performance. This great address not only ended the Republican attack upon the Administration, but settled American law as to Executive power in carrying out extradition treaties. Marshall's argument was a mingling of impressive oratory and judicial finality. It had in it the fire of the debater and the calmness of the judge.

It is the highest of Marshall's efforts as a public speaker. For many decades it continued to be published in books containing the masterpieces of American oratory as one of the best examples of the art.[3] It is a landmark in Marshall's career and a monument in the development of the law of the land. They go far who assert that Marshall's address is

[1] *Annals*, 6th Cong., 1st Sess., 595–96.

[2] Pickering to James Winchester, March 17, 1800; Pickering MSS., Mass. Hist. Soc. Also Binney, in Dillon, iii, 312.

[3] See Moore: *American Eloquence*, ii, 20–23. The speech also appears in full in *Annals*, 6th Cong., 1st Sess., 596–619; in Benton: *Abridgment of the Debates of Congress;* in Bee's *Reports*, 266; and in the Appendix to Wharton: *State Trials*, 443.

a greater performance than any of the speeches of Webster, Clay, Sumner, or other American orators of the first class; and yet so perfect is this speech that the commendation is not extreme.

The success of a democratic government, said Marshall, depended not only on its right administration, but also on the public's right understanding of its measures; public opinion must be "rescued from those numerous prejudices which . . . surround it." Bayard and others had so ably defended the Administration's course that he would only "reëstablish" and "confirm" what they had so well said.

Marshall read the section of the Jay Treaty under which the President acted: This provided, said he, that a murderer of either nation, fleeing for "asylum" to the other, when charged with the crime, and his delivery demanded on such proof as would justify his seizure under local laws if the murder had been committed in that jurisdiction, must be surrendered to the aggrieved nation. Thus Great Britain had required Thomas Nash at the hands of the American Government. He had committed murder on a British ship and escaped to America.

Was this criminal deed done in British jurisdiction? Yes; for "the jurisdiction of a nation extends to the whole of its territory, and to its own citizens in every part of the world. . . . The nature of civil union" involves the "principle" that "the laws of a nation are rightfully obligatory on its own citizens in every situation where those laws are really extended to them."

This "is particularly recognized with respect to the fleets of a nation on the high seas." By "the opinion of the world . . . a fleet at sea is within the jurisdiction of the nation to which it belongs," and crimes there committed are punishable by that nation's laws. This is not contradicted by the right of search for contraband, as Gallatin had contended, for "in the sea itself no nation has any jurisdiction," and a belligerent has a right to prevent aid being carried to its enemy. But, as to its crew, every ship carried the law of its flag.

Marshall denied that the United States had jurisdiction, concurrent or otherwise, over the place of the murder; "on the contrary, no nation has any jurisdiction at sea but over its own citizens or vessels or offenses against itself." Such "jurisdiction . . . is personal, reaching its own citizens only"; therefore American authority "cannot extend to a murder committed by a British sailor on board a British frigate navigating the high seas." There is no such thing as "common [international] jurisdiction" at sea, said Marshall; and he exhaustively illustrated this principle by hypothetical cases of contract, dueling, theft, etc., upon the ocean. "A common jurisdiction . . . at sea . . . would involve the power of punishing the offenses . . . stated." Piracy was the one exception, because "against all and every nation . . . and therefore punishable by all alike." For "a pirate . . . is an enemy of the human race."

Any nation, however, may by statute declare an act to be piratical which is not so by the law of nations; and such an act is punishable only by that particular state and not by other governments. But an act universally recognized as criminal, such as robbery, murder, and the like, "is an offense against the community of nations."

The Republican contention was that murder and robbery (seizure of ships) constituted piracy "by the law of nations," and that, therefore, Nash should have been indicted and tried by American authority as a pirate; whereas he had been delivered to Great Britain as a criminal against that nation.

But, said Marshall, a single act does not necessarily indicate piratical intent unless it "manifests general hostility against the world"; if it shows an "intention to rob generally, then it is piracy." If, however, "it be merely mutiny and murder in a vessel with the intention of delivering it up to the enemy, it" is "an offense against a single nation and not piracy." It was only for such murder and "not piracy" that "Nash was delivered." And, indisputably, this was covered by the treaty. Even if Nash had been tried and acquitted for piracy, there still would have remained the crime of murder over which American courts had no jurisdiction, because it was not a crime punishable by international law, but only by the law of the nation in whose jurisdiction the crime was committed, and to which the criminal belonged.

American law and American courts could not deal with such a condition, insisted Marshall, but British law and courts could and the treaty bound America to deliver the criminal into British hands. "It was an act to which the American Nation was bound by a most solemn compact." For an American court to have convicted Nash and American authorities to have executed him "would have been murder"; while for them to have "acquitted and discharged him would have been a breach of faith and a violation of national duty."

It was plain, then, said he, that Nash should have been delivered to the British officers. By whom? The Republicans insisted that this authority was in the courts. Marshall demonstrated that the President alone could exercise such power. It was, he said, "a case for Executive and not for judicial decision." The Republican resolutions declared that the judicial power extends to *all* questions arising under the Constitution, treaties, and laws of the United States; but the Constitution itself provided that the judicial power extends only to all cases "*in law and equity*" arising under the Constitution, laws, and treaties of the United States.

"The difference was material and apparent," said Marshall. "A case in law or equity was a term well understood and of limited signification. It was a controversy between parties which had taken a shape for judicial decision. If the judicial power extended to every question under the Constitution, it would involve almost every subject proper for Legislative discussion and decision; if to every question under the laws and treaties of the United States, it would involve almost every subject on which the Executive could act. The division of power . . . could exist no longer, and the other departments would be swallowed up in the Judiciary."

The Constitution did not confer on the Judiciary "any political power whatever." The judicial power covered only cases where there are "parties to come into court, who can be reached by its process and bound by its power; whose rights admit of ultimate decision by a tribunal to which they are bound to submit." Such a case, said Marshall, "may arise under a treaty where the rights of individuals acquired or secured by a treaty are to be asserted or defended in court"; and he gave examples. "But the judicial power cannot extend to political compacts; as the establishment of the boundary line between American and British Dominions . . . or the case of the delivery of a murderer under the twenty-seventh article of our present Treaty with Britain. . . .

"The clause of the Constitution which declares that 'the trial of all crimes . . . shall be by jury'" did not apply to the decision of a case like that of Robins. "Certainly this clause . . . cannot be thought obligatory on . . . the whole world. It is not designed to secure the rights of the people of Europe or Asia or to direct and control proceedings against criminals throughout the universe. It can, then, be designed only to guide the proceedings of our own courts" in cases "to which the jurisdiction of the nation may rightfully extend." And the courts could not "try the crime for which Thomas Nash was delivered up to justice." The sole question was "whether he should be delivered up to a foreign tribunal which was alone capable of trying and punishing him." A provision for the trial of crimes in the courts of the United States is clearly "not a provision for the surrender to a foreign Government of an offender against that Government."

If the murder by Nash were a crime, it is one "not provided for by the Constitution"; if it were not a crime, "yet it is the precise case in which his surrender was stipulated by treaty" which the President, alone, must execute. That in the Executive decision "judicial questions" must also be determined, argued nothing; for this often must be the case, as, for instance, in so simple and ordinary matter as issuing patents for public lands, or in settling whether vessels have been captured within three miles of our coasts, or in declaring the legality of prizes taken by privateers or the restoration of such vessels — all such questions, of which these are familiar examples, are, said Marshall, "questions of political law proper to be decided by the Executive and not by the courts."

This was the Nash case. Suppose that a murder were "committed within the United States and the murderer should seek an asylum in Great Britain!" The treaty covered such a case; but no man would say "that the British courts should decide" it. It is, in its nature, a National demand made upon the Nation. The parties are two nations. They cannot come into court to litigate their claims, nor can a court decide on them. "Of consequence," declares Marshall, "the demand is not a case for judicial cognizance."

"The President is the sole organ of the nation in its external relations"; therefore "the demand of a foreign nation can only be made on him. He possesses the whole Executive power. He holds and directs the force of the nation. Of consequence, any act to be performed by the force of the nation is to be performed through him. He is charged to execute the laws. A treaty is . . . a law. He must, then, execute a treaty, where he, and he alone, possesses the means of executing it."

This, in rough outline, is Marshall's historic speech which helped to direct a new nation, groping blindly and with infinite clamoring, to a straight and safe pathway. Pickering immediately reported to Hamilton: "Mr. Marshall delivered a very luminous argument on the case, placing the 27th article of the treaty in a clear point of view and giving constructions on the questions arising out of it perfectly satisfactory, but, as it would seem, wholly unthought of when the meaning of the article was heretofore considered. His argument will, I hope, be fully and correctly published; it illustrates an important national question."[1]

The Republicans were discomfited; but they were not without the power to sting. Though Marshall had silenced them in Congress, the Republican press kept up the attack. "*Mr. Marshall* made an ingenious and *specious* defence of the administration, in relation to executive interference in the case of *Robbins*," [*sic*] says the "Aurora," "but he was compelled to admit, what certainly implicates both the President and Judge Bee. . . . He admitted that an American seaman was justifiable, in rescuing him-

[1] Pickering to Hamilton, March 10, 1800; Pickering MSS., Mass. Hist. Soc.

self from impressment, to put to death those who kept him in durance. . . . Robbins [*sic*] claimed to be an American citizen, and asserted upon his oath, that he had been impressed and yet his claim was not examined into by the Judge, neither did the President *advise* and *request* that this should be a subject of enquiry. The enquiry into his citizenship was made *after* his surrender and execution, and the evidence exhibited has a very suspicious aspect. . . . Town clerks may be found to certify to anything that Timothy Pickering shall desire." [1] Nevertheless, even the "Aurora" could not resist an indirect tribute to Marshall, though paying it by way of a sneer at Samuel W. Dana of Connecticut, who ineffectually followed him.

"In the debate on *Mr. Livingston's* resolutions, on Friday last," says the "Aurora," "Mr. Marshall made, in the minds of some people, a very satisfactory defense of the conduct of the *President* and *Judge Bee* in the case of *Jonathan Robbins* [*sic*]. Mr. Dana, however, thought the subject exhausted, and very *modestly* (who does not know his *modesty*) resolved with his inward man to shed a few more rays of light on the subject; a federal judge, much admired for his wit and humour, happened to be present, when Mr. Dana began his flourishes.

"The judge thought the seal of conviction had been put upon the case by Mr. Marshall, and discovered symptoms of uneasiness when our little Connecticut Cicero displayed himself to catch Mr. Speaker's vacant eye — 'Sir,' said the wit to a bye-

[1] *Aurora*, March 10, 1800.

stander, 'what can induce that man to rise, he is nothing but a shakebag, and can only shake out the ideas that have been put into the members' heads by Mr. Marshall.'"[1]

Marshall's argument was conclusive. It is one of the few speeches ever delivered in Congress that actually changed votes from one party to the other in a straight-out party fight. Justice Story says that Marshall's speech "is one of the most consummate juridical arguments which was ever pronounced in the halls of legislation; . . . equally remarkable for the lucid order of its topics, the profoundness of its logic, the extent of its research,[2] and the force of its illustrations. It may be said of that speech . . . that it was '*Réponse sans réplique*,' an answer so irresistible that it admitted of no reply. It silenced opposition and settled then and forever the points of international law on which the controversy hinged. . . . An unequivocal demonstration of public opinion followed. The denunciations of the Executive, which had hitherto been harsh and clamorous everywhere throughout the land, sunk away at once into cold and cautious whispers only of disapprobation.

"Whoever reads that speech, even at this distance of time, when the topics have lost much of their interest, will be struck with the prodigious

[1] *Aurora*, March 14, 1800.

[2] Marshall's speech on the Robins case shows some study, but not so much as the florid encomium of Story indicates. The speeches of Bayard, Gallatin, Nicholas, and others display evidence of much more research than that of Marshall, who briefly refers to only two authorities.

powers of analysis and reasoning which it displays, and which are enhanced by the consideration that the whole subject was then confessedly new in many of its aspects." [1]

The Republican leaders found their own members declaring themselves convinced by Marshall's demonstration and announcing their intentions of voting with the Administration. Gallatin, Livingston, and Randolph had hard work to hold their followers in line. Even the strongest efforts of these resourceful men would not rally all of their shattered forces. Many Republican members ignored the pleadings of their leaders and supported Marshall's position.

This is not to be wondered at, for Marshall had convinced even Gallatin himself. This gifted native of Switzerland was the Republican leader of the House. Unusually well-educated, perfectly upright, thorough in his industry, and careful in his thinking, Gallatin is the most admirable of all the characters attracted to the Republican ranks. He had made the most effective argument on the anti-Administration side in the debate over the Livingston resolutions, and had been chosen to answer Marshall's speech. He took a place near Marshall and began making notes for his reply; but soon he put his pencil and paper aside and became absorbed in Marshall's reasoning. After a while he arose, went to the space back of the seats, and paced up and down while Marshall proceeded.

When the Virginian closed, Gallatin did not come

[1] Story, in Dillon, iii, 357–58.

forward to answer him as his fellow partisans had expected. His Republican colleagues crowded around the brilliant little Pennsylvania Swiss and pleaded with him to answer Marshall's speech without delay. But Gallatin would not do it. "Answer it yourself," exclaimed the Republican leader in his quaint foreign accent; "for my part, I think it unan*swer*able," laying the accent on the *swer*.[1]

Nicholas of Virginia then tried to reply, but made no impression; Dana spoke to no better purpose, and the House ended the discussion by a vote which was admitted to be a distinctively personal triumph for Marshall. The Republican resolutions were defeated by 61 to 35, in a House where the parties were nearly equal in numbers.[2]

For once even Jefferson could not withhold his applause for Marshall's ability. "Livingston, Nicholas & Gallatin distinguished themselves on one side & J. Marshall greatly on the other," he writes in his curt account of the debate and its result.[3] And this grudging tribute of the Republican chieftain is higher praise of Marshall's efforts than the flood of eulogy which poured in upon him; Jefferson's virulence toward an enemy, and especially toward Marshall, was such that he could not see, except on rare occasions, and this was one, any merit whatever in an opponent, much less express it.

[1] Grigsby, i, 177; Adams: *Gallatin*, 232.

[2] *Annals*, 6th Cong., 1st Sess., 619.

[3] Jefferson to Madison, March 8, 1800; *Works:* Ford, ix, 121. In sending the speeches on both sides to his brother, Levin Powell, a Virginia Federalist Representative, says: "When you get to Marshall's it will be worth a perusal." (Levin Powell to Major Burr Powell, March 26, 1800; *Branch Historical Papers*, ii, 241.)

Marshall's defense of the army law was scarcely less powerful than his speech in the Robins case; and it reveals much more clearly Marshall's distinctively military temper of mind.

Congress had scarcely organized when the question came up of the reduction of the army. On this there was extended debate. Nicholas of Virginia offered a resolution to repeal the act for the provisional army of which Washington had been the Commander-in-Chief. The expense of this military establishment greatly alarmed Nicholas, who presented an array of figures on which his anxieties fed.[1] It was nonsense, he held, to keep this army law on the statute books for its effect on the negotiations with France.

Marshall promptly answered. "If it was true," said he, "that America, commencing her negotiation with her present military force would appear in the armor which she could only wear for a day, the situation of our country was lamentable indeed. If our debility was really such . . . our situation was truly desperate." There was "no cheaper mode of self-defense"; to abandon it "amounted to a declaration that we were unable to defend ourselves." It was not necessary to repeal the law entirely or to put it, "not modified," in full effect. Marshall suggested a middle ground by which "the law might be modified so as to diminish the estimated expense, without dismissing the troops already in actual service."[2]

Answering the favorite argument made by the opponents of the army, that no power can invade

[1] *Annals*, 6th Cong., 1st Sess., 247–50. [2] *Ib.*, 252.

America, he asked: "What assurance have gentlemen that invasion is impracticable?" Who knows the real conditions in Europe? — the "effect of the late decisive victories of France? . . . It was by no means certain" that these had not resulted in the release of forces which she "may send across the Atlantic."

Why be precipitate? asked Marshall; by the opening of the next campaign in Europe we should have more information. Let us look the situation in the face: "We are, in fact, at war with France, though it is not declared in form"; commerce is suspended; naval battles are being fought; property is "captured and confiscated"; prisoners are taken and incarcerated. America is of "vast importance to France"; indeed, "the monopoly of our commerce in time of peace" is invaluable to both France and England "for the formation of a naval power."

The Republicans, he said, had "urged not only that the army is useless," but that we could not afford the expense of maintaining it. "Suppose this had been the language of '75!" exclaimed Marshall. "Suppose a gentleman had risen on the floor of Congress, to compare our revenues with our expenses— what would have been the result of the calculation?" It would have shown that we could not afford to strike for our independence! Yet we did strike and successfully. "If vast exertions were then made to acquire independence, will not the same exertions be now made to maintain it?"

The question was, "whether self-government and national liberty be worth the money which must be expended to preserve them?"[1] He exposed the sophistry of an expensive economy. It should never be forgotten that true economy did not content itself with inquiring into the mere saving of the present moment; it should take an enlarged view of the subject, and determine, on correct calculations, whether the consequence of a present saving might not be a much more considerable future expenditure.

Marshall admitted that the reduction of the army would certainly diminish the expense of the present year, but contended that the present saving would bear no proportion to the immense waste of blood, as well as treasure, which it might occasion.[2] "And consider," he exclaimed, "the effect the army already had produced on the mind and conduct of France. While America was humbly supplicating for peace, and that her complaints might be heard, France spurned her contemptuously and refused to enter on a discussion of differences, unless that discussion was preceded by a substantial surrender of the essential attributes of independence."

"America was at length goaded into resistance," asserted Marshall, "and resolved on the system of defense, of which the army now sought to be disbanded forms a part." What was the result? "Immediately the tone of France was changed, and she consented to treat us as an independent nation. Her depredations indeed did not cease; she continued still to bring war upon us; but although peace was not granted, the door to peace was opened."

If "a French army should be crossing the Atlantic

[1] *Annals*, 6th Cong., 1st Sess., 253–54. [2] *Ib.*

to invade our territory," would anybody insist on disbanding our army? "Was it wise, then, to do so while such a probability existed?" In a few months we should know; and, if danger should disappear, "the army expires by the law which gave it being." Meantime the expense would be trifling.[1]

In a private letter Marshall states, with even more balance, his views of the conflicting questions of the expense involved in, and the necessity for, military equipment. He regrets that a loan is "absolutely unavoidable"; but "attention must be paid to our defenses": —

"The whole world is in arms and no rights are respected but those that [are] maintained by force. In such a state of things we dare not be totally unmindful of ourselves or totally neglectful of that military position to which, in spite of the prudence and pacific disposition of our government, we may be driven for the preservation of our liberty and national independence.

"Altho' we ought never to make a loan if it be avoidable, yet when forc'd to it much real consolation is to be deriv'd from the future resources of America. These resources, if we do not throw them away [by] dissolving the union, are invaluable. It is not to be doubted that in twenty years from this time the United States would be less burthen'd by a revenue of twenty millions than now by a revenue of ten. It is the plain & certain consequence of our increasing population & our increasing wealth. . . .

"The system of defence which has rendered this

[1] *Annals*, 6th Cong., 1st Sess., 254, 255.

measure necessary was not [only] essential to our character as an independent nation, but it has actually sav'd more money to the body of the people than has been expended & has very probably prevented either open war or such national degradation as would make us the objects of general contempt and injury.

"A bill to stop recruiting in the twelve additional regiments has been brought in and will pass without opposition. An attempt was made absolutely to disband them, but [it] was negativ'd. It has been so plainly prov'd to us that french aggression has been greatly increased, & that their contemptuous refusal even to treat with us as an independent nation has been entirely occasioned by a belief that we could not resist them; & it is so clear that their present willingness to treat is occasioned by perceiving our determination to defend ourselves, that it was thought unwise to change materially our system at the commencement of negotiation.

"In addition to this it had much weight, that we should know in a few months the facts of our negotiation & should then be able to judge whether the situation & temper of France rendered an invasion pro[bable]. Then would be the time to decide on diminishing [or] augmenting our military forces. A French 64 has it is said arrived in the west indies & three frigates expected."[1]

Although the debate dragged on and the army

[1] Marshall to Dabney, Jan. 20, 1800; MS. Colonel Charles Dabney of Virginia was commander of "Dabney's Legion" in the Revolution. He was an ardent Federalist and a close personal and political friend of Marshall.

was attacked and defended with brilliant ability, Marshall's argument remained the Gibraltar of the Administration, upon which all the assaults of the Republicans were centered unavailingly. For his army speech was never answered. Only once more during this debate did Marshall rise and then but briefly, to bring his common sense to bear upon the familiar contention that, if the country is in danger, its citizens will rise spontaneously to defend it. He said that it would be absurd to call men to arms, as had been done, and then "dismiss them before the service was performed . . . merely because their zeal could be depended on" hereafter. He "hoped the national spirit would never yield to that false policy."[1]

The fourth important subject in which Marshall was a decisive influence was the National Bankruptcy Law, passed at this session of Congress. He was the second member of the committee that drafted this legislation.[2] For an entire month the committee worked on the bill and reported it on January 6, 1800.[3] After much debate, which is not given in the official reports, the bill passed the House on February 21 and the Senate March 28.[4]

While the "Annals" do not show it, we know from the testimony of the Speaker of the House that Marshall was the vital force that shaped this first National Bankruptcy Act. He was insistent that the law should not be too extensive in its provisions for the curing of bankruptcy, and it was he who

[1] *Annals*, 6th Cong., 1st Sess., 395–96. [2] *Ib.*, 191.
[3] *Ib.*, 247. [4] *Ib.*, 126; see law as passed, 1452–71.

secured the trial by jury as to the fact of bankruptcy.

"It [the Bankruptcy Law] is far from being such an one as I wished," writes Sedgwick. "The *acts* in curing bankruptcy are too restricted, and the trial of the question Bankrupt or not, by jury, will be found inconvenient, embarrassing & dilatory. The mischief was occasioned by Virginia Theory. It was the whim of General Marshall; with him a *sine qua non* of assent to the measure, & without him the bill must have been lost, for it passed the House by my casting vote."

"Besides the bankrupt bill, we have passed [only] one more of great importance," writes the Speaker of the House in a review of the work of the session.[1] Much of the Speaker's summary is devoted to Marshall. Sedgwick was greatly disappointed with the laws passed, with the exception of the Bankruptcy Bill "and one other."[2] "All the rest we have made here are, as to any permanently beneficial effects, hardly worth the parchment on which they are written. The reason of this feebleness is a real feebleness of character in the house." Sedg-

[1] Sedgwick to King, May 11, 1800; King, iii, 236.

[2] The act requiring the Secretary of the Treasury to lay before Congress at each session a report of financial conditions with his recommendations. (*Annals*, 6th Cong., 1st Sess., Appendix, 1523.) The Speaker thought this law important because it "will give splendor to the officer [Secretary of the Treasury] and respectability to the Executive Department of the Govt." (Sedgwick to King, *supra.*) Yet the session passed several very important laws, among them the act accepting the cession of the Western Reserve (*Annals*, 6th Cong., 1st Sess., Appendix, 1495–98) and the act prohibiting American citizens "or other persons residing within the United States" to engage in the slave trade between foreign countries (*ib.*, 1511–14.)

wick lays most of this at Marshall's door, and in doing so, draws a vivid picture of Marshall the man, as well as of Marshall the legislator: —

"Marshall was looked up to as the man whose great and commanding genius was to enlighten & direct the national councils. This was the general sentiment, while some, and those of no inconsiderable importance, calculating on his foolish declaration, relative to the alien & sedition laws, thought him temporizing while others deemed him feeble.

"None had in my opinion justly appreciated his character. As his character has stamped itself on the measures of the present session, I am desirous of letting you know how I view it.

"He is a man of a very affectionate disposition, of great simplicity of manners and honest & honorable in all his conduct.

"He is attached to pleasures, with convivial habits strongly fixed.

"He is indolent, therefore; and indisposed to take part in the common business of the house.

"He has a strong attachment to popularity but indisposed to sacrifice to it his integrity; hence it is that he is disposed on all popular subjects to feel the public pulse and hence results indecision and *an expression* of doubt.

"Doubts suggested by him create in more feeble minds those which are irremovable. He is disposed . . . to express great respect for the sovereign people, and to quote their opinions as an evidence of truth.

"The latter is of all things the most destructive

of personal independence & of that weight of character which a great man ought to possess.

"This gentleman, when aroused, has strong reasoning powers; they are almost unequalled. But before they are excited, he has frequently, nearly, destroyed any impression from them." [1]

Such was Marshall's work during his six months' service in Congress, the impression he made, and the estimate of him by his party friends. His "convivial habits, strongly fixed," his great good nature, his personal lovableness, were noted by his associates in the National House of Representatives quite as much as they had been observed and commented on by his fellow members in the Virginia Legislature and by his friends and neighbors in Richmond.

The public qualities which his work in Congress again revealed in brilliant light were his extraordinary independence of thought and action, his utter fearlessness, and his commanding mental power. But his personal character and daily manners applied a soothing ointment to any irritation which his official attitude and conduct on public questions created in the feelings of his associates.

So came the day of adjournment of Congress; and with it the next step which Fate had arranged for John Marshall.

[1] Sedgwick to King, May 11, 1800; King, iii, 237.

CHAPTER XII

CHIEF JUSTICE OF THE UNITED STATES

I consider General Marshall as more than a secretary — as a state conservator. (Oliver Wolcott.)

To Mr. Jefferson I have felt insuperable objections. The morals of the author of the letter to Mazzei cannot be pure. (Marshall.)

You have given an opinion in exact conformity with the wishes of your party. Come forward and defend it. (George Hay to Marshall.)

"THE P. requests Mr. McHenry's company for one minute," wrote President Adams to his Secretary of War on the morning of May 5, 1800.[1] The unsuspicious McHenry at once responded. The President mentioned an unimportant departmental matter; and then, suddenly flying into a rage, abused his astounded Cabinet adviser in "outrageous"[2] fashion and finally demanded his resignation.[3] The meek McHenry resigned. To the place thus made vacant, the harried President, without even consulting him, immediately appointed Marshall, who "as immediately declined."[4] Then Adams tendered the office to Dexter, who accepted.

And resign, too, demanded Adams of his Secretary

[1] Adams to McHenry, May 5, 1800; Steiner, 453.

[2] McHenry to John McHenry, May 20, 1800; Gibbs, ii, 348.

[3] According to McHenry, Adams's complaints were that the Secretary of War had opposed the sending of the second mission to France, had not appointed as captain a North Carolina elector who had voted for Adams, had "EULOGIZED GENERAL WASHINGTON . . . attempted to praise Hamilton," etc. (McHenry to John McHenry, May 20, 1800; Gibbs, ii, 348; and see Hamilton's "Public Conduct, etc., of John Adams"; Hamilton: *Works:* Lodge, vii, 347–49.)

[4] Gore to King, May 14, 1800; King, iii, 242–43; also Sedgwick to Hamilton, May 7, 1800; *Works:* Hamilton, vi, 437–38.

of State.[1] The doughty Pickering refused[2] — "I did not incline to accept this insidious favor,"[3] he reported to Hamilton. Adams dismissed him.[4] Again the President turned to Marshall, who, deeply troubled, considered the offer. The Federalist Cabinet was broken to pieces, and a presidential election was at hand which would settle the fate of the first great political party in American history.

The campaign had already started. The political outlook was dark enough before the President's outburst; this shattering of his Cabinet was a wicked tongue of lightning from the threatening clouds which, after the flash, made them blacker still.[5]

Few Presidents have ever faced a more difficult party condition than did John Adams when, by a humiliating majority of only three votes, he was elected in 1796. He succeeded Washington; the ruling Federalist politicians looked to Hamilton as their party chieftain; even Adams's Cabinet, inherited from Washington, was personally unfriendly to the President and considered the imperious New York statesman as their supreme and real commander. "I had all the officers and half the crew always ready to throw me overboard," accurately declared Adams some years later.[6]

Adams's temperament was the opposite of Washington's, to which the Federalist leaders had so long

[1] Adams to Pickering, May 10, 1800; *Works:* Adams, ix, 53.
[2] Pickering to Adams, May 11, 1800; *ib.*, 54.
[3] Pickering to Hamilton, May 15, 1800; *Works:* Hamilton, vi, 443.
[4] Adams to Pickering, May 12, 1800; *Works:* Adams, ix, 55.
[5] Sedgwick to Hamilton, May 13, 1800; *Works:* Hamilton, vi, 442.
[6] Adams to Rush, March 4, 1809; *Old Family Letters*, 219.

been accustomed that the change exasperated them.[1] From the very beginning they bound his hands. The new President had cherished the purpose of calling to his aid the ablest of the Republicans, but found himself helpless. "When I first took the Chair," bitterly records Adams, "I was extremely desirous of availing myself of Mr. Madison's abilities, . . . and experience. But the violent Party Spirit of Hamilton's Friends, jealous of every man who possessed qualifications to eclipse him, prevented it. I could not do it without quarreling outright with my Ministers whom Washington's appointment had made my Masters." [2]

On the other hand, the high Federalist politicians, most of whom were Hamilton's adherents, felt that Adams entertained for their leader exactly the same sentiments which the President ascribed to them. "The jealousy which the P.[resident] has felt of H.[amilton] he now indulges toward P.[inckney], W.[olcott] & to'd *very many of their friends* who are suspected of having too much influence in the Community, & of not knowing how to appreciate his

[1] "There never was perhaps a greater contrast between two characters than between those of the present President & his predecessor. . . . The one [Washington] cool, considerate, & cautious, the other [Adams] headlong & kindled into flame by every spark that lights on his passions; the one ever scrutinizing into the public opinion and ready to follow where he could not lead it; the other insulting it by the most adverse sentiments & pursuits; W. a hero in the field, yet overweighing every danger in the Cabinet — A. without a single pretension to the character of a soldier, a perfect Quixotte as a statesman." (Madison to Jefferson, Feb., 1798; *Writings:* Hunt, vi, 310.) And [Adams] "always an honest man, often a wise one, but sometimes wholly out of his senses." (Madison to Jefferson, June 10, 1798; *ib.*, 325.)

[2] Adams to Rush, Aug. 23, 1805; *Old Family Letters*, 76.

[Adams's] merits. . . . The Consequence is that his ears are shut to his best real friends & open to Flatterers, to Time servers & even to some Jacobins." [1]

Adams, the scholar and statesman, but never the politician, was the last man to harmonize these differences. And Hamilton proved to be as inept as Adams.

After the President had dispatched the second mission to France, Hamilton's followers, including Adams's Cabinet, began intriguing in a furtive and vicious fashion to replace him with some other Federalist at the ensuing election. While, therefore, the President, as a personal matter, was more than justified in dismissing McHenry and Pickering (and Wolcott also [2]), he chose a fatal moment for the blow; as a matter of political strategy he should have struck sooner or not at all.

At this late hour the great party task and duty of the President was, by any and every honorable means, to unite all Federalist factions for the impending battle with the eager, powerful, and disciplined Republicans. Frank and full conference, tolerance, and conciliation, were the methods now required. These might not have succeeded, but at least they would not have irritated still more the ragged edges of party dissension. Not only did the exasperated President take the opposite course, but his manner and conduct were acid instead of ointment to the raw and angry wounds.[3]

[1] Cabot to King, April 26, 1799; King, iii, 8.

[2] Wolcott was as malicious as, but more cautious than, Pickering in his opposition to the President.

[3] "He [Adams] is liable to gusts of passion little short of frenzy. . . . I speak of what I have seen." (Bayard to Hamilton, Aug. 18, 1800;

This, then, was the state of the Federalist Party, the frame of mind of the President, and the distracted condition of the Cabinet, when Marshall was asked to become Secretary of State in the late spring of 1800. He was minded to refuse this high station as he had that of Secretary of War. "I incline to think Mr. Marshall will decline this office also," wrote McHenry to his brother.[1] If he accepted, he would be loyal to the President — his nature made anything else impossible. But he was the personal friend of all the Federalist leaders, who, in spite of his disapproval of the Alien and Sedition Laws and of his dissent from his party's plans in Congress, in spite, even, of his support of the President's detested second mission to France,[2] nevertheless trusted and liked him.

The President's selection of Marshall had been anticipated by the Republicans. "General Marshall . . . has been nominated to hold the station of Secretary of War," said the "Aurora," in an article heavy with abuse of Pickering. "This . . . however, is said to be but preparatory to General Marshall's appointment to succeed Mr. Pickering who is expected to resign." [3]

Works: Hamilton, vi, 457.) "He would speak in such a manner . . . as to persuade one that he was actually insane." (McHenry to John McHenry, May 20, 1800; Gibbs, ii, 347.) "Mr. Adams had conducted strangely and unaccountably." (Ames to Hamilton, Aug. 26, 1800; *Works:* Ames, i, 280.) These men were Adams's enemies; but the extreme irritability of the President at this time was noted by everybody. Undoubtedly this was increased by his distress over the illness of his wife.

[1] McHenry to John McHenry, May 20, 1800; Gibbs, ii, 347.

[2] See preceding chapter.

[3] *Aurora*, May 9, 1800; the *Aurora* had been attacking Pickering with all the animosity of partisanship.

Strangely enough the news of his elevation to the head of the Cabinet called forth only gentle criticism from the Republican press. "From what is said of Mr. Marshall," the "Aurora" thought that he was "as little likely to conciliate" France as Pickering. He "is well known to have been the disingenuous writer of all the X. Y. Z. Dispatches," which the Federalists had "confessed to be one of the best and most successful political *tricks* that was ever *played off*. . . . General Marshall's fineering and var[ni]shing capacity" was "well known," said the "Aurora." "General Marshall consequently has been nominated and appointed. . . . In genuine federal principles, General Marshall is as inflexible as Mr. Pickering; but in the negotiation with France, the General may not have imbibed so strong prejudices — and, having been one of the Envoys to that Republic, he may be supposed to be more conversant with some of the points in dispute, than Col. Pickering, and consequently to be preferred.

"We find him very well spoken of in the *reformed Gazettes of France*," continues the "Aurora," "which being now under guardianship [1] may be considered as speaking the language of the government — '*Le Bien Informé*,' after mentioning the motion Gen. M. made in announcing to Congress the death of Gen. Washington, adds — 'This is the gentleman who some time since came as Envoy from the *United States;* and who so virtuously and so spiritedly re-

[1] The French press had been quite as much under the control of the Revolutionary authorities as it was under that of Bonaparte as First Consul or even under his rule when he had become Napoleon I.

fused to fill the pockets of some of *our gentry* with Dutch inscriptions, and millions of livres.'"[1]

For nearly two weeks Marshall pondered over the President's offer. The prospect was not inviting. It was unlikely that he could hold the place longer than three quarters of a year, for Federalist defeat in the presidential election was more than probable; and it seemed certain that the head of the Cabinet would gather political cypress instead of laurel in this brief and troubled period. Marshall consulted his friends among the Federalist leaders; and, finally, accepted the proffered portfolio. Thereupon the "Aurora," quoting Pickering's statement that the office of Secretary of State "was never better filled than by General Marshall," hopes that "Gen. Marshall will take care of his *accounts*," which that Republican paper had falsely charged that Pickering had manipulated corruptly.[2]

Expressing the Republican temper the "Aurora" thus analyzes the new Federalist Cabinet: "The Secretary of the Treasury [Oliver Wolcott]" was "scarcely qualified to hold the second desk in a

[1] *Aurora*, May 27, 1800.

[2] *Ib.*, June 4, 1800; and June 17, 1800. The *Aurora* now made a systematic campaign against Pickering. It had "*substantial and damning facts*" which it threatened to publish if Adams did not subject Pickering to a "scrutiny" (*ib.*, May 21, 1800). Pickering was a "disgrace to his station" (*ib.*, May 23); several hundred thousand dollars were "unaccounted for" (*ib.*, June 4, and 17).

The attack of the Republican newspaper was entirely political, every charge and innuendo being wholly false. Adams's dismissal of his Secretary of State was not because of these charges, but on account of the Secretary's personal and political disloyalty. Adams also declared, afterwards, that Pickering lacked ability to handle the grave questions then pending and likely to arise. (*Cunningham Letters*, nos. xii, xiii, and xiv.) But that was merely a pretense.

Mercantile Counting-House"; the Attorney-General [Charles Lee] was "without talents"; the Secretary of the Navy [Benjamin Stoddert] was "a small Georgetown politician . . . cunning, gossiping, . . . of no . . . character or . . . principles"; the Secretary of War [Samuel Dexter] was no more fit for the place than "his MOTHER"; and Marshall, Secretary of State, was "more distinguished as a *rhetorician* and a *sophist* than as a *lawyer* and a *statesman* — sufficiently pliant to succeed in a corrupt court, too insincere to command respect, or confidence in a republic." However, said the "Aurora," Adams was "able to teach Mr. Marshall 'l'art diplomatique.'"[1]

Some of the Federalist leaders were not yet convinced, it appears, of Marshall's party orthodoxy. Pinckney reassures them. Writing from Virginia, he informs McHenry that "Marshall with reluctance accepts, but you may rely on his federalism, & be certain that he will not unite with Jefferson & the Jacobins."[2] Two months later even the Guy Fawkes of the Adams Cabinet declares himself more than satisfied: "If the gentlemen now in office [Marshall and Dexter] had declined," declares Wolcott, "rage, vexation & despair would probably have occasioned the most extravagant conduct[3] [on the part of the President]." After Marshall had been at the head of the Cabinet for four months, Cabot writes that "Mr. Wolcott thinks Mr. Marshall accepted the secretaryship from good motives, and

[1] *Aurora*, June 12, 1800.
[2] Pinckney to McHenry, June 10, 1800; Steiner, 460.
[3] Wolcott to Ames, Aug. 10, 1800; Gibbs, ii, 402.

with a view of preserving union, and that he and Dexter, *by accepting*, have rendered the nation great service; for, if they had refused, we should have had — *Heaven alone knows whom!* He thinks, however, as all must, that under the present chief they will be disappointed in their hopes, and that if Jefferson is President they will probably resign." [1]

In view of "the temper of his [Adams's] mind," which, asserts the unfaithful Wolcott, was "revolutionary, violent, and vindictive, . . . their [Marshall's and Dexter's] acceptance of their offices is the best evidence of their patriotism. . . . I consider Gen. Marshall and Mr. Dexter as more than secretaries — as state conservators — the value of whose services ought to be estimated, not only by the good they do, but by the mischief they have prevented. If I am not mistaken, however, Gen. Marshall will find himself out of his proper element." [2]

No sooner was Marshall in the Secretary's chair than the President hastened to his Massachusetts home and his afflicted wife. Adams's part in directing the Government was done by correspondence.[3] Marshall took up his duties with his characteristically serious, yet nonchalant, patience.

The National Capital had now been removed to Washington; and here, during the long, hot summer

[1] Cabot to Gore, Sept. 30, 1800; Lodge: *Cabot*, 291.

[2] Wolcott to Ames, Aug. 10, 1800; Gibbs, ii, 401–02.

[3] Adams's correspondence shows that the shortest time for a letter to go from Washington to Quincy, Massachusetts, was seven days, although usually nine days were required. "Last night I received your favor of the 4th." (Adams at Quincy to Dexter at Washington, Aug. 13, 1800; *Works:* Adams, ix, 76; and to Marshall, Aug. 14; *ib.*, 77; and Aug. 26; *ib.*, 78; and Aug. 30; *ib.*, 80.)

of 1800, Marshall remained amidst the steaming swamps and forests where the "Federal City" was yet to be built.[1] Not till October did he leave his post, and then but briefly and on urgent private business.[2]

The work of the State Department during this period was not onerous. Marshall's chief occupation at the Capital, it would appear, was to act as the practical head of the Government; and even his political enemies admitted that he did this well. Jefferson's most partial biographer says that "under the firm and steady lead [of Marshall and Dexter] . . . the Government soon acquired an order, system, and character which it never had before possessed." [3] Still, enough routine business came to his desk to give the new Secretary of State something to do in his own department.

Office-seeking, which had so annoyed Washington, still vexed Adams, although but few of these hornets' nests remained for him to deal with. "Your knowledge of persons, characters, and circumstances," wrote the President to Marshall concerning the applications for the office of United States Marshal for Maryland, "are so much better than mine, and my confidence in your judgment and

[1] Washington at this time was forest, swamp, and morass, with only an occasional and incommodious house. Georgetown contained the only comfortable residences. For a description of Washington at this period, see chap. I, vol. III, of this work.

[2] Marshall to Adams, Sept. 17, 1800; Adams MSS. This trip was to argue the case of Mayo *vs.* Bentley (4 Call, 528), before the Court of Appeals of Virginia. (See *supra,* chap. VI.)

[3] Randall, ii, 547. Although Randall includes Dexter, this tribute is really to Marshall who was the one dominating character in Adams's reconstructed Cabinet.

impartiality so entire, that I pray you . . . give the commission to him whom you may prefer." [1] Adams favored the son of Judge Chase; but, on the advice of Stoddert of Maryland, who was Secretary of the Navy, Marshall decided against him: "Mr. Chase is a young man who has not yet acquired the public confidence and to appoint him in preference to others who are generally known and esteem'd, might be deem'd a mere act of favor to his Father. Mr. Stoddert supposes it ineligible to accumulate, without superior pretensions, offices in the same family." [2]

Marshall generally trimmed his sails, however, to the winds of presidential preference. He undoubtedly influenced the Cabinet, in harmony with the President's wish, to concur in the pardon of Isaac Williams, convicted, under the Jay Treaty, of waging war on the high seas against Great Britain. Williams, though sailing under a French commission, was a pirate, and accumulated much wealth from his indiscriminate buccaneering.[3] But the President wrote Marshall that because of "the man's generosity to American prisoners," and "his present poverty and great distress," he desired to pardon Williams.[4]

Marshall informed the President that "repeated

[1] Adams to Marshall, July 30, 1800; *Works:* Adams, ix, 66; also Marshall to Adams, Aug. 1, Aug. 2, and July 29, 1800; Adams MSS.

[2] Marshall to Adams, July 29, 1800; Adams MSS. This cost Adams the support of young Chase's powerful father. (McHenry to John McHenry, Aug. 24, 1800; Gibbs, ii, 408.)

[3] McMaster, ii, 448.

[4] Adams to Marshall, Aug. 7, 1800; *Works:* Adams, ix, 72; and Marshall to Adams, Aug. 16, 1800; Adams MSS. Chief Justice

complaints are made to this department of the depredations committed by the Spaniards on the American commerce."[1] The French outrages were continuing; indeed, our naval war with France had been going on for months and Spain was aiding the French. An American vessel, the Rebecca Henry, had been captured by a French privateer. Two Yankee sailors killed the French prize master in recapturing the vessel, which was taken again by another French sea rover and conveyed into a Spanish port. The daring Americans were imprisoned and threatened with death. Marshall thought "proper to remonstrate and to threaten retaliation if the prisoners should be executed."[2]

The French ship Sandwich was captured by Captain Talbot, an American officer, in a Spanish port which Spain had agreed to transfer to France. Marshall considered this a violation of our treaty with Spain. "I have therefore directed the Sandwich to be given up to the minister of his Catholic Majesty,"[3] he advised the President. The Spanish Minister thanked Marshall for his "justice" and "punctuality."[4]

But Talbot would not yield his prize; the United

Ellsworth presided at the trial of Williams, who was fairly convicted. (Wharton: *State Trials*, 652–58.) The Republicans, however, charged that it was another "political" conviction. It seems probable that Adams's habitual inclination to grant the request of any one who was his personal friend (Adams's closest friend, Governor Trumbull, had urged the pardon) caused the President to wish to extend clemency to Williams.

[1] Marshall to Adams, June 24, 1800; Adams MSS.

[2] Marshall to Adams, Aug. 2, 1800; *ib.*

[3] Marshall to Adams, July 26, 1800; *ib.*

[4] De Yrujo to Marshall, July 31, 1800; *ib.*

States Marshal declined to act. Marshall took "measures[1] which will," he reported to the President, "I presume occasion the delivery of this vessel, unless . . . the government has no right to interpose, so far as captors are interested." Talbot's attitude perplexed Marshall; for, wrote he, "if the Executive of the United States cannot restore a vessel captured by a national ship, in violation of the law of nations, . . . cause for war may be given by those who, of all others, are, perhaps, most apt to give it, and that department of the government, under whose orders they are plac'd will be unable to correct the mischief."[2]

That picturesque adventurer, Bowles, whose plots and activities among the Indians had been a thorn to the National Government since the early part of Washington's Administration,[3] again became annoying. He was stirring up the Indians against the Spanish possessions in Florida and repeated his claim of having the support of Great Britain. The Spaniards eagerly seized on this as another pretext for annoying the American Government. Measures were taken to break Bowles's influence with the Indians and to suppress the adventurer's party.[4]

But, although the President was of the opinion that "the military forces . . . should join [the Span-

[1] Marshall does not state what these measures were.

[2] Marshall to Adams, Sept. 6, 1800; Adams MSS.

[3] *Am. St. Prs.*, v, *Indian Affairs*, i, 184, 187, 246. For picturesque description of Bowles and his claim of British support see Craig's report, *ib.*, 264; also, 305. Bowles was still active in 1801. (*Ib.*, 651.)

[4] Adams to Marshall, July 31, 1800; *Works:* Adams, ix, 67; Marshall to De Yrujo, Aug. 15, 1800; Adams MSS.

iards] in an expedition against Bowles,"[1] Marshall did not think "that the Spaniards require any military aid; nor," continues he, "do I suppose they would be willing to receive it. . . . American troops in either of the Floridas wou'd excite very much their jealousy, especially when no specific requisition for them has been made, and when their own force is entirely competent to the object."[2]

Liston, the British Minister, assured Marshall that the British Government had no connection with Bowles.[3] But, irritated by gossip and newspaper stories, he offensively demanded that Marshall "meet these insidious calumnies by a flat and formal contradiction."[4] Without waiting for the President's approval, Marshall quickly retorted:[5] the "suspicions . . . were not entirely unsupported by appearances." Newspaper "charges and surmises . . . are always causes of infinite regret" to the Government "and wou'd be prevented if the means of prevention existed." But, said Marshall, the British Government itself was not blameless in that respect; "without going far back you may find examples in your own of the impunity with which a foreign friendly nation [America] may be grossly libel'd." As to the people's hostility to Great Britain, he tartly reminded the British Minister that "in examining the practice of your officers employ'd in the business of impressment, and of your courts of Vice Admiralty, you will perceive at least some

[1] Adams to Marshall, Aug. 11, 1800; *Works:* Adams, ix, 73.

[2] Marshall to Adams, Aug. 12, 1800; Adams MSS. [3] *Ib.*

[4] Liston to Marshall, Aug. 25, 1800; *ib.*

[5] Marshall to Adams, Sept. 6, 1800; *ib.*

of the causes, by which this temper may have been produc'd."[1]

Sweden and Denmark proposed to maintain, jointly with the United States, a naval force in the Mediterranean to protect their mutual commerce from the Barbary Powers. Marshall declined because of our treaties with those piratical Governments; and also because, "until . . . actual hostilities shall cease between" France and America, "to station American frigates in the Mediterranean would be a hazard, to which our infant Navy ought not perhaps to be exposed."[2]

Incidents amusing, pathetic, and absurd arose, such as announcements of the birth of princes, to which the Secretary of State must prepare answers;[3]

[1] Marshall to Liston, Sept. 6, 1800; Adams MSS.

[2] Marshall to J. Q. Adams, July 24, 1800; MS. It is incredible that the Barbary corsairs held the whole of Europe and America under tribute for many years. Although our part in this general submission to these brigands of the seas was shameful, America was the first to move against them. One of Jefferson's earliest official letters after becoming President was to the Bey of Tripoli, whom Jefferson addressed as "Great and Respected Friend . . . Illustrious & honored . . . whom God preserve." Jefferson's letter ends with this fervent invocation: "I pray God, very great and respected friend, to have you always in his holy keeping." (Jefferson to Bey of Tripoli, May 21, 1801; *Am. St. Prs., For. Rel.*, ii, 349.)

And see Jefferson to Bey of Tunis (Sept. 9, 1801; *ib.*, 358), in which the American President addresses this sea robber and holder of Americans in slavery, as "Great and Good Friend" and apologizes for delay in sending our tribute. In Jefferson's time, no notice was taken of such expressions, which were recognized as mere forms. But ninety years later the use of this exact expression, "Great and Good Friend," addressed to the Queen of the Hawaiian Islands, was urged on the stump and in the press against President Cleveland in his campaign for reelection. For an accurate and entertaining account of our relations with the Barbary pirates see Allen: *Our Navy and the Barbary Corsairs.*

[3] Marshall to Adams, Aug. 1, 1800; Adams MSS.

the stranding of foreign sailors on our shores, whose plight we must relieve; [1] the purchase of jewels for the Bey of Tunis, who was clamoring for the glittering bribes.[2]

In such fashion went on the daily routine work of his department while Marshall was at the head of the Cabinet.

The only grave matters requiring Marshall's attention were the perplexing tangle of the British debts and the associated questions of British impressment of American seamen and interference with American commerce.

Under the sixth article of the Jay Treaty a joint commission of five members had been appointed to determine the debts due British subjects. Two of the Commissioners were British, two Americans, and the fifth chosen by lot. Chance made this deciding member British also. This Commission, sitting at Philadelphia, failed to agree. The treaty provided, as we have seen, that the United States should pay such British debts existing at the outbreak of the Revolutionary War as the creditors were not able to collect because of the sequestration laws and other "legal impediments," or because, during the operation of these statutes, the debtor had become insolvent.

Having a majority of the Commission, the British members made rules which threw the doors wide

[1] Marshall to Adams, June 24, 1800; Adams MSS.

[2] Marshall to Adams, Aug. 16, 1800; July 24, 1800; *Ib.* and see Adams to Marshall, Aug. 2, and to Secretary of State, May 25; King, iii, 243–46. The jewels were part of our tribute to the Barbary pirates.

open.[1] "They go the length to make the United States at once the debtor for all the *outstanding* debts of British subjects contracted before the peace of 1783. . . . The amount of the claims presented exceeds nineteen millions of dollars." [2] And this was done by the British representatives with overbearing personal insolence. Aside from the injustice of the British contention, this bullying of the American members [3] made the work of the Commission all but impossible.

A righteous popular indignation arose. "The construction put upon the Treaty by the British Commissioners . . . will never be submitted to by this country. . . . The [British] demand . . . excites much ill blood." [4] The American Commissioners refused to attend further sittings of the Board. Thereupon, the British Government withdrew its members of the associate Commission sitting in London, under the seventh article of the treaty, to pass upon claims of American citizens for property destroyed by the British.

The situation was acute. It was made still sharper by the appointment of our second mission to France. For, just as France had regarded Jay's mission and treaty as offensive, so now Great Britain looked upon

[1] King to Secretary of State, Oct. 11, 1799; note to Grenville; King, iii, 129.

[2] Secretary of State to King, Feb. 5, 1799; *Am. St. Prs., For. Rel.*, ii, 383. Hildreth says that the total amount of claims filed was twenty-four million dollars. (Hildreth, v, 331; and see Marshall to King, *infra.*)

[3] Secretary of State to King, Sept. 4, 1799; *Am. St. Prs., For. Rel.*, ii, 383.

[4] Troup to King, Sept. 2, 1799; King, iii, 91.

the Ellsworth mission as unfriendly. As a way out of the difficulty, the American Government insisted upon articles explanatory of the sixth article of the Jay Treaty which would define exactly what claims the Commission should consider.[1] The British Government refused and suggested a new commission.[2]

This was the condition that faced Marshall when he became Secretary of State. War with Great Britain was in the air from other causes and the rupture of the two Commissions made the atmosphere thicker. On June 24, 1800, Marshall wrote the President that we ought "still to press an amicable explanation of the sixth article of our treaty"; perhaps during the summer or autumn the British Cabinet might feel "more favorable to an accommodation." But he "cannot help fearing that . . . the British Ministry" intends "to put such a construction on the law of nations . . . as to throw into their hands some equivalent to the probable claims of British creditors on the United States." [3]

Lord Grenville then suggested to Rufus King, our Minister at London, that the United States pay a gross sum to Great Britain in settlement of the whole controversy.[4] Marshall wondered whether this simple way out of the tangle could "afford just cause of discontent to France?" [5] Adams thought not. "We surely have a right to pay our honest debts in the

[1] Secretary of State to King, Dec. 31, 1799; *Am. St. Prs., For. Rel.*, ii, 384–85.

[2] King to Secretary of State, April 7, 1800; King, iii, 215.

[3] Marshall to Adams, June 24, 1800; Adams MSS.

[4] King to Secretary of State, April 22, 1800; King, iii, 222.

[5] Marshall to Adams, July 21, 1800; Adams MSS.

manner least inconvenient to ourselves and no foreign power has anything to do with it," said the President. Adams, however, foresaw many other difficulties; [1] but Marshall concluded that, on the whole, a gross payment was the best solution in case the British Government could not be induced to agree to explanatory articles.[2]

Thereupon Marshall wrote his memorable instructions to our Minister to Great Britain. In this, as in his letters to Talleyrand two years earlier, and in the notable one on British impressment, contraband, and freedom of the seas,[3] he shows himself an American in a manner unusual at that period. Not the least partiality does he display for any foreign country; he treats them with exact equality and demands from all that they shall deal with the American Government as a *Nation*, independent of and unconnected with any of them.[4]

The United States, writes Marshall, "can never submit to" the resolutions adopted by the British Commissioners, which put "new and injurious burthens" upon the United States "unwarranted by compact," and to which, if they had been stated in the treaty, "this Government never could and never would have assented." Unless the two Governments can "forget the past," arbitration cannot be successful; it is idle to discuss who committed the first fault, he says, when two nations are trying to adjust their differences.

[1] Adams to Marshall, Aug. 1, 1800; *Works:* Adams, ix, 68–69.

[2] Marshall to Adams, Aug. 12, 1800; Adams MSS.

[3] *Infra*, 507 *et seq.*

[4] *Am. St. Prs., For. Rel.*, ii, 386.

The American Commissioners, declares Marshall, withdrew from the Board because the hostile majority established rules under which "a vast mass of cases never submitted to their consideration" could and would be brought in against American citizens. The proceedings of the British Commissioners were not only "totally unauthorized," but "were conducted in terms and in a spirit only calculated to destroy all harmony between the two nations."

The cases which the Board could consider were distinctly and specifically stated in the fifth article of the treaty. Let the two Governments agree to an explanation, instead of leaving the matter to wrangling commissioners. But, if Minister King finds that the British Government will not agree to explanatory articles, he is authorized to substitute "a gross sum in full compensation of all claims made or to be made on this Government."

It would, of course, be difficult to agree upon the amount. "The extravagant claims which the British creditors have been induced to file," among which "are cases . . . so notoriously unfounded that no commissioners retaining the slightest degree of self-respect can establish them; . . . others where the debt has been fairly and voluntarily compromised by agreement between creditor and debtor"; others "where the money has been paid in specie, and receipts in full given"; and still others even worse, all composing that "enormous mass of imagined debt," will, says Marshall, make it hard to agree on a stated amount.[1]

[1] *Am. St. Prs., For. Rel.*, ii, 387.

The British creditors, he asserts, had been and then were proceeding to collect their debts through the American courts, and "had they not been seduced into the opinion that the trouble and expense inseparable from the pursuit of the old debts, might be avoided by one general resort to the United States, it is believed they would have been still more rapidly proceeding in the collection of the very claims, so far as they are just, which have been filed with the commissioners. They meet with no objection, either of law or fact, which are not common to every description of creditors, in every country. . . . Our judges are even liberal in their construction of the 4th article of the treaty of peace" and have shown "no sort of partiality for the debtors."

Marshall urges this point with great vigor, and concludes that, if a gross amount can be agreed upon, the American Minister must see to it, of course, that this sum is made as small as possible, not "to exceed one million sterling" in any event.[1] In a private letter, Marshall informs King that "the best opinion here is that not more than two million Dollars could justly be chargeable to the United States under the treaty."[2]

Adams was elated by Marshall's letter. "I know not," he wrote, "how the subject could have been better digested."[3]

[1] *Am. St. Prs., For. Rel.*, ii, 387.

[2] Marshall to Adams, Sept. 9, 1800; Adams MSS.

[3] Adams to Marshall, Sept. 18, 1800; *Works:* Adams, ix, 84. After Jefferson became President and Madison Secretary of State, King settled the controversy according to these instructions of Marshall. But the Republicans, being then in power, claimed the credit.

Almost from the exchange of ratifications of the Jay compact, impressment of American seamen by the British and their taking from American ships, as contraband, merchandise which, under the treaty, was exempt from seizure, had injured American commerce and increasingly irritated the American people.[1] The brutality with which the British practiced these depredations had heated still more American resentment, already greatly inflamed.[2]

In June, 1799, Marshall's predecessor had instructed King "to persevere . . . in denying the right of British Men of War to take from our Ships of War any men whatever, and from our merchant vessels any Americans, or foreigners, or even Englishmen." [3] But the British had disregarded the American Minister's protests and these had now been entirely silenced by the break-up of the British Debts Commissions.

Nevertheless, Marshall directed our Minister at

[1] Secretary of State to King, Oct. 26, 1796; King, ii, 102.

[2] For a comprehensive though prejudiced review of British policy during this period see Tench Coxe: *Examination of the Conduct of Great Britain Respecting Neutrals.* Coxe declares that the purpose and policy of Great Britain were to "monopolize the commerce of the world. . . . She denies the lawfulness of supplying and buying from her enemies, and, in the face of the world, enacts statutes to enable her own subjects to do these things. (*Ib.*, 62.) . . . She now aims at the Monarchy of the ocean. . . . Her trade is war. . . . The spoils of neutrals fill her warehouses, while she incarcerates their bodies in her floating castles. She seizes their persons and property as the rich fruit of bloodless victories over her unarmed friends." (*Ib.*, 72.)

This was the accepted American view at the time Marshall wrote his protest; and it continued to be such until the War of 1812. Coxe's book is packed closely with citations and statistics sustaining his position.

[3] Secretary of State to King, June 14, 1799; King, iii, 47; and see King to Secretary of State, July 15, 1799; *ib.*, 58–59; and King to Grenville, Oct. 7, 1799; *ib.*, 115–21.

the Court of St. James to renew the negotiations. In a state paper which, in ability, dignity, and eloquence, suggests his famous Jonathan Robins speech and equals his memorial to Talleyrand, he examines the vital subjects of impressment, contraband, and the rights of neutral commerce.

It was a difficult situation that confronted the American Secretary of State. He had to meet and if possible modify the offensive, determined, and wholly unjust British position by a statement of principles based on fundamental right; and by an assertion of America's just place in the world.

The spirit of Marshall's protest to the British Government is that America is an independent nation, a separate and distinct political entity, with equal rights, power, and dignity with all other nations [1] — a conception then in its weak infancy even in America and, apparently, not entertained by Great Britain or France. These Powers seemed to regard America, not as a sovereign nation, but as a sort of subordinate state, to be used as they saw fit for their plans and purposes.

But, asserts Marshall, "the United States do not hold themselves in any degree responsible to France or to Britain for their negotiations with the one or the other of these Powers, but are ready to make amicable and reasonable explanations with either. . . . An exact neutrality . . . between the belligerent Powers" is the "object of the American Government. . . . Separated far from Europe, we mean not to mingle in their quarrels. . . . We have avoided

[1] This complete paper is in *Am. St. Prs., For. Rel.*, ii, 486–90.

and we shall continue to avoid any . . . connections not compatible with the neutrality we profess. . . . The aggressions, sometimes of one and sometimes of another belligerent power have forced us to contemplate and prepare for war as a probable event. . . . But this is a situation of necessity, not of choice." France had compelled us to resort to force against her, but in doing so "our preference for peace was manifest"; and now that France makes friendly advances, "America meets those overtures, and, in doing so, only adheres to her pacific system."

Marshall lays down those principles of international conduct which have become the traditional American policy. Reviewing our course during the war between France and Great Britain, he says: "When the combination against France was most formidable, when, if ever, it was dangerous to acknowledge her new Government" and maintain friendly relations with the new Republic, "the American Government openly declared its determination to adhere to that state of impartial neutrality which it has ever since sought to maintain; nor did the clouds which, for a time, lowered over the fortunes of the [French] Republic, in any degree shake this resolution. When victory changed sides and France, in turn, threatened those who did not arrange themselves under her banners, America, pursuing with undeviating step the same steady course," nevertheless made a treaty with Great Britain; "nor could either threats or artifices prevent its ratification."

"At no period of the war," Marshall reminds the British Government, "has France occupied such elevated ground as at the very point of time when America armed to resist her: triumphant and victorious everywhere, she had dictated a peace to her enemies on the continent and had refused one to Britain." On the other hand, "in the reverse of her fortune, when defeated both in Italy and on the Rhine, in danger of losing Holland, before the victory of Massena had changed the face of the last campaign, and before Russia had receded from the coalition against her, the present negotiation [between America and France] was resolved on. During this pendency," says Marshall, "the state of the war has changed, but the conduct of the United States" has not.

"Our terms remain the same: we still pursue peace. We still embrace it, if it can be obtained without violating our national honor or our national faith; but we will reject without hesitation all propositions which may compromit the one or the other."

All this, he declares, "shows how steadily it [the American Government] pursues its system [Neutrality and peace] without regarding the dangers from the one side or the other, to which the pursuit may be exposed. The present negotiation with France is a part of this system, and ought, therefore, to excite in Great Britain no feelings unfriendly to the United States."

Marshall then takes up the British position as to contraband of war. He declares that even under the law of nations, "neutrals have a right to carry on their usual commerce; belligerents have a right to prevent them from supplying the enemy with instruments of war." But the eighteenth article of the treaty itself covered the matter in express terms, and specifically enumerated certain things as contraband and also "generally whatever may serve *directly* to the equipment of vessels." Yet Great Britain had ruthlessly seized and condemned American vessels regardless of the treaty — had actually plundered American ships of farming material upon the pretense that these articles might, by some remote possibility, be used "to equip vessels." The British contention erased the word "*directly*"[1] from the express terms of the treaty. "This construction we deem alike unfriendly and unjust," he says. Such "garbling a compact . . . is to substitute another agreement for that of the parties. . . ."

"It would swell the list of contraband to" suit British convenience, contrary to "the laws and usages of nations. . . . It would prohibit . . . articles . . . necessary for the ordinary occupations of men in peace" and require "a surrender, on the part of the United States, of rights in themselves unquestionable, and the exercise of which is essential to themselves. . . . A construction so absurd and so odious ought to be rejected."[2]

Articles, "even if contraband," should not be confiscated, insists Marshall, except when "they are attempted to be carried to an enemy." For instance,

[1] At one place the word "distinctly" is used and at another the word "directly," in the *American State Papers* (ii, 487 and 488). The word "directly" is correct, the word "distinctly" being a misprint. This is an example of the inaccuracies of these official volumes, which must be used with careful scrutiny.

[2] *Am. St. Prs., For. Rel.*, ii, 488.

"vessels bound to New Orleans and laden with cargoes proper for the ordinary use of the citizens of the United States who inhabit the Mississippi and its waters . . . cannot be justly said to carry those cargoes to an enemy. . . . Such a cargo is not a just object of confiscation, although a part of it should also be deemed proper for the equipment of vessels, because it is not attempted to be carried to an enemy."

On the subject of blockade, Marshall questions whether "the right to confiscate vessels bound to a blockaded port . . . can be applied to a place not completely invested by land as well as by sea." But waiving "this departure from principle," the American complaint "is that ports not effectually blockaded by a force capable of completely investing them, have yet been declared in a state of blockage, and vessels attempting to enter therein have been seized, and, on that account, confiscated." This "vexation . . . may be carried, if not resisted, to a very injurious extent."

If neutrals submit to it, "then every port of the belligerent powers may at all times be declared in that [blockaded] state and the commerce of neutrals be thereby subjected to universal capture." But if complete blockage be required, then "the capacity to blockade will be limited by the naval force of the belligerent, and, of consequence, the mischief to neutral commerce can not be very extensive. It is therefore of the last importance to neutrals that this principle be maintained unimpaired."

The British Courts of Vice-Admiralty, says

Marshall, render "unjust decisions" in the case of captures. "The temptation which a rich neutral commerce offers to unprincipled avarice, at all times powerful, becomes irresistible unless strong and efficient restraints be imposed by the Government which employs it." If such restraints are not imposed, the belligerent Government thereby "causes the injuries it tolerates." Just this, says Marshall, is the case with the British Government.

For "the most effectual restraint is an impartial judiciary, which will decide impartially between the parties and uniformly condemn the captor in costs and damages, where the seizure has been made without probable cause." If this is not done, "indiscriminate captures will be made." If an "unjust judge" condemns the captured vessel, the profit is the captor's; if the vessel is discharged, the loss falls upon the owner. Yet this has been and still is the indefensible course pursued against American commerce.

"The British Courts of Vice Admiralty, whatever may be the case, seldom acquit and when they do, costs and damages for detention are never awarded." Marshall demands that the British Government shall "infuse a spirit of justice and respect for law into the Courts of Vice Admiralty"—this alone, he insists, can check "their excessive and irritating vexations. . . . This spirit can only be infused by uniformly discountenancing and punishing those who tarnish alike the seat of justice and the honor of their country, by converting themselves from judges into mere instruments of plunder." And Marshall broadly intimates that these courts are corrupt.

As to British impressment, "no right has been asserted to impress" Americans; "yet they are impressed, they are dragged on board British ships of war with the evidence of citizenship in their hands, and forced by violence there to serve until conclusive testimonials of their birth can be obtained." He demands that the British Government stop this lawless, violent practice "by punishing and frowning upon those who perpetrate it. The mere release of the injured, after a long course of service and of suffering, is no compensation for the past and no security for the future. . . . The United States therefore require positively that their seamen . . . be exempt from impressments." Even "alien seamen, not British subjects, engaged in our merchant service ought to be equally exempt with citizens from impressments. . . . Britain has no pretext of right to their persons or to their service. To tear them, then, from our possession is, at the same time, an insult and an injury. It is an act of violence for which there exists no palliative."

Suppose, says Marshall, that America should do the things Great Britain was doing? "Should we impress from the merchant service of Britain not only Americans but foreigners, and even British subjects, how long would such a course of injury, unredressed, be permitted to pass unrevenged? How long would the [British] Government be content with unsuccessful remonstrance and unavailing memorials?"

Or, were America to retaliate by inducing British sailors to enter the more attractive American service, as America might lawfully do, how would Great Britain look upon it? Therefore, concludes Marshall, "is it not more advisable to desist from, and to take effectual measures to prevent an acknowledged wrong, than be perseverant in that wrong, to excite against themselves the well founded resentment of America, and to force our Government into measures which may possibly terminate in an open rupture?"[1]

Thus boldly and in justifiably harsh language did Marshall assert American rights as against British violation of them, just as he had similarly upheld those rights against French assault. Although France desisted from her lawless practices after Adams's second mission negotiated with Bonaparte an adjustment of our grievances,[2] Great Britain persisted in the ruthless conduct which Marshall and his successors denounced until, twelve years later, America was driven to armed resistance.

Working patiently in his stuffy office amidst the Potomac miasma and mosquitoes during the sweltering months, it was Marshall's unhappy fate to behold the beginning of the break-up of that great party which had built our ship of state, set it upon the waters, navigated it for twelve tempestuous years, through the storms of domestic trouble and foreign danger.[3] He was powerless to stay the

[1] *Am. St. Prs., For. Rel.*, ii, 490. [2] *Infra*, 524.

[3] While political parties, as such, did not appear until the close of Washington's first Administration, the Federalist Party of 1800 was made up, for the most part, of substantially the same men and interests that forced the adoption of the Constitution and originated all the policies and measures, foreign and domestic, of the first three Administrations.

Federalist disintegration. Even in his home district Marshall's personal strength had turned to water, and at the election of his successor in Congress, his party was utterly crushed. "Mr. Mayo, who was proposed to succeed Gen. Marshall, lost his election by an immense majority," writes the alert Wolcott; "was grossly insulted in public by a brother-in-law of the late Senator Taylor, and was afterwards wounded by him in a duel. This is a specimen of the political influence of the Secretary of State in his own district." [1]

Marshall himself was extremely depressed. "Ill news from Virginia," he writes Otis. "To succeed me has been elected by an immense majority one of the most decided democrats [2] in the union." Upon the political horizon Marshall beheld only storm and blackness: "In Jersey, too, I am afraid things are going badly. In Maryland the full force of parties will be tried but the issue I should feel confident would be right if there did not appear to be a current setting against us of which the force is incalculable. There is a tide in the affairs of nations, of parties, and of individuals. I fear that of real Americanism is on the ebb." [3] Never, perhaps, in the history of political parties was calm, dispassionate judgment and steady courage needed more than they were now required to avert Federalist defeat.

Yet in all the States revenge, apprehension, and

[1] Wolcott to Ames, Aug. 10, 1800; Gibbs, ii, 404.

[2] During this period, the word "Democrat" was used by the Federalists as a term of extreme condemnation, even more opprobrious than the word "Jacobin." For many years most Republicans hotly resented the appellation of "Democrat."

[3] Marshall to Otis, Aug. 5, 1800; Otis MSS.

despair blinded the eyes and deranged the councils of the supreme Federalist managers.[1] The voters in the party were confused and angered by the dissensions of those to whom they looked for guidance.[2] The leaders agreed that Jefferson was the bearer of the flag of "anarchy and sedition," captain of the hordes of "lawlessness," and, above all, the remorseless antagonist of Nationalism. What should be done "by the friends of order and true liberty to keep the [presidential] chair from being occupied by an enemy [Jefferson] of both?" was the question which the distressed Federalist politicians asked one another.[3]

In May, Hamilton thought that "to support *Adams* and *Pinckney* equally is the only thing that can save us from the fangs of *Jefferson*." [4] Yet, six days later, Hamilton wrote that "*most* of the most *influential men* of that [Federalist] party consider him [Adams] as a very *unfit* and *incapable* character. . . . My mind is made up. I will never more be responsible for him by any direct support, even though the consequence should be the election of *Jefferson*. . . . If the cause is to be sacrificed to a weak and perverse man, I withdraw from the party." [5]

As the summer wore on, so acrimonious grew the feeling of Hamilton's supporters toward the Presi-

[1] For a vivid review of factional causes of the Federalists' decline see Sedgwick to King, Sept. 26, 1800; King, iii, 307–10; and Ames to King, Sept. 24, 1800; *ib.*, 304.

[2] "The Public mind is puzzled and fretted. People don't know what to think of measures or men; they are mad because they are in the dark." (Goodrich to Wolcott, July 28, 1800; Gibbs, ii, 394.)

[3] Ames to Hamilton, Aug. 26, 1800; *Works:* Ames, i, 280.

[4] Hamilton to Sedgwick, May 4, 1800; *Works:* Lodge, x, 371.

[5] Same to same, May 10, 1800; *ib.*, 375.

dent that they seriously considered whether his reëlection would not be as great a misfortune as the success of the Republican Party.[1] Although the Federalist caucus had agreed to support Adams and Pinckney equally as the party's candidates for President,[2] yet the Hamiltonian faction decided to place Pinckney in the presidential chair.[3]

But, blindly as they groped, their failing vision was still clear enough to discern that the small local leaders in New England, which was the strong Federalist section of the country, were for Adams;[4] and that everywhere the party's rank and file, though irri-

[1] "In our untoward situation we should do as well with Jefferson for President and Mr. Pinckney Vice President as with anything we can now expect. Such an issue of the election, if fairly produced, is the only one that will keep the Federal Party together." (Cabot to Wolcott, Oct. 5, 1800; Lodge: *Cabot*, 295.)

"If Mr. Adams should be reëlected, I fear our constitution would be more injured by his unruly passions, antipathies, & jealousy, than by the whimsies of Jefferson." (Carroll to McHenry, Nov. 4, 1800; Steiner, 473.)

"He [Adams] has palsied the sinews of the party, and" another four years of his administration "would give it its death wound." (Bayard to Hamilton, Aug. 18, 1800; *Works:* Hamilton, vi, 457.)

[2] McHenry to John McHenry, May 20, 1800; Gibbs, ii, 347. According to the caucus custom, two candidates were named for President, one of whom was understood really to stand for Vice-President, the Constitution at that time not providing for a separate vote for the latter officer.

[3] "You may rely upon my co-operation in every reasonable measure for effecting the election of General Pinckney." (Wolcott to Hamilton, July 7, 1800; *Works:* Hamilton, vi, 447–48.)

"The affairs of this government will not only be ruined but . . . the disgrace will attach to the federal party if they permit the re-election of Mr. Adams." (*Ib.*) "In Massachusetts almost all the leaders of the first class are dissatisfied with Mr. Adams and enter heartily into the policy of supporting General Pinckney." (Hamilton to Bayard, Aug. 6, *ib.*, 452 (also in *Works:* Lodge, x, 384); and see Jefferson to Butler, Aug. 11, 1800; *Works:* Ford, ix, 138.)

[4] Hamilton to Carroll, July 1, 1800; *Works:* Lodge, x, 378; and see Hamilton to Bayard, Aug. 6, 1800; *ib.*, 384.

tated and perplexed, were standing by the President. His real statesmanship had made an impression on the masses of his party: Dayton declared that Adams was "the most popular man in the United States." [1] Knox assured the President that "the great body of the federal sentiment confide implicitly in your knowledge and virtue. . . . They will . . . cling to you in preference to all others." [2]

Some urged Adams to overthrow the Hamiltonian cabal which opposed him. "Cunning half Jacobins assure the President that he can combine the virtuous and moderate men of both parties, and that all our difficulties are owing to an oligarchy which it is in his power to crush, and thus acquire the general support of the nation," [3] testifies Wolcott.

The President heeded this mad counsel. Hamilton and his crew were not the party, said Adams; they were only a faction and a "British faction" at that.[4]

[1] Sedgwick to Hamilton, May 7, 1800, quoting "our friend D.[ayton] who is not perfectly right" (*Works:* Hamilton, vi, 437; and see Cabot to Hamilton, Aug. 10, 1800; *ib.*, 454); also Cabot to Wolcott, July 20, 1800; Lodge: *Cabot*, 282.)

[2] Knox to Adams, March 5, 1799; *Works:* Adams, viii, 626–27. Knox had held higher rank than Hamilton in the Revolutionary War and Adams had tried to place him above Hamilton in the provisional army in 1798. But upon the demand of Washington Knox was given an inferior rank and indignantly declined to serve. (Hildreth, v, 242–44. And see Washington to Knox, July 16, 1798; *Writings:* Ford, xiv, 43–46.) Thereafter he became the enemy of Hamilton and the ardent supporter of Adams.

[3] Wolcott to Ames, Dec. 29, 1799; Gibbs, ii, 315.

[4] Hamilton to Adams, Aug. 1, 1800; *Works:* Lodge, x, 382, and see 390; Ames to Wolcott, Aug. 3, 1800; Gibbs, ii, 396; Wolcott to Ames, Dec. 29, 1799; *ib.*, 315.

The public discussion of Adams's charge of a "British faction" against his party enemies began with the publication of a foolish letter he had written to Coxe, in May of 1792, insinuating that Pinckney's appointment to the British Court had been secured by "much British

He would "rip it up."[1] The justly angered President, it appears, thought of founding a new party, an American Party, "a constitutionalist party."[2] It was said that the astute Jefferson so played upon him that Adams came to think the engaging but crafty Virginian aspired only to be and to be known as the first lieutenant of the Massachusetts statesman.[3] Adams concluded that he could make up any Federalist loss at the polls by courting the Republicans, whose "friendship," wrote Ames, "he seeks for himself."[4]

But the Republicans had almost recovered from the effect of the X. Y. Z. disclosures. "The *rabies canina* of Jacobinism has gradually spread . . . from the cities, where it was confined to docks and mob, to the country,"[5] was the tidings of woe that Ames sent to Gore. The Hamiltonian leaders despaired of the continuance of the Government and saw "a

influence." (Adams to Coxe, May, 1792; Gibbs, ii, 424.) The President gave vitality to the gossip by talking of the Hamiltonian Federalists as a "British faction." He should have charged it publicly and formally or else kept perfectly silent. He did neither, and thus only enraged his foe within the party without getting the advantage of an open and aggressive attack. (See Steiner, footnote 3, to 468.)

[1] Phelps to Wolcott, July 15, 1800; relating Noah Webster's endorsement of Adams's opinions; Gibbs, ii, 380.

[2] Ames to Wolcott, Aug. 3, 1800; Gibbs, ii, 396.

[3] In the summer of 1800, Jefferson dined with the President. Adams was utterly unreserved to the Republican leader. After dinner, General Henry Lee, also a guest, remonstrated with the President, who responded that "he believed Mr. Jefferson never had the ambition, or desire to aspire to any higher distinction than to be his [Adams's] first Lieutenant." (Lee to Pickering, 1802; Pickering MSS., Mass. Hist. Soc.; also partly quoted in Gibbs, ii, 366; and see Ames to Wolcott, June 12, 1800; Gibbs, ii, 368; and to King, Sept. 24, 1800; King, iii, 304.)

[4] Ames to Pickering, Nov. 5, 1799; *Works:* Ames, i, 261.

[5] Ames to Gore, Nov. 10, 1799; *ib.*, 265.

convulsion of revolution" as the result of "excessive democracy."[1] The union of all Federalist votes was "the only measure by which the government can be preserved."[2] But Federalist union! As well ask shattered glass to remould itself!

The harmonious and disciplined Republicans were superbly led. Jefferson combined their battle-cries of the last two years into one mighty appeal — simple, affirmative, popular. Peace, economy, "freedom of the press, freedom of religion, trial by jury, . . . no standing armies," were the issues he announced, together with the supreme issue of all, States' Rights. Upon this latter doctrine Jefferson planted all the Republican guns and directed their fire on "centralization" which, said he, would "monarchise" our Government and make it "the most corrupt on earth," with increased "stock-jobbing, speculating, plundering, office-holding, and office-hunting."[3]

The Federalists could reply but feebly. The tax-gatherer's fingers were in every man's pockets; and Adams had pardoned the men who had resisted the collectors of tribute. The increased revenue was required for the army and navy, which, thought the people, were worse than needless[4] if there were to be no war and the President's second mission made hostilities improbable (they had forgotten that this very preparation had been the principal means of

[1] Ames to Gore, Nov. 10, 1799; Ames, i, 268.

[2] Cabot to Wolcott, June 14, 1800; Lodge: *Cabot*, 274.

[3] Jefferson to Granger, Aug. 13, 1800; *Works:* Ford, ix, 138–41; and see Jefferson to Gerry, January 26, 1799; *ib.*, 17–19.

[4] "The Jacobins and the half federalists are ripe for attacking the permanent force, as expensive, and unnecessary, and dangerous to liberty." (Ames to Pickering, Oct. 19, 1799; *Works:* Ames, i, 258.)

changing the haughty attitude of France). The Alien and Sedition Laws had infuriated the "foreign" voters[1] and alarmed thousands of American-born citizens. Even that potent bribe of free institutions, the expectation of office, could no longer be employed effectively with the party workers, who, testifies Ebenezer Huntington, were going over "to Jefferson in hopes to partake of the loaves and fishes, which are to be distributed by the new President." [2]

The Federalist leaders did nothing, therefore, but write letters to one another denouncing the "Jacobins" and prophesying "anarchy." "Behold France — what is theory here is fact there." [3] Even the tractable McHenry was disgusted with his stronger associates. "Their conduct," said he, "is tremulous, timid, feeble, deceptive & cowardly. They write private letters. To whom? To each other. But they do nothing. . . . If the party recover its pristine energy & splendor, shall I ascribe it to such cunning, paltry, indecisive, backdoor conduct?" [4]

[1] "In my lengthy journey through this State [Pennsylvania] I have seen many, very many Irishmen and with very few exceptions, they are United Irishmen, Free Masons, and the most God-provoking Democrats on this side of Hell," who, "with the joy and ferocity of the damned, are enjoying the mortification of the few remaining honest men and Federalists, and exalting their own hopes of preferment, and that of their friends, in proportion as they dismiss the fears of the gallows. . . . The Democrats are, without doubt, increasing." (Uriah Tracy to Wolcott, Aug. 7, 1800; Gibbs, ii, 399.)

[2] Huntington to Wolcott, Aug. 6, 1800; *ib.*, 398.

[3] Ames to Wolcott, June 12, 1800; *ib.*, 369.

[4] McHenry to Wolcott, July 22, 1800; Steiner, 462. "Your very wise political correspondents will tell you anything sooner than the truth. For not one of them will look for anything but profound reasons of state at the bottom of the odd superstructure of parties here. There is nothing of the kind at the bottom." (Ames to King, Aug. 19, 1800; King, iii, 294.)

What had become of the French mission? [1] Would to God it might fail! That outcome might yet save the Federalist fortunes. "If Mr. Marshall has any [news of the second French mission] beg him to let it out," implored Chauncey Goodrich.[2] But Marshall had none for public inspection. The envoys' dispatches of May 17,[3] which had reached him nearly seven weeks afterward, were perplexing. Indeed, Marshall was "much inclined to think that . . . the French government may be inclined to protract it [the negotiation] in the expectation that events in America[4] may place them on higher ground than that which they now occupy." [5] To Hamilton, he cautiously wrote that the dispatches contained nothing "on which a positive opinion respecting the result of that negotiation can be formed." [6]

But he told the President that he feared "the impression which will probably be made by the New York Election," [7] and that European military developments might defeat the mission's purpose. He advised Adams to consider what then should be done. Should "hostilities against France with the exception of their West India privateers . . . be continued if on their part a change of conduct shall be

[1] The Republicans were making much political capital out of the second mission. They had "saved the country from war," they said, by forcing Adams to send the envoys: "What a roaring and bellowing did this excite among all the hungry gang that panted for blood only to obtain pelf in every part of the country." (*Aurora*, March 4, 1800.)

[2] Goodrich to Wolcott, Aug. 26, 1800; Gibbs, ii, 412.

[3] *Am. St. Prs., For. Rel.*, ii, 325.

[4] Republican success in the approaching election.

[5] Marshall to Adams, July 21, 1800; Adams MSS.

[6] Marshall to Hamilton, Aug. 23, 1800; *Works:* Hamilton, vi, 460.

[7] A Republican victory.

manifest?" [1] Adams was so perturbed that he asked Marshall whether, in case the envoys returned without a treaty, Congress ought not to be asked to declare war, which already it had done in effect. For, said Adams, "the public mind cannot be held in a state of suspense; public opinion must be always a decided one whether right or not." [2]

Marshall counseled patience and moderation. Indeed, he finally informed Adams that he hoped for an adjustment: "I am greatly disposed to think," he advised the President, "that the present [French] government is much inclined to correct, at least in part, the follies of the past. Of these, none were perhaps more conspicuous or more injurious to the french nation, than their haughty and hostile conduct to neutrals. Considerable retrograde steps in this respect have already been taken, and I expect the same course will be continued." If so, "there will exist no cause for war, but to obtain compensation for past injuries"; and this, Marshall is persuaded, is not "a sufficient motive" for war.[3]

To others, however, Marshall was apprehensive: "It is probable that their [the French] late victories and the hope which many of our papers [Republican] are well calculated to inspire, that America is disposed once more to crouch at her [France's] feet may render ineffectual our endeavors to obtain peace." [4]

[1] Marshall to Adams, Aug. 25, 1800; Adams MSS.

[2] Adams to Marshall, Sept. 4 and 5, 1800; *Works:* Adams, ix, 80–82.

[3] Marshall to Adams, Sept. 17, 1800; Adams MSS. The "retrograde steps" to which Marshall refers were the modification of the French *arrêts* and decrees concerning attacks on our commerce.

[4] Marshall to Tinsley, Sept. 13, 1800; MS., Mass. Hist. Soc.

But the second American mission to France had dealt with Bonaparte himself, who was now First Consul. The man on horseback had arrived, as Marshall had foreseen; a statesman as well as a soldier was now the supreme power in France. Also, as we have seen, the American Government had provided for an army and was building a navy which, indeed, was even then attacking and defeating French ships. "America in arms was treated with some respect," as Marshall expresses it.[1] At any rate, the American envoys did not have to overcome the obstacles that lay in the way two years earlier and the negotiations began without difficulty and proceeded without friction.

Finally a treaty was made and copies sent to Marshall, October 4, 1800.[2] The Republicans were rejoiced; the Federalist politicians chagrined.[3] Hamilton felt that in "the general politics of the world" it "is a make-weight in the wrong scale," but he favored its ratification because "the contrary ... would . . . utterly ruin the federal party," and "moreover it is better to close the thing where it is than to leave it to a Jacobin to do much worse." [4]

Marshall also advised ratification, although he was "far, very far, from approving" [5] the treaty.

[1] Marshall, ii, 438.

[2] *Am. St. Prs., For. Rel.*, ii, 342 *et seq.*

[3] Gunn to Hamilton, Dec. 18, 1800; *Works:* Hamilton, vi, 492; and Rutledge to Hamilton, Jan. 10, 1801; *ib.*, 511; Ames to Gore, Nov. 10, 1799; *Works:* Ames, i, 265.

[4] Hamilton to Sedgwick, Dec. 22, 1800; *Works:* Lodge, x, 397; also, to Morris, Dec. 24, 1800; *ib.*, 398.

[5] Marshall to Hamilton, Jan. 1, 1801; *Works:* Hamilton, vi, 502–03; and see Brown: *Ellsworth*, 314–15. The principal American demand was compensation for the immense spoliation of American commerce

The Federalists in the Senate, however, were resolved not to ratify it; they were willing to approve only with impossible amendments. They could not learn the President's opinion of this course; as to that, even Marshall was in the dark. "The Secretary of State knows as little of the intentions of the President as any other person connected with the government."[1] Finally the Senate rejected the convention; but it was so "extremely popular," said the Republicans, that the Federalist Senators were "frightened" to "recant."[2] They reversed their action and approved the compact. The strongest influence to change their attitude, however, was not the popularity of the treaty, but the pressure of the mercantile interests which wanted the business-destroying conflict settled.[3]

The Hamiltonian group daily became more wrathful with the President. In addition to what they considered his mistakes of policy and party blunders, Adams's charge that they were a "British faction" angered them more and more as the circulation of it spread and the public credited it. Even "General

by the French. The treaty not only failed to grant this, but provided that we should restore the French ships captured by American vessels during our two years' maritime war with France, which, though formally undeclared, was vigorous and successful. "One part of the treaty abandons all our rights, and the other part makes us the dupes of France in the game she means to play against the maritime power of England. . . . We lose our honor, by restoring the ships we have taken, and by so doing, perhaps, make an implicit acknowledgment of the injustice of our hostile operations." (Rutledge to Hamilton, Jan. 10, 1801; *Works:* Hamilton, vi, 511.)

[1] Bayard to Andrew Bayard, Jan. 26, 1801; *Bayard Papers:* Donnan, 121.

[2] Gallatin to his wife, Feb. 5, 1801; Adams: *Gallatin*, 259.

[3] *Ib.*, 254.

M[arshall] said that the hardest thing for the Federalists to bear was the charge of British influence." [1] That was just what the "Jacobins" had been saying all along.[2] "If this cannot be counteracted, our characters are the sacrifice," wrote Hamilton in anger and despair.[3] Adams's adherents were quite as vengeful against his party enemies. The rank and file of the Federalists were more and more disgusted with the quarrels of the party leaders. "I cannot describe . . . how broken and scattered your federal friends are!" lamented Troup. "We have no rallying-point; and no mortal can divine where and when we shall again collect our strength. . . . Shadows, clouds, and darkness rest on our future prospects." [4] The "Aurora" chronicles that "the disorganized state of the anti-Republican [Federalist] party . . . is scarcely describable." [5]

Marshall, alone, was trusted by all; a faith which deepened, as we shall see, during the perplexing months that follow. He strove for Federalist union, but without avail. Even the most savage of the President's party enemies felt that "there is not a man in the U. S. of better intentions [than Marshall] and he has the confidence of all good men — no man regrets more than he does the disunion which has

[1] Ames to Gore, Dec. 29, 1800; reviewing political events of the year; *Works:* Ames, i, 286–87.

[2] Hamilton to Wolcott, Aug. 3, 1800; *Works:* Lodge, x, 383; and Wolcott to Ames, Aug. 10, 1800; Gibbs, ii, 400.

[3] Hamilton to Wolcott, Sept. 26, 1800; *Works:* Lodge, x, 389 (also in Gibbs, ii, 422); and see same to same, Aug. 3, 1800; *Works:* Lodge, x, 383.

[4] Troup to King, Oct. 1, 1800; King, iii, 315.

[5] *Aurora,* May 20, 1800.

taken place and no one would do more to heal the wounds inflicted by it. In a letter . . . he says 'by union we can securely maintain our ground — without it we must sink & with us all sound correct American principle.' His efforts will . . . prove ineffectual." [1]

It seems certain, then, that Hamilton did not consult the one strong man in his party who kept his head in this hour of anger-induced madness. Yet, if ever any man needed the advice of a cool, far-seeing mind, lighted by a sincere and friendly heart, Hamilton required it then. And Marshall could and would have given it. But the New York Federalist chieftain conferred only with those who were as blinded by hate as he was himself. At last, in the midst of an absurd and pathetic confusion of counsels,[2] Hamilton decided to attack the President, and, in October, wrote his fateful and fatal tirade against Adams.[3] It was an extravaganza of party folly. It denounced Adams's "extreme egotism," "terrible jealousy," "eccentric tendencies," "violent rage";

[1] Sedgwick to King, Sept. 26, 1800; King, iii, 309.

[2] Ames to Hamilton, Aug. 26, 1800; *Works:* Hamilton, vi, 463; also Cabot to Hamilton, Aug. 21, 1800; *ib.*, 458; and Aug. 23, 1800; *ib.*, 460 (also in Lodge: *Cabot*, 284–88); and to Wolcott, Aug. 23, 1800; Lodge: *Cabot*, 288–89.

The local politicians were loyal to the President; Ames bitterly complains of "the small talk among the small politicians, about disrespect to the President, &c., &c." (Ames to Pickering, Nov. 23, 1799; *Works:* Ames, i, 272.)

[3] Hamilton to Adams, Aug. 1, 1800; *Works:* Lodge, x, 382; and same to same, Oct. 1, 1800; *ib.*, 390. Wolcott supplied most of the material and revised Hamilton's manuscript. (Wolcott to Hamilton, Oct. 1, 2, 1800; *Works:* Hamilton, vi, 470–71.) For entire attack see Hamilton: "Public Conduct and Character of John Adams"; *Works:* vii, 687–726 (also in *Works:* Lodge, vii, 309–65.)

and questioned "the solidity of his understanding." Hamilton's screed went back to the Revolution to discover faults in the President. Every act of his Administration was arraigned as a foolish or wicked mistake.

This stupid pamphlet was not to be made public, but to be circulated privately among the Federalist leaders in the various States. The watchful Burr secured a copy [1] and published broadcast its bitterest passages. The Republican politicians shook with laughter; the Republican masses roared with glee.[2] The rank and file of the Federalists were dazed, stunned, angered; the party leaders were in despair. Thus exposed, Hamilton made public his whole pamphlet. Although its purpose was to further the plan to secure for Pinckney more votes than would be given Adams, it ended with the apparent advice to support both. Absurd conclusion! There might be intellects profound enough to understand why it was necessary to show that Adams was not fit to be President and yet that he should be voted for; but the mind of the average citizen could not fathom such ratiocination. Hamilton's influence was irreparably impaired.[3] The "Washington Federalist"

[1] Parton: *Burr*, 256–57; Davis: *Burr*, ii, 65 *et seq.*

[2] "This pamphlet has done more mischief to the parties concerned than all the labors of the *Aurora!*" (Duane to Collot; Parton: *Burr*, 258.)

[3] "Our friends . . . lamented the publication. . . . Not a man . . . but condemns it. . . . Our enemies are universally in triumph. . . . His [Hamilton's] usefulness hereafter will be greatly lessened." (Troup to King, Nov. 9, 1800; King, iii, 331.) "All . . . blame . . . Mr. Hamilton." (Carroll to McHenry, Nov. 4, 1800; Steiner, 476.)

Some Federalist politicians, however, observed Hamilton's wishes. For example: "You must at all events secure to the Genr. [Pinckney] a majority in Cong., it may there be done with *safety*, his success depends

denounced his attack as "the production of a disappointed man" and declared that Adams was "much his superior as a statesman." [1]

The campaign was a havoc of virulence. The Federalists' hatred for one another increased their fury toward the compact Republicans, who assailed their quarreling foes with a savage and unrestrained ferocity. The newspapers, whose excesses had whipped even the placid Franklin into a rage a few years before, now became geysers spouting slander, vituperation, and unsavory [2] insinuations. "The venal,

on the accomplishment of this measure. You know a friend of ours who can arrange this necessary business with the utmost perfect suavity." (Dickinson to McHenry, Oct. 7, 1800; Steiner, 471.)

Again Dickinson writes of "the absolute necessity of obtaining a *majority* (if it should only be by a *single* vote) in Cong. to favor the man who interests us most" and hopes "Hamilton's publication . . . will produce the desired effect." (Oct. 31, 1800; *ib.*, 472.)

[1] *Washington Federalist*, Nov. 29, 1800.

[2] For instance see the *Aurora's* editorial on women in the army, January 14, 1800; and see titles of imaginary books editorially suggested for use by the various Federalist leaders, especially Hamilton, Harper, and Gouverneur Morris, in *ib.*, May 10, 1800. On August 21 it described some Federalist leaders as "completely bankrupt of character as well as fortune."

Although it did not equal the extravagance of the Republican newspapers, the Federalist press was also violent. See, for instance, a satirical poem "by an Hibernian and an Alien" in the *Alexandria Advertiser*, reprinted in the *Washington Federalist* of February 12, 1801, of which the last verse runs: —

"With J[effer]son, greatest of men,
Our President next we will dash on.
Republican marriages then,
And drowning boats will be in fashion.
Co-alitions, tri-color we'll form
'T wixt white Men, Mulattos, and Negroes.
The banks of the treasury we'll storm —
Oh! how we'll squeeze the old Quakers,
Philosophy is a fine thing!"

The familiar campaign arguments were, of course, incessantly reiterated as: "The Government" cost only "FIVE MILLION dollars

servile, base and stupid"[1] "newspapers are an overmatch for any government," cried Ames. "They will first overawe and then usurp it."[2] And Noah Webster felt that "no government can be durable . . . under the licentiousness of the press that now disgraces our country."[3] Discordant Federalists and harmonious Republicans resorted to shameful methods.[4] "Never . . . was there such an Election in America."[5]

As autumn was painting the New England trees, Adams, still tarrying at his Massachusetts home, wrote Marshall to give his "sentiments as soon as possible in writing" as to what the President should say to Congress when it met December 3.[6] Three days later, when his first request was not yet halfway to Washington, Adams, apparently forgetful of his first letter, again urged Marshall to advise him as President in regard to his forthcoming farewell address to the National Legislature.[7]

Marshall not only favored the President with his "sentiments" — he wrote every word of the speech which Adams delivered to Congress and sent it to

. . . before the British treaty"; now it costs "FIFTEEN MILLIONS. Therefore every man who paid *one dollar* taxes then pays *three* dollars now." (*Aurora*, Oct. 30, 1800.)

[1] Ames to Pickering, Nov. 5, 1799; *Works:* Ames, i, 264.

[2] Ames to Dwight, March 19, 1801; *ib.*, 294.

[3] Webster to Wolcott, June 23, 1800; Gibbs, ii, 374.

[4] The *Washington Federalist*, Jan. 12, 1801, charged that, in Virginia, public money was used at the election and that a resolution to inquire into its expenditures was defeated in the Legislature.

[5] Charles Pinckney to Jefferson, Oct. 12, 1800; *Amer. Hist. Rev.*, iv, 117. For election arguments and methods see McMaster, ii, 499 *et seq.*

[6] Adams to Marshall, Sept. 27, 1800; *Works:* Adams, ix, 85; and see Graydon, footnote to 362.

[7] Adams to Marshall, Sept. 30, 1800; Adams MSS.

the distressed Chief Magistrate in such haste that he did not even make a copy.[1] This presidential address, the first ever made to Congress in Washington, was delivered exactly as Marshall wrote it, with a change of only one word "much" for "such" and the omission of an adjective "great." [2]

The address is strong on the necessity for military and naval preparation. It would be "a dangerous imprudence to abandon those measures of self-protection . . . to which . . . violence and the injustice of others may again compel us to resort. . . . Seasonable and systematic arrangements . . . for a defensive war" are "a wise and true economy." The navy is described as particularly important, coast defenses are urged, and the manufacture of domestic arms is recommended in order to "supercede the necessity of future importations." The extension of the national Judiciary is pressed as of "primary importance . . . to the public happiness." [3]

The election, at last, was over. The Republicans won, but only by a dangerously narrow margin. Indeed, outside of New York, the Federalists secured more electoral votes in 1800 than in the election of

[1] Marshall to Adams, without date; Adams MSS.

[2] Adams MSS. Marshall wrote two speeches for Adams. Both are in Marshall's handwriting. The President selected and delivered the one which appears in Adams's *Works* and in Richardson. The undelivered speech was the better, although it was written before the French treaty arrived, and was not applicable to the state of our relations with France when Congress convened. Marshall also wrote for Adams the two brief separate addresses to the Senate and the House. (*Ib.*)

[3] The original manuscripts of these speeches, in Marshall's handwriting, are in the Adams MSS. They are notable only as an evidence of Adams's confidence in Marshall at this, the most irritating period of his life.

Adams four years earlier.[1] The great constructive work of the Federalist Party still so impressed conservative people; the mercantile and financial interests were still so well banded together; the Federalist revival of 1798, brought about by Marshall's dispatches, was, as yet, so strong; the genuine worth of Adams's statesmanship [2] was so generally recognized in spite of his unhappy manner, that it would seem as though the Federalists might have succeeded but for the quarrels of their leaders and Burr's skillful conduct of the Republican campaign in New York.

Jefferson and Burr each had seventy-three votes

[1] Beard: *Econ. O. J. D.*, chap. xiii.

[2] When it was certain that Adams had been defeated, "Solon," in the *Washington Federalist* of Jan. 9, 1801, thus eulogized him: —

"The die is cast! . . . Our beloved ADAMS will now close his bright career. . . . Immortal sage! May thy counsels continue to be our saving Angel! Retire and receive . . . the . . . blessings of all *good* men. . . .

"Sons of faction [party]! demagogues and high priests of anarchy, now have you cause to triumph. Despots and tyrants! now may you safely pronounce 'ingratitude is the common vice of all republics. Envy and neglect are the only reward of superior merit. Calumny, persecution and banishment are the laurels of the hoary patriot.' . . .

". . . We have to contend . . . for national existence. Magistrates and rulers, be firm. . . . Our constitution is our last fortress. Let us entrench it against every innovation. When this falls, our country is lost forever."

This editorial, as well as all political matter appearing in the *Washington Federalist* during 1800–01, is important because of Marshall's reputed influence over that paper. (See *infra*, 541.)

At news of Jefferson's success the leading Federalist journal declared that some Republicans in Philadelphia "huzzaed until they were seized with lockjaw . . . and three hundred are now drunk beyond hope of recovery. Gin and whiskey are said to have risen in price 50 per cent since nine o'clock this morning. The bells have been ringing, guns firing, dogs barking, cats meuling, children crying, and jacobins getting drunk, ever since the news of Mr. Jefferson's election arrived in this city." (*Gazette of the United States*, Feb. 19, 1801.)

for President. Under the Constitution, as it stood at that time, the final choice for President was thus thrown into the House of Representatives.[1] By united and persistent effort, it was possible for the Federalists to elect Burr, or at least prevent any choice and, by law, give the Presidency to one of their own number until the next election. This, Jefferson advises Burr, "they are strong enough to do."[2] The Federalists saw their chance; the Republicans realized their danger.[3] Jefferson writes of the "great dismay and gloom on the republican gentlemen here and equal exultation on the federalists who openly declare they will prevent an election."[4] This "opens upon us an abyss, at which every sincere patriot must shudder."[5]

Although Hamilton hated Burr venomously, he advised the Federalist managers in Washington "to throw out a lure for him, in order to tempt him to start for the plate, and then lay the foundation of

[1] At that time, the presidential electors did not vote for a Vice-President, but only for President. The person receiving the largest number of electoral votes became President and the one for whom the second largest number of votes were cast became Vice-President. When Jefferson and Burr each had seventy-three votes for President, the election was thrown into the House of Representatives.

Thus, although, in casting their ballots for electors, the people really voted for Jefferson for President and for Burr for Vice-President, the equal number of votes received by each created a situation where it was possible to defeat the will of the people. Indeed, as appears in the text, that result was almost accomplished. It was this constitutional defect that led to the Twelfth Amendment which places the election of President and Vice-President on its present basis. (See "The Fifth Wheel in our Government"; Beveridge: *Century Magazine*, December, 1909.)

[2] Jefferson to Burr, Dec. 15, 1800; *Works:* Ford, ix, 155.

[3] "Jefferson & Burr have each 73 votes and . . . the Democrats are in a sweat." (Uriah Tracy to McHenry, Dec. 30, 1800; Steiner, 483.)

[4] Jefferson to Madison, Dec. 19, 1800; *Works:* Ford, ix, 158.

[5] Jefferson to Breckenridge, Dec. 18, 1800; *ib.*, 157.

dissension between" him and Jefferson.[1] The Federalists, however, already were turning to Burr, not according to Hamilton's unworthy suggestion, but in deadly earnest. At news of this, the fast-weakening New York Federalist chieftain became frantic. He showered letters upon the party leaders in Congress, and upon all who might have influence, appealing, arguing, persuading, threatening.[2]

But the Federalists in Congress were not to be influenced, even by the once omnipotent Hamilton. "The Federalists, almost with one Mind, from every Quarter of the Union, say elect Burr" because "they must be disgraced in the Estimation of the People if they vote for Jefferson having told Them that He was a Man without Religion, the Writer of the Letter to Mazzei, a Coward, &c., &c."[3] Hamilton's fierce warnings against Burr and his black prophecies of "the *Cataline* of America"[4] did not frighten them. They knew little of Burr, personally, and the coun-

[1] Hamilton to Wolcott, Dec. 16, 1800; *Works:* Lodge, x, 392.

[2] See these letters in *ib.*, 392 *et seq.*; and to Bayard, Jan. 16, 1801; *ib.*, 412 (also in *Works:* Hamilton, vi, 419, but misplaced and misdated).

[3] Hindman to McHenry, Jan. 17, 1801; Steiner, 489–90; and see Carroll to Hamilton, April 18, 1800; *Works:* Hamilton, vi, 434–35.

The *Washington Federalist*, even when the balloting was in progress, thus stimulated the members of its party in the House: "*Unworthy* will he be and consecrate his name to infamy, who . . . has hitherto opposed . . . Mr. Jefferson . . . and shall now meanly and inconsistently lend his aid to promote it [Jefferson's election]. . . . Will they confer on Mr. Jefferson the Federal suffrage in reward for the calumnies he has indiscriminately cast upon the Federal character; or will they remunerate him . . . for the very honorable epithets of *pander, to the whore of England,* '*timid men, office hunters, monocrats, speculators and plunderers*' which he has missed no opportunity to bestow upon them." (*Washington Federalist*, Feb. 12, 1801.)

[4] Hamilton to Wolcott, Dec. 17, 1800; *Works:* Lodge, x, 395.

try knew less. What was popularly known of this extraordinary man was not unattractive to the Federalists.

Burr was the son of the President of Princeton and the grandson of the celebrated Jonathan Edwards, the greatest theologian America had produced. He had been an intrepid and efficient officer in the Revolutionary War, and an able and brilliant Senator of the United States. He was an excellent lawyer and a well-educated, polished man of the world. He was a politician of energy, resourcefulness, and decision. And he was a practical man of affairs. If he were elected by Federalist votes, the fury with which Jefferson and his friends were certain to assail Burr [1] would drive that practical politician openly into their camp; and, as President, he would bring with him a considerable Republican following. Thus the Federalists would be united and strengthened and the Republicans divided and weakened.[2]

This was the reasoning which drew and bound the Federalists together in their last historic folly; and they felt that they might succeed. "It is . . . certainly within the compass of possibility that Burr

[1] Jefferson rightly attributed to Burr Republican success in the election. "He has certainly greatly merited of his country, & the Republicans in particular, to whose efforts his have given a chance of success." (Jefferson to Butler, Aug. 11, 1800; *Works:* Ford, ix, 138.)

[2] Sedgwick to Hamilton, Jan. 10, 1800; *Works:* Hamilton, vi, 511–14; Cabot to Hamilton, Aug. 10, 1800; *ib.*, 453 (also in Lodge: *Cabot*, 284); Hindman to McHenry, Jan. 17, 1801; Steiner, 489–90; Morris to Hamilton, Jan. 5, 1801; Morris, ii, 398; and same to same, Jan. 26, 1801; *ib.*, 402 (also in *Works:* Hamilton, vi, 503); Carroll to McHenry, Nov. 4, 1800; Steiner, 473–76; Rutledge to Hamilton, Jan. 10, 1801; *Works:* Hamilton, vi, 510.

may ultimately obtain nine States," writes Bayard.[1] In addition to the solid Federalist strength in the House, there were at least three Republican members, two corrupt and the other light-minded, who might by "management" be secured for Burr.[2] The Federalist managers felt that "the high Destinies . . . of this United & enlightened people are up";[3] and resolved upon the hazard. Thus the election of Burr, or, at least, a deadlock, faced the Republican chieftain.

At this critical hour there was just one man who still had the confidence of all Federalists from Adams to Hamilton. John Marshall, Secretary of State, had enough influence to turn the scales of Federalist action. Hamilton approached Marshall indirectly at first. "You may communicate this letter to *Marshall*," he instructed Wolcott, in one of his most savage denunciations of Burr.[4] Wolcott obeyed and reported that Marshall "has yet expressed no opinion."[5] Thereupon Hamilton wrote Marshall personally.

This letter is lost; but undoubtedly it was in the same vein as were those to Wolcott, Bayard, Sedgwick, Morris, and other Federalists. But Hamilton could not persuade Marshall to throw his influence to Jefferson. The most Marshall would do was to agree to keep hands off.

[1] Bayard to Andrew Bayard, Jan. 26, 1801; *Bayard Papers:* Donnan, 121.

[2] Bayard to Hamilton, March 8, 1801; *Works:* Hamilton, vi, 524.

[3] Tracy to McHenry, Jan. 15, 1801; Steiner, 488–99; and see Bayard to Andrew Bayard, Jan. 26, 1801; *supra.*

[4] Hamilton to Wolcott, Dec. 16, 1800; *Works:* Lodge, x, 392.

[5] Wolcott to Hamilton, Dec. 25, 1800; *Works:* Hamilton, vi, 498.

"To Mr. Jefferson," replies Marshall, "whose political character is better known than that of Mr. Burr, I have felt almost insuperable objections. His foreign prejudices seem to me totally to unfit him for the chief magistracy of a nation which cannot indulge those prejudices without sustaining deep and permanent injury.

"In addition to this solid and immovable objection, Mr. Jefferson appears to me to be a man, who will embody himself with the House of Representatives.[1] By weakening the office of President, he will increase his personal power. He will diminish his responsibility, sap the fundamental principles of the government, and become the leader of that party which is about to constitute the majority of the legislature. The morals of the author of the letter to Mazzei [2] cannot be pure. . . .

[1] See Chief Justice Ellsworth's statement of the conservative opinion of Jefferson. (Brown: *Ellsworth*, 324–25.)

[2] Jefferson to Mazzei, April 24, 1796; *Works:* Ford, viii, 237–41. The letter as published in America, although it had undergone three translations (from English into Italian, from Italian into French, and from French into English again), does not materially differ from Jefferson's original.

It greatly angered the Federalist leaders. Jefferson calls the Federalists "an Anglican, monarchical & aristocratical party." The Republicans had "the landed interests and men of talent"; the Federalists had "the Executive, the Judiciary," the office-holders and office-seekers — "all timid men who prefer the calm of despotism to the boisterous sea of liberty, British merchants & Americans trading on British capital, speculators & holders in the banks & public funds, a contrivance invented for the purposes of corruption," etc.

Jefferson thus refers to Washington: "It would give you a fever were I to name to you the apostates who have gone over to these heresies, men who were Samsons in the field & Solomons in the council, but who have had their heads shorn by the whore England." It was this insult to Washington which Marshall resented most bitterly.

Jefferson must have known that Mazzei would probably publish this

"Your representation of Mr. Burr, with whom I am totally unacquainted, shows that from him still greater danger than even from Mr. Jefferson may be apprehended. Such a man as you describe is more to be feared, and may do more immediate, if not greater mischief.

"Believing that you know him well, and are impartial, my preference would certainly not be for him, but I can take no part in this business. I cannot bring myself to aid Mr. Jefferson. Perhaps respect for myself should, in my present situation, deter me from using any influence (if, indeed I possessed any) in support of either gentleman.

"Although no consideration could induce me to be the Secretary of State while there was a President whose political system I believed to be at variance with my own; yet this cannot be so well known to others, and it might be suspected that a desire to be well with the successful candidate had, in some degree, governed my conduct." [1]

Marshall had good personal reasons for wishing Burr to be elected, or at least that a deadlock should be produced. He did not dream that the Chief Justiceship was to be offered to him; his law practice,

letter. Writing at Paris, in 1788, of Mazzei's appointment by the French King as "intelligencer," Jefferson said: "The danger is that he will overact his part." (Jefferson to Madison, July 31, 1788; *Works:* Ford, v, 425.)

The Republicans frankly defended the Mazzei letter; both its facts and "predictions" were correct, said the *Aurora,* which found scarcely "a line in it which does not contain something to admire for elegance of expression, striking fact, and profound and accurate penetration." (*Aurora,* May 26, 1800.)

[1] Marshall to Hamilton, January 1, 1801; *Works:* Hamilton, vi, 501–03.

neglected for three years, had passed into other hands; the head of the Cabinet was then the most important [1] office in the Government, excepting only the Presidency itself; and rumor had it that Marshall would remain Secretary of State in case Burr was chosen as Chief Magistrate. If the tie between Jefferson and Burr were not broken, Marshall might even be chosen President.[2]

"I am rather inclined to think that Mr. Burr will be preferred. . . . General Marshall will then remain in the department of state; but if Mr. Jefferson be chosen, Mr. Marshall will retire," writes Pickering.[3] But if Marshall cherished the ambition to continue as Secretary of State, as seems likely, he finally stifled it and stood aloof from the struggle. It was a decision which changed Marshall's whole life and affected the future of the Republic. Had Marshall openly worked for Burr, or even insisted upon a

[1] Following is a list of the annual salaries of different officers: —

President	$25,000
Vice-President	5,000
Chief Justice	4,000
Associate Justices	3,500
Attorney-General	1,500
Secretary of the Treasury	3,500
Secretary of State	3,500
Secretary of War	3,000

(*Annals*, 1st Cong., 1st Sess., Appendix, 2233–38.)

[2] At the very beginning of the movement in his favor, Burr refused to encourage it. "Every man who knows me ought to know that I disclaim all competition. Be assured that the Federalist party can entertain no wish for such a change. . . . My friends would dishonor my views and insult my feelings by a suspicion that I would submit to be instrumental in counteracting the wishes and expectations of the United States. And I now constitute you my proxy to declare these sentiments if the occasion shall require." (Burr to Smith, Dec. 16, 1800; *Washington Federalist*, Dec. 31, 1800.)

[3] Pickering to King, Jan. 5, 1801; King, iii, 366.

permanent deadlock, it is reasonably certain that the Federalists would have achieved one of their alternate purposes.

Although Marshall refrained from assisting the Federalists in their plan to elect Burr, he did not oppose it. The "Washington Federalist," which was the Administration organ [1] in the Capital, presented in glowing terms the superior qualifications of Burr over Jefferson for the Presidency, three weeks after Marshall's letter to Hamilton.[2]

[1] See *Aurora*, Jan. 21, 1801.

[2] "Lucius," of Fredericksburg, Virginia, in the *Washington Federalist*, Jan. 21, 25, and Feb. 6, 1801.

The following extracts from the first of these articles reveal the temper and beliefs of the Federalists: "Burr never *penned* a declaration of independence; . . . but he . . . has *engraved that declaration* in *capitals* with the point of his sword: It is yet *legible* on the *walls of Quebeck.* He has *fought* for that *independency,* for which Mr. *Jefferson* only *wrote. He* has gallantly exposed his life in support of that declaration and for the *protection* of its *penn-man.* He has been *liberal* of his *blood, while* Mr. *Jefferson* has *only hazarded* his *ink.* . . .

"*He never shrank from the post of danger. He* is *equally fitted for* service in the *field* and in the *public counsels:* He has been *tried* in *both:* in the one we have seen him *an able and distinguished Senator;* — in the *other* a *brave* and *gallant officer.* . . .

"*Mr. Jefferson* is better qualified to give the description of a butterfly's wing or to write an essay on the bones of the Mammouth; . . . but Mr. Burr . . . in . . . knowledge . . . necessary to form the *great and enlightened statesman,* is *much superior* to Mr. Jefferson. . . .

"Mr. Burr is not . . . *consecrated* to the *French;* . . . nor has he unquenchable hatred to . . . Great Britain. Unlike the *penn-man* of the declaration he feels the *full force* of the expression, '*in war enemies,* in *peace friends*' . . . Mr. Burr . . . will *only* consult *national honor* and *national* happiness, having no improper passions to gratify.

"Mr. Burr is . . . a friend of the Constitution . . . a friend of the commercial interests . . . the firm and decided friend of the *navy* . . . the *Eastern* States have had a President and Vice President; So have the *Southern.* It is proper that the *middle* states should also be respected. . . .

"Mr. Burr has never procured or encouraged those infamous Calumnies against those who have filled the Executive departments . . .

The Republicans said that Marshall wrote much that appeared in this newspaper.[1] If he was influential with the editor, he did not exercise his power to exclude the paper's laudation of the New York Republican leader.

It was reported that Marshall had declared that, in case of a deadlock, Congress "may appoint a Presidt. till another election is made." [2] The rumor

which we long have witnessed: Nor have those polluted *Sinks*, the Aurora, the Argus, the Press, the Richmond Examiner, and the like, poured forth their *impure* and *fœtid streams* at the influence of Mr. Burr, or to subserve his vanity or his ambition.

"If Mr. Burr is elected, the *Federalists* have nothing to *fear*. . . . The vile calumniators . . . of all who have . . . supported our government, and the *foreign incendiaries*, who, having no interest in *Heaven*, have called *Hell* to their assistance, . . . from Mr. Burr have nothing to *hope*. . . .

"Mr. Burr can be raised to the Presidency without any *insult* to the feelings of the Federalists, the friends of Government; . . . WITHOUT an *insult* to the *Memory* of *our* Washington; for it was not by Mr. *Burr*, nor was it by *his* friends, nor to *serve him that the great, the good, the immortal* Washington was charged with having, by his name, given a sanction to corruption, with being meanly jealous of the fame of even that contemptible wretch Tom Paine, with being an unprincipled Hypocrite and with being a foul murderer! a murderer under circumstances of such peculiar atrocity as to shock with horror the merciless savages, and to cause them indignantly to fly from his blood polluted banner!"

[1] "John Marshall . . . is the reputed author of a great part of the [rubbish] in the Washington Federalist." (Scots Correspondent [Callender] in *Richmond Examiner*, Feb. 24, 1801.) There is no proof of Callender's assertion; but some of the matter appearing in the *Washington Federalist* is characteristic of Marshall's style and opinions. See, for instance, the editorial on the prosecution of Theodore Dwight, denouncing "party spirit" (*Washington Federalist*, March 1, 1801). The *Aurora* of March 26, 1801, denounced "John Marshall's Federal Gazette at Washington."

[2] Monroe to Jefferson, Jan. 18, 1801; Monroe's *Writings:* Hamilton, iii, 256. An article signed "Horatius" in the *Washington Federalist* of Jan. 6, 1801, stated this position with great ability. The argument is able and convincing; and it is so perfectly in Marshall's method of

increased Republican alarm and fanned Republican anger. From Richmond came the first tidings of the spirit of popular resistance to "such a usurpation,"[1] even though it might result in the election of Marshall himself to the Presidency. If they could not elect Burr, said Jefferson, the Federalists planned to make Marshall or Jay the Chief Executive by a law to be passed by the expiring Federalist Congress.[2]

Monroe's son-in-law, George Hay, under the *nom de guerre* of "Hortensius," attacked Marshall in an open letter in the "Richmond Examiner," which was copied far and wide in the Republican press. Whether Congress will act on Marshall's opinion, says Hay, "is a question which has already diffused throughout America anxiety and alarm; a question on the decision of which depends not only the peace of the nation, but the existence of the Union." Hay recounts the many indications of the Federalists' purpose and says: "I understand that you, Sir, have not only examined the Constitution, but have given an opinion in exact conformity with the wishes of your party." He challenges Marshall to "come forward ... and defend it." If a majority of the House choose Burr the people will submit, says Hay, because such an election, though contrary to their wishes,

reasoning and peculiar style of expression that his authorship would appear to be reasonably certain.

"Horatius's" opinion concluded that the power of Congress "is completely adequate . . . to provide by law for the vacancy that may happen by the removal of both President and Vice President on the 3d of March next, and the non-election of a successor in the manner prescribed by the constitution."

[1] Monroe to Jefferson, Jan. 18, 1801; Monroe's *Writings:* Hamilton, iii, 256.

[2] Jefferson to Madison, Dec. 26, 1800; *Works:* Ford, ix, 161-62.

would be constitutional. But if, disregarding the popular will and also violating the Constitution, Congress "shall elect a stranger to rule over us, peace and union are driven from the land. . . . The usurpation . . . will be instantly and firmly repelled. The government will be at an end." [1]

Although the "Washington Federalist" denounced as "a lie" [2] the opinion attributed to him, Marshall, personally, paid no attention to this bold and menacing challenge. But Jefferson did. After waiting a sufficient time to make sure that this open threat of armed revolt expressed the feeling of the country, he asserted that "we thought best to declare openly and firmly, one & all, that the day such an act passed, the Middle States would arm, & that no such usurpation, even for a single day, should be

[1] "Hortensius" to John Marshall, Secretary of State, in the *Richmond Examiner;* reprinted in the *Aurora,* Feb. 9, 1801. George Hay, the writer of this letter, was a lawyer in Richmond. Jefferson appointed him United States Attorney for the District of Virginia, and, as such, he conducted the prosecution of Aaron Burr for treason before John Marshall, who, as Chief Justice of the United States, presided at the trial. (See vol. III of this work.)

Marshall was again attacked in two open letters, signed "Lucius," in the *Richmond Examiner,* Feb. 10, 13, 1801. His reported opinion, said "Lucius," alarmed "the active friends of freedom"; Marshall was "the Idol of his party" and knew the influence of his views: unless he publicly disclaimed the one now attributed to him, "Lucius" proposed to "unveil" Marshall's "motives" and "expose" him "uncovered to the sight of the people" — his "depravity shall excite their odium," etc. "Lucius's" attacks ended with Jefferson's election.

[2] The paper criticized "the intemperate counsel of a certain *would be attorney-general* of the United States (George Hay, *Esq.* of the antient dominion) . . . under the signature of Hortensius, and addressed to General Marshall, in consequence of a lie fabricated against him relative to an opinion said to have been given by him upon the late presidential election, which the honorable attorney knew to be a lie as well as we did, but was fearful of being forgot, and despaired of getting a better opportunity to shew himself!!!" (*Washington Federalist,* Feb. 12, 1801.)

submitted to."[1] The Republicans determined not only to resist the "usurpation . . . by arms," but to set aside the Constitution entirely and call "a convention to reorganize and amend the government."[2]

The drums of civil war were beating. Between Washington and Richmond "a chain of expresses" was established, the messengers riding "day and night."[3] In Maryland and elsewhere, armed men, wrought up to the point of bloodshed, made ready to march on the rude Capital, sprawling among the Potomac hills and thickets. Threats were openly made that any man appointed President by act of Congress, pursuant to Marshall's reputed opinion, would be instantly assassinated. The Governor of Pennsylvania prepared to lead the militia into Washington by the 3d of March.[4]

To this militant attitude Jefferson ascribed the final decision of the Federalists to permit his election. But no evidence exists that they were intimidated in the least, or in any manner influenced, by the ravings of Jefferson's adherents. On the contrary, the Federalists defied and denounced the Republicans and met their threats of armed interference with declarations that they, too, would resort to the sword.[5]

[1] Jefferson to Monroe, Feb. 15, 1801; *Works:* Ford, ix, 178–79; and see Jefferson to McKean, March 9, 1801; *ib.*, 206.

[2] Jefferson to Madison, Feb. 18, 1801; *ib.*, 182.

[3] Monroe to Hoomes, Feb. 14, 1801; Monroe's *Writings:* Hamilton, iii, 259; and Monroe to Nicholas, Feb. 18, 1801; *ib.*, 260.

[4] For these incidents and reports see Gallatin to his wife, May 8, 1801; Adams: *Gallatin*, 249.

[5] Thus, for example, the *Washington Federalist* of Feb. 12, 1801, after the House had balloted "upwards of 30 times": —

"But say the bold and impetuous partisans of Mr. Jefferson, and

The proof is overwhelming and decisive that nothing but Burr's refusal to help the Federalists in his own behalf,[1] his rejection of their proposals,[2] and

that, too, *in the Teeth of the Assembled Congress of America* — '*Dare* to designate any officer whatever, even temporarily, to administer the government in the event of a non-agreement on the part of the House of Representatives, and we will march and *dethrone him as an usurper. Dare* (*in fact*) to exercise the right of opinion, and place in the presidential chair any other than the philosopher of Monticello, and ten thousand republican *swords will instantly leap from their scabbards*, in defence of the violated rights of the *People!!!*

"Can our Countrymen be caught by so flimsy a pretext?

"Can it possibly interest either their feelings or their judgment?

"Are they, then, ripe for civil war, and ready to imbrue their hands in kindred blood?

"If the tumultuous meetings of a set of factious foreigners in Pennsylvania or a few *fighting* bacchanals of Virginia, mean the *people*, and are to dictate to the Congress of the United States whom to elect as President — if the constitutional rights of this body are so soon to become the prey of anarchy and faction — . . . it would be prudent to prepare for the contest: the woeful experiment if tried at all could never be tried at a more favorable conjuncture!

"With the militia of Massachusetts consisting of 70,000 (*regulars let us call them*) in arms — with those of New Hampshire and Connecticut united almost to a man, with half the number at least of the citizens of eleven other States ranged under the federal banner in support of the Constitution, what could Pennsylvania aided by Virginia — the militia of the latter untrained and farcically performing the manual exercise with *corn-stalks* instead of muskets — . . . What, may it be asked, would be the issue of the struggle?"

[1] "The means existed of electing Burr, but this required his cooperation. By deceiving one man (a great blockhead) and tempting two (not incorruptible) he might have secured a majority of the States." (Bayard to Hamilton, March 8, 1801; *Works:* Hamilton, vi, 522–24.)

"The Federalists were confident at first, they could debauch Col. B.[urr] . . . His conduct has been honorable and decisive, and greatly embarrasses them." (Jefferson to his daughter, Jan. 4, 1801; *Works:* Ford, ix, 166.)

[2] "I was enabled soon to discover that he [Burr] was determined not to shackle himself with federal principles. . . . When the experiment was fully made, and acknowledged upon all hands, . . . that Burr was resolved not to commit himself, . . . I came out . . for Jefferson." (Bayard to Hamilton, March 8, 1801; *Works:* Hamilton, vi, 523.)

his determination, if chosen, to go in as a Republican untainted by any promises;[1] and, on the other hand, the assurances which Jefferson gave Federalists as to offices and the principal Federalist policies — Neutrality, the Finances, and the Navy[2] — only all of these circumstances combined finally made Jefferson president. Indeed, so stubborn was the opposition that, in spite of his bargain with the Federalists and Burr's repulsion of their advances, nearly all of them, through the long and thrillingly dramatic days and nights of balloting,[3] with the menace of physical violence hanging over them, voted against Jefferson and for Burr to the very end.

[1] The Federalist managers were disgusted with Burr because he refused to aid them in their plot to elect him. "Burr has acted a miserable paultry part," writes Bayard. "The election was in his power, but he was determined to come in as a Democrat. . . . We have been counteracted in the whole business by letters he has written to this place." (Bayard to Bassett, Feb. 16, 1801; *Bayard Papers:* Donnan; 126.)

Burr had not "used the least influence" to be elected. (Bayard's Deposition; Davis: *Burr*, ii, 127.)

"*Had Burr done anything, for himself, he would, long ere this, have been President.*" (Cooper to Morris, Feb. 13, 1801; Davis: *Burr*, ii, 113.)

[2] Depositions of Bayard and Smith, in Gillespie *vs.* Smith; Randall, ii, 613–17; and Davis: *Burr*, ii, 135–37; also Baer to Bayard, April 19, 1830; *ib.*, 118; and see Bayard's account; Remarks in the Senate, Jan. 31, 1835; also, Bayard to McLane, Feb. 17, 1801; *Bayard Papers:* Donnan, 126 *et seq.*

In his "Anas" (*Works:* Ford, i, 392–93) Jefferson flatly denied his deal with the Federalists, and this, afterwards, provoked much controversy. It now is established that the bargain was made. See Professor McMaster's conclusion: "The price settled . . . the Republicans secured ten states." (McMaster, ii, 526.)

[3] For accounts by participants in this exciting and historic contest, see Gallatin's letters to his wife and to Nicholson from Feb. 5 to Feb. 19, 1801; Adams: *Gallatin*, 257–63; Dana to Wolcott, Feb. 11, 1801; Gibbs, ii, 489–90; Bayard to several friends, Feb. 22, 1801; *Bayard Papers, supra.*

The terms concluded with Jefferson, enough Federalists cast blank ballots[1] to permit his election; and so the curtain dropped on this comedy of shame.[2] "Thus has ended the most wicked and absurd attempt ever tried by the Federalists," said the innocent Gallatin.[3] So it came about that the party of Washington, as a dominant and governing force in the development of the American Nation, went down forever in a welter of passion, tawdry politics, and disgraceful intrigue. All was lost, including honor.

But no! All was not lost. The Judiciary remained. The newly elected House and President were Republican and in two years the Senate also would be "Jacobin"; but no Republican was as yet a member of the National Judiciary. Let that branch of the Government be extended; let new judgeships be created, and let new judges be made while Federalists could be appointed and confirmed, so that, by means, at least, of the National Courts, States' Rights might be opposed and retarded, and Nationalism defended and advanced — thus ran the thoughts and the plans of the Federalist leaders.

Adams, in the speech to Congress in December of the previous year, had urged the enactment of a law to this end as "indispensably necessary." [4] In the

[1] Jefferson to Madison, Feb. 18, 1801; *Works:* Ford, ix, 183.

[2] After Jefferson's election, for many days the *Washington Federalist* carried in italics at the head of its editorial columns a sentiment characteristic of Marshall: "*May he discharge its duties in such a manner as to merit and receive the blessings of all good men and without redding the cheek of the American Patriot with blushes for his country!!!*"

[3] Gallatin to his wife, Feb. 17, 1801; Adams: *Gallatin*, 262.

[4] Adams to Congress, Dec. 3, 1799; *Annals*, 6th Cong., 1st Sess.,

President's address to the expiring Federalist Congress on December 3, 1800, which Marshall wrote, the extension of the National Judiciary, as we have seen, was again insistently urged.[1] Upon that measure, at least, Adams and all Federalists agreed. "Permit me," wrote General Gunn to Hamilton, "to offer for your consideration, the policy of the federal party *extending the influence of our judiciary;* if neglected by the federalists the ground will be occupied by the enemy, the very next session of Congress, and, sir, we shall see —— and many other scoundrels placed on the seat of justice." [2]

Indeed, extension of the National Judiciary was now the most cherished purpose of Federalism.[3] A year earlier, after Adams's first recommendation of it, Wolcott narrates that "the steady men" in the Senate and House were bent upon it, because "there is no other way to combat the state opposition [to National action] but by an efficient and extended organization of judges." [4]

Two weeks after Congress convened, Roger Griswold of Connecticut reported the eventful bill to

187–88; and Richardson, i, 289. Yet at this period the business of the courts was actually decreasing. (See Brown: *Ellsworth*, 198.) But the measure was demanded by the bar generally and insisted upon by the Justices of the Supreme Court. (See Gibbs, ii, 486.)

[1] Adams to Congress, Dec. 3, 1799; as written by Marshall; Adams MSS.

[2] Gunn to Hamilton, Dec. 13, 1800; *Works:* Hamilton, vi, 483.

[3] The Federalist attitude is perfectly expressed in the following toast drunk at a banquet to Wolcott, attended by "the heads of departments" and the Justices of the Supreme Court: "*The Judiciary of the United States! Independent of party, independent of power and independent of popularity.*" (*Gazette of the United States,* Feb. 7, 1801.)

[4] Wolcott to Ames, Dec. 29, 1799; Gibbs, ii, 316.

carry out this Federalist plan.[1] It was carefully and ably drawn and greatly widened the practical effectiveness of the National Courts. The Supreme Court was reduced, after the next vacancy, to five members — to prevent, said the Republicans, the appointment of one of their party to the Nation's highest tribunal.[2] Many new judgeships were created. The Justices of the Supreme Court, who had sat as circuit judges, were relieved of this itinerant labor and three circuit judges for each circuit were to assume these duties. At first, even the watchful and suspicious Jefferson thought that "the judiciary system will not be pushed, as the appointments, if made, by the present administration, could not fall on those who create them."[3]

[1] *Annals*, 6th Cong., 1st Sess., Dec. 19, 837–38.

[2] *Richmond Examiner*, Feb. 6, 1801.

[3] Jefferson to Madison, Dec. 19, 1800; *Works:* Ford, ix, 159. The Republicans were chiefly alarmed because, in the extension of the National Judiciary, offices would be provided for Federalists. Even Jefferson then saw nothing but patronage in the Judiciary Act.

The "evident" purpose of the bill, said the *Aurora*, Feb. 4, 1801, was to "increase the influence of the present Executive and provide a *comfortable retreat* for some of those *good federalists* who have found it convenient to resign from their offices or been dismissed from them by the people."

In comparison to this objection little attention was paid to the more solid ground that the National Judiciary would be used to "force the introduction of the common law of England as a part of the law of the United States"; or even to the objection that, if the Judiciary was extended, it would "strengthen the system of terror by the increase of prosecutions under the Sedition law"; or to the increase of the "enormous influence" given the National Courts by the Bankruptcy Law.

The *Aurora*, March 18, 1801, sounded the alarm on these and other points in a clanging editorial, bidding "*the people beware*," for "the hell hounds of persecution may be let loose . . . and the people be ROASTED into implicit acquiescence with every measure of the 'powers that be.'" But at this time it was the creation of offices that the Federalists would fill to which the Republicans chiefly objected.

But Jefferson underestimated the determination of the Federalists. Because they felt that the bill would "greatly extend the judiciary power and of course widen the basis of government," they were resolved, writes Rutledge, to "profit of our short-lived majority, and do as much good as we can before the end of this session"[1] by passing the Judiciary Bill.

In a single week Jefferson changed from confidence to alarm. After all, he reflected, Adams could fill the new judgeships, and these were life appointments. "I dread this above all the measures meditated, because appointments in the nature of freehold render it difficult to undo what is done,"[2] was Jefferson's second thought.

The Republicans fought the measure, though not with the vigor or animosity justified by the political importance they afterwards attached to it. Among the many new districts created was an additional one in Virginia. The representatives from that State dissented; but, in the terms of that period, even their opposition was not strenuous. They said that, in Virginia, litigation was declining instead of increasing. "At the last term the docket was so completely cleared in . . . ten days . . . that the court . . . had actually decided on several [suits] returnable to the ensuing term."[3]

That, replied the Federalists, was because the courts were too far away from the citizens. As for the National revenues, they could be collected only

[1] Rutledge to Hamilton, Jan. 10, 1801; *Works:* Hamilton, vi, 511.
[2] Jefferson to Madison, Dec. 26, 1800; *Works:* Ford, ix, 161.
[3] *Annals*, 6th Cong., 1st Sess., 878.

through National tribunals; for this purpose,[1] two Federal Courts in Virginia, as provided by the bill, were essential. But, of course, sneered the Federalists, "Virginia would be well satisfied with one court in preference to two or with no court whatever in preference to one."[2]

But there was a defect in the bill, intimated the Virginia Republicans, that affected tenants and landowners of the Northern Neck. A clause of section thirteen gave the newly established National Court jurisdiction of all causes arising under the Constitution where original or exclusive jurisdiction was not conferred upon the Supreme Court or Admiralty Courts.[3] The National Court of the new Virginia District was to be held at Fredericksburg. Thus all suits for quitrents or other claims against those holding their lands under the Fairfax title could be brought in this near-by National Court, instead of in State Courts. This criticism was so attenuated and so plainly based on the assumption that the State Courts would not observe the law in such actions, that it was not pressed with ardor even by the impetuous and vindictive Giles.

But Nicholas went so far as to move that the jurisdiction of National Courts should be limited to causes exceeding five hundred dollars. This would cut out the great mass of claims which the present holders of the Fairfax title might lawfully have against tenants or owners. The Marshalls were the Fairfax assign-

[1] *Annals*, 6th Cong., 1st Sess., 879.

[2] *Ib.* The person who made this absurd speech is not named in the official report.

[3] *Ib.*, 896.

ees, as we have seen. No Republican, however, mentioned them in debate; but some one procured the insertion in the record of an insinuation which nobody made on the floor. In brackets, the "Annals," after the brief note of Nicholas's objection, states: "[It is understood that the present assignees of the claims of Lord Fairfax, are General Marshall, General Lee, and a third individual and that they maintain their claims under the British Treaty.]"[1]

For three weeks the debate in the House dragged along. Republican opposition, though united, was languid.[2] At last, without much Republican resistance, the bill passed the House on January 20, 1801, and reached the Senate the next day.[3] Two weeks later the Senate Republicans moved a substitute providing for fewer circuits, fewer judges, and a larger Supreme Court, the members of which were to act as circuit judges as formerly.[4] It was defeated by a vote of 17 to 13.[5] The next day the bill was passed by a vote of 16 to 11.[6]

When the debate began, the National Judiciary was without a head. Ellsworth, broken in health, had resigned. Adams turned to Jay, the first Chief Justice, and, without asking his consent, reappointed him. "I have nominated you to your old station,"[7]

[1] *Annals*, 6th Cong., 1st Sess., 897. This curious entry is, plainly, the work of some person who wished to injure Marshall and Lee. Nicholas's motion was lost, but only by the deciding vote of the Speaker. (*Ib.*) The bill, as finally passed, limited the jurisdiction of the National Courts to causes exceeding four hundred dollars. (*Ib.*)

[2] *Ib.*, 900, 901, 903, and 905.

[3] *Ib.*, 734. [4] *Ib.*, 740–41. [5] *Ib.*, 741. [6] *Ib.*, 742.

[7] Adams to Jay, Dec. 19, 1800; *Works:* Adams, ix, 91.

wrote the President. "This is as independent of the inconstancy of the people, as it is of the will of a President." But Jay declined.[1] Some of the Federalist leaders were disgruntled at Jay's appointment. "Either Judge Paterson [of New Jersey] or General Pinckney ought to have been appointed; but both these worthies were your friends," [2] Gunn reported to Hamilton. The Republicans were relieved by Jay's nomination — they "were afraid of something worse." [3]

Then, on January 20, 1801, with no herald announcing the event, no trumpet sounding, suddenly, and without previous notification even to himself, John Marshall was nominated as Chief Justice of the United States a few weeks before the Federalists went out of power forever. His appointment was totally unexpected. It was generally thought that Judge Paterson was the logical successor to Ellsworth.[4] Marshall, indeed, had recommended his selection.[5] The letters of the Federalist leaders, who at this period were lynx-eyed for any office, do not so much as mention Marshall's name in connection with the position of Chief Justice.

Doubtless the President's choice of Marshall was influenced by the fact that his "new minister,

[1] Jay to Adams, Jan. 2, 1801; *Jay:* Johnston, iv, 284. Jay refused the reappointment because he believed the Supreme Court to be fatally lacking in power. See chap. I, vol. III, of this work.

[2] Gunn to Hamilton, Dec. 18, 1800; *Works:* Hamilton, vi, 492.

[3] Jefferson to Madison, Dec. 19, 1800; *Works:* Ford, ix, 159. It is impossible to imagine what this "something worse" was. It surely was not Marshall, who was in nobody's mind for the Chief Justiceship when Jay was named.

[4] Pickering to King, Jan. 12, 1801; King, iii, 367.

[5] Story, in Dillon, iii, 359.

Marshall, did all to" his "entire satisfaction."[1] Federalist politicians afterward caviled at this statement of Adams. It was quite the other way around, they declared. "Every one who knew that great man [Marshall] knew that he possessed to an extraordinary degree the faculty of putting his own ideas into the minds of others, unconsciously to them. The secret of Mr. Adams's satisfaction [with Marshall] was, that he obeyed his Secretary of State without suspecting it."[2]

The President gave Marshall's qualifications as the reason of his elevation. Boudinot reported to Adams that the New Jersey bar hailed with "the greatest pleasure" a rumor that "the office of Chief Justice . . . may be filled by" Adams himself "after the month of March next." The President, who admitted that he was flattered, answered: "I have already, by the nomination of a gentleman in the full vigor of middle age, in the full habits of business, and whose reading of the science is fresh in his head,[3] to this office, put it wholly out of my power as it never was in my hopes or wishes."[4]

Marshall's appointment as Chief Justice was not

[1] Adams to William Cunningham, Nov. 7, 1808; *Cunningham Letters*, no. xiv, 44; also mentioned in Gibbs, ii, 349.

[2] Gibbs, ii, 349, 350.

[3] As we have seen, Marshall's "reading of the science," "fresh" or stale, was extremely limited.

[4] Adams to Boudinot, Jan. 26, 1801; *Works:* Adams, ix, 93–94. Adams's description of Marshall's qualifications for the Chief Justiceship is by way of contrast to his own. "The office of Chief Justice is too important for any man to hold of sixty-five years of age who has wholly neglected the study of the law for six and twenty years." (*Ib.*) Boudinot's "rumor" presupposes an understanding between Jefferson and Adams.

greeted with applause from any quarter; there was even a hint of Federalist resentment because Paterson had not been chosen. "I see it denied in your paper that Mr. Marshall was nominated Chief Justice of the U.S. The fact is so and he will without doubt have the concurrence of the Senate, tho' some hesitation was at first expressed from respect for the pretensions of Mr. Paterson."[1] The Republican politicians were utterly indifferent; and the masses of both parties neither knew nor cared about Marshall's elevation.

The Republican press, of course, criticized the appointment, as it felt bound to attack any and every thing, good or bad, that the Federalists did. But its protests against Marshall were so mild that, in view of the recklessness of the period, this was a notable compliment. "The vacant Chief Justiceship is to be conferred on John Marshall, one time General, afterwards ambassador to X. Y. and Z., and for a short time incumbent of the office of Secretary of State. . . . Who is to receive the salary of the Secretary of State, after Mr. Marshall's resignation, we cannot foretell, because the wisdom of our wise men surpasseth understanding."[2] Some days later the "Aurora," in a long article, denounced the Judiciary Law as a device for furnishing defeated Federalist politicians with offices,[3]

[1] Bayard to Andrew Bayard, Jan. 26, 1801; *Bayard Papers:* Donnan, 122.

[2] *Aurora*, Jan. 22, 1801.

[3] It is worthy of repetition that practically all the emphasis in their attacks on this act was laid by the Republicans on the point that offices were provided for Federalists whose characters were bitterly assailed. The question of the law's enlargement of National power was, com-

and declared that the act would never be "carried into execution, . . . unless" the Federalists still meant to usurp the Presidency. But it goes on to say: —

"We cannot permit ourselves to believe that *John Marshall* has been called to the bench to foster such a plot. . . . Still, how can we account for the strange mutations which have passed before us — Marshall for a few weeks Secretary of State ascends the bench of the Chief Justice."[1] The principal objection of the Republican newspapers to Marshall, however, was that he, "before he left the office [of Secretary of State], made provision for all the Federal printers to the extent of his power. . . . He employed the *aristocratic presses alone* to publish laws . . . for . . . one year."[2]

Only the dissipated and venomous Callender, from his cell in prison, displayed that virulent hatred of Marshall with which an increasing number of Jefferson's followers were now obsessed. "We are to have that precious acquisition John Marshall as Chief Justice. . . . The very sound of this man's name is an insult upon truth and justice"; and the dissolute scribbler then pours the contents of his ink-pot over Marshall's X. Y. Z. dispatches, bespatters his campaign for election to Congress, and continues thus:—

"John Adams first appointed John Jay in the room of Ellsworth. A strong suspicion exists that

paratively, but little mentioned; and the objections enlarged upon in recent years were not noticed by the fierce partisans of the time.

[1] *Aurora*, Feb. 3, 1801.

[2] *Baltimore American;* reprinted in the *Aurora*, April 2, 1801.

John did this with the previous certainty that John Jay would refuse the nomination. It was then in view to name John Marshall: first, because President Jefferson will not be able to turn him out of office, unless by impeachment; and in the second place that the faction [Federalist Party] who burnt the war office might, with better grace, attempt, forsooth, to set him up as a sort of president himself. *Sus ad Minervam!*"[1]

That the voice of this depraved man, so soon to be turned against his patron Jefferson, who had not yet cast him off, was the only one raised against Marshall's appointment to the highest judicial office in the Nation, is a striking tribute, when we consider the extreme partisanship and unrestrained abuse common to the times.

Marshall himself, it appears, was none too eager to accept the position which Ellsworth had resigned and Jay refused; the Senate delayed the confirmation of his nomination;[2] and it was not until the last day of the month that his commission was executed.

On January 31, 1801, the President directed Dexter "to execute the office of Secretary of State so far as to affix the seal of the United States to the inclosed commission to the present Secretary of State, John Marshall, of Virginia, to be Chief Justice of the United States, and to certify in your own

[1] *Richmond Examiner*, Feb. 6, 1801.

[2] Marshall's nomination was confirmed January 27, 1801, a week after the Senate received it. Compare with the Senate's quick action on the nomination of Marshall as Secretary of State, May 12, 1800, confirmed May 13. (Executive Journal of the Senate, iii.)

name on the commission as executing the office of Secretary of State *pro hac vice*." [1]

It was almost a week before Marshall formally acknowledged and accepted the appointment. "I pray you to accept my grateful acknowledgments for the honor conferred on me in appointing me Chief Justice of the United States. This additional and flattering mark of your good opinion has made an impression on my mind which time will not efface. I shall enter immediately on the duties of the office, and hope never to give you occasion to regret having made this appointment." [2] Marshall's acceptance greatly relieved the President, who instantly acknowledged his letter: "I have this moment received your letter of this morning, and am happy in your acceptance of the office of Chief Justice." [3]

Who should be Secretary of State for the remaining fateful four weeks? Adams could think of no one but Marshall, who still held that office although he had been appointed, confirmed, and commissioned as Chief Justice. Therefore, wrote Adams, "the circumstances of the times . . . render it necessary that I should request and authorize you, as I do by this letter, to continue to discharge all the duties of Secretary of State until ulterior arrangements can be made." [4]

Thus Marshall was at the same time Chief Jus-

[1] Adams to Dexter, Jan. 31, 1801; *Works:* Adams, ix, 95–96
[2] Marshall to Adams, Feb. 4, 1801; *ib.*, 96.
[3] Adams to Marshall, Feb. 4, 1801; *ib.*, 96.
[4] Same to same, Feb. 4, 1801; *ib.*, 96–97.

tice of the Supreme Court and Secretary of State. Thus for the second time these two highest appointive offices of the National Government were held simultaneously by the same man.[1] He drew but one salary, of course, during this period, that of Chief Justice,[2] the salary of Secretary of State remaining unpaid.

The President rapidly filled the newly created places on the Federal Bench. Marshall, it appears, was influential in deciding these appointments. "I wrote for you to Dexter, requesting him to show it to Marshall,"[3] was Ames's reassuring message to an aspirant to the Federal Bench. With astounding magnanimity or blindness, Adams bestowed one of these judicial positions upon Wolcott, and Marshall "transmits . . . the commission . . . with peculiar pleasure. Permit me," he adds, "to express my sincere wish that it may be acceptable to you." His anxiety to make peace between Adams and Wolcott suggests that he induced the President to make this appointment. For, says Marshall, "I will allow myself the hope that this high and public evidence, given by the President, of his respect for your services and character, will efface every unpleasant sensation respecting the past, and smooth the way to a perfect reconciliation."[4]

[1] Jay held both offices for six months.

[2] Auditor's Files, Treasury Department, no. 12, 166. This fact is worthy of mention only because Marshall's implacable enemies intimated that he drew both salaries. He could have done so, as a legal matter, and would have been entirely justified in doing so for services actually rendered. But he refused to take the salary of Secretary of State.

[3] Ames to Smith, Feb. 16, 1801; *Works:* Ames, i, 292.

[4] Marshall to Wolcott, Feb. 24, 1801; Gibbs, ii, 495.

Wolcott "cordially thanks" Marshall for "the obliging expressions of" his "friendship." He accepts the office "with sentiments of gratitude and good will," and agrees to Marshall's wish for reconciliation with Adams, "not only without reluctance or reserve but with the highest satisfaction." [1] Thus did Marshall end one of the feuds which so embarrassed the Administration of John Adams.[2]

Until nine o'clock [3] of the night before Jefferson's inauguration, Adams continued to nominate officers, including judges, and the Senate to confirm them. Marshall, as Secretary of State, signed and sealed the commissions. Although Adams was legally within his rights, the only moral excuse for his conduct was that, if it was delayed, Jefferson would make the appointments, control the National Judiciary, and through it carry out his States' Rights doctrine which the Federalists believed would dissolve the

[1] Wolcott to Marshall, March 2, 1801; Gibbs, ii, 496.

[2] The irresponsible and scurrilous Callender, hard-pressed for some pretext to assail Marshall, complained of his having procured the appointment of relatives to the Judiciary establishment. "Mr. John Marshall has taken particular care of his family," writes Jefferson's newspaper hack, in a characteristically partisan attack upon Adams's judicial appointments. (Scots Correspondent, in *Richmond Examiner*, March 13, 1801.)

Joseph Hamilton Davies, a brother-in-law of Marshall's, was appointed United States Attorney for the District of Kentucky; George Keith Taylor, another brother-in-law, was appointed United States Judge of the Fourth Circuit; and Marshall's brother, James M. Marshall, was appointed Assistant Judge of the Territory (District) of Columbia. These appointments were made, however, before the new Judiciary Act was passed. (Executive Journal of the Senate, i, 357, 381, 387.) Callender appears to have been the only person to criticize these appointments. Even Jefferson did not complain of them or blame Marshall for them. The three appointees were competent men, well fitted for the positions; and their appointment, it seems, was commended by all.

[3] Jefferson to Rush, March 24, 1801; *Works:* Ford, ix, 231.

Union; if Adams acted, the most the Republicans could do would be to oust his appointees by repealing the law.[1]

The angry but victorious Republicans denounced Adams's appointees as "midnight judges." It was a catchy and clever phrase. It flew from tongue to tongue, and, as it traveled, it gathered force and volume. Soon a story grew up around the expression. Levi Lincoln, the incoming Attorney-General, it was said, went, Jefferson's watch in his hand, to Marshall's room at midnight and found him signing and sealing commissions. Pointing to the timepiece, Lincoln told Marshall that, by the President's watch, the 4th of March had come, and bade him instantly lay down his nefarious pen; covered with humiliation, Marshall rose from his desk and departed.[2]

[1] The Republicans did so later. "This outrage on decency should not have its effect, except in life appointments [judges] which are irremovable." (Jefferson to Knox, March 27, 1801; *Works:* Ford, ix, 237.)

[2] Parton: *Jefferson,* 585–86. Parton relates this absurd tale on the authority of Jefferson's great-granddaughter. Yet this third-hand household gossip has been perpetuated by serious historians. The only contemporary reference is in the address of John Fowler of Kentucky to his constituents published in the *Aurora* of April 9, 1801: "This disgraceful abuse was continued to the latest hour of the President's holding his office." The "shameful abuse" was thus set forth: "It [Judiciary Law of 1801] creates a host of judges, marshalls, attorneys, clerks, &c, &c, and is calculated, if it could endure, to unhinge the state governments and render the state courts contemptible, while it places the courts of law in the hands of creatures of those who have lost the confidence of the people by their misconduct. The insidiousness of its design has been equalled only by the shameless manner of its being carried into execution. The Constitution disables any member of Congress from filling an office created during his period of service. The late President [Adams] removed persons from other branches of the Judiciary, to the offices created

This tale is, probably, a myth. Jefferson never spared an enemy, and Marshall was his especial aversion. Yet in his letters denouncing these appointments, while he savagely assails Adams, he does not mention Marshall.[1] Jefferson's "Anas," inspired by Marshall's "Life of Washington," omits no circumstance, no rumor, no second, third, or fourth hand tale that could reflect upon an enemy. Yet he never once refers to the imaginary part played by Marshall in the "midnight judges" legend.[2]

Jefferson asked Marshall to administer to him the presidential oath of office on the following day. Considering his curiously vindictive nature, it is unthinkable that Jefferson would have done this had he sent his newly appointed Attorney-General, at the hour of midnight, to stop Marshall's consummation of Adams's "indecent"[3] plot.

Indeed, in the flush of victory and the multitude of practical and weighty matters that immediately claimed his entire attention, it is probable that Jefferson never imagined that Marshall would prove to

by this law & then put members of Congress into the thus vacated offices. . . . This law can be considered in no other light than as providing pensions for the principals and adherents of a party [Federalist]. The evil however will not I trust be durable and as it was founded in fraud the return of a wiser system will release the country from the shame and imposition." (Fowler to his constituents in the *Aurora*, April 9, 1801.)

[1] Jefferson to Rush, March 24, 1801; *Works:* Ford, ix, 230–31; to Knox, March 27, 1801; *ib.*, 237; to Mrs. Adams, June 13, 1804; *ib.*, x, 85.

[2] Neither Randall nor Tucker, Jefferson's most complete and detailed biographers, both partisans of the great Republican, mentions the Lincoln-Marshall story, although, if it had even been current at the time they wrote, it is likely that they would have noticed it.

[3] Jefferson to Knox, *supra*.

be anything more than the learned but gentle Jay or the able but innocuous Ellsworth had been. Also, as yet, the Supreme Court was, comparatively, powerless, and the Republican President had little cause to fear from it that stern and effective resistance to his anti-national principles, which he was so soon to experience. Nor did the Federalists themselves suspect that the Virginia lawyer and politician would reveal on the Supreme Bench the determination, courage, and constructive genius which was presently to endow that great tribunal with life and strength and give to it the place it deserved in our scheme of government.

In the opinions of those who thought they knew him, both friend and foe, Marshall's character was well understood. All were agreed as to his extraordinary ability. No respectable person, even among his enemies, questioned his uprightness. The charm of his personality was admitted by everybody. But no one had, as yet, been impressed by the fact that commanding will and unyielding purpose were Marshall's chief characteristics. His agreeable qualities tended to conceal his masterfulness. Who could discern in this kindly person, with "lax, lounging manners," indolent, and fond of jokes, the heart that dared all things? And all overlooked the influence of Marshall's youth, his determinative army life, his experience during the disintegrating years after Independence was achieved and before the Constitution was adopted, the effect of the French Revolution on his naturally orderly mind, and the part he had taken and the ineffaceable impressions necessarily made upon him by the tremendous events of the first three Administrations of the National Government.

Thus it was that, unobtrusively and in modest guise, Marshall took that station which, as long as he lived, he was to make the chief of all among the high places in the Government of the American Nation.

END OF VOLUME II

APPENDIX

APPENDIX

I. LIST OF CASES

Argued by Marshall before the Court of Appeals of Virginia

Case	*Date*	*Reported*
Joseph Cutchin *v.* William Wilkinson	Spring Term, 1797	1 Call, 1
William Fairclaim, lessee, *v.* Richard and Elizabeth Guthrie	Spring Term, 1797	1 Call, 5
Cabell *et al.* *v.* Hardwick	Fall Term, 1798	1 Call, 301
Hopkins *v.* Blane	Fall Term, 1798	1 Call, 315
Pryor *v.* Adams	Fall Term, 1798	1 Call, 332
Proudfit *v.* Murray	Fall Term, 1798	1 Call, 343
Harrison *v.* Harrison, *et al.*	Fall Term, 1798	1 Call, 364
Shaw *et al.* *v.* Clements	Fall Term, 1798	1 Call, 373
Graves *v.* Webb	Fall Term, 1798	1 Call, 385
Jones *v.* Jones	Fall Term, 1798	1 Call, 396
Auditor of Public Accounts *v.* Graham	Fall Term, 1798	1 Call, 411
Beverley *v.* Fogg	Spring Term, 1799	1 Call, 421
Rowe *et al.* *v.* Smith	Spring Term, 1799	1 Call, 423
Ritchie & Co. *v.* Lyne	Spring Term, 1799	1 Call, 425
Eckhols *v.* Graham, *et al.*	Spring Term, 1799	1 Call, 428
Noel *v.* Sale	Spring Term, 1799	1 Call, 431
Lee *v.* Love & Co.	Spring Term, 1799	1 Call, 432
Wilson *v.* Rucker	Spring Term, 1799	1 Call, 435
Garlington *v.* Clutton	Spring Term, 1799	1 Call, 452
Taliaferro *v.* Minor	Spring Term, 1799	1 Call, 456
Hacket *v.* Alcock	Spring Term, 1799	1 Call, 463
Rose *v.* Shore	Spring Term, 1799	1 Call, 469
Smith *v.* Dyer	Spring Term, 1799	1 Call, 488
Macon *v.* Crump	Spring Term, 1799	1 Call, 500
Flemings *v.* Willis *et ux.*	Fall Term, 1799	2 Call, 5
Eppes, Ex'r, *v.* DeMoville, Adm'r.	Fall Term, 1799	2 Call, 19
Cooke *v.* Simms	Fall Term, 1799	2 Call, 33
Lawrason, Adm'r *v.* Davenport *et al.*	Fall Term, 1799	2 Call, 79
Price *et al.* *v.* Campbell	Fall Term, 1799	2 Call, 92
Eppes *et al.*, Ex'rs, *v.* Randolph	Fall Term, 1799	2 Call, 103
Taliaferro *v.* Minor	Fall Term, 1799	2 Call, 156

Case	*Date*	*Reported*
Anderson *v.* Anderson	Fall Term, 1799	2 Call, 163
Crump *et al. v* Dudley *et ux*	June, 1790	3 Call, 439
Beall *v.* Edmondson	June, 1790	3 Call, 446
Johnsons *v.* Meriwether	July, 1790	3 Call, 454
Barrett *et al. v.* Floyd *et al.*	July, 1790	3 Call, 460
Syme *v.* Johnston	December, 1790	3 Call, 482
Ross *v.* Pynes	December, 1790	3 Call, 490
Rev. John Bracken *v.* The Visitors of William and Mary College	December, 1790	3 Call, 495
Hite *et al. v.* Fairfax *et al.*	May, 1786	4 Call, 42
Pickett *v.* Claiborne	October, 1787	4 Call, 99
Beall *v.* Cockburn	July, 1790	4 Call, 162
Hamilton *v.* Maze	June, 1791	4 Call, 196
Calvert *v.* Bowdoin	June, 1791	4 Call, 217
Tabb *v.* Gregory	April, 1792	4 Call, 225
Ross *v.* Gill *et ux.*	April, 1794	4 Call, 250
White *v.* Jones	October, 1792	4 Call, 253
Marshall *et al. v.* Clark	November, 1791	4 Call, 268
Foushee *v.* Lea	April, 1795	4 Call, 279
Braxton *et al. v.* Winslow *et al.*	April, 1791	4 Call, 308
Commonwealth *v.* Cunningham & Co.	October, 1793	4 Call, 331
Johnston *v.* Macon	December, 1790	4 Call, 367
Hooe *v.* Marquess	October, 1798	4 Call, 416
Chapman *v.* Chapman	April, 1799	4 Call, 430
Mayo *v.* Bentley	October, 1800	4 Call, 528
Turberville *v.* Self	April, 1795	4 Call, 580
Executors of William Hunter and the Executors of Herndon *v.* Alexander Spotswood	Fall Term, 1792	1 Wash. 145
Stevens *v.* Taliaferro, Adm'r.	Spring Term, 1793	1 Wash. 155
Kennedy *v.* Baylor	Spring Term, 1793	1 Wash. 162
Baird and Briggs *v.* Blaigove, Ex'r.	Spring Term, 1793	1 Wash. 170
Bannister's Ex'rs *v.* Shore	Spring Term, 1793	1 Wash. 173
Clayborn, Ex'r *v.* Hill	Spring Term, 1793	1 Wash. 177
Anderson *v.* Bernard	Spring Term, 1793	1 Wash. 186
Johnson *v.* Bourn	Spring Term, 1793	1 Wash. 187
Eustace *v.* Gaskins, Ex'r	Spring Term, 1793	1 Wash. 188
Wilson and McRae *v.* Keeling	Fall Term, 1793	1 Wash. 195
Payne, Ex'r, *v.* Dudley, Ex'r	Fall Term, 1793	1 Wash. 196
Hawkins *v.* Berkley	Fall Term, 1793	1 Wash. 204
Hooe & Harrison *et al. v.* Mason	Fall Term, 1793	1 Wash. 207
Thweat & Hinton *v.* Finch	Fall Term, 1793	1 Wash. 217
Brown's Adm'r *v.* Garland *et al.*	Fall Term, 1793	1 Wash. 221
Jones *v.* Williams & Tomlinson	Fall Term, 1793	1 Wash. 230

Case	*Date*	*Reported*
Coleman *v.* Dick & Pat.	Fall Term, 1793	1 Wash. 233
Taylor's Adm'rs *v.* Peyton's Adm'rs	Spring Term, 1794	1 Wash. 252
Smith and Moreton *v.* Wallace	Spring Term, 1794	1 Wash. 254
Carr *v.* Gooch	Spring Term, 1794	1 Wash. 260
Cole *v.* Clayborn	Spring Term, 1794	1 Wash. 262
Shermer *v.* Shermer	Fall Term, 1794	1 Wash. 266
Ward *v.* Webber *et ux.*	Fall Term, 1794	1 Wash. 274
Applebury *et al. v.* Anthony's Ex'rs	Fall Term, 1794	1 Wash. 287
Smallwood *v.* Mercer *et al.*	Fall Term, 1794	1 Wash. 290
Minnis Ex'r, *v.* Philip Aylett	Fall Term, 1794	1 Wash. 300
Brown's Ex'rs *v.* Putney	Fall Term, 1794	1 Wash. 302
Leftwitch *et ux. v.* Stovall	Fall Term, 1794	1 Wash. 303
Lee, Ex'r, *v.* Cooke	Fall Term, 1794	1 Wash. 306
Burnley *v.* Lambert	Fall Term, 1794	1 Wash. 308
Cooke *v.* Beale's Ex'rs	Fall Term, 1794	1 Wash. 313
Dandridge *v.* Harris	Fall Term, 1794	1 Wash. 326
Nicolas *v.* Fletcher	Fall Term, 1794	1 Wash. 330
Watson & Hartshorne *v.* Alexander	Fall Term, 1794	1 Wash. 340
Wroe *v.* Washington *et al.*	Fall Term, 1794	1 Wash. 357
Cosby, Ex'r, *v.* Hite	Fall Term, 1794	1 Wash. 365
Hewlett *v.* Chamberlayne	Fall Term, 1794	1 Wash. 367
Pendleton *v.* Vandevier	Fall Term, 1794	1 Wash. 381
Walden, Ex'r, *v.* Payne	Fall Term, 1794	2 Wash. 1
James Roy *et al. v.* Muscoe Garnett	Fall Term, 1794	2 Wash. 9
James Ferguson *et al. v.* Moore	Spring Term, 1795	2 Wash. 54
Currie *v.* Donald	Spring Term, 1795	2 Wash. 58
Shelton *v.* Barbour	Spring Term, 1795	2 Wash. 64
Brock *et al. v.* Philips	Spring Term, 1795	2 Wash. 68
Turner *v.* Moffett	Spring Term, 1795	2 Wash. 70
Turberville *v.* Self	Spring Term, 1795	2 Wash. 71
Brydie *v.* Langham	Spring Term, 1795	2 Wash. 72
Bernard *v.* Brewer	Fall Term, 1795	2 Wash. 76
Philip McRae *v.* Richard Woods	Fall Term, 1795	2 Wash. 80
Newell *v.* The Commonwealth	Fall Term, 1795	2 Wash. 88
White *v.* Atkinson	Fall Term, 1795	2 Wash. 94
Martin & William Picket *v.* James Dowdall	Fall Term, 1795	2 Wash. 106
Claiborne *v.* Parrish	Fall Term, 1795	2 Wash. 146
Brown *et al. v.* Adm'r, Thomas Brown, dec'd	Fall Term, 1795	2 Wash. 151
Harrison, Ex'r, *v.* Sampson	Fall Term, 1795	2 Wash. 155
Harvey *et ux. v.* Borden	Fall Term, 1795	2 Wash. 156
Lee *v.* Turberville	Fall Term, 1795	2 Wash. 162

Case	Date	Reported
Jordan *v.* Neilson	Fall Term, 1795	2 Wash. 164
Ruffin *v.* Pendleton & Courtney	Spring Term, 1796	2 Wash. 184
Pearpoint *v.* Henry	Spring Term, 1796	2 Wash. 192
Sarah Walker & Thomas Walker, Ex'rs, *v.* Thomas Walke[r]	Spring Term, 1796	2 Wash. 195
Davenport *v.* Mason	Spring Term, 1796	2 Wash. 200
Lewis Stephens *v.* Alexander White	Fall Term, 1796	2 Wash. 203
Picket *v.* Morris	Fall Term, 1796	2 Wash. 255
Booth's Ex'rs *v.* Armstrong	Fall Term, 1796	2 Wash. 301

II. GENERAL MARSHALL'S ANSWER TO AN ADDRESS OF THE CITIZENS OF RICHMOND, VIRGINIA

I WILL not, Gentlemen, attempt to describe the emotions of joy which my return to my native country, and particularly to this city, has excited in my mind; nor can I paint the sentiments of affection and gratitude towards you which my heart has ever felt, and which the kind and partial reception now given me by my fellow citizens cannot fail to increase. He only who has been . . . absent from a much loved country, and from friends greatly and deservedly esteemed — whose return is welcomed with expressions, which, di[rec]ted by friendship, surpass his merits or his ho[pes,] will judge of feelings to which I cannot do justice.

The situation in which the late Envoys from [the] United States to the *French Republic* found themselves in *Paris* was, indeed, attended with the unpleasant circumstances which you have traced. — Removed far from the councils of their country, and receiving no intelligence concerning it, the scene before them could not fail to produce the most anxious and disquieting sensations. Neither the ambition, the power, nor the hostile temper of *France*, was concealed from them; nor could they be unacquainted with the earnest and unceasing solicitude felt by the government and people of the *United States* for peace. But midst these difficulties, they possessed, as guides, clear and explicit instructions, a conviction of the firmness and magnanimity, as well as of the justice and pacific temper of their government, and a strong reliance on that patriotism and love of liberty, which can never cease to glow in the American bosom. With these guides, however thorny the path of duty might be, they could not mistake it. It was their duty, unmindful of personal considerations, to pursue peace with unabating zeal, through all the difficulties with which the pursuit was embarrassed by a haughty and victorious government, holding in perfect contempt the rights of others, but to repel, with unhesitating decision, any propositions, an acceptance of which would subvert the independence of the *United States*. — This they have endeavoured to do. I delight to believe that their endeavours have not dissatisfied their government or country, and it is most grateful to my mind to be assured that they receive the approbation of my fellow-citizens in *Richmond*, and its vicinity.

I rejoice that I was not mistaken in the opinion I had formed of my countrymen. I rejoice to find, though they know how to estimate, and therefore seek to avoid the horrors and dangers of war, yet they know also how to value the blessings of liberty and national independence: — They know that peace would be purchased at too high a price by bending beneath a foreign yoke, and that peace so purchased could be but of short duration. The nation thus submitting would be soon involved in the quarrels of its master, and would be compelled to exhaust its blood and its treasure, not for its own liberty, its own independence, or its own rights, but for the aggrandizement of its oppressor. The modern world unhappily exhibits but too plain a demonstration of this proposition. I pray heaven that *America* may never contribute its still further elucidation.

Terrible to her neighbors on the continent of *Europe*, as all must admit *France* to be, I believe that the *United States*, if indeed united, if awake to the impending danger, if capable of employing their whole, their undivided force — are so situated as to be able to preserve their independence. An immense ocean placed by a gracious Providence, which seems to watch over this rising empire, between us and the European world, opposes of itself such an obstacle to an invading ambition, must so diminish the force which can be brought to bear upon us, that our resources, if duly exerted, must be adequate to our protection, and we shall remain free if we do not deserve to be slaves.

You do me justice, gentlemen, when you suppose that consolation must be derived from a comparison of the Administration of the American Government, with that which I have lately witnessed. To a citizen of the *United States*, so familiarly habituated to the actual possession of liberty, that he almost considers it as the inseparable companion of man, a view of the despotism, which borrowing the garb and usurping the name of freedom, tyrannizes over so large and so fair a proportion of the earth, must teach the value which he ought to place on the solid safety and real security he enjoys at home. In support of these, all temporary difficulties, however great, ought to be encountered, and I agree with you that the loss of them would poison and embitter every other joy; and that deprived of them, men who aspire to the exalted character of freemen, would turn with loathing and disgust from every other comfort of life.

To me, gentlemen, the attachment you manifest to the government of your choice affords the most sincere satisfaction. Having no interests separate from or opposed to those of the people, being themselves subject in common with others, to the laws they make, being soon to return to that mass from which they are selected for a time in order to conduct the affairs of the nation, it is by no means probable that those who administer the government of the *United States* can be actuated by other motives than the sincere desire of promoting the real prosperity of those, whose destiny involves their own, and in whose ruin they must participate. Desirable as it is at all times, a due confidence in our government, it is peculiarly so in a moment of peril like the present, in a moment when the want of that confidence must impair the means of self defence, must increase a danger already but too great, and furnish, or at least give the appearance of furnishing, to a foreign real enemy, those weapons, which have so often been so successfully used.

Accept, gentlemen, my grateful acknowledgments for your kind expressions concerning myself, and do me the justice to believe, that your prosperity, and that of the city of *Richmond* and its vicinity, will ever be among the first wishes of my heart.

(From *Columbian Centinel*, Saturday, Sept. 22, 1798.)

III. FREEHOLDER'S QUESTIONS TO GENERAL MARSHALL

VIRGINIA. Fredericksburg, Oct. 2

POLITICAL QUESTIONS

Addressed to General* MARSHALL *with his Answer thereto

To J. MARSHALL, Esq.

RICHMOND, Sept. 12.

DEAR SIR,

Under a conviction that it will be of utility, should the answers to the following questions be such as I anticipate, I state them with a confidence of your readiness to give replies. They will, at all events, greatly satisfy my mind.

1st. Do you not in heart, and sentiment, profess yourself an American — attached to the genuine principles of the Constitution, as sanctioned by the will of the people, for their general liberty, prosperity and happiness?

2d. Do you conceive that the true interest and prosperity of *America*, is materially, or at all, dependent upon an alliance with any foreign nation? If you do, please state the causes, and a preference, if any exists, with the reasons for that preference.

3d. Are you in favor of an alliance, offensive and defensive, with *Great Britain?* In fine, are you disposed to advocate any other, or a closer connection with that nation, than exists at the ratification of the treaty of 1794? If so, please state your reasons.

4th. By what general principles, in your view, have the measures of our Administration and Government, in respect to *France*, been consistent with true policy or necessity? And could not the consequences have been avoided by a different line of conduct on our part?

5th. Are you an advocate for the Alien and Sedition Bills? Or, in the event of your election, will you use your influence to obtain a appeal of these laws?

A FREEHOLDER

(*Columbian Centinel*, Boston, Mass., Saturday, October 20, 1798.)

MARSHALL'S ANSWERS TO FREEHOLDER'S QUESTIONS

RICHMOND, Sept. 20, '98.

DEAR SIR: —

I have just received your letter of yesterday, [*sic*] and shall with equal candor and satisfaction, answer all your queries. Every citizen has a right to know the political sentiments of the man who is proposed as his representative; and mine have never been of a nature to shun examination. To those who think another gentleman more capable of serving the district than myself, it would be useless to explain my opinions because whatever my opinions may be, they will, and ought, to vote for that other; but I cannot help wishing that those who think differently, would know my real principles, and not attribute to me those I never possessed; and with which active calumny has been pleased to asperse me.

Answ. 1. In heart and sentiment, as well as by birth and interest, I am an American, attached to the genuine principles of the constitution, as sanctioned by the will of the people, for their general liberty, prosperity and happiness. I consider that constitution as the rock of our political salvation, which has preserved us from misery, division and civil wars; and which will yet preserve us if we value it rightly and support it firmly.

2. I do not think the interest and prosperity of America, at all dependent on the alliance with any foreign nation; nor does the man exist who would regret more than myself the formation of such an alliance. In truth, America has, in my opinion, no motive for forming such connection, and very powerful motives for avoiding them. Europe is eternally engaged in wars in which we have no interest; and with which the fondest policy forbids us to intermeddle.

We ought to avoid any compact which may endanger our being involved in them. My sentiments on this subject are detailed at large in the beginning of the memorial addressed by the late envoys from the United States to the minister of foreign affairs of the French Republic, where the neutrality of the United States is justified, and the reasons for that neutrality stated.

3rd. I am not in favor of an alliance offensive and defensive with Great Britain nor for closer connection with that nation than already exists. No man in existence is more decidedly opposed to such an alliance, or more fully convinced of the evils that would result from it. I never have, in thought, word, or deed, given the smallest reason to suspect I wished it; nor do I believe any man acquainted with me does suspect it. Those who originate and countenance such an idea, may (if they know me) design to impose on others, but they do not impose on themselves.

The whole of my politics respecting foreign nations are reducible to this single position. We ought to have commercial intercourse with all, but political ties with none. Let us buy cheap and sell as dear as possible. Let commerce go wherever individual, and consequently national interest, will carry it; but let us never connect ourselves politically with any nation whatever.

I have not a right to say, nor can I say positively, what are the opinions of those who administer the Government of the United States; but I believe firmly that neither the President, nor any one of those with whom he advises, would consent to form a close and permanent political connection with any nation upon earth.

Should France continue to wage an unprovoked war against us, while she is also at war with Britain, it would be madness and folly not to endeavor to make such temporary arrangements as would give us the aid of the British fleets to prevent our being invaded; but I would not, even to obtain so obvious a good, make such a sacrifice as I think we should make, by forming a permanent political connection with that, or any other nation on earth.

4th. The measures of the administration and government of the United States with respect to France have in my opinion been uniformly directed by a sincere and unequivocal desire to observe, faithfully, the treaties existing between the two nations and to preserve the neutrality and independence of our country. — Had it been possible to maintain peace with France without sacrificing those great objects, I am convinced that our government would have maintained it.

Unfortunately it has been impossible. I do not believe that any different line of conduct on our part, unless we would have relinquished the rights of self government, and have become the colonies of France, could have preserved peace with that nation. — But be assured that the primary object of France is and for a long time past has been, dominion over others. This is a truth only to be disbelieved by those who shut their eyes on the history and conduct of that nation.

The grand instruments by which they effect this end, to which all their measures tend, are immense armies on their part, and divisions, which a variety of circumstances have enabled them to create, among those whom they wish to subdue. Whenever France has exhibited a disposition to be just toward the United States, an accurate attention to facts now in possession of the public, will prove that this disposition was manifest in the hope of involving us in her wars, as a dependent and subordinate nation.

5th. I am not an advocate for the alien and sedition bills; had I been in Congress when they passed, I should, unless my judgment could have been changed, certainly have opposed them. Yet, I do not think them fraught with all those mischiefs which many gentlemen ascribe to them. I should have opposed them because I think them useless; and because they are calculated to create unnecessary discontents and jealousies at a time when our very existence, as a nation, may depend on our union —

I believe that these laws, had they been opposed on these principles by a man, not suspected of intending to destroy the government, or being hostile to it, would never have been enacted. With respect to their repeal, the effort will be made before I can become a member of Congress.

If it succeeds there will be an end of the business — if it fails, I shall on the question of renewing the effort, should I be chosen to represent the district, obey the voice of my constituents. My own private opinion is, that it will be unwise to renew it for this reason: the laws will expire of themselves, if I recollect rightly the time for which they are enacted, during the term of the ensuing Congress. I shall indisputably oppose their revival; and I believe that opposition will be more successful, if men's minds are not too much irritated by the struggle about a repeal of laws which will, at the time, be expiring of themselves.

J. MARSHALL.

(From *Times and Virginia Advertiser,* Alexandria, Va., Oct. 11, 1798.)

that nation. — But be assured that the primary object of France is and for a long time past has been, dominion over others. This is a truth only to be disbelieved by those who shut their eyes on the history and conduct of that nation.

The grand instruments by which they effect this end, to which all their measures lead, are immense armies on their part, and divisions, which a variety of circumstances have enabled them to create among those whom they wish to subdue. Whenever France has evinced a disposition to be just toward the United States, an accurate attention to facts now in possession of the public, will prove that the disposition was manifest in the hope of involving us in her wars as a dependent and subordinate nation.

3d. I am not an advocate for the alien and sedition bills: had I been in Congress when they passed, I should, unless my judgment could have been changed, certainly have opposed them. Yet, I do not think them fraught with all those mischiefs which many gentlemen ascribe to them. I should have opposed them because I think them useless; and because they are calculated to create unnecessary discontents and jealousies at a time when our very existence, as a nation, may depend on our union.

I believe that these laws, had they been opposed on these principles by a man not suspected of intending to destroy the government, or being hostile to it, would never have been enacted. With respect to their repeal, the effort will be made before I can become a member of Congress.

If it succeeds there will be an end of the business — if it fails, I shall on the question of renewing the effort, should I be chosen to represent the district, obey the voice of my constituents. My own private opinion is, that it will be unwise to renew it for this reason: the laws will expire of themselves, if I recollect rightly the time for which they are enacted, during the term of the ensuing Congress. I shall indisputably oppose their revival; and I believe that opposition will be more successful, if men's minds are not too much irritated by the struggle about a repeal of laws which will, at the time, be expiring of themselves.

J. Marshall.

(From *Times and Virginia Advertiser*, Alexandria, Va., Oct. 11, 1798.)

WORKS CITED IN THIS VOLUME

WORKS CITED IN THIS VOLUME

The material given in parentheses and following certain titles indicates the form in which those titles have been cited in the footnotes.

Adams, Charles Francis, *editor*. *See* Adams, John. Works.

Adams, Henry. The Life of Albert Gallatin. Philadelphia. 1879. (Adams: *Gallatin.*)

See also Gallatin, Albert. Writings.

Adams, John. Works. Edited by Charles Francis Adams. 10 vols. Boston. 1856. (*Works:* Adams.)

—— Old Family Letters. Copied from the originals for Alexander Biddle. Philadelphia. 1892. (*Old Family Letters.*)

—— Correspondence between the Honorable John Adams, late President of the United States, and the late William Cunningham. Boston. 1823. (*Cunningham Letters.*)

See also Wood, John. History of Administration of John Adams.

Adams, John Quincy. Writings. Edited by Worthington Chauncey Ford. 5 vols. New York. 1913. (*Writings, J. Q. A.*: Ford.)

Allen, Gardner Weld. Our Naval War with France. Boston. 1909. (Allen: *Our Naval War With France.*)

—— Our Navy and the Barbary Corsairs, Boston. 1905. (Allen: *Our Navy and the Barbary Corsairs.*)

Ambler, Charles Henry. Sectionalism in Virginia, from 1776 to 1861. Chicago. 1910. (Ambler.)

American Historical and Literary Curiosities. See Smith, John Jay, and Watson, John Fanning, *joint editors.*

American Historical Review. Managing editor, J. Franklin Jameson. Vols. 1–21. New York. 1896–1916. (*Amer. Hist. Rev.*)

American Remembrancer, The; or An Impartial Collection of Essays, Resolves, Speeches, &c., Relative, or Having Affinity to, the Treaty with Great Britain. 3 vols. Philadelphia. 1795. (*American Remembrancer.*)

American State Papers. Documents, Legislative and Executive, of Congress of the United States. Selected and

Edited under the Authority of Congress. 38 vols. Washington, D.C. 1832–61. [All citations in this work are from Foreign Relations, Class I, unless otherwise stated in the notes.] (*Am. St. Prs.*)

Ames, Fisher. Works, from his Speeches and Correspondence. Edited by his son, Seth Ames. 2 vols. Boston. 1854. (*Works:* Ames.)

Anderson, Dice Robins. William Branch Giles: A Study in the Politics of Virginia and the Nation from 1790 to 1830. Menasha, Wisconsin. 1914. (Anderson.)

Austin, James T. The Life of Elbridge Gerry, with Contemporary Letters. 2 vols. Boston. 1828–29. (Austin: *Gerry.*)

Avery, Elroy McKendree. A History of the United States and its people. 7 vols. Cleveland. 1904–10. (Avery.)

Bassett, John Spencer. The Federalist System, 1789–1801. [Volume 2 of The American Nation.] New York. 1906. (Bassett.)

Bayard, James A. Papers, from 1796 to 1815. Edited by Elizabeth Donnan. Washington. 1915. [Volume 2 of *Annual Report of the American Historical Association* for 1913.] (*Bayard Papers:* Donnan.)

Beard, Charles A. An Economic Interpretation of the Constitution of the United States. New York. 1913. (Beard: *Econ. I. C.*)

—— Economic Origins of Jeffersonian Democracy. New York. 1915. (Beard: *Econ. O. J. D.*)

Beaumarchais, Pierre Augustin Caron de. Beaumarchais et son temps. *See* Loménie, Louis de.

Bee, Thomas. Reports of Cases Decided in the District Court of South Carolina and Cases Determined in Other Districts of the United States. Philadelphia. 1810. (Bee's *Reports.*)

Benton, Thomas Hart. *See* United States. Congress. Abridgment of the Debates.

Binney, Horace. Eulogy on John Marshall, reprinted. *See* Dillon, John F.

Blennerhassett, Charlotte Julia [von Leyden], *Lady.* Talleyrand. By Lady Blennerhassett (Gräfin Leyden). Translated from the German by Frederick Clarke. 2 vols. London. 1894. (Blennerhassett: *Talleyrand.*)

BONAPARTE, NAPOLEON. Life. *See* Sloane, William Milligan. *Also see* Lanfrey, Pierre. History of Napoleon First.

BRACKENRIDGE, HENRY M. History of the Western Insurrection in Pennsylvania, commonly called the Whiskey Insurrection, 1794. Pittsburgh. 1859. (Brackenridge: *History of the Western Insurrection.*)

BRANCH, JOHN P. Historical Papers, issued by the Randolph-Macon College, Ashland, Virginia. Richmond. 1901. (*Branch Historical Papers.*)

BRISSOT DE WARVILLE, JEAN PIERRE. New Travels in the United States of America, performed in 1788. Dublin. 1792. (De Warville.)

BROGLIE, *Duc* DE, *editor*. *See* Talleyrand, Prince de. Memoirs.

BROWN, WILLIAM GARROTT. The Life of Oliver Ellsworth. New York. 1905. (Brown: *Ellsworth.*)

BURK, JOHN DALY. The History of Virginia, from its First Settlement to the Present Day. Continued by Skelton Jones and Louis Hue Girardin. 4 vols. Richmond. 1804–16. (Burk.)

BURKE, EDMUND. Works, with a Memoir. 3 vols. New York. 1849. (*Works:* Burke.)

BURR, AARON. Memoirs. *See* Davis, Matthew L. *Also see* Parton, James. Life and Times of Aaron Burr.

CABOT, GEORGE. *See* Lodge, Henry Cabot. Life and Letters of George Cabot.

Calendar of Virginia State Papers and Other Manuscripts. Preserved in the Capitol at Richmond. Vols. 1–11. Richmond. 1875–93. (*Cal. Va. St. Prs.*)

CALLENDER, JOHN THOMAS. The Prospect Before Us. Richmond. 1800. (Callender: *The Prospect Before Us.*)

CHANNING, EDWARD. A History of the United States. [Vols. 1–3.] New York. 1912–16. (Channing.)

CHASTELLUX, *Marquis* F. J. DE. Travels in North America in the years 1780–81–82. New York. 1828. (Chastellux.)

CHRISTIAN, WILLIAM ASBURY. Richmond, Her Past and Present. Richmond. 1912. (Christian.)

COBBETT, WILLIAM. Porcupine's Works, 1783 to 1801. 12 vols. London. 1801. (Cobbett.)

CONWAY, MONCURE DANIEL. Omitted Chapters of History, disclosed in the Life and Papers of Edmund Randolph. New York. 1888. (Conway.) *Also see* Paine, Thomas. Writings.

Coxe, Tench. An Examination of the Conduct of Great Britain Respecting Neutrals. Philadelphia. 1807. (Coxe: *An Examination of the Conduct of Great Britain Respecting Neutrals.*)

Cunningham, William. *See* Adams, John. Correspondence.

Dallas, A. J. *See* United States. Supreme Court Reports.

Davis, John. Travels of Four Years and a half in the United States of America. 1798–1802. London. 1803. (Davis.)

Davis, Matthew L. Memoirs of Aaron Burr, with miscellaneous selections from his correspondence. 2 vols. New York. 1838. (Davis: *Burr.*)

Dedham [Mass.] Historical Register. Vols. 1–14. Dedham Historical Society, Dedham, Mass. 1890–1903. (*Dedham Historical Register.*)

De Warville. *See* Brissot de Warville, Jean Pierre.

Dillon, John F., *compiler*. John Marshall, Life, Character, and Judicial Services. (Including the Classic Orations of Binney, Story, Phelps, Waite, and Rawle.) 3 vols. Chicago. 1903. (Story, in Dillon; and Binney, in Dillon.)

Dodd, William E. Statesmen of the Old South, or From Radicalism to Conservative Revolt. New York. 1911. (Dodd.)

Donnan, Elizabeth, *editor*. *See* Bayard, James A. Papers.

Eckenrode, H. J. The Revolution in Virginia. Boston. 1916. (Eckenrode: *R. V.*)

—— Separation of Church and State in Virginia. A Study in the Development of the Revolution. Richmond. 1910. [Special Report of the Department of Archives and History of the Virginia State Library.] (Eckenrode: *S. of C. and S.*)

Ellsworth, *Chief Justice* Oliver. Life. *See* Brown, William Garrott.

Findley, William. History of the Insurrection, in the Four Western Counties of Pennsylvania, in the year 1794. Philadelphia. 1796. (Findley: *History of the Western Insurrection.*)

Flanders, Henry. The Lives and Times of the Chief Justices of the Supreme Court of the United States. 2 vols. Philadelphia. 1881. (Flanders.)

FORD, PAUL LEICESTER, *editor. See* Jefferson, Thomas. Works.

FORD, WORTHINGTON CHAUNCEY, *editor. See* Jefferson, Thomas. Correspondence.
Also see Washington, George. Writings.
And *see also* Adams, John Quincy. Writings.
Also see Vans Murray, William. Letters.

FRENEAU, PHILIP. Poems of Philip Freneau. Edited by Fred Lewis Pattee. 3 vols. Princeton. 1902–07. (Freneau.)

FUNCK-BRENTANO, FRANTZ. Legends of the Bastille, translated by George Maidment. London. 1899. (Funck-Brentano: *Legends of the Bastille.*)

GALLATIN, ALBERT. Writings. Edited by Henry Adams. 3 vols. Philadelphia. 1879. (Gallatin's *Writings:* Adams.)
See also Adams, Henry. Life of Albert Gallatin.

GARLAND, HUGH A. Life of John Randolph of Roanoke. 2 vols. New York. 1851. (Garland: *Randolph.*)

GAY, SYDNEY HOWARD. James Madison. [American Statesmen Series.] Boston. 1895.

GIBBS, GEORGE, *editor. See* Wolcott, Oliver. Memoirs of the Administrations of Washington and John Adams. (Gibbs.)

GILMAN, DANIEL C. James Monroe, in his Relations to the Public Service During Half a Century. 1776 to 1826. [American Statesmen Series.] Boston. 1895.

GILMER, FRANCIS WALKER. Sketches, Essays, and Translations. Baltimore, 1828. (Gilmer.)

GRAYDON, ALEXANDER. Memoirs of His Own Time, with Reminiscences of the Men and Events of the Revolution. Edited by John Stockton Littell. Philadelphia. 1846. (Graydon.)

Green Bag, The; an Entertaining Magazine for Lawyers. Edited by Horace W. Fuller. Vols. 1–26. Boston. 1889–1914. [After 1914 consolidated with *The Central Law Journal.*] (*Green Bag.*)

GRIGSBY, HUGH BLAIR. The History of the Virginia Federal Convention of 1788. Virginia Historical Society. Richmond. 1815. [Volume 1 is volume 9, new series. Volume 2 is volume 10, new series.] (Grigsby.)

HAMILTON, ALEXANDER. Works. Edited by John C. Hamilton. 7 vols. New York. 1851. (*Works:* Hamilton.)

—— Works. Edited by Henry Cabot Lodge. [Federal Edition.] 12 vols. New York. 1904. (*Works:* Lodge.)

HAMILTON, JOHN C., *editor*. History of the Republic of the United States, as traced in the Writings of Alexander Hamilton and his Contemporaries. 6 vols. New York. 1857–60. (Hamilton: *History of the Republic.*)

See also Hamilton, Alexander. Works.

HAMILTON, STANISLAUS MURRAY, *editor*. *See* Monroe, James. Writings.

HAZEN, CHARLES DOWNER. Contemporary American Opinion of the French Revolution. Baltimore. 1897. (Hazen.)

HENING, WILLIAM WALLER. *See* Virginia. Laws.

HENRY, PATRICK. Life, Correspondence, and Speeches. Edited by William Wirt Henry. 3 vols. New York. 1891. (Henry.)

See also Wirt, William. Sketches of Life and Character of Patrick Henry.

HENRY, WILLIAM WIRT, *editor*. *See* Henry, Patrick. Life, Correspondence, and Speeches.

HILDRETH, RICHARD. History of the United States. 6 vols. New York. 1854–55. (Hildreth.)

Historical Magazine and Notes and Queries Concerning the Antiquities, History, and Biography of America. [1st Series.] Vols. 1–10. New York. 1857–75. (*Hist. Mag.*)

HOWE, HENRY. Historical Collections of Virginia. Charleston, S.C. 1845. (Howe.)

HUDSON, FREDERIC. Journalism in the United States from 1690 to 1872. New York. 1873. (Hudson: *Journalism in the United States.*)

HUNT, GAILLARD, *editor*. *See* Madison, James. Writings.

Interesting State Papers, from President Washington, M. Fauchet, and M. Adet, etc.; quoted by Edmund Randolph, Secretary of State, in his Defense of his Resignation of that Office. Philadelphia. 1796. (*Interesting State Papers.*)

IREDELL, JAMES. *See* McRee, Griffith J. Life and Correspondence of James Iredell.

JAY, JOHN. Correspondence and Public Papers. Edited by Henry P. Johnston. 4 vols. New York. 1890 (*Jay: Johnston.*)

JEFFERSON, THOMAS. Works. Edited by Paul Leicester Ford.

Federal Edition. 12 vols. New York. 1904. (*Works: Ford.*)
See Morse, John T. Thomas Jefferson.
And see Randall, Henry S. Life of Thomas Jefferson.
Also see Tucker, George. Life of Thomas Jefferson.
And see Parton, James. Life of Thomas Jefferson.

JOHNSTON, HENRY P., *editor*. *See* Jay, John. Correspondence and Public Papers.

JOHNSTON, MARY. Lewis Rand. Boston. 1908.

JONES, HUGH. The Present State of Virginia. London. 1724. (Jones.)

KENNEDY, JOHN P. Memoirs of the Life of William Wirt. 2 vols. Philadelphia. 1860. (Kennedy.)

KING, CHARLES R., *editor*. *See* King, Rufus. Life and Correspondence.

KING, RUFUS. Life and Correspondence. Edited by Charles R. King. 6 vols. New York. 1894. (King.)

LANCASTER, ROBERT A., JR. Historic Virginia Homes and Churches, with 316 Illustrations. Philadelphia. 1915.

LANFREY, PIERRE. The History of Napoleon the First. 4 vols. London. 1871–79. (Lanfrey: *Napoleon.*)

LA ROCHEFOUCAULD-LIANCOURT, FRANÇOIS ALEXANDRE FRÉDÉRIC, *Duc* DE. Travels through the United States of North America. 4 vols. London. 1800. (La Rochefoucauld.)

Lippincott's Monthly Magazine. A Popular Journal of General Literature. [1st Series.] Vols. 1–62. Philadelphia. 1868–98. (*Lippincott's Magazine.*)

LODGE, HENRY CABOT. Life and Letters of George Cabot. Boston. 1878. (Lodge: *Cabot.*)
—— George Washington. 2 vols. Boston. 1889. [American Statesmen.] (Lodge: *Washington.*)
See also Hamilton, Alexander. Works.

LOLIÉE, FRÉDÉRIC. Prince Talleyrand and His Times. Adapted by Bryan O'Donnell. London. 1911. (Loliée: *Talleyrand and His Times.*)

LOMÉNIE, LOUIS DE. Beaumarchais et son temps. 2 vols. Paris. 1856. (Loménie: *Beaumarchais et son temps.*)

LORING, JAMES SPEAR. The Hundred Boston Orators. Boston. 1855. (Loring: *Hundred Boston Orators.*)

Louisiana Law Journal. Edited by Gustavus Schmidt. [1 vol.] New Orleans. 1841–42.

LYMAN, THEODORE, JR. The Diplomacy of the United States. 2 vols. Boston. 1828. (Lyman: *Diplomacy of the United States.*)

MACCABE, JOSEPH. Talleyrand, A Biographical Study. London. 1906. (MacCabe: *Talleyrand.*)

MCHENRY, JAMES. Life and Correspondence. *See* Steiner, Bernard C.

MCMASTER, JOHN BACH. A History of the People of the United States. 8 vols. New York. 1914. (McMaster.)

MCREE, GRIFFITH, J. Life and Correspondence of James Iredell. 2 vols. New York. 1857. (McRee.)

MADISON, JAMES. Writings. Edited by Gaillard Hunt. 9 vols. New York. 1900. (*Writings:* Hunt.)

See also Rives, William C. History of Life and Times.

And see Gay, Sydney Howard. James Madison.

MARSHALL, HUMPHREY. The History of Kentucky. 2 vols. Frankfort. 1824. (Humphrey Marshall.)

MARSHALL, JOHN. Autobiography. *See* Smith, John Jay *and* Watson, John Fanning, *joint editors.* American Historical and Literary Curiosities. (*Autobiography.*)

—— Same. In National Portrait Gallery of Eminent Americans. Paintings by Alonzo Chappel, and Biographical and Historical Narratives by Evert A. Duyckinck. 2 vols. New York. 1862.

—— Same, reprinted. *See* Dillon, John F.

—— Life of George Washington. [1st Edition.] 5 vols. Philadelphia. 1805. [2d Edition.] 2 vols. Philadelphia. 1840. [The 2d Edition is cited in this work unless otherwise stated in the notes.] (Marshall.)

See also Thayer, James Bradley. John Marshall.

And see Flanders, Henry. Lives of the Chief Justices.

Also see Van Santvoord, George. Sketches of the Lives of the Chief-Justices.

MASON, GEORGE. Life. *See* Rowland, Kate Mason.

Massachusetts Historical Society. Collections. [Series vii.] Vols. 1–10. Boston. 1792–1915. (Mass. Hist. Soc. Coll.)

MEADE, *Bishop* WILLIAM. Old Churches, Ministers, and Families of Virginia. 2 vols. Richmond. 1910. (Meade.)

Monroe, James. Writings. Edited by Stanislaus Murray Hamilton. 7 vols. [Unfinished work.] New York. 1898–1903. (Monroe's *Writings:* Hamilton.)

Moore, Frank. American Eloquence, A Collection of Speeches and Addresses by the most Eminent Orators of America. 2 vols. New York. 1857. (Moore: *American Eloquence.*)

Mordecai, Samuel. Richmond in By-Gone Days, Being Reminiscences of An Old Citizen. Richmond. 1856. (Mordecai.)

Morison, Samuel Eliot. The Life and Letters of Harrison Gray Otis, Federalist, 1765–1848. 2 vols. Boston. 1913. (Morison.)

Morris, Gouverneur. Diary and Letters. Edited by Anne Cary Morris. 2 vols. London. 1889. (Morris.)

Morris, Robert. *See* Oberholtzer, Ellis Paxton. Robert Morris.

Morse, John T. Thomas Jefferson. Boston. 1795. [American Statesmen.] (Morse.)

Munford, George Wythe. The Two Parsons; Cupid's Sports; The Dream; and the Jewels of Virginia. Richmond. 1884. (Munford.)

New Jersey Historical Society. Proceedings. Vols. 1–10. Newark. 1847–1905. (*Proc.*, N.J. Hist. Soc.)

North American Review. Vols. 1–202. Boston. 1815–1915.

Oberholtzer, Ellis Paxton. Robert Morris, Patriot and Financier. New York. 1903. (Oberholtzer.)

Otis, Harrison Gray. Life and Letters. *See* Morison, Samuel Eliot.

Paine, Robert Treat, Jr. Works, in Verse and Prose, with Sketches of His Life, Character, and Writings. Boston. 1812. (*Works of Robert Treat Paine.*)

Paine, Thomas. Writings. Edited by Moncure Daniel Conway. 4 vols. New York. 1894–96. (*Writings:* Conway.)

Parton, James. The Life and Times of Aaron Burr. [Fourteenth Edition.] New York. 1861. (Parton: *Burr.*)

—— Life of Thomas Jefferson. Boston. 1874.

Paulding, James K. A Life of Washington. 2 vols. 1835. [Harper's Family Library. Stereotype Edition, 1836.] (Paulding.)

PAXTON, WILLIAM M. The Marshall Family, or a Genealogical Chart of the Descendants of John Marshall and Elizabeth Markham. Cincinnati. 1885. (Paxton.)

PECQUET DU BELLET, LOUISE. Some Prominent Virginia Families. 4 vols. Lynchburg, Va. 1909. (Pecquet du Bellet.)

Pennsylvania Magazine of History and Biography. Published by the Historical Society of Pennsylvania. Vols. 1–40. Philadelphia. 1877–1916. (*Pa. Mag. Hist. and Biog.*)

PERKINS, JAMES BRECK. France in the American Revolution. Boston. 1911. (Perkins: *France in the American Revolution.*)

PICKERING, OCTAVIUS. Life of Timothy Pickering, by his son and continued by Charles W. Upham. 4 vols. Boston. 1867–73. (Pickering: *Pickering.*)

PICKERING, TIMOTHY. Life. *See* Pickering, Octavius.

RANDALL, HENRY S. Life of Thomas Jefferson. 3 vols. New York. 1858. (Randall.)

RANDOLPH, EDMUND. Life and Papers. *See* Conway, Moncure Daniel.

RANDOLPH, JOHN. Life. *See* Garland, Hugh A.

RICHARDSON, JAMES D. A Compilation of the Messages and Papers of the Presidents. 1789–1897. 10 vols. Washington, D.C. 1896–99. (Richardson.)

RIVES, WILLIAM C. The History of the Life and Times of James Madison. 3 vols. Boston. 1859. (Rives.)

ROWLAND, KATE MASON. Life of George Mason. 2 vols. New York. 1892. (Rowland.)

SCHMIDT, GUSTAVUS, *editor*. *See* Louisiana Law Journal.

SCHOEPF, JOHANN DAVID. Travels in the Confederation, 1783–1784. Translated and edited by Alfred J. Morrison. 2 vols. Philadelphia. 1911. (Schoepf.)

SCHOULER, JAMES. History of the United States of America under the Constitution. 1783–1877. 7 vols. Washington, D.C. 1895–1913. (Schouler.)

SCOTT, JOHN, of Fauquier County, Va. The Lost Principle. By "Barbarossa" [*pseud.*]. Richmond. 1860. (Scott.)

SLOANE, WILLIAM MILLIGAN. Life of Napoleon Bonaparte. 4 vols. New York. 1796–1897. (Sloane: *Life of Napoleon.*)

SMITH, JOHN JAY, *and* WATSON, JOHN FANNING, *joint editors. American Historical and Literary Curiosities.* New York. 1852. (*Am. Hist. and Lit. Curiosities.*)

Southern Literary Messenger. Vols. 1–38. New York and Washington. 1834–64.

SPARKS, JARED. Correspondence of the American Revolution [being letters of eminent men to George Washington]. 4 vols. Boston. 1853. (*Cor. Rev.*: Sparks.)
See also Washington, George. Writings.

STEINER, BERNARD C. The Life and Correspondence of James McHenry. Cleveland. 1907. (Steiner.)

STORY, JOSEPH. Discourse on John Marshall, reprinted.
See Dillon, John F.
Also see Story, William Wirt.

STORY, WILLIAM WIRT. Life and Letters of Joseph Story. 2 vols. Boston. 1851. (Story.)

TALLEYRAND-PÉRIGORD, CHARLES MAURICE DE, *Prince* DE BÉNÉVENT. Memoirs. Edited by the Duc de Broglie. 5 vols. New York. 1891. (*Memoirs of Talleyrand:* Broglie's Ed.)

—— Memoirs. [Edited] by [—— Stewarton] the author of the Revolutionary Plutarch. 2 vols. London. 1805. (*Memoirs of Talleyrand:* Stewarton.)
See Loliée, Frédéric. Talleyrand and His Times.
Also see Blennerhassett, Charlotte Julia, *Lady.* Talleyrand.
And see MacCabe, Joseph. Life.

THAYER, JAMES BRADLEY. John Marshall. Boston. 1904. [Riverside Biographical Series, No. 9.] (Thayer.)

THOMPSON, JOHN, of Petersburg, Virginia. The Letters of Curtius. Richmond. 1804. (Thompson: *Letters of Curtius.*)

TICKNOR, ANNA, *and* HILLARD, GEORGE S. *joint editors. See* Ticknor, George. Life, Letters, and Journals.

TICKNOR, GEORGE. Life, Letters, and Journals. Edited by Anna Ticknor and George S. Hillard. 2 vols. Boston. 1876. (Ticknor.)

TUCKER, GEORGE. Life of Thomas Jefferson. 2 vols. Philadelphia. 1837. (Tucker.)

United States. Congress. Debates and Proceedings in the Congress of the United States. [1st Congress, 1st Session, to 18th Congress, 1st Session; Mar. 3, 1789 to May 27, 1824.] 41 vols. Washington, D.C. 1834–56.

—— Benton, Thomas Hart. Abridgment of the Debates of Congress from 1789 to 1856. 16 vols. New York. 1857–61.

UNITED STATES. State Trials. State Trials of the United States during the Administrations of Washington and Adams. By Francis Wharton. Philadelphia. 1849. (Wharton: *State Trials.*)

UNITED STATES. Supreme Court Reports. Dallas, A. J. Reports of the Cases Ruled and Adjudged in the Courts of Pennsylvania before and since the Revolution. Philadelphia. 4 vols. 1806–07.

VAN SANTVOORD, GEORGE. Sketches of the Lives and Judicial Services of the Chief-Justices of the Supreme Court of United States. New York. 1854. (Van Santvoord.)

VAN TYNE, CLAUDE HALSTEAD. The Loyalists in the American Revolution. New York. 1902.

VANS MURRAY, WILLIAM. Letters to John Quincy Adams, 1797–1803. Edited by Worthington Chauncey Ford. [Reprinted from the *Annual Report of the American Historical Association* for 1912, pp. 341–715.] Washington. 1914. (*Letters:* Ford.)

VIRGINIA. House of Delegates. Journal of the Virginia House of Delegates. 1776–1916. Now in the Archives of the Virginia State Library. (Journal, H.D.)

VIRGINIA. Laws. Hening, William Waller. The Statutes at Large. Being a Collection of the Laws of Virginia from 1619 to 1808. 13 vols. New York. 1819–23. (Hening.)

VIRGINIA. Laws. Revised Code, of the Laws of Virginia, being a Collection of all such Acts of the General Assembly. [By William Waller Hening.] 2 vols. Richmond. 1819. (Laws of Virginia, Revised Code, 1819.)

VIRGINIA. Law Reports. Call, Daniel. Reports of Cases Argued and Adjudged in the Court of Appeals of Virginia. 6 vols. Richmond. 1824–33. (Call.)

VIRGINIA. Law Reports. Washington, Bushrod. Reports of Cases Argued and Determined in the Court of Appeals of Virginia. 2 vols. Richmond. 1798–99.

Virginia Magazine of History and Biography. Published by the Virginia Historical Society. Vols. 1–24. Richmond. 1893–1916. (*Va. Mag. Hist. and Biog.*)

VON HOLST, H. The Constitutional and Political History of the United States, by Dr. H. von Holst. [Translated from the German by John J. Lalor, and Alfred B. Mason.] 7 vols. Chicago. 1876. (Von Holst: *Constitutional History of the United States.*)

WARVILLE. *See* Brissot de Warville.

WASHINGTON, BUSHROD. *See* Virginia. Law Reports.

WASHINGTON, GEORGE. Diary from 1789 to 1791. Edited by Benson J. Lossing. New York. 1860. (Washington's *Diary:* Lossing.)

—— Writings. Edited by Worthington Chauncey Ford. 14 vols. New York. 1889–93. (*Writings:* Ford.)

—— Writings. Edited by Jared Sparks. 12 vols. Boston. 1834–37. (*Writings:* Sparks.)

And Lodge, Henry Cabot. George Washington.

Also Marshall, John. Life of George Washington.

Also see Paulding, James K. Life of Washington.

WASHINGTON, H. A., *editor.* *See* Jefferson, Thomas. Writings.

WATSON, JOHN FANNING. Annals of Philadelphia and Pennsylvania, In the Olden Time. 3 vols. Philadelphia. 1877–79. (Watson: *Annals of Philadelphia.*)

WELD, ISAAC. Travels Through the States of North America, and the Provinces of Upper and Lower Canada During the Years 1795, 1796, and 1797. [3d Edition.] 2 vols. London. 1800. (Weld.)

WHARTON, FRANCIS. *See* United States. State Trials.

WIRT, WILLIAM. The Letters of the British Spy. [9th Edition.] Baltimore. 1831. (Wirt: *British Spy.*)

—— Sketches of the Life and Character of Patrick Henry. Philadelphia. 1818. (Wirt.)

See Kennedy, John P. Memoirs of William Wirt.

WISE, JOHN SERGEANT. The End of An Era. Boston. 1899. (Wise: *The End of An Era.*)

WOLCOTT, OLIVER. Memoirs of the Administrations of Washington and John Adams. Edited from the papers of Oliver Wolcott, by George Gibbs. 2 vols. New York. 1846. (Gibbs.)

WOOD, JOHN. History of Administration of John Adams, Esq. Late President of the United States. New York. 1802. (Wood.)